The new Islamic dynasties

The New Edinburgh Islamic Surveys
Series Editor: Carole Hillenbrand

TITLES AVAILABLE OR FORTHCOMING

The New Islamic Dynasties Clifford Edmund Bosworth
Media Arabic Julia Ashtiany Bray
An Introduction to the Hadith John Burton
A History of Islamic Law Noel Coulson
A Short History of the Ismailis Farhad Daftary
Islam: An Historical Introduction (2nd Edition) Gerhard Endress
A History of Christian–Muslim Relations Hugh Goddard
Shi'ism (2nd Edition) Heinz Halm
Islamic Science and Engineering Donald Hill
Islamic Law: From Historical Foundations to Contemporary Practice Mawil Izzi Dien
Sufism: An Historical Introduction Ahmet T. Karamustafa
Islamic Aesthetics Oliver Leaman
Persian Historiography Julie Scott Meisami
The Muslims of Medieval Italy Alex Metcalfe
Muslims in Western Europe (3rd Edition) Jørgen Nielsen
Medieval Islamic Medicine Peter Pormann and Emilie Savage-Smith
Islamic Jurisprudence Kevin Reinhart and Aron Zysow
Islamic Names Annemarie Schimmel
Modern Arabic Literature Paul Starkey
Islamic Medicine Manfred Ullman
Islam and Economics Ibrahim Warde
A History of Islamic Spain W. Montgomery Watt and Pierre Cachia
Introduction to the Qur'an W. Montgomery Watt
Islamic Creeds W. Montgomery Watt
Islamic Philosophy and Theology W. Montgomery Watt
Islamic Political Thought W. Montgomery Watt
Understanding the Qur'an Alford Welch

The new Islamic dynasties

A chronological and genealogical manual

CLIFFORD EDMUND BOSWORTH

EDINBURGH UNIVERSITY PRESS

Transferred to digital print 2012

Edinburgh University Press Ltd
22 George Square, Edinburgh

Typeset in Linotype Trump Medieval by
Koinonia, Manchester, and
printed and bound by CPI Group (UK) Ltd, Croydon, CR0 4YY

A CIP Record for this book is available from the British Library

ISBN 0 7486 2137 7 (paperback)

Published with the support of the
Edinburgh University Scholarly
Publishing Initiatives Fund.

CONTENTS

Abbreviations used xiv
Introduction xv

CHAPTER ONE The Caliphs
1. The Rightly-Guided or 'Patriarchal' or 'Orthodox' Caliphs (*al-Khulafā' al-Rāshidūn*) 1
2. The Umayyad Caliphs 3
 1. The Sufyānids
 2. The Marwānids
3. The 'Abbāsid Caliphs 6
 1. The caliphs in Iraq and Baghdad
 2. The caliph in Aleppo, Ḥarrān and northern Syria
 3. The caliphs in Cairo

CHAPTER TWO Spain
4. The Spanish Umayyads 11
5. The Mulūk al-Ṭawā'if or Reyes de Taifas in Spain 14
 1. The Ḥammūdids of Málaga
 2. The Ḥammūdids of Ceuta
 3. The 'Abbādids of Seville
 4. The Banū Birzāl in Carmona
 5. The Banū Khazrūn in Arcos
 6. The Zīrids of Granada
 7. The Banū Ṣumādiḥ of Almería
 8. The Banū Mujāhid of Denia and Majorca
 9. The rulers in Majorca during the eleventh and early twelfth centuries
 10. The Jahwarids of Cordova
 11. The rulers in Cordova of the Almoravid-Almohad interregnum
 12. The Afṭasids of Badajoz
 13. The Dhu 'l-Nūnids of Toledo
 14. The 'Āmirids of Valencia
 15. The rulers in Valencia of the Almoravid-Almohad interregnum
 16. The Tujībids in Saragossa
 17. The Hūdids in Saragossa, Huesca, Tudela and Lérida, and, subsequently, Denia, Tortosa and Calatayud
 18. The rulers of Murcia, including the Ṭāhirids and Hūdids
6. The Banū Ghāniya 21
7. The Naṣrids or Banu 'l-Aḥmar 22

CHAPTER THREE North Africa
8. The Idrīsids 25
9. The Rustamids 27
10. The Midrārids 29
11. The Aghlabids 31

12. The Kalbids 33
13. The Zīrids and Ḥammādids 35
14. The Almoravids or al-Murābiṭūn 37
15. The Almohads or al-Muwaḥḥidūn 39
16. The Marīnids 41
17. The 'Abd al-Wādids or Zayyānids or Ziyānids 43
18. The Ḥafṣids 45
19. The Waṭṭāsids 48
20. The Sa'did Sharīfs 50
21. The 'Alawid or Filālī Sharīfs 53
22. The Ḥusaynid Beys 55
23. The Qaramānlīs 57
24. The Sanūsī Chiefs and Rulers 58

CHAPTER FOUR Egypt and Syria
25. The Ṭūlūnids 60
26. The Ikhshīdids 62
27. The Fāṭimids 63
28. The Mirdāsids 66
29. The chief *dā'īs* of the Nizārī Ismā'īlīs or Assassins in Syria 68
30. The Ayyūbids 70
1. The line in Egypt
2. The line in Damascus
3. The line in Aleppo
4. The line in Ḥimṣ
5. The line in Ḥamāt
6. The line in Diyār Bakr (Mayyāfāriqīn and Jabal Sinjār)
7. The line in Diyār Bakr (Ḥiṣn Kayfā, Āmid and Akhlāṭ)
8. The line in Yemen
9. The minor branches of the family in Ba'lbakk, Karak, Bāniyās and Subayba, and Buṣrā
31. The Mamlūks 76
1. The Baḥrī line
2. The Burjī line
32. The Ma'n Amīrs of Lebanon 81
33. The Shihāb Amīrs of Lebanon 82
34. The house of Muḥammad 'Alī 83

CHAPTER FIVE Iraq and Jazīra before the Seljuqs
35. The Ḥamdānids 85
1. The line in Mosul and Jazīra
2. The line in Aleppo and northern Syria
36. The Mazyadids 87
37. The Marwānids 89
38. The 'Uqaylids 91
1. The line in Jazīrat Ibn 'Umar, Niṣībīn and Balad of Muḥammad b. al-Musayyab al-'Uqaylī
2. The line in Mosul and later in Jazīrat Ibn 'Umar, Niṣībīn and

Balad, also of the al-Musayyab line
3. The line in Takrīt of Ma'n b. al-Muqallad's descendants
4. The line in Hīt
5. The line in 'Ukbarā of Ma'n b. al-Muqallad's descendants
6. The other minor branches at Āna and al-Ḥadītha and at Qal'at Ja'bar
39. The Numayrids 93

CHAPTER SIX The Arabian Peninsula
40. The Carmathian or Qarmaṭī Rulers of the line of Abū Sa'īd al-Jannābī 94
41. The Zaydī Imāms of Yemen 96
1. The early period: the Rassid line
2. The more recent period: the Qāsimid line
42. The Ziyādids 99
43. The Yu'firids or Ya'furids 100
44. The Najāḥids 101
45. The Ṣulayḥids 102
46. The Zuray'ids or Banu 'l-Karam 104
47. The Hamdānids 106
1. The first line of the Banū Ḥātim
2. The line of the Banu 'l-Qubayb
3. The second line of the Banū Ḥātim
48. The Mahdids 107
49. The Rasūlids 108
50. The Ṭāhirids 110
51. The Āl al-Julandā 111
52. The Mukramids 112
53. The Ya'rubids 113
54. The Āl Bū Sa'īd 114
1. The united sultanate
2. The line of sultans in Oman
3. The line of sultans in Zanzibar
55. The Āl Su'ūd (Sa'ūd) 116
56. The Hāshimite Sharīfs of Mecca from the 'Awn family 118
1. The original line in Western Arabia
2. The post-First World War branches of the Hāshimite family in the Fertile Crescent countries
(a) The line in Syria
(b) The line in Iraq
(c) The line in Transjordan and then Jordan
57. The Āl Rashīd 120

CHAPTER SEVEN West Africa
58. The Keita Kings of Mali 122
59. The Kings of Songhay 124
1. The Zas or Zuwas of Gao
2. The Sis or Sonnis
3. The Askiyas

60. The Rulers of Kanem and Bornu or Borno 126
1. The 'red' (i.e. white) Sayfī (Sefuwa) or Yazanī rulers of Kanem
2. The 'black' Sultans of Kanem
3. The new line of Sultans in Bornu, the Mais or rulers, claiming Sayfī descent
4. The Kanembu line of Shaykhs or Shehus of Bornu and Dikwa
(a) The Shehus in Bornu, reinstated by the British
(b) The Shehus and Mais in Dikwa, reinstated by the French
61. The Fulani Rulers in Hausaland, as Sultans and Caliphs of Sokoto 130

CHAPTER EIGHT East Africa and the Horn of Africa
62. The Sultans of Kilwa 132
1. The Shīrāzī dynasty
2. The Mahdali Sayyids
63. The Nabhānī Rulers of Pate 134
64. The Mazrui (Mazrū'ī) *Liwali*s or Governors of Mombasa 136
65. The Āl Bū Sa'īd in East Africa 137
66. The Sultans of Harar 138
1. The line of Aḥmad Grāñ in Harar and Ausa
2. The line of 'Alī b. Dāwūd in Harar, independent of Ausa

CHAPTER NINE The Caucasus and the Western Persian Lands before the Seljuqs
67. The Sharwān Shāhs 140
1. The first line of Yazīdī Shāhs
2. The second line of Shāhs
68. The Hāshimids 143
69. The Justānids 145
70. The Sājids 147
71. The Musāfirids or Sallārids 148
1. The line in Azerbaijan
2. The line in Daylam
72. The Rawwādids 150
73. The Shaddādids 151
1. The main line in Ganja and Dvīn
2. The line in Ānī
74. The Dulafids 153
75. The Būyids or Buwayhids 154
1. The line in Jibāl
(a) The branch in Hamadan and Isfahan
(b) The branch in Rayy
2. The line in Fars (Fārs) and Khūzistān
3. The line in Kirman (Kirmān)
4. The line in Iraq
5. The rulers of the dynasty acknowledged by local chiefs in Oman
76. The Ḥasanūyids or Ḥasanawayhids 158
77. The 'Annāzids 159

78. The Kākūyids or Kākawayhids 160
79. The Dābūyid Ispahbadhs 162
80. The Bāwandid Ispahbadhs 164
1. The line of the Kāwūsiyya (Ṭabaristān), with their centre at Firrīm
2. The line of the Ispahbadhiyya (Ṭabaristān and Gīlān), with their centre at Sārī
3. The line of the Kīnkhwāriyya (vassals of the Il Khānids), with their centre at Āmul
81. The Ziyārids 166

CHAPTER TEN The Eastern Persian Lands, Transoxania and Khwārazm before the Seljuqs
82. The Ṭāhirids and Muṣʿabids 168
1. The governors in Khurasan and its administrative dependencies
2. The military governors (*Aṣḥāb al-Shurṭa*) in Baghdad and Iraq
83. The Sāmānids 170
84. The Ṣaffārids 172
1. The Laythid branch
2. The Khalafid branch
85. The Bānījūrids or Abū Dāwūdids 174
86. The Sīmjūrids 175
87. The Ilyāsids 176
88. The Muḥtājids 177
89. The Khwārazm Shāhs 178
1. The Afrīghids of Kāth
2. The Ma'mūnids of Gurgānj
3. The Ghaznawid governors with the title of Khwārazm Shāh
4. The line of Anūshtigin Shiḥna, originally as governors for the Seljuqs with the title of Khwārazm Shāh, from towards the mid-twelfth century often in practice largely independent rulers in Khwārazm and, at times, in Transoxania and Persia
90. The Qarakhānids 181
1. The Great Qaghans of the united kingdom
2. The Great Qaghans of the western kingdom (Transoxania, including Bukhara and Samarkand, and Farghāna at times), with its centre at Samarkand
3. The Great Qaghans of the eastern kingdom (Īlāq, Talas, Shāsh, at times Farghāna, Semirechye, Kāshghar and Khotan), with its centre at Balāsāghūn, later Kāshghar
4. The Qaghans in Farghāna, with their centre in Uzgend

CHAPTER ELEVEN The Seljuqs, Their Dependants and the Atabegs
91. The Seljuqs 185
1. The Great Seljuqs in Persia and Iraq
2. The Seljuqs of Syria
3. The Seljuqs of Kirman
92. The Börids or Būrids 189

93. The Zangids 190
1. The main line in Mosul and Aleppo
2. The line in Damascus and then Aleppo
3. The line in Sinjār
4. The line in Jazīra
5. The line in Shahrazūr
94. The Begtiginids 192
95. The Lu'lu'ids 193
96. The Artuqids 194
1. The line in Ḥiṣn Kayfā and Āmid
2. The line in Khartpert
3. The line in Mārdīn and Mayyāfāriqīn
97. The Shāh-i Armanids 197
1. The Sökmenids
2. The Sökmenid slave commanders
98. The Aḥmadīlīs 198
99. The Eldigüzids or Ildegizids 199
100. The Bādūspānids 201
1. The rulers of the united principality
2. The rulers in Kujūr (with the title of Malik)
3. The rulers in Nūr (with the title of Malik)
101. The Nizārī Ismā'īlīs or Assassins in Persia 203
102. The Hazāraspids 205
103. The Salghurids 207
104. The Atabegs of Yazd 209
105. The Qutlughkhānids 210
106. The Maliks of Nīmrūz 211
1. The Naṣrids
2. The Mihrabānids

CHAPTER TWELVE The Turks in Anatolia
107. The Seljuqs of Rūm 213
108. The Dānishmendids 215
1. The line in Sivas
2. The line in Malatya and Elbistan
109. The Mengüjekids 217
1. The line in Erzincan and Kemakh
2. The line in Divriği
110. The Saltuqids 218
111. The Qarasï (Karasï) Oghullarï 219
112. The Ṣarukhān Oghullarï 220
113. The Aydïn Oghullarï 221
114. The Menteshe Oghullarï 222
115. The Inanj Oghullarï 223
116. The Germiyān Oghullarï 224
117. The Ṣāḥib Atā Oghullarï 225
118. The Ḥamīd Oghullarï and the Tekke Oghullarï 226
1. The Ḥamīd Oghullarï line in Eğridir

2. The Tekke Oghullarï line in Antalya
119. The Beys of Alanya 227
120. The Ashraf (Eshref) Oghullarï 228
121. The Jāndār Oghullarï or Isfandiyār (Isfendiyār) Oghullarï 229
122. The Parwāna Oghullarï 230
123. The Chobān Oghullarï 231
124. The Qaramān Oghullarï or Qaramānids 232
125. The Eretna Oghullarï 234
126. The Qāḍī Burhān al-Dīn Oghullarï 235
127. The Tāj al-Dīn Oghullarï 236
128. The Ramaḍān Oghullarï 237
129. The Dulghadïr Oghullarï or Dhu 'l-Qadrids 238
130. The Ottomans or Osmanlis 239

CHAPTER THIRTEEN The Mongols and their Central Asian and Eastern European Successors
The Mongols or Chingizids 243
131. The Mongol Great Khāns, Descendants of Ögedey and Toluy, later the Yüan Dynasty of China 246
132. The Chaghatayids, Descendants of Chaghatay 248
133. The Il Khānids, Descendants of Qubilay's brother Hülegü 250
134. The Khāns of the Golden Horde, Descendants of Jochi 252
1. The line of Batu'ids, Khāns of the Blue Horde in South Russia, Khwārazm and the western part of the Qïpchaq steppe
2. The line of Orda, Khāns of the White Horde in western Siberia and the eastern part of the Qïpchaq steppe, and, after 780/1378, of the Blue and White Hordes united into the Golden Horde of South Russia
135. The Giray Khāns of the Crimea, Descendants of Jochi 255
1. The Khāns of the Crimea
2. The Khāns of the Tatars of Bujaq or Bessarabia, as Ottoman nominees
136. The Khāns of Astrakhan (Astrakhān, Ashtarkhān) 258
137. The Khāns of Kazan (Qāzān) 259
1. The line of Ulugh Muḥammad
2. Khāns from various outside lines
138. The Khāns of Qāsimov 261
1. The Khāns from the line of rulers of Kazan
2. The Khāns from the line of the rulers of the Crimea
3. The Khāns from the line of the rulers of Astrakhan
4. Kazakh Khān
5. The Khāns from the line of the rulers of Siberia

CHAPTER FOURTEEN Persia after the Mongols
139. The Karts or Kurts 263
140. The Muẓaffarids 264
141. The Inju'ids 266
142. The Jalāyirids 267

143. The Sarbadārids 269
144. The Tīmūrids 270
1. The rulers in Samarkand
2. The rulers in Khurasan after Ulugh Beg's death
3. The rulers in western Persia and Iraq after Tīmūr
145. The Qara Qoyunlu 273
146. The Aq Qoyunlu 275
147. The Musha'sha'ids 277
148. The Ṣafawids 279
149. The Afshārids 281
150. The Zands 283
151. The Qājārs 285
152. The Pahlawīs 287

CHAPTER FIFTEEN Central Asia after the Mongols
153. The Shībānids (Shaybānids) or Abu 'l-Khayrids 288
154. The Toqay Temürids or Jānids or Ashtarkhānids 290
155. The Mangïts 292
156. The Qungrats or Inaqids 293
157. The Mings 295

CHAPTER SIXTEEN Afghanistan and the Indian Subcontinent
158. The Ghaznawids 296
159. The Ghūrids 298
1. The main line in Ghūr and then also in Ghazna
2. The line in Bāmiyān, Ṭukhāristān and Badakhshān
160. The Delhi Sultans 300
1. The Mu'izzī or Shamsī Slave Kings
2. The Khaljīs
3. The Tughluqids
4. The Sayyids
5. The Lōdīs
6. The Sūrīs
161. The Governors and Sultans of Bengal 306
1. The governors for the Delhi Sultans, often ruling as independent sovereigns
2. The governors, and then independent rulers, of Balban's line
3. The line of Ilyās Shāh
4. The line of Rājā Gaṇeśa (Ganesh)
5. The line of Ilyās Shāh restored
6. The domination of the Ḥabashīs
7. The line of Sayyid Ḥusayn Shāh
8. The Sūrīs
9. The Kararānīs
162. The Sultans of Kashmīr 310
1. The line of Shāh Mīr Swātī
2. The line of Ghāzī Shāh Chak
163. The Sultans of Gujarāt 312

164. The Sharqī Sultans of Jawnpur 314
165. The Sultans and Rulers of Mālwa 316
1. The line of the Ghūrīs
2. The line of the Khaljīs
3. Various governors and independent rulers
166. The Sultans of Maʿbar or Madura 318
167. The Bahmanids 319
1. The rulers at Aḥsanābād-Gulbargā
2. The rulers in Muḥammadābād-Bīdar
168. The Fārūqī Rulers of Khāndesh 322
169. The Barīd Shāhīs 324
170. The ʿĀdil Shāhis 325
171. The Niẓām Shāhīs 326
172. The ʿImād Shāhīs 327
173. The Quṭb Shāhīs 328
174. The Arghūns 329
1. The line of Dhu 'l-Nūn Beg
2. The line of Muḥammad ʿĪsā Tarkhān
175. The Mughal Emperors 331
176. The Nawwāb-Viziers and Nawwāb-Nāẓims of Bengal 335
177. The Nawwāb-Viziers and Kings of Oudh (Awadh) 337
178. The Nāẓims of Hyderabad (Ḥaydarābād) 339
179. The Muslim Rulers in Mysore (Mahisur, Maysūr) 340
180. The Abdālī or Durrānī Rulers and Kings of Afghanistan 341
1. The Sadōzays or Popalzays
2. The Bārakzays or Muḥammadzays

CHAPTER SEVENTEEN South-East Asia and Indonesia
181. The Rulers of Malacca (Melaka) 344
182. The Sultans of Acheh (Atjèh, Aceh) 346
183. The Rulers of Mataram 348
184. The Susuhunans of Surakarta 350
185. The Sultans of Jogjakarta 351
186. The Sultans of Brunei 353

Indexes: (a) Personal names; (b) Dynasties, peoples, tribes, etc. (c) Places 357

ABBREVIATIONS USED

Album = Stephen Album, *A Checklist of Popular Islamic Coins*, Santa Rosa, CA 1993

AIEO Alger = *Annales de l'Institut d'Etudes Orientales, Alger*

AMI = *Archäologische Mitteilungen aus Iran*

ANS = *The American Numismatic Society*

BIFAO = *Bulletin de l'Institut Français d'Archéologie Orientale du Caire*

Bosworth–Merçil–İpşirli = C. E. Bosworth, tr. Erdoğan Merçil and Mehmet İpşirli, *Islâm devletleri tarihi (kronoloji ve soykütüğü elkitabı)*, Istanbul 1980

CT = *Cahiers de Tunisie*

*EI*¹ = *Encyclopaedia of Islam*, 1st edn, Leiden 1913–36

*EI*² = *Encyclopaedia of Islam*, 2nd edn, Leiden 1960–

EIr = *Encyclopaedia Iranica*, London, etc. 1985–

HJAS = *Harvard Journal of Asiatic Studies*

İA = *İslam Ansiklopedisi*, Istanbul 1940–85

IC = *Islamic Culture*

Iran, JBIPS = *Iran, Journal of the British Institute of Persian Studies*

JA = *Journal Asiatique*

JAOS = *Journal of the American Oriental Society*

JASB = *Journal of the Asiatic Society of Bengal*

JBBRAS = *Journal of the Bombay Branch of the Royal Asiatic Society*

JRAS = *Journal of the Royal Asiatic Society*

Justi = F. Justi, *Iranisches Namenbuch*, Marburg 1895

Khalīl Ed'hem = Khalīl Ed'hem, *Düwel-i Islāmiyye*, Istanbul 1345/1927

Lane-Poole = Stanley Lane-Poole, *The Mohammadan Dynasties. Chronological and Genealogical Tables with Historical Introductions*, London 1893

Méms DAFA = Mémoires de la Délégation Archéologique Française en Afghanistan

NC = *Numismatic Chronicle*

NZ = *Numismatische Zeitschrift*

REI = *Revue des Etudes Islamiques*

Sachau = Eduard Sachau, 'Ein Verzeichnis Muhammedanischer Dynastien', *Abhandlungen der Preussischen Akademie der Wissenschaften*, Phil.-hist. Klasse (Berlin 1923), no. 1

SAD = *Selçuklu Araştırmalar Dergisi (Journal of Seljuk Studies)*

SBWAW = *Sitzungsberichte der Wiener Akademie der Wissenschaften*, Phil.-hist. Klasse

TP = *T'oung-Pao*

Zambaur = E. de Zambaur, *Manuel de généalogie et de chronologie pour l'histoire de l'Islam*, Hanover 1927

ZfN = *Zeitschrift für Numismatik*

INTRODUCTION

The precursor of this present book, *The Islamic Dynasties: A Chronological and Genealogical Handbook*, was published by Edinburgh University Press in 1967 as no. 5 in the *Islamic Surveys* series, and speedily established itself as a convenient reference work for the chronology of Islamic dynasties of the Middle Eastern and North African heartlands and of Central and South Asia and for their historical backgrounds. It has proved useful not only for Islamic historians but also for Islamic art historians and numismatists. Nevertheless, all these groups of scholars remain much less well provided with such *Hilfsmittel* as chronologies of events, genealogical tables, historical atlases, etc., than their colleagues in the fields of British or European history.[1] Some of the subsequent writers of general histories of the Islamic world or its component regions and peoples, and writers of reference works covering the world in general or the Islamic lands in particular, who have given lists of dynasties and rulers, have obviously drawn upon the original *Islamic Dynasties* – sometimes with due acknowledgement,[2] sometimes not.

To my knowledge, four translations into East European and Middle Eastern languages have been made. In 1971, there appeared in Moscow an authorised translation by P. A. Gryaznevich, under the overall editorship of I. P. Petrushevskiy, *Musulmanskie dynastii. Spravochnik po khronologii i genealogii*, Izdatel'stvo <<Nauka>> Glavnaya Redaktsiya Vostochnoi Literaturï, 324 pp., to which I contributed a Preface. The text is a straight translation, but the bibliographical indications at the end of each dynasty's entry have been enriched by references to works in Russian, obviously valuable for such regions as the Caucasus, Central Asia and the Iranian world in general. In 1980, there appeared in Istanbul *Islâm devletleri tarihi (kronoloji ve soykütüğü elkitabı)*, Oğuz Press, xxvii + 385 pp., an authorised Turkish translation by Erdoğan Merçil and Mehmet İpşirli. This has additional material in that Dr Merçil appended an additional, eleventh chapter 'Anadolu beylikleri' dealing in detail with the principalities of Anatolia during the interim between the decay of the Rūm Seljuqs and the rise of the Ottomans. I have, in fact, drawn upon this useful additional chapter for my own, widely expanded Chapter Twelve 'The Turks in Anatolia'. In 1371/1982 there appeared *Silsilahā-yi Islāmī*, an unauthorised Persian translation by one Farīdūn Badra'ī, Mu'assasa-yi Muṭāla'at wa Taḥqīqāt Farhangī, 358 pp. In 1994, there appeared at Kuwait an authorised Arabic translation by the late Ḥusayn ʿAlī al-Lubūdī, under the general supervision of Dr Sulaymān Ibrāhīm al-ʿAskarī, *al-Usar al-ḥākima fi 'l-Islām. Dirāsa fi 'l-ta'rīkh wa 'l-ansāb*, Mu'assasat al-Shirāʿ al-ʿArabī, 293 pp.

The original book is thus still proving useful in these parts of the world through translations, although the Edinburgh University Press original is now out of print in both the original hardback and the paperback versions (the latter, of 1980, contained some slight corrections, all that the process of largely verbatim reproduction allowed). But well before the book became finally out of print, I had been noting corrections and gathering fresh information for a new, considerably expanded version. It would be strange if the explosion of knowledge over the last thirty years had not brought much fresh information for the Islamic chronologist and genealogist, from such disciplines as historical research, epigraphy and numismatics. Much of the relevant information is, however, scattered, and, in regard to epigraphy and numismatics in particular, often appears in the local publications of the countries concerned and is not easily accessible in Britain and Western Europe. I have nevertheless endeavoured, with assistance and advice from specialist colleagues and friends (who are detailed and appropriately thanked at the end of this Introduction), to incorporate as much of this new information as possible, though certain periods and areas remain – and perhaps always will remain – dark.

Most obvious to the reader of this present book will be the fact that it is much bigger than the 1967 book. There are now seventeen chapters, covering 186 dynasties, whereas the original *Islamic Dynasties* had only ten chapters, covering 82 dynasties. The new or vastly expanded chapters include ones dealing with Muslim Spain, with much more detailed coverage of the Mulūk al-Ṭawā'if (Chapter Two); the Arabian peninsula, again with much greater detail (Chapter Six); West Africa, and East Africa and the Horn of Africa, both entirely new chapters (Chapters Seven and Eight); the Turks of Anatolia, now with detailed coverage of the Beyliks there (Chapter Twelve); Central Asia after the Mongols, a substantially new chapter which includes the Khanates arising there out of the Turco-Mongol domination of Inner Asia and persisting until the extension of Russian imperial power through Central Asia (Chapter Fifteen); Afghanistan and the Indian Subcontinent, with increased coverage of, for example, the Sultanates of the Deccan and the Indian dynasties of the eighteenth and nineteenth centuries (Chapter Sixteen); and South-East Asia and Indonesia, again dealing with an entirely new region (Chapter Seventeen). But apart from these ones specifically mentioned, virtually all chapters are enlarged to some extent or other.

Thus the coverage of the new book approaches much more closely to coverage of the whole Islamic world, from Senegal to Borneo, than did the 1967 book, since it has often in the past been noted that works purporting to deal with Islam or the Islamic world have tended to concentrate on the Arab-Persian-Turkish heartlands to the neglect of the fringes, even though such peripheral regions as South and South-East Asia and Indonesia now contain the majority of Muslim peoples. Yet somewhat in extenuation of this concentration in the past on the heartlands, it must be admitted that the historian and chronologist of the peripheries is on much shakier ground. The heartlands have been long Islamised; many of their lands possess ancient historiographical traditions, with reliable dynastic histories and clearly-dated coins inscribed with a plethora of information on names and titulature. Whereas in regions far from the heartlands such as sub-Saharan Africa, South-East Asia and Indonesia, there may well be a care for local tribal or dynastic traditions, their recording in clearly-dated written form has nevertheless been patchy, and the task of making such records has often been complicated by attempts, of a mythic nature, to prove the ancient reception of the Islamic faith by families and classes ruling over lands and subjects which remained largely pagan for lengthy periods subsequently. The coinage of such ruling strata is nearly always much less complete in dated series, and in actual information on the coins, than for the Islamic heartlands and the Indian Subcontinent. The difficulties involved in constructing king-lists and chronologies in such circumstances may be discerned below, with reference to, for example, the kings of

Songhay (no. 59), the rulers of Kanem and Bornu (no. 60), the Sultans of Kilwa (no. 62) and the Sultans of Brunei (no. 186).

Even so, the position in such a region, comparatively near to the heartlands, as early Islamic Central Asia is far from crystal-clear. Zambaur confessed seventy years ago regarding the Qarakhanids of Transoxania and eastern Turkestan that this was 'la seule grande dynastie musulmane dont la généalogie est restée obscure' (*Manuel*, 206 n. 1). Much elucidation has meanwhile come from such scholars as Omeljan Pritsak and Elena A. Davidovich, but significant problems remain; the substantially increased numbers of coins now finding their way from Central Asia and Afghanistan to the West since the demise of the USSR may possibly resolve some of these remaining obscurities.

In the Introduction to the 1967 book, I traced the development of Islamic chronological and genealogical studies and listings from Stanley Lane-Poole's seminal *The Mohammadan Dynasties* (1893), through the more specific work of F. Justi in his *Iranisches Namenbuch* (1895) and the expansions and improvements upon Lane-Poole by W. Barthold in his *Musulmanskiy dynastii* (1899), E. Sachau in his 'Ein Verzeichnis Muhammedanischer Dynastien' (1923), and Khalīl Ed'hem in his *Düwel-i Islāmiyye* (1345/1927), to E. de Zambaur's almost entirely new and monumental *Manuel de généalogie et de chronologie pour l'histoire de l'Islam* (1927).[3] It does not seem necessary to repeat here all these details, except to note that no-one has attempted since the publication of Zambaur's work to update it as a whole; although a stupendous work for its time, its inaccuracies and erroneous renderings of names appear more and more obvious with the lapse of time.

I opined in 1967 that such an updating and rewriting could probably only be done as a cooperative effort by historians who are specialists in various sectors of the Islamic world, aided by epigraphists and numismatists. The prospects of such a collaboration seem no nearer in 1995 than they did twenty-nine years ago. Hence my *New Islamic Dynasties*, here presented to the scholarly world, does not aim at such overall completeness as Zambaur essayed (although he did not in fact achieve it; his attempts at covering dynasties in sub-Saharan Africa, the Indian Ocean islands and Indonesia were fragmentary and feeble to the point of uselessness); but I think I may venture to say that it represents as extensive a coverage of Islamic dynasties as one person is likely to achieve in our present day. I have endeavoured to cover what might be termed the first, second and third ranks of dynasties and to give as up-to-date and accurate information on them as possible. There remains the fourth rank and beyond, and readers may well have pet dynasties and ruling houses in which they are especially interested and which they consider ought to have been included. I can only plead that one must draw the line somewhere, and that I have left plenty of opportunities for other researchers; such readers might, for instance, care to get their teeth into elucidating the *Ṣudūr* of Bukhara, the *Wālī*s of Badakhshān, the Khāns of Sibir, the sultans of the Sulu archipelago and the Moro rulers of Mindanão in the southern Philippines, etc. Moreover, an extensive field remains open for future scholars, one which Zambaur tackled valiantly and to some extent successfully, namely that of elucidating the lines of viziers to the rulers of such dynasties as the 'Abbāsids, the Fāṭimids, the Būyids, the Great Seljuqs and their related branches, and the Ottomans. Zambaur also set forth the series of provincial governors in the *amṣār* or military concentration-points of the Arab caliphate, and he tentatively envisaged a second edition of his *Manuel* (which never appeared, although the author did not die until 1941) in which he would tackle the local governors of a host of other cities of the east, such as Tabriz, Isfahan, Hamadhan, Marw, Bukhara and Samarkand. Certainly, in regard to the viziers, our increased knowledge of the ʿAbbāsid and Seljuq vizierates, for instance, and the chronological researches of such Turkish scholars as İsmail Hami Danişmendli in his *İzahlı Osmanlı tarihi kronolojisi*, Istanbul 1947–71, in regard to the Ottoman viziers, should enable fuller and more accurate lists to be compiled, above all, of the innumerable, rapidly-changing Ottoman viziers. Similarly, the publication of many texts out of the rich genre of local histories, which has flourished in the Iranian and Central Asian lands from classical times virtually until the present day, would enable us to reconstruct the history and chronology of the ruling strata in many of the cities mentioned above by Zambaur.

A feature of Lane-Poole's *The Mohammadan Dynasties* was the short historical account of each dynasty prefixed to its relevant entry, accounts which, he said,

> do not attempt to relate the internal history of each dynasty: they merely show its place in relation to other dynasties, and trace its origin, its principal extensions, and its downfall; they seek to define the boundaries of its dominions, and to describe the chief steps in its aggrandisement and in its decline. (p. vi)

Zambaur agreed that 'Il eût été agréable de trouver, en tête de chaque dynastie, un aperçu succinct de ses origines, de son développement et de sa fin', but, for reasons of space and economy, renounced 'ses introductions qui forment un attrait séduisant du livre de M. St. Lane-Poole' (*Manuel*, p. vii). Nevertheless, the accounts here of Lane-Poole were most useful, especially in pre-*Encyclopaedia of Islam* days, and have still seemed to me eminently desirable for a work on Islamic dynastic chronology. A bare list of rulers and their dates would admittedly be of use to specialist Islamic historians and numismatists, who would know where to look for historical information on the dynasties in question (though this might well take them down some obscure pathways). But historical introductions to the dynasties seem to me essential for students and non-specialists. My own aim, as in 1967, has been similar to that of Lane-Poole: not so much to give a potted history as to place the dynasty in the broad context of Islamic history; to outline some of the major trends of its period; and, where relevant, to indicate some of the dynasty's achievements. I have tried to make the bibliographical references at the end of each section fuller than in the 1967 book. As well as including works specifically useful for illuminating the chronology and titulature of the dynasty, I have given references to a series of general works dealing with the dynasty concerned, and to a selection at least of specific studies, where such general works and special studies exist. But the references here are not meant to be in any way exhaustive, nor are they meant to replace the detailed information available in the bibliographies to the various dynasties in the new edition of the *Encyclopaedia of Islam* entries, or set forth in the latest French version (*Introduction à l'histoire du monde musulman médiéval VIIe–XVe siècle. Méthodologie et éléments de bibliographie*, Paris 1982) of the late Claude Cahen's *refonte*, expansion and updating of Jean Sauvaget's *Introduction à l'histoire de l'Orient Musulman: éléments de bibliographie* (with additions and corrections, Paris 1946) (English version, unfortunately with rather more cursory bibliographical references, *Introduction to the History of the Muslim East: A Bibliographical Guide*, Berkeley and Los Angeles 1965). Also, there has very recently appeared *Etats, sociétés et cultures du monde musulman médiéval X^e^–XVe siècles, Tome 1*, Paris 1995, written by a team of specialists (Jean-Claude Garçin, Michel Ballivet, Thierry Bianquis, Henri Bresc, Jean Calmard, Marc Gaborieau, Pierre Guichard and Jean-Louis Triaud) and containing a very extensive section *Les outils de travail* with up-to-date bibliographical references, maps and genealogical tables (pp. vii–ccxi). For the more recent history of the Islamic lands, there are also bibliographical references in general histories such as Ira Lapidus's *A History of Islamic Societies* (Cambridge 1988) and in such encyclopaedic works as Francis Robinson, *Atlas of the Islamic World since 1500*, Oxford 1982; Trevor Mostyn and Albert Hourani (eds), *The Cambridge Encyclopedia of the Middle East and North Africa*, Cambridge 1988; Francis Robinson (ed.), *The Cambridge History of India, Pakistan, Bangladesh, Sri Lanka*, Cambridge 1989; and John L. Esposito (ed.), *The Oxford Encyclopedia of the Modern Islamic World*, Oxford 1995. These are all recently published and contain presumably up-to-date bibliographical information. For the classical period of Islamic history, however, such works mentioned above as those of Lapidus, and of Robinson in his *Atlas of the Islamic World* (whose timespan covers both the later mediaeval and the modern periods), can profitably be consulted, but it is a matter of alphabetical chance whether the entry in the new edition of the *Encyclopaedia of Islam* dates from the late 1940s or 1950s, when the second edition was conceived and first published (as in the case of , for example, the ʿAbbāsids and the Būyids), or from the last few years (as in the case, for example, of the Mamlūks, the Mughals, the Ottomans and the Ṣafawids). If the former, then the bibliographical references are distinctly out of date, and I have endeavoured here to supply some more recent ones.

Since various numismatic colleagues have, over the years, told me how useful they have found the 1967 book, it has seemed to that more information might be included in this new book for the numismatist. The study of coins, and the information which their legends yield on titulature, accession dates, periods of power, extent of territories ruled over, etc., have long been recognised as constituting an invaluable ancillary discipline for the Islamic dynastic and political historian (and equally, for different reasons, for the economic and social one).[4] I have tried to use, wherever possible, numismatic evidence in compiling the present lists of rulers and their dates, and have listed significant numismatic sources in the bibliographies for each dynasty where such sources exist. Also, as an innovatory feature of the present book, in the dynastic lists I have marked those rulers who issued coins, following the convention established by Zambaur in his *Manuel* of prefixing a small circle to their dates and name, in the hope that this will be a worthwhile extra feature for the numismatist and historian alike. In general, I have disregarded the numismatic information given by Zambaur, which was not free from coin misattributions, and have derived my own information, where possible, from coin catalogues, the various studies on the coinages of specific dynasties, such as exist, for example, for the Idrīsids, the Spanish Muslim dynasties, the Fāṭimids, the Ayyūbids and the Mamlūks, and from the monthly lists of coins offered for sale by Mr Stephen Album of Santa Rosa, California. I am aware of the difficulties involved in deciding whether a specific dynasty or ruler issued its or his own coins, with personal names and titles on them, or whether a ruler was content to issue coins in the name of his suzerain, as were, for example, the Beys of Tunis up to the later nineteenth century, the Qaramānlī governors of Tripoli, and the rulers from the house of Muḥammad ʿAlī in Egypt until the early twentieth century, all of which rulers for long minted coins in the names of their suzerains (however nominal this suzerainty might ultimately become), the Ottoman Sultan-Caliphs. On the whole, I have tended to regard only those coins with the full names and titles of the actual minting authority as evidence for the independent issue of coins by the dynasty or ruler in question, but am conscious that some inconsistencies may have crept in here.

Following Lane-Poole, I have given dates in both the Muslim *Hijrī* and the Christian eras. It should be noted by those unfamiliar with the Muslim system of dating that the pre-Islamic Arabs used a lunar calendar of twelve months (because observation of the moon's phases was the only possible basis for time-reckoning in a desert environment) with intercalation (*nasī'*) of an extra month every two or three years in order to keep some relation with the solar year and with the rhythm of the agricultural seasons, and in order to fix the great annual fairs of Arabia at the same time each year. The Prophet Muḥammad introduced a lunar year, forbidding intercalation and thus throwing the old Arabian system out of gear. It was the second caliph ʿUmar b. al-Khaṭṭāb who tactfully regulated the system. He decreed that the lunar year of twelve months should continue, beginning it now, however, on the first day of the Arabian year in which Muḥammad had made his *Hijra* or migration from Mecca to Medina, namely 16 July AD 622. Furthermore, ʿUmar added days to the alternate lunar months, and also an additional day to the final month of the year every three years (such a leap year being called a *sana kabīsa*). Thus the lunar year normally consisted of 354 days grouped into twelve months alternately of twenty-nine and thirty days, but, in a *kabīsa* year, it consisted of 355 days. The *Hijrī* months therefore do not correspond with the four seasons of the year, as do the Christian Gregorian or the Jewish months, but begin slightly earlier, by approximately eleven days each solar year. For instance, the month of Ramaḍān 1387 began on 3 December 1967. Because of the eleven days' disparity, the next Ramaḍān began on 22 November 1968. It is taking about thirty-two and a half Christian-era years before Ramaḍān will begin again in early December (in fact, 9 December 1999 = 1 Ramaḍān 1420). In this way, the 100 years in a Muslim-era century are approximately equal to ninety-seven Christian years.

It has been difficult and tedious to convert quickly from Christian to *Hijrī* dates and vice versa by arithmetical means, so recourse has traditionally been made to conversion tables.[5] (The present availability of instantaneous computer programs for converting dates now makes this easy for the scholar sitting in his study with a computer, but tables in book form will doubtless continue to be the most convenient way of finding equivalents for the traveller or the worker in the field viewing such epigraphic texts as inscriptions on tombstones or dedications on buildings.) In fact, a shifting lunar calendar has obvious disadvantages for the fixing of recurrent agricultural operations or financial transactions, and solar calendars soon came into use in the Islamic world for these practical purposes. Today, most of the Islamic world follows the European Gregorian calendar for purely secular and everyday purposes. Iran and Afghanistan, however, have since the earlier decades of the twentieth century used a solar *Hijrī* year, namely one having as its starting point the year of Muḥammad's *Hijra* (AD 622) but calculated thereafter on a solar basis. However, the primary records for Islamic history up to the nineteenth century (and, in certain regions, into the twentieth century), whether written in manuscripts and produced in the shape of early printed or lithographed books, or in numismatic and epigraphic legends, are almost invariably dated in the *Hijrī* system, so that dates of accessions, deaths, durations of reigns, etc., are here given in it.

Since the Christian and Muslim years hardly ever correspond, it follows that it is impossible to give equivalent Christian dates for historical events in the Islamic world with complete accuracy unless the month and day of the *Hijrī* year are known (strictly speaking, one needs also to know the exact time of day for an event, given the fact that Muslims, like Jews, calculated the beginning of a day not from midnight but from sunset on the previous evening). But although some mediaeval Islamic historians were remarkably accurate over the pinpointing of events, others were not, and might give only the year of an occurrence; inscriptions are usually exactly dated, but coins only occasionally give the month of their minting. Hence in this book, I have followed two basic principles in giving the Christian equivalent of Muslim dates (and in a very few cases – see below – when giving the Muslim equivalent of Christian dates).

First, where possible I have ascertained from my sources the exact day, or at least the month, of the event during the year in question, and have converted to the Christian era on this basis. Zambaur gave only Muslim-era dates, with citation of the exact day and month where possible, and did not give Christian-era equivalents; Lane-Poole gave dates in both eras, and explained that his basic principle was to cite the Christian year in which the *Hijrī* year in question began, except that when the *Hijrī* year began towards the close of a Christian year he gave the following AD year (*The Mohammadan Dynasties*, p. vii n.*), and this he regarded as adequate for practical purposes. Second, where exact information on the day or month is lacking in my sources, I have simply taken the equivalent Christian year as the one in which the greater part of the Muslim year fell; and if the Muslim year began halfway through the Christian year (i.e. at the end of June or the beginning of July), I have taken the Christian year as the one in which the first half of the Muslim year fell. As with Lane-Poole's system, the equivalents arrived at this way are clearly not always going to be right, but this procedure seems to me in the present context preferable to the cumbersome citation of two Christian years. Thus I have written 741/1340 instead of the more exact 741/1340–1.

The difficulties of correctly setting forth the Christian- and Muslim-era dates are one thorny aspect of Islamic chronology. Another one arises from the often confused circumstances of rulers' succession to power. The great Arabic chroniclers, such as al-Ṭabarī and ʿIzz al-Dīn Ibn al-Athīr (on the latter of whom Zambaur relied heavily for his dating of pre-thirteenth-century dynasties of the Middle Eastern heartlands – cf. his *Manuel*, pp. v–vi), were often wonderfully exact in recording dates, on occasion down to the very time of day when events occurred; but, when one goes out beyond the major dynasties of the heartlands, sources often grow sparse and at times barely exist. Sometimes the literary evidence contradicts that of coin legends and of inscriptions; in this connection, it is well known that such monetary and epigraphic texts do not always reflect reality but might be struck or carved for tendentious, propaganda purposes, and hence be at variance with what was really happening. Even when all the relevant dates are known, it may be difficult to decide which one to choose as an exact accession date. In mediaeval Christendom, the actual accession of a monarch was usually followed by a formal coronation. In mediaeval England, it came to involve both the secular and religious sealing of approval (the Recognition and the Anointing, followed by the Crowning), and the whole act might take place several months after actual accession (in regard to Edgar of Mercia during Anglo-Saxon times, fourteen years later!). The Islamic equivalent of such a ceremony was the official offering by the great men of state and representatives of the religious institution of the *bayʿa*, literally 'hand clasping' (cf. the mediaeval European *manumissio*), by which fealty was pledged (the act of *mubāyaʿa*). Or such pledging might take place at the formal ceremony of *julūs*, the ruler's 'seating' on his throne (*ʿarsh, sarīr*), often accompanied by his publicly taking up and flourishing such insignia of royalty as a sword (*al-taqlīd bi 'l-sayf*, in Ottoman Turkish *qīlīch qushanmasī*), or a sceptre/rod (*qaḍīb, khayzurān*) or staff (*ʿaṣā*), in the case of the Umayyad and ʿAbbāsid caliphs, with whom the rod or staff in question was assumed to be a legacy from the Prophet Muḥammad himself.[6] The date when a claimant first seized power, occupying the capital or a major part of the kingdom, would obviously be anterior to such ceremonies; is this, then, to be considered as the start of a reign? Also, among the early Ottomans, up to c. AD 1600, for instance, there was often a slight interregnum between the death of a sultan, during which the throne was technically unoccupied, and the new incumbent taking the throne. The demise of the previous ruler was meanwhile concealed from the public until the heir to the throne, the *walī 'l-ʿahd*, could return from his provincial governorship and assume power in the capital, the great fear being of an outbreak of disorder and civil strife between rival claimants.[7] Moreover, a first *julūs* might be followed by a second ceremony, as sometimes happened among the Il Khānids of Persia, when the Great Khān in distant Qaraqorum or Peking signified his approval and assent to the succession to power of the provincial Khāns, his theoretical subordinates; thus the Il Khān Arghun was enthroned in 683/1284 after the execution of his uncle Aḥmad Tegüder, but a second ceremony took place twenty months later in 685/1286 when a *yarligh* or document containing the Great Khān Qubilay's agreement had arrived.[8]

Nor can one always rely on having *Hijrī* dates available for constructing a dynastic chronology. Several of the dates of the Naṣrid kings of Granada during the last century of that dynasty's existence, the fifteenth century, are known only from Castilian Spanish chronicles, coins being known for only a few of the rulers of that time. For the chronology of some of the minor states of the Indian Ocean shores, peninsular India, Malaysia and Indonesia, Portuguese and then Dutch and British historical information is important. West African dynasties like Mali, Songhay and the sultans in Hausaland often handed down king-lists which have to be correlated, as far as possible, with the *Hijrī* dates.

Yet another difficulty in setting down the names of rulers in a consistent yet intelligible form arises from the complex system of Arabic and Islamic nomenclature, especially where rulers and great men of state were concerned. As well as the given name (*ism*) – these names being rather limited in number – all Muslims (even children, before they could biologically become fathers or mothers) could have a patronymic (*kunya*), composed of Abū 'father of …' or Umm 'mother of …'. They might further have a *nisba*, indicating profession, religious or legal affiliation, place of origin of the holder or of his family, etc., for example al-Sarrāj 'the saddler', al-Ḥanafī 'follower of the law school of Abū Ḥanīfa', al-Dimashqī 'the man from Damascus', etc. Any Muslim might also have a nickname (*nabaz*, *laqab*), such as Ta'abbaṭa Sharran 'he who carries an evil under his arm', or al-Akhṭal 'having a fleshy and pendulous ear, a cauliflower ear'. Additionally, as time went on, the ruler himself, and members of the ruling classes, military or civilian, would almost certainly have an honorific title or nickname, also called a *laqab*, for example Dhu 'l-Riyāsatayn 'possessor of the two functions [civil and military]' or Jalāl al-Dawla 'exalted one of the state'. Any one or other of all these elements might be the one by which a person was generally or best known (his or her *shuhra*), and the *shuhra*s of mediaeval times might not always be the ones by which a person is best known today; thus classical Arabic sources more often refer to the poet al-Mutanabbī by his *kunya* of Abu 'l-Ṭayyib.[9]

From the tenth century AD onwards, honorific titles of this type began to proliferate among the holders of power, eventually extending to religious scholars and literary figures, with an inevitable cheapening of their significance. The study of this titulature is a fascinating one for the historian or epigrapher or numismatist, and can often throw significant light on historical events and trends.[10] But the piling-up of increasingly grandiloquent honorifics in the titulature of a single ruler poses problems for the Islamic chronologer. Not infrequently, these titles become so long-winded and numerous that a choice has to be made: which one(s) to include in a book such as the present one? One factor involved is the question of the names by which a ruler was and still is best known. In some instances, the choice is easy; thus Maḥmūd of Ghazna is best known as holder of the *laqab* Yamīn al-Dawla. For others, the choice is less obvious. In the 1967 *Islamic Dynasties*, I tended to give simplified versions of long strings of titles, setting down the one or ones which seemed to me the most familiar and the most significant for identification and differentiation purposes. In the *New Islamic Dynasties*, I have been more generous in recording honorifics; and, as well as giving the *ism* in the first place, I have always added the *kunya*, where known, and have endeavoured to display the *nasab* or string of filiation for at least one generation back, for example Aḥmad b. al-Ḥasan, or for more than one generation back when this is necessary for clarity or identificatory purposes, for example Aḥmad b. al-Ḥasan b. Jaʿfar. This should in many cases enable the construction of a *nasab* for a dynasty, always assuming that there is father–son or grandfather–son or ruler–brother, etc., succession. Of course, such neat succession is far from general in Islam, and questions of succession might frequently be settled by the interposition of the sword. Also, at the outset of the new faith and society, there still survived the feeling that the inheritance of power should be by any capable male relative within a clan or family; only with the ʿAbbāsid caliphs did father–son succession beome more usual, though by no means universal. When Turkish and then Turco-Mongol dynasties appeared in later mediaeval times, tribal customs and a patrimonial conception of the sharing of power often led to succession not necessarily by a son but possibly by other members of the ruling family. When this occurred within a dynasty, I have tried to indicate the relationship of the new ruler to his predecessor by giving the kin connection, where this is known.

Clearly, the ideal would be to have genealogical tables, as had Lane-Poole, Barthold, Zambaur and Khalīl Ed'hem. Alas, the days when publishers were willing to lavish space and to swallow the typographical complications involved in the construction of genealogical stemmas, let alone to countenance hand-inserted fold-out tables, are now past. The attempt which I have made to show genealogical filiation by giving two or more terms in a *nasab* represents a second-best compared with the provision of spaciously set-out tables, but I hope that my practice here will go some way to obviate the sort of criticism made, with some justice, of the 1967 book, that it was a chronological handbook but not a genealogical one.

The Arabic-type names of the early lines of rulers in the Arabic heartlands of the Middle East and North Africa present the problems of arrangement and choice touched upon above. The Iranian names found among many of the Kurdish, Daylamī and Caucasian dynasties which rose to prominence during what the late V. Minorsky called 'the Iranian intermezzo' of the tenth to the twelfth centuries AD at times present problems where dialectical and hypocoristic forms of names are involved; here, recourse to such a work as Justi's *Iranisches Namenbuch* is available. From the eleventh century onwards, dynasties of Turkish military slave or tribal origin, followed by Turco-Mongol ones from the thirteenth century onwards, rapidly spread across the northern tier of the Islamic world of Western and South Asia and of North Africa, so that rulers of Turkish origin eventually ruled most of the Islamic lands between Algiers in the west and Bengal and Assam in the east, extending as far south as Yemen in the Arabian peninsula and the Deccan in South India. The rendering of the Turkish names by which many of these holders of power were known involves yet more problems, for these names often appear in Arabic script in deformed, at times barely recognisable, versions. I have set down the correct Turkish and Mongol forms where this has been ascertainable; but, where there is considerable divergence between them and the Arabic orthography, this last is noted in parentheses, thus Hülegü (Hūlākū), Öljeytü (Ūljāytū), Negübey (Nīkpāy). However, I have left the familiar transliteration of the Turkish name Tīmūr as applied to the great conqueror, although the more correct rendering Temür is used for other possessors of this name, as in, for example, Toqay Temürids. Where Ottoman Turkish pronunciation of Arabic names produced forms somewhat divergent from the standard Arabic pronunciation of these names, these are likewise noted in parentheses, thus Muḥammad (Meḥemmed), 'Uthmān ('Othmān), Bāyazīd (Bāyezīd), Sulaymān (Süleymān). For the dynasties of sub-Saharan West and East Africa, the renderings of Arabic names in the indigenous languages have often been followed, thus Bukaru for Abū Bakr, Aliyu for 'Ālī. A similar procedure for the names of some of the Malaysian and Indonesian dynasties has been adopted.

I have attempted to make the indexes as full as possible, in order to facilitate identifying rulers, with cross-referencing where necessary; and I have further given standard, Europeanised forms such as Saladin and Tamerlane.

There remains the pleasant task of thanking various colleagues who have patiently answered queries or provided information from their own special fields in Islamic history. They include Professor Barbara Watson Andaya (Indonesia and Malaysia); Dr Mohamed Ben Madani (the Beys of Tunis); Professor A. D. H. Bivar (West Africa); Dr Peter Carey (Java); Dr E. van Donzel (Harar); Professor Antonio Fernández-Puertas (Muslim Spain); Dr Greville Freeman-Grenville (East Africa); Dr Peter Jackson (the Delhi Sultanate); Professor Irfan Habib (the Nawwābs of Bengal); Professor Alexander Knysh (post-Mongol Central Asia); Dr David Morgan (the Mongols); Professor Giovanni Oman (Sicily); Dr C. E. R. Pennell (Indonesia and Malaysia); Dr Muhammad Yusuf Siddiq (Bengal); and Professor G. Rex Smith (the Arabian peninsula). For help on numismatics, I am equally indebted to Mr Stephen Album, Mrs Helen Mitchell Brown, Dr J. Leyten and Mr William F. Spengler. Such libraries as the John Rylands University Library at Manchester, the Library of the School of Oriental and African Studies, London, the Indian Institute Library, Oxford, and the Heberden Coin Room Library in the Ashmolean Museum, Oxford, have provided much of the background literature. Dr Freeman-Grenville has also provided much wisdom in the thorny field of eras and chronology. Finally, it is a pleasure to have this new version of an old book, which was part of the Islamic Surveys series, appear from Edinburgh University Press, and I am grateful for much general encouragement from the series adviser, Dr Carole Hillenbrand and for the skill of the Press staff and their typesetters in coping with such a complex manuscript.

NOTES

1. See *The Islamic Dynasties*, Introduction, p. xi and n. 1.
2. It is duly acknowledged in what are now the two fullest and most up-to-date, standard works on world rulers and governments, G. C. Allen (ed.), *Rulers and Governments of the World*, 3 vols, London 1978 (chronological arrangement), and Peter Truhart, *Regents of Nations. Systematic Chronology of States and their Political Representatives in Past and Present: A Biographical Reference Book*, 3 vols. in 4 parts, Munich 1984–8 (arrangement by areas; vol. II covers Asia and Australia-Oceania). It may be noted that these works replace the pioneer, but largely outdated, book by A. M. H. J. Stokvis, *Manuel d'histoire, de généalogie et de chronologie de tous les états du globe*, 3 vols, Leiden 1888–91, and also B. Spuler (ed.), *Regenten und Regierungen der Welt*, 2nd edn, Würzburg 1962.
3. *The Islamic Dynasties*, pp. xi–xiii.
4. The brief general study by Philip Grierson, *Numismatics and History*, Historical Association pamphlets, General series no. G19, London 1951, is still well worth consulting.
5. These are accessible in several places, for example in C. H. Philips (ed.), *Handbook of Oriental History*, The Royal Historical Society, London 1951, 33–40; Sir Thomas W. Haig, *Comparative Tables of Muhammadan and Christian Dates*, London 1932; H. G. Cattenoz, *Tables de concordance des ères chrétiennes et hégiriennes*, Rabat 1954; V. V. Tsybulskiy, *Sovremennye kalendari stran blizhnetsa i srednogo vostoka*, Moscow 1964; G. S. P. Freeman-Grenville, *The Islamic and Christian Calendars* AD *622–2222 (*AH*1–1650). A Complete Guide for Converting Christian and Islamic Dates and Dates of Festivals*, Garnet Publishing, Reading 1995 (= a new version of his *The Muslim and Christian Calendars*, first published London 1963, including corrections which the author was not allowed to make to the first edition and its reprint). The fullest

treatment, including not only the *Hijrī* calendar but also the various other eras in use in the Middle East and the Iranian lands at various times, is by F. Wüstenfeld and E. Mahler, *Vergleichungs-Tabellen zur islamischen und iranischen Zeitrechnung*, 3rd edn, revised by J. Mayr and B. Spuler, Wiesbaden 1961.

6. Dr Freeman-Grenville has pointed out to me that, at Kilwa in East Africa (see below, no. 62), the formal Recognition was by mention in the Friday *khuṭba*.
7. See A. D. Alderson, *The Structure of the Ottoman Dynasty*, Oxford 1956, 37–45.
8. See EIr, art. 'Argūn Khan' (Peter Jackson).
9. An excellent survey of the Arabic name and its component parts was begun by L. Caetani and G. Gabrieli in their *Onomasticon arabicum ossia repertorio alfabetico dei nomi di persona e di luogo contenuti nelle principali opere storiche, biografiche e geographiche, stampate e manoscritto, relative all'Islām. I Fonti – Introduzione*, Rome 1915, but unfortunately the project lapsed for over half a century. It has now happily been taken up again by an international team based in Paris, under the direction of Mme Jacqueline Sublet, who are producing fascicules of the new *Onomasticon* and a series of *Cahiers d'onomastique arabe*. For the most up-to-date, detailed and scholarly treatment of the name in Arabic, including the cultural, literary and historical aspects, see now Jacqueline Sublet, *Le voile du nom. Essai sur le nom propre arabe*, Paris 1991, and, in a rather briefer compass, Annemarie Schimmel, *Islamic Names*, Edinburgh 1989. For the *laqab* in particular, see the article s.v. in EI[2] (C. E. Bosworth).
10. Thus P. Guichard has recently suggested that the form of the favoured *laqab* of the ʿĀmirid *ḥājib* Ibn Abī ʿĀmir in late tenth-century Muslim Spain, al-Manṣūr *tout court*, and of the similar honorifics of the members of the ʿĀmirid family who followed him (see below, Chapter Two, no. 4), reflects their limited pretensions to fully legitimate sovereignty in the Umayyad caliphate; the later Spanish Umayyads, like their rivals the ʿAbbāsids, used honorifics of this type, but with such complements expressing divine help or dependence on God as *bi 'llāh* or *ʿalā 'llāh*. See his '*Al-Manṣūr* ou *al-Manṣūr bi llāh*? Les *laqab*/s des ʿĀmirides d'après la numismatique et les documents officiels', *Archéologie Islamique*, 5 (1995), 47–53.

Post-scriptum

A French translation of the original *Islamic Dynasties* by Yves Thoraval, *Les dynasties musulmanes*, has recently appeared from Editions Sindbad, Paris 1996, 340 pp., with some slight updating of the entries on dynasties surviving into the last third of the present century and some new bibliographical references, mainly intended for a Francophone readership.

ONE
The Caliphs
1

THE RIGHTLY-GUIDED OR 'PATRIARCHAL' OR 'ORTHODOX' CALIPHS (AL-KHULAFĀ' AL-RĀSHIDŪN)
11–40/632–61

11/632	Abū Bakr ʿAtīq, Ibn Abī Quḥāfa, al-Ṣiddīq
13/634	Abū Ḥafṣ ʿUmar (I) b. al-Khaṭṭāb, al-Fārūq
23/644	Abū ʿAmr or Abū ʿAbdallāh or Abū Laylā ʿUthmān b. ʿAffān, Dhu 'l-Nūrayn
35–40/656–61	Abu 'l-Ḥasan ʿAlī b. Abī Ṭālib, al-Imām al-Murtaḍā
40/661	*Umayyad caliphs*

On the Prophet Muḥammad's death at Medina in 11/632, four of his Companions, all closely related to him either through marriage or through blood, succeeded him as temporal leaders of the infant Muslim *umma* or community. They assumed the title of *Khalīfa* or Caliph (literally, 'he who follows behind, successor'), with responsibility for the upholding and spreading of the new faith and the well-being of Muḥammad's people, and – at least in the case of the first three of these caliphs – general recognition as the interpreters of the faith and religious leaders of the community.

Abū Bakr was the father of the Prophet's virgin wife and favourite, ʿĀ'isha, and was one of his oldest and most trusted supporters. It was he who imposed the authority of the capital Medina over the outlying parts of the Arabian peninsula, such as Najd, Baḥrayn, Oman (ʿUmān) and Yemen, after many of the Bedouin tribes had renounced their personal allegiance to Muḥammad (the *Ridda* Wars). ʿUmar's daughter Ḥafṣa was also a wife of the Prophet, and it was under ʿUmar's vigorous direction that the martial energies of the desert Arabs were turned outside the peninsula against the Byzantine territories of Syria, Palestine and Egypt and against the Sāsānid Persian ones of Iraq and Persia. ʿUmar was also a capable organiser, and both the introduction of a rudimentary civil administration for the conquered provinces and the invention of the register or *dīwān* system for paying the Arab warriors' stipends are attributed to him. It was he who abandoned the increasingly clumsy title of 'Successor of the Successor of the Messenger of God' in favour of the simple term 'caliph' and who further adopted the designation of *Amīr al-Mu'minīn* 'Commander of the Faithful', perhaps implying a spiritual as well as a purely secular, political element in his leadership.

ʿUthmān was, through his wife Ruqayya, the Prophet's son-in-law, and was elected caliph after ʿUmar's murder by a small council (*shūrā*) of the leading Companions, but his reign ended in a rebellion by discontented elements and his death in 35/656. This assassination inaugurated a period of strife and counter-strife (*fitna*, literally 'temptation, trial [of the believer's faith]'), and for this reason it was later often referred to as *al-Bāb al-maftūḥ* 'the door opened [to civil warfare]'. The last of the Rightly-Guided Caliphs, 'Alī, was doubly related to Muḥammad as his cousin and, through his marriage to Fāṭima, as his son-in-law, and as a child had been brought up with the Prophet. Thus in the eyes of certain pious circles, those who later formed the nucleus of the *shīʿat ʿAlī* or 'party of ʿAlī' (or simply, the Shīʿa), he was particularly well fitted to succeed to the Prophet's heritage. But he was never able to enforce his authority all though the Islamic lands, for Syria and then Egypt were controlled by Muʿāwiya, governor of Syria (see below, no. 2). ʿAlī moved his capital out of the Arabian peninsula to Kūfa in Iraq, and attempted to rally the Arab tribesmen of Iraq to his side. He confronted Muʿāwiya in battle at Ṣiffīn on the upper Euphrates in 37/657, but had no decisive success. He was murdered in 40/661 by one of the Khārijīs, a radical, egalitarian group which had seceded from ʿAlī's army; his son al-Ḥasan half-heartedly succeeded to the caliphate in Iraq, but was speedily bought out by Muʿāwiya and renounced his rights to the caliphate, which now passed to the Umayyads (see below, no. 2).

In later centuries, the age of the first four caliphs came to be regarded, through a somewhat romantic and pious haze, as a Golden Age when faith, justice and the pristine Islamic virtues flourished. Hence the title 'rightly-guided' was applied to them, thereby distinguishing them from their successors the Umayyads, who in the eyes of the religious classes came to be regarded as impious and worldly *mulūk* 'kings' rather than religiously-inspired leaders of the community.

Lane-Poole, 3–5, 9; Zambaur, 3.

EI[1] 'ʿOmar b. al-Khaṭṭāb', 'ʿOthmān b. ʿAffān' (G. Levi Della Vida), *EI*[2] 'Abū Bakr' (W. Montgomery Watt), 'ʿAlī b. Abī Ṭālib' (L. Veccia Vaglieri).

L. Veccia Vaglieri, 'The Patriarchal and Umayyad caliphates', in P. M. Holt, A. K. S. Lambton and B. Lewis (eds), *The Cambridge History of Islam*, Cambridge 1970, I, 57–103.

H. Kennedy, *The Prophet and the Age of the Caliphs, The Islamic Near East from the Sixth to the Eleventh Century*, London 1986, 50–81, with genealogical table at p. 402.

A. Noth, 'Früher Islam', in U. Haarmann (ed.), *Geschichte der arabischen Welt*, Munich 1987, 11–100.

2

THE UMAYYAD CALIPHS
41–132/661–750

1. The Sufyānids

⌀ 41/661	Abū ʿAbd al-Raḥmān Muʿāwiya I b. Abī Sufyān
60/680	Abū Khālid Yazīd I b. Muʿāwiya
64/683	Muʿāwiya II b. Yazīd I

2. The Marwānids

64/684	Abū ʿAbd al-Malik Marwān I b. al-Ḥakam
⌀ 65/685	Abu ʾl-Walīd ʿAbd al-Malik b. Marwān I, Abu ʾl-Mulūk
⌀ 86/705	Abu ʾl-ʿAbbās al-Walīd I b. ʿAbd al-Malik
⌀ 96/715	Abū Ayyūb Sulaymān b. ʿAbd al-Malik
⌀ 99/717	Abū Ḥafṣ ʿUmar (II) b. ʿAbd al-ʿAzīz
⌀ 101/720	Abu Khālid Yazīd II b. ʿAbd al-Malik,
⌀ 105/724	Abu ʾl-Walīd Hishām b. ʿAbd al-Malik
⌀ 125/743	Abu ʾl-ʿAbbās al-Walīd II b. Yazīd II
⌀ 126/744	Abū Khālid Yazīd III b. al-Walīd I
⌀ 126/744	Ibrāhīm b. al-Walīd I, k. 132/750
⌀ 127–32/744–50	Abū ʿAbd al-Malik Marwān II b. Muḥammad, al-Jaʿdī al-Ḥimār
132/750	*ʿAbbāsid caliphs*

Muʿāwiya followed ʿAlī and al-Ḥasan as caliph of the Muslims, having adopted the cry of 'Vengeance for ʿUthmān' against ʿAlī and his regicide supporters (Muʿāwiya and ʿUthmān were kinsmen, both of them belonging to the Meccan clan of Umayya or ʿAbd Shams). Muʿāwiya had governed Syria for twenty years, and had led the warfare by land and sea against the Byzantines; he consequently had a disciplined and well-trained army to set against the anarchic Bedouins of Iraq who formed the bulk of ʿAlī's support. He thus inaugurates the first branch of the Umayyads, the Sufyānids; on the death of the ephemeral caliph Muʿāwiya II, the caliphate passed – after a period of crisis when it seemed that leadership of the community might go to the Zubayrids, the family of another of Muḥammad's most prominent Companions – to Marwān I, belonging to a parallel branch of the Umayyads, from whom all the subsequent caliphs of the dynasty (and also the Spanish Umayyads: see below, no. 4) descended.

The three greatest caliphs of the dynasty, Muʿāwiya, ʿAbd al-Malik and Hishām, each reigned for some twenty years from their capital Damascus, and proved first-class administrators of the empire which the Arabs were conquering. With no precedents for a theory of Islamic government over vast territories and ethnically and confessionally heterogeneous populations, but with a dynamic leadership and a system of society which moved from early rigidity to a more flexible form, the Umayyads were necessarily innovators here. Among other things, they were concerned to adapt and to incorporate within their system of government the administrative practices of the Greeks and Persians whose former lands they now ruled over; the later Umayyad period seems to witness the introduction of several Sāsānid techniques and manners, a process which was to accelerate under the ʿAbbāsids. Military expansion proceeded apace, above all, in the reign of al-Walīd I, even though the easiest conquests had now been made and the Arab troops had to campaign in remote, often mountainous regions and in harsh climatic conditions; nor did plunder come in so easily as in the first stages of Arab conquest. All of North Africa west of Egypt was occupied, and Muslim raiders passed across the Straits of Gibraltar into Spain, subsequently surmounting the Pyrenees and raiding into late Merovingian and Carolingian France. From Egypt, pressure was exerted against the Christian kingdoms of Nubia. Beyond the Caucasus, contact was made with the Turkish Khazars, and the Greek frontiers in south-eastern Anatolia and Armenia were harried. On the eastern Persian fringes, Khwārazm was invaded and Transoxania gradually conquered for Islam against the strenuous opposition of native Iranian rulers and their Turkish allies. Finally, an Arab governor penetrated through Makrān into Sind, implanting Islam for the first time on Indian soil. All these conquests not only increased the taxative resources of the empire but also brought in large numbers of slaves and clients; the use of this labour enabled the minority of Arabs in the empire to live off the conquered lands as a rentier class and to exploit some of the economic potential of regions like the Fertile Crescent.

Yet territorial expansion and economic and administrative progress did not prevent the fall of the Umayyad régime. Within the heartlands, the caliphs faced the unceasing opposition of the Arab tribesmen of Iraq and of sectarian activists like the Khārijīs. The formation of a religious institution centred on Medina made the two Holy Cities of Arabia centres of pious opposition, especially as some of these elements favoured the claims to headship of the community of ʿAlī's descendants, the *Ahl al-Bayt* or 'House of the Prophet', who regarded themselves as the Imāms or divinely-designated inheritors of the prophetic charge. It was not, as anti-Umayyad views which emerged under their supplanters, the ʿAbbāsids, were later to allege, that the Umayyad caliphs were mere kings, hostile to Islamic religion and introducers of the foreign practice of hereditary succession in the state. We can now discern that the Umayyads had an exalted view of the religious nature of their charge, not just as successors of the Prophet but as God's own deputies, implied by their title *Khalīfat Allāh* 'God's Caliph', and considered themselves fully competent to form and to interpret the nascent Islamic doctrine. But social tensions appeared within the caliphate at large. New classes, such as the *Mawālī* or clients, converts to Islam from the formerly subject populations, began to seek a more satisfactory social and political role within the *umma* commensurate with their numbers and their skills. Various discontents were skilfully exploited by members of a rival Meccan clan to the Umayyads, that of the descendants of the Prophet's uncle al-ʿAbbās. Hence after 128/746 there began in the Khurasan or eastern Persia a revolutionary movement led by an agitator of genius, Abū Muslim. The anti-Umayyad forces gained military victory and, with the claims of the ʿAlids to the imamate speedily elbowed aside, the ʿAbbāsids succeeded to the caliphate in 132/750 (see below, no. 3). In a general massacre of the defeated Umayyads, one of the few members of the family to survive was Hishām's grandson ʿAbd al-Raḥmān; he escaped to North Africa and eventually founded in Spain a fresh, much longer-lived line of Umayyads (see below, no. 4).

Lane-Poole, 4–6, 9; Zambaur, 3 and Table F; Album, 7–11.
EI[1] 'Umaiyads' (G. Levi Della Vida).
Veccia Vaglieri, 'The Patriarchal and Umayyad caliphates', in *The Cambridge History of Islam*, I, 57–103.
H. Kennedy, *The Prophet and the Age of the Caliphates. The Islamic Near East from the Sixth to the Eleventh Century*, 82–123, with genealogical table at p. 403.
G. R. Hawting, *The First Dynasty of Islam. The Umayyad Caliphate AD 661–750*, London 1986, with genealogical table at p. xv.
A. Noth, 'Früher Islam', in Haarmann (ed.), *Geschichte der arabischen Welt*, 11–100.

3

THE ʿABBĀSID CALIPHS
132–923/750–1517

1. The caliphs in Iraq and Baghdad 132–656/749–1258

⊘ 132/749	ʿAbdallāh b. Muḥammad al-Imām, Abu ʾl-ʿAbbās al-Saffāḥ
⊘ 136/754	ʿAbdallāh b. Muḥammad al-Imām, Abū Jaʿfar al-Manṣur
⊘ 158/775	Muḥammad b. al-Manṣūr, Abū ʿAbdallāh al-Mahdī
⊘ 169/785	Mūsā b. al-Mahdī, Abū Muḥammad al-Hādī
⊘ 170/786	Hārūn b. al-Mahdī, Abū Jaʿfar al-Rashīd
⊘ 193/809	Muḥammad b. al-Rashīd, Abū Mūsā al-Amīn
⊘ 189/813	ʿAbdallāh b. al-Rashīd, Abū Jaʿfar al-Maʾmūn
⊘ *201–3/817–19*	*Ibrāhīm b. al-Mahdī, in Baghdad, d. 224/839*
⊘ 218/833	Muḥammad b. al-Rashīd, Abū Isḥāq al-Muʿtaṣim
⊘ 227/842	Hārūn b. al-Muʿtaṣim, Abū Jaʿfar al-Wāthiq
⊘ 232/847	Jaʿfar b. al-Muʿtaṣim, Abu ʾl-Faḍl al-Mutawakkil
⊘ 247/861	Muḥammad b. al-Mutawakkil, Abū Jaʿfar al-Muntaṣir
⊘ 248/862	Aḥmad b. Muḥammad, Abu ʾl-ʿAbbās al-Mustaʿīn
⊘ 252/866	Muḥammad b. al-Mutawakkil, Abū ʿAbdallāh al-Muʿtazz
⊘ 255/869	Muḥammad b. al-Wāthiq, Abū Isḥāq al-Muhtadī
⊘ 256/870	Aḥmad b. al-Mutawakkil, Abu ʾl-ʿAbbās al-Muʿtamid
⊘ 279/892	Aḥmad b. al-Muwaffaq, Abu ʾl-ʿAbbās al-Muʿtaḍid
⊘ 289/902	ʿAlī b. al-Muʿtaḍid, Abū Muḥammad al-Muktafī
295/908	Jaʿfar b. al-Muʿtaḍid, Abu ʾl-Faḍl al-Muqtadir, first reign
296/908	*Ibn al-Muʿtazz al-Murtaḍā al-Muntaṣif, in Baghdad*
⊘ 296/908	Jaʿfar al-Muqtadir, second reign
317/929	Muḥammad b. al-Muʿtaḍid, Abū Manṣūr al-Qāhir, first reign, in Baghdad
317/929	Jaʿfar al-Muqtadir, third reign
⊘ 320/932	Muḥammad al-Qāhir, second reign, d. 339/950
⊘ 322/934	Aḥmad b. al-Muqtadir, Abu ʾl-ʿAbbās al-Rāḍī
⊘ 329/940	Ibrāhīm b. al-Muqtadir, Abū Isḥāq al-Muttaqī, d. 357/968
⊘ 333/944	ʿAbdallāh b. al-Muktafī, Abu ʾl-Qāsim al-Mustakfī, d. 338/949
⊘ 334/946	al-Faḍl b. al-Muqtadir, Abu ʾl-Qāsim al-Muṭīʿ, d. 364/974
⊘ 363/974	ʿAbd al-Karīm b. al-Muṭīʿ, Abu ʾl-Faḍl al-Ṭāʾiʿ, d. 393/1003
⊘ 381/991	Aḥmad b. Isḥāq, Abu ʾl-ʿAbbās al-Qādir
⊘ 422/1031	ʿAbdallāh b. al-Qādir, Abū Jaʿfar al-Qāʾim
⊘ 467/1075	ʿAbdallāh b. Muḥammad, Abu ʾl-Qāsim al-Muqtadī
⊘ 487/1094	Aḥmad b. al-Muqtadī, Abu ʾl-ʿAbbās al-Mustaẓhir
⊘ 512/1118	al-Faḍl b. al-Mustaẓhir, Abū Manṣūr al-Mustarshid
⊘ 529/1135	al-Manṣūr b. al-Mustarshid, Abū Jaʿfar al-Rāshid
⊘ 530/1136	Muḥammad b. al-Mustaẓhir, Abū ʿAbdallāh al-Muqtafī
⊘ 555/1160	Yūsuf b. al-Muqtafī, Abu ʾl-Muẓaffar al-Mustanjid
⊘ 566/1170	al-Ḥasan b. al-Mustanjid, Abū Muḥammad al-Mustaḍīʾ
⊘ 575/1180	Aḥmad b. al-Mustaḍīʾ, Abu ʾl-ʿAbbās al-Nāṣir

⊘ 622/1225	Muḥammad b. al-Nāṣir, Abū Naṣr al-Ẓāhir
⊘ 623/1226	al-Manṣūr b. al-Ẓāhir, Abū Ja'far al-Mustanṣir
⊘ 640–56/1242–58	'Abdallāh b. al-Mustanṣir, Abū Aḥmad al-Musta'ṣim
⊘ *656/1258*	*Mongol sack of Baghdad*

2. The caliph in Aleppo, Ḥarrān and northern Syria 659–60/1261

⊘ 659–60/1261	Aḥmad b. al-Ḥasan, Abu 'l-'Abbās al-Ḥākim I
661/1262	*Transfer to Cairo*

3. The caliphs in Cairo 659–923/1261–1517

659–60/1261	Aḥmad b. al-Ẓāhir, Abu 'l-Qāsim al-Mustanṣir
661/1262	Aḥmad b. al-Ḥasan, Abu 'l-'Abbās al-Ḥākim I
701/1302	Sulaymān b. al-Ḥākim I, Abū Rabī'a al-Mustakfī I
740/1340	Ibrāhīm b. Muḥammad al-Mustamsik, Abū Isḥāq al-Wāthiq I
741/1341	Aḥmad b. al-Mustakfī I, Abu 'l-'Abbās al-Ḥākim II
753/1352	Abū Bakr b. al-Mustakfī I, Abu 'l-Fatḥ al-Mu'taḍid I
763/1362	Muḥammad b. al-Mu'taḍid I, Abū 'Abdallāh al-Mutawakkil I, first reign
779/1377	Zakariyyā' b. al-Wāthiq I, Abū Yaḥyā al-Mu'taṣim, first reign
779/1377	Muḥammad al-Mutawakkil I, second reign
785/1383	'Umar b. al-Wāthiq I, Abū Ḥafṣ al-Wāthiq II
788/1386	Zakariyyā' al-Mu'taṣim, second reign
791/1389	Muḥammad al-Mutawakkil I, third reign
808/1406	'Abbās or Ya'qūb b. al-Mutawakkil I, Abu 'l-Faḍl al-Musta'īn (also in 815/1412 proclaimed sultan, see below, no. 31, 2)
816/1414	Dāwūd b. al-Mutawakkil I, Abu 'l-Fatḥ al-Mu'taḍid II
845/1441	Sulaymān b. al-Mutawakkil I, Abū Rabī'a al-Mustakfī II
855/1451	Ḥamza b. al-Mutawakkil I, Abū Bakr al-Qā'im
859/1455	Yūsuf b. al-Mutawakkil I, Abu 'l-Maḥāsin al-Mustanjid
884/1479	'Abd al-'Azīz b. al-Musta'īn, Abu 'l-'Izz al-Mutawakkil II
903/1497	Ya'qūb b. al-Mutawakkil II, Abu 'l-Ṣabr al-Mustamsik, first reign
914/1508	al-Mutawakkil III b. al-Mustamsik, first reign
922/1516	Ya'qūb al-Mustamsik, second reign
923/1517	al-Mutawakkil III, second reign, d. in Istanbul
923/1517	*Ottoman conquest of Egypt*

The 'Abbāsids acquired the caliphate through what might be considered from one aspect as a power-struggle between rival Meccan families, since they stemmed from the family of the Prophet's uncle al-'Abbās, of the Meccan clan of Hāshim; and because of this descent they were able to claim a legitimacy in the eyes of the orthodox Sunnī religious classes which the Umayyads had lacked. Even so, during the first century of their power the 'Abbāsids had to contend with frequent revolts of the 'Alids, descendants of the two sons of 'Alī, al-Ḥasan and al-Ḥusayn, who were grandsons of Muḥammad and whom their partisans the Shī'a considered as having a better title to the caliphate and imamate, one based on a specific act of divinely-inspired designation by the Prophet. In self-defence, the apologists of the ʿAbbāsids stressed the superiority of descent through males over descent through females (since the ʿAlid claim was through Muḥammad's daughter Fāṭima), and the caliphs themselves soon adopted a system of honorific titles (*alqāb*, sing. *laqab*) when they each ascended the throne, a practice unknown to their Umayyad predecessors; these titles proclaimed dependence on God and claimed divine support for ʿAbbāsid rule. The theocratic nature of the new dynasty's power was gradually emphasised in other ways, and the orthodox religious institution enlisted as far as possible on the side of the ʿAbbāsids. Spreading into the sphere of practical government, there were also influences from the older Persian traditions of divine rulership and statecraft; for the ʿAbbāsid Revolution, while in origin an Arab movement, began on Persian soil and took advantage of certain Persian discontents. The shifting of the capital from Damascus in Syria to Iraq, eventually to Baghdad, symbolised the new eastward orientation of the caliphate, and over the next centuries Persian material and cultural practices and influences became increasingly evident within it.

The Islamic empire had virtually reached its full extent under the Umayyads, and, under the early ʿAbbāsids, the borders of the *Dār al-Islām* were almost static. Only a few of the caliphs distinguished themselves as military commanders in the field – al-Ma'mūn and al-Muʿtaṣim led successful expeditions into Anatolia against the Byzantines – and in the tenth and early eleventh centuries it was the Muslims who were forced on to the defensive by the vigorous Greek emperors of the Macedonian dynasty. Already in the ninth century, the political unity of the caliphate began to dissolve. A branch of the Umayyads, *a priori* hostile to the ʿAbbāsids, ruled in Spain (see below, no. 4), and North Africa was in general too distant to be controlled properly. Such lines of governors as the Ṭūlūnids in Egypt (see below, no. 25) and the Ṭāhirids and Sājids in Persia (see below, nos 82, 70) still behaved as faithful vassals of Baghdad, but their existence nevertheless paved the way for largely autonomous dynasties on the far eastern fringes of the Persian world, like the Sāmānids of Transoxania and the Ṣaffārids of Sistan (see below, nos 83, 84), who forwarded taxation to Baghdad only rarely or not at all. The effective authority of the ʿAbbāsids became reduced to central Iraq, above all, in the tenth century, when an aggressive political Shīʿism triumphed temporarily over a large part of the central and eastern lands of the caliphate. The Fāṭimids seized first North Africa and then Egypt and southern Syria (see below, no. 27), setting themselves up in Cairo as rival caliphs. In Iraq and western Persia, the Daylamī Būyids rose to power (see below, no. 75), entering Baghdad in 334/945 and reducing the ʿAbbāsids to the status of puppets, with almost nothing left save their moral and spiritual influence as heads of Sunnī Islam.

The situation was saved for the ʿAbbāsids and for Sunnī orthodoxy in general by the appearance in the Middle East in the eleventh century of the Turkish Seljuqs (see below, no. 91), but the Seljuqs, while upholders of the Sunna from the religious point of view, did not intend to let the political power of the caliphs revive to the detriment of the sultanate which they had just established. It was only in the twelfth century, when the family solidarity of the Great Seljuqs was impaired and their authority thereby enfeebled, that the fortunes of the ʿAbbāsids began to rise under such vigorous caliphs as al-Muqtafī and al-Nāṣir. This recovery in the effective power and moral influence was, however, cut short by the Mongol cataclysm, and in 656/1258 Hülegü's Mongol troops murdered the last ʿAbbāsid caliph to rule in Baghdad (see below, no. 133).

The first three centuries of ʿAbbāsid rule (eighth to eleventh centuries AD) saw the full flowering of mediaeval Islamic civilisation. Literature, theology, philosophy and the natural sciences all flourished, with fertilising influences coming in from Persia and the Hellenistic and Byzantine cultures. Economic and commercial progress was widespread, above all in the older, long-settled lands of Persia, the Fertile Crescent and Egypt, and trade links were established with outside regions like the Eurasian steppes, the Far East, India and black Africa. Despite political breakdown at the centre and tribal and sectarian violence during the tenth and eleventh centuries, this progress in the material and cultural fields continued, and it was in this regard apt for the Swiss orientalist Adam Mez to designate the tenth century that of the 'Renaissance of Islam'. Within the northern tier of the Middle East, incoming Turkmen nomads and subsequently-established Turkish dynasties brought extensive changes in such spheres as land utilisation and economic life, but were largely absorbed into the cultural and religious fabric of Islam; it was the Mongols, for several decades fierce enemies of Islam and bringers of a steppe way of life alien to the settled agricultural economies of the Middle East, who dealt more serious blows to the economic and social stability of Iraq and the Persian lands.

The Baghdad caliphate was thus extinguished by the Mongols, but soon afterwards the Mamlūk sultan of Egypt, Baybars (see below, no. 31, 1), himself decided to install a caliph, and invited Aḥmad al-Mustanṣir, an ostensible uncle of the last ʿAbbāsid of Baghdad, who had been held prisoner there but had been then released by the Mongols, to Cairo (659/1261), This caliph led an army in an unsuccessful bid to reconquer Baghdad, possibly dying in the attempt and certainly disappearing from further mention. Meanwhile, a further ʿAbbāsid, who seems genuinely to have been a descendant of al-Mustarshid, had in this same year been proclaimed caliph at Aleppo, with the backing of the Amīr Aqqush, as al-Ḥākim, subsequently installed in Cairo in 661/1262. The establishment of a caliph in Cairo served to legitimise Mamlūk rule and to increase Mamluk prestige in places as far apart as North Africa and Muslim India, and it was a moral weapon in the warfare against the Crusaders and the Mongols; furthermore the caliphs continued, as they had done in late ʿAbbāsid Baghdad, to act as heads of the *Futuwwa* or chivalric orders. But they had no practical power in the Mamlūk state, and there was certainly no idea of a division of power with the sultans. The last caliph, al-Mutawakkil III, was carried off to Istanbul in 923/1517 by the Ottoman conqueror Selīm the Grim, but the story that he then transferred his rights in the caliphate to the Turkish sultans is a piece of fiction originating in the nineteenth century.

The advent of the ʿAbbāsids in 132/749 saw a general elevation of the ruler's status and a formalising of the court ceremonial surrounding him, possibly as a reflection of the increased permeation of Persian cultural influences into ʿAbbāsid society mentioned above. Whereas the Umayyad caliphs had been content with their simple names as ruling designations, from the accession of al-Manṣūr onwards, the ʿAbbāsid caliphs adopted honorific titles expressing divine support for their rule, for example al-Mahdī 'the divinely-guided one' or emphasising the ruler's leading role in implementing God's plan for His world, for example al-Qā'im 'he who arises, undertakes [something]' or al-Ẓāhir 'he who makes prevail', usually with a complement such as *li-dīn Allāh* 'to/for God's religion' or *bi-amr Allāh* 'in the furtherance of God's affair/command'. Once the unity of the caliphate began to dissolve and provincial dynasties arose, lesser, local rulers began to emulate the caliphs and adorn themselves with high-flown, sonorous titles of this type, not infrequently ludicrously at variance with the actual significance of the bearers of them.

Lane-Poole, 6–8, 12–13; Zambaur, 4–5 and Table G; Album, 11–13.
EI[2] "'Abbāsids' (B. Lewis).
D. and J. Sourdel, *La civilisation de l'Islam classique*, Paris 1968, chs 2 and 3, 61–126.
D. Sourdel, 'The 'Abbāsid caliphate', in *The Cambridge History of Islam*, I, 104–39.
H. Kennedy, *The Early Abbasid Caliphate: A Political History*, London 1981.
idem, *The Prophet and the Age of the Caliphs. The Islamic Near East from the Sixth to the Eleventh Century*, 124–99, with genealogical table at p. 404.
T. Nagel, 'Das Kalifat der Abbasiden', in Haarmann (ed.), *Geschichte der arabischen Welt*, 101–65.
P. M. Holt, 'Some observations on the 'Abbāsid caliphate of Cairo', *Bulletin of the School of Oriental [and African] Studies*, 47 (1984), 501–7.
S. Heidemann, *Das Aleppiner Kalifat (A.D. 1261). Vom Ende des Kalifates in Bagdad über Aleppo zu den Restaurationen in Kairo*, Leiden 1994.

TWO
Spain
4

THE SPANISH UMAYYADS
138–422/756–1031

The Iberian peninsula, excepting the Christian kingdoms of the north

⌀ 138/756	ʿAbd al-Raḥmān I b. Muʿāwiya, Abu ʾl-Muṭarrif al-Dākhil
⌀ 172/788	Hishām I b. ʿAbd al-Raḥmān I, Abu ʾl-Walīd
⌀ 180/796	al-Ḥakam I b. Hishām I, Abu ʾl-ʿĀṣ
⌀ 206/822	ʿAbd al-Raḥmān II b. al-Ḥakam I, Abu ʾl-Muṭarrif al-Mutawassiṭ
⌀ 238/852	Muḥammad I b. ʿAbd al-Raḥmān II, Abū ʿAbdallāh
⌀ 273/886	al-Mundhir b. Muḥammad I, Abu ʾl-Ḥakam
⌀ 275/888	ʿAbdallāh b. Muḥammad I, Abū Muḥammad
⌀ 300/912	ʿAbd al-Raḥmān III b. Muḥammad, Abu ʾl-Muṭarrif al-Nāṣir
⌀ 350/961	al-Ḥakam II b. ʿAbd al-Raḥmān III, Abu ʾl-Muṭarrif al-Mustanṣir
⌀ 366/976	Hishām II b. al-Ḥakam II, Abu ʾl-Walīd al-Muʾayyad, first reign
⌀ 399/1009	Muḥammad II b. Hishām II, al-Mahdī, first reign
⌀ 400/1009	Sulaymān b. al-Ḥakam, al-Mustaʿīn, first reign
⌀ 400/1010	Hishām II, second reign
⌀ 403/1013	Sulaymān, second reign
407/1016	*ʿAlī Ibn Ḥammūd, al-Nāṣir, Ḥammūdid*
⌀ 408/1018	ʿAbd al-Raḥmān IV b. Muḥammad, al-Murtaḍā
408/1018	*al-Qāsim Ibn Ḥammūd, al-Maʾmūn, Ḥammūdid,* first time
412/1021	*Yaḥyā b. ʿAlī, al-Muʿtalī, Ḥammūdid,* first time
413/1023	*al-Qāsim, Ḥammūdid,* second time
⌀ 414/1023	ʿAbd al-Raḥmān V b. Hishām, al-Mustaẓhir
⌀ 414/1024	Muḥammad III b. ʿAbd al-Raḥmān, al-Mustakfī, k. 416/1025
416/1025	*Yaḥyā, Ḥammūdid,* second time
⌀ 418–22/1027–31	Hishām III b. Muḥammad, al-Muʿtadd, d. 428/1036
	Mulūk al-Ṭawāʾif

Arab and Berber troops crossed over the Straits of Gibraltar from Morocco to Spain in 92/711 and speedily overthrew the Visigoths, the Germanic military aristocracy who had ruled Spain until then. Over the next decades, the Muslim forces drove the remnants of the Visigoths into the Cantabrian Mountains of the extreme north of the Iberian peninsula, and even penetrated across the Pyrenees into Frankish Gaul, until Charles Martel defeated them just to the north of Poitiers, in the battle called by the Arabs that of Balāṭ al-Shuhadāʾ, in 114/732.

During these early years, Spain was ruled by a succession of Arab governors sent out from the east, as the most westerly province of the Islamic empire, called in the Arabic sources al-Andalus (almost certainly *not* from *Vandalicia, the land of the Vandals, whose passage through Spain over two centuries before had left virtually no traces, but more probably from a Germanic expression meaning 'share, parcel of land'). But in 138/756, ʿAbd al-Raḥmān I, later called *al-Dākhil* 'the Incomer', and one of the few Umayyads to have escaped slaughter in the ʿAbbāsid Revolution, appeared in Spain and founded the Umayyad amirate there.

In a peninsula where the facts of geography militated against central control and firm rule, the establishment of the Umayyad state was an achievement indeed. The amirate was based on Seville (Ishbīliya) and Cordova (Qurṭuba), but the Amīrs' hold on the outlying provinces was less secure. Although a good proportion of the Hispano-Roman population became Muslim (the *Muwalladūn*), a substantial number remained Christian (the *Mustaʿrabūn*, Mozarabs), and looked to the independent Christian north for moral and religious support. In particular, Toledo (Ṭulayṭila), the ancient capital of the Visigoths and the ecclesiastical centre of Spain, was a centre of rebelliousness. Among the Muslims, there were many local princes whose military strength as marcher lords enabled them to live virtually independently of the capital Cordova; these flourished above all in the Ebro valley of the north-east, the later Aragon and Catalonia (e.g. the Tujībids of Saragossa and the Banū Qasī of Tudela). In the later ninth century, there were two centres of prolonged rebellion against the central government by its own Muslim subjects, one around Badajoz under Ibn Marwān the Galician, and the other in the mountains of Granada under Ibn Ḥafṣūn.

Despite these weaknesses, and despite the continued existence of the petty Christian kingdoms of the north, the Spanish Umayyads made Cordova a remarkable centre of craft industries and trade, and as a home for Arabic culture, learning and artistic production it was inferior only to Baghdad and Cairo. The tenth century was dominated by ʿAbd al-Raḥmān III, called al-Nāṣir 'the Victorious', who reigned for fifty years (300–50/912–61). He raised the power of the monarchy to a new pitch; court ceremonial was made more elaborate, possibly with Byzantine practice in mind, and ʿAbd al-Raḥmān countered the pretensions of his enemies the Fāṭimids by himself adopting the titles of Caliph and Commander of the Faithful in place of the simple previous designation of Amīr. In this way, the rather vague ideological basis of the state, which had prevailed for over 150 years – in which the Umayyads had never been able to decide whether they were still a part, albeit peripheral, of the Islamic oecumene, or whether they were ruling over a localised, Iberian principality, Muslim in faith but turned inwards politically – was relinquished. ʿAbd al-Raḥmān now clearly set aside the doctrine of orthodox religious theory that the caliphate was one and indivisible. No longer relying primarily on the Andalusian Arab *jund*s or territorially-based military contingents, the Caliph built up the army's strength with fresh Berber tribesmen from North Africa and with slave troops brought from various parts of Christian Europe (the Ṣaqāliba). The Christians of the north were humbled and an anti-Fāṭimid policy pursued in North Africa. But after the death of al-Ḥakam II in 366/976, the succession devolved on minors and weaker candidates, so that real power in the state passed to the *Ḥājib* or chief minister Ibn Abī ʿAmir, called al-Manṣūr 'the Victorious' (the Almanzor of Christian sources); it was he who captured Barcelona and who on one occasion sacked the shrine of St James of Compostella in Galicia.

Yet early in the eleventh century, the ʿĀmirid *Ḥājib*s lost control and the Umayyad caliphate fell apart. Possible reasons for this have been much discussed by historians. It has been argued, for instance, that the numbers of Muslims in al-Andalus had increased by conversion from Christianity in ʿAbd al-Raḥmān III's reign so that the Muslims were perhaps for the first time a majority there and felt a new confidence from this strength and a greater feeling of control over the land; hence they no longer saw the necessity of a strong, central government as vital for the preservation of Islam in the Iberian peninsula. If this was the case, such confidence was misplaced. The last, ephemeral Umayyads could not maintain the primacy in the state of the old Andalusian Muslims, essentially Arabs and *Muwalladūn*, in face of the military strength of the Berbers and Ṣaqāliba. Their short reigns alternated with periods of rule by the Berberised Arab Ḥammūdids, local rulers in Malaga, Ceuta, Tangier and Algeciras (see below, no. 5, Taifas nos 1, 2). The Umayyads finally disappeared in 422/1031, and Muslim Spain fell into a period of political fragmentation, in the course of which various local chiefs and ethnic groups held power (the age of the *Mulūk al-Ṭawāʾif* or Reyes de Taifas: see below, no. 5); not until the coming of the Almoravids (see below, no. 14) at the end of the century did al-Andalus experience unity again.

Lane-Poole, 19–22; Zambaur, 3–4 and Table F; Album, 13–14.

EI[1] 'Umaiyads. II' (E. Lévi-Provençal).

G. C. Miles, *The Coinage of the Umayyads of Spain*, ANS Hispanic Numismatic Series, Monographs, no. 1, New York 1950.

E. Lévi-Provençal, *Histoire de l'Espagne musulmane*, Paris 1950–67, I–II, with Table at II, 346.

5

THE MULŪK AL-ṬAWĀ'IF OR REYES DE TAIFAS IN SPAIN

Fifth to early seventh century/eleventh to early thirteenth century

Central and southern Spain, Ceuta and the Balearic Islands

The seventy or eighty years or so between the end of the line of 'Āmirid *Ḥājib*s and the coming of the Almoravids saw the final collapse of the Umayyad dynasty and the formation of local principalities across Muslim Spain; yet, as has not infrequently happened in world history, political fragmentation was accompanied by great cultural brilliance.

The process began in the post-'Āmirid period of *fitna* or chaos, well before the disappearance of the Umayyads in 422/1031, with the main Taifa principalities firmly established by then. The former capital Cordova was never able to establish more than a local authority during these decades of the Taifas. Instead, there arose a mosaic of local powers, whose geographical centres David Wasserstein has listed as amounting to in effect thirty-nine, as follows (in alphabetical order):

1. Algeciras/al-Jazīra al-Khaḍrā' (the Ḥammūdids)
2. Almería/al-Mariya (the Banū Ṣumādiḥ)
3. Alpuente/al-Bunt (the Banu 'l-Qāsim)
4. Arcos/Arkush (the Banū Khazrūn)
5. Badajoz/Baṭalyaws (the Afṭasids)
6. Baza/Basṭa
7. Calatayud/Qal'at Ayyūb (the Hūdids)
8. Calatrava/Qal'at Rabāḥ
9. Carmona/Qarmūna (the Banū Birzāl)
10. Ceuta/Sabta (the Ḥammūdids)
11. Cordova/(Qurṭuba (the Jahwarids)
12. Denia/Dāniya (the Banū Mujāhid)
13. Majorca/Mayūrqa and the Balearic Islands/al-Jazā'ir al-Sharqiyya (the Banū Mujāhid and then governors for the North African dynasties and independent rulers of the Banū Ghāniya: see below, no. 6)
14. Granada/Gharnāṭa (the Zīrids)
15. Huelva/Walba or Awnaba and Saltes/Shaltīsh
16. Huesca/Washqa (the Hūdids)
17. Jaén/Jayyān
18. Lérida/Lārida (the Hūdids)
19. Majorca/Mayūrqa (the Banū Mujāhid)
20. Málaga/Mālaqa (the Ḥammūdids)
21. Medinaceli/Madīnat Sālim
22. Mértola/Martula
23. Morón/Mawrūr (the Banū Nūḥ)
24. Murcia/Mursiya (various rulers, including the Ṭāhirids)
25. Murviedro/Murbayṭar
26. Niebla/Labla and Gibraleón/Jabal al-'Uyūn (the Yaḥṣubids)

27. Ronda/Runda
28. La Sahla or Albarracin/al-Sahla (the Banū Razīn)
29. Santa Maria de Algarve/Shantamariya al-Gharb or Ocsonoba/Ukshūnuba (the Banū Hārūn)
30. Saragossa/Saraquṣṭa (the Tujībids and then Hūdids)
31. Segura/Shaqūra
32. Seville/Ishbīliya (the ʿAbbādids)
33. Silves/Shilb (the Banū Muzayn)
34. Toledo/Ṭulayṭila (the Dhu 'l-Nūnids)
35. Tortosa/Ṭurṭūsha
36. Tudela/Tuṭīla (the Hūdids)
37. Valencia/Balansiya (the ʿĀmirids)
38. Vilches/Bilj
39. Ḥiṣn al-Ashrāf

Some of these, especially in the more prosperous and settled south, south-east and east, were little more than city states, but others, like the Afṭasids of Badajoz in the south-west of the peninsula, the Dhu 'l-Nūnids of Toledo, on the far northern edge of Muslim territory, and the Hūdids in the Ebro valley, ruled large tracts of territory. The dynasties were of varying official background and race, reflecting the trends of later Umayyad times and of the ethnic rivalries of the various groups. Several sprang out of the old ʿĀmirid military élite and their clients. Some were from long-established Arab families, like the ʿAbbādids of Seville, the Banū Qāsim of Alpuente and the Hūdids of Saragossa. Others were Berber, like the Miknāsa Afṭasids and the Ḥawwāra Dhu 'l-Nūnids (whose original name was the Berber one of Zennun), or were Berberised Arabs like the Ḥammūdids (ultimately of Idrīsid origin) of Algeciras, Ceuta and Málaga; in several cases, these Berber Taifas sprang from the great influx of troops from North Africa brought about by Ibn Abī ʿĀmir towards the end of the tenth century, such as the Ṣanhāja Zīrids in Granada. In certain towns of the south-east and east, Ṣaqlabī commanders seized power, such as the initial rulers in Almeria, Badajoz, Murcia, Valencia and Tortosa, although the role of the Ṣaqāliba in Spain tended to fade out after the mid-eleventh century.

The larger Taifas pursued aggressive policies at the expense of their neighbours. The ʿAbbādids expanded almost to Toledo, and to further their designs at one stage resuscitated a man who claimed to be the last Umayyad caliph, Hishām III, thought to have died in obscurity after his deposition. Several of the Taifas were quite content to intrigue with or even to call in the Christians against their fellow-Muslims; the last Afṭasid, ʿUmar al-Mutawakkil, was ready, after the arrival in Spain of the Almoravids, to cede his possessions in central Portugal to Alfonso VI of Léon and Castile in return for help against the threatening Berber power.

Towards the end of the eleventh century, the tide was clearly flowing against the Muslims in Spain, a complete reversal of the situation a century or so before when the weak, petty kingdoms of northern Spain had paid tribute to the mighty Cordovan caliphate; now many of the Taifas were paying tribute, *parias*, to the Christian states and were in varying relations of vassalage to them. Toledo fell to Alfonso in 478/1085 as much through internal dissensions as through external attack. Appeals to the greatest Muslim power in the West, the Almoravids of Mauritania and Morocco, both from Taifa rulers and from the religious classes in Spain, seemed to be the only way out, but the victory of the Almoravids at Sagrajas or al-Zallāqa in 479/1086 proved to be the prelude to the sweeping-away of almost all the Taifas within a few years, the Hūdids in Saragossa alone preserving a tenuous independence until 503/1110.

In the interval between the collapse of Almoravid power in Spain and the assertion of Almohad control there after 540/1145 (see below, nos. 14, 15), short-lived Taifas were constituted in some places, e.g. at Valencia, Cordova, Murcia and Mértola; and after the decline of Almohad authority in Spain, local commanders were able to seize power in certain places, for example at Valencia, Niebla and, somewhat more enduringly, Murcia, until these towns were recovered by the Christians.

1. The Ḥammūdids of Málaga

⊘ 404/1014	or
405/1015	ʿAlī b. Ḥammūd, al-Nāṣir
⊘ 408/1017	al-Qāsim b. Ḥammūd, al-Maʾmūn, first reign
⊘ 412/1021	Yaḥyā I b. ʿAlī, al-Muʿtalī, first reign
413/1022	al-Qāsim I, second reign
417/1026	Yaḥyā I al-Muʿtalī, second reign
⊘ 427/1036	Idrīs I b. ʿAlī, al-Mutaʾayyad
431/1039	Yaḥyā II b. Idrīs, al-Qāʾim
⊘ 431/1040	al-Ḥasan b. Yāhyā I, al-Mustanṣir
⊘ 434/1043	Idrīs II b. Yaḥyā I, al-ʿAlī, first reign
⊘ 438/1046	Muḥammad I b. Idrīs, al-Mahdī
444/1052	Idrīs III b. Yaḥyā II, al-Sāmī al-Muwaffaq
⊘ 445/1053	Idrīs II al-ʿAlī al-Ẓāfir, second reign
? to 448/1056	Muḥammad II b. Idrīs, al-Mustaʿlī
	The main Ḥammūdid line in Málaga extinguished by the Zīrids of Granada, the branch in Alcegiras being extinguished also in 446/1054 or 451/1059 by the ʿAbbādids of Seville.

2. The Ḥammūdids of Ceuta

400/1010	ʿAlī b. Ḥammūd, al-Nāṣir
408/1017	al-Qāsim b Ḥammūd, al-Maʾmūn
412/1021 or 414/1023 to 427/1036	Yaḥyā I b. ʿAlī, al-Muʿtalī
426/1035	Idrīs I b. ʿAlī, al-Mutaʾayyad
431/1039	Yaḥyā II b. Idrīs, al-Qāʾim
431/1040	Ḥasan b. Yaḥyā I, al-Mustanṣir
c. 442/c. 1050	Idrīs II b. Yaḥyā I, al-ʿAlī
by 453/1061	*Governors for the Ḥammūdids and then independent rulers from the Barghawāṭa Berbers*

3. The ʿAbbādids of Seville

414/1023	Muḥammad I b. Ismāʿīl Ibn ʿAbbād, Abu ʾl-Qāsim, initially as member of a triumvirate
⊘ 433/1042	ʿAbbād b. Muḥammad I, Abu ʿAmr Fakhr al-Dawla al-Muʿtaḍid
⊘ 461–84/1069–91	Muḥammad II b. ʿAbbād, Abu ʾl-Qāsim al-Muʿtamid, d. 487/1095
484/1091	*Almoravid conquest*

4. The Banū Birzāl in Carmona

414/1023	Muḥammad b. ʿAbdallāh al-Birzālī, Abū ʿAbdallāh
434/1043	Isḥāq b. Muḥammad
444–59/1052–67	al-ʿAzīz or al-ʿIzz b. Isḥāq, al-Mustaẓhir
459/1067	*ʿAbbādid annexation*

5. The Banū Khazrūn in Arcos

402/1012	Muḥammad Ibn Khazrūn, Abū ʿAbdallāh ʿImād al-Dawla
?	ʿAbdūn Ibn Khazrūn
448–58/1056–66	Muḥammad b. ʿAbdūn
459/1067	*ʿAbbādid annexation*

6. The Zīrids of Granada

403/1013	Zāwī b. Zīrī al-Ṣanhājī	
410/1019	Ḥabbūs b. Māksan	
⊘ 429/1038	Bādīs b. Ḥabbūs, al-Muẓaffar al-Nāṣir	
465–83/1073–90	⊘ ʿAbdallāh b. Buluggīn b. Bādīs, Sayf al-Dawla, in Granada, died in exile Tamīm b. Buluggīn, in Málaga, d. 488/1095	co-rulers
483/1090	*Almoravid conquest*	

7. The Banū Ṣumādiḥ of Almería

c. 403/c. 1013	*Khayrān al-Ṣaqlabī*
419/1028	*Zuhayr al-Ṣaqlabī*
429–33/1038–42	*ʿAbd al-ʿAzīz b. ʿAbd al-Raḥmān Ibn Abī ʿĀmir, al-Manṣūr of Valencia*
429/1038	Governors from the Banū Ṣumādiḥ for the ʿĀmirids of Valencia
433/1042	Maʿn b. Muḥammad Ibn Ṣumādiḥ
⊘ 443/1051	Muḥammad b. Maʿn, Abū Yaḥyā al-Muʿtaṣim
484/1091	Aḥmad b. Muḥammad, Muʿizz al-Dawla, died in exile
484/1091	*Almoravid conquest*

8. The Banū Mujāhid of Denia and Majorca

⊘ c. 403/c. 1012	Mujāhid b. ʿAbdallāh al-ʿĀmirī, al-Muwaffaq
⊘ 436–68/1045–76	ʿAlī b. Mujāhid, Iqbāl al-Dawla
468/1076	*Annexation by the Hūdids*

9. The rulers in Majorca during the eleventh and early twelfth centuries

405–68/1015–76	*Governors of the Banū Mujāhid of Denia*
⊘ 468/1076	ʿAbdallāh al-Murtaḍā
⊘ 486–508/1093–1114	Mubashshir b. Sulaymān, Nāṣir al-Dawla
508/1114	*Almoravid annexation*

10. The Jahwarids of Cordova

422/1031	Jahwar b. Muḥammad Ibn Jahwar, Abu 'l-Ḥazm, formally as member of a triumvirate
⊘ 435/1043	Muḥammad b. Jahwar, Abu 'l-Walīd al-Rashīd
450-61/1058-69	ʿAbd al-Malik b. Muḥammad, Dhu 'l-Siyādatayn al-Manṣur al-Ẓāfir, died in exile
461/1069	*ʿAbbādid conquest*

11. The rulers in Cordova of the Almoravid-Almohad interregnum

⊘ 538/1144	Ḥamdīn b. Muḥammad, al-Manṣūr, first reign
⊘ 539/1145	Aḥmad III b. ʿAbd al-Malik, Sayf al-Dawla, Hūdid, d. 540/1146
540/1146	Ḥamdīn b. Muḥammad, second reign
541/1146	Yaḥyā b. ʿAlī, Ibn Ghāniya
543/1148	*Almohad conquest*

12. The Afṭasids of Badajoz

403/1012–13	*Sābūr al-Ṣaqlabī*
413/1022	ʿAbdallāh b. Muḥammad Ibn al-Afṭas, Abū Muḥammad al-Manṣūr
437/1045	Muḥammad b. ʿAbdallāh, Abū Bakr al-Muẓaffar
⊘ 460/1068	Yaḥyā b. Muḥammad
⊘ 460–87/1068–94	ʿUmar b. Muḥammad, Abū Ḥafṣ al-Mutawakkil, k. 487/1094 or 488/1095
487/1094	*Almoravid conquest*

13. The Dhu 'l-Nūnids of Toledo

c. 403/c. 1012	*Yaʿīsh b. Muḥammad, Abū Bakr al-Qāḍī*
⊘ 409/1018	Ismāʿīl b. ʿAbd al-Raḥmān Ibn Dhi 'l-Nūn, Abū Muḥammad Dhu 'l-Riyāsatayn al-Ẓāfir
⊘ 435/1043	Yaḥyā I b. Ismāʿīl, Abu 'l-Ḥasan Sharaf al-Dawla al-Ma'mūn Dhu 'l-Majdayn
⊘ 467/1075	Yaḥyā II b. Ismāʿīl b. Yaḥyā I, al-Qādir, first reign
472/1080	*Occupation by the Afṭasid ʿUmar al-Mutawakkil*
⊘ 473–8/1081–5	Yaḥyā II al-Qādir, second reign, k. 485/1092
478/1085	*Conquest by Alfonso VI of León and Castile, with Yaḥyā installed in Valencia as a puppet ruler*

14. The ʿĀmirids of Valencia

401/1010–11	*Mubārak al-Ṣaqlabī and Muẓaffar al-Ṣaqlabī*
408 or 409/1017–18	*Labīb al-Ṣaqlabī*
⊘ 411/1020 or 412/1021	ʿAbd al-ʿAzīz b. ʿAbd al-Raḥmān (Sanchuelo) Ibn Abī ʿĀmir, al-Manṣūr
⊘ 452/1060	ʿAbd al-Malik b. ʿAbd al-ʿAzīz, Niẓām al-Dawla al-Muẓaffar
457–68/1065–76	*Dhu ʾl-Nūnid occupation*
468/1076	Abū Bakr b. ʿAbd al-ʿAzīz, al-Manṣūr
478/1085	ʿUthmān b. Abī Bakr, al-Qāḍī
478–85/1085–92	*Dhu ʾl-Nūnid Yaḥyā b. Ismāʿīl al-Qādir installed as puppet ruler by Alfonso VI*
487–92/1094–9	*Valencia occupied by the Cid*
495/1102	*Almoravid conquest*

15. The rulers in Valencia of the Almoravid-Almohad interregnum

539/1144	Manṣūr b. ʿAbdallāh, Qāḍī
⊘ 542/1147	Abū ʿAbdallāh Muḥammad b. Saʿd, Ibn Mardanīsh, *Rey Lobo* or *Lope*
567/1172	Hilāl b. Muḥammad, Ibn Mardanīsh, submitted to the Almohads

16. The Tujībids in Saragossa

400/1010	*al-Mundhir I b. Yaḥyā al-Tujībī, governor for the Umayyads*
⊘ 414/1023	Yaḥyā b. al-Mundhir I, al-Muẓaffar
⊘ 420/1029	al-Mundhir II b. Yaḥyā, Muʿizz al-Dawla al-Manṣūr
⊘ 430–1/1039–40	ʿAbdallāh b. al-Ḥakam, al-Muẓaffar
431/1040	*Succession of the Hūdids*

17. The Hūdids in Saragossa, Huesca, Tudela and Lérida, and, subsequently, Denia, Tortosa and Calatayud

⊘ 431/1040	Sulaymān b. Muḥammad Ibn Hūd al-Judhāmī, Abū Ayyūb al-Mustaʿīn I, d. 438/1046
⊘ c. 439/c. 1047	Sulaymān b. Yūsuf, Tāj al-Dawla
⊘ (c. 439–40/ c. 1047–8	Muḥammad b. Sulaymān, ʿAḍud al-Dawla, in Calatayud
⊘ c. 439–42/c. 1047–50	? al-Mundhir b. Sulaymān, in Tudela)
⊘ 441–75/1049–82	Aḥmad I b. Sulaymān, Sayf al-Dawla ʿImād al-Dawla al-Muqtadir
⊘ 474/1081	Yūsuf b. Aḥmad I, al-Muʾtamin
⊘ (474–83/1081–90	al-Mundhir b. Aḥmad, ʿImād al-Dawla, in Denia and Tortosa)
⊘ 476/1083	Aḥmad II b. Yūsuf, Sayf al-Dawla al-Mustaʿīn
⊘ (483–c. 492/ 1090–c. 1099	Sulaymān b. al-Mundhir, Sayyid al-Dawla, in Denia and then Tortosa)
503/1110	ʿAbd al-Malik b. Aḥmad II, ʿImād al-Dawla, after this same year in Rueda de Jalón/Rūṭa

503/1110	*Almoravid occupation of Saragossa*
512/1118	*Christian occupation of Saragossa*
524–40/1130–46	Aḥmad III b. ʿAbd al-Malik, Sayf al-Dawla, in Rueda and then in central Spain
540/1146	*Former Hūdid territories in central Spain taken over by Alfonso I el Batallador and Ramiro II of Aragon*

18. The rulers of Murcia, including the Ṭāhirids and Hūdids

403/1012–13	*Khayrān al-Ṣaqlabī of Almería*
419/1028	*Zuhayr al-Ṣaqlabī of Almería*
429/1038	*ʿAbd al-ʿAzīz b. ʿAbd al-Raḥmān Ibn Abī ʿĀmir, al-Manṣūr, of Valencia*
436/1045	*Mujāhid b. ʿAbdallāh al-ʿĀmirī of Denia*
c. 440/c. 1049	Aḥmad, Abū Bakr Ibn Ṭāhir
455/1063	Muḥammad b. Aḥmad Ibn Ṭāhir
471/1078	*Governors on behalf of the ʿAbbādids of Seville*
484/1091	*Almoravid conquest*
489–90/1096–7	Aḥmad b. Abī Jaʿfar ʿAbd al-Raḥmān Ibn Ṭāhir, Abū Jaʿfar
	Resumption of Almoravid control
540/1145	⊘ ʿAbdallāh b. ʿIyāḍ and ⊘ ʿAbdallāh b. Faraj al-Thaghrī as rivals for power
⊘ 543/1148	Muḥammad b. Saʿd, Abū ʿAbdallāh Ibn Mardanīsh, *Rey Lobo* or *Lope*, of Valencia
567/1172	*Almohad occupation*
⊘ 625/1228	Muḥammad b. Yūsuf Ibn Hūd, Abū ʿAbdallāh al-Mutawakkil, also in Valencia till the Christian reconquest of Valencia in 636/1238
⊘ 635/1238	Muḥammad b. Muḥammad, Abū Bakr al-Wāthiq, first reign
636/1239	al-ʿAzīz b. ʿAbd al-Malik, Ḍiyāʾ al-Dawla
⊘ 638/1241	Muḥammad Ibn Hūd, Abū Jaʿfar Bahāʾ al-Dawla
660/1262	Muḥammad b. Abī Jaʿfar Muḥammad
662/1264	Muḥammad b. Muḥammad, Abu Bakr, second reign
?	ʿAbdallāh b. ʿAlī, Ibn Ashqīlūla, of the Naṣrids of Granada
(664/1266	*Aragonese conquest)*

Zambaur, 53–8 and Map 1; Lane-Poole, 23–6; Album, 14–15.

A. Prieto y Vives, *Los Reyes de Taifas, estudio histórico-numismático de los Musulmanes españoles en el siglo V de la Hégira (XI de J.C.)*, Madrid 1926.

H. W. Hazard, *The Numismatic History of Late Medieval North Africa*, ANS Numismatic Studies, no. 8, New York 1952, 57–8, 96, 233–6, 281–2 (for the Ḥammūdids of Málaga, Algeciras and Ceuta), 68–9, 158–9, 272–3 (for the later Hūdids of Murcia and Ceuta).

G. C. Miles, *Coins of the Spanish Mulūk al-Ṭawāʾif*, ANS Hispanic Numismatic Series, Monographs, no. 3, New York 1954.

D. Wasserstein, *The Rise and Fall of the Party Kings. Politics and Society in Islamic Spain 1002–1086*, Princeton 1985.

EI[1] art. 'Tudjīb (Banū)', 'Zīrids' (E. Lévi-Provençal)

EI[2] arts 'ʿAbbādids', 'Afṭasids', 'Balansiya' (Lévi-Provençal), 'Dhu 'l-Nūnids' (D. M. Dunlop), 'Djahwarids', 'Ḥammūdids' (A. Huici Miranda), 'Hūdids' (Dunlop), 'Ibn Mardanīsh', 'Ḳarmūna', 'Mayūrḳa' (J. Bosch-Vilá), 'Saraḳusṭa' (M. J. Viguera).

6

THE BANŪ GHĀNIYA

520–99/1126–1203

The Balearic Islands

520/1126	Muḥammad b. ʿAlī b. Yūsuf al-Massūfī, Ibn Ghāniya, governor of the Balearics for the Almoravids
550/1155	ʿAbdallāh b. Muḥammad
550/1155	Abū Ibrāhīm Isḥāq b. Muḥammad
579/1183	Muḥammad b. Isḥāq, under Almohad suzerainty
580/1184	ʿAlī b. Isḥāq
583–600/1187–1203	ʿAbdallāh b. Isḥāq
600/1203	*Almohad occupation of the Balearics, and Almohad governors*
627–8/1230–1	*Aragonese conquest of Majorca*

The founder of this petty Ṣanhāja Berber dynasty, which controlled the Balearic Islands for eighty years and also played a significant role during the period of later Almohad rule in the eastern Maghrib, was an Almoravid descendant on the female side, deriving his name Ibn Ghāniya from the name of an Almoravid princess, the wife of ʿAlī b. Yūsuf. ʿAlī's son Yaḥyā defended the Almoravid possessions in Spain against the incoming Almohads (see below, no. 15), and then remnants of the Ibn Ghāniya family withdrew to the Balearic Islands. There they founded their own independent line as a post-Almoravid principality which grew rich on, *inter alia*, piracy against the Christians. One member of the family, ʿAlī b. Isḥāq, decided to leave the Balearics and carry on the struggle against the Almohads in the eastern Maghrib. He and his successor there, Yaḥyā b. Isḥāq, were for several decades destabilising influences in the affairs of Ifrīqiya and what is now eastern Algeria until ʿAlī's defeat and death in 633/1227 and Yaḥyā's loss of Ifrīqiya and subsequent death in 635/1236; the activities here of the Banū Ghāniya were a potent factor in the decline of Almohad power in the eastern Maghrib. Meanwhile, the Almohad caliph al-Nāṣir had invaded Majorca and installed his own governor there, ending the rule of the Banū Ghāniya in the Balearics; the Almohads and their epigoni held the islands for nearly thirty years until James I of Aragon conquered Majorca, with Ibiza and Minorca following it into Christian hands by 686/1287.

Zambaur, 57.

EI² 'G͟hāniya, Banū' (G. Marçais); 'Mayūrḳa' (J. Bosch-Vilá).

A. Bel, *Les Benou Ghânya, derniers représentants de l'empire almoravide et leur lutte contre l'empire almohade*, Publications de l'Ecole des Lettres d'Alger, Bull. de Correspondance Africaine, XXVII, Paris 1903, with a genealogical table at p. 26.

7

THE NAṢRIDS OR BANU 'L-AḤMAR
629–897/1232–1492
Granada

⊘ 629/1232	Muḥammad I b. Yūsuf, Abū ʿAbdallāh al-Ghālib or al-Shaykh, called Ibn al-Aḥmar
671/1273	Muḥammad II b. Muḥammad I, Abū ʿAbdallāh al-Faqīh
701/1302	Muḥammad III b. Muḥammad II, Abū ʿAbdallāh al-Makhlūʿ
708/1309	Naṣr b. Muḥammad II, Abu 'l-Juyūsh, after 713/1314 governor in Guadix
713/1314	Ismāʿīl I b. Faraj, Abu 'l-Walīd
⊘ 725/1325	Muḥammad IV b. Ismāʿīl, Abū ʿAbdallāh
⊘ 733/1333	Yūsuf I b. Ismāʿīl I, Abu 'l-Ḥajjāj al-Mu'ayyad
⊘ 755/1354	Muḥammad V b. Yūsuf I, Abū ʿAbdallāh, first reign
760/1359	Ismāʿīl II b. Yūsuf I, Abu 'l-Walīd
761/1360	Muḥammad VI b. Ismāʿīl, Abū ʿAbdallāh al-Ghālib (el Bermejo in Christian chronicles)
⊘ 763/1362	Muḥammad V, al-Ghani, second reign
793/1391	Yūsuf II b. Muḥammad V, Abu 'l-Ḥajjāj al-Mustaghnī
794/1392	Muḥammad VII b. Yūsuf II, Abū ʿAbdallāh al-Mustaʿīn
810–20/1408–17	Yūsuf III b. Yūsuf II, Abu 'l-Ḥajjāj al-Nāṣir
⊘ 1417	Muḥammad VIII b. Yūsuf III, Abū ʿAbdallāh al-Mutamassik (al-Ṣaghīr/el Pequeño), first reign
⊘ 1419	Muḥammad IX b. Naṣr, Abū ʿAbdallāh al-Ghālib (al-Aysar/el Zurdo), first reign
1427	Muḥammad VIII, second reign
1429	Muḥammad IX, second reign
1432	Yūsuf IV, Abu 'l-Ḥajjāj (Ibn al-Mawl/Abenalmao)
1432	Muḥammad IX, third reign
1445	Muḥammad X b. ʿUthmān, Abū ʿAbdallāh (al-Aḥnaf/el Cojo), first reign
1445	Yūsuf V b. Aḥmad b. Muḥammad V, Abu 'l-Ḥajjāj (Ibn Ismāʿīl/Aben Ismael), first reign
1446	Muḥammad X, second reign
1447–53	Muḥammad IX, fourth reign (1451–3 in association with Muḥammad XI)
1451-5	Muḥammad XI b. Muḥammad VIII, (el Chiquito) (1454–5 in competition with Saʿd)
1454-64	Abū Naṣr Saʿd b. ʿAli b. Yūsuf II, al-Mustaʿīn (Ciriza < Sīdī Saʿd, Muley Zad, Çah) (1462 in competition with Yūsuf V), second reign
⊘ 1464	ʿAlī b. Saʿd, Abu 'l-Ḥasan (Muley Hácen), first reign
⊘ 887/1482	Muḥammad XII b. Abi 'l-Ḥasan ʿAlī, Abū ʿAbdallāh al-Zughūbī (Boabdil el Chico), first reign
1483	ʿAli b. Saʿd, second reign

1485	Muḥammad b. Sa'd, al-Zaghal, from 1486 in competition with his nephew Muḥammad XII's second reign
8967/1490–2	Muḥammad XII, third reign, d. 940/1533
897/1492	*Spanish reconquest*

After the Almohads (see below, no. 15) were defeated in Spain, most of the Muslim towns fell speedily into Christian hands: Cordova fell in 633/1236 and Seville in 646/1248. One Muslim chief, Muḥammad (I) al-Ghālib, who claimed descent from a Medinan Companion of the Prophet, managed to gain control of the mountainous and thus defensible extreme south of the Iberian peninsula covering the present provinces of Granada, Málaga and Almería with parts of Cádiz, Jaén and Murcia. He made Granada his capital and its citadel, known as the Alhambra (*al-Ḥamrā'* 'the Red [fortress]'), his centre, agreeing to pay *parias* or tribute first to Ferdinand III of Castile and León and then to his successor Alfonso X. The Naṣrid sultans were rivals with the Marīnids of Morocco (see below, no. 16) for control of the Straits of Gibraltar, and Muḥammad II and Muḥammad V actually controlled Ceuta during 705–9/1305–9 and 786–9/1384–7, minting coins there. But they eventually had to seek help from the Marīnids against pressure from the Christian kingdoms of Castile and Aragon; yet Muslim hopes of successful Marīnid intervention in the Iberian peninsula were dashed when the Marinīd sultan Abu 'l Ḥasan 'Alī and the Naṣrid sultan Yūsuf I were defeated by the Castilians and Portuguese at the battle of Tarifa (known in Christian sources as that of the Rio Salado) in 741/1340.

Despite its precarious position, partly because of instability and disturbances within the kingdom of Castile-Léon, the Naṣrid sultanate remained for two and a half centuries a centre for Islamic civilisation, attracting scholars and literary men from all over the Muslim West. The historian Ibn Khaldūn served as a diplomat for Muḥammad V on a mission to Pedro I of Castile at Seville, and in the vizier Lisān al-Dīn Ibn al-Khaṭīb, whose history of Granada is a source of prime importance, Naṣrid Granada produced a major literary figure. But in the fifteenth century the internal unity of Granada was impaired by internecine rivalries among the ruling family, aided and abetted by powerful families like that of the Banu 'l-Sarrāj (the 'Abencerrajes'). The marriage of Ferdinand II of Aragon (subsequently Ferdinand V of Castile-Aragon) to Isabella of Castile in 1469 brought about the unification of the greater part of Christian Spain under one crown, and the prospects for the sultanate's survival darkened. Dynastic strife grew worse under the last Naṣrids, until in 897/1492 Granada was handed over to the Christians by Muḥammad XII (Boabdil), who remained as lord of Mondújar and the Alpujarras for one year and some months before crossing over to Morocco.

The history and the chronology of the last Naṣrid amīrs are extremely confused; where Christian era dates alone are given in the above list of rulers, this indicates that the chronology has to be constructed from Christian sources alone and that regnal dates are not provided by the Arabic ones.

Lane-Poole, 28–9; Zambaur, 58–9; Album, 15.
The lists of Lane-Poole and Zambaur are, in our present state of knowledge, very inaccurate and misleading. See now EI[2] 'Naṣrids' (J. D. Latham), with a much more

accurate chronology, utilising the standard histories of Rachel Arié, *L'Espagne musulmane au temps des Naṣrides (1232–1492)*, enlarged 2nd edn, Paris 1990, with table after plate XII; eadem, *El reino naṣrí de Granada*, Madrid 1992; and L. P. Harvey, *Islamic Spain 1250–1500*, Chicago and London 1990, with tables at pp. 17–19.

F. Codera y Zaydín, *Tratado de numismática arábigo-española*, Madrid 1879.

A. Vives y Escudero, *Monedas de las dinastías arábigo-españolas*, Madrid 1893.

H. W. Hazard, *The Numismatic History of Late Medieval North Africa*, 84–5, 228, 279, 285 (for coins minted by the Naṣrids at Ceuta).

M. A. Ladero Quesada, *Granada, historia de un país islámico (1232–1571)*, 2nd edn, Madrid 1979.

J. J. Rodriguez Lorente, *Numismática nasrí*, Madrid 1983.

THREE
North Africa
8

THE IDRĪSIDS
172–375/789–985
Morocco

⊘ 172/789	Idrīs I (al-Akbar) b. ʿAbdallāh
(175/791	Regency for his posthumous son Idrīs)
⊘ 187/803	Idrīs II (al-Aṣghar or al-Azhar) b. Idrīs I
⊘ 213/828	Muḥammad b. Idrīs II, al-Muntaṣir
⊘ 221/836	ʿAlī I Ḥaydara b. Muḥammad
⊘ 234/849	Yaḥyā I b. Muḥammad
⊘ 249/863	Yaḥyā II b. Yaḥyā I
⊘ 252/866	ʿAlī II b. ʿUmar
?	Yaḥyā III b. al-Qāsim, al-Miqdām al-Jūṭī
292/905	Yaḥyā IV b. Idrīs, deposed in 307/919
305/917 onwards	*Tributary to the Fāṭimids, with the Fāṭimid governor Mūsā b. Abi 'l-ʿĀfiya installed*
313–15/925–7	al-Ḥasan b. Muḥammad, al-Ḥajjām
326/938	al-Qāsim Gannūn b. Muḥammad (at Ḥajar al-Naṣr, in the Rīf and north-western Morocco)
337/948	Aḥmad b. al-Qāsim, Abu 'l-ʿAysh (at Aṣīlā)
343–63/954–74	al-Ḥasan b. al-Qāsim (at Ḥajar al-Nasr), first reign
375/985	al-Ḥasan, second reign, k. 375/985
375/985	*Incorporation of the Western Maghrib into the Fāṭimid empire*

The Idrīsids were the first dynasty who attempted to introduce the doctrines of Shīʿism, albeit in a very attenuated form, into the Maghrib, where the most vigorous form of Islam – in a region where there was still much paganism and Christianity surviving – was that of the radical and egalitarian Khārijism. Idrīs I was a great-grandson of al-Ḥasan b. ʿAlī b. Abī Ṭālib, hence connected with the line of Shīʿī Imāms. He took part in the ʿAlid rising in the Ḥijāz of his nephew al-Ḥusayn, the *ṣāḥib Fakhkh*, against the ʿAbbāsids in 169/786, and was compelled to flee to Egypt and then to North Africa, where the prestige of his ʿAlid descent led several Zanāta Berber chiefs of northern Morocco to recognise him as their leader. There he settled at Walīla, the Roman Volubilis, but it seems that he also began the laying-out of a military camp, Madīnat Fās, nucleus of the later city of Fez. This last soon grew populous, attracting emigrants from Muslim Spain and Ifrīqiya, the eastern Maghrib, and became the Idrīsids' capital. Its role as a holy city, home of the *Shorfā* (< *shurafā*' 'noble ones'), privileged descendants of the Prophet's grandsons al-Ḥasan and al-Ḥusayn, also begins now, and henceforth these *Shorfā* play an important role in Moroccan history (see below, nos 20, 21).

The Idrīsid period is also important for the diffusion of Islamic culture over the recently-converted Berber tribesmen of the interior.

However, during the reign of Muḥammad al-Muntaṣir, the Idrīsid dominions became politically fragmented as a result of his decision to divide out the family's various towns – the Idrīsids' hold on Morocco was essentially urban-based rather than on the countryside – as appanages for several of his numerous brothers. The Idrīsids thus fell prey to attacks from their Berber enemies, but in the early tenth century a more determined and dangerous foe appeared in the shape of the radical Shīʿī Fāṭimids of Ifrīqiya. Yaḥyā IV had to recognise the suzerainty of the Mahdī ʿUbaydallāh, and much of his territory was detached and given to the Miknāsa Berber chief Mūsā b. Abi 'l-ʿAfiya. The Idrīsids were subsequently driven to the peripheries of Morocco, so that there were minor branches at places like Tamdult in the south, but the main line was established among the Ghumāra Berbers in the Rīf of northern Morocco. These last gave their allegiance variously to the Spanish Umayyads, who were now, under their caliph ʿAbd al-Raḥmān III, attempting to extend their influence in North Africa, and to the Fāṭimids. In 353/974, the Idrīsid al-Ḥasan had to surrender to the Umayyads and was carried off to Cordova. Some years later, he managed to reappear, with Fāṭimid support, but was killed by Umayyad forces and the Idrīsid dynasty in North Africa ended.

However, during the period of Umayyad decadence in the early eleventh century, a distant branch of the Idrīsids, the Ḥammūdids, succeeded in establishing Taifa principalities in Málaga and Algeciras (see above, no. 5, Taifas nos 1, 2).

Lane-Poole, 35; Zambaur, 65 and Table 4; Album, 15.

*EI*² 'Idrīs I', 'Idrīs II', 'Idrīsids' (D. Eustache).

H. Terrasse, *Histoire du Maroc des origines à l'établissement du Protectorat français*, Casablanca 1949–50, I, 107–34.

D. Eustache, *Corpus de dirhams idrīsides et contemporains. Collection de la Banque du Maroc et autres collections mondiales, publiques et privées*, Rabat 1970–1, with a list of rulers and genealogical tables at pp. 3ff. and with notes at pp. 17–24.

9

THE RUSTAMIDS

161–296/778–909

Tahert (Tāhart), in western Algeria

161/778	ʿAbd al-Raḥmān b. Rustam
171/788	ʿAbd al-Wahhāb b. ʿAbd al-Raḥmān
208/824	Aflaḥ b. ʿAbd al-Wahhāb, Abū Saʿīd
258/872	Abū Bakr b. Aflaḥ
260/874	Muḥammad b. Aflah, Abu ʾl-Yaqẓān
281/894	Yūsuf b. Muḥammad, Abū Ḥātim, first reign
282/895	Yaʿqūb b. Aflaḥ, first reign
286/899	Yūsuf b. Muḥammad, second reign
?	Yaʿqūb b. Aflaḥ, second reign
294–6/907–9	Yaqẓān b. Muḥammad
296/909	*Destruction of Tahert by the Fāṭimids*

The Rustamids have an importance for the history of Islam in North Africa disproportionate to the duration and limited extent of their political power. In the eighth century, the majority of the Berbers of North Africa adopted the radical, egalitarian religio-political sect of Khārijism, perhaps as an expression of their own ethnic solidarity against domination by their orthodox Sunnī Arab masters. Whereas in the east, except for certain areas of concentration, Khārijism tended to be an extremist, savagely violent minority faith, in North Africa, though equally violent, it was more of a mass movement. The Khārijī sub-sect of the Ibāḍiyya, the followers of one ʿAbdallāh b. Ibāḍ of Baṣra, had their original North African centre among the Zanāta Berbers of the Jabal Nafūsa in modern Tripolitania; and, after a temporary capture of Kairouan (Qayrawān) in central Ifrīqiya or Tunisia, the bastion of Arab religious orthodoxy and military power, these Ibāḍīs controlled a vast region from Barca to the fringes of Morocco. When Arab dominion was largely re-established, a group of the Ibāḍīs under the leadership of ʿAbd al-Raḥmān b. Rustam (whose name would indicate Persian descent; he was later provided with a doubtless fictitious genealogy back to Sāsānid royalty) fled to what is now western Algeria.

Here, ʿAbd al-Raḥmān in 144/761 founded a Khārijī principality based on the newly-founded town of Tahert (Tāhart) (near modern Tiaret), and some fifteen years later he was offered the imamate of all the Ibāḍiyya of North Africa. This nucleus in Tahert was linked with Ibāḍī communities in the Aurès, southern Tunisia and the Jabal Nafūsa, and groups as far south as the Fezzān oasis acknowledged the spiritual headship of the Ibāḍī Imāms. Surrounded as they were by enemies, including the Shīʿī Idrīsids (see above, no. 8) to the west and the Sunnī ʿAbbāsid governors and then the Aghlabids to the east, the Rustamids sought the alliance of the Spanish Umayyads, and received subsidies from them. But the rise of the messianic Shīʿī Fāṭimids in Morocco was fatal for them, as for other local dynasties of the Maghrib like the Ṣufrī Khārijī Midrārids (see below, no. 10) and the Aghlabids. The later Rustamids were cut off in the course of the ninth century through schisms within Khārijism from their co-religionists in Tripolitania, and in 296/909 Tahert fell to the Kutāma Berber followers of the Fāṭimid *dāʿī* or propagandist Abū ʿAbdallāh; many of the Rustamids were massacred, and the rest fled southwards to the oasis of Ouargla (Wargla).

Tahert under the Rustamids enjoyed a great material prosperity, being one of the northern termini, like Sijilmāsa, of the trans-Saharan caravan routes, and it acquired the name of 'the Iraq of the Maghrib'. It attracted a cosmopolitan population, among whom were appreciable Persian and Christian elements, and was a centre of scholarship. Its great historical role was as a rallying-point and nerve-centre for Khārijism throughout North Africa; although Tahert succumbed to the Fāṭimids, Ibāḍī doctrines long remained potent in the Maghrib, and have indeed survived to this day in a few places like the Mzāb oasis in Algeria, the Tunisian island of Djerba (Jarba) and in the Jabal Nafūsa.

It is somewhat remarkable that no coins of the Rustamids have yet been found.

Sachau, 24–5 no. 55; Zambaur, 64.
EI[1] 'Tāhert' (G. Marçais), EI[2] 'Ibāḍiyya' (T. Lewicki), 'Rustamids' (M. Talbi).
Chikh Békri, 'Le Kharijisme berbère: quelques aspects du royaume rustumide', AIEO *Alger*, 15 (1957), 55–108.

10

THE MIDRĀRIDS
208–366/823–977
Sijilmāsa in south-eastern Morocco

208/823	al-Muntaṣir b. Ilyasaʿ, Abū Mālik, called Midrār
253/867	Maymūn b. al-Muntaṣir, Ibn Thaqiyya, al-Amīr
263/877	Muḥammad b. Maymūn
270/884	Ilyasaʿ b. al-Muntaṣir, Abu ʾl-Manṣūr
296/909	Wāsūl al-Fatḥ b. Maymūn al-Amīr
300/913	Aḥmad b. Maymūn al-Amīr
309/921	Muḥammad b. (?) Sārū, Abu ʾl-Muntaṣir al-Muʿtazz
321/933	Samgū b. Abi ʾl-Muntaṣir, al-Muntaṣir, first reign
⊘ 331/943	Muḥammad b. Wāsūl al-Fatḥ, al-Shākir
347/958	Samgū al-Muntaṣir, second reign
352 to 366 or 369/963 to 977 or 980	(?) ʿAbdallāh b. Muḥammad, Abū Muḥammad
c. 366/c. 977	*Deposition of the Midrārids*

The Banū Midrār were a Berber family from the Miknāsa tribe who arose in the town of Sijilmāsa on the Sahara fringes of Morocco, either at roughly the same time as the town was founded (or refounded) or shortly afterwards, in the second half of the eighth century. The town, which seems originally to have been a settlement of Ṣufrī Khārijīs, now flourished as the northern terminus of trans-Saharan caravan trade coming from West Africa; the Midrārids came to levy transit dues and taxes on the products of the mines of southern Morocco and Mauritania (we know virtually nothing, however, of any corresponding cultural activity in the town under their rule). The chiefs of the Midrārid family had become prominent there, but it is difficult to pin down the date of the actual dynasty's beginning. A convenient date, however, is 208/823, when Abū Mālik al-Muntaṣir, called Midrār ('copiously flowing' [with milk, largesse, etc.]), achieved power.

At first, the Midrārids were nominal vassals of the ʿAbbāsid caliphs, but had some connections with the Rustamids of Tahert (see above, no. 9), who were also Khārijī in faith. But in the early tenth century, following a prediction according to which the expected Mahdī or Divinely-Guided One of the Shīʿa was to appear at Sijilmāsa, the partisans of the future founder of the Fāṭimid dynasty (see below, no. 27), ʿUbaydallāh al-Mahdī, took over Sijilmāsa in 296/909. The Midrārids were henceforth generally vassals of the Fāṭimids. But Muḥammad b. Wāsūl's repudiation of Ṣufrī Khārijism and adoption of Mālikī Sunnism involved adherence to the cause of the Spanish Umayyads, and this change of loyalties, plus his assumption, like the Umayyads, of the exalted title of caliph, provoked a Fāṭimid reconquest of Sijilmāsa. The Midrārids returned to control the town briefly, but their dominion was ended around 366/977 or shortly thereafter, when Khazrūn, the chief of the Berber Maghrāwa tribe, which was allied with the Spanish

Umayyads, killed the last Midrārid and put an end to the dynasty (the descendants of Khazrūn were in the early eleventh century to establish a Taifa principality at Arcos in Spain: see above, no. 5, Taifa no. 5).

Sachau, 25 no. 56; Zambaur, 64–5, 66; Album, 16.
EI[1] 'Sidjilmāsa' (G. S. Colin); EI[2] 'Midrār, Banū' (Ch. Pellat).

11

THE AGHLABIDS
184–296/800–909
Ifrīqiya, Algeria, Sicily

⊘ 184/800	Ibrāhīm I b. al-Aghlab
⊘ 197/812	ʿAbdallāh I b. Ibrāhīm I, Abu ʾl-ʿAbbās
⊘ 201/817	Ziyādat Allāh I b. Ibrāhīm I, Abū Muḥammad
⊘ 223/838	al-Aghlab b. Ibrāhīm I, Abū ʿIqāl
⊘ 226/841	Muḥammad I b. al-Aghlab, Abu ʾl-ʿAbbās
⊘ 242/856	Aḥmad b. Muḥammad I, Abū Ibrāhīm
⊘ 249/863	Ziyādat Allāh II b. Muḥammad I
⊘ 250/863	Muḥammad II b. Aḥmad, Abū ʿAbdallāh Abu ʾl-Gharānīq
⊘ 261/875	Ibrāhīm II b. Aḥmad, Abū Isḥāq
⊘ 289/902	ʿAbdallāh II b. Ibrāhīm II, Abu ʾl-ʿAbbās
⊘ 290–6/903–9	Ziyādat Allāh III b. ʿAbdallāh II, Abū Muḍar, died in exile
290/909	*Fāṭimid conquest*

Ibrāhīm b. al-Aghlab's father was a Khurāsānian Arab commander in the ʿAbbāsid army, and in 184/800 the son was granted the province of Ifrīqiya by Hārūn al-Rashīd in return for an annual tribute of 40,000 dīnārs. The grant involved considerable rights of autonomy, and the great distance of North Africa from Baghdad ensured that none of the Aghlabids was much disturbed by the caliphal government, itself increasingly racked by succession disputes and internal strife after the mid-ninth century. Nevertheless, the Aghlabids always remained theoretical vassals of the caliphs, retaining the caliphs' names in the *khuṭba* or Friday sermon though never on Aghlabid coins after the time of Ibrāhīm I. The first Aghlabids suppressed outbreaks of Berber Khārijism in their territories; and then, under Ziyādat Allāh I, one of the most capable and energetic members of the family, the great project of the conquest of Sicily from the Byzantines was begun in 217/827. An extensive corsair fleet was launched, making the Aghlabids masters of the central Mediterranean and enabling them to harry the coasts of southern Italy, Sardinia, Corsica and even that of the Maritime Alps. Malta was captured before 256/870 and occupied by the Muslims for over two centuries until the Norman reconquest. It is probable that the conquest of Sicily was begun in order to divert religious bellicosity into *jihād* against the infidels, for the early Aghlabid amīrs had to cope with strong internal opposition in Ifrīqiya from the Mālikī *fuqahā'* or religious lawyers in Kairouan. By the opening of the tenth century the conquest of Sicily was virtually complete, and the island remained under Muslim rule, at first under governors appointed by the Aghlabids and then under those of the Fāṭimids, including the Kalbids (see below, no. 12), until the Norman reconquest of the later eleventh century, forming an important centre for the diffusion of Islamic culture to Christian Europe.

However, the Aghlabids' hold on Ifrīqiya became loosened towards the end of the ninth century. The Shīʿī propaganda of the *dāʿī* Abū ʿAbdallāh had a powerful effect among the Kutāma Berbers of the mountainous region of what is now north-eastern Algeria. Kutāma forces inflicted several defeats on the Aghlabid army, and the last of the line, Ziyādat Allāh III, was compelled in 296/909 to abandon the capital al-Raqqāda, founded by his grandfather Ibrāhīm II, and fled to Egypt after fruitless attempts to secure help from the ʿAbbāsids, subsequently dying in the East. Ifrīqiya now became the nucleus of the Fāṭimids' North African possessions, where they constructed their capital al-Mahdiyya, which then replaced al-Raqqāda.

Lane-Poole, 36–8; Zambaur, 67–8; Album, 15–16.
EI[2] 'Ag͟hlabids' (G. Marçais).
M. Vonderheyden, *La Berbérie orientale sous la dynastie des Benoû Aṛlab 800–909*, Paris 1927, with genealogical table at p. 332.
O. Grabar, *The Coinage of the Ṭūlūnids*, ANS Numismatic Notes and Monographs, no. 139, New York 1957, 51–4.
M. Talbi, *L'émirat aghlabide*, Paris 1966.

12

THE KALBIDS
337–445/948–1053
Governors in Sicily

337/948	al-Hasan b. ʿAbdallāh b. Abi ʾl-Ḥusayn al-Kalbī
342/953	Aḥmad b. al-Ḥasan, Abu ʾl-Ḥusayn
359/970	ʿAlī b. al-Ḥasan, Abu ʾl-Qāsim
372/982	Jāhir b. ʿAlī
373/983	Jaʿfar b. Muḥammad b. ʿAlī
	375/985 ʿAbdallāh b. Muḥammad b. ʿAlī
379/989	Yūsuf b. ʿAbdallāh, Abu ʾl-Futūḥ Thiqat al-Dawla
388/998	Jaʿfar b. Yūsuf, Tāj al-Dawla
410/1019	Aḥmad al-Akḥal b. Yūsuf, Abū Jaʿfar Taʾyīd al-Dawla, d. 429/1038
431–c. 445/1040–c. 1053	al-Ḥasan al-Ṣamṣām b. Yūsuf, Ṣamṣām al-Dawla
436–/1044–	*Disintegration of Arab Sicily into various principalities, with the Norman conquest beginning from 452/1060 onwards*

The Byzantine province of Sicily was conquered by Arab forces sent by the Aghlabids of Ifrīqiya (see above, no. 11) over a period of more than seventy years from 212/827 onwards, culminating in the capture of Taormina in 289/902. The Aghlabids appointed their own governors to the island, as did their successors in North Africa after 296/909, the Fāṭimids (see below, no. 27). The lengthy period of rule by the Kalbid governors began with the caliph al-Manṣūr's nomination of al-Ḥasan b. ʿAlī al-Kalbī, although their succession was not recognised as implicitly hereditary until al-Muʿizz's caliphate in 359/970. The Fāṭimids' transfer of their centre of power to Egypt meant, in practice, more freedom of action for the Kalbids, who nevertheless remained firmly loyal to their masters, receiving from them honorific titles and, latterly, resisting pressure from the Zīrids (see below, no. 13) in North Africa. In the early decades of their rule, the Kalbids combated the Byzantines and led frequent raids on Calabria and other parts of the Italian mainland, reaching as far as Naples. After c. 421/c. 1040, however, the power of the Kalbids was in decline, with attacks from the Byzantines and from Italian city-states like Pisa. All these led to a period of disintegration of Arab rule in Sicily into a series of *ṭawāʾif* resembling those in Spain (see above, no. 5), paving the way for the first appearance of the Normans in 1060 and the subsequent reincorporation of Sicily into Christendom.

It does not seem that the Kalbid governors ever minted coins in Sicily on behalf of their suzerains, but a puzzling point is the large number of glass weights of their period which have been found in Sicily, these being far more numerous than would have been needed for weighing out small quantities of precious metals. It has accordingly been suggested that these glass weights may have served as a purely local currency for minor transactions.

Sachau, 26 no. 64; Zambaur, 67–9.
EI[2] 'Kalbids' (U. Rizzitano); 'Sikilliya' (R. Traini, G. Oman and V. Grassi).
M. Amari, *Storia dei Musulmani di Sicilia*, 2nd edn, C. A. Nallino, Catania 1933–9, II, 241–490.
Aziz Ahmad, *A History of Muslim Sicily*, Edinburgh 1975, 30–40.

13

THE ZĪRIDS AND ḤAMMĀDIDS
361–547/972–1152
Tunisia and eastern Algeria

1. Zīrid governors of the Maghrib for the Fāṭimids

after 336/947	Zīrī b. Manād
361/972	Yūsuf Buluggīn I b. Zīrī
373/984	al-Manṣūr b. Buluggīn I
386/996	Bādīs b. al-Manṣūr, Nāṣir al-Dawla
	Division of authority

2. Zīrids of Kairouan

405/1015	Bādīs
⊘ 406/1016	al-Muʿizz b. Bādīs
454/1062	Tamīm b. al-Muʿizz
501/1108	Yaḥyā b. Tamīm
509/1116	ʿAlī b. Yaḥyā
515–43/1121–48	al-Ḥasan b. ʿAlī
	Norman and then Almohad conquest, with al-Ḥasan as Almohad governor until 558/1163, d. 563/1168

3. Ḥammādids of Qalʿat Banī Ḥammād

405/1015	Ḥammād b. Buluggīn I
419/1028	al-Qā'id b. Ḥammād, Sharaf al-Dawla
446/1054	Muḥsin b. al-Qā'id
447/1055	Buluggīn II b. Muḥammad
454/1062	al-Nāṣir b. ʿAlannās
481/1088	al-Manṣūr b. al-Nāṣir
498/1105	Bādīs b. al-Manṣūr
498/1105	al-ʿAzīz b. al-Manṣūr
⊘ 515 or 518–47/ 1121 or 1124–52	Yaḥyā b. al-ʿAzīz, d. 557/1162
547/1152	*Almohad conquest*

The Zīrids were Ṣanhāja Berbers inhabiting the central part of the Maghrib, who early identified themselves with the Fāṭimid cause in North Africa, bringing military relief to the Fāṭimid capital of al-Mahdiyya when in 334/945 it was besieged by the Khārijī rebel Abū Yazīd al-Nukkarī 'the Man on the Donkey'. Accordingly, when the Fāṭimid caliph al-Muʿizz left for Egypt, he appointed Buluggīn I b. Zīrī, whose family had already served the dynasty as governors, to be viceroy of Ifrīqiya. Buluggīn kept up the traditional enmity of his people with the nomadic Zanāta Berbers, and overran all the Maghrib as far west as Ceuta. A branch of the family under another son of Zīrī, Zāwī, took service in Spain under the Ḥājib al-Muẓaffar b. al-Manṣūr Ibn Abī ʿAmir, and after 403/1013 was able to found a Taifa in Granada (see above, no. 5, Taifa no. 6).

Buluggīn's grandson Bādīs entrusted the more westerly part of his governorship to his uncle Ḥammād b. Buluggīn I, and the latter built a capital for himself and his family at Qalʿat Banī Ḥammād, in the upland plain of the Hodna near Msila in the central Maghrib. After discord broke out in 405/1015 between Ḥammād and Bādīs, in which the former temporarily transferred his allegiance to the ʿAbbāsids, there was a *divisio imperii*: the Zīrid main branch of North Africa remained in Ifrīqiya, with its capital at Kairouan, while Ḥammād's line took over the lands further west.

The rich resources and wealth of Ifrīqiya tempted the Zīrid al-Muʿizz b. Bādīs to rebel against his Fāṭimid overlords, and in 433/1041 he gave his allegiance to the ʿAbbāsids (the Ḥammādid al-Qā'id, after temporarily recognising the Baghdad caliphs, returned to Fāṭimid allegiance). Hence shortly afterwards, the Fāṭimids in Egypt released against the Zīrids bands of unassimilated, barbarian Bedouins of the Hilāl and Sulaym tribes, who migrated from Lower Egypt to the Maghrib. These Arabs gradually worked their way across the countryside, terrorising the towns and forcing the Zīrids to evacuate Kairouan for al-Mahdiyya on the coast and the Ḥammādids to withdraw to the less accessible port of Bougie (Bijāya), renamed al-Nāṣiriyya after its founder al-Nāṣir b. ʿAlannās. Having lost control of the land, the two sister lines turned to the sea and built up a fleet; it is, indeed, this period which inaugurates the age of the Barbary corsairs. But they were unable to prevent Muslim Sicily from falling to the Normans, even though peaceful commercial relations were later established with the Norman kings. By the twelfth century, the Zīrids were hard pressed; Roger II of Sicily captured al-Mahdiyya and the Tunisian coast, forcing the Zīrid al-Ḥasan b. ʿAlī to pay tribute. Also, within the Maghrib, the Almohads (see below, no. 15) were now advancing relentlessly eastwards. The Ḥammādids were overrun, and the last ruler, Yaḥyā, surrendered at Constantine and ended his days in exile in Morocco. The last Zīrid, al-Ḥasan, was at one point reinstated as Almohad governor of al-Mahdiyya, functioning there until the Almohad sultan ʿAbd al-Mu'min's death in 558/1163, but died also in Morocco eight years later.

Lane-Poole, 39–40; Zambaur, 70–1; Album, 16.

EI[1] 'Zīrids' (G. Marçais); EI[2] 'Ḥammādids' (H. R. Idris).

H. W. Hazard, *The Numismatic History of Late Medieval North Africa*, ANS Numismatic Studies, no. 8, New York 1952, 53–7, 89–96, 233.

H. R. Idris, *La Berbérie orientale sous les Zīrīdes X^{e}–XIIe siècles*, 2 vols, Paris 1962, with detailed genealogical and chronological tables at II, 830ff., making many corrections to Zambaur.

Amin T. Tibi, *The Tibyān. Memoirs of ʿAbd Allāh b. Buluggīn, last Zīrid Amīr of Granada*, Leiden 1986, with table of the Zīrids of Muslim Spain, showing connections with the North African lines, at p. 30.

14

THE ALMORAVIDS OR AL-MURĀBIṬŪN

454–541/1062–1147

North-west Africa and Spain

Yaḥyā b. Ibrāhīm al-Gudālī or al-Jaddālī Yaḥyā b. ʿUmar al-Lamtūnī, d. 447 or 448/1055–6 ⊘ Abū Bakr b. ʿUmar al-Lamtūnī, d. 480/1087	Berber chiefs in the Sahara acknowledging the spiritual authority of ʿAbdallāh b. Yāsīn

⊘ 453/1061	Yūsuf b. Tāshufīn
⊘ (462–7/1070–5	Ibrāhīm b. Abī Bakr, ruler in Sijilmāsa)
⊘ 500/1107	ʿAlī b. Yūsuf
⊘ 537/1142	Tāshufīn b. ʿAlī
⊘ 540/1146	Ibrāhīm b. Tāshufīn
⊘ 540–1/1146–7	Isḥāq b. ʿAlī
541/1147	*Almohad conquest*

The Almoravids arose from one of the waves of spiritual exaltation which have from time to time in the history of the Maghrib come over the Berber peoples there. In the early part of the eleventh century, the Ṣanhāja chief Yaḥyā b. Ibrāhīm of the Gudāla tribe, whose territories extended over parts of what became in modern times the Spanish Sahara and Mauritania, made the Pilgrimage to Mecca. Fired with enthusiasm, he came back to his own people with a Moroccan scholar, ʿAbdallāh b. Yāsīn, with the intention of propagating a strict form of Mālikī Sunnism. The militant and expansionist ideology which ʿAbdallāh b. Yāsīn now brought into being was, according to later local historians, given impetus by the community of *murābiṭūn*, dwellers in a *ribāṭ* or hermitage situated near the mouth of the Senegal River or along the Mauritanian coast; but if this *dār al-murābiṭīn* did in fact exist, its importance may well have been exaggerated. At all events, the term for these warriors, *murābiṭūn* 'those dwelling in a hermitage or frontier fortress', was to yield the Spanish form *Almorávides* by which the subsequent dynasty was to be called, and also the French word *marabout* 'holy man, saint', a figure especially characteristic of North African Muslim piety. These Berber warriors of the Sahara wore veils over their faces against the sand and wind (as do their modern descendants the Tuaregs), hence were also known as *al-mutalaththimūn* 'the veiled ones'.

Led by the Lamtunā chiefs Yaḥyā and Abū Bakr and then by the latter's lieutenant Yūsuf b. Tāshufīn, the Almoravids moved northwards against Morocco and conquered North Africa as far as the central part of what is now Algeria. With Abū Bakr now deflected southwards into the western Sahara, Yūsuf founded Marrakech (Marrākush) as his capital in 454/1062; from this event may be dated the formal beginning of the Almoravid dynasty in Morocco, explicitly designated on some coins, after Yūsuf's death, as the Banū Tāshufīn. The Almoravids recognised the ʿAbbāsid caliphs as spiritual heads of Islam and followed the conservative Mālikī law school, dominant in Spain and North Africa after the virtual demise of Khārijism.

Muslim Spain was at this time in the fragmented condition of the age of the *Mulūk al-Ṭawā'if* (see above, no. 5), and, now that the Christian Reconquista was gathering momentum, it became clear that only the rising power and enthusiasm of the Almoravids could save the divided and squabbling princelings there. Yūsuf b. Tāshufīn crossed over from Africa in 479/1086 and won a great victory over Alfonso VI of Léon and Castile at Zallāqa near Badajoz. Much Muslim territory was recovered or made secure in the western marches, although the recently-lost city of Toledo remained in Christian hands. Over the next few years, Yūsuf suppressed almost all the Taifas, only the Hūdids being allowed to remain in Saragossa (see above, no. 5, Taifa no. 17), and a fierce form of puritanical Islam, in which the works of the great theologian of eastern Islam, al-Ghazālī, were publicly burned, was introduced into Spain.

But in the early years of the twelfth century, the Almoravid position in the Maghrib was threatened by the rise there of a fresh religio-political movement, that of the Almohads and their Maṣmūda supporters in southern Morocco (see below, no. 15). It was because of this pressure in their rear that the Almoravids were unable to save Saragossa from the Christians in 512/1118. In 541/1147, the last Almoravid ruler in Marrakech, Isḥāq b. ʿAlī, was killed by ʿAbd al-Mu'min's troops, and the Almohads now began crossing into Spain. When the last Almoravid governor there, Yaḥyā b. Ghāniya al-Massūfī, whose family was related by marriage to the Almoravid ruling house, died in 543/1148, Almoravid power was ended. However, the post-Almoravid line of this Berber family, the Banū Ghāniya, continued, and held power in the Balearic Islands until the beginning of the thirteenth century (see above, no. 6).

The Almoravids of Morocco, and the Maghrib in general, rapidly assimilated Andalusian culture at this time. Abu Bakr b. ʿUmar and Yūsuf b. Tāshufīn came to disclaim their Berber origins and instead pretended to a Qaḥṭānī, South Arabian, royal pedigree. The dominance of Mālikism in North Africa was given a great fillip by their patronage, and the study of Māliki legal manuals was exalted above that of the Qur'ān and Ḥadīth, while *kalām*, scholastic theology, was regarded as positively inimical to the faith. Perhaps the most lasting legacy, however, of the Almoravid movement was the impetus which it gave to the spread of Islam, and of Almoravid religious doctrines in particular, southwards across the Sahara to the Sāḥil and Savannah zones of West Africa, namely to modern Senegal, Niger, Mali and northern Nigeria.

Lane-Poole, 41–4; Zambaur, 73–4; Album, 16.

EI[2] 'al-Murābiṭūn' (H. T. Norris and P. Chalmeta).

H. Terrasse, *Histoire du Maroc*, I, 211–60.

J. Bosch Vilá, *Los Almorávides*, Instituto General Franco de Estudios y investigación hispano-árabe, Historia de Marruecos, Tetouan 1950.

H. W. Hazard, *The Numismatic History of Late Medieval North Africa*, 59–64, 95–143, 236–63, 282–3.

15

THE ALMOHADS OR AL-MUWAḤḤIDŪN
524–668/1130–1269
North Africa and Spain

	Muḥammad b. Tūmart, d. 524/1130
⊘ 524/1130	ʿAbd al-Muʾmin b. ʿAlī al-Kūmī
⊘ 558/1163	Yūsuf I b. ʿAbd al-Muʾmin, Abū Yaʿqūb
⊘ 580/1184	Yaʿqūb b. Yūsuf I, Abū Yūsuf al-Manṣūr
⊘ 595/1199	Muḥammad b. Yaʿqūb, Abū ʿAbdallāh al-Nāṣir
⊘ 610/1213	Yūsuf II b. Muḥammad, Abū Yaʿqūb al-Mustanṣir
621/1224	ʿAbd al-Wāḥid b. Yūsuf I, Abū Muḥammad al-Makhlūʿ
⊘ 621/1224	ʿAbdallāh b. Yaʿqūb, Abū Muḥammad al-ʿĀdil
⊘ 624–33/1227–35	Yaḥyā b. Muḥammad, Abū Zakariyyāʾ al-Muʿtaṣim. Authority in Morocco disputed by ⊘ Idrīs I b. Yaʿqūb, Abu ʾl-ʿUlā al-Maʾmūn, 624–30/1227–32, and ⊘ ʿAbd al-Wāḥid b. Idrīs I, Abū Muḥammad al-Rashīd, 630/1232 onwards
⊘ 633/1235	ʿAbd al-Wāḥid b. Idrīs I, al-Rashīd
⊘ 640/1242	ʿAlī b. Idrīs I, Abu ʾl-Ḥasan al-Saʿīd
⊘ 646/1248	ʿUmar b. Isḥāq, Abū Ḥafṣ al-Murtaḍā
⊘ 665–8/1266–9	Idrīs II b. Muḥammad, Abu ʾl-ʿUlā Abū Dabbūs al-Wāthiq *Christian conquest of all mainland Spain, except Granada, by the mid-seventh/thirteenth century; the Almohad North African territories divided among the Ḥafṣids, ʿAbd al-Wādids and Marīnids*

The Almohads (an originally Spanish form from *al-Muwaḥḥidūn* 'those who proclaim God's unity') represented, intellectually and theologically, a protest against the rigidly conservative and legalistic Mālikism prevalent in North Africa and against the social laxity of life under the later Almoravids (see above, no. 14). Their founder, the Maṣmūda Berber Ibn Tūmart, had studied in the East and had acquired ascetic, reformist views. On returning to Morocco, he was in 515/1121 hailed by his followers as the Mahdī or promised charismatic leader who would restore and cause to triumph the true and universal Islam. For his fellow-Berbers of southern Morocco, he made available in their own language Muslim creeds and other theological and legal works, so that one aspect of his mission may have been to express the religious feelings of the mountain Berbers against the essentially urban attitudes of the Mālikī lawyers who were the mainstay of Almoravid religious authority. His lieutenant ʿAbd al-Muʾmin assumed leadership of the movement on Ibn Tūmart's death; he carried on the war against the Almoravids, gradually taking over Morocco from them, and after 542/1147 he made the Almoravid capital of Marrakech his own.

In Spain, there was a vacuum of power after the decline of the Almoravids there, in which some local groups like the Taifas of the previous century reappeared, for example at Valencia, Cordova, Murcia and Mértola (see above, no. 5, Taifas nos 11, 15, 18). Then, in 540/1145, ʿAbd al-Muʾmin despatched an army to Spain and soon occupied the greater part of the Muslim-held territory there. A powerful Almohad kingdom, with its capital at Seville, was now constituted on both sides of the Straits of Gibraltar. The countryside of the central and eastern Maghrib had become economically disrupted, and socially and politically disturbed, by influxes of nomadic Arabs from the East, and the coastlands were being harried by Norman Christian raiders. With his highly effective military and naval forces, ʿAbd al-Muʾmin conquered as far as Tunis and Tripoli, thus uniting the whole of North Africa under Almohad rule; the Ayyūbid sultan Ṣalāḥ al-Dīn or Saladin (see below, no. 30) sought – in vain, as it proved – Almohad ships for his war against the Frankish Crusaders. The Almohad rulers now assumed the lofty titles of caliph and 'Commander of the Faithful'.

The structure of the Almohad state reflected the messianic, authoritarian nature of Ibn Tūmart's original teaching, and was built around a closely-knit hierarchy of the caliphs' advisers and intimates. Their court was a splendid centre of art and learning, above all, for the last flowering of Islamic philosophy associated with such scholars as Ibn Ṭufayl (Abubacer) and Ibn Rushd (Averroes), both of whom acted as court physicians to the Almohad rulers; and the Almohad period saw a remarkable florescence of a simple but monumental style of architecture in North Africa and at Seville. Intellectual speculation was nevertheless confined to the narrow court circles, and elsewhere in the Almohad empire a rigid and repressive orthodoxy prevailed. The *Dhimmīs* or 'Protected Peoples', Jews and Christians, suffered extreme hostility and persecution, seen in the massacres of Jews in Spain and Morocco, which triggered an exodus of Jews to Christian Europe and to the Near East; those to the latter destination included the physician and philosopher Maimonides, who fled from Cordova and settled in Cairo.

Abū Yūsuf Yaʿqūb won a victory over the Christians of Spain at Alarcos (al-Arak) in 591/1195, and his successor freed the eastern Maghrib as far as Libya and the Balearic Islands from the control of the Banū Ghāniya (see above, no. 6). But Muḥammad al-Nāṣir's catastrophic defeat in 609/1212 at Las Navas de Tolosa (al-ʿIqāb), at the hands of most of the Christian kings of the peninsula, led to a decline of Almohad authority in Spain and Morocco, with internal revolts and dynastic quarrels, and with Idrīs al-Maʾmūn repudiating the Almohad doctrine. Spain was abandoned, to face alone the impetus of the Reconquista, and the Almohad grip on North Africa began also to loosen. In 627/1230, the Ḥafṣid governor of Ifrīqiya proclaimed his independence (see below, no. 18), and a decade later the rising of Yaghmurāsan b. Zayyān or Ziyān in the central Maghrib led to the formation of the ʿAbd al-Wādid kingdom based on Tlemcen (Tilimsān) (see below, no. 17). Within Morocco, the Marīnids (see below, no. 16) began to wear down what remained of Almohad authority, culminating in their capture of Marrākush in 668/1269 and of Tinmallal, cradle of the Almohad movement, eight years later; the capital of Morocco now moved to Fez.

Lane-Poole, 45–7; Zambaur, 73–4; Album, 16–17.
EI[2] 'al-Muwaḥḥidūn' (M. Shatzmiller).
H. Terrasse, *Histoire du Maroc*, I, 261–367.
H. W. Hazard, *The Numismatic History of Late Medieval North Africa*, 64–8, 143–58, 262–73, 283.
A. Huici Miranda, *Historia politica del imperio Almohade*, 2 vols, Instituto General Franco de Estudios y investigación hispano-árabe, Tetouan 1956–7.

16

THE MARĪNIDS
614–869/1217–1465
North Africa

	ʿAbd al-Ḥaqq I al-Marīnī, Abū Muḥammad
614/1217	ʿUthmān I b. ʿAbd al-Ḥaqq I, Abū Saʿīd
638/1240	Muḥammad I b. ʿAbd al-Ḥaqq I, Abū Maʿrūf
⊘ 642/1244	Abū Bakr b. ʿAbd al-Ḥaqq I, Abū Yaḥyā
⊘ 656/1258	Yaʿqūb b. ʿAbd al-Ḥaqq I, Abū Yūsuf
⊘ 685/1286	Yūsuf b. Yaʿqūb, Abū Yaʿqūb al-Nāṣir
706/1307	ʿAmr b. Yūsuf, Abū Thābit
708/1308	Sulaymān b. Yūsuf, Abu ʾl-Rabīʿ
⊘ 710/1310	ʿUthmān II b. Yaʿqūb, Abū Saʿīd
⊘ 731/1331	ʿAlī b. ʿUthmān II, Abu ʾl-Ḥasan
⊘ 749/1348	Fāris b. ʿAlī, Abū ʿInān al-Mutawakkil
759/1358	Muḥammad II b. Fāris, Abū Zayyān or Ziyān al-Saʿīd, first reign
759/1358	Abū Bakr b. Fāris, Abū Yaḥyā
⊘ 760/1359	Ibrāhīm b. ʿAli, Abū Sālim
762/1361	Tāshufīn b. ʿAlī, Abū ʿAmr
⊘ 763/1362	Muḥammad II b. Fāris, al-Muntaṣir, second reign
(763/1362	ʿAbd al-Ḥalīm b. ʿUmar, Abū Muḥammad, in Sijilmāsa only)
⊘ (764–5/1363–4	ʿAbd al-Muʾmin b. ʿUmar, Abū Mālik in Sijilmāsa only)
⊘ 767/1366	ʿAbd al-ʿAzīz I b. ʿAlī, Abū Fāris al-Mustanṣir
⊘ 774/1372	Muḥammad III b. ʿAbd al-ʿAzīz, Abū Zayyān or Ziyān al-Saʿīd
⊘ 775/1373	Aḥmad I b. Ibrāhīm, Abu ʾl-ʿAbbās al-Mustanṣir
⊘ (776–84/1374–82	ʿAbd al-Raḥmān b. Abī Ifallūsin, Abū Zayd, ruler in Marrakech)
⊘ 786/1384	Mūsā b. Fāris, Abū Fāris
⊘ 788/1386	Muḥammad IV b. Aḥmad I, Abū Zayyān or Ziyān al-Muntaṣir
788/1386	Muḥammad V b. ʿAlī, Abū Zayyān or Ziyān al-Wāthiq
789/1387	Aḥmad II b. Aḥmad I, Abu ʾl-ʿAbbās
⊘ 796/1393	ʿAbd al-ʿAzīz II b. Aḥmad II, Abū Fāris
⊘ 799/1397	ʿAbdallāh b. Aḥmad II, Abū ʿAmir
⊘ 800/1398	ʿUthmān III b. Aḥmad II, Abū Saʿīd
823–69/1420–65	ʿAbd al-Ḥaqq II b. ʿUthmān III, Abū Muḥammad, *under the regency of the Waṭṭāsids and then as nominal ruler under their control*

The Marīnids succeeded to the heritage of the Almohads (see above, no. 15) in Morocco and much of the lands of the Maghrib lying to the east. The Banū Marīn were a tribe of Zanāta Berbers who nomadised on the north-western fringes of the Sahara, where there now runs in a north-east to south-west direction the modern border between Algeria and Morocco. It seems that they were sheep herders and that they gave their name to the fine-quality merino wool exported from an early date via mediaeval Italy to Europe. The cultural level of the Banū Marīn was probably low; they were uninspired in their bid for power by any of the religious enthusiasms which had given impetus to the movements of the Almoravids and Almohads, and may not have been long converted to Islam. These facts, combined with what seem to have been comparatively restricted numbers, doubtless account for the protracted nature of their struggles in the mid-thirteenth century with the later Almohads. They first invaded Morocco from the Sahara in 613/1216, but were halted by the Almohad rulers, and did not capture the latter's capital Marrakech until 668/1269 and Sijilmāsa until four years later.

Once established in their capital at Fez, the Marīnids acquired a strong sense of being heirs to the Almohads, and attempted, with considerable success, to rebuild their empire in the Maghrib. They further nurtured the spirit of *jihād* and utilised popular religious fervour in the Maghrib for a desired reconquest of Spain. Several Marīnid sultans fought personally in the Iberian peninsula. Abū Yūsuf Yaʿqūb crossed over in answer to an appeal from the Naṣrids of Granada (see above, no. 7) and won the battle of Ecija in 674/1275. After the Christian capture of Gibraltar in 709/1309, Marīnid troops again appeared in Spain, but Abu 'l-Ḥasan ʿAlī was routed at the Rio Salado in 741/1340 by the forces of Alfonso XI of Castile and his brother-in-law Alfonso IV of Portugal, and the Marīnids never again tried to intervene directly in Spain. Within North Africa, the Marīnids wore down their neighbours the ʿAbd al-Wādids (see below, no. 17), occupying their capital Tlemcen in 737/1337 and 753/1352 and temporarily dislodging the Ḥafṣids from Tunis in 748/1347, for a while controlling the whole Maghrib. These years of the later thirteenth and the first two-thirds of the fourteenth century also saw a remarkable cultural and artistic efflorescence in Morocco, seen in the extensive building of mosques, madrasas and other public buildings which gave concrete expression to the strength of a restored Mālikism and an increased trend towards popular Ṣūfism and maraboutism.

Towards the end of the fourteenth century, the decline of the Marīnids began to be apparent. In 803/1401, Henry III of Castile attacked Tetouan (Tiṭṭāwīn) and in 818/1415 the Portuguese took Ceuta (Sabta), and this extension of the Reconquista to North Africa provoked a further wave of religious sentiment and calls for *jihād* in the Maghrib against the infidels. Within the Marīnid sultanate, there was a prolonged series of succession crises, with Marīnid princes placed on the throne for short reigns by palace coups or by Arab and Berber tribal revolts. After the assassination of sultan Abū Saʿīd ʿUthmān III in 823/1420, *de facto* power in the western Maghrib was assumed by a family related to the Marīnids, the Banū Waṭṭās (see below, no. 19), acting at first as regents for the infant Abū Muḥammad ʿAbd al-Ḥaqq II; but after the latter's murder in 869/1465, the Waṭṭāsids shortly afterwards succeeded in form as well as name to the heritage of the Marīnids in Morocco.

Lane-Poole, 57–9; Zambaur, 79–80; Album, 18.

EI[1] 'Merīnids' (G. Marçais); *EI*[2] 'Marīnids' (Maya Shatzmiller), with detailed genealogical table, correcting and replacing that of Zambaur.

H. Terrasse, *Histoire du Maroc*, II, 3–104.

H. W. Hazard, *The Numismatic History of Late Medieval North Africa*, 79–84, 192–227, 275–8, 284–5.

17

THE ʿABD AL-WĀDIDS OR ZAYYĀNIDS OR ZIYĀNIDS
633–962/1236–1555
Western Algeria

⊘	633/1236	Yaghmurāsan b. Zayyān or Ziyān, Abū Yaḥyā
	681/1283	ʿUthmān I b. Yaghmurāsan, Abū Saʿīd
	703/1304	Muḥammad I b. ʿUthmān, Abū Zayyān or Ziyān
⊘	707/1308	Mūsā I b. ʿUthmān, Abū Ḥammū
⊘	718/1318	ʿAbd al-Raḥmān I b. Mūsa I, Abū Tāshufīn
	737/1337	*First Marīnid conquest*
	749/1348	ʿUthmān II b. ʿAbd al-Raḥmān I,Abū Saʿīd al-Zaʿīm b. ʿAbd al-Raḥmān I, Abū Thābit } co-rulers
	753/1352	*Second Marīnid conquest*
⊘	760/1359	Mūsā II b. Yūsuf, Abū Ḥammū
⊘	791/1389	ʿAbd al-Raḥmān II b. Mūsā II, Abū Tāshufīn
	796/1394	Yūsuf I b. ʿAbd al-Raḥmān II, Abū Thābit
	796/1394	Yūsuf II b. Mūsa II, Abu ʾl-Ḥajjāj
⊘	797/1395	Muḥammad II b. Mūsā II, Abū Zayyān or Ziyān
⊘	802/1400	ʿAbdallāh I b. Mūsā II, Abū Muḥammad
⊘	804/1402	Muḥammad III b. Mūsā II, Abū ʿAbd Allāh al-Wāthiq
	813/1411	ʿAbd al-Raḥmān III b. Muḥammad III, Abū Tāshufīn
	814/1411	Saʿīd b. Mūsā II
⊘	814/1411	ʿAbd al-Wāḥid b. Mūsā II, Abū Mālik, first reign
⊘	827/1424	Muḥammad IV b. ʿAbd al-Raḥmān III, Abū ʿAbdallāh
	831/1428	ʿAbd al-Wāḥid b. Mūsā II, second reign
⊘	833/1430	Aḥmad I b. Mūsā II, Abu ʾl-ʿAbbās
⊘	866/1462	Muḥammad V b. Muḥammad, Abū ʿAbdallāh al-Mutawakkil
	873/1469	Abū Tāshufīn b. Muḥammad V
	873/1469	Muḥammad VI b. Muḥammad V, Abū ʿAbdallāh al-Thābitī
⊘	910/1504	Muḥammad VII b. Muḥammad VI, Abū ʿAbdallāh al-Thābitī, after 918/1512 as a vassal of Ferdinand II of Aragon
	923/1517	Mūsā III b. Muḥammad V, Abū Ḥammū
	934/1528	ʿAbdallāh II b. Muḥammad V, Abū Muḥammad
⊘	947/1540	Muḥammad VIII b. ʿAbdallāh II, Abū ʿAbdallāh
	947/1541	Aḥmad II b. ʿAbdallāh II, Abū Zayyān or Ziyān, first reign
	949/1543	*Spanish occupation*
	951/1544	Aḥmad II b. ʿAbdallāh II, second reign, as an Ottoman vassal
	957/1550	al-Ḥasan b. ʿAbdallāh II
	962/1555	*Conquest of Tlemcen by Ṣalāḥ Reʾīs Pasha of Algiers*

The ʿAbd al-Wādids or Zayyānids or Ziyānids were originally from the Wāsīn tribe of Zanāta Berbers, hence kin to the Marīnids (see above, no. 16). They rose to prominence in what is now north-western Algeria through their support to the Almohads, so that their chief, Yaghmurāsan (? Yaghamrāsan), was able to found a principality of his own based on Tlemcen (Tilimsān). The decay of his Almohad suzerains left him exposed to attack by the Marīnids of Fez, and after his death the latter were twice to occupy Tlemcen. The ʿAbd al-Wādid princes endeavoured to stem Marīnid ambitions against Tlemcen through alliances with Christian Castile and the Naṣrids of Granada (see above, no. 7), common foes of the Marīnids, although, having inherited lands which had been devastated by the incoming nomadic Arabs of the Banū Hilāl and Banū Sulaym, their economic and military resources were limited. The only direction in which the ʿAbd al-Wādids could themselves contemplate expansion was eastwards, although their raids here were generally checked by the Ḥafṣids (see below, no. 18). The ʿAbd al-Wādid principality never fully recovered from the Marīnid occupations, although the decline of the Marīnid rulers of Fez and their replacement by the less formidably aggressive Waṭṭāsids (see below, no. 19) relieved pressure from the direction of Morocco. It was the Ḥafṣids who were the main threat to Tlemcen in the fifteenth century, at one point successfully attacking the town and imposing vassal ʿAbd al-Wādid princes on the throne there; but this threat was succeeded in the sixteenth century by ones from the Spaniards in Oran and the Turkish pashas in Algiers, and it was from the pressure of these last two powers that the ʿAbd al-Wādids finally succumbed in 962/1555, the son of the last ruler, al-Ḥasan, becoming a Christian convert under the name of Carlos.

Tlemcen owed much of its mediaeval florescence and splendour to the ʿAbd al-Wādids. It lay on the main east–west route through Algeria to Morocco, with a caravan route southwards to the Sahara and with its own port at nearby Hunayn, which traded with the Christian powers of the western Mediterranean. The fine public buildings of Tlemcen attest the encouragement of learning and enlightened patronage of its princes.

Lane-Poole, 51, 54; Sachau, 25 no. 57; Zambaur, 77–8; Album, 17.

EI[1] 'Tlemcen' (A. Bel); EI[2] 'ʿAbd al-Wādids' (G. Marçais).

H. W. Hazard, *The Numismatic History of Late Medieval North Africa*, 75–9, 181–92, 274–5, 284.

18

THE ḤAFṢIDS

627–982/1229–1574

Tunisia and eastern Algeria

⊘ 627/1229	Yaḥyā I b. 'Abd al-Wāḥid, Abū Zakariyyā'
⊘ 647/1249	Muḥammad I b. Yaḥyā I, Abū 'Abdallāh al-Mustanṣir
⊘ 675/1277	Yaḥyā II b. Muḥammad I, Abū Zakariyyā' al-Wāthiq
⊘ 678/1279	Ibrāhīm I b. Yaḥyā I, Abū Isḥāq, k. 682/1283
681/1282	*Usurpation of Aḥmad b. Abī 'Umāra*
⊘ 683/1284	'Umar I b. Yaḥyā I, Abū Ḥafṣ (after 684/1285 in Tunis only)
⊘ 684/1285	Yaḥyā III b. Ibrāhīm I, Abū Zakariyyā' al-Muntakhab (in Bougie and Constantine until 689/1299)
⊘ 694/1295	Muḥammad II b. Yaḥyā II, Abū 'Abdallāh (or Abū 'Aṣīda)
⊘ 709/1309	Abū Bakr I b. 'Abd al-Raḥmān, Abū Yaḥyā al-Shahīd (after 709/1309 in Constantine and after 712/1312 in Bougie)
⊘ 709/1309	Khālid I b. Yaḥyā III, Abu 'l-Baqā'
⊘ 711/1311	Zakariyyā' I b. Aḥmad, al-Liḥyānī, Abū Yaḥyā (in Tunis)
⊘ 717/1317	Muḥammad III b. Zakariyyā' I, Abū 'Abdallāh or Abū Ḍarba al-Liḥyānī al-Mustanṣir (in Tunis)
⊘ 718/1318	Abū Bakr II b. Yaḥyā III, Abū Yaḥyā al-Mutawakkil
⊘ 747/1346	'Umar II b. Abī Bakr II, Abū Ḥafṣ
748/1348	*First Marīnid occupation of Tunis*
⊘ 750/1350	Aḥmad I b. Abī Bakr II, Abu 'l-'Abbās al-Faḍl al-Mutawakkil
⊘ 750/1350	Ibrāhīm II b. Abī Bakr II, Abū Isḥāq al-Mustanṣir, first reign
758/1357	*Second Marīnid occupation of Constantine and Tunis*
⊘ 758/1357	Ibrāhīm II b. Abī Bakr II, second reign (in Tunis until 770/1369; other Ḥafṣid princes in Bougie and Constantine)
770/1369	Khālid II b. Ibrāhīm II, Abu 'l-Baqā' (in Tunis)
⊘ 772/1370	Aḥmad II b. Muḥammad, Abu 'l-'Abbās al-Mustanṣir (previously in Bougie and Constantine)
⊘ 796/1394	'Abd al-'Azīz b. Aḥmad II, Abū Fāris al-Mutawakkil
837/1434	Muḥammad IV b. Muḥammad al-Manṣūr, Abū 'Abdallāh al-Muntaṣir
⊘ 839/1435	'Uthmān b. Muḥammad al-Manṣūr, Abū 'Amr or 'Umar
893/1488	IV b. Muḥammad al-Mas'ūd, Abū Zakariyyā' Yaḥyā
894/1489	'Abd al-Mu'min b. Abī Sālim Ibrāhīm, Abū Muḥammad
895/1490	Zakariyyā' II b. Yaḥyā IV, Abū Yaḥyā
⊘ 899/1494	Muḥammad V b. Abī Muḥammad al-Ḥasan, Abū 'Abdallāh al-Mutawakkil
⊘ 932/1526	al-Ḥasan b. Muḥammad V, Abū 'Abdallāh, first reign
941/1534	*First Turkish conquest of Tunis by Khayr al-Dīn Barbarossa*
942/1535	al-Ḥasan b. Muḥammad V, second reign (as a vassal of the Emperor Charles V)
⊘ 950/1543	Aḥmad III b. al-Ḥasan, Abū Zayyān or Ziyān
977/1569	*Second Turkish conquest of Tunis by 'Ulūj 'Alī*

981/1573 Muḥammad VI b. al-Ḥasan, Abū ʿAbdallāh (as a vassal of Spain)
982/1574 Third and definitive Turkish conquest of Tunis from Don John of Austria by Sinān Pasha

The Ḥafṣids, the most important dynasty in the history of later mediaeval Ifrīqiya, derived their name from Shaykh Abū Ḥafṣ ʿUmar al-Hintātī (d. 571/1176), a disciple of the founder of the Almohad movement, Ibn Tūmart (see above, no. 15), and one of ʿAbd al-Muʾmin's commanders. His offspring filled various important offices under the Almohads, including the governorship of Ifrīqiya, and, once established as a separate dynasty, the early Ḥafṣids were to continue Almohad traditions in many ways. One of these Ḥafṣid governors, Abū Zakariyyāʾ Yaḥyā I, in 627/1229 threw off the authority of the Almohad caliph, alleging that the latter had abandoned the true Muʾminid traditions, and proclaimed himself an independent amīr. He now expanded westwards into the central Maghrib, taking Constantine, Bougie and Algiers, making the ʿAbd al-Wādids of Tlemcen (see above, no. 17) his tributaries, compelling the Marīnids of Morocco to acknowledge him and receiving appeals for help from the beleaguered Muslims of southern Spain. He further began the tradition of close commercial relations in the western Mediterranean with such powers as Angevin Sicily and Aragon. The power of the Ḥafṣids was equally great under his son Abū ʿAbdallāh Muḥammad I, who repelled the attacks of Louis IX of France and Charles of Anjou (the Crusade of 668/1270), and assumed the titles of caliph and 'Commander of the Faithful' plus the grandiose honorific of al-Mustanṣir, obtaining these titles from the Sharīf of Mecca and claiming to be the heir of the recently-defunct Baghdad ʿAbbāsids (see above, no. 3, 1).

Towards the end of the thirteenth century, however, the unity of the Ḥafṣid amirate became loosened, with Bougie and Constantine, in particular, tending to fall under the authority of separate rulers from the Ḥafṣid family, and with southern Tunisia and the Djerid region also throwing off the control of Tunis during periods of weak rule. At times, there were several contenders for the throne in Tunis, with claimants ruling in various towns, and during the course of the fourteenth century the Ḥafṣid capital was twice occupied temporarily by the Marīnids (see above, no. 16). The dynasty rallied in the fifteenth century under such strong rulers as Abū Fāris ʿAbd al-ʿAzīz al-Mutawakkil and his grandson Abū ʿUmar ʿUthmān, but in the early sixteenth century the establishment of the Turks in Algiers and other ports and the inability of the Ḥafṣids to curb corsair depredations in the western Mediterranean invited attacks and reprisals by the Christians. A Turkish occupation of Tunis in 941/1535 drove out the Ḥafṣid ruler, who was only restored after the Emperor Charles V had planted a Spanish garrison at La Goletta later in that year. The last Ḥafṣids retained a precarious authority with Spanish help against the Turks; in 981/1573 Don John of Austria took Tunis, but in the following year the Ottoman commander Sinān Pasha recaptured it and carried off the last Ḥafṣid captive to Istanbul.

Tunis under the Ḥafṣids enjoyed a great resurgence of prosperity. Before the disruptive activity of the Barbary pirates caused a deterioration in relations, the Ḥafṣids had fruitful commercial treaties with Anjevin Sicily, with the Italian and southern French cities and with Aragon. Both the economy and the culture of the land also benefited from the influx of Spanish Muslim refugees (among whom were the forebears of the historian Ibn Khaldūn). Tunis became a great artistic and intellectual centre, and it was the Ḥafṣids who in the thirteenth century introduced the madrasa system of education already flourishing in the central and eastern lands of Islam.

Lane-Poole, 49–50, 52–3; Zambaur, 74–6; Album, 17.
EI^2 'Ḥafṣids' (H. R. Idris).
R. Brunschvig, *La Berbérie orientale sous les Ḥafṣides des origines à la fin du XVe siècle*, 2 vols, Paris 1940–7, with genealogical tables at II, 446.
H. W. Hazard, *The Numismatic History of Late Medieval North Africa*, 69–75, 159–81, 273–4, 284.

19

THE WAṬṬĀSIDS

831–946/1428–1549
Morocco and the central Maghrib

831/1428	Yaḥyā I b. Zayyān al-Waṭṭāsī, Abū Zakariyyā', at first regent for the Marīnids and then as *de facto* ruler for them
852/1448	'Alī b. Yūsuf } *de facto* rulers for the Marīnids
863/1458–9	Yaḥyā II b. Yaḥyā I }
863–9/1459–65	*Direct rule of the Marīnid 'Abd al-Ḥaqq II*
869–75/1465–71	*Rule of the Idrīsid* Shorfā *in Fez*
⊘ 876/1472	Muḥammad I b. Yaḥyā I, Abū 'Abdallāh al-Shaykh
⊘ 910/1504	Muḥammad II b. Muḥammad I, Abū 'Abdallāh al-Burtuqālī
⊘ 932/1526	'Alī b. Muḥammad II, Abu 'l-Ḥasan or Abū Ḥassūn, as rival ruler, first reign
⊘ 932/1526	Aḥmad b. Muḥammad II, first reign
⊘ 952/1545	Muḥammad III b. Aḥmad, al-Qaṣrī, Nāṣir al-Dīn
954–6/1547–9	Aḥmad b. Muḥammad II, second reign
956/1549	*Sa'did Sharīfs*
961/1554	'Alī b. Muḥammad II, temporary occupation of Fez, second reign
961/1554	*Sa'did Sharīfs*

The decline of the Marīnids (see above, no. 16) facilitated the rise of the Banū Waṭṭās, a collateral branch of the Berber Banū Marīn from which the family of 'Abd al-Ḥaqq I, founder of the Marīnid fortunes, had sprung. The Banū Waṭṭās settled in north-eastern Morocco and the Rīf as virtually autonomous governors for their Marīnid kinsmen, with whose rule they were always closely linked, receiving high offices and other favours from the sultans.

When Morocco fell into anarchy in the 1420s, with extensive Christian attacks on its coasts and with the murder of the Marīnid Abū Sa'īd 'Uthmān III, the Waṭṭāsid Abū Zakariyyā' Yaḥyā, governor of Salé (Salā), proclaimed a young son of the dead sultan as the new ruler (as events proved, the last of the Marīnid line), 'Abd al-Ḥaqq II, with himself acting as regent. This regency of the Waṭṭāsids in fact lasted until well after the Marīnid reached his majority, and only latterly did 'Abd al-Ḥaqq manage to throw off their tutelage. However, the Waṭṭāsids returned to power at Fez in 876/1472, now as independent rulers; under them, the city's splendour to some extent continued as under the Marīnids, and it was during their time that Leo Africanus visited Fez.

Pressure from the Christian powers of the Iberian peninsula was meanwhile growing apace, and the fall of Granada in 897/1492 aroused a fresh wave of Islamic fervour in Morocco, spearheaded by the Sa'did *Shorfā* from southern Morocco (see below, no. 20), who moved northwards and seized Marrakech in 929/1523 and Fez in 956/1549. The Waṭṭāsids even tried, in vain, to get help from the Emperor Charles V and from the Portuguese, but were unable to check the Sa'did advance. A revanche with Ottoman Turkish help from Tlemcen achieved only a momentary success, with its ultimate failure sealing the fate of the dynasty permanently;

some of the last Waṭṭāsids left for the Iberian peninsula and became converts to Christianity.

Lane-Poole, 58; Sachau, 26 no. 62; Zambaur, 79–80; Album, 18.
EI[1] 'Waṭṭāsids' (E. Lévi-Provençal).
A. Cour, *La dynastie marocaine des Beni Waṭṭās (1420–1534)*, Constantine 1920.
H. De Castries (ed.), *Les sources inédites de l'histoire du Maroc de 1530 à 1845, Série 1, Dynastie saadienne 1530–1660*, vol. IV, part I, Paris 1921, with detailed genealogical tables of the Waṭṭāsids at pp. 162–3.
H. Terrasse, *Histoire du Maroc*, II, 105–57.
H. W. Hazard, *The Numismatic History of Late Medieval North Africa*, 85–6, 229–30, 279–80, 285.

20

THE SAʿDID SHARĪFS
916–1069/1510–1659
Morocco

916/1510	Muḥammad I b. ʿAbd al-Raḥmān, Abū ʿAbdallāh al-Qāʾim al-Mahdī, in the Sūs	
923/1517	Aḥmad al-Aʿraj b. Muḥammad al-Mahdī, north of the Atlas, then in Marrakech after 930/1524 until 950/1543	
⊘ 923/1517	Maḥammad al-Shaykh b. Muḥammad al-Mahdi, Abū ʿAbdallāh al-Mahdī al-Imām, in the Sūs, then in Marrakech after 950/1543, and then in Fez after 956/1549 as sole Saʿdī ruler in Morocco	
⊘ 964/1557	ʿAbdallāh b. Maḥammad al-Shaykh, Abū Muḥammad al-Ghālib	
⊘ 981/1574	Muḥammad II b. ʿAbdallāh, al-Mutawakkil al-Maslūkh	
⊘ 983/1576	ʿAbd al-Malik b. Maḥammad al-Shaykh, Abū Marwān	
⊘ 986/1578	Aḥmad b. Maḥammad al-Shaykh, Abu ʾl-ʿAbbās al-Manṣūr al-Dhahabī	
⊘ 1012/1603	Zaydān, Abu ʾl-Maʿālī al-Nāṣir, in Fez until 1013/1604, then in the Sūs, then in Marrakech after 1018/1609 until his death in 1036/1627	sons of Aḥmad al-Manṣūr, in rivalry for the sultanate
	⊘ ʿAbdallāh, Abū Fāris al-Wāthiq, in Marrakech until 1015/1606, then in Fez until his death in 1018/1609	
	⊘ Maḥammad al-Shaykh al-Maʾmūn, in Fez from 1015/1606; killed in 1022/1613	
⊘ 1015/1606	ʿAbdallāh b. Maḥammad al-Shaykh al-Maʾmūn, al-Ghālib, at first in Marrakech, then after 1018/1609 in Fez until his death in 1032/1623	
⊘ 1032/1623	ʿAbd al-Malik b. Maḥammad al-Shaykh, al-Muʿtaṣim, in Fez until 1036/1627	
⊘ 1036/1627	ʿAbd al-Malik b. Zaydān al-Nāṣir, Abū Marwān, successor to his father in Marrakech until his death in 1040/1631	
⊘ (1037–8/1628–9	Aḥmad b. Zaydān al-Nāṣir, Abu ʾl-ʿAbbās, claimant)	
⊘ 1040/1631	Muḥammad al-Walīd b. Zaydān al-Nāṣir, in Marrakech	
⊘ 1045/1636	Maḥammad al-Shaykh al-Aṣghar or al-Ṣaghīr b. Zaydān al-Nāṣir, in Marrakech	
1065/1655	Aḥmad al-ʿAbbās b. Maḥammad al-Shaykh al-Aṣghar	
1069–79/1659–68	*Power in Morocco divided between the Filālī or ʿAlawī* Sharīfs *of Tafilalt and the Dilāʾī marabouts of the Atlas*	

From mediaeval times onwards, the *Shorfā* of Morocco (classical form *Shurafāʾ*, sing. *Sharīf*) have played an outstanding part in the country's history. The Maghrib has often been receptive to the leadership of messianic or charismatic figures, and some of the most characteristic forms of popular Islam there have been the cult of holy men, saints and marabouts (< *murābiṭ*: see above, no. 14) and the formation of religious fraternities organised round the religio-military centres of the *zāwiyas*. The strength of maraboutism and the rise to social pre-eminence of the *Shorfā* have been especially characteristic of Moroccan Islam, for Morocco, with its Mediterranean and Atlantic seaboards and its proximity to Spain and Portugal, bore the brunt of crusading Christian naval and military attacks from the thirteenth century onwards, provoking a Muslim reaction of commensurate intensity.

The *Sharīfs* are the descendants in general of the Prophet Muḥammad, but in Morocco most of the lines of *Shorfā* have traced their descent from the Prophet's grandson al-Ḥasan b. ʿAlī, and the Saʿdids and their successors the ʿAlawīs or Filālīs (see below, no. 21) claimed descent thus, specifically via al-Ḥasan's grandson Muḥammad b. ʿAbdallāh, called *al-Nafs al-Zakiyya* 'the Pure Soul' (killed at Medina in 145/767). The Idrīsids (see above, no. 8) were the first line of *Sharīfs* to achieve power in Morocco, but in ensuing centuries various Berber dynasties from the Midrārids and Almoravids onwards (see above, nos 10, 14) dominated the history of the land. However, the chance of the *Shorfā* came in the sixteenth century when the power of the Berber Waṭṭāsids of Fez (see above, no. 19) was clearly waning. From a base in the Sūs of southern Morocco, the Saʿdid line of *Shorfā* – who had been quietly consolidating their position in southern Morocco for some two centuries – gradually extended northwards, seizing Marrakech in 930/1524 and Fez from the last Waṭṭāsids in 956/1549.

The full titles of the founder of the line's fortunes, Sīdī Muḥammad al-Mahdī al-Qā'im bi-amr Allāh, show how messianic expectations in Morocco and feelings of religious exaltation and *jihād* against the Christians were utilised by the early Saʿdīs. Their authority was now imposed over almost the whole of Morocco, and the *Bilād al-Makhzan*, or area where the sultan's writ ran and from which taxation and troops were raised, reached its maximum extent. In the east, the Saʿdids had a determined enemy in the Turks of Algiers, who aimed at extending Ottoman suzerainty over as much of the Maghrib as possible. Hence the Saʿdids did not hesitate in the sixteenth century to ally with powers like Spain and Navarre against the Turks, but a long-term aim of theirs was ejection of the Portuguese from their *presidios* or garrison towns on the Atlantic coast. Under the greatest ruler of the dynasty, Mawlāy Aḥmad al-Manṣūr, trading relations were established with Christian powers as far afield as England, with the Barbary Company receiving commercial privileges within Morocco. But his greatest achievement was a vast expansion southwards in 999/1590 through the Sudan to the Niger valley, defeating the local ruler or *Askia* of Gao (in modern Mali) and extending Moroccan dominion over the *Sāḥil* and Savannah belt of West Africa from Senegal to Bornu. The gold which now accrued to al-Manṣūr from the Sudan earned him his further honorific of *al-Dhahabī* 'the Golden One', while control of the salt-pans of the Western Sahara brought further economic benefits to Morocco. The social and fiscal privileges of the *Shorfā* were now further consolidated and confirmed by each new sultan on his accession, and it was the *Shorfā* also who, at this time, played a leading role in the formation of a Moroccan feeling, strongly xenophobic and imbued with feelings of *jihād*, and concerned to preserve the land against Christian and Turkish encroachments.

However, in the early seventeenth century the Saʿdids were rent by succession disputes, with anarchy over much of Morocco and with various local adventurers and marabouts striving for power. The last *Sharīf*s tended to be confined to the Marrakech region, and, despite help at times from outside powers like the English and Dutch, the Saʿdids disappeared in 1069/1659 as the authority of the ʿAlawī or Filālī *Sharīf*s of Tafilalt (see below, no. 21) rose *pari passu* with their decline and finally displaced them.

It should be noted that the honorific title *Mawlāy* 'My Lord' was frequently borne by and prefixed to the names of the Sharīfī sultans, both Saʿdī and Filālī, with the exception of those who were called Muḥammad and were therefore called *Sayyidī/Sīdī* (with the same meaning), although the variant form Maḥammad (colloquial form M'ḥammed, used in the Maghrib with a hope of sharing in the *baraka* or charisma attached to the Prophet's name without risk of the original form Muḥammad being profaned in any way) did not exclude the usage of *Mawlāy*.

Lane-Poole, 60–2; Zambaur, 81 and Table C; Album, 18.

EI[1] 'S̲h̲orfā'' (E. Lévi-Provençal); *EI*[2] 'Ḥasanī' (G. Deverdun), with a genealogical table; 'al-Mag̲h̲rib, al-Mamlaka al-Mag̲h̲ribiyya II. History' (G. Yver*), 'Saʿdids' (Chantal de La Véronne), with a genealogical table.

H. Terrasse, *Histoire du Maroc*, II, 158–235.

H. de Castries (ed.), *Les sources inédites de l'histoire du Maroc de 1530 à 1845*, Series I, *Dynastie saadienne 1530–1660*, vol. I, part 1, Paris 1905, with detailed genealogical table between pp. 382–3.

21

THE ʿALAWID OR FILĀLĪ SHARĪFS
1041– /1631–
Morocco

1041/1631 Muḥammad I al-Sharīf, in Tafilalt, died 1069/1659
1045/1635 Maḥammad or Muḥammad II b. Muḥammad I al-Sharīf, in eastern Morocco, k. 1075/1664
⊘ 1076/1666 al-Rashīd b. Muḥammad I al-Sharīf, in Fez, originally in Oujda (Wajda)
⊘ 1082/1672 Ismāʿīl b. Muḥammad I al-Sharīf, al-Samīn, governor in Meknès (Miknāsa), then sultan in Fez
1139/1727 Aḥmad b. Ismāʿīl, al-Dhahabī, reigned on two occasions, died, at the end of the second reign, in 1171/1757; his power contested by several of his brothers, immediately in 1139/1727 by ʿAbd al-Malik b. Ismāʿīl, and subsequently by ⊘ ʿAbdallāh (reigned on five occasions, beginning 1141/1729 and ending with his death in 1171/1757); ʿAlī Zayn al-ʿAbidīn (reigned on two occasions); Muḥammad b. al-ʿArabiyya, al-Mustaḍīʾ; etc.
⊘ 1171/1757 Muḥammad III b. ʿAbdallāh
⊘ 1204/1790 Yazīd b. Muḥammad III
⊘ (1205–9/1790–4 Ḥusayn, in Marrakech)
⊘ 1206/1792 Hishām b. Muḥammad III
⊘ 1207/1793 Sulaymān b. Muḥammad III
⊘ 1238/1822 ʿAbd al-Raḥmān b. Hishām
⊘ 1276/1859 Muḥammad IV b. ʿAbd al-Raḥmān
⊘ 1290/1873 al-Ḥasan I b. Muḥammad IV, Abū ʿAlī
⊘ 1311/1894 ʿAbd al-ʿAzīz b. al-Ḥasan I, abdicated 1326/1908
⊘ 1325/1907 (ʿAbd) al-Ḥafīẓ b. al-Ḥasan I
⊘ 1330/1912 Yūsuf b. al-Ḥasan I
⊘ 1346/1927 Muḥammad V b. Yūsuf, first reign
⊘ 1372/1953 Muḥammad b. ʿArafa
⊘ 1375/1955 Muḥammad V b. Yūsuf, second reign
⊘ 1380–/1961– al-Ḥasan II b. Muḥammad V

As the two Saʿdid *makhzan*s based on Marrakech and Fez crumbled in the middle years of the seventeenth century (see above, no. 20), Morocco was rent by internal factions, usually with strong religious, maraboutic bases. It was the ʿAlawids or Filālī *Shorfā*, of the same Ḥasanī descent as the declining Saʿdids, who finally succeeded in imposing order from an original centre in Tafilalt, the valley of the Wādī Zīz in south-eastern Morocco (whence the name Filālī). Mawlāy al-Rashīd was the first of the family to assume the title of sultan. He began the work of pacification and attempted a restoration of central authority throughout Morocco, but this proved an extremely lengthy process, so deep-rooted had become provincialism and anarchy. A strong figure like Mawlāy Ismāʿīl tried in vain to solve these problems by recruiting, in addition to the *gīsh* (< Class. Ar. *jaysh*) or the sultans' military guard of Arabs, a standing army which included among other elements black slave troops, the *ʿabīd al-Bukhārī* (colloquially known as the *Bwākher*), descendants of black slaves imported by the Saʿdids; it was also Ismāʿīl who developed Meknès as the capital and the favoured place of residence for himself and his eighteenth-century successors. But he failed to dislodge the Christians from the ports held by them, and, after his death, Morocco was plunged into its nadir of anarchy and brigandage, with a succession of rival, ephemeral rulers.

Some degree of order and prosperity was restored towards the end of the century; the last foothold of the Portuguese on the Atlantic coast at Mazagan (al-Jadīda) was taken over in 1182/1769, but the Spanish could not be dislodged from Ceuta and Melilla. Morocco was opened up to a limited extent for trade with Europe, and the new town of Mogador or Essouaira (al-Suwayra) was founded to accommodate and isolate the infidel merchants and consuls whom the sultans were compelled reluctantly to admit. However, with an essentially mediaeval polity, hardly touched by the influences which during the course of the nineteenth century affected such Islamic lands as those of Egypt, the Ottoman empire and Persia, Morocco was ill-prepared for the two disastrous wars which she fought with France (1260/1844) and Spain (1277/1859–60). By the end of the century, the ʿAlawid dynasty was tottering, with the sultans' power challenged by various pretenders and the country forming the locale for such international incidents as that of Agadir (1911). The French Protectorate proclaimed in 1330/1912 saved the ʿAlawid dynasty itself from disappearing and Morocco from disintegration and possible dismemberment by outside powers, although the work of pacification and restoration of the sultan's authority took twenty years; it was 1930 before the *makhzan* was fully in control and before the modernisation of Morocco's infrastructure could proceed properly. Sīdī Muḥammad V in 1934 aligned himself with the growing Moroccan nationalism of the Istiqlāl or Independence Party. After the end of the Second World War, friction between Moroccan nationalism, eager for independence, and the more cautious attitude of the French Protectorate authorities, grew. Conservative, traditionalist Moroccan forces lent support to the decision in 1953 to depose Muḥammad V, but it was soon apparent that the overwhelming mass of Moroccan opinion was behind the sultan and the desire for full independence, and he had to be restored two years later. Morocco became independent in 1956, and in 1957 Sīdī Muḥammad assumed the title of king, so that Morocco under his son and successor al-Ḥasan II is one of the few monarchies surviving today in the Arab world.

Lane-Poole, 60–2; Zambaur, 81 and Table C; Album, 18–19.

EI[2] 'ʿAlawīs' (H. Terrasse), 'Ḥasanī' (G. Deverdun), with a genealogical table; 'al-Maghrib, al-Mamlaka al-Maghribiyya. II. History' (G. Yver*), 'Shurafāʾ' (E. Lévi-Provençal and Chantal de La Véronne).

H. de Castries and Pierre de Cenival (eds), *Les sources inédites de l'histoire du Maroc ...*, Series II, *Dynastie filalienne. Archives et bibliothèques de France*, Paris 1922–31.

H. Terrasse, *Histoire du Maroc*, II, 239–406.

22

THE ḤUSAYNID BEYS

1117–1376/1705–1957

Tunisia

1117/1705	al-Ḥusayn I b. ʿAlī al-Turki, k. 1152/1746
1148/1735	ʿAlī I b. Muḥammad
1170/1756	Muḥammad I b. al-Ḥusayn I
1172/1759	ʿAlī II b. al-Ḥusayn I
1196/1782	Ḥam(m)ūda Pasha b. ʿAlī II
1229/1814	ʿUthmān b. ʿAlī II
1229/1814	Maḥmūd b. Muḥammad I
1239/1824	al-Ḥusayn II b. Maḥmūd
1251/1835	Muṣṭafā b Maḥmūd
1253/1837	Aḥmad I b. Muṣṭafā
⊘ 1271/1855	Muḥammad II b. al-Ḥusayn II
⊘ 1276/1859	Muḥammad III al-Ṣādiq b. al-Ḥusayn II
⊘ 1299/1882	ʿAlī III b. al-Ḥusayn II
⊘ 1320/1902	Muḥammad IV al-Hādī b. ʿAlī III
⊘ 1324/1906	Muḥammad V al-Nāṣir b. Muḥammad II
⊘ 1341/1922	Muḥammad VI al-Ḥabīb b. Muḥammad V
⊘ 1347/1929	Aḥmad II b. ʿAlī III
⊘ 1361/1942	Muḥammad VII al-Munṣif (Moncef) b. Muḥammad V
⊘ 1362/1943	Muḥammad VIII al-Amīn (Lamine) b. Muḥammad VI, d. 1382/1962
⊘ 1376/1957	Ḥusayn al-Naṣr b. Muḥammad V
1376/1957	Rashād al-Mahdī b. Ḥusayn, King of the Tunisians
1376/1957	*Republican régime*

The Ḥusaynid Beys arose out of the Turkish garrison for the Ottomans in Algiers. The commander al-Ḥusayn b. ʿAlī was raised to the Beylicate after the military defeat and deposition of the previous Bey of Tunis in 1117/1705. While the suzerainty of the Ottomans was to be acknowledged, with the sultans in their turn regarding the Ḥusaynids as provincial goverors or *beylerbeyi*s, al-Ḥusayn and his descendants were granted by the local Ottoman commanders hereditary succession by male primogeniture. In practice, this form of succession did not always happen, and latterly the succession tended to go to elderly collateral members of the family who were no longer fully competent to deal with affairs. But the Ḥusaynids were nevertheless to rule for two and a half centuries, though latterly under French protection. In an absence of Turkish interference, the Beys were able to make diplomatic agreements with European powers like France, England and the Italian states, and their power within Tunisia became somewhat firmer once Ḥam(m)ūda Pasha had suppressed the local corps of Janissaries in 1226/1811.

During the nineteenth century, there were signs that the Beys aimed at a policy more independent of their suzerains in Istanbul. The relationship, with the possibility of Ottoman diplomatic and military protection, still had advantages for Tunis, as in 1259–60/1843–4 when there was tension with Sardinia. Tunisian contingents joined the Ottoman forces during the Greek Revolt and the Crimean War, but in 1261/1845 Aḥmad I Bey managed, with French diplomatic backing, to throw off the obligation to send tribute to Istanbul. The Porte still regarded the Ḥusaynids as linked with themselves, as local *müshīrs*, marshals of the army, and *wālīs*, governors, but the link was largely symbolic and was in any case ended in 1298/1881. Reckless spending by the Beys, abolition of the lucrative slave trade, an increased European commercial penetration of Tunisia plus administrative malpractices, brought Muḥammad Ṣādiq Bey to the verge of bankruptcy in 1286/1869, leading to the imposition of an international financial commission in order to regulate Tunisia's debt. French pressure led to a military occupation of Tunisia in 1298/1881 followed by a Protectorate in 1300/1883, so that subsequent Beys functioned under a French Resident-General. At times, the Beys were able to give some impression of representing Tunisian national interests, despite their foreign origin; but in the twentieth century the nationalist movements of the Destour or Constitutionalists and then the Néo-Destour Parties became strong. In 1956, France agreed to the full independence of Tunisia, but the last Ḥusaynid, who was hailed as King of the Tunisians at Kairouan, ruled for only two months before he was forced out of his homeland by the Néo-Destour Party led by Habib Bourgiba (Ḥabīb Bū Ruqayba) and a republic was proclaimed.

The Beys displayed their dependence on the Ottoman by minting coins at Tunis only in the names of the Ottoman sultans, until in 1272/1856 Muḥammad II b. Ḥusayn II started the practice of adding his own name to that of the sultan; with the French occupation, the Beys and, later, the kings issued their own coins.

Zambaur, 84–5.

EI[1] 'Tunisia. 2. History' (R. Brunschvig); *EI*[2] 'Ḥusaynids' (R. Mantran).

P. Grandchamp, 'Arbre généalogique de la famille hassanite (1705–1941)', *Rev. Tunisienne*, nos 45–7 (1941), 233.

R. Mantran, 'La titulature des beys de Tunis au XIXe siècle d'après les documents d'archives turcs du Dar-el-Bey (Tunis)', *CT*, nos 19–20 (1957), 341–8.

L. Carl Brown, *The Tunisia of Ahmad Bey 1837–1855*, Princeton 1974, with a chronological table of events at pp. xv–xviii.

Hugh Montgomery-Massingberd (ed.), *Burke's Royal Families of the World. II. Africa and the Middle East*, London 1980, 225–9.

23

THE QARAMĀNLĪS
1123–1251/1711–1835
Tripolitania

1123/1711	Aḥmad Bey I b. Yūsuf, Qaramānlī
1157/1745	Muḥammad b. Aḥmad
1167/1754	ʿAlī I b. Muḥammad
1209/1795	Aḥmad II b. ʿAlī
1210/1796	Yūsuf b. ʿAlī, d. 1254/1838
1248–51/1832–5	ʿAlī II b. Yūsuf
1251/1835	*Re-establishment of Ottoman direct rule*

The Qaramānlīs were a line of Turkish soldiers apparently arising out of the Qulughlīs or products of mixed marriages between the Turkish Janissary units in North Africa and local women. In the prevailing chaos and internal strife characterising early eighteenth-century Ottoman Tripolitania, Aḥmad Qaramānlī (whose name may derive from the fact that he or his forebears came originally from Qaramān in Anatolia) seized power, eventually receiving from the sultan in Istanbul the titles of *Beylerbey* or governor and Pasha and establishing what was virtually an independent line. From Tripoli (Ṭarābulus al-Gharb), he extended his control over most of what is now Libya. He and his sons managed to control the local factions of the Turks and the Arabs, and, despite the fact that Tripoli was notoriously a base of the Barbary corsairs, concluded trade agreements with countries like Britain and France. In the early nineteenth century, various rivals for the succession within the ruling family were to seek support from one or other of these two powers. But the appearance of the French in Algeria after 1830 alarmed the Sublime Porte and, taking advantage of Qaramānlī dissensions, sultan Maḥmūd II sent an expedition against Tripoli which removed the Qaramānlīs and imposed a rule from Istanbul which lasted until the Italian seizure of Libya in the early twentieth century.

The Qaramānlīs used only coins in the names of the Ottoman sultans issued by the Tripoli mint.

Zambaur, 85.
EI[2] 'Ḳaramānlī' (R. Mantran).

24

THE SANŪSĪ CHIEFS AND RULERS
1253–1389/1837–1969
Eastern Sudan and Libya

1253/1837	Sayyid Muḥammad b. ʿAlī, al-Idrīsi al-Sanūsī al-Kabīr, founder of the Sanūsiyya dervish order, d. 1275/1859
1276/1859	Sayyid Muḥammad al-Mahdī b. Muḥammad b.ʿAlī al-Sanūsī
1320/1902	Sayyid Aḥmad al-Sharīf b. Muḥammad al-Sharīf (in 1336/ 1918 gave up military and political leadership, but retained spiritual primacy until his death at Medina in 1351/1933)
⊘ 1336–89/1969	Sayyid Muḥammad Idrīs b. Muḥammad al-Mahdī (initially as military and political leader; 1371/1951 King of Libya), d. 1401/1982
1389/1969	*Republican régime*

Muḥammad b. ʿAlī, known as the 'Great Sanūsī', was born in Algeria towards the end of the eighteenth century. While studying in Fez, he was much influenced by Moroccan Ṣūfism, especially that of the Tijāniyya order; and later, while further studying in Ḥijāz, he joined several dervish orders himself and became an adherent of the Moroccan Ṣūfī and Sharīf Aḥmad b. Idrīs. In addition to this inclination towards mysticism, he developed reformist and innovatory ideas, and, after Aḥmad b. Idrīs's death in 1253/1837, organised in Mecca his own *ṭarīqa* or order, the Sanūsiyya. Finding his homeland Algeria in the process of being taken over by the French, he settled in Cyrenaica, where direct Ottoman Turkish rule had recently been imposed in place of the local line of Qaramānlī Pashas (see above, no. 23). Moving into the desert interior rather than the coastlands, several *zāwiya*s or religious, educational and social centres for the Sanūsiyya were now founded there, including in 1272/1856 that of Jaghbūb near the Egyptian border. This was to be the headquarters of the order until 1313/1895, when it was moved southwards to the less accessible oasis of Kufra and, soon afterwards, to what is now northern Chad. The Sanūsī message appealed to the desert-dwellers of North Africa and the eastern Sudan. Veneration for the person of the Great Sanūsī accorded with the maraboutism and saint-worship of those regions, but the firm organisation of the order gave these enthusiasms effect and purpose. Expectations of a coming Mahdī, who would restore Islam to its pristine simplicity, were also rife, as events in Dongola were to show in the Mahdiyya movement there of the late nineteenth century. The Sanūsīs hoped for a reunion and regeneration of all Islamic peoples, and the Ottoman sultan ʿAbd al-Ḥamīd II (see below, no. 130) hoped to recruit their support for his Pan-Islamic policies. The Sanūsiyya did, in fact, have a strong missionary zeal, and *zāwiya*s were founded in Ḥijāz, Egypt, Fezzān and as far south as Wadai and Lake Chad, the faith in this case following the trans-Saharan caravan routes.

The Sanūsīs were in the forefront of opposition to the French advance into Chad and the central Sudan, and for some twenty years after 1911 provided the driving power behind local Libyan resistance to the Italian invaders, especially in Cyrenaica. Italy's entry into the First World War on the Allied side in 1915 inevitably inclined the Sanūsiyya to the Turkish cause, and the head of the order, Sayyid Aḥmad, had to leave for Istanbul in 1918; thereafter, the military struggle in Cyrenaica was left largely to local Sanūsī leaders. During the Second World War, the British government recognised Muḥammad Idrīs, who had been in exile in Egypt for twenty years, not merely as a spiritual head but also as Amīr or political head of the Sanūsīs of Cyrenaica. In 1371/1951 he became ruler of the independent federated kingdom of Libya, comprising Cyrenaica, Tripolitania and Fezzān; in 1382/1963 it became a unitary state. So far, the process of the Sanūsī family's development from being heads of a religious movement to the headship of a modern Arab state had been somewhat reminiscent of the development of the Suʿūdī state in Arabia (see below, no. 55) out of the Wahhābiyya, but the Idrīsid monarchy of Libya was destined to have only a short life. The new state failed to develop a political system which could accommodate the aspirations of the new classes and a social one which could cope with the new stresses resulting from the unprecedented Libyan oil boom of 1955 onwards. In 1969, King Idrīs was deposed by an army coup, and Libya became a republic under Colonel Muʿammar Gaddafi (Qadhdhāfī).

Zambaur, 89; *EI*[2] 'al-Sanūsī, Muḥammad b. ʿAlī', 'Sanūsiyya' (J.-C. Triaud).

E. E. Evans-Pritchard, *The Sanusi of Cyrenaica*, Oxford 1949, with a genealogical table at p. 20.

N. A. Ziadeh, *Sanūsīyah: A Study of a Revivalist Movement in Islam*, Leiden 1959.

J. Wright, *Libya: A Modern History*, London 1981.

FOUR
Egypt and Syria
25

THE ṬŪLŪNIDS
254–92/868–905
Egypt and Syria

⊘ 254/868 Aḥmad b. Ṭūlūn
⊘ 270/884 Khumārawayh b. Aḥmad, Abu 'l-Jaysh
⊘ 282/896 Jaysh b. Khumārawayh, Abu 'l-ʿAsākir
⊘ 283/896 Hārūn b. Khumārawayh, Abū Mūsā
292/904 Shaybān b. Aḥmad, Abu 'l-Manāqib
292/905 Conquest by the ʿAbbāsid general Muḥammad b. Sulaymān

The Ṭūlūnids represent the first local dynasty of Egypt and Syria to secure some degree of autonomy from the caliphate in Baghdad. Aḥmad b. Ṭūlūn (Ṭūlūn < Turkish *dolun* 'full [moon]', the equivalent of Ar. *badr*) was a Turkish soldier whose father had been sent in the tribute from Bukhara in the early ninth century. Aḥmad first came to Egypt as deputy of the ʿAbbāsid governor there, but then acquired the governorship himself, extending his power into Palestine and Syria also. His ambitions were facilitated by the preoccupation of al-Muwaffaq – brother of the caliph al-Muʿtamid (see above, no. 3, 1) and virtual ruler – with the Zanj rebels in Lower Iraq, which meant that Aḥmad could not be dislodged militarily from the west. Under Aḥmad's son Khumārawayh, the Ṭūlūnids' fortunes continued to be high. The new caliph al-Muʿtaḍid (see above, no. 3, 1) had on his accession in 279/892 to grant to Khumārawayh and his heirs for thirty years Egypt, Syria up to the Taurus Mountains and Jazīra (northern Mesopotamia) with the exception of Mosul (Mawṣil), in return for an annual tribute of 300,000 dinars. The treaty was later revised in a form less favourable to the Ṭūlūnids, but it was not until Khumārawayh's death in 282/896 that the fabric of the Ṭūlūnid empire, weakened by Khumārawayh's luxurious living and extravagance – he left behind an empty treasury – began to crack. The inability of the last Ṭūlūnids to keep the Carmathian radical religious sectaries of the Syrian desert in check led the caliph to despatch an army which conquered Syria and then seized the Ṭūlūnid capital of Fusṭāṭ or Old Cairo, carrying off the remaining members of the family to Baghdad and imposing a direct ʿAbbāsid rule over Egypt which was to last for thirty years.

For the mediaeval Egyptian historians, the age of the Ṭūlūnids was a golden one. Aḥmad held power by means of a large multi-ethnic army, which included Bedouins, Greeks and black Nubians, but the resultant financial burden was alleviated for the people of Egypt by the ending of governmental malpractices; only under Khumārawayh did administrative chaos and insubordination in the army appear. Since Syria can best be held from Egypt by sea, Aḥmad also built a strong fleet. He was a great builder in his capital Fusṭāṭ, laying out there the military quarter of al-Qaṭā'iʿ and constructing his famous mosque in order to accommodate all those troops who could not find room in the mosque of the conqueror of Egypt ʿAmr b. al-ʿĀṣ.

Lane-Poole, 68; Zambaur, 93; Album, 20.

EI[1] 'Ṭūlūnids' (H. A. R. Gibb)

Z. M. Hassan, *Les Tulunides; étude de l'Egypte musulmane à la fin du IXe siècle*, Paris 1933.

O. Grabar, *The Coinage of the Ṭūlūnids*, ANS Numismatic Notes and Monographs, no. 139, New York 1957.

26

THE IKHSHĪDIDS
323–58/935–69
Egypt and southern Syria

⌀ 323/935	Muḥammad b. Ṭughj, Abū Bakr al-Ikhshīd
⌀ 334/946	Ūnūjūr (? On Uyghur) b. Muḥammad, Abu 'l-Qāsim
⌀ 349/961	ʿAlī b. Muḥammad, Abu 'l-Ḥasan
⌀ *355/966*	*Kāfūr al-Lābī, Abu 'l-Misk, originally regent for ʿAlī, then sole ruler until his death in 357/968*
⌀ 357/968	Aḥmad b. ʿAlī, Abu 'l-Fawāris, d. 371/981
358/969	*Conquest of Egypt by the Fāṭimid general Jawhar*

Muḥammad b. Ṭughj came of a Turkish military family which had already been in the service of the ʿAbbāsids for two generations. He was appointed governor of Egypt in 323/935 and remained a faithful vassal of the caliphs. He also secured from al-Rāḍī (see above, no. 3, 1) the title of *al-Ikhshīd*. The Arabic sources are unclear about the meaning of this title, but it is obvious that Muḥammad b. Ṭughj knew that it was a title of honour in the Central Asian homeland of his forefathers (it is in fact an Iranian title meaning 'prince, ruler', and had been borne by the local Iranian rulers of Soghdia and Farghāna). Muḥammad b. Ṭughj defended himself against the caliph's *Amīr al-Umarā'* or Commander-in-Chief, Muḥammad b. Rā'iq, and against the Ḥamdānids in Syria (see below, no. 35, 2), holding on to Damascus. The two sons who succeeded him were, however, mere puppets, and real power in the state passed to Muḥammad b. Ṭughj's Nubian slave Kāfūr (*kāfūr* = 'camphor', a reference by antiphrasis to his black colour), whom he appointed regent for his sons just before he died.

On ʿAlī's death in 355/956, Kāfūr became unrestricted ruler. To him belongs the credit for holding up the threatened Fāṭimid advance along the North African coast (see below, no. 27) and for containing the Ḥamdānids in northern Syria. It was only after his death that a weak and ephemeral grandson of Muḥammad b. Ṭughj was installed in Fusṭāṭ, to go down almost immediately before the Fāṭimid invasion, this time successful. Kāfūr was famed as a liberal patron of literature and the arts, and it was at his court that the poet al-Mutanabbī spent some time.

Lane-Poole, 69; Zambaur, 93; Album, 20.
EI[1] 'Ikhshīdids' (C. H. Becker); EI[2] 'Kāfūr' (A. S. Ehrenkreutz), 'Muḥammad b. Ṭughdj' (J. L. Bacharach).
P. Balog, 'Tables de référence des monnaies ikhchidites', *Revue Belge de Numismatique*, 103 (1957), 107–34.
J. L. Bacharach, 'The career of Muḥammad b. Ṭughj al-Ikhshīd, a tenth-century governor of Egypt', *Speculum*, 50 (1975), 586–612.

27

THE FĀṬIMIDS

297–567/909–1171

North Africa, then Egypt and southern Syria

The dāʿī *or propagandist Abū ʿAbdallāh al-Shīʿī, active in North Africa preparing the way for:*

⊘ 297/909	ʿAbdallāh (or ʿUbaydallāh) b. Ḥusayn, Abū Muḥammad al-Mahdī
⊘ 322/934	Muḥammad b. (?) al-Mahdī, Abu ʾl-Qāsim al-Qāʾim
⊘ 334/946	Ismāʿīl b. al-Qāʾim, Abū Ṭāhir al-Manṣūr
⊘ 341/953	Maʿadd b. al-Manṣūr, Abū Tamīm al-Muʿizz
⊘ 365/975	Nizār b. al-Muʿizz, Abū Manṣūr al-ʿAzīz
⊘ 386/996	al-Manṣūr b. al-ʿAzīz, Abū ʿAlī al-Ḥākim
⊘ 411/1021	ʿAlī b. al-Ḥākim, Abu ʾl-Ḥasan al-Ẓāhir
⊘ 427/1036	Maʿadd b. al-Ẓāhir, Abū Tamīm al-Mustanṣir
⊘ 487/1094	Aḥmad b. al-Mustanṣir, Abu ʾl-Qāsim al-Mustaʿlī
⊘ 495/1101	al-Manṣūr b. al-Mustaʿlī, Abū ʿAlī al-Āmir
⊘ *524/1130*	*Interregnum; rule by al-Ḥāfiẓ as regent but not yet as caliph; coins in the name of al-Muntaẓar 'the Expected One'*
⊘ 525/1131	ʿAbd al-Majīd b. Muḥammad, Abu ʾl-Maymūn al-Ḥāfiẓ
⊘ 544/1149	Ismāʿīl b. al-Ḥāfiẓ, Abu ʾl-Manṣūr al-Ẓāfir
⊘ 549/1154	ʿĪsā b. al-Ẓāfir, Abu ʾl-Qāsim al-Fāʾiz
⊘ 555–67/1160–71	ʿAbdallāh b. Yūsuf, Abū Muḥammad al-ʿĀḍid
	Conquest by the Ayyūbid Ṣalāḥ al-Dīn (Saladin)

The Fāṭimids claimed ʿAlid descent, and their name derives from Fāṭima, daughter of the Prophet and wife of the fourth caliph ʿAlī (see above, no. 1). Sunnī and mainstream Shīʿī opponents usually referred to them as the ʿUbaydiyyūn, descendants of ʿAbdallāh (or ʿUbaydallāh, as they termed him) al-Mahdī, explicitly rejecting any ʿAlid connection; it is unclear whether the Fāṭimid caliphs ever in fact referred to themselves as 'the Fāṭimids'. Some of the Fāṭimids' enemies even accused them of Jewish origins (this being, however, a standard form of calumny in mediaeval Islam). A connection with the main line of ʿAlid Imāms, through Ismāʿīl, son of the Sixth Imām Jaʿfar al-Ṣādiq, certainly seems dubious, and it is more likely that the forebears of ʿAbdallāh al-Mahdī stemmed either from *ghulāt* or extremist Shīʿī circles in Kūfa or else from ʿAlī's half-brother ʿAqīl b. Abī Ṭālib. At all events, the constituting of the Fāṭimid state represents the most successful and enduring political achievement of radical, Ismāʿīlī Shīʿism at this time.

The first Fāṭimid caliph came from Salamiya in Syria to North Africa, where the dissemination of Shīʿī propaganda had already made conditions propitious for his arrival. With the support of the sedentary Kutāma Berbers, his agent, the *dāʿī* Abū ʿAbdallāh al-Shīʿī, overthrew the Aghlabid goverors of Ifrīqiya (see above, no. 11) and the Khārijī Rustamids of Tahert (see above, no. 9); subsequently, the Idrīsids of Fez (see above, no. 8) became tributaries of the Fāṭimids. In 297/909 the Mahdī was proclaimed caliph, in rivalry to the ʿAbbāsids of Baghdad, at al-

Raqqāda in Ifrīqiya. Subsequently, Sicily was occupied and naval operations were undertaken against the Byzantines. From their Ifrīqiyan base of al-Mahdiyya, the Fāṭimids amassed supplies and treasure in preparation for an advance eastwards, and in 358/969 their general Jawhar entered Old Cairo or Fusṭāṭ, removing the last Ikhshīdid (see above, no. 26). As they had done in the case of al-Mahdiyya in Ifrīqiya, the Fāṭimids began to build for themselves a new capital in Egypt, that of New Cairo (*al-Qāhira* 'the Victorious').

From Egypt, the Fāṭimids extended into Palestine and Syria. During the long reign of al-Mustanṣir, spanning much of the eleventh century, they reached the zenith of their power. After initially clashing with the Byzantines over Syria, the caliphs in general enjoyed peaceful relations with the Greeks; later in the century, the common threat of the Seljuqs and the Turkmen adventurers in Syria and Anatolia further drew them close together. The Ismā'īlī *dā'ī*s of the Fāṭimids worked as far afield as the Yemen and Sind, and in 451/1059 Baghdad was temporarily held in the name of al-Mustanṣir. The appearance of the First Crusade at the end of the century brought about the wresting of Jerusalem from its Fāṭimid governor, but by then the Fāṭimid presence in Palestine and Syria had become essentially one in only the coastal towns there; yet on the whole, the Crusaders posed a greater threat to the various Turkish rulers of Syria than to the Fāṭimids. Certain Sunnī Muslim historians allege that the Fāṭimids encouraged the Franks to land in the Levant, but this is improbable. The Fāṭimid viziers of the mid-twelfth century cooperated with the Zangid Nūr al-Dīn of Aleppo and Damascus (see below, no. 93, 2) against the Crusaders, but nevertheless lost Ascalon ('Asqalān) to them in 548/1153. Soon afterwards, the Fāṭimid caliphate began to crumble internally; the caliphs had by now lost much of their power, and the viziers had assumed much of the executive and military leadership. Accordingly, it was not difficult for the Ayyūbid Ṣalāḥ al-Dīn (see below, no. 30) to end Fāṭimid rule altogether in 567/1171 as the last caliph lay dying.

In rivalry with the 'Abbāsids, the Fāṭimids had proclaimed themselves the true caliphs and had assumed regnal titles which expressed the messianic nature of their original movement and the theocratic nature of their established rule, for example al-Mahdī, al-Qā'im and al-Ẓāfir. Yet the majority of their subjects remained Sunnīs and, under the Fāṭimids' generally tolerant rule, retained most of their religious liberty. Many of the *dā'ī*s who were trained at the newly-founded college of al-Azhar in Cairo went to work outside the Fāṭimid dominions. Except during the first part of the unbalanced caliph al-Ḥākim's reign, the Christians and Jews were comparatively well treated, and some of them occupied high offices in the state up to the level of the vizierate. It was during al-Ḥākim's reign that the extremist Shī'ī religious movement of the Druzes became implanted in southern Lebanon and Syria; because of al-Ḥākim's encouragement of the *dā'ī* al-Duruzī, the Druzes came to revere that caliph as an incarnation of God. On the death of al-Mustanṣir, there was a serious split in the Ismā'īlī movement, with two opposing parties ranged behind his sons Nizār and al-Musta'lī. The partisans of the former, the more activist and extreme of the two groups, became the Assassins or Ismā'īlīs of Syria and Persia (see below, nos 29, 101), while al-Musta'lī's more moderate followers are the spiritual ancestors of the modern Bohrā Ismā'īlīs of Bombay and Gujarāt. Al-Musta'lī retained the caliphate, but the spiritual basis of the Fāṭimid movement was to some extent impaired, above all after a further religio-political crisis on the death of al-Āmir in 525/1130 (the split of the Ṭayyibī Ismāʿīlīs, who were subsequently influential in Yemen and India).

Egypt and Cairo enjoyed under the Fāṭimids an economic prosperity and cultural vitality which eclipsed those of contemporary Iraq and Baghdad. Trade links were maintained with the non-Islamic world, including India and the Christian Mediterranean countries; in this commercial activity, Jewish merchants seem to have played an important role, as also perhaps the forerunners of the Muslim Kārimī merchants known from subsequent Ayyūbid and Mamlūk times. It is from the workshops of Egypt at this time, too, that some of the finest products of Islamic art – metalwork, ceramics, textiles and glassware – were produced, while the architectural heritage of the Fāṭimids is still visible in both North Africa and Egypt.

Lane-Poole, 70–3; Zambaur, 94–5; Album, 20–1.
EI[2] 'Fāṭimids' (M. Canard).
G. C. Miles, *Fatimid Coins in the Collections of the University Museum, Philadelphia, and the American Numismatic Society*, ANS Numismatic Notes and Monographs, no. 121, New York 1951.
H. W. Hazard, *The Numismatic History of Late Medieval North Africa*, 52–3.
Ḥusayn b. Faḍl Allāh al-Hamdānī and Ḥasan Sulaymān Maḥmūd al-Juhanī, *al-Ṣulayḥiyyūn wa 'l-ḥaraka al-Fāṭimiyya fi 'l-Yaman (min sanat 628 h. ilā sanat 626 h.)*, Cairo 1955, with detailed table at p. 343.
F. Dachraoui, *Le califat fatimide au Maghreb 296–362/909–973. Histoire politique et institutions*, Tunis 1981.
H. Halm, 'Die Fatimiden', in Haarmann (ed.), *Geschichte der arabischen Welt*, 166–99.
idem, *Das Reich der Mahdi. Der Aufstieg der Fatimiden (875–973)*, Munich 1991.

28

THE MIRDĀSIDS
415–72/1024–80
Northern and central Syria

⊘ 415/1024	Ṣāliḥ b. Mirdās, Asad al-Dawla, previously Amīr of Raḥba since 399/1009
⊘ 420/1029	Naṣr I b. Ṣāliḥ, Abū Kāmil Shibl al-Dawla
⊘ *429/1038*	*First Fāṭimid occupation of Aleppo*
⊘ 433/1042	Thimāl b. Ṣāliḥ, Abu ʿUlwān Muʿizz al-Dawla, first reign
⊘ *449/1057*	*Second Fāṭimid occupation of Aleppo*
⊘ 452/1060	Maḥmūd b. Naṣr I, Rashīd al-Dawla, first reign
⊘ 453/1061	Thimāl b. Ṣāliḥ, second reign
454/1062	ʿAṭiyya b. Ṣāliḥ, Abū Dhu'āba (in Raḥba and Raqqa until 463/1071)
457/1065	Maḥmūd b. Naṣr I, second reign
467 or 468/1075–6	Naṣr II b. Maḥmūd, Abu 'l-Muẓaffar Jalāl al-Dawla
⊘ 468–72/1076–80	Sābiq b. Maḥmūd, Abu 'l-Faḍā'il
472/1080	*ʿUqaylid occupation of Aleppo*

The Mirdāsids were part of the North Arab tribe of Kilāb, who in the early years of the eleventh century migrated from the lands along the Euphrates in north-eastern Syria to Aleppo, which their leader Ṣāliḥ b. Mirdās captured in 415/1024, thereby succeeding substantially to the heritage of the Ḥamdānids (see below, no. 35, 2). The Mirdāsid migration formed part of a general movement of Bedouins – many of them (although not the Mirdāsids) at least nominally Shīʿī in faith – into the settled fringes of Iraq and Syria during the tenth and early eleventh centuries; it is possible that the unsettled conditions in the Syrian Desert brought about by the Carmathian risings there were one of the stimuli to this process.

Once established in Aleppo, Ṣāliḥ and his sons Naṣr and Thimāl had to defend themselves on one side against the Fāṭimids, who were attempting to restore their control over northern Syria, and on the other against the resurgent Byzantines under Basil II Bulgaroctonus and Romanus III Argyrus, although, in general, the favourable attitude of the Greeks towards them was one of the factors enabling the Mirdāsids to survive as an independent power for half a century. For four years, 429–33/1038–42, Aleppo was occupied by the Fāṭimid governor of Damascus, Anūshtigin, and on a second occasion Thimāl was obliged to abandon Aleppo and exchange it for towns on the Syro-Palestinian littoral, on account of pressure from undisciplined Kilābī tribesmen on his position within Aleppo. The westward advance of the Seljuqs, and the appearance in northern Syria of bands of Turkmens and various military adventurers, together with the waning of Fāṭimid influence there, confronted the Mirdāsids with a new situation. They found it expedient to transfer allegiance from the Fāṭimids to the Sunnī ʿAbbāsids and to submit to the Seljuq sultan Alp Arslan. Latterly, Mirdāsid influence in Aleppo was undermined by disputes between the Turkish mercenaries whom the amīrs had been compelled to recruit and the Kilābī tribesmen, and in 468/1076 a civil war broke out between the two Mirdāsid brothers Sābiq and Waththāb.

Pressure on Aleppo from the Seljuq Tutush, who was trying to carve out a principality for himself in Syria (see below, no. 91, 2), drove Sābiq in 472/1080 to offer the city to the ʿUqaylid Muslim b. Quraysh (see below, no. 38). The surviving members of the Mirdāsid family were compensated by the grant of various towns in Syria, and they played some part in the affairs of the region up to the arrival of the First Crusade.

Lane-Poole, 114–15; Zambaur, 133, 135; Album, 22.
EI[2] 'Mirdās, Banū' (Th. Bianquis).
Suhayl Zakkār, *The Emirate of Aleppo 1004–1094*, Beirut 1391/1971.
Th. Bianquis, *Damas et la Syrie sous la domination fatimide (359–468/969–1076). Essai d'interpretation de chroniques arabes médiévales*, Damascus 1986–9.

29

THE CHIEF *DĀʿĪS* OF THE NIZĀRĪ ISMĀʿĪLĪS OR ASSASSINS IN SYRIA

Early sixth/twelfth century to the mid-eighth/fourteenth century

The mountains of western Syria

c. 493/c. 1100	al-Ḥakīm al-Munajjim, d. 496/1103
496/1103	Abū Ṭāhir al-Ṣāʾigh, d. 507/1113
c. 507/c. 1113	Bahrām, leader of the Syrian Ismāʿīlī community, d. 522/1128
522/1128	Ismāʿīl al-ʿAjamī, d. 524/1130
524/1131	Abu ʾl-Fatḥ
?	Abū Muḥammad
?	Khwāja ʿAlī b. Masʿūd
557/1162	Sinān b. Salmān or Sulaymān al-Baṣrī, Abu ʾl-Ḥasan Rashīd al-Dīn, d. 588/1192 or 589/1193
589/1193 or 590/1194	Abū Manṣūr b. Muḥammad or Naṣr, al-ʿAjamī
620–56/1223–58	al-Ḥasan b. Masʿūd, Kamāl al-Dīn, together with Majd al-Dīn; Muẓaffar b. al-Ḥusayn, Sirāj al-Dīn; Abu ʾl-Futūḥ b. Muḥammad, Tāj al-Dīn; and Abu ʾl-Maʿālī, Raḍī ʾl-Dīn
660/1262	Ismāʿīl b. al-Shaʿrānī, Najm al-Dīn, d. 672/1274, aided by Shams al-Dīn b. Najm al-Dīn and Mubārak b. Raḍī ʾl-Dīn, Ṣārim al-Dīn
669/1271	Shams al-Dīn b. Najm al-Dīn
	Submission of the Ismāʿīlī fortresses to the Mamlūk Baybars by 671/1273

The Nizārī *daʿwa* arose out of a split within the Fāṭimid caliphate at the death in 487/1094 of al-Mustanṣir, when his heir Nizār was set aside in a putsch in favour of his brother, who became the caliph al-Mustaʿlī and continued the Fāṭimid line (see above, no. 27). Nizār's cause was taken up by the *dāʿī* Ḥasan-i Ṣabbāḥ, who had already towards the end of al-Mustanṣir's lifetime established Ismāʿīlī power in certain regions of Persia (see below, no. 101, for the heads of this *daʿwa*, the subsequent Grand Masters and the history of the movement in Persia). The now independent Nizārī *daʿwa jadīda* or 'new mission' was then implanted in Syria by agents from Alamūt, and Ismāʿīlism henceforth played a role in the tortuous political rivalries and strife of the Syrian cities, although it was not until the mid-twelfth century that the Syrian Ismāʿīlīs succeeded in acquiring fortresses, as in Persia, but here in the mountains of western Syria, the later Jabal Anṣāriyya.

These garrisons and communities at times played a role in the struggles of the Crusaders and the Muslim principalities. Under their greatest head, the Iraqi *dāʿī* Rashīd al-Dīn Sinān, they achieved in effect independence from the Persian Ismāʿīlī leadership which normally controlled the Syrian movement. The leaders of the latter tended to have friendly relations with the Ayyūbids (see below, no. 30). They survived the Mongol onslaught on Syria but became tributary to the

Mamlūks, and their fortresses were gradually reduced by Baybars, that of Kahf surrendering in 671/1273. Nevertheless, the Syrian Ismāʿīlī community itself survived largely intact, though with its centre subsequently at Salamiya to the east of the Syrian mountains, maintaining its cohesion and traditions through the succeeding centuries, whereas the Persian Ismāʿīlī communities never really recovered from the violence of the Mongol invasions.

Zambaur, 103.
EI^2 'Ismāʿīliyya' (W. Madelung).
Farhad Daftary, *The Ismāʿīlīs: Their History and Doctrines*, Cambridge 1990, 357–61, 374–80, 396–403, 419–21, 430–4.

30

THE AYYŪBIDS

564 to end of the ninth century/1169 to end of the fifteenth century

Egypt, Syria, Diyār Bakr, western Jazīra and Yemen

1. The line in Egypt

⌀ 564/1169	al-Malik al-Nāṣir I Yūsuf b. Najm al-Dīn Ayyūb b. Shādhī, Abu 'l-Muẓaffar Ṣalāḥ al-Dīn (Saladin)
⌀ 589/1193	al-Malik al-ʿAzīz I ʿUthmān b. al-Nāṣir I Ṣalāḥ al-Dīn Yūsuf, Abu 'l-Fatḥ ʿImād al-Dīn
⌀ 595/1198	al-Malik al-Manṣūr Muḥammad b. al-ʿAzīz ʿImād al-Dīn ʿUthmān, Nāṣir al-Dīn
⌀ 596/1200	al-Malik al-ʿĀdil I Muḥammad or Aḥmad b. Najm al-Dīn Ayyūb, Abū Bakr Sayf al-Dīn, of Damascus
⌀ 615/1218	al-Malik al-Kāmil I Muḥammad b. al-ʿĀdil I Muḥammad or Aḥmad Sayf al-Dīn, Abu 'l-Maʿālī Nāṣir al-Dīn, of Damascus
⌀ 635/1238	al-Malik al-ʿĀdil II Abū Bakr b. al-Kāmil Muḥammad Nāṣir al-Dīn, Sayf al-Dīn, of Damascus, d. 645/1248
⌀ 637/1240	al-Malik al-Ṣāliḥ II Ayyūb b. al-Kāmil Muḥammad Nāṣir al-Dīn, Najm al-Dīn, of Damascus
⌀ 647/1249	al-Malik al-Muʿaẓẓam Tūrān Shāh b. Yūsuf Ṣalāḥ al-Dīn II b. Muḥammad Ghiyāth al-Dīn, of Damascus
⌀ 648–50/1250–2	al-Malik al-Ashraf II Mūsā b. al-Masʿūd Yūsuf Ṣalāḥ al-Dīn b. al-Kāmil Muḥammad Nāṣir al-Dīn, Muẓaffar al-Dīn
650/1252	*Power seized by the Mamlūk Aybak, but with al-Malik al-Ashraf II's name retained in the* khuṭba *until 652/1254*

2. The line in Damascus

⌀ 582/1186	al-Malik al-Afḍal ʿAlī b. al-Nāṣir Yūsuf Ṣalāḥ al-Dīn I, Abu 'l-Ḥasan Nūr al-Dīn
⌀ 592/1196	al Malik al-ʿĀdil I Muḥammad or Aḥmad b. Ayyūb Najm al-Dīn, Abū Bakr Sayf al-Dīn, of Egypt and Aleppo
(597–615/1201–18	*al-Malik al-Muʿaẓẓam ʿĪsā, Sharaf al-Dīn, as governor)*
615/1218	al-Malik al-Muʿaẓẓam ʿĪsā b. al-ʿĀdil I Muḥammad or Aḥmad Sayf al-Dīn, Sharaf al-Dīn
624/1227	al-Malik al-Nāṣir II Dāwūd b. al-Muʿaẓẓam ʿĪsā Sharaf al-Dīn, Ṣalāḥ al-Dīn
626/1229	al-Malik al-Ashraf I Mūsā b. al-ʿĀdil II Abū Bakr Sayf al-Dīn, Abu 'l-Fatḥ Muẓaffar al-Dīn, of Diyār Bakr
⌀ 635/1237	al-Malik al-Ṣāliḥ I Ismāʿīl b. al-ʿĀdil II Abū Bakr Sayf al-Dīn, ʿImād al-Dīn, first reign
⌀ 635/1238	al-Malik al-Kāmil I Muḥammad b. al-ʿĀdil I Muḥammad or Aḥmad Sayf al-Dīn, Abu 'l-Maʿālī Nāṣir al-Dīn
635/1238	al-Malik al-ʿĀdil II Abū Bakr b. al-Kāmil Muḥammad Nāṣir al-Dīn

⊘ 636/1239 al-Malik al-Ṣāliḥ II Ayyūb b. al-Kāmil Muḥammad Nāṣir al-Dīn, Najm al-Dīn, first reign

⊘ 637/1239 al-Malik al-Ṣāliḥ I Ismāʿīl, ʿImād al-Dīn, second reign

⊘ 643/1245 al-Malik al-Ṣāliḥ II Ayyūb, Najm al-Dīn, of Egypt, second reign

⊘ 647/1249 al-Malik al-Muʿaẓẓam Tūrān Shāh b. al-Ṣāliḥ II Ayyūb Najm al-Dīn, Ghiyāth al-Dīn, together with Egypt

648–58/1250–60 al-Malik al-Nāṣir II Yūsuf b. al-ʿAzīz Muḥammad Ghiyāth al-Dīn, Ṣalāḥ al-Dīn, of Aleppo

658/1260 Temporary Mongol conquest, followed by rule of the Mamlūk Baybars

3. The line in Aleppo

⊘ 579/1183 al-Malik al-Zāhir Ghāzī b. al-Nāṣir I Yūsuf Ṣalāḥ al-Dīn, Abu ʾl-Fatḥ or Abū Manṣūr Ghiyāth al-Dīn I, as governor for his father

579/1183 al-Malik al-ʿĀdil I Muḥammad or Aḥmad b. Ayyūb Najm al-Dīn, Abū Bakr Sayf al-Dīn

⊘ 582/1186 al-Malik al-Ẓāhir Ghāzī b. al-Nāṣir I Yūsuf Ṣalāḥ al-Dīn, Abu'l-Fatḥ or Abu Manṣūr Ghiyāth al-Dīn I

⊘ 613/1216 al-Malik al-ʿAzīz Muḥammad b. al-Ẓāhir Ghāzī Ghiyāth al-Dīn I, Ghiyāth al-Dīn II

634–40/1236–42 Regency of Ḍayfa Khātūn bt. al-Malik al-ʿĀdil I Muḥammad or Aḥmad Sayf al-Dīn

⊘ 634–58/1236–60 al-Malik al-Nāṣir II Yūsuf b. al-ʿAzīz Muḥammad Ghiyāth al-Dīn II, Ṣalāḥ al-Dīn

658/1260 Mongol and then Mamlūk conquests

4. The line in Ḥimṣ

574/1178 al-Malik al-Qāhir Muḥammad b. Shīrkūh I Asad al-Dīn b. Shādhī, Nāṣir al-Dīn

581/1186 al-Malik al-Mujāhid Shīrkūh II b. al-Qāhir Muḥammad Nāṣir al-Dīn, Ṣalāḥ al-Dīn

637/1240 al-Malik al-Manṣūr Ibrāhīm b. al-Mujāhid Shīrkūh II Ṣalāḥ al-Dīn, Nāṣir al-Dīn

644–62/1246–63 al-Malik al-Ashraf Mūsā b. al-Manṣur Ibrāhīm Nāṣir al-Dīn, Muẓaffar al-Dīn, also lord of Tell Bashīr 646–8/1248–50

Direct rule by the Mamlūks

5. The line in Ḥamāt

574/1178 al-Malik al-Muẓaffar I ʿUmar b. Shāhanshāh Nūr al-Dīn, Abū Saʿīd Taqī ʾl-Dīn

⊘ 587/1191 al-Malik al-Manṣūr I Muḥammad b. al-Muẓaffar I ʿUmar Taqī ʾl-Dīn, Abu ʾl-Maʿālī Nāṣir al-Dīn

617/1221 al-Malik al-Nāṣir Qilij Arslan b. al-Manṣūr, Ṣalāḥ al-Dīn

⊘ 626/1229	al-Malik al-Muẓaffar II Maḥmūd b. al-Manṣūr I Muḥammad Nāṣir al-Dīn, Taqī 'l-Dīn
⊘ 642/1244	al-Malik al-Manṣūr II Muḥammad b. al-Muẓaffar II Maḥmūd Taqī 'l-Dīn, Sayf al-Dīn
658/1260	*Mongol and then Mamlūk occupations; the subsequent Ayyūbids of Ḥamāt as vassals of the Mamlūks*
683/1284	al-Malik al-Muẓaffar III Maḥmūd b. al-Mansūr II Muḥammad Sayf al-Dīn, Taqī 'l-Dīn
698/1299	*Direct rule by amīrs of the Mamlūk al-Nāṣir Muḥammad Nāsir al-Dīn*
710/1310	al-Malik al-Ṣāliḥ al-Mu'ayyad Ismā'īl b. al-Afḍal 'Alī Nūr al-Dīn, Abu 'l-Fidā' 'Imād al-Dīn
732/1332	al-Malik al-Afḍal Muḥammad b. al-Ṣāliḥ Ismā'īl 'Imād al-Dīn, removed by the Mamlūks shortly afterwards and died in 742/1342

6. The line in Diyār Bakr (Mayyāfāriqīn and Jabal Sinjār)

⊘ 581/1185	al-Malik al-Nāṣir I Ṣalāḥ al-Dīn (Saladin) b. Ayyūb Najm al-Dīn
⊘ 591/1195	al-Malik al-'Ādil I Muḥammad or Aḥmad b. Ayyūb Najm al-Dīn, Abū Bakr Sayf al-Dīn, of Damascus
⊘ 596/1200	al-Malik al-Awḥad Ayyūb b. al-'Ādil I Muḥammad or Aḥmad Sayf al-Dīn, Najm al-Dīn
⊘ 607/1210	al-Malik al-Ashraf I Mūsā b. al-'Ādil I Muḥammad or Aḥmad Sayf al-Dīn, Abu 'l-Fatḥ Muẓaffar al-Dīn
⊘ 617/1220	al-Malik al-Muẓaffar Ghāzī b. al-'Ādil I Muḥammad or Aḥmad Sayf al-Dīn, Shihāb al-Dīn
(628/1231	*Temporary Mongol conquest)*
⊘ 642–58/1244–60	al-Malik al-Kāmil II Muḥammad b. al-Muẓaffar Ghāzī Shihāb al-Dīn, Nāṣir al-Dīn
	Definitive Mongol conquest

7. The line in Diyār Bakr (Ḥiṣn Kayfā, Āmid and Akhlāṭ)

⊘ 629/1232	al-Malik al-Ṣāliḥ II Ayyūb b. al-Kāmil I Maḥmūd Nāṣir al-Dīn, Najm al-Dīn
636/1239	al-Malik al-Mu'aẓẓam Tūrān Shāh b. al-Ṣāliḥ II Ayyūb Najm al-Dīn
⊘ 647/1249	al-Malik al-Muwaḥḥid 'Abdallāh b. al-Mu'aẓẓam Tūrān Shāh, Taqi 'l-Dīn
beginning 657/1259	*Mongol conquest of Diyār Bakr; the remaining Ayyūbids in Ḥiṣn Kayfā under the suzerainty of the Mongol Il Khānids and then of the Turkmen dynasties*
⊘ 682/1283	al-Malik al-Kāmil III Muḥammad b. al-Muwaḥḥid 'Abdallāh Taqi 'l-Dīn, Abū Bakr
?	al-Malik al-'Ādil III Muḥammad b. al-Kāmil III Muḥammad, Mujīr al-Dīn
?	al-Malik al-'Ādil IV Ghāzī b. al-'Ādil III Muḥammad Mujīr al-Dīn, Shihāb al-Dīn

? al-Malik al-Ṣāliḥ III Abū Bakr b. al-ʿĀdil IV Ghāzī Shihāb al-Dīn
⊘ 780/1378 al-Malik al-ʿĀdil V Sulaymān I b. al-ʿĀdil IV Ghāzī Shihāb al-Dīn, Fakhr al-Dīn
⊘ 828/1425 al-Malik al-Ashraf II Aḥmad b. al-ʿĀdil V Sulaymān, Sharaf al-Dīn
836/1433 al-Malik al-Ṣāliḥ IV Khalīl b. al-Ashraf II
⊘ 856/1452 al-Malik al-Kāmil or al-ʿĀdil Aḥmad b. al-Ṣāliḥ IV Khalīl, Nāṣir al-Dīn
⊘ ? al-Malik al-ʿĀdil VI Khalaf b. Muḥammad b. al-Ashraf II
⊘ 866/1462 al-Malik al-Kāmil Khalīl II b. Sulaymān I b. al-Ashraf II (?)
? Sulaymān II b. Khalīl II
? al-Ḥusayn b. Khalīl II
Conquest in the later fifteenth century by the Aq Qoyunlu

8. The line in Yemen

⊘ 569/1174 al-Malik al-Muʿaẓẓam Tūrān Shāh I b. Ayyūb Najm al-Dīn, Shams al-Dīn
⊘ 577/1181 al-Malik al-ʿAzīz Tughtigin b. Ayyūb Najm al-Dīn, Abu 'l-Fawāris Ẓahīr al-Dīn Sayf al-Islam
⊘ 593/1197 Ismāʿīl b. al-ʿAzīz Tughtigin, Muʿizz al-Dīn
⊘ 598/1202 al-Malik al-Nāṣir Ayyūb b. al-ʿAzīz Tughtigin
611/1214 al-Malik al-Muʿaẓẓam (? al-Muẓaffar) Sulaymān b. Shāhanshāh Saʿd al-Dīn, d. 649/1251
⊘ 612–26/1215–29 al-Malik al-Masʿūd Yūsuf b. al-Kāmil I Muḥammad Nāṣir al-Dīn, Ṣalāḥ al-Dīn
627/1229 Succession of the Rasūlids, apparently maintaining during 628/1230 at least the nominal authority of the Ayyūbids, including mention of them on coins

9. The minor branches of the family in Baʿlbakk, Karak, Bāniyās and Subayba, and Buṣrā (for details, see Zambaur, 98–9)

Najm al-Dīn Ayyūb and Asad al-Dīn Shīrkūh b. Shādhī, the progenitors of the dynasty, were from the Hadhbānī tribe of Kurds, although the family seems to have become considerably Turkicised from their service at the side of Turkish soldiers. The Turkish commander of Mosul and Aleppo, Zangī b. Aq Sonqur (see below, no. 93, 1) recruited large numbers of bellicose Kurds into his following, including in 532/1138 Ayyūb, and soon afterwards his brother Shīrkūh entered the service of Zangī's famous son Nūr al-Dīn. In 564/1169, Shīrkūh gained control of Egypt on the demise of the last Fāṭimid caliph al-ʿĀḍid (see above, no. 27) but died almost immediately, and his nephew Ṣalāḥ al-Dīn b. Najm al-Dīn Ayyūb (Saladin) was recognised by his troops as Shīrkūh's successor.

The celebrated foe of the Frankish Crusaders, Saladin, was accordingly the real founder of the dynasty. He extinguished the last vestiges of Fāṭimid rule in Egypt and replaced the Ismāʿīlī Shīʿism which had prevailed there for two centuries by a strongly orthodox Sunnī religious and educational policy; the great wave of Ayyūbid mosque- and madrasa-building in Egypt and Syria was one aspect of this. The Ayyūbids were in this way continuing the policy of the Zangids in Syria and were acting in a parallel manner to the Great Saljuqs before them, who had inaugurated a Sunnī reaction in the Iraqi and Persian lands taken over from the Shīʿī Būyids (see below, no. 75). Although the Ayyūbids were in fact less enthusiastic pursuers of *jihād* than the Zangids had been, Saladin is associated in Western scholarship with his successes in Palestine, for his enthusiasm enabled him to weld together armies of Kurds, Turks and Arabs in a common cause. With his victory at Ḥaṭṭīn in 583/1187, the holy city of Jerusalem again became Muslim after eighty years in Christian hands; the Franks were driven back essentially to the cities and fortresses of the Syro-Palestinian littoral, and, apart from their briefly restored rule in Jerusalem and the other lost districts, mentioned below, were unable to recover most of their losses.

Before his death in 589/1193, Saladin granted out various parts of the Ayyūbid empire, including the cities of Syria, Diyār Bakr, western Jazīra and Yemen, as appanages for various members of the family, the intention being that the supreme sultan should normally reside in Egypt. A reasonable sense of family solidarity was maintained under al-Malik al-ʿĀdil Sayf al-Dīn Muḥammad or Aḥmad and his son al-Kāmil Nāṣir al-Dīn Muḥammad until the latter's death in 635/1238. Under these two sultans, Saladin's activist policies gave place to ones of détente and peaceful relations with the Franks, especially as the northern branches of the Ayyūbids in Diyār Bakr and Jazīra were now feeling pressure from the Rūm Seljuqs and the Khwārazm Shāhs (see below, nos 107, 89). The culmination of these new policies was al-Kāmil's offer of Jerusalem and the territories conquered by Saladin a generation before to the Emperor Frederick II (626/1229); in fact, the Crusaders recovered only the Holy City and one or two other towns, including Nazareth, and ten years later al-Nāṣir Dāwūd b. al-Muʿaẓẓam ʿĪsā of Damascus was to regain it. The period of peace did, however, bring economic benefits to Egypt and Syria, including a revival of trade with the Christian powers of the western Mediterranean.

After al-Kāmil, internal quarrels among the Ayyūbids intensified. The supreme sultan in Egypt had never been an autocrat, and the Ayyūbid empire was more a confederation of local principalities, those in Syria and Diyār Bakr often with unstable and shifting borders; these principalities resisted attempts by the supreme sultans to impose a more centralised authority. The Franks' Sixth Crusade was mastered and its leader, the French King St Louis (IX), captured, but soon after al-Ṣāliḥ Najm al-Dīn Ayyūb's death the Turkish Baḥrī slave troops seized power in Egypt, making their leader Aybak first Atabeg and then sultan in 648/1250. Al-ʿĀdil I Sayf al-Dīn Muḥammad or Aḥmad had sent out his young grandson al-Masʿūd Ṣalāḥ al-Dīn Yūsuf with an Atabeg or tutor to continue Ayyūbid rule over Yemen, but the dynasty were unable to maintain themselves there and the region passed to their former servants, the Turkish Rasūlids (see below, no. 49).

The appearance of the Mongol armies of Hülegü (see below, no. 133) was disastrous for the northern petty lines of Ayyūbids, and the Il Khān personally killed the prince of Mayyāfāriqīn and his brother. In Syria, only the branch at Ḥamāt survived, because of its obscurity and docility, until the mid-fourteenth century, although it did produce, as its penultimate amīr, the historian and geographer Abu 'l-Fidā'. However, in Diyār Bakr a local Kurdicised Ayyūbid principality around Ḥiṣn Kayfā survived the Il Khānids and Tīmūrids, and these amīrs were only extinguished by the 'White Sheep' Turkmens in the later fifteenth century.

A striking feature of Ayyūbid titulature was the rulers' adoption of titles comprising *al-Malik* 'prince, ruler' plus a qualifying adjective expressing such qualities as power, honour, piety, justice, etc., hence *al-Malik al-Muʿaẓẓam, al-Malik al-Kāmil,* etc. These usually appear on the coins minted by ruling princes, but the use of such titles extended to distinctly minor members of the Ayyūbid family also. This practice was inherited, together with much other Ayyūbid administrative and ceremonial practice, by their successors the Mamlūks (see below, no. 31).

Justi, 462–3; Lane-Poole, 74–9; Sachau, 19 nos 36–8 (branches in Baʿlbakk, Karak and Ḥiṣn Kayfā); Zambaur, 97–101 and Table H; Album, 22–3.

EI[2] 'Ayyūbids' (Cl. Cahen), 'Ḥamāt' (D. Sourdel), 'Ḥimṣ' (N. Elisséeff), 'Mayyāfārikīn. 2' (Carole Hillenbrand).

H. A. R. Gibb, 'The Aiyūbids', in K. M. Setton et al. (eds), *A History of the Crusades. II. The Later Crusades 1189–1311,* Philadelphia 1962, 693–714.

Ḥ .F. A. al-Hamdānī and Ḥ. S. M. al-Juhanī, *al-Ṣulayḥiyyūn wa 'l-ḥaraka al-Fāṭimiyya fi 'l-Yaman,* table of the Yemen Ayyūbids at p. 347.

G. R. Smith, *The Ayyūbids and Early Rasūlids in the Yemen (567–694/1173–1295),* 2 vols, London 1974–8, with a table of the Yemen Ayyūbids at II, 50.

R. S. Humphreys, *From Saladin to the Mongols. The Ayyubids of Damascus, 1193–1260,* Albany 1977, with tables at 88–91.

P. Balog, *The Coinage of the Ayyūbids,* Royal Numismatic Society, Special Publication, no. 12, London 1980.

N. D. Nicol, 'Paul Balog's The coinage of the Ayyubids: additions and corrections', NC, 9th series, vol. 146 (1986), 119–54.

H. Halm, 'Die Ayyubiden', in Haarmann (ed.), *Geschichte der arabischen Welt,* 200–16.

31

THE MAMLŪKS
648–92/1250–1517
Egypt and Syria

1. The Baḥrī line 648–792/1250–1390

⊘ *648/1250*	*Shajar al-Durr, Umm Khalīl ʿIṣmat al-Dunyā wa ʾl-Dīn, widow of the Ayyūbid al-Malik al-Ṣāliḥ II Ayyūb b. Muḥammad Nāṣir al-Dīn, Najm al-Dīn*
648/1250	al-Malik al-Muʿizz Aybak al-Turkumānī, ʿIzz al-Dīn, first reign
⊘ *648/1250*	*al-Malik al-Ashraf Mūsā, Ayyūbid nominal sultan*
⊘ 652/1254	Aybak, ʿIzz al-Dīn, second reign
⊘ 655/1257	al-Malik al-Manṣūr ʿAlī I b. Aybak ʿIzz al-Dīn, Nūr al-Dīn
⊘ 657/1259	al-Malik al-Muẓaffar Quṭuz al-Muʿizzī, Sayf al-Dīn
⊘ 658/1260	al-Malik al-Ẓāhir Baybars I al-Bunduqdārī, Rukn al-Dīn
(658–9/1260–1	al-Malik al-Mujāhid Sanjar, ʿAlam al-Dīn, rebel in Damascus)
⊘ 676/1277	al-Malik al-Saʿīd Baraka or Berke Khān b. Baybars I Rukn al-Dīn, Nāṣir al-Dīn
⊘ 678/1279	al-Malik al-ʿĀdil Salāmish or Süleymish b. Baybars I Rukn al-Dīn, Badr al-Dīn
⊘ 678/1279	al-Malik al-Manṣūr Qalāwūn al-Alfī, Abu ʾl-Maʿālī Sayf al-Dīn
⊘ (678–9/1279–80	al-Malik al-Kāmil Sunqur al-Ashqar, Sayf al-Dīn, rebel in Damascus)
⊘ 689/1290	al-Malik al-Ashraf Khalīl b. Qalāwūn Sayf al-Dīn, Ṣalāḥ al-Dīn
693/1293	(?) al-Malik al-ʿĀdil Baydarā, Badr al-Dīn
⊘ 693/1293	al-Malik al-Nāṣir Muḥammad I b. Qalāwūn Sayf al-Dīn, Nāṣir al-Dīn first reign
⊘ 694/1294	al-Malik al-ʿĀdil Kitbughā, Zayn al-Dīn
⊘ 696/1296	al-Malik al-Manṣūr Lāchīn or Lājīn al-Ashqar, Ḥusām al-Dīn
⊘ 698/1299	Muḥammad I b. Qalāwūn, Nāṣir al-Dīn, second reign
⊘ 708/1309	al-Malik al-Muzaffar Baybars II al-Jāshnakīr, Rukn al-Dīn (Burjī)
⊘ 709/1310	Muḥammad I b. Qalāwūn, Nāṣir al-Dīn, third reign
⊘ 741/1341	al-Malik al-Manṣūr Abū Bakr b. Muḥammad Nāṣir al-Dīn, Sayf al-Dīn
⊘ 742/1341	al-Malik al-Ashraf Kūjūk or Küchük b. Muḥammad Nāṣir al-Dīn, ʿAlāʾ al-Dīn
⊘ 742/1342	al-Malik al-Nāṣir Aḥmad I b. Muḥammad Nāṣir al-Dīn, Shihāb al-Dīn
⊘ 743/1342	al-Malik al-Ṣāliḥ Ismāʿīl b. Muḥammad Nāṣir al-Dīn, ʿImād al-Dīn

⊘ 746/1345 al-Malik al-Kāmil Sha'bān I b. Muḥammad Nāṣir al-Dīn, Sayf al-Dīn

⊘ 747/1346 al-Malik al-Muẓaffar Ḥājjī I b. Muḥammad Nāṣir al-Dīn, Sayf al-Dīn

⊘ 748/1347 al-Malik al-Nāṣir al-Ḥasan b. Muḥammad Nāṣir al-Dīn, Nāṣir al-Dīn, first reign

⊘ 752/1351 al-Malik al-Ṣāliḥ Ṣāliḥ b. Muḥammad Nāṣir al-Dīn, Ṣalāḥ al-Dīn

⊘ 755/1354 al-Ḥasan b. Muḥammad Nāṣir al-Dīn, Nāṣir al-Dīn, second reign

⊘ 762/1361 al-Malik al-Manṣūr Muḥammad II b. Ḥājjī I Sayf al-Dīn, Ṣalāḥ al-Dīn

⊘ 764/1363 al-Malik al-Ashraf Sha'bān II b. al-Malik al-Amjad Ḥusayn, Nāṣir al-Dīn

⊘ 778/1377 al-Malik al-Manṣūr 'Alī II b. Sha'bān II Nāṣir al-Dīn, 'Alā' al-Dīn

⊘ 783/1382 al-Malik al-Ṣāliḥ or al-Manṣūr Ḥājjī II b. Sha'bān II Nāṣir al-Dīn, Ṣalāḥ al-Dīn, first reign

⊘ 784/1382 al-Malik al-Ẓāhir Barqūq al-Yalbughāwī, Sayf al-Din (Burjī), first reign

⊘ 791–2/1389–90 al-Malik al-Muẓaffar Ḥājjī II b. Sha'bān II Nāṣir al-Dīn, Ṣalāḥ al-Dīn, second reign, d. 814/1411

2. The Burjī line 784–922/1382–1517

⊘ 784/1382 al-Malik al-Ẓāhir Barqūq al-Yalbughāwī, Sayf al-Dīn, first reign

⊘ 791/1389 Ḥājjī II b. Sha'bān II Nāṣir al-Dīn, Ṣalāḥ al-Dīn (Baḥrī), second reign

⊘ 792/1390 Barqūq, Sayf al-Dīn, second reign

⊘ 801/1399 al-Malik al-Nāṣir Faraj b. Barqūq Sayf al-Dīn, Nāṣir al-Dīn, first reign

⊘ 808/1405 al-Malik al-Manṣūr 'Abd al-'Azīz b. Barqūq Sayf al-Dīn, 'Izz al-Dīn, d. 809/1406

⊘ 808/1405 Faraj b. Barqūq Sayf al-Din, Nāṣir al-Dīn, second reign

⊘ (809/1407 al-Malik al-'Ādil 'Abdallāh Jakam, rebel in Aleppo)

⊘ *815/1412 al-Malik al-'Ādil al-'Abbās or Ya'qūb b. al-Mutawakkil I, Abu 'l-Faḍl al-Musta'īn, 'Abbāsid caliph, proclaimed sultan*

⊘ 815/1412 al-Malik al-Mu'ayyad Shaykh al-Maḥmūdī al-Ẓāhirī, Sayf al-Dīn

⊘ 824/1421 al-Malik al-Muẓaffar Aḥmad II b. Shaykh Sayf al-Dīn

⊘ 824/1421 al-Malik al-Ẓāhir Ṭaṭār, Sayf al-Dīn

⊘ 824/1421 al-Malik al-Ṣāliḥ Muḥammad III b. Ṭaṭār Sayf al-Dīn, Nāṣir al-Dīn

⊘ 825/1422 al-Malik al-Ashraf Barsbay, Abu 'l-Naṣr Sayf al-Dīn

⊘ 841/1438 al-Malik al-'Azīz Yūsuf b. Barsbay Sayf al-Dīn, Jamāl al-Dīn

⊘ 842/1438 al-Malik al-Ẓāhir Chaqmaq or Jaqmaq, Sayf al-Dīn

⊘ 857/1453 al-Malik al-Manṣūr 'Uthmān, Fakhr al-Dīn

⊘ 857/1453	al-Malik al-Ashraf Ināl al-ʿAlāʾī al-Ẓāhirī, Abu 'l-Naṣr Sayf al-Dīn
⊘ 865/1461	al-Malik al-Muʾayyad Aḥmad III b. Ināl Sayf al-Dīn, Shihāb al-Dīn
⊘ 865/1461	al-Malik al-Ẓāhir Khushqadam, Sayf al-Dīn
⊘ 872/1467	al-Malik al-Ẓāhir Yalbay, Sayf al-Dīn
⊘ 872/1467	al-Malik al-Ẓāhir Timurbughā
⊘ 872/1468	al-Malik al-Ashraf Qāyit Bay al-Ẓāhirī, Abu 'l-Naṣr Sayf al-Dīn
⊘ 901/1496	al-Malik al-Nāṣir Muḥammad IV b. Qāyit Bay
⊘ 904/1498	al-Malik al-Ẓāhir Qānṣawh I
⊘ 905/1500	al-Malik al-Ashraf Jānbulāṭ
⊘ 906/1501	al-Malik al-ʿĀdil Ṭūmān Bay I, Sayf al-Dīn
⊘ 906/1501	al-Malik al-Ashraf Qānṣawh II al-Ghawrī
⊘ 922-3/1516-17	al-Malik al-Ashraf Ṭūmān Bay II
923/1517	*Ottoman conquest*

The Mamlūks succeeded to the dominant position formerly held by the Ayyūbids in Egypt and Syria. Like most major Islamic dynasties of the age, the Ayyūbids had found it necessary to buttress their power with professional slave soldiers inherited from the Zangids (see below, no. 93) and other local powers of the Fertile Crescent, and the Mamlūks (*mamlūk*, literally 'one possessed, slave') arose from the Turkish troops of al-Malik al-Ṣāliḥ Najm al-Dīn Ayyūb of Egypt and Damascus (see above, no. 30, 1–2). Within the two and a half centuries of independent Mamlūk rule, two lines of sultans are somewhat artificially distinguished: the Baḥrī ones, so-called because these guards of the Ayyūbids originally had their barracks on the island of al-Rawḍa in the Nile (*al-Baḥr*), and the Burjī ones, thus named because Sultan Qalāwūn had quartered his guards in the citadel (*al-Burj*) of Cairo. Various of the Baḥrī sultans, such as Baybars I and Qalāwūn (whose descendants managed to succeed him over three generations), tried to establish personal, hereditary dynasties, but not with much success, and in the last fifty years or so of Baḥrī rule a dozen sultans followed in rapid succession. Within the Burjīs, the pattern of rule tended to be that a great Mamlūk commander would usurp the throne and then at his death pass it on to his son; but within a few years another usurper would take it over. These leading commanders came mostly from the military households of previous sultans, with the followings of Barqūq and Qāyit Bay being especially productive of subsequent rulers.

Ethnically, the Baḥrīs were mainly Qïpchaq Turks from the South Russian steppes, with an admixture of other races, including from the *Wāfidiyya*, Kurds, other Turks and even Mongols arriving from the East to join the Mamlūk army. The Burjīs, on the other hand, were primarily Circassians (*Charkas*, *Jarkas*) from the Christian areas of the northern Caucasus. Up to the end of the Mamlūks as a social group in Egypt in the early nineteenth century, Circassia provided most of their manpower. *Pace* the assertions of some earlier historians of the Mamlūks that this class failed to perpetuate itself more than two or three generations, it seems that Mamlūk families reproduced themselves all right but that succeeding generations from them no longer followed a military career; instead, they fell back into civilian life, seeking careers in the ranks of groups like the *'ulamā'* and religious lawyers and the administrators of *awqāf* or charitable endowments. Fresh importations of slave soldiers were accordingly necessary to maintain the ruling élite of Mamlūk military leaders.

The slave origins of the Mamlūks were reflected in the rather complex system of nomenclature which evolved for them, the sultans included. The mamlūk fresh from the South Russian steppes started off with simply a personal name, generally a Turkish one, such as Azdamur/Özdemür, 'choice iron' = 'best-quality iron', or Mankūbars/Mengü-bars 'eternal tiger', or Taghrībirdī/ Tangrï-verdi 'God gave'. But once within the Islamic military hierarchy, he could acquire a *nisba* relating to the slave merchant who had imported him into Egypt, such as al-Mujīrī, from the name Mujīr al-Dīn, or the circumstances of his purchase, such as al-Alfī 'bought for 1,000 [dinars]'; then a *nisba* relating to the amīr of whose household or nexus of clientage he formed part, such as al-Sayfī, from Sayf al-Dīn, or al-Ṣāliḥī, from al-Malik al-Ṣāliḥ' and finally, if he rose to eminence, a *laqab* or honorific of his own, such as Ḥusām al-Dīn 'sword of religion' or Badr al-Dīn 'full moon of religion'.

This ruling institution was a hierarchical construction, with the sultan's own mamlūks at the apex of the structure. An origin in the non-Muslim lands of the north and slave status were essential for success in the power struggle, for the free elements, including the progeny of former mamlūks, had only an inferior place in the armed forces (a similar position obtained regarding the Ottoman Turkish slave institution, where in the heyday of the empire the *Qapï Qullarï* or 'Slaves of the Porte' had superior opportunities for advancement compared with free elements). The sultans' arbitrary power was checked by the chief amīrs and the bureacracy, and the basic instability of the sultanate is seen in the rapid turnover of rulers at most periods and the three separate reigns of a sultan like Nāṣir al-Dīn Muḥammad b. Qalāwūn.

The Mamlūks continued the strongly Sunnī policy of the Ayyubids, with sultans, governors and amīrs founding numerous mosques, madrasas and other religious and charitable buildings in Cairo, Damascus, Aleppo and other towns. They derived great prestige from their role as defenders of Islam against the infidel Mongols, against the remnants of the Frankish Crusaders (see below) and against heterodox Muslims like the Nuṣayrīs and Ismā'īlīs of the mountains of western Syria. The Mamlūks' maintenance in Cairo of a line of *fainéant* 'Abbāsid caliphs (see above, no. 3, 3) is probably to be connected with this zeal for the Sunna.

The might and the achievements of the Mamlūk state were impressive and were lauded by contemporary historians, who stressed the role of the Turks as a people sent by God to preserve the fabric of the *Dār al-Islām*. Qutuz defeated Hülegü's Mongols at 'Ayn Jālūt in Palestine in 658/1260, and his successors consolidated the victory and set the new régime on its feet, although the threat from the Mongol Il Khānids did not recede until early in the fourteenth century. By the end of the thirteenth century, the last Crusader fortresses of the Syro-Palestinian coast had been mopped up; in the next one the Rupenid kingdom of Little Armenia or Cilicia was ended; and in the fifteenth century the Christian kingdom of Cyprus was made tributary for a time. The territories of the Mamlūks extended to Cyrenaica in the west, to Nubia and Massawa (Maṣawwa') in the south and to the Taurus Mountains in the north, while in Arabia they claimed to be protectors of the Holy Cities. In the course of the fifteenth century, however, the Ottomans emerged as the Mamlūks' main enemies in place of the Mongols. Foes of the Ottomans like the Qaramānids (see below, no. 124) were supported and the Turkmen principality of the Dulghadïr Oghullarï or Dhu 'l-Qadrids (see below, no. 129) maintained in western Diyār Bakr as a buffer-state. But the superior élan and vigour of the Ottomans, and their well-developed use of artillery and hand-guns, worked in their favour, while the Mamlūks were still wedded to the ideal of the armed cavalryman with his lance and sword. The penultimate Mamlūk sultan, Qānṣawh II al-Ghawrī, died in battle with the Ottomans at Marj Dābiq near Aleppo in 922/1516, and in the next year Sultan Selīm I defeated the last Mamlūk ruler in Egypt. Syria and Egypt now became governorates of the Ottoman empire, although the military and social caste of the Mamlūks continued virtually to control Egypt internally until Muḥammad ʿAlī Pasha (see below, no. 34) destroyed their power in 1226/1811.

Certainly until the economic and demographic crisis of the fifteenth century, Egypt and Syria under the Mamlūks enjoyed considerable prosperity, and there was a great cultural and artistic efflorescence, with special achievements in the fields of architecture, ceramics and metalwork; the development of the science of heraldry goes back to Ayyūbid and especially Mamlūk times. There were close commercial links with the Christian powers of the Mediterranean, such as Aragon, Sicily and other Italian states, despite strongly anti-Christian policies in the Near East, so that the Mamlūk period as a whole saw a distinct worsening of the position of the *Dhimmī*s in Egypt, above all, of the Christians. However, the reckless spending and ambitious building policies in Cairo of al-Nāṣir Muḥammad b. Qalāwūn overstretched the state's resources for the future, and the Black Death affected Egypt and Syria particularly severely. Under the later Baḥrī and then the Circassian sultans, the revenue from land taxation shrank, while public security declined in the face of Bedouin depredations. The Mamlūks had further to bear expenses in the Arabian Sea and Indian Ocean region in a fruitless endeavour to check Portuguese expansion there and to preserve Mamlūk trade connections with India and the lands beyond, so that the failure of the once mighty Mamlūk state to withstand the onslaught of Ottoman imperialism becomes understandable.

Lane-Poole, 803; Zambaur, 103–6; Album, 23–6.

EI² 'Mamlūks' (P. M. Holt).

P. Balog, *The Coinage of the Mamlūk Sultans of Egypt and Syria*, ANS Numismatic Studies, no. 12, New York 1964.

idem, *Supplement to The Coinage of the Mamlūk Sultans of Egypt and Syria*, in *ANS Museum Notes*, 16 (1970), 113–71.

P. M. Holt, *The Age of the Crusades. The Near East from the Eleventh Century to 1517*, London 1986, with genealogical tables at pp. 229–31.

R. Irwin, *The Middle East in the Middle Ages. The Early Mamluk Sultanate 1250–1382*, London 1986, with a list of rulers at p. 161.

U. Haarmann, 'Der arabische Osten im späten Mittelalter 1250–1517', in idem (ed.), *Geschichte der arabischen Welt*, 217–52.

32

THE MAʿN AMĪRS OF LEBANON

Tenth century to 1109/sixteenth century to 1697

Southern Lebanon

	ʿUthmān Maʿn b. al-Ḥājj Yūnus, Fakhr al-Dīn I, d. 912/1506
	Yūnus Maʿn b. ? ʿUthmān Fakhr al-Dīn, d. 917/1511
c. 922/c. 1516	Qorqmaz I b. ? Yūnus Maʿn Maʿn, ʿAlam al-Dīn Maʿn, Zayn al-Dīn } chiefs under Ottoman suzerainty
?	Qorqmaz II b. Fulān b. ? Qorqmaz I, d. 993/1585
993/1585	Fakhr al-Dīn II b. Qorqmaz II
1042/1633	Mulḥim b. Yūnus
1068–1108/1658–97	Aḥmad b. Mulḥim
1108/1697	*End of the direct Maʿnid line and succession of the Shihāb family*

The Banū Maʿn were an Arab Druze family of feudal chiefs in the Shūf region of southern Lebanon who were prominent in political life under the Ottomans in the sixteenth and seventeenth centuries. The Maʿnids replaced the Buḥtur family of the Gharb when the Ottomans took over Syria in 922/1516, and members of the family now begin to have firm historical attestation. Fakhr al-Dīn II was a tax-farmer for the Ottomans and governor of the *sanjaq*s of Sidon-Beirut and of Ṣafad. Through skilful political manoeuvring, in which he enlisted the help of the Maronites of Kisrawān and even of an external power like the Medici Dukes of Tuscany (he spent several years in exile in Italy), he eventually became master of most of Syria as far east as Palmyra and as far north as the fringes of Anatolia. These ambitions inevitably provoked an Ottoman reaction, leading to his military defeat and execution. Although a bloody tyrant, Fakhr al-Dīn II did improve agriculture and trade, with the aim of raising more revenue, and his inauguration of a tradition of Druze–Maronite cooperation was a factor in the subsequent formation of a Lebanese national identity, so that Lebanese have come to regard him, somewhat anachronistically, as the founder of their modern country.

After his death, his descendants retained what was in effect autonomy in Mount Lebanon by acting as governors there for the Ottomans, but the direct line of the Maʿnids ended with Aḥmad b. Mulḥim in 1108/1697, their power in the region being replaced by that of their kinsmen, the Banū Shihāb (see below, no. 33).

Zambaur, 109.

EI² 'Fakhr al-Dīn', 'Maʿn, Banū' (K. S. Salibi).

Adel Ismail, *Histoire du Liban du XVIIe siècle à nos jours. Le Liban au temps de Fakhr-ed-Din II (1590–1633)*, Paris 1955.

P. K. Hitti, *Lebanon in History*, London 1957.

P. M. Holt, *Egypt and the Fertile Crescent 1516–1922: A Political History*, Ithaca and London 1966, with a genealogical table at p. 311.

33

THE SHIHĀB AMĪRS OF LEBANON
1109–1257/1697–1842
Lebanon

1109/1697	Bashīr I b. Ḥusayn, of Rāshayyā
1118/1707	Ḥaydar b. Mūsā, of Ḥāṣbayyā
1144/1732	Mulḥim b. Ḥaydar
1167/1754	Manṣūr b. Ḥaydar
1184/1770	Yūsuf b. Mulḥim
1203/1788	Bashīr II b. Qāsim b. Mulḥim
1256/1840	*Intervention by the Allies and Turkey against Ibrāhīm Pasha of Egypt*
1256–7/1840–2	Bashīr III b. Qāsim b. ʿUmar as amīr under Allied aegis
1257/1842	*Imposition of direct Ottoman rule*

The Shihāb family of Sunnī Muslim notables rose to power as amīrs of Lebanon when the main line of the Maʿns (see above, no. 32) came to an end in 1109/1697, Bashīr I Shihāb being a maternal grandson of Aḥmad Maʿn b. Mulḥim. The amirate which the Shihābs ruled was in fact largely controlled by Druze feudal lords, increasingly rent by rival factions, while from the later eighteenth century onwards the numbers and strength of the Maronites increased; a reflex of these processes was the adoption of Christianity by Mulḥim's sons and the accession of Yūsuf b. Mulḥim as the first Maronite Shihāb amīr. The Shihābs managed to maintain themselves in Mount Lebanon against Aḥmad Jazzār Pasha, the Ottoman governor of Sidon and the coastal towns. Bashīr II operated within the increasingly complex politics of the Near East after the Napoleonic invasion and carefully conciliated Muḥammad ʿAlī Pasha (see below, no. 34), but became isolated in his own land by 1840 and fell from power when the Egyptian cause in Syria was lost; after a brief interlude, Ottoman direct rule in Lebanon was restored in 1257/1842.

Zambaur, 108 and Table K.
EI[2] 'Bashīr Shihāb II' (A. J. Rustum).
P. M. Holt, *Egypt and the Fertile Crescent 1516–1922: A Political History*, with a genealogical table at p. 312.
K. S. Salibi, *The Modern History of Lebanon*, London 1965.

34

THE HOUSE OF MUḤAMMAD ʿALĪ
1220–1372/1805–1953
Egypt

1220/1805	Muḥammad ʿAlī Pasha
1264/1848	Ibrāhīm Pasha b. Muḥammad ʿAlī
1264/1848	ʿAbbās Ḥilmī I Pasha b. Ṭūsūn Pasha
1270/1854	Muḥammad Saʿīd Pasha b. Muḥammad ʿAlī
1280/1863	Ismāʿīl Pasha b. Ibrāhīm (assumed the title of Khedive in 1284/1867), d. 1312/1895
1296/1879	Muḥammad Tawfīq b. Ismāʿīl
1309/1892	ʿAbbās Ḥilmī II b. Tawfīq, d. 1364/1944
⊘ 1333/1914	Ḥusayn Kāmil b. Ismāʿīl (asumed the title of Sultan), d. 1335/1917
⊘ 1335/1917	Aḥmad Fu'ād I b. Ismāʿīl (assumed the title of King in 1340/1922)
⊘ 1355/1936	Fārūq b. Fu'ād I, d. 1384/1965
1371–2/1952–3	Aḥmad Fu'ād II b. Fārūq
1371/1953	*Republican régime established*

Muḥammad ʿAlī (b. c. 1180/late 1760s) was a commander from Kavalla in Macedonia who went with local forces as part of the Ottoman–Albanian army sent by the Porte to dislodge the occupying French from Egypt. With great adeptness he contrived to stay there as *de facto* ruler, forcing the sultan to recognise him as governor or pasha and bloodily disposing of the old ruling class of the Circassian Mamlūks (see above, no. 31, 2). Muḥammad ʿAlī was thus one of a type which had been not uncommon in the eighteenth-century Ottoman empire, that is, a governor who tried to establish the hereditary rule of his family in his governorship; but he was unusual in successfully founding an autonomous and hereditary dynasty, with an increasingly centralised administration, in a century when the Porte was successfully reasserting its authority in many other parts of the Turkish and Arab lands of the empire. Once firmly in power, Muḥammad ʿAlī realised that Egypt could best flourish and progress if the military and technical advances of the West, and its educational practices, could be emulated; he therefore ranks with his contemporaries the Ottoman sultans Selīm III and Maḥmūd II as a pioneer westerniser in the Middle East. A newly-raised conscript army was raised to subjugate the Sudan and tap the rich slave markets there; higher educational institutions were set up, with European staff and advisers; fiscal policy was reformed and modified to meet the increased revenue needs. Externally, Muḥammad ʿAlī and his capable son Ibrāhīm intervened on the Ottoman side in the Greek War of Independence and carried on successful campaigns against the Wahhābī rulers in eastern and central Arabia, overthrowing the first Suʿūdī state and almost annihilating the Suʿūd dynasty (see below, no. 55) there.

But by the end of Muḥammad ʿAlī's reign, Egypt was already acquiring a burden of indebtedness, despite his immediate successors' abandonment of attempts to maintain the pace of reform. This burden was accentuated by extravagance and the desire of rulers in the mid-nineteenth century to imitate European royal standards. Ismā'īl was the first of his family to secure from the sultan the title of khedive, one of ancient Iranian origin, and also the promise of his descendants' hereditary succession in Egypt. It was under Ismā'īl also that work on the Suez Canal was completed, but imperialist Egyptian ventures in Ethiopia and the Sudan shattered Egypt's financial stability. Like Turkey itself, Egypt now came under the financial control of European creditor nations. After the proto-nationalist revolt of 'Urābī Pasha in 1299/1882, Britain assumed control of Egyptian finances and installed a permanent garrison there; not until 1340/1922 did the British Protectorate end.

The reigns of the last two significant members of the dynasty, Fu'ād I and Fārūq, were dominated internally by struggles with the majority political party of the Wafd and, externally, by the struggle to throw off the remaining vestiges of British control. Just before the end of the monarchy, Naḥḥās Pasha abrogated the Condominium Agreement over the Sudan and proclaimed Fārūq 'King of Egypt and the Sudan'. Nevertheless, discontent mounted, especially after the Arab–Israeli débâcle of 1947, widely attributed to royal corruption and incompetence. The monarch had always been felt as more Turkish than truly Arab, and in 1952 Fārūq was forced by the Free Officers' movement under Muḥammad Najīb (Neguib) and Jamāl 'Abd al-Nāṣir (Nasser) to abdicate. His infant son remained nominally on the throne under a regency, until the monarchy was finally abolished in June 1953.

Muḥammad 'Alī and his descendants minted Ottoman coins in Egypt, with the names on them of their suzerains the sultans alone, right up to the First World War and the final severing of all constitutional links with Istanbul, after which Ḥusayn Kāmil and his successors placed their own names on the Egyptian coinage.

Lane-Poole, 84–5; Zambaur, 107.

EI² 'Muḥammad 'Alī Pasha' (E. R. Toledano).

P. M. Holt, *Egypt and the Fertile Crescent 1516–1922: A Political History*, with a genealogical table at p. 312.

P. J. Vatikiotis, *The History of Egypt from Muhammad Ali to Sadat*, London 1980.

FIVE

Iraq and Jazīra before the Seljuqs

35

THE ḤAMDĀNIDS
293–394/906–1004
Jazīra and northern Syria

1. The line in Mosul and Jazīra

c. 254/868	Ḥamdān b. Ḥamdūn al-Taghlibī, chief in Mārdīn and the Mosul region
282–303/895–916	al-Ḥusayn b. Ḥamdān, caliphal governor in Jibāl and Diyār Rabīʿa, d. 306/918
293/906	ʿAbdallāh b. Ḥamdān, Abu 'l-Hayjā', caliphal governor in Mosul
⊘ 317/929	al-Ḥasan b. Abi 'l-Hayjā' ʿAbdallāh, Abū Muḥammad Nāṣir al-Dawla, d. 358/969
⊘ 356/967	Faḍl Allāh b. al-Ḥasan, Abū Taghlib ʿUddat al-Dawla al-Ghaḍanfar
369/979	*Būyid conquest*
379–87/981–9	al-Ḥusayn b. al-Ḥasan, Abū ʿAbdallāh, and Ibrāhīm b. al-Ḥasan, Abū Ṭāhir, vassals of the Būyids
387/989	*Conquest of Mosul by the ʿUqaylids and of Diyār Bakr by the Marwānids*

2. The line in Aleppo and northern Syria

⊘ 333/944	ʿAlī I b. Abi 'l-Hayjā' ʿAbdallāh, Abu 'l-Ḥasan Sayf al-Dawla
⊘ 356/967	Sharīf I b. ʿAlī, Abu 'l-Maʿālī Saʿd al-Dawla
⊘ 381/991	Saʿīd b. Sharīf, Abu 'l-Faḍā'il Saʿīd al-Dawla
⊘ 392–-4/1002–4	ʿAlī II b. Saʿīd, Abu 'l-Ḥasan, and Sharīf II b. Saʿīd, Abu 'l-Maʿālī, under the regency of Lu'lu'
394–406/1004–15	*Rule of Lu'lu', d. 399/1009, and then of his son ⊘ Manṣūr, Abū Naṣr Murtaḍā 'l-Dawla, as vassals of the Fāṭimids*

The Ḥamdānids came from the Arab tribe of Taghlib, long settled in Jazīra (although certain authorities alleged that they were only *mawālī* or clients of the Banū Taghlib). The founder of the family's fortunes, Ḥamdān b. Ḥamdūn, appears in the later years of the ninth century as an ally of the Khārijīs of Jazīra, in rebellion against caliphal authority; later, the Ḥamdānids tended to follow the Shīʿī inclinations of the majority of Arab tribes on the Syrian Desert fringes at that time. However, Ḥamdān's son al-Ḥusayn became a commander in the service of the ʿAbbāsids, and distinguished himself against the Carmathians or Qarāmiṭa of the Syrian Desert (see below, no. 40). Another son, Abu 'l-Hayjā'

ʿAbdallāh, was in 293/905 appointed governor of Mosul, and ʿAbdallāh's own son, al-Ḥasan, eventually followed him there as Nāṣir al-Dawla, behaving as an independent ruler and extending his power westwards from the Ḥamdānids' original centre of Diyār Rabīʿa into northern Syria. His son Abū Taghlib, called *al-Ghaḍanfar* 'the Lion', was unfortunate enough to confront the great Būyid amīr ʿAḍud al-Dawla at the height of the latter's power, when he had just in 376/978 taken over Iraq from his cousin ʿIzz al-Dawla (see below, no. 75). ʿAḍud al-Dawla marched northwards and drove out Abū Taghlib, who fled to the Fāṭimids in a vain search for help. His two brothers were afterwards restored in Mosul by the Būyids, and reigned there for a while until another family of Arab amīrs, the ʿUqaylids (see below, no. 38), took over the city.

Nevertheless, the junior branch of the Ḥamdānids remained in Syria, with Abū Taghlib's famous uncle, Sayf al-Dawla, ruling there in the middle decades of the tenth century after capturing Aleppo, Ḥimṣ and other towns from the Ikhshīdids (see above, no. 26). The establishment of the Ḥamdānid amirate in Syria coincided with a great resurgence of Byzantine fortunes under the energetic Macedonian emperors, and much of Sayf al-Dawla's reign was occupied in defending his territories from the Greeks. His son Saʿd al-Dawla was unable to prevent the Byzantines from several times invading Syria and temporarily capturing Aleppo and Ḥimṣ, although these were left to the Ḥamdānids as tribute-payers; moreover, a fresh threat arose in southern Syria from the appearance of the Fāṭimids and their expansionist policies. Finally, Saʿd al-Dawla's son Saʿīd al-Dawla was killed, probably at the instigation of the former slave general of Sayf al-Dawla's, Lu'lu'. Lu'lu' at first ruled as regent for Saʿīd al-Dawla's two sons, but later assumed power independently as a vassal of the Fāṭimids; his own son and successor Murtaḍā 'l-Dawla Manṣūr had to flee and ended his days as a refugee in Byzantium.

The Ḥamdānids achieved renown as patrons of Arabic literature, above all for Sayf al-Dawla's encouragement of the poet al-Mutanabbī; and this last amīr also secured a great contemporary reputation – though he was as often unsuccessful as successful in war – as a leader in the holy war against the Greeks. Yet although they came to rule over prosperous regions, with many centres of urban commercial activity, the Ḥamdānids still retained a considerable admixture of the irresponsibility and destructiveness of Bedouins. Syria and Jazīra inevitably suffered from the ravages of war, but these were aggravated by their tyranny and rapacity, as recorded by the traveller and geographer Ibn Ḥawqal, and the latter years of the Ḥamdānids were ones of decline and impotence.

Lane-Poole, 111–13; Zambaur, 133–4; Album, 21.
EI[2] 'Ḥamdānids' (M. Canard).
M. Canard, *Histoire de la dynastie des H'amdanides de Jazîra et de Syrie*, I, Algiers 1951.
Ramzi J. Bikhazi, *The Ḥamdānid Dynasty of Mesopotamia and Northern Syria 254–404/868–1014*, University Microfilms, Ann Arbor 1981.

36

THE MAZYADIDS

c. 350–c. 545/c. 961–c. 1150

Ḥilla and central Iraq

c. 350/c. 961	ʿAlī I b. Mazyad al-Asadī al-Nāshirī, Sanāʾ al-Dawla, governor for the Būyids in central Iraq
408/1017	Dubays I b. ʿAlī I, Abu ʾl-Aʿazz (al-Agharr?) Nūr al-Dawla
474/1082	Manṣūr b. Dubays I, Abū Kāmil Bahāʾ al-Dawla
479/1086	Ṣadaqa I b. Manṣūr, Abu ʾl-Ḥasan Sayf al-Dawla Fakhr al-Dīn, 'Malik al-ʿArab'
501/1108	Dubays II b. Ṣadaqa I, Abu ʾl-Aʿazz (al-Agharr?) Nūr al-Dawla
529/1135	Ṣadaqa II b. Dubays II, Sayf al-Dawla
532/1138	Muḥammad b. Dubays II
540/1145	ʿAlī II b. Dubays II
545– ?/1150– ?	Muhalhil b. ʿAlī II
558/1163	*Occupation of Ḥilla by caliphal forces*

The Mazyadids belonged to the North Arab Asad tribe, and were strongly Shīʿī in sympathy. The family acquired a hold on the region between Hīt and Kūfa when lands there were conveyed to them during the reign of the Būyid amīr Muʿizz al-Dawla at some date between 345/956 and 352/963. The beginnings of ʿAlī b. Mazyad's reign there must be put back, according to George Makdisi, to well before the date in the early eleventh century usually given in older Western sources. It seems also that the Mazyadid capital Ḥilla was already in the early eleventh century a permanent settlement and not a mere encampment, and that it gradually merged with and replaced the former Jāmiʿayn; under the great Ṣadaqa I b. Manṣūr, the town was enclosed by a strong wall and became the fortified centre of Mazyadid power in Iraq.

Despite their Bedouin origins, the Mazyadids showed themselves skilful organisers and diplomatists, making themselves a significant power in the shifting pattern of alliances in the Iraq of the Seljuq period. Their early rivals were the ʿUqaylids of Mosul and Jazīra (see below, no. 38), who in the reign of Dubays I b. ʿAlī I supported Dubays's brother Muqallad in the latter's bid for the Mazyadid amirate. When Ṭoghrïl and the Seljuqs appeared in Iraq, Dubays feared the Turkish invaders and supported the pro-Fāṭimid, Turkish general Arslan Basāsīrī in Baghdad. During the troubled reign of the Seljuq Berk-yaruq, Ṣadaqa I, the so-called 'King of the Arabs' (*Rex Arabum* in the Latin Crusader sources), acquired a position of great influence; but once sultan Muḥammad b. Malik Shāh (see below, no. 91, 1) was firmly on the throne, he moved against his overmighty vassal, and in 501/1108 defeated and killed Ṣadaqa in battle. The later Mazyadids allied with various Turkish amīrs against sultan Masʿūd b. Muḥammad, and Ḥilla was occupied on various occasions by Seljuq and caliphal troops. Ṣadaqa's son Dubays II achieved great fame in the eyes of the Frankish Crusaders, among others, and was a great patron of the Arabic poets of his time, but was murdered by one of the Assassins (see above, no. 29 and below, no. 101) at the same time as the caliph al-Mustarshid was killed.

ʿAlī II b. Dubays II died in 545/1150, and seems to have been succeeded in Ḥilla by his son Muhalhil. But the latter is a shadowy figure, and nothing is known of his reign in Ḥilla or of the length of this tenure of power; the town was in 558/1163 definitively incorporated in the territories of the resurgent ʿAbbāsid caliph al-Mustanjid, and the power there of both the Mazyadids and the Banū Asad ended.

The Mazyadids do not appear to have minted coins of their own.

Lane-Poole, 119–20; Zambaur, 137.

EI[2] 'Asad' (W. Caskel), 'Mazyad, Banū' (C. E. Bosworth).

G. Makdisi, 'Notes on Ḥilla and the Mazyadids in medieval Islam', JAOS, 74 (1954), 249–62.

ʿAbd al-Jabbār Nājī, *al-Imāra al-Mazyadiyya, dirāsa fī waḍʿihā al-siyāsī wa 'l-iqtiṣādī wa 'l-ijtimāʿī*, Basra 1970.

37

THE MARWĀNIDS
372–478/983–1085
Diyār Bakr

(372/983	*Bādh al-Kurdī, seized various towns of Diyār Bakr from the Ḥamdānids)*
⊘ 380/990	al-Ḥasan b. Marwān, Abū ʿAlī
⊘ 387/997	Saʿīd b. Marwān, Abū Manṣūr Mumahhid al-Dawla
⊘ 401/1011	Aḥmad b. Marwān, Abū Naṣr Naṣr al-Dawla
453/1061	Naṣr b. Aḥmad, Abu ʾl-Qāsim Niẓām al-Dīn
472–8/1079–85	Manṣūr b. Naṣr, Nāṣir al-Dawla, d. 489/1096
478/1085	*Seljuq conquest*

The Marwānids of Diyār Bakr, Khilāṭ and Malāzgird were Kurdish in origin. The founder Bādh was a Kurdish chief who seized various strongholds on the frontiers of Armenia and Kurdistan; taking advantage of the decline of Būyid influence there after ʿAḍud al-Dawla's death in 372/983 (see below, no. 75), he took over Diyār Bakr from the Ḥamdānids (see above, no. 35), held Mosul for a time and even threatened Baghdad at one point.

His nephew al-Ḥasan b. Marwān firmly based the dynasty in the captured towns of Mayyāfāriqīn and Āmid, but it was his younger brother Naṣr al-Dawla Aḥmad, Ibn Marwān, who ruled for over fifty years and who raised the Marwānid principality to a height of splendour and affluence. The strategic position of Diyār Bakr, commanding as it did the routes from Syria and Anatolia to Iraq and the east, meant that Ibn Marwān needed a skilful diplomatic policy to survive between powerful neighbours, all struggling for influence in the area. He recognised the ʿAbbāsid caliph at the outset, but he also had the Fāṭimids as neighbours in northern Syria; Fāṭimid cultural influence was strong in his domains, and he may for a while have acknowledged the Fāṭimid caliph al-Mustanṣir (see above, no. 27) as his suzerain. Before this, he had been forced for a time to pay tribute to the ʿUqaylids of Mosul (see below, no. 38) and in 421/1030 to cede to them Niṣībīn. Reigning as he did over a numerous Christian population in Diyār Bakr, he had amicable relations with the Byzantines, and the Emperor Constantine X Ducas used Ibn Marwān's good offices to get the captured Georgian prince Liparit freed by the Seljuq sultan Ṭoghrïl. The Oghuz nomads and their flocks were ejected from Diyār Bakr in 433/1041–2, and Ṭoghrïl himself did not appear there until 448/1056, when Ibn Marwān became his vassal. Within his lands, such towns as Āmid, Mayyāfāriqīn and Ḥiṣn Kayfā enjoyed much prosperity under Marwānid rule and there was a vigorous cultural life; the local historian of Mayyāfāriqīn, Ibn al-Azraq, describes how Ibn Marwān lightened taxes and carried out many public and charitable works there.

On his death in 453/1061, his territories were divided between his sons Naṣr and Saʿīd, but the power of the Marwānids was now waning. The cupidity of the caliphal vizier Fakhr al-Dawla Ibn Jahīr (who had previously been in Ibn Marwān's service) was now aroused; although the Marwānids had done the Seljuqs no harm, Fakhr al-Dawla and his son ʿAmīd al-Dawla secured permission from the sultan, Malik Shāh, to invade the Marwānid lands with a Seljuq army. In 478/1085, after stiff fighting, the attackers were victorious and the Marwānid principality was incorporated in the Seljuq empire. The last Marwānid, Manṣūr b. Naṣr, lived on in Jazīrat Ibn ʿUmar for another decade or so, but over the next centuries Diyār Bakr was to be predominantly under the control of Turkmen dynasties and to become increasingly Turkicised.

Lane-Poole, 118; Zambaur, 136; Album, 21.
EI² 'Djahīr (Banū)' (Cl. Cahen), 'Marwānids' (Carole Hillenbrand), 'Naṣr al-Dawla' (H. Bowen).
H. F. Amedroz, 'The Marwānid dynasty at Mayyāfāriqīn in the tenth and eleventh centuries A.D.', *JRAS* (1903), 123–54.

38

THE ʿUQAYLIDS

c. 380–564/c. 990–1169

Iraq, Jazīra and northern Syria

1. The line in Jazīrat Ibn ʿUmar, Niṣībīn and Balad of Muḥammad b. al-Musayyab al-ʿUqaylī

⊘ c.380/c. 990	Muḥammad b. al-Musayyab, Abu ʾl-Dhawwād
⊘ 386/996	ʿAlī b. Muḥammad, Abu ʾl-Ḥasan Janāḥ al-Dawla
⊘ 390/1000	al-Ḥasan b. Muḥammad, Abū ʿAmr Sinān al-Dawla
⊘ 393/1003	Muṣʿab b. Muḥammad, Abū Maraḥ Nūr al-Dawla

2. The line in Mosul and later in Jazīrat Ibn ʿUmar, Niṣībīn and Balad, also of the al-Musayyab line

c. 382/c. 992	Muḥammad b. al-Musayyab, Abu ʾl-Dhawwād
⊘ 386/996	al-Muqallad b. al-Musayyab, Abū Ḥassān Ḥusām al-Dawla
⊘ 391/1001	Qirwāsh b. al-Muqallad, Abu ʾl-Manīʿ Muʿtamid al-Dawla
442/1050	Baraka b. al-Muqallad, Abū Kāmil Zaʿīm al-Dawla
443/1052	Quraysh b. Abi ʾl-Faḍl Badrān, Abu ʾl-Maʿālī ʿAlam al-Dīn
⊘ 453/1061	Muslim b. Quraysh, Abu ʾl-Makārim Sharaf al-Dawla
478/1085	Ibrāhīm b. Quraysh, Abū Muslim
486–9/1093–6	ʿAlī b. Muslim
489/1096	*Seljuq conquest*

3. The line in Takrīt of Maʿn b. al-Muqallad's descendants

?	Rāfiʿ b. al-Ḥusayn b. Maʿn, Abu ʾl-Musayyab
427/1036	Khamīs b. Taghlib, Abu Manʿa
435/1044	Abū Ghashshām b. Khamīs
444/1052	ʿĪsā b. Khamīs
448/1056	Naṣr b. ʿĪsā
449– ?/1057– ?	*Rule of Abu ʾl-Ghanāʾim as governor on behalf of ʿĪsā's widow, and then Seljuq occupation*

4. The line in Hīt

487/1094	Tharwān b. Wahb, Bahāʾ al-Dawla
?	Kathīr b. Wahb
?	al-Manṣūr b. Kathīr
496– ?/1103– ?	Muḥammad b. Rāfiʿ

5. The line in ʿUkbarā of Maʿn b. al-Muqallad's descendants

⊘ 401/1011	Gharīb b. Muḥammad, Abū Sinān Sayf al-Dīn Kamāl al-Dawla
425– ?/1034– ?	Abu ʾl-Rayyān b. Gharīb

6. The other minor branches at Āna and al-Ḥadītha and at Qalʿat Jaʿbar (for details, see Lane Poole and Zambaur, *loc. cit.*)

The ʿUqaylids came from the great North Arab Bedouin tribal group of ʿĀmir b. Ṣaʿṣaʿa, which also included the Khafāja of the Iraq desert fringes and the Muntafiq of the Baṭāʾiḥ or marshlands of lower Iraq. With the decay of the last Ḥamdānids of Mosul (see above, no. 35, 1), the town passed to the ʿUqaylid Muḥammad b. al-Musayyab, who held it as a nominal vassal of the Būyid amīr Bahāʾ al-Dawla. After Muḥammad's death, there were internecine struggles for power among his sons, but control over Mosul and the other ʿUqaylid towns and fortresses in Jazīra eventually came to his nephew Qirwāsh b. al-Muqallad. At a time when Būyid influence in Iraq was weakening, Qirwāsh's main problem was to preserve intact his dominions in face of the new threat from the Turkmen invaders of western Persia and Iraq during the third and fourth decades of the eleventh century, and this work of defence necessitated alliances with another threatened power in Iraq, the Mazyadids of Ḥilla (see above, no. 36).

Under Qirwāsh's great-nephew Muslim b. Quraysh, the ʿUqaylid dominions reached their greatest extent and stretched almost from Baghdad as far as Aleppo. As a Shīʿī, Muslim's natural inclination was to support the Fāṭimids against the strongly Sunnī Seljuqs, but he allied with the Seljuq sultans Alp Arslan and Malik Shāh in order to secure the Mirdāsid territories in northern Syria (see above, no. 28). But a further switch to the Fāṭimids brought Seljuq armies to Mosul, forcing Muslim to flee to Āmid and Aleppo, where he was eventually killed fighting the Seljuq rebel Sulaymān b. Qutalmïsh (478/1085). ʿUqaylids survived in Mosul as governors on behalf of the Seljuqs until Tutush b. Alp Arslan in 486/1093 imposed on the town his own ʿUqaylid nominee, and shortly afterwards the line there was extinguished. Other branches of the ʿUqaylids persisted, however, as local lords in central Iraq and Diyār Muḍar for several more decades, the branch at Raqqa and Qalʿat Jaʿbar lasting up to 564/1169 under a descendant of Badrān b. al-Muqallad, when Nūr al-Dīn Maḥmūd b. Zangī (see below, no. 93) took over there. After the general loss of their power in Iraq, the Banū ʿUqayl moved southwards to their former eastern Arabian pasture grounds in Hajar and Yamāma, and established there a line of the Shaykhs of the Banū ʿUṣfūr.

It seems that the ʿUqaylids were not entirely a predatory Bedouin dynasty, but had introduced some features at least of the standard pattern of ʿAbbāsid administration into their land; thus it is mentioned that Muslim b. Quraysh had a postmaster or intelligence officer (*ṣāḥib al-khabar*) in every village of his principality. Several members of the dynasty were famed as poets. The passing of the ʿUqaylids and the Mazyadids marks the end of a period during which Arab amirates had held power over large stretches of Iraq and Syria, maintaining themselves between the great powers of the Fāṭimids, the Būyids and the Seljuqs. The generally Shīʿī sympathies of these amirates, and their strategic positions commanding the routes westwards into Diyār Bakr and Anatolia, inevitably brought them up against the expanding Sunnī Seljuqs and their Turkmen followers needing pasture land for their herds. Henceforth, political and military leadership in Iraq, Jazīra and Syria was to be almost exclusively in Turkish hands.

Lane-Poole, 116–17, with a genealogical table; Zambaur, 37, 135; Album, 21.
EI[1] 'ʿOḳailids' (K. V. Zettersteen).
H. C. Kay, 'Notes on the history of the Banu ʿOḳayl', JRAS, new series, 18 (1886), 491–526, with a genealogical table facing p. 526.

39

THE NUMAYRIDS
380–c. 474/990–c. 1081
Ḥarrān, Sarūj, Qal'at Ja'bar and Raqqa

⊘ 380/990	Waththāb b. Sābiq al-Numayrī, Abū Qawām Mu'ayyid al-Dawla	
⊘ 410/1019	Shabīb b. Waththāb, Abū Naṣr Ṣanī'at al-Dawla	
⊘ 431/1040	Muṭā'in b. Waththāb, in Raqqa Ḥasan b. Waththāb, in Sarūj Qawām b. Waththāb, in Ḥarrān	brief division of power
⊘ 431–55/1040–63	Manī' b. Shabīb, Abu 'l-Zimām Najīb al-Dawla Raḍī 'l-Dawla, eventually sole ruler	
	Numayrids in Ḥarrān until c. 474/c. 1081, but the names of these rulers unrecorded	

The Numayrids were a line of amīrs who flourished during the late tenth and the eleventh centuries in several towns of Diyār Muḍar: briefly at Edessa, more continuously at Ḥarrān, Sarūj, Qal'at Ja'bar and Raqqa. Their name derives from the North Arab tribal group to which they belonged, hence their origins were parallel to those of the Mirdāsids of Aleppo (see above, no. 28). Tribesmen of Numayr were early involved in the fighting in northern Syria and Jazīra as auxiliaries of such powers as the Ḥamdānids, until Waththāb in 380/990 made himself independent of the Ḥamdānids at Ḥarrān, from where he conquered other fortresses of the region. The first Numayrids found themselves forced to pay tribute to the Greeks on their western borders, and were unable to hold on to Byzantine Edessa, which they had temporarily captured. As the Fāṭimids expanded into northern Syria, Shabīb b. Waththāb in 430/1038 recognised the Fāṭimid caliph al-Mustanṣir, although after the Fāṭimid attempt to hold Baghdad, made by Arslan Basāsīrī, failed in 452/1060, the Numayrids probably changed allegiance to the 'Abbāsids. But the advent of the Seljuqs was fatal for the Numayrids, as for other petty principalities of the region, like that of the Marwānids (see above, no. 37). The names of the last Numayrid rulers in Ḥarrān are unknown to us. Their town fell in the end to the Seljuqs' allies, the 'Uqaylids (see above, no. 38), although members of the family were still to be found holding fortresses into the next century.

Zambaur, 138 (vague and inaccurate); Album, 22.
D. S. Rice, 'Medieval Ḥarrān. Studies on its topography and monuments. I', *Anatolian Studies*, 2 (1952), 36–84, with a genealogical table at p. 84.

SIX

The Arabian Peninsula

40

THE CARMATHIAN OR QARMAṬĪ RULERS OF THE LINE OF ABŪ SAʿĪD AL-JANNĀBĪ
c. 273–470/c. 886–1078
Originally in the Syrian Desert region and Iraq, then in eastern Arabia

273/886 or 281/894	al-Ḥasan b. Bahrām al-Jannābī, Abū Saʿīd	
301/913	Saʿīd b. Abī Saʿīd al-Jannābī, Abu 'l-Qāsim	
305/917	Sulaymān b. Abī Saʿīd, Abū Ṭāhir	
332/944	⊘ Aḥmad, Abū Manṣūr Saʿīd, Abu 'l-Qāsim al-Faḍl, Abu 'l-ʿAbbās Yūsuf, Abū Yaʿqūb	four sons of Abū Sa'īd al-Ḥasan, ruling jointly with Sābūr b. Abī Ṭāhir Sulaymān
⊘ (by 351/962	al-Ḥasan b. Aḥmad b. Abī Saʿīd, Abū ʿAlī al-Aʿṣam, in Syria, d. 366/977)	
361/972	Yūsuf, Abū Yaʿqūb, d. 366/977	
366/977	joint rule of six of Abū Saʿīd al-Ḥasan's grandsons, *al-sāda al-ru'asā'*	
470/1078	*Conquest of al-Aḥsā by the ʿUyūnid family of the Banū Murra*	

The Carmathian or Qarmaṭī movement was one of the manifestations of messianic, radical Shīʿism arousing out of the Ismāʿīlism which took shape in the later eighth and ninth centuries, towards the end of which period a *dāʿī* or missionary called Ḥamdān Qarmaṭ allegedly worked in Iraq. At the opening of the tenth century, the Syrian Desert fringes were agitated by the revolutionary movement of Zakarūya or Zakrawayh until it was suppressed in 293/906. This Carmathian *daʿwa* had split from the main Ismāʿīlī group in Syria in 186/899, unwilling to recognise the claims of the Fāṭimids (see above, no. 27), with the 'Old Believer' Carmathians now claiming to represent the claims of Ismāʿīl, son of the Sixth Imām Jaʿfar al-Ṣādiq, as conveyed through Ismāʿīl's son Muḥammad; the split with the Fāṭimids was never to be really healed.

Instead, the Carmathians established themselves in lower Iraq, where the Zanj or black slave rebellion of the later ninth century had left behind much social and religious discontent, and among the Bedouin of north-eastern Arabia, in the region of al-Aḥsā or Baḥrayn. Here, Abū Saʿīd al-Jannābī built up an enduring principality, often described later as that of the Abū Saʿīdīs. The organisation of the Carmathian community there was sufficiently different from the norm of Islamic states at that time to excite the deep suspicion of orthodox Sunnī observers. It seems that there were tentative experients with the communal ownership of property and goods, soon abandoned; in any case, the economic foundation of the Carmathian principality rested on black slave labour. The rulers of Abū Sa'īd's family were backed by a council of elders, the *'Iqdāniyya* 'those who have power to bind [and loose]'; contemporary travellers and visitors to al-Aḥsā praised the justice and good order prevailing there.

The relations of the Carmathians, in their earlier, activist phase, with the Fāṭimids continued to be tense. They raided into Iraq and as far as the coast of Fars (Fārs) and harried the fringes of Syria and Palestine; they had adherents in Yemen, and at one point conquered Oman ('Umān). Their greatest coup of all was in 317/930 carrying off the Black Stone from the Ka'ba in Mecca, considering it to be a mere object of superstitious reverence; it was twenty years later before, at the Fāṭimid caliph al-Manṣūr's pleading, they agreed to replace it. Towards the end of the tenth century, the Carmathians grew more moderate in tone, and their principality evolved into something like a republic, with a council of elders in which the house of Abū Sa'īd al-Jannābī was still notable. It seems to have lasted thus until the later eleventh century and the end of the Carmathian state as an independent entity through joint operations by a Seljuq–'Abbāsid army from Iraq and a local Bedouin chief, founder of the subsequent line of 'Uyūnids in eastern Arabia. The surviving Carmathians probably then gave their adherence to the Fāṭimids, but descendants of Abū Sa'īd, called *sayyid*s, were to be found in al-Aḥsā two or three centuries later.

Ismā'īlism has long disappeared from eastern Arabia, but it may have left a distant legacy in the present existence there, within modern Saudi Arabia, Qaṭar and Baḥrayn Island, of significant Twelver Shī'ī communities.

Coins of the Carmathians are extant from the second half of the tenth century, but seem to have been minted by their governors and commanders on the borders of Palestine and Syria rather than in al-Aḥsā.

Zambaur, 116; Album, 20.

EI[2] 'Ismā'īliyya', 'Ḳarmaṭī' (W. Madelung).

M. J. de Goeje, 'La fin de l'empire des Carmathes du Bahraïn', *JA*, 9th series, 5 (1895), 1–30.

W. Madelung, 'Fatimiden und Baḥrainqarmaten', *Der Islam*, 34 (1959), 34–88, English tr. 'The Fatimids and the Qarmaṭīs of Baḥrayn', in F. Daftary (ed.), *Medieval Isma'ili History and Thought*, Cambridge 1996, 21–83.

George T. Scanlon, 'Leadership in the Qarmaṭian sect', *BIFAO*, 59 (1959), 29–48, with a provisional genealogical table at p. 35.

François de Blois, 'The 'Abu Sa'īdīs or so-called "Qarmatians" of Bahrayn', *Proceedings of the Seminar for Arabian Studies*, 16 (1986), 13–21.

F. Daftary, *The Ismā'īlīs, their History and Doctrines*, Cambridge 1990, 103–34, 160–5, 17–6, 220–2.

H. Halm, *Shiism*, Edinburgh 1991, 166–77.

41

THE ZAYDĪ IMĀMS OF YEMEN

284–1382/897–1962

Generally in Highland Yemen, with seats in Ṣaʿda or Ṣanʿāʾ; in the twentieth century uniting all Yemen

1. The early period: the Rassid line

	al-Qāsim b. Ibrāhīm al-Ḥasanī al-Rassī, d. 246/860 in Medina
	al-Ḥusayn b. al-Qāsim, also resident in Medina
⊘ 284/897	Yaḥyā b. al-Ḥusayn, al-Hādī ilā ʾl-Ḥaqq, in Ṣaʿda
298/911	Muḥammad b. Yaḥyā, al-Murtaḍā, d. 310/922
⊘ 301/913	Aḥmad b. Yaḥyā, al-Nāṣir
322/934	Yaḥyā b. Aḥmad, d. 345/956
358/968	Yūsuf b. Yaḥyā, al-Manṣūr al-Dāʿī, d. 403/10122
389/998	al-Qāsim b. ʿAlī al-ʿIyānī, Abu ʾl-Ḥusayn al-Manṣūr, d. 393/1003
401/1010	al-Ḥusayn b. al-Qāsim, al-Mahdī, d. 404/1013
413/1022	Jaʿfar b. al-Qāsim
426/1035	al-Ḥasan b. ʿAbd al-Raḥmān, Abū Hāshim d. 431/1040
437/1045	Abu ʾl-Fatḥ b. al-Ḥusayn, al-Daylamī al-Nāṣir
	Period of weakness for the Zaydī Imāms, with the Ṣulayḥids capturing Ṣanʿāʾ in 454/1062 and the Hamdānid line of Ḥātim b. al-Ghashīm ruling there in 492/1099
?	Ḥamza b. Abī Hāshim, d. 458/1066
458/1067	al-Fāḍil b. Jaʿfar, d. 460/1068
?	Muḥammad b. Jaʿfar, d. 478/1085
511/1117	Yaḥyā b. Muḥammad, Abū Ṭālib
531/1137	ʿAlī b. Zayd
532/1138	Aḥmad b Sulaymān, al-Mutawakkil, d. 566/1171
566/1171	*Hamdānid occupation of Ṣanʿāʾ*
569–626/1174–1229	*Ayyūbid conquest and occupation of Yemen*
⊘ 583/1187	ʿAbdallāh b. Ḥamza, al-Manṣūr, d. 614/1217
614/1217	Yaḥyā b. Ḥamza, Najm al-Dīn al-Hādī ilā ʾl-Ḥaqq, in Ṣaʿda
614/1217	Muḥammad b. ʿAbdallāh, ʿIzz al-Dīn al-Nāṣir, in the southern districts until 623/1226
626– /1229–	*Rasūlid rule established in Ṣanʿāʾ*
⊘ 646–56/1248–58	Aḥmad b. al-Ḥusayn, al-Mahdī al-Mūṭiʾ
	The Zaydī imamate held by members of a collateral branch

2. The more recent period: the Qāsimid line

c. 1000/c. 1592	al-Qāsim b. Muḥammad, al-Manṣūr
⊘ 1029/1620	Muḥammad b. al-Qāsim, al-Muʾayyad

⊘ 1054/1644	Ismā'īl b. al-Qāsim, al-Mutawakkil
⊘ 1087/1676	Aḥmad b. al-Ḥasan, al-Mahdī
	(al-Qāsim b. Muḥammad, al-Mu'ayyad, rival Imām in southern Yemen)
⊘ 1092/1681	Muḥammad b. Aḥmad, al-Mutawakkil
⊘ 1097/1686	Muḥammad b. Muḥammad, al-Nāṣir al-Hādi al-Mahdī
⊘ 1128/1716	al-Qāsim b. al-Ḥusayn, al-Mutawakkil
⊘ 1139/1726	al-Ḥusayn al-Manṣūr
⊘ 1160/1747	al-'Abbās b. al-Ḥusayn, al-Mahdī
⊘ 1189/1775	'Alī b. al-'Abbās, al-Manṣūr
1221/1806	Aḥmad b. al-Ḥusayn, al-Mahdī
⊘ 1223/1808	Aḥmad b. 'Alī, al-Mutawakkil
⊘ 1231/1816	'Abdallāh b. Aḥmad, al-Mahdī
1257/1841	al-Qāsim al-Mahdī
⊘ 1261/1845	Muḥammad Yaḥya, al-Mutawakkil
1265/1849	*First Ottoman attack on Ṣan'ā'*
1288–1336/1871–1918	*Ottoman occupation of Yemen*
1308/1890	Muḥammad b. Yaḥyā, Ḥamīd al-Dīn al-Manṣūr
⊘ 1322/1904	Yaḥyā b. Muḥammad al-Manṣūr, al-Mutawakkil
⊘ 1367–82/1948–62	Aḥmad b. Yaḥyā, Sayf al-Islām, d. 1382/1962
⊘ 1382/1962	Badr b. Aḥmad, in conflict with republican forces until 1970, when the Yemen Arab Republic was established

The Zaydīs are a moderate branch of the Shī'a, and they held that the caliph 'Alī had been designated by the Prophet Muḥammad as Imām of the Community of the Faithful through his personal merits rather than through a divine ordinance or *naṣṣ*, and also that the Fifth Imām of the Shī'a should rightfully have been not Muḥammad al-Bāqir but his brother Zayd, martyred during the reign of the Umayyad caliph Hishām (see above, no. 2). The descendants and partisans of Zayd later won over by their propaganda the Persian peoples of Daylam and the south-western coastlands of the Caspian Sea, a region sufficiently inaccessible (and, indeed, hardly at that time Islamised) for this work to be carried out without impediment.

The region of Yemen in the south-western corner of the Arabian peninsula was likewise remote from control by the 'Abbāsid caliphs, and here Tarjumān al-Dīn al-Qasim b. Ibrāhīm Ṭabāṭabā, a descendant of the Second 'Alid Imām al-Ḥasan, came from Medina and established himself during al-Ma'mūn's caliphate; it was he who founded the legal and theological school of the Zaydiyya. The name 'Rassids', conveniently used by Western scholars to designate the ensuing line of Imāms, is geographical in origin and derived from al-Rass, a place in the Ḥijāz; the term is not commonly used by indigenous Yemeni historians.

The Rassids thus settled at Ṣa'da in northern Yemen, and maintained themselves there against the local Khārijīs, Qarmaṭīs and other opponents of their rule. As well as possessing Ṣa'da, they frequently held Ṣan'ā' also. Over the next century, Yemen remained the centre of the Zaydī *da'wa*, with missionaries going to the Caspian provinces and to other parts of the Islamic world. Ṣan'ā' was taken by the Ṣulayḥids (see below, no. 45) in the second half of the eleventh century, and in the next century it was held by Arab chiefs of the Banū Hamdān (see below, no. 47) for fifty years; only briefly were Zaydī fortunes restored under Aḥmad b. Sulaymān, al-Mutawakkil, a descendant of the tenth-century Imām Aḥmad b. Yaḥyā, al-Nāṣir. The Ayyūbid conquest of Yemen in 569/1174 and their domination there for over half a century (see above, no. 30, 8) considerably restricted the authority of the Imāms; they revived somewhat under the first Rasūlid rulers of Yemen (see below, no. 49), until internal disputes and civil strife brought about the eclipse of their power in Yemen.

After this time, the names of various Imāms are known, but the succession seems to have been interrupted by the intrusion of several Imāms from other Ḥasanid lines and of various claimants and counter-Imāms. A more definitely-known sequence appears after around 1000/1592 with the line of al-Qāsim b. Muḥammad. Before this, Yemen had been conquered by the Turks, with Özdemir Pasha entering Ṣan'ā' in 954/1547, after which Yemen became a province of the Ottoman empire, with the Zaydī Imāms recognising Ottoman suzerainty and left with considerable internal freedom of action. But the Turkish yoke was thrown off by 1045/1635, the Imāms having been reinstalled at Ṣan'ā' after 1038/1629. The internal history of Yemen over the next two and a half centuries continued to be confused until the Ottomans returned in the later nineteenth century to 'Asīr, the region immediately to the north of Yemen, and then in 1288/1871 took Ṣan'ā'. The hold of the Zaydī Imāms on the countryside of highland Yemen remained, however, firm, and on occasion they occupied Ṣan'ā' temporarily. The Turks left Yemen at the end of the First World War, and the Imāms were able to impose their authority over the whole country and enjoy an internationally-recognised independence. But a closed society and a traditional type of autocratic rule became increasingly difficult to maintain after the Second World War, and in 1962 a military coup brought with it the proclamation of a republic. A protracted and bloody civil war followed, until in 1970 the rule of the Ḥamīd al-Dīn family was replaced by a coalition republican régime.

Sachau, 22 no. 45; Zambaur, 122–4 and Table B.
EI[1] 'Zaidīya' (R. Strothmann); EI[2] 'Ṣan'ā'' (G. R. Smith).
H. C. Kay, *Yaman: Its Early Mediaeval History*, London 1892, with a detailed genealogical table at p. 302.
'Abd al-Wāsi' b. Yaḥyā al-Wāsi'ī, *Furjat al-humūm wa 'l-ḥuzn fī ḥawādith wa-ta'rīkh al-Yaman*, Cairo 1346/1927–8.
Ramzi J. Bikhazi, 'Coins of al-Yaman 139–569 A.H.', *al-Abḥāth*, 23 (1970), 17–127.
G. R. Smith, *The Ayyūbids and Early Rasūlids in the Yemen (567–694/1173–1295)*, London 1974–8, II, 76–81, with a list of Imāms and a genealogical table at pp. 76–7, 81.

42

THE ZIYĀDIDS

203–409/818–1018

Yemen, with their capital at Zabīd

203/818	Muḥammad b. Ziyād
245/859	Ibrāhīm b. Muḥammad
283/896	Ziyād b. Ibrāhīm
289/902	(Ibn) Ziyād
⊘ 299/911	Isḥāq b. Ibrāhīm, Abu 'l-Jaysh
371/981	'Abdallāh or Ziyād (?) b. Isḥāq
402–9/1012–18	Ibrāhīm or 'Abdallāh b. 'Abdallāh
409/1018	*Succession of the Ziyādids' slave ministers, including the Najāḥids, in the northern territories of the Ziyādids*

The founder of this line, Muḥammad b. Ziyād, claimed descent from the great Umayyad governor of Iraq, Ziyād b. Abīhi, but such a connection is speculative. He was appointed by the 'Abbāsid caliph al-Ma'mūn as governor of Yemen, in the hope of restraining Shī'ī dissent there, and the Ziyādids always recognised the overlordship of Baghdad. Muḥammad's centre of power was Zabīd in Tihāma or coastal lowlands of Yemen, and he managed to extend his authority eastwards into Ḥaḍramawt and over some parts of highland Yemen, although the Yu'firids (see below, no. 43) eventually established themselves in Ṣan'ā'. The subsequent Ziyādids were threatened by the Yu'firids and other local potentates, and only with the long reign of Abu 'l-Jaysh Isḥāq did Ziyādid fortunes revive somewhat. The last Ziyādids, whose dates are uncertain, were really *fainéants*, and in the early eleventh century power passed in Zabīd to their black Ḥabashī slave ministers, one of whom was to found the dynasty of the Najāḥids (see below, no. 44).

Lane-Poole, 90–1; Zambaur, 115; Album, 26.

EI[1] 'Ziyādīs' (R. Strothmann).

H. C. Kay, *Yaman: Its Early Mediaeval History*, 2–18, 234ff.

Ramzi J. Bikhazi, 'Coins of al-Yaman 139–569 A.H.', 64ff.

G. R. Smith, in W. Daum (ed.), *Yemen: 3000 Years of Art and Civilisation in Arabia Felix*, Innsbruck n.d. [c. 1988], 130, 138, with a list of rulers.

43

THE YUʿFIRIDS OR YAʿFURIDS

232–387/847–997

Yemen, with their centres at Ṣanʿāʾ and Janad

232/847	Yuʿfir b. ʿAbd al-Raḥmān al-Ḥiwālī al-Ḥimyarī
258/872	Muḥammad b. Yuʿfir, d. 269/882
	(Ibrāhīm b. Muḥammad, Abū Yuʿfir, as deputy ruler)
269/882	Ibrāhīm b. Muḥammad, as sole ruler, d. 273/886
273/886	*Period of confusion*
c. 285/c. 898	Asʿad b. Ibrāhīm, Abū Ḥassān, first reign
	Period of confusion, with power in Ṣanʿāʾ seized at times by the Zaydī Imāms and pro-Fāṭimid chiefs
⊘ 303/915	Asʿad b. Ibrāhīm, second reign
332/944	? Muḥammad b. Ibrāhīm
344–87/955–97	ʿAbdallāh b. Qaḥṭān, with his power disputed
387/997	*The Yuʿfirids reduced to the status of petty, local chiefs*

In the mid-ninth century, Yuʿfir b. ʿAbd al-Raḥmān assrted his independence of the ʿAbbāsid governors in the Yemen highlands, occupying Ṣanʿāʾ and Janad and becoming the first local dynasty to achieve power there. His family came from Shibām to the north-west of Ṣanʿāʾ, and claimed a distant descent from the Tubbaʿ kings of pre-Islamic times. Yuʿfir was still, however, careful to maintain his own allegiance to the ʿAbbāsid caliphs. Subsequent members of the family became involved with rival powers in confused struggles for the control of Ṣanʿāʾ and northern Yemen; a new element here was the arrival in 284/897 of the Zaydī Imāms (see above, no. 41) and, shortly afterwards, the appearance of the Qarmaṭīs, supporters of the Fāṭimids (see above, nos 27, 40). Relative stability was achieved under Asʿad b. Ibrāhīm, but after his death the family was rent by dissensions and by 387/997 lost their ruling power, though apparently surviving in Yemen as obscure, local lords.

Lane-Poole, 91; Zambaur, 116;

EI[1] 'Yaʿfur b. ʿAbd al-Raḥmān' (R. Strothmann).

H. C. King, *Yaman: Its Early Mediaeval History*, 5–6, 223ff.

Ḥ. F. al-Hamdānī and Ḥ. S. M. al-Juhanī, *al-Ṣulayḥiyyūn wa 'l-ḥaraka al-Fāṭimiyya fi 'l-Yaman*, with a genealogical table at p. 333.

G. R. Smith, in W. Daum (ed.), *Yemen: 3000 Years of Art and Civilisation in Arabia Felix*, 130–1, 138.

44

THE NAJĀḤIDS

412–553/1022–1158

Yemen, with their capital at Zabīd

⊘ 412/1022	Najāḥ, al-Mu'ayyad Nāṣir al-Dīn
c. 452/c. 1060	*Ṣulayḥid occupation of Zabīd*
473/1081	Sa'īd b.Najāḥ, al-Aḥwal, first reign
475/1083	*Ṣulayḥid revanche*
479/1086	Sa'īd b. Najāḥ, second reign
⊘ 482/1089	Jayyāsh b. Najāḥ, Abū Ṭāmī
c. 500/c. 1107	Fātik I b. Jayyāsh
503/1109	al-Manṣūr b. Fātik I
518/1124	Fātik II b. al-Manṣūr
531/1137	Fātik III b. Muḥammad
c. 553/c. 1158	*Fātik III deposed by tḥe Zaydī Imām, and Zabīd seized by the Mahdids in 554/1159*

With the demise of the Ziyādids (see above, no. 42), one of their black Ḥabashī viziers, Najāḥ, managed to kill a rival and establish himself in Zabīd as an independent ruler, acquiring honorifics from the 'Abbāsid caliph, whom he acknowledged, and extending his dominion northwards through Tihāma. Najāḥ and his successors, like the Ziyādids before them, imported into Yemen contingents of Abyssinian military slaves to support their power, thereby contributing to the mixture of races to be found until today in lowland Yemen. Sa'īd b. Najāḥ was on more than one occasion dispossessed by the Ṣulayḥids (see below, no. 45), and al-Manṣūr b. Fātik I reigned as one of their vassals. The Najāḥids of the twelfth century ruled amid growing confusion and under increasing pressure, latterly from the Mahdids (see below, no. 48), and despite the deposition of Fātik III b. Muḥammad as the price of military help from the Zaydī Imām Aḥmad b. Sulaymān al-Mutawakkil, the Mahdids entered Zabīd in 554/1159.

Lane-Poole, 92–3; Zambaur. 117–18; Album, 26.

EI² 'Nadjāḥids' (G. R. Smith).

H. C. Kay, *Yaman: Its Early Mediaeval History*, 14ff.

Ḥ. F. A. al-Hamdānī and Ḥ. S. M. al-Juhanī, *al-Ṣulayḥiyyūn wa 'l-ḥaraka al-Fāṭimiyya fi 'l-Yaman*, with a genealogical table at p. 339.

G. R. Smith, *The Ayyūbids and Early Rasūlids in the Yemen (567–694/1173–1295)*, II, 55–9.

idem, in W. Daum (ed.), *Yemen: 3000 Years of Art and Civilisation in Arabia Felix*, 131–2, 138.

45

THE ṢULAYḤIDS

439–532/1047–1138

Yemen, with their capital at Ṣanʿāʾ and then at Dhū Jibla

⊘ 439/1047	ʿAlī b. Muḥammad al-Ṣulayḥī, Abū Kāmil al-Dāʿī	
⊘ 459/1067 or 473/1080	Aḥmad b. ʿAlī, al-Mukarram	
⊘ 467/1075 or 479/1086	ʿAlī b. Aḥmad b. ʿAli, al-Mukarram al-Aṣghar	under the supreme rule of al-Sayyida Arwā bt. Aḥmad b. Jaʿfar
c. 484/c. 1091	al-Manṣūr Sabaʾ b. Aḥmad b. al-Muẓaffar, d. 492/1099	
⊘ 492–532/1099–1138	al-Sayyida Arwā bt. Aḥmad	
532/1138	*Power assumed by the Zurayʿids of Aden*	

As well as becoming, because of its remoteness from the centre of the caliphate in Iraq, a centre for Zaydī Shīʿism (see above, no. 41), Yemen also proved fertile ground for the Ismāʿīlī Shīʿī *daʿwa*, and Carmathian or Qarmaṭī activity (see above, no. 40) is mentioned there from the early tenth century onwards. Once the Fāṭimids became established in Egypt in the second half of the tenth century (see above, no. 27), with the Holy Cities of the Ḥijāz acknowledging the new caliphs in Cairo, relations between Egypt and Yemen became close.

The Ṣulayḥids ruled in Yemen as adherents of Ismāʿīlism and as nominal vassals of the Fāṭimids. ʿAlī b. Muḥammad, a member of the South Arabian tribe of Hamdān and the son of a local Shāfiʿī *qāḍī* or judge, became the *khalīfa* or deputy of the chief Fāṭimid *dāʿī* in Yemen, Sulaymān b. ʿAbdallāh al-Zawāḥī, and was thus able to set up a principality in the Yemen highlands. He defeated the Abyssinian slave dynasty of the Najāḥids of Tihāma (see above, no. 44); by 455/1063 he had captured Ṣanʿāʾ from the Zaydī Imāms and invaded the Ḥijāz; and in the next year, he took Aden from the Banū Maʿn. Under his son al-Mukarram Aḥmad, the Ṣulayḥid dominions reached their maximum extent. Yet these conquests could not be held beyond the eleventh century. The Najāḥids revived, Aden was usually independent, and the Zaydī Imāms remained at their centre of Ṣaʿda in northern Yemen. From the latter part of Aḥmad's reign until her own death in 532/1138, effective authority was exercised by his capable and energetic consort, al-Sayyida Arwā. It was she who moved the Ṣulayḥid capital to Dhū Jibla, controlling from there southern Yemen and Tihāma in a reign of some brilliance as the 'Second Bilqīs'.

After her death at the advanced age of 92, power passed to the Zurayʿids, who were to hold it until the advent in 569/1174 of the Ayyūbid Tūrān Shāh (see above, no. 30, 8), although some Ṣulayḥid princes continued to hold fortresses in Yemen down to the end of the twelfth century.

Lane-Poole, 94; Zambaur, 118–19 (both very inaccurate); Album, 26.

*EI*² 'Ṣulayḥids' (G. R. Smith).

H. C. Kay, *Yaman: Its Early Mediaeval History*, 19–64, with a detailed genealogical table at p. 335.

Ḥ. F. A. al-Hamdānī and Ḥ. S. M. al-Juhanī, *al-Ṣulayḥiyyūn wa 'l-ḥaraka al-Fāṭimiyya fi 'l-Yaman*, with a detailed genealogical table at p. 335.
Ramzi J. Bikhazi, 'Coins of al-Yaman 139–569', 77ff.
G. R. Smith, in W. Daum (ed.), *Yemen: 3000 Years of Art and Civilisation in Arabia Felix*, 132, 138.

46

THE ZURAYʿIDS OR BANU 'L-KARAM

473–571/1080–1175

Southern Yemen, with their capital at Aden

473/1080	al-ʿAbbās b. al-Mukarram or al-Makram or al-Karam b. al-Dhi'b and al-Masʿūd b. al-Mukarram, joint vassals of the Ṣulayḥids
477/1084	al-Masʿūd b. al-Mukarram and Zurayʿ b. al-ʿAbbās, joint rulers
504–32/1110–38	Confused period of rivalry between the two branches of the family, the sons of al-Masʿūd and the sons of Zurayʿ: rule at unspecified dates of Abu 'l-Suʿūd b. Zurayʿ and Abu 'l-Ghārāt b. al-Masʿūd, ⊘ Saba' b. Abi 'l-Suʿūd and Muḥammad b. Abi 'l-Ghārāt, and then ʿAlī b. Muḥammad
c. 532/c. 1138	Saba' b. Abi 'l-Suʿūd, sole ruler in Aden, d. 533/1139
533/1139	ʿAlī b. Saba', al-Aʿazz (? al-Agharr)
⊘ 534/1140	Muḥammad b. Saba', al-Muʿaẓẓam
⊘ c. 548/c. 1153	ʿImrān b. Muḥammad, d. 561/1166
561/1166	*Rule of Ḥabashī viziers, including Jawhar al-Muʿaẓẓamī as regent for ʿImrān's young sons*
571/1175	*Ayyūbid conquest of Aden*

The Zurayʿids belonged to the Jusham branch of the Banū Yām, and were, like the Ṣulayḥids (see above, no. 45), partisans of the Ismāʿīliyya, acknowledging the overlordship of the Fāṭimids. Their fortunes came from the Ṣulayḥid Aḥmad al-Mukarram's driving out the Banū Maʿn from Aden and his then installing the two brothers al-ʿAbbās and al-Masʿūd as joint rulers there in return for their services to the Fāṭimid cause. They paid tribute to the Ṣulayḥid queen, al-Sayyida Arwā, until, when she was distracted by internal problems after al-Mukarram Aḥmad's death in 484/1091, the two cousins Abu 'l-Ghārāt and Zurayʿ (after whom the dynasty is usually named, though some Yemeni historians use the designation Banu 'l-Karam for the family) threw off Ṣulayḥid control. Henceforth, the Zurayʿids ruled over their principality around Aden as, in effect, an independent power, while still under the distant overlordship of the Fāṭimids.

The ensuing decades were, however, filled with dispute and civil warfare between the two branches of the family, the descendants of al-Masʿūd on one side and those of al-ʿAbbās and Zurayʿ on the other. The names of successive rulers are known, but not the exact dates when they exercised power. It was not until c. 532/c. 1138 that Saba' b. Abi 'l-Suʿūd b. Zurayʿ managed to impose a unified authority over the region of Aden, and this authority henceforth remained within his branch of the family. A marriage alliance with al-Sayyida Arwā brought to the Zurayʿids various Ṣulayḥid towns and fortresses, but when ʿImrān, head of the dynasty and chief *dāʿī* in Yemen, died, his young sons came under the tutelage of Abyssinian slave viziers. The Ayyūbids occupied Aden in 571/1175 (see above, no. 30, 8) and effectively ended the independent power of the Zurayʿids.

Lane-Poole, 97; Zambaur, 117; Album, 26.
H. C. Kay, *Yaman: Its Early Mediaeval History*, 158–61, 307–8, with a genealogical table at p. 307.
Ramzi J. Bikhazi, 'Coins of al-Yaman 139–569 A.H.', 102ff.
G. R. Smith, *The Ayyūbids and the Early Rasūlids in the Yemen*, II, 63–7, with a genealogical table at p. 63.
idem, in W. Daum (ed.), *Yemen: 3000 Years of Art and Civilisation in Arabia Felix*, 133, 138, with a list at p. 138.

47

THE HAMDĀNIDS

492–570/1099–1174

Northern Yemen, with their capital at Ṣanʿā'

1. The first line of the Banū Ḥātim

492/1099	Ḥātim b. al-Ghashīm al-Hamdānī
502/1109	ʿAbdallāh b. Ḥātim
504–10/1111–16	Maʿn b. Ḥātim

2. The line of the Banu 'l-Qubayb

510/1116	Hishām b. al-Qubayb b. Rusaḥ
518/1124	al-Ḥumās b. al-Qubayb
527–33/1132–9	Ḥātim b. al-Ḥumās

3. The second line of the Banū Ḥātim

533/1139	Ḥātim b. Aḥmad, Ḥamīd al-Dawla
556–70/1161–74	ʿAlī b. Ḥātim, al-Waḥīd
570/1174	*Ayyūbid conquest of Ṣanʿā'*

This dynastic title includes three short lines, all stemming from the tribe of Hamdān, the first two of which were probably adherents of the Fāṭimids and the third line certainly so. Ḥātim b. al-Ghashīm, a powerful tribal chief, took over Ṣanʿā' when in 492/1099 the Ṣulayḥids lost effective control of the city (see above, no. 45). Subsequently, Hamdānī tribal discontent led to the deposition of Maʿn and the end of the first line, and the coming to power of the sons of al-Qubayb, forming the second line.

However, when the sons of Ḥātim b. al-Ḥumās fell into dissension after his death, the tribal leaders of Hamdān raised to power Ḥātim b. Aḥmad, who became the greatest leader of the dynasty, defending Ṣanʿā' against the Zaydī Imām Aḥmad b. Sulaymān al-Mutawakkil. His line succeeded in retaining control of much of northern Yemen and in 569/1174 drove back the Mahdids (see below, no. 48) from Aden. Like other Yemeni lines, they were however threatened by the arrival of the Ayyūbids, who entered Ṣanʿā' in 570/1174 and took it over (see above, no. 30, 8), although Hamdānī tribal elements continued to be a factor in the military history of northern Yemen for at least the next twenty years.

Lane-Poole, 94; Zambaur, 119.

*EI*² 'Hamdānids' (C. L. Geddes).

G. R. Smith, *The Ayyūbids and Early Rasūlids in the Yemen*, II, 68–75, with a genealogical table at pp. 68–9.

idem, in W. Daum (ed.), *Yemen: 3000 Years of Art and Civilisation in Arabia Felix*, 133–4, 138, with a list of rulers at p. 138.

48

THE MAHDIDS

554–69/1159–73

Yemen, with their capital at Zabīd

531/1137	ʿAlī b. Mahdī al-Ruʿaynī al-Ḥimyarī, Abu ʾl-Ḥasan, with his own *daʿwa* in Tihāma, 554/1159 in Zabīd
554/1159	Mahdī b. ʿAlī (? jointly with his brother ʿAbd al-Nabī)
⊘ 559–69/1163–74	ʿAbd al-Nabī b. ʿAli, k. 571/11762
569/1174	*Ayyūbid capture of Zabīd*

ʿAlī b. Mahdī traced his ancestry back, like so many other Yemeni leaders, to the pre-Islamic Tubbaʿ kings. He acquired a reputation in Tihāma as the preacher of an ascetic and rigorist Islamic message, although it does not seem correct to describe him – somewhat anachronistically, anyway – as a Khārijī. ʿAlī designated his followers Anṣār and Muhājirūn, and with them he began a series of violent attacks, including on the by now declining Najāḥids (see above, no. 44), finally capturing Zabīd and toppling the older dynasty. The expansionary ambitions of ʿAlī and his sons led them into a series of attacks in both lowland Yemen, including on Aden, and in the southern part of the highlands, including Taʿizz. Mahdid excesses may have been one of the factors inducing the Ayyūbid Tūrān Shāh to intervene in Yemen (see above, no. 30, 8). At all events, the Ayyūbid army speedily defeated the Mahdids, and in 571/1176 ʿAbd al-Nabī and one of his brothers were executed by the Ayyūbids after an apparent Mahdid attempt to regain Zabīd.

Lane-Poole, 96; Zambaur, 118; Album, 26.

*EI*² 'Mahdids' (G. R. Smith).

H. C. Kay, *Yaman: Its Early Mediaeval History*, 124–34.

G. R. Smith, *The Ayyūbids and Early Rasūlids in the Yemen*, II, 56–62, with a genealogical table at p. 56.

idem, in W. Daum (ed.), *Yemen: 3000 Years of Art and Civilisation in Arabia Felix*, 134–5, 138, with a list of rulers at p. 138.

49

THE RASŪLIDS

626–858/1228–1454

Southern Yemen and Tihāma, with their capital at Taʿizz

⊘ 626/1229	al-Malik al-Manṣūr ʿUmar I b. ʿAlī b. Rasūl, Nūr al-Dīn al-Ghassānī	
⊘ 647/1250	al-Malik al-Muẓaffar Yūsuf I b. ʿUmar I, Shams al-Dīn	
⊘ 694/1295	al-Malik al-Ashraf ʿUmar II b. al-Muẓaffar, Abu ʾl-Fatḥ Mumahhid al-Dīn	
⊘ 696/1296	al-Malik al-Muʾayyad Dāwūd b. Yūsuf I, Ḥizabr al-Dīn	
⊘ 721/1321	al-Malik al-Mujāhid ʿAlī b. Dāwūd, Sayf al-Dīn	
⊘ 764/1363	al-Malik al-Afḍal al-ʿAbbās b. ʿAlī, Ḍirghām al-Dīn	
⊘ 778/1377	al-Malik al-Ashraf Ismāʿīl I b. al-ʿAbbās	
⊘ 803/1400	al-Malik al-Nāṣir Aḥmad b. Ismāʿīl I, Ṣalāḥ al-Dīn	
⊘ 827/1424	al-Malik al-Manṣūr ʿAbdallāh b. Aḥmad	
⊘ 830/1427	al-Malik al-Ashraf Ismāʿīl II b. ʿAbdallāh	
⊘ 831/1428	al-Malik al-Ẓāhir Yaḥyā b. Ismāʿīl II	
842/1439	al-Malik al-Ashraf Ismāʿīl III b. Yaḥyā	
845–58/1442–54	al-Muẓaffar Yūsuf II b. ʿUmar	
846/1442	al-Malik al-Afḍal Muḥammad b. Ismāʿīl b. ʿUthmān	rival claimants to the Rasūlid throne
846/1442	al-Malik al-Nāṣir Aḥmad b. Yaḥyā	
847–58/1443–54	al-Malik al-Masʿūd b. Ismāʿīl III, Ṣalāḥ al-Dīn	
855–8/1451–4	al-Malik al-Muʾayyad al-Ḥusayn b. Ṭāhir	
858/1454	*Ṭāhirid capture of Aden*	

Obliging historians and genealogists concocted for the Rasūlids a descent from the royal house of the pre-Islamic Ghassānids and, ultimately, from Qaḥṭān, progenitor of the South Arabs. But it is more probable that they came from the Menjik clan of the Oghuz Turks, who had participated in the Turkish invasions of the Middle East under the Saljuqs, and that the original Rasūl had been employed as an envoy (*rasūl*) by the ʿAbbāsid caliphs.

A number of amīrs from the Rasūlid family accompanied the first Ayyūbids to Yemen (see above, no. 30, 8), and, when the last Ayyūbid, al-Malik al-Kāmil's son al-Malik al-Masʿūd Ṣalāḥ al-Dīn Yūsuf, left Yemen for Syria in 626/1229, he left Nūr al-Dīn ʿUmar al-Rasūlī as his deputy. In the event, no Ayyūbid ever reappeared in Yemen, so the Rasūlids now began to rule independently in Tihāma and the southern highlands, acknowledging the Ayyūbids and the ʿAbbāsid caliphs as their overlords; Ayyūbid traditions remained strong in the new state, seen for example in their royal titulature. Very soon, the strongly Sunnī Rasūlids were able to extend their power and to capture Ṣanʿāʾ from the Zaydī Imāms, holding it for a few decades, and as far eastwards in Ḥaḍramawt and Ẓufār as modern Salāla in the southern part of the sultanate of Oman. The later thirteenth and fourteenth centuries saw the zenith of Rasūlid political power and cultural splendour. The sultans were great builders in such cities as Taʿizz and Zabīd, and were munificent patrons of Arabic literature, with not a few of the sultans themselves proficient authors. From Aden, a far-flung trade was conducted to India, South-East Asia, China and East Africa, and an embassy from Yemen to China is recorded, doubtless stimulated by these trade links with the Far East. But after the death of Ṣalāḥ al-Dīn Aḥmad in 827/1424, the Rasūlid state began to show signs of disintegration, with indiscipline among the Rasūlids' slave troops, a series of short-reigned rulers and internecine warfare among several pretenders. Thus when the Rasūlid amīr of Aden, al-Ḥusayn b. Ṭāhir, surrendered his city to the Ṭāhirids (see below, no. 50) and Ṣalāḥ al-Dīn b. Ismāʿīl III left for Mecca, the rule of the family came to an end after more than two centuries.

Lane-Poole, 99–100; Zambaur, 120; Album, 27.
EI[2] 'Rasūlids' (G. R. Smith).
G. R. Smith, *The Ayyūbids and Early Rasūlids in the Yemen*, II, 83–90, with genealogical tables at pp. 83–4.
idem, in W. Daum (ed.), *Yemen: 3000 Years of Art and Civilisation in Arabia Felix*, 136–7, 139, with a list of rulers at p. 139.

50

THE ṬĀHIRIDS
858–923/1454–1517
Southern Yemen and Tihāma, with their capitals at al-Miqrāna and Juban

858/1454	al-Malik al-Ẓāfir ʿĀmir I b. Ṭāhir, Ṣalāḥ al-Dīn al-Malik al-Mujāhid ʿAlī b. Ṭāhir, Shams al-Dīn	two brothers ruling jointly
864/1460	al-Malik al-Mujāhid ʿAlī b. Ṭāhir, Shams al-Dīn, as sole ruler	
⊘ 883/1478	al-Malik al-Manṣūr ʿAbd al-Wahhāb b. Dāwūd b. Ṭāhir, Tāj al-Dīn	
⊘ 894–923/1489–1517	al-Malik al-Ẓāfir ʿĀmir II b. ʿAbd al-Wahhāb, Ṣalāḥ al-Dīn	
923/1517	*Conquest of the Yemen by the Egyptian Mamlūks*	
(924–45/1518–38	*Persistence of some Ṭāhirid princes in fortresses of the highlands of Yemen; five of them are mentioned, from Aḥmad b. ʿĀmir II to ⊘ ʿĀmir III b. Dāwūd)*	

The Ṭāhirids were a native Yemeni, Sunnī family who rose to prominence in the last days of the Rasūlids (see above, no. 49) and took over the Rasūlid lands in southern Yemen and Tihāma on the demise of that dynasty. Four sultans ruled jointly or succeeded each other, maintaining the administrative traditions of their former patrons. They also inherited the Rasūlids' role as great builders: in such towns as Zabīd, the religious centre of Yemeni Sunnism, they erected mosques and madrasas; in Aden, the principal port of Yemen and bastion against the Egyptian Mamlūks and the Portuguese (it was first besieged by Afonso d'Albuquerque in 919/1513), they built commercial premises and fortifications. In highland Yemen, they extended their power against the Zaydī Imāms and captured Ṣanʿāʾ. But the Egyptian Mamlūks wished to control Yemen as a base for operations in the Indian Ocean against the Portuguese, and after 921/1515 Egyptian attacks began, leading to the Mamlūks' occupation of much of Yemen and the end of the Ṭāhirids. Only a few Ṭāhirid chiefs seem to have survived in the highland zone until the Ottoman governor Süleymān Pasha executed the last one, ʿĀmir III b. Dāwūd, in 945/1538.

Lane-Poole, 101; Zambaur, 121; Album, 27.
G. R. Smith, in W. Daum (ed.), *Yemen: 3000 Years of Art and Civilisation in Arabia Felix*, 137–9, with a list of rulers at p. 139.
Venetia A. Porter, *The History and Monuments of the Tahirid Dynasty of the Yemen 858–923/1454–1517*, University of Durham Ph.D. thesis 1992, unpubl., I, with genealogical tables at pp. 295–7.

51

THE ĀL AL-JULANDĀ
First to second/seventh to eighth centuries
Oman

	Sa'īd and Sulaymān b. 'Abbād b. 'Abd b. al-Julandā, joint rulers, abandoned Oman during the caliphate of 'Abd al-Malik
131–3/748–51	al-Julandā b. Mas'ūd b. Ja'far b. al-Julandā, first Ibāḍī Imām in Oman
? –177/? –793	Rashīd b. al-Naẓr and Muḥammad b. Zā'ida, joint rulers on behalf of the 'Abbāsids
	End of the second century/beginning of the ninth centuryDecline of Julandī power in Oman

The Āl al-Julandā were a line of obvious importance in the pre-Islamic and early Islamic history of Oman, but one for which it seems impossible to construct a firm chronology of rule, since they impinged on the Islamic historical sources at only a few key points in their history. The line was of Azdī origin, and must have arrived in Oman as part of the general migrations of the Azd from Ḥijāz in pre-Islamic times, reaching there at a time when the coastlands at least of Oman were controlled by Sāsānid Persia, After the extension of Arab-Muslim control over eastern Arabia, the Julandā chiefs became representatives of the Medinan government. But Oman's role as a refuge area for Khārijīs and other dissidents provoked an expedition during al-Ḥajjāj b. Yūsuf's governorship of Iraq and the East which ejected the Julandī brothers Sa'īd and Sulaymān and forced them to flee to East Africa.

Al-Julandā b. Mas'ūd was won over by the local Ibāḍī Khārijīs (see on the Ibāḍiyya, above, no. 9) and became their first Imām in Oman (the beginning of what was to be a tradition of allegiance to Ibāḍī doctrines there which has lasted to this day), but he was killed in 133/751 by a punitive expedition sent by the 'Abbāsid caliph al-Saffāḥ (see above, no. 3, 1). Thereafter, the Āl al-Julandā seem to have abandoned leadership of the Ibāḍiyya, but the joint rulers Rashīd and Muḥammad were overthrown in a tribal revolt in 177/793, and Julandī power then declined, after having been influential in Oman for three centuries; only odd members of the family are mentioned in the ninth century.

Zambaur, 125–6.

G. P. Badger, *History of the Imâms and Seyyids of 'Omân, by Salîl Ibn Razîk, from A.D. 661–1856*, London 1871.

J. C. Wilkinson, 'The Julanda of Oman', *Journal of Oman Studies*, 1 (1975), 97–108, with a genealogical table at p. 106.

'Isam 'Ali Ahmed al-Rawas, *Early Islamic Oman (ca. 622–1280/893)*, Durham University Ph.D. thesis 1992, unpubl., 166ff.

52

THE MUKRAMIDS
c. 390–443/c. 1000–40
Coastal Oman

between 390 and 394/ between 1000 and 1004	al-Ḥusayn b. Mukram, Abū Muḥammad I
⊘ before 415/1024	ʿAlī b. al-Ḥusayn, Abu ʾl-Qāsim Nāṣir al-Dīn, d. 428/1037
⊘ 428/1037	Abu ʾl-Jaysh b. ʿAlī, Nāṣir al-Dīn, d. soon after becoming governor
431–3/1040–2	Abū Muḥammad II b. ʿAlī
433/1042	*Assumption of direct rule by the Būyids*

The Mukramids were presumably a local Omani family, who around the beginning of the eleventh century were appointed governors in coastal Oman, with their capital at Ṣuḥār, by the Būyids of Persia (see below, no. 75). The interior of Oman must have been held by the Imāms elected by the Ibāḍī Khārijī community there. The Mukramid Abū Muḥammad I al-Ḥusayn subsequently served the Būyid Amīrs in Fars. The end of this brief line of hereditary governors came after a revolt against his suzerain by Abū Muḥammad II, so that in 433/1042 a Būyid prince was installed as governor in Oman.

S. M. Stern and A. D. H. Bivar, 'The coinage of Oman under Abū Kālījār the Buwayhid', *NC*, 6th series, 18 (1958), 147–56, with a genealogical table of the Mukramids at p. 149.

53

THE YA'RUBIDS

1034–1156/1625–1743

Oman, with their centre at al-Rustāq

1034/1625	Nāṣir b. Murshid
1059/1649	Sulṭān I b. Sayf
c. 1091–1103/c. 1680–92	Abu 'l-'Arab b. Sayf, in Jabrīn
1103/1692	Sayf I b. Sulṭān I, in al-Rustāq
1123/1711	Sulṭān II b. Sayf I, in al-Ḥazm
1131/1719	Sayf II b. Sulṭān II, d. 1156/1743 } rivals for power
1134/1722	Ya'rub b. Abi 'l-'Arab } rivals for power
1137–40/1724–8	Muḥammad b. Nāṣir al-Ghāfirī, guardian of Sayf II, proclaimed Imām
1151/1738	Sulṭān b. Murshid, rival Imām
1167/1754	*Succession to power of the Āl Bū Sa'īd*

The Ya'rubī chiefs rose to prominence as Imāms of the Ibāḍīs at a time when coastal Oman was threatened by the Portuguese and when interior Oman had been largely taken over by other, non-Ibāḍī Arab groups like the Nabhānīs and immigrants from Baḥrayn and Persia. In the two or three decades after Nāṣir b. Murshid's accession in 1034/1625, the Ya'rubīs secured their power against external enemies like the Portuguese and the Persian Ṣafawids. But in the early eighteenth century, the succession of a minor, Sayf II b. Sulṭān II, led to internal disputes between the tribal groups of the Ḥināwīs and the Ghāfirīs, with rival candidates for the imamate and intervention by the Persians at Muscat (Masqaṭ) and Ṣuḥār. It now fell to the rising power of the Āl Bū Sa'īdīs to eject the intruders, replace the quarrelling last Ya'rubids and make firm their own authority in both Oman and the East African coast (see below, nos 54, 65).

Zambaur, 128.

EI[1] 'Ya'rub' (A. Grohmann).

R. D. Bathurst, *The Ya'rubī Dynasty of Oman*, Oxford University D.Phil. thesis 1967, unpubl.

J. C. Wilkinson, *The Imamite Tradition of Oman*, Cambridge 1987, 12–13, with a genealogical table at p. 13.

54

THE ĀL BŪ SAʿĪD
c. 1167– /c. 1754–
Muscat and then Zanzibar, at present in Oman

1. The united sultanate

c. 1167/c. 1754	Aḥmad b. Saʿīd, elected Imām of the Ibāḍiyya
1198/1783	Saʿīd b. Aḥmad, Imām
c. 1200/c. 1786	Ḥāmid b. Saʿīd, Sayyid, regent
1206/1792	Sulṭān b. Aḥmad
1220/1806	Sālim b. Sulṭān, jointly with Saʿīd b. Sulṭān until the former's death in 1236/1821
1236/1821	Saʿīd b. Sulṭān, sole ruler
1273/1856	*Division of the sultanate on Saʿīd's death*

2. The line of sultans in Oman

1273/1856	Thuwaynī b. Saʿīd
1282/1866	Sālim b. Thuwaynī
1285/1868	ʿAzzān b. Qays
1287/1870	Turkī b. Saʿīd
⊘ 1305/1888	Fayṣal b. Turkī
1331/1913	Taymūr b. Fayṣal
⊘ 1350/1932	Saʿīd b. Taymūr
⊘ 1390– /1970–	Qābūs b. Saʿīd

3. The line of sultans in Zanzibar (see below, no. 65)

The Bū Saʿīdīs succeeded to the heritage of the preceding line of Yaʿrubid Imāms (see above, no. 53) in both Oman and the East African coastlands. Aḥmad b. Saʿīd began as governor of Ṣuḥār in coastal Oman when the last Yaʿrubids were embroiled in their family quarrels, and soon became de facto ruler of Oman. Hence the Ibāḍī 'ulamā' formally elected him Imām in c. 1167/c. 1754. His son and successor Saʿīd also had the title of Imām, but thereafter the Bū Saʿīdī rulers styled themselves Sayyids, while being generally known to the outside world as Sultans.

Muscat, which eventually became the Bū Saʿīdī capital, had long been a port of international significance and had played an important role in the struggles of the Portuguese and then the Dutch for the commercial control of the Persian Gulf. Sulṭān b. Aḥmad pursued an expansionist policy there as far as Baḥrayn island and as far as Bandar ʿAbbās, Kishm and Hurmuz along the southern coasts of Fars. However, the Sayyids' position was menaced in the early nineteenth century by the aggressive Wahhābīs of Najd. They countered this by an alliance with Britain, which was concerned that Muscat, lying as it did near the route to India, should remain in friendly hands. In 1212/1798, the first treaty with the East India Company was made; later, in the nineteenth century, Britain used her influence at Muscat to control and then end the slave trade in the Gulf.

The Yaʿrubid possessions on the East African coast had been largely lost in the wars with Persia of the late eighteenth century, with virtually only Zanzibar, Pemba and Kilwa remaining to the Bū Saʿīdīs. But Saʿīd b. Sulṭān during his long reign extended his suzerainty over all the Arab and Swahili colonies from Mogadishu in the north to Cape Delgado in the south, effectively ruling in Zanzibar from 1242/1827 onwards. After his death in 1273/1856, the Bū Saʿīdī dominions were divided into two separate sultanates, with Thuwaynī ruling over Oman from Muscat and his brother Mājid ruling over Zanzibar and the East African coastland respectively; for this last branch of the family, see below, no. 65.

Oman itself was then racked by family discord, and in the early twentieth century the rigorist Ibāḍī *ʿulamāʾ* of the interior dissociated themselves from what they regarded as the corrupt rule of the Bū Saʿīdīs in the coastal regions. They restored the imamate in 1331/1913 and erupted into rebellion against the Sultan and what they regarded as his British protectors. But confined as it was to the interior, and with a totally backward-looking aspect which contrasted with the adaptability to new conditions of the Suʿūdīs and their Wahhābī followers, the imamate represented a last stand of tribal elements. The armed insurrection of the 1950s, in which the Imām Ghālib b. ʿAlī had Suʿūdī and Egyptian backing, was largely extinguished by the end of the decade; and the deposition of the reactionary and parsimonious Saʿīd b. Taymūr by his son Qābūs in 1390/1970 at last opened up Oman to the world around it and, eventually, led to a reconciliation of elements within the country.

Zambaur, 129 and Table M.

*EI*² 'Bū Saʿīd' (C. F. Beckingham), with a genealogical table which corrects Zambaur's list in several places; 'Masḳaṭ' (J. C. Wilkinson).

J. C. Wilkinson, *The Imamate Tradition of Oman*, with a genealogical table at p. 14.

55

THE ĀL SUʿŪD (SAʿŪD)

1148– /1735–

Originally in south-eastern Najd; in the twentieth century kings of Ḥijāz and Najd and then of Suʿūdī (Saudi) Arabia

1148/1735	Muḥammad b. Suʿūd b. Muḥammad, amīr of Dirʿiyya
1179/1765	ʿAbd al-ʿAzīz I b. Muḥammad
1218/1803	Suʿūd I b. ʿAbd al-ʿAzīz
1229/1814	ʿAbdallāh I b. Suʿūd I, k. 1234/1819
1233–8/1818–22	*First Turco-Egyptian occupation*
1237/1822	Turkī b. ʿAbdallāh b. Muḥammad
1249/1834	Mushārī b. ʿAbd al-Raḥmān
1249/1834	Fayṣal I b. Turkī, first reign
1254–9/1838–43	*Second Turco-Egyptian occupation*
1254/1838	Khālid b. Suʿūd I } as vassals of Egypt
1257/1841	ʿAbdallāh II b. Thunayyān b. Suʿūd b. Muḥammad } as vassals of Egypt
1259/1843	Fayṣal I, second reign
1282/1865	ʿAbdallāh III b. Fayṣal I, first reign
1288/1871	Suʿūd II b. Fayṣal I
1291/1874 (? 1288/1871)	ʿAbdallāh III b. Fayṣal I, second reign
1305/1887	Muḥammad b. Suʿūd II
1305/1887	*Conquest of Riyāḍ by Muḥammad b. ʿAbdallāh Ibn Rashīd of Ḥāʾil, with ʿAbdallāh III as governor of Riyāḍ until 1307/1889*
1307/1889	ʿAbd al-Raḥmān b. Fayṣal I as governor in Riyāḍ under the Āl Rashīd
1309/1891	Muḥammad b. Fayṣal I, al-Muṭawwiʿ, as vassal governor under the Āl Rashīd
1309/1891	*Direct rule in Riyāḍ of Muḥammad Ibn Rashīd*
⊘ 1319/1902	ʿAbd al-ʿAzīz II b. ʿAbd al-Raḥmān, amīr in Riyāḍ, King of Ḥijāz and Najd 1344/1926 and King of Suʿūdī Arabia in 1350 or 1351/1932
⊘ 1373/1952	Suʿūd III b. ʿAbd al-ʿAzīz
⊘ 1384/1964	Fayṣal II b. ʿAbd al-ʿAzīz
⊘ 1395/1975	Khālid b. ʿAbd al-ʿAzīz
⊘ 1401– /1982–	Fahd b. ʿAbd al-ʿAzīz

Suʿūd b. Muḥammad b. Muqrin (d. 1148/1735), from the ʿAnaza tribe, was amīr of Dirʿiyya in the Wādī Ḥanīfa district of Najd, and Dirʿiyya remained the seat of the Suʿūd family until its destruction by Ibrāhīm Pasha in the early nineteenth century and the end of the first Suʿūdī state. The rise of the family was connected with the movement of Muḥammad b. ʿAbd al-Wahhāb, a puritanical reformer in the conservative legal tradition of Ḥanbalism and the thirteenth-fourteenth-century religious leader in Damascus, Ibn Taymiyya. He stressed the unity and transcendence of God and the duty of avoiding all forms of *shirk*, associating other persons or things with God, one practical effect of this being hostility to such aspects of popular religion in Arabia as the cult of saints and their shrines; when the Su'ūdī-led Wahhābīs extended their power through much of the peninsula, they systematically destroyed such manifestations of (to them) *bid'a*, heretical innovation. It seems that the Su'ūdī amīrs saw the material advantages of harnessing Wahhābī enthusiasm for their plans of political expansion in Najd. By the end of the eighteenth century, all Najd was controlled by them, and raids were made against Ottoman Syria and Iraq, culminating in the sack of the Shī'ī holy city of Karbalā' in 1218/1803, regarded as an object of superstitious veneration; and the Holy Cities of Mecca and Medina were seized and purged of idolatrous features.

The collapse of this power and of the first Su'ūdī state came as a result of these Su'ūdī provocations of the Ottomans. The sultan deputed the governor of Egypt, Muḥammad 'Alī Pasha (see above, no. 34), to deal with the Arabian situation. Hence in 1233/1818 the latter's son Ibrāhīm took Dir'iyya and destroyed it utterly, carrying off the Su'ūdī amīr for execution in Istanbul. The second Su'ūdī amirate revived cautiously in eastern Arabia during the middle years of the century. From his capital Riyāḍ, Fayṣal I extended his power over al-Aḥsā in the eastern Arabian coastland, but a second Turco-Egyptian occupation took place in 1254–9/1838–43, with Fayṣal carried off to Egypt and Su'ūdī vassals of the Ottomans placed on the throne. Fayṣal escaped from captivity, and in 1259/1843 successfully regained power in his homeland, with this second reign marking a high point in Su'ūdī fortunes. But after his death, the family was rent by internal disputes; al-Aḥsā was occupied by the Ottoman governor of Iraq, Midḥat Pasha; and the second Su'ūdī state came to an end in 1305/1887 when the Su'ūdīs' rival Muḥammad Ibn Rashīd of Ḥā'il (see below, no. 57) occupied Riyāḍ, so that the Su'ūdīs had to take refuge in Kuwait.

The establishment of the third, and present, Su'ūdī state in the twentieth century is connected with the long-lived and remarkable figure of 'Abd al-'Azīz Ibn Su'ūd, who, with tacit British support, eventually subdued the pro-Ottoman Āl Rashīd, annexed 'Asīr, prevented the Sharīf Ḥusayn from setting himself up as caliph in 1924 (see below, no. 56), took over Ḥijāz shortly afterwards, and became King of Ḥijāz and Najd and then of Su'ūdī Arabia, controlling by then nearly three-quarters of the peninsula. The large-scale exploitation of oil in eastern Arabia, begun in Ibn Su'ūd's time, has transformed what was originally a desert state into a power of international economic significance, especially after the 1970s' oil-price boom, but has also brought to the country internal religious and social tensions.

Zambaur, 124 and Table L.

EI[1] 'Ibn Sa'ūd' (J. H. Mordtmann); EI[2] 'Su'ūd, Āl' (Elizabeth M. Sirriyyeh).

Naval Intelligence Division, Geographical Handbook series, *Western Arabia and the Red Sea*, London 1946, 265–70, 283–6, with a genealogical table at p. 286.

H. St J. Philby, *Arabian Jubilee*, London 1952, with detailed genealogical tables at pp. 250–71.

idem, *Saudi Arabia*, London 1955.

R. Bayley Winder, *Saudi Arabia in the Nineteenth Century*, London 1965.

56

THE HĀSHIMITE SHARĪFS OF MECCA FROM THE ʿAWN FAMILY

1243–1344/1827–1925

Mecca and Ḥijāz latterly, with branches in the Fertile Crescent countries

1. The original line in Western Arabia

(1243/1827	ʿAbd al-Muṭṭalib b. Ghālib, of the Zayd branch of Sharīfs, first reign)
1243/1827	Muḥammad b. ʿAbd al-Muʿīn b. ʿAwn, first Sharīfian Amīr in Mecca of the ʿAbādila branch of the ʿAwn family, first reign
(1267/1851	ʿAbd al-Muṭṭalib b. Ghālib, second reign)
1272/1856	Muḥammad b. ʿAbd al-Muʿīn, second reign
1274/1858	ʿAbdallāh b. Muḥammad
1294/1877	al-Ḥusayn b. Muḥammad
(1297/1880	ʿAbd al-Muṭṭalib b. Ghālib, third reign)
1299/1882	ʿAwn al-Rafīq b. Muḥammad
1323/1905	ʿAlī b. ʿAbdallāh
⊘ 1326/1908	Ḥusayn b. ʿAlī, until 1335/1916 Sharīf of Mecca and Ḥijāz, thereafter King of Ḥijāz, assumed the title of caliph in 1343/1924, d. 1350/1931
1343/1925	ʿAlī b. Ḥusayn, d. 1353/1934
1344/1925	*Conquest of Ḥijāz by ʿAbd al-ʿAzīz Ibn Suʿūd*

2. The post-First World War branches of the Hāshimite family in the Fertile Crescent countries

(a) The line in Syria

⊘ 1338/1920	Fayṣal b. Ḥusayn b. ʿAlī, elected King of Greater Syria, subsequently King of Iraq
1338/1920	*French Mandate imposed on Syria*

(b) The line in Iraq

⊘ 1340/1921	Fayṣal I b. Ḥusayn, appointed King of Iraq
⊘ 1352/1933	Ghāzī b. Fayṣal
⊘ 1358–77/1939–58	Fayṣal II b. Ghāzī
1377/1958	*Overthrow of the monarchy and its replacement by a republican régime*

(c) The line in Transjordan and then Jordan

⊘ 1339/1921	ʿAbdallāh b. Ḥusayn, declared Amīr of Transjordan, and in 1365/1946 King of Transjordan, later Jordan
1370/1951	Ṭalāl b. ʿAbdallāh, d. 1392/1972
⊘ 1371– /1952–	Ḥusayn b. Ṭalāl

The Hāshimite Sharīfs ('noble ones') of Mecca traced their descent directly back to the Prophet Muḥammad and his clan in Mecca of Hāshim. The Sharīfs held power in the Holy City from the tenth century onwards, in later times under Mamlūk and then Ottoman protection. In the early nineteenth century they were subjected to attacks by the Wahhābīs of Najd under the Amīr Su'ūd b. 'Abd al-'Azīz, who captured Mecca in 1218/1803 (see above, no. 55). Liberated in 1228/1813 by Ibrāhīm b. Muḥammad 'Alī of Egypt's army, the Sharīfate alternated during the nineteenth century between the Zayd and 'Awn branches, not finally settled in favour of the 'Abādila of the 'Awn until 1299/1882, by which time the Ottomans had for some four decades been controlling Ḥijāz as a province of their empire.

With Turkey's involvement in the First World War on the side of the Central Powers, the Sharīf Ḥusayn became caught up in the Arab Revolt of 1916 which cleared all Ḥijāz except Medina of Ottoman troops and which, in concert with the British army advance from Egypt, eventually freed Greater Syria from Turkish control. Early in the Revolt, Ḥusayn proclaimed himself 'King of the Arab lands', but the Allies would only recognise him as King of Ḥijāz. After 1918 his authority was confined to Ḥijāz, where he came to arouse much Arab hostility by an ill-judged attempt in 1924 to assume the caliphate personally after Muṣṭafā Kemāl's abolition of that institution in Turkey. His eldest son and successor 'Alī had to abandon Ḥijāz to the Su'ūdī invader 'Abd al-'Azīz b Su'ūd, who soon afterwards formed his united kingdom of Ḥijāz and Najd (see above, no. 55).

In the post-First World War arrangements for the Arab lands of the former Ottoman empire, other sons of Ḥusayn were, however, to play a prominent role. The third son Fayṣal from 1918 onwards endeavoured to assume power in the Greater Syria region, and in 1920 was elected King of a united Syria by the Second Syrian General Arab Congress, but had to leave there shortly afterwards when Syria passed under French Mandatary tutelage. Instead, in 1921 and with British support, he became King of Iraq, under a British Mandate; the Hāshimites had no particular connection with Iraq, but no more suitable candidate presented himself. The Hāshimite monarchy in Iraq, although ruling the first Arab country to free itself from Mandatary control, never put down deep roots, and in 1958 was overthrown by a bloody army coup led by 'Abd al-Karīm al-Qāsim in which Fayṣal II was killed. More successful and enduring was the establishment of Ḥusayn's second son 'Abdallāh as Amīr of the Transjordanian lands separate from Mandatary Palestine, which after the Second World War became the independent Hāshimite Kingdom of Jordan, still ruled until today by one of the great survivors of Middle Eastern politics, 'Abdallāh's grandson King Ḥusayn.

Zambaur, 23.

*EI*² 'Hā<u>sh</u>imids' (C. E. Dawn); 'Ḥusayn b. 'Alī' (S. H. Longrigg); 'Makka. 2. From the 'Abbāsid to the modern period' (A. J. Wensinck and C. E. Bosworth).

C. Snouck Hurgronje, *Mecca in the Later Part of the Nineteenth Century*, Leiden 1931.

Naval Intelligence Division, Geographical Handbook series, *Western Arabia and the Red Sea*, 268ff., with a genealogical table at p. 282.

Gerald de Gaury, *Rulers of Mecca*, London 1951, with a list of rulers of Mecca at pp. 288–93.

57

THE ĀL RASHĪD
1252–1340/1836–1921
Northern Najd

(c. 1248/c. 1832	ʿAbdallāh b. ʿAlī b. Rashīd, as governor for the Wahhābīs)
1252/1836	ʿAbdallāh b. ʿAlī, as independent ruler
1264/1848	Ṭalāl b. ʿAbdallāh
1285/1868	Mutʿab (colloquially, Mitʿab) I b. ʿAbdallāh
1286/1869	Bandar b. Ṭalāl
1286/1869	Muḥammad b. ʿAbdallāh
1315/1897	ʿAbd al-ʿAzīz b. Mutʿab
1324/1906	Mutʿab (Mitʿab) II b. ʿAbd al-ʿAzīz, k. 1324/1906
1325/1907	Sulṭān b. Ḥammūd
1325/1908	Suʿūd I b. Ḥammūd
1328/1910	Suʿūd II b. ʿAbd al-ʿAzīz, k. 1338/1920
1339/1920	ʿAbdallāh b. Mutʿab II, d.
1339/1921	Muḥammad b. Ṭalāl, d.
1340/1921	*Suʿūdī conquest*

The Rashīd family were chiefs of the ʿAbda clan of the Shammar tribal confederation in the Jabal Shammar region of northern Arabia, with their centre at Ḥā'il. ʿAbdallāh b. ʿAlī achieved power in Ḥā'il with the support of Fayṣal b. Turkī of the Suʿūdī rulers of Riyāḍ (see above, no. 55), displacing his kinsmen of the Āl Ibn ʿAlī, and he was, like the Suʿūdīs, an adherent of Wahhābism, but in its religious rather than political aspect. The Rashīdī shaykhdom reached a peak of prosperity in the mid-nineteenth century, with a prosperous caravan trade based on Ḥā'il, and Muḥammad b. ʿAbdallāh extended his authority northwestwards through the Wādī Sirḥān and as far as Palmyra in Syria, and southeastwards to Qaṣīm in the heart of Najd. He temporarily captured Riyāḍ from the Suʿūdīs and expelled them altogether from Najd to Kuwait in 1309/1891; the port of Kuwait was itself coveted by the Rashīdīs for the import of arms into their landlocked principality.

The whole history of the Āl Rashīd was marked by violence and fratricidal strife (the great majority of the amīrs died either by assassination or in battle), and after Muḥammad's death their power declined because of savage internal quarrels plus pressure from the renascent power of the Suʿūdīs under ʿAbd al-ʿAzīz b. ʿAbd al-Raḥmān Ibn Suʿūd. The general backing of the Ottomans, including the despatch of regular Turkish troops to support them in Najd, did not save them, and Ibn Suʿūd was finally able to capture Ḥā'il in 1340/1921. The Rashīdī territories were incorporated into what now became the united principality of Najd and, soon afterwards, the Suʿūdī kingdom of Ḥijāz and Najd (see above, no. 55), and the members of the Āl Rashīd were exiled to Riyāḍ.

None of the amīrs of the Āl Rashīd issued coins.

Zambaur, 125–6.
EI[2] 'Ḥāyil' (J. Mandaville); 'Rashīd, Āl' (Elizabeth M. Sirriyyeh).

Naval Intelligence Division, Geographical Handbooks Series, *Western Arabia and the Red Sea*, 269ff., with a genealogical table at p. 286.
H. St J. Philby, *Saudi Arabia*, London 1955.
Madawi Al-Rasheed, *Politics in an Arabian Oasis: The Rashidi Tribal Dynasty*, London 1991, with a genealogical table and list of the amīrs at pp. 55–6.

SEVEN

West Africa

58

THE KEITA KINGS OF MALI

Early seventh century to mid-ninth century/early thirteenth century to mid-fifteenth century

The central and western parts of modern Mali; northern Guinea; Gambia; and Senegal

627/1230	Mari Sun Dyāta (Mārī Jāṭa) I, son of Nare fa Maghan
653/1255	Mansā Ulī or Ule, son of Mari Sun Dyāta
668/1270	Mansā Wātī, son of Mari Sun Dyāta
672/1274	Mansā Khalīfa, son of Mari Sun Dyāta
673/1275	Mansā Abū Bakr I, called Bata-Mande-Bori, grandson of Mari Sun Dyāta by one of his daughters and adopted son of Mari Sun Dyāta
684/1285	*Sabakura or Sākūra, freed slave of the royal family*
699/1300	Mansā Gaw or Qū, son of Mansā Ulī
704/1305	Mansā Mamadu or Muḥammad, son of Mansā Gaw, d. 712/1312
709/1310	Mansā Abū Bakr II, descendant of Sun Mari Dyāta I's brother Bakari or Abū Bakr
712/1312	Mansā Mūsā I, son of Abū Bakr II
737/1337	Mansā Maghan or Maghā I, Muḥammad, son of Mūsā I
742/1341	Mansā Sulaymān, brother of Mūsā I
761/1360	Mansā Kamba or Qanba or Qāsā, son of Sulaymān
762/1361	Mansā Mari Dyāta or Mārī Jāṭa II, son of Maghan I
775/1374	Mansā Mūsā II, son of Mari Dyāta II
789/1382	Mansā Maghan II, son of Mari Dyāta II
790 or 791/ 1388 or 1389	Usurpation of the Sandigi or Ṣandiki, i.e. vizier
792/1390	Mansā Maghan III, Maḥmūd, descendant of Gaw
	Succession strife and chaos, ended by the ascendancy of the Songhay kingdom in the mid-ninth/mid-fifteenth century

Mali was the successor, as dominant power in West Africa, to the Soninke kingdom of Ghana, which lay mainly in the Sāḥil to the north of the upper Niger (in the western part of modern Mali and in the south-eastern corner of Mauritania), with its capital, Ghana, possibly to be identified with Kumbi Ṣāliḥ (in the extreme south of modern Mauritania). Ghana had been famed among the Muslim geographers and historians since the eighth century as a prime source of gold. It does not seem that, as was earlier thought, Ghana was directly conquered in the later eleventh century by the Berber Almoravids (see above, no. 14), but it may have been other Berbers from the direction of the Sahara who, in collusion with indigenous Black African opposition elements, brought about the undoubted decline of Ghana in the twelfth century and the spread of Islam in this originally totally pagan land. At the beginning of the next century, the pagan Soninkes of Soso captured the capital of Ghana. The rule of the Soso represented an anti-Islamic reaction in the upper Niger region, but it was followed by a successful Malinke or Mandinka struggle against Soso domination led by Sun Mari Dyāta, a chief of the Keita clan, who then became head of all the Malinke with the title of Mansā.

It was Sun Dyāta's successors who made Mali into a powerful kingdom, with its capital probably located at Nyane on the Sankarani, a right-bank affluent of the upper Niger (although the site of the capital of Mali apparently varied at different times). It developed strong cultural and religious links with the Islamic lands of North Africa and Egypt, with diplomatic and religious connections with the Marīnids of Morocco (see above, no. 16) and the Mamlūks of Egypt (see above, no. 31). Several of the kings of Mali made the Pilgrimage to Arabia, with that of Mansā Mūsā I (in whose reign Mali was visited by the Moroccan traveller Ibn Baṭṭūṭa) achieving special fame. Even so, animist concepts remained strong beneath the veneer of official and ruling-class Islam, and the local form of Islam developed clear syncretist elements within it. There was a flourishing trans-Saharan commerce in such items as gold and slaves, with Timbuktu, near the northernmost point of the Niger bend and probably in origin a Touareg settlement, developing in the fourteenth century as a terminus for the caravan traffic and as a significant intellectual centre of Islamic learning.

In the later fourteenth century, Mali was weakened by succession disputes, Early in the next century, it lost Timbuktu and much of the Sāḥil zone to the Touaregs, and was threatened by the rise of Songhay (see below, no. 59), which stripped Mali of its eastern and central lands, so that it became confined to the Malinke heartland in approximately what is now western Mali and Guinea, where it survived as a power of only local significance; it withstood Moroccan pressure at the end of the sixteenth century, but by 1081/1670 it was eclipsed by the rising Bambara states of Segu and Karta.

EI[1] 'Soso' (Maurice Delafosse); *EI*[2] 'Ghāna' (R. Cornevin), 'Mali' (N. Levtzion).
J. Spencer Trimingham, *A History of Islam in West Africa*, London 1962, 47–83, with a chronological table at p. 236.
Nehemia Levtzion, 'The thirteenth- and fourteenth-century kings of Mali', *Journal of African History*, 3 (1963), 341–53, with a genealogical table at p. 353.
idem, *Ancient Ghana and Mali*, London 1973, chs 5–7, with a genealogical table at p. 71.
M. Ly Tall, *L'empire du Mali*, Dakar 1977.

59

THE KINGS OF SONGHAY

? third century to 1000/? ninth century to 1592

The Savannah zone of Mali along the Niger bend and to its west

1. The Zas or Zuwas of Gao

? third/ninth century	Alyaman
fifth/eleventh century	Kosoy or Kosay Muslim Dam.
	Some fourteen or sixteen further rulers, often with divergent names, enumerated in the Arabic chronicles, that by the family of Maḥmūd al-Kātī, the *Ta'rīkh al-Fattāsh*, and that by 'Abd al-Raḥmān al-Sa'dī's *Ta'rīkh al-Sūdan*, ending with the Za Bisi Baro or Ber.

2. The Sis or Sonnis

? c. 674/c. 1275	'Alī Golom or Kolon
?	Salmān Nari
?	Ibrāhīm Kabayao
c. 720/c. 1320	'Uthmān Gifo or Kanafa
	Some twelve or fifteen successive rulers, often with divergent names, enumerated in the *Ta'rīkh al-Fattāsh* and the *Ta'rīkh al-Sūdān*, but both ending with:
?	Sulaymān Dama or Dandi
868 or 869/ 1464 or 1465	'Alī, son of Si Ma Gogo or Maḥmūd Da'o, called Ber 'the Great'
897–8/1492–3	Abū Bakr or Bakari or Baru, son of 'Alī Ber

3. The Askiyas

898/1493	Muḥammad Ture, son of Abū Bakr, called Askiya or Sikiya, d. 945/1538
934/1528	Mūsā, son of Muḥammad Ture
937/1531	Muḥammad II Benkan, son of 'Umar Kamdiagu
943/1537	Ismā'īl, son of Muḥammad Ture
946/1539	Isḥāq I
956/1549	Dāwūd, son of Muḥammad Ture
990/1582	Muḥammad III
994/1586	Muḥammad IV Bani, son of Dāwūd
996/1588	Isḥāq II
999/1591	*Moroccan conquest*
999–1000/1591–2	Muḥammad Gao or Kawkaw, killed by the Moroccans, who then set up puppet Askiyas

The Songhay (a name of unknown origin) are a group of peoples of mixed origins living along the shores of the northern part of the Niger bend, where a town, possibly on the right bank of the river, and a principality of Gao or Kawkaw are mentioned in Arabic historical sources of the ninth century. Al-Saʿdī relates a tradition that it was the fifteenth Za, Kosoy, who in the eleventh century became the first convert to Islam, being called Muslim Dam 'the voluntary Muslim'. After c. 674/c. 1275 there came a new line of the Sis or Sonnis, begun by ʿAlī Golom, who freed Gao from the domination of Mali (see above, no. 58). However, when Ibn Baṭṭūṭa was in Kawkaw in 754/1353, he implied that it came within the political sphere of Mali at that time; it seems from his account that in Kawkaw, as elsewhere it was the ruling classes and the merchants who were Muslim, while the mass of people were still animists.

At the end of the fourteenth century, Songhay became completely independent of Mali, and a powerful empire, with both military and naval forces, was built up by Sonni ʿAlī the Great, penultimate ruler of the Si line and the real founder of the Songhay empire. Shortly after Sonni ʿAlī's death, his commander Muḥammad Ture, of Soninke origin, seized the throne and founded a new dynasty of his own, that of the Askiyas. Under him, Islam became the imperial cult, and Timbuktu developed as a centre of Islamic learning. Like the rulers of Mali, Muḥammad Ture made the Pilgrimage to Mecca in 901–2/1496–7, and there received from the Sharīf ʿAbbās investiture as ruler of Takrūr (*stricto sensu*, a region on the Senegal River, but extensively used also in mediaeval Islamic usage for the western Sudan, *bilād al-Takrūr*, in general). He extended Songhay power westwards to Senegal and the old lands of Ghana, and in the east raided Hausaland, and set up a flexible, decentralised provincial administration for his empire. His successors proved quarrelsome and less capable. After the reign of his son Dāwūd, the kingdom fell victim to the disciplined army, using its firearms to good effect, sent against Gao by the Saʿdid sultan of Morocco Aḥmad al-Manṣūr al-Dhahabī (see above, no. 20), covetous of the famed wealth of the Sudan (999/1591). The three main towns of Gao, Timbuktu and Jenne fell to the invaders. The middle Niger region fell into political fragmentation and disorder. The Moroccan pashas or governors of Timbuktu ruled over only a limited area, and after c. 1070/c. 1660 direct Moroccan authority there seems to have lapsed.

EI² 'Songhay' (J. O. Hunwick).
J. Spencer Trimingham, *A History of Islam in West Africa*, 83–103.
Nehemia Levtzion, *Ancient Ghana and Mali*, 84–93.

60

THE RULERS OF KANEM AND BORNU OR BORNO

? third century–/? ninth century–
East-central Sudan

1. The 'red' (i.e. white) Sayfī (Sefuwa) or Yazanī rulers of Kanem

c. 478/c. 1085	Hume or Ume Jilmi son of Selema, the first Muslim ruler of his line, according to the Bornu King List
490/1097	Dunama Umemi Muḥammad, son of Hume
546/1151	'Uthmān Biri, son of Dunama
569/1174	'Abdallāh Bikur b. 'Uthmān
590/1194	'Abd al-Jalīl (Jīl) or Selema b. 'Abdallāh
618–57/1221–59	Dunama Dibalemi, Muḥammad, son of Selema, the first Muslim ruler of his line according to al-Maqrīzī

2. The 'black' Sultans of Kanem

?	Kade b. Dunama
?	Biri, Ibrāhīm or 'Uthmān, Kachim Biri b. Dunama
?	Jalīl or Jil b. Dunama
?	Dirke Kelem b. Dunama
689/1290	Ibrāhīm Nikale b. Biri
711/1311	'Abdallāh b. Kade
722/1322	Selema b. 'Abdallāh
726/1326	Kure Gana b. 'Abdallāh
727/1327	Kure Kura b. 'Abdallāh
728/1328	Muḥammad b. 'Abdallāh
729/1329	Idrīs b. Ibrāhīm Nikale
754/1353	Dāwūd b. Ibrāhīm Nikale
764/1363	'Uthmān b. Dāwūd
767/1366	'Uthmān b. Idrīs
769/1368	Abū Bakr b. Dāwūd
770/1369	Idrīs b. Dāwūd and/or Dunama b. Ibrāhīm
778/1376	'Umar b. Idrīs
789/1387	Sa'īd b. Idrīs
790/1388	Muḥammad b. Idrīs
791/1389	Kade Afunu b. Idrīs
792/1390	'Uthmān b. Idrīs
825/1422	'Uthmān Kalinumuwa b. Dāwūd
826/1423	Dunama b. 'Umar
828/1425	'Abdallāh b. 'Umar
836/1433	Ibrāhīm b. 'Uthmān
844/1440	Kade b. 'Uthmān
848/1444	Biri b. Dunama
849/1445	Dunama b. Biri
853/1449	Muḥammad

854/1450	Ume or Amer or Amarma
855/1451	Muḥammad b. Kade
860/1456	Ghāzī
865/1461	ʿUthmān b. Kade
870/1466	ʿUmar b. ʿAbdallāh
871–6/1467–72	Muḥammad b. Muḥammad

3. The new line of Sultans in Bornu, the Mais or rulers, claiming Sayfī descent

875/1470	ʿAlī Ghāzī Kanuri b. Dunama
908/1503	Idrīs Katagarmabe b. ʿAlī, with suzerainty over Kanem also
931/1525	Muḥammad b. Idrīs
951/1544	ʿAlī b. Idrīs
953/1546	Dunama Muḥammad b. Muḥammad, brother of ʿAlī
970/1563	ʿAbdallāh b. Dunama Muḥammad (? initially with ʿAlī Fannami b. Muḥammad as regent)
977/1569	Idrīs Alawma b. ʿAlī, in Kanem also (? initially with ʿĀʾisha (Aisa) Kili Ngirmarama, as Magira or Queen-Mother)
c. 1012/c. 1603	Muḥammad b. Idrīs
c. 1027/c. 1618	Ibrāhīm b. Idrīs
c. 1034/c. 1625	ʿUmar b. Idrīs
1055–95/1645–84	ʿAlī
c. 1110/c. 1699	Dunama b. ʿAlī
c. 1138/c. 1726	Ḥamdūn b. Dunama
c. 1143/c. 1731	Muḥammad Ergama b. Ḥamdūn
1160/1747	Dunama Gana b. ? Muḥammad
1163/1750	ʿAlī b. Ḥamdūn
1205/1791	Aḥmad b. ʿAlī, dispossessed from Bornu by the Fulani *jihād* 1223/1808, fled to Kanem and restored with Kanemi help
1223/1808	Dunama Lefiami b. Aḥmad, under Kanemi suzerainty, first reign
1226/1811	Muḥammad Ngileruma b. ʿAlī b. Ḥamdūn
1229/1814	Dunama Lefiami, second reign
1232/1817	Ibrāhīm b. Aḥmad, k. by the Kanemis 1262/1846
1262/1846	ʿAlī b. Ibrāhīm, k. in battle, last of the Sayfī Mais

4. The Kanembu line of Shaykhs or Shehus of Bornu and Dikwa

	(Muḥammad Amīn al-Kānemī, Shehu Laminu, *de facto* ruler in Bornu from Dunama Lefiami of Bornu's reign onwards, d. 1251/1835)
1251/1835	ʿUmar b. Muḥammad Amīn, first *de jure* Shehu of Bornu, first reign
1269/1853	ʿAbd al-Raḥmān b. Muḥammad Amīn
1270/1854	ʿUmar b. Muḥammad Amīn, second reign
1297/1880	Abū Bakr or Bukar I Kura b. ʿUmar
1301/1884	Ibrāhīm b. ʿUmar

1302/1885	Hāshim b. 'Umar, k. 1311/1893
1311/1893	Muḥammad Amīn Kiari b. Bukar Kura, k. 1311/1893
1311/1893	Sanda Limanambe Wuduroma b. Bukar Kura, k. 1311/1893
1311–19/1893–1901	*Conquest of Bornu and Dikwa by Rābiḥ b. Faḍl Allāh, k. 1319/1901*

(a) The Shehus in Bornu, reinstated by the British

1320/1902	Bukar Garbai b. Ibrāhīm (previously, Shehu of Dikwa)
1340/1922	'Umar Sanda Kura b. Ibrāhīm
1354-?/1937-?	'Umar Sanda Kiarimi b. Muḥammad Amīn Kiari (previously, Shehu of Dikwa)

(b) The Shehus and Mais in Dikwa, reinstated by the French

1318/1900	Shehu 'Umar Sanda Kura b. Ibrāhīm, first reign
1319/1901	Shehu Bukar Garbai b. Ibrāhīm (later, Shehu of Bornu)
1320/1902	Shehu 'Umar Sanda Mandarama b. Bukar I Kura, first reign
1323/1905	Shehu Ibrāhīm b. Bukar I Kura
1324/1906	Shehu 'Umar Sanda Mandarama b. Bukar I Kura, second reign
1335/1917	Shehu 'Umar Sanda Kiarimi b. Muḥammad Amīn Kiari (later, Shehu of Bornu)
1356/1937	Mai Abba Muṣṭafā I or Masta b. Muḥammad Amīn Kiari
1369/1950	Mai Bukar b. Shehu 'Umar Sanda Kiarimi
1371/1952	Mai Abba Muṣṭafā II or Masta b. Shehu Sanda Mandarama
1373–?/1954–?	Mai 'Umar Abba Yarema b. Shehu Ibrāhīm

During Islamic times, the histories of Kanem and Bornu have been intertwined, but together they have formed one of the oldest and certainly the most enduring of Muslim states in West Africa. Kanem lay to the east of Lake Chad, in what is now the Republic of Chad, while Bornu lay to the south-west of the lake, in what is now north-eastern Nigeria.

Already in Umayyad times, Arab raiders are reputed to have penetrated to Fezzan in southern Libya and to Tibesti and the region of the Tubu people in what is now northern Chad, but Kanem seems to have been founded by the Saharan nomadic people of the Zaghāwa. Islam was probably introduced into Kanem from the north by the Tubu during the eleventh century, when we find a dynasty ruling there which apparently claimed a spurious descent from the pre-Islamic Ḥimyarite prince of South Arabia, Sayf b. Dhī Yazan. There were connections across the Sahara with Egypt and North Africa, with a traffic in black slaves, and Dunama Dabalemi in 655/1257 sent a famed present of a giraffe to the Ḥafṣid ruler in Tunis (see above, no. 18).

By the end of the fourteenth century, these Sayfī rulers of Kanem had been forced to move to Bornu by the ascendancy in Kanem of a rival clan, the Bulālas (? Bilālīs). The Sayfīs, now in Bornu, were refounded as the Mais or rulers by 'Alī Ghāzī, with their new capital at N'gazargamu (Qaṣr Gomo) to the west of Lake Chad, and this remained the capital until 1811. The rulers of Bornu subsequently regained Kanem, and extended their power westwards into Hausaland, north-westwards to the Aïr and north-eastwards against the Tubu. In the later sixteenth century they discovered the value in warfare of firearms, and imported Turkish musketeers, and they also began to make their state more consciously Islamic by introducing the prescriptions of the *Sharīʿa* in certain spheres. Over the next two centuries, however, Bornu remained either static or in a state of decline, under pressure from the Hausas and the Touaregs of the Sahara. At the beginning of the nineteenth century, the Fulani *jihād* (see below, no. 61) affected Bornu adversely, with the Mais being denounced as inadequate Muslims, so that in 1224/1809 Aḥmad b. ʿAlī had to appeal to Muḥammad Amīn al-Kānemī for help against the Fulbe. Al-Kānemī's intervention marked the reduction of the Sayfīs of Bornu to the status of *fainéants*, and after 1262/1846 the line of the Kanembu Shaykhs or Shehus, religious scholars in origin, assumed legitimate power there. Bornu was occupied by the invader from Wadai, Rābiḥ, for several years, but soon after the restoration of the Kanembus in Bornu and the sister-sultanate of Dikwa after Rābiḥ's death in 1318/1900, its territory was divided between the colonial powers of Britain, Germany and France. The Shehus of Bornu and the Mais of Dikwa still survive as local potentates within the North-eastern State of the present Nigerian Republic, which has its administrative centre at Maiduguru.

Complete harmonisation of the lists of Bornu kings, prepared by various Western scholars (German, French and British, starting with Barth in the 1850s) from the records of court scribes in Bornu, is not easy, although there is a remarkable degree of agreement as to names of rulers, if not of lengths of their rule. The list and dates given above follow such sources as those in the Bibliography below, with especial use of the work of Hogben and Kirk-Greene and of the concordance of dates and names prepared by Cohen.

EI[1] 'Bornū' (G. Yver); *EI*[2] 'Bornū' (C. E. J. Whitting), 'Kanem' (G. Yver*).
Y. Urvoy, *Histoire de l'empire de Bornou*, Paris 1949.
J. Spencer Trimingham, *A History of Islam in West Africa*, 104–26, 207–13.
S. J. Hogben and A. H. M. Kirk-Greene, *The Emirates of Northern Nigeria: A Preliminary Survey of their Historical Traditions*, London 1966, 307–42, with a list of rulers and a genealogical table for Bornu at pp. 341–2 and a genealogical table for Dikwa at p. 353.
Ronald Cohen, 'The Bornu king lists', in *Boston University Papers on Africa. II. African history*, ed. Jeffrey Butler, Boston 1966, 41–83, with a list of rulers at pp. 80–3.
J. F. A. Ajayi and M. Crowder, *History of West Africa*, 2nd edn, London 1976, I, chs 6 (J. O. Hunwick) and 13 (R. A. Adeleye), II, ch. 4 (R. Cohen and L. Brenner).
H. Montgomery-Massingberd (ed.), *Burke's Royal Families of the World. II. Africa and the Middle East*, London 1980, 178–80.

61

THE FULANI RULERS IN HAUSALAND, AS SULTANS AND CALIPHS OF SOKOTO

1218– /1804–

Northern Nigeria and the adjacent Niger valley

1218/1804	ʿUthmān b. Fūdī (Usumanu dan Fodio), proclaimed his *hijra* and *jihād* in this year, d. 1232/1817
1223/1808	ʿAbdallāh (Abdallahi) b. Fūdī, as vizier of his brother, in the western part of Hausaland, with his capital at Gwandu Muḥammad Bello b. ʿUthmān, as vizier of his father, in the eastern part, with his capital at Sokoto
1232/1817	Muḥammad Bello, called Mai Wurno, with ʿAbdallāh, d. 1243/1828, as co-ruler
1253/1837	Abū Bakr ʿAtīq (Atiku) b. ʿUthmān, called Mai Katuru
1258/1842	ʿAlī (Aliyu) Babba b. Muḥammad Bello, called Mai Cinaka
1275/1859	Aḥmad (Ahmadu) or Zaraku b. Abī Bakr ʿAtīq, called Mai Cimola
1283/1866	ʿAlī Karām (Aliyu Karami) b. Muḥammad Bello
1284/1867	Aḥmad (Ahmadu Rafaye) b. ʿUthmān b. Fūdī
1290/1873	Abū Bakr ʿAtīq (Atiku na Rabah) b. Muḥammad Bello
1294/1877	Muʿādh (Mu'azu, Moyasa) Ahmadu b. Muḥammad Bello
1298/1881	ʿUmar (Umaru) b. ʿAlī Babba
1308/1891	ʿAbd al-Raḥmān (Danyen Kasko) b. Abū Bakr ʿAtīq
1320/1902	Muḥammad Ṭāhir I b. Aḥmad ʿAtīq
1321/1903	Muḥammad Ṭāhir II b. ʿAlī Babba
(1322/1904	*British capture of Sokoto)*
1333/1915	Muḥammad b. Aḥmad ʿAtīq, called Mai Turare
1342/1924	Muḥammad b. Muḥammad b. Aḥmad ʿAtīq, called Tambari
1349/1930	Ḥasan b. Muʿādh Aḥmad
1357–/1938–	Abū Bakr b. Shehu b. Muʿādh Aḥmad

From the later eighteenth century, the position of Islam in West Africa began to be transformed by the appearance of militant, puritanical movements, sometimes with millenarian elements, among the Fulani or Fulbe of western Sudan, in the Futa Jallon plateau region where the Niger and Senegal Rivers rise. This revivalist current was taken up by the Tokolors of Futa Toro, to the south of the Senegal River, where various Imāms or *almami*s of the Tokolor religious classes established their secular power until the arrival of the French at the end of the nineteenth century; notable among these were Ḥamadu Bari of Masina on the upper Niger and al-Ḥājj ʿUmar b. Saʿīd Tal in the upper Niger–upper Senegal region. Within these religious movements, the motivating power of Ṣūfī orders, such as the Qādiriyya and the Tijāniyya, was notable.

From Gobir in Hausaland there arose the Tokolor religious leader ʿUthmān b. Fūdī (*fodio* 'learned, holy man'), who began to preach *jihād* against those whom he regarded as lax Muslims, those compromised, in his view, with the surrounding paganism, and against the animist majority of black Africans. He assumed the ancient title implying political and religious leadership of the Muslim community, 'Commander of the Faithful', *Amīr al-Mu'minīn*, in Hausa *Sarkin Musulmi*, a title still born by his descendants in Sokoto (who have been also known as 'caliphs', following 'Uthmān's designation of himself as 'Commander of the Faithful', and sultans). With his Fulani followers, 'Uthmān wore down the uncoordinated resistance of most of the Hausa states, and individual Fulani leaders carved out for themselves principalities as far east as the Adamwa plateau of northern Cameroons, often adopting the title of *amīr* or *lamidu*.

His descendants, beginning with Muḥammad Bello, erected a states system which was inevitably based on the old Hausa ones which they had dispossessed, but with new centres of power such as Sokoto or Sakwato, founded in 1224/1909, and where 'Uthmān's tomb became a noted place of pilgrimage. The original religious impetus of the *jihād* was gradually lost, and Fulani rule degenerated into an undisguised slave-raiding economy, causing devastation, depopulation and misery. With power in the hands of local governors, only the religious authority of the rulers in Sokoto was acknowledged. At the end of the nineteenth century, the colonial powers Britain, France and Germany converged on Hausaland and divided it up. British troops entered Sokoto without resistance in 1322/1904, and it thereafter came within the Protectorate of Northern Nigeria which had been set up four years previously. The line of sultans in Sokoto continued, however, under the British policy of indirect rule, namely maintenance of the ruling structures in Nigeria, and into the present Republican period. Sokoto is now the administrative capital of the North-western State of the Nigerian Republic.

EI² 'Sokoto' D. M. Last, 'Fulbe' (R. Cornevin).

J. Spencer Trimingham, *A History of Islam in West Africa*, 160–207.

S. J. Hogben and A. H. M. Kirk-Greene, *The Emirates of Northern Nigeria: A Preliminary Survey of their Historical Traditions*, 367–417, with a genealogical table at p. 414.

D. Murray Last, *The Sokoto Caliphate*, London 1967.

H. A. S. Johnston, *The Fulani Empire of Sokoto*, London 1967.

J. F. A. Ajayi and M. Crowder (eds), *History of West Africa*, 2nd edn, II, ch. 3 (R. A. Adeleye̩).

H. Montgomery-Massingberd (ed.), *Burke's Royal Families of the World. II. Africa and the Middle East*, 192–4.

EIGHT

East Africa and the Horn of Africa

62

THE SULTANS OF KILWA

? fourth century to c. 957/? tenth century to c. 1550

The modern Tanzanian coastland

1. The Shīrāzī dynasty

⊘ ? c. 346/? c. 957	ʿAlī b. al-Ḥusayn b. ʿAlī
?	Muḥammad b. ʿAlī
386/996	ʿAlī b. Basḥat b. ʿAlī
389–93/999–1003	Dāwūd b. ʿAlī
395/1005	al-Ḥasan b. Sulaymān
433–93/1042–1110	ʿAlī b. Dāwūd
499/1106	al-Ḥasan b. Dāwūd
523/1129	Sulaymān
525/1131	Dāwūd b. Sulaymān
565/1170	Sulaymān b. al-Ḥasan b. Dāwūd
585/1189	Dāwūd b. Sulaymān
586/1190	Ṭālūt b. Sulaymān
587/1191	al-Ḥasan b. Sulaymān
612/1215	Khālid b. Sulaymān
622/1225	? b. Sulaymān
661–5/1263–7	ʿAlī b. Dāwūd
	Transfer of power to the Mahdalis

2. The Mahdali Sayyids

⊘ 676/1277	al-Ḥasan b. Ṭālūt
⊘ 693/1294	Sulaymān b. al-Ḥasan
708/1308	Dāwūd b. Sulaymān, first reign
⊘ 710/1310	al-Ḥasan b. Sulaymān, Abu 'l-Mawāhib
⊘ 733/1333	Dāwūd b. Sulaymān, second reign
757/1356	Sulaymān b. Dāwūd
757/1356	al-Ḥusayn b. Sulaymān
763/1362	Ṭālūt b. al-Ḥusayn
⊘ 765/1364	Sulaymān b. al-Ḥusayn
767/1366	Sulaymān b. Sulaymān b. al-Ḥasan
791/1389	al-Ḥusayn b. Sulaymān
⊘ 815/1412	Muḥammad b. Sulaymān, al-ʿĀdil
824/1421	Sulaymān b. Muḥammad

46/1442	Ismāʿīl b. al-Ḥusayn b. Sulaymān
858/1454	Muḥammad b. al-Ḥusayn b. Muḥammad b. Sulayman, al-Maẓlūm
859/1455	Aḥmad b. Sulaymān b. Muḥammad
860/1456	al-Ḥasan b. Ismāʿīl, al-Khaṭīb
870/1466	Saʿīd b. al-Ḥusayn
881/1476	Sulaymān b. Muḥammad b. al-Ḥusayn
882/1477	ʿAbdallāh b. al-Ḥasan
883/1478	ʿAlī b. al-Ḥasan
884/1479	al-Ḥasan b. Sulaymān, first reign
890/1485	Sabḥat b. Muḥammad b. Sulaymān
891–4/1486–9	al-Ḥasan b. Sulaymān, second reign
895/1490	Ibrāhīm b. Muḥammad
900/1495	Muḥammad b. Kiwāb, brother of Sulaymān b. Muḥammad, usurper
900–4/1495–9	Fuḍayl b. Sulaymān
	Six further rulers, either usurpers or Portuguese appointees, until c. 957/c. 1550

The island of Kilwa (the Quiloa of the Portuguese seafarers, modern Kilwa Kisawani), off the east coast of modern Tanzania and some 140 miles south of Dar es Salaam, was the seat of a series of Muslim sultans who came to control much of the trade along the East African coast until the coming of the Portuguese in the sixteenth century. The first, so-called Shīrāzī line of these (any origin for them in the Persian city of Shiraz is, however, very improbable) may have begun to rule in the tenth century, but they emerge more clearly into the light of history during the twelfth century. They were succeeded towards the end of the thirteenth century by a line of Mahdali Sayyids, who continued until the decline of Kilwa and its trade as the Portuguese assumed control of the East African coastland trade. This latter line in Kilwa included rulers of what the Kilwa Chronicle calls 'the family of Abu 'l-Mawāhib'. Obscure sultans continued in Kilwa as vassals of the Portuguese and then of the Omanis, until the Bū Saʿīdīs of Zanzibar (see below, no. 65) deposed the last one in 1843.

A good number of the coins of the sultans, and especially of the Mahdalis, have come to light through discoveries of hoards and through archaeological investigation. But dates are sparse, and the genealogy and chronology of the sultans remain distinctly obscure; the dates given in the table above, reckoned from the regnal years given in the Kilwa Chronicle, are in all cases only approximate.

Zambaur, 309 (very fragmentary); Album, 28–9.

EI² 'Kilwa' (G. S. P. Freeman-Grenville).

J. Walker, 'History and coinage of the Sultans of Kilwa', NC, 5th series, 16 (1936), 41–8.

idem, 'Some new coins from Kilwa', NC, 5th series, 19 (1939), 223–7.

G. S. P. Freeman-Grenville, *The Medieval History of the Coast of Tanganyika, with Special Reference to Recent Archaeological Discoveries*, London 1962, with genealogical tables at the end.

idem, *The French at Kilwa Island*, Oxford 1965, 28ff.

Elias Saad, 'Kilwa dynastic historiography: a critical study', *History in Africa*, 6 (1979), 177–207.

63

THE NABHĀNĪ RULERS OF PATE

600–1312/1203–1894

The island of Pate, off the modern Kenyan coastland

600/1203	Sulaymān b. Muẓaffar
628/1227	Muḥammad b. Sulaymān
650/1252	Aḥmad b. Sulaymān
670/1272	Aḥmad b. Muḥammad b. Sulaymān
705/1305	Muḥammad b. Aḥmad
732/1332	ʿUmar b. Muḥammad
749/1348	Muḥammad b. ʿUmar
797/1395	Aḥmad b. ʿUmar
840/1436	Abū Bakr b. Muḥammad
875/1470	Muḥammad b. Abī Bakr
900/1495	Abū Bakr b. Muḥammad
945/1538	Bwana Mkuu I b. Muḥammad
973/1565	Muḥammad b. Abī Bakr
1002/1594	Bwana Bakari I b. Bwana Mkuu I
1011/1602	Abū Bakr Bwana Gogo b. Muḥammad
1061/1651	Bwana Mkuu II b. Bwana Bakari I
1100/1689	Bwana Bakari II b. Bwana Mkuu II
1103/1692	Aḥmad b. Abī Bakr
1111/1699	Bwana Tamu Mkuu, Abū Bakr b. Muḥammad Bwana Mtiti
1152/1739	Aḥmad b. Abī Bakr b. Muḥammad
1160/1747	Bwana Tamu Mtoto, Abū Bakr
1177/1763	Mwana Khadīja bt. Bwana Mkuu b. Abī Bakr Bwana Gogo
1187/1773	Bwana Mkuu b. Shehe b. Abī Bakr Bwana Tamu Mkuu
1191/1777	Bwana Fumo Madi, Muḥammad b. Abī Bakr Bwana Tamu Mtoto
1224/1809	Aḥmad b. Shehe b. Fumo Luti
1230/1815	Fumo Luti Kipanga b. Bwana Fumo Madi
1236/1821	Fumo Luti b. Shehe b. Fumo Luti
1236/1821	Bwana Shehe b. Muḥammad Bwana Fumo Madi, first reign
1239/1824	Aḥmad, Bwana Waziri b. Bwana Tamu b. Shehe, first reign
1241/1826	Bwana Shehe, second reign
1247/1831	Aḥmad, Bwana Waziri, second reign
1250/1835	Fumo Bakari b. Bwana Shehe
1262/1846	Aḥmad b. Shehe b. Fumo Luti
1273/1857	Aḥmad Simba b. Fumo Luti b. Shehe
1306/1889	Fumo Bakari b. Aḥmad, d. 1308/1891, ruler in Witu
1308/1890	Bwana Shehe b. Aḥmad b. Shehe
1308–12/1890–4	Fumo Omari b. Aḥmad b. Shehe, last ruler in Pate
1312/1894	*British rule*
1312–after 1326/ 1894–after 1908	Omar Madi, under British suzerainty

This line of rulers apparently stemmed from the same tribal group as the Nabhānīs ruling in Oman before the Ya'rubids (see above, no. 53), though probably not from the Nabhānī ruling family. They ruled the island of Pate in the Lamu archipelago off the Kenyan coast from the thirteenth century onwards under Omani suzerainty, after 1109/1698 (the date when the Omanis took Mombasa from the Portuguese) paying customs dues to Zanzibar. The rulers of Pate also controlled Witu on the mainland, but came under British control at the end of the nineteenth century. A remarkably full list of the rulers of Pate is to be found in the Swahili oral traditional history of the family, only written down at the end of the nineteenth century (see the bibliography below); the dates in it, followed *faute de mieux* in the above table, should obviously be regarded as very approximate.

EI² 'Lamu', 'Pate' (G. S. P. Freeman-Grenville).
G. S. P. Freeman-Grenville (tr. and introd.), *Habari za Pate: the History of Pate ...*, unpublished paper.
J. S. Kirkman, 'The early history of Oman in East Africa', *Journal of Oman Studies* VI (1980), 41–58, with lists of the rulers of Pate and the Nabhānīs at pp. 56–7.

64

THE MAZRUI (MAZRŪʿĪ) *LIWALIS* OR GOVERNORS OF MOMBASA
c. 1109–1253/c. 1698–1837
Mombasa and Pemba island in the East African coastland

c. 1109/c. 1698	Nāṣir b. ʿAbdallāh Mazrūʿī	
1141/1729	*Muḥammad b. Saʿīd al-Maʿāmirī*	*non-Mazrūʿī governors*
1142/1730	*Ṣāliḥ b. Muḥammad al-Ḥaḍramī*	
1146/1734	Muḥammad b. ʿUthmān b. ʿAbdallāh	
1159/1746	*Sayf b. Khalaf, non-Mazrūʿī governor*	
1160/1747	ʿAlī b. ʿUthmān	
1167/1754	Masʿūd b. Nāṣir	
1193/1779	ʿAbdallāh b. Muḥammad b. ʿUthmān	
1196/1782	Aḥmad b. Muḥammad b. ʿUthmān	
1227/1812	ʿAbdallāh b. Aḥmad	
1238/1823	Sulaymān b. ʿAlī	
1240/1825	Sālim b. Aḥmad	
1253/1837	*Assertion of authority by the Bū Saʿīdīs*	

The Mazrūʿī family (Swahili Wamazrui) originally stemmed from eastern Arabia, having migrated from Oman at the end of the seventeenth century. Over nearly a century and a half, they provided an almost unbroken line of governors (Swa. *liwali* < Ar. *al-wālī*) in Mombasa, with branches on Pemba island and elsewhere. At times they were strong enough to attack the Bū Saʿīdīs in Zanzibar (see below, no. 65), and they intervened in the affairs of Pate (see above, no. 63). The Bū Saʿīdī ruler of Zanzibar Saʿīd b. Sulṭān nevertheless suppressed the Mombasa line in 1253/1837, but members of the Mazrūʿī family continued to hold positions of power and of religious and intellectual eminence on the coastland, and the family has remained influential to this day. As with the rulers of Kilwa and Pate, a local chronicle exists for the Mazrūʿīs, but this was compiled as recently as c. 1946.

EI[2] 'Mazrūʿī', 'Mombasa' (G. S. P. Freeman-Grenville).

G. S. P. Freeman-Grenville and B. G. Martin, 'A preliminary handlist of the Arabic inscriptions of the eastern African coast', *JRAS* (1973), 98–122.

Shaykh al-Amīn b. ʿAlī al-Mazrūʿī, *History of the Mazrui*, ed. and tr. J. McL. Ritchie, The British Academy, Fontes Historiae Africanae, London 1995.

65

THE ĀL BŪ SAʿĪD IN EAST AFRICA

1256–1383/1840–1964

Zanzibar and the East African coastland

1256/1840	Saʿīd b. Sulṭān b. Aḥmad, permanently established in Zanzibar, having been sporadically ruling there since 1242/1827
1273/1856	Majīd b. Saʿīd b. Sulṭān
⊘ 1287/1870	Barghash b. Saʿīd
1305/1888	Khalīfa b. Barghash
1307/1890	ʿAlī b. Saʿīd
1310/1893	Ḥāmid b. Thuwaynī
1314/1896	Ḥammūd b. Muḥammad
⊘ 1320/1902	ʿAlī b. Ḥammūd
1329/1911	Khalīfa b. Kharūb
1380/1960	ʿAbdallāh b. Khalīfa
1383/1963–4	Jamshīd b. ʿAbdallāh
1383/1964	*Overthrow of the Bū Saʿīdī family and a republican régime established in Zanzibar*

As noted in no. 54 above, the Āl Bū Saʿīd of Oman came, like their predecessors the Yaʿrubids (see above, no. 53) to control either directly or indirectly much of the East African coastland. The vigorous and forceful Saʿīd b. Sulṭān divided his time in the 1830s equally between Muscat and Zanzibar, but in 1256/1840 settled permanently in Zanzibar, primarily for commercial reasons. He introduced the cultivation of cloves on Zanzibar and the neighbouring island of Pemba as an export crop, so that he became very rich from this trade; it was during these years that Western European powers and the USA established consulates in Zanzibar. After his death, the Bū Saʿīdī dominions became permanently divided into two separate sultanates, one in Oman based on Muscat and the other based on Zanzibar.

In 1307/1890, Zanzibar and Pemba became a British protectorate, one lying off the coast of German East Africa. The Bū Saʿīdī sultanate achieved a momentary independence once more in December 1963. But in January 1964 a coup d'état ended Sultan Jamshīd's rule, and in April 1964 Zanzibar was linked with Tanganyika in what was at first called the United Republic of Tanganyika and Zanzibar and then the Republic of Tanzania.

See the bibliography to no. 54 above, to which should be added EI[2] 'Saʿīd b. Sulṭān' (G. S. P. Freeman-Grenville).

66

THE SULTANS OF HARAR

912–1304/1506–1887

Harar, in south-eastern Ethiopia

1. The line of Aḥmad Grāñ in Harar and Ausa

912/1506	Aḥmad Grāñ b. Ibrāhīm, Imām, Ṣāḥib al-Fatḥ
950/1543	(Bat'iah) Dēl Wanbarā, Aḥmad Grāñ's widow, and his son 'Alī Jarād, jointly
959/1552	Nūr b. Mujāhid, nephew of Aḥmad Grāñ, Ṣāḥib al-Fatḥ al-Thānī, d. 975/1567
975/1567	'Uthmān
977/1569	Ṭalḥa b. 'Abbās al-Wazīr, with the title of sultan
979/1571	Nāṣir b. 'Uthmān
980/1572	Muḥammad b. Nāṣir, k. 985/1577
985/1577	Muḥammad Jāsā, Imām, transferred his capital to Ausa, leaving his brother in Harar as his vizier there, k. 991/1583
993/1585	Sa'd al-Dīn
1022/1613	Ṣabr al-Dīn b. Ādam, d. 1034/1625 or 1041/1632
1041/1632	Ṣādiq
1056/1646	Malāq Ādam b. Ṣādiq
1057/1647	Aḥmad b. al-Wazīr Abrām
1083–?/1672–?	Imām 'Umar Dīn b. Ādam, overthrown by the 'Afar at an unknown date

2. The line of 'Alī b. Dāwūd in Harar, independent of Ausa

1057/1647	'Alī b. Dāwūd
1073/1662	Hāshim b. 'Alī
1081/1671	'Abdallāh I b. 'Alī
1111/1700	Ṭalḥa b. 'Abdallāh
1134/1721	Abū Bakr I b. 'Abdallāh
1144/1732	Khalaf b. Abī Bakr
1146/1733	Ḥāmid b. Abī Bakr
1160/1747	Yūsuf b. Abī Bakr
1169/1755	Aḥmad I b. Abī Bakr
⊘ 1197/1782	'Abd al-Shakūr Muḥammad I b. Yūsuf
⊘ 1209/1794	Aḥmad II b. Muḥammad
1236/1820	'Abd al-Raḥmān b. Muḥammad
⊘ 1240/1825	'Abd al-Karīm b. Abī Bakr
⊘ 1250/1834	Abū Bakr II b. Aftal Jarād
⊘ 1268/1852	Aḥmad III b. Abī Bakr
⊘ 1272–92/1856–75	Muḥammad II b. 'Alī
1292–1302/1875–85	*Egyptian occupation*
⊘ 1302–4/1885–6	'Abdallāh II b. Muḥammad b. 'Alī
1304/1887	*Conquest by the Emperor Menelik of Ethiopia*

Harar has been an ancient centre for Islam and its diffusion within the interior of the Horn of Africa, mainly among the Galla and Somali there, whereas the coastal areas have been Islamised from such maritime centres as Maqdishū (Mogadishu). (The names of many sultans of Mogadishu are known from coins, but their genealogical connections and their chronology are almost wholly obscure.) The Walashmaʿ (Amharic, Walasma) sultanate of Ifat transferred itself to Harar in the early sixteenth century, and it was one of the commanders of the Walasma, Aḥmad Grāñ (Amharic, 'left-handed'), who upheld the Muslim cause in Ethiopia until his death in battle with Christian Ethiopian and Portuguese forces in 950/1543. Thereafter, various of his descendants ruled in Harar and Ausa until the mid-seventeenth century, when a new line of sultans, that of ʿAlī b. Dāwūd, took over power at Harar for over two centuries. The connection of the last sultans of this line, from ʿAbd al-Karīm b. Abī Bakr onwards, with the original line of ʿAlī Dāwūd is uncertain.

A Turco-Egyptian force occupied Harar in 1292/1875 and executed its sultan, and in 1304/1887 the Emperor Menelik captured Harar and incorporated it into the Ethiopian kingdom.

Zambaur, 89, 309 (fragmentary).

EI[2] 'Harar' (E. Ullendorff).

R. Basset, 'Chronologie des rois de Harar (1637–1887)', *JA*, 11th series, 3 (March–April 1914), 245–58.

E. Cerulli, 'Gli emiri di Harar dal secolo XVI alla conquista egiziana (1875)', *Rassegna di Studi Etiopici*, 2 (1942), 3–20.

E. Wagner, *Legende und Geschichte. Der Fatḥ madīnat Harar von Yaḥyā Naṣrallāh*, Wiesbaden 1978.

Ahmed Zakaria, 'Harari coins: a preliminary survey', *Journal of Ethiopian Studies*, Institute of Ethiopian Studies, Addis Ababa University, 24 (November 1991), 23–46.

NINE

The Caucasus and the Western Persian Lands before the Seljuqs

67

THE SHARWĀN SHĀHS

183 to early eleventh century /799 to early seventeenth century

Sharwān in eastern Transcaucasia, with their original centre at Yazīdiyya

1. The first line of Yazīdī Shāhs

183/799	Yazīd b. Mazyad al-Shaybānī, governor of Armenia, Azerbaijan, Arrān, Sharwān and Bāb al-Abwāb, d. 185/801
⊘ 205/820	Khālid b. Yazīd, d. 228/843 or 230/845
230/845	Muḥammad b. Khālid, governor of Armenia, Azerbaijan, Arrān and Sharwān, resident in Arrān
247/861	Haytham b. Khālid, independent in Sharwān as the Sharwān Shāh
?	Muḥammad b. Haytham, in Layzān
⊘ ?	Haytham b. Muḥammad, in Layzān
before 300/913	ʿAlī b. Haytham, in Layzān, deposed 305/917
304/916	Yazīd b. Muḥammad b. Yazīd, Abū Ṭāhir, in Sharwān, latterly also in Bāb al-Abwāb
337/948	Muḥammad b. Yazīd
345/956	Aḥmad b. Muḥammad
370/981	Muḥammad b. Aḥmad
⊘ 381/991	Yazīd b. Aḥmad
418/1028	Manuchihr I b. Yazīd
⊘ 425/1034	ʿAlī b. Yazīd, Abū Manṣūr
435/1043	Qubādh b. Yazīd
441/1049	Bukhtnaṣṣar ʿAlī b. Aḥmad b. Yazīd
⊘ by 445/1053	Sallār b. Yazīd
⊘ 455/1063	Farīburz b. Sallār b. Yazīd
c. 487/c. 1094	Farīdūn I b. Farīburz, d. 514/1120
⊘ c. 487/c. 1094	Manūchihr II b. Farīburz, immediate predecessor or successor of Farīburz, or contemporaneous ruler of Sharwān during Farīdūn's time?
⊘ c. 514/c. 1120	Manūchihr III b. Farīdūn
⊘ c. 555/c. 1160	Akhsitān I b. Manūchihr III, d. between 593/1197 and 600/1204
⊘ c. 575/c. 1179	Shāhanshāh b. Manūchihr III, ? contemporaneous ruler with Aksitān, to c. 600/c. 1204
583/1187	Farīdūn II b. Manūchihr III, ? also a contemporaneous ruler with his brothers, to c. 600/c. 1204

after 583/after 1187	Farīburz II b. Farīdūn II, ? also a contemporaneous ruler with his father and/or uncles
after 583/after1187	Farrukhzād I b. Manūchihr III, ? also a contemporaneous ruler with his nephew and/or brothers, to before 622/1225
⌀ after 600/after 1204	Garshāsp I b. Farrukhzād I
⌀ c. 622/c. 1225	Farīburz III b. Garshāsp I, to ʻAlāʼ al-Dīn, 641/1243
⌀ by 653/1255	Akhsitān II b. Farīburz III
656/1258	Garshāsp II or Gushnāsp b. Akhsitān II
c. 663/c. 1265	Farrukhzād II b. Akhsitān II
....	....
c. 746/c. 1345	Kay Qubādh
⌀ 749/1348	Kay Kāwūs b. Kay Qubādh
c. 774–c. 780 or c. 784/c. 1372–c. 1378 or c. 1382	Hūshang b. Kay Kāwūs

2. The second line of Shāhs

⌀ 780/1378	Ibrāhīm I b. Muḥammad b. Kay Qubādh
⌀ 821/1418	Khalīl I b. Ibrāhīm I
⌀ 867/1463	Farrukhsiyar b. Khalīl I
905/1500	Bayram b. Farrukhsiyar
907/1502	Ghāzī b. Farrukhsiyar
⌀ 908/1503	Maḥmūd b. Ghāzī
⌀ 908/1503	Ibrāhīm II or Shaykh Shāh, uncle of Maḥmūd b. Ghāzī
⌀ 930/1524	Khalīl II b. Ibrāhīm II
⌀ 942/1535	Shāh Rukh b. Farrukh b. Ibrāhīm II, k. 946/1539
945/1538	*Ṣafawid occupation*
951/1544	Abortive revanche by Burhān ʻAlī b. Khalīl II, d. 958/1551
958/1551	*Ṣafawid occupation*
987–?/1579–?	Abū Bakr b. Burhān ʻAlī, as governor for the Ottomans
1016/1607	*Ṣafawid rule definitively established*

The title of Sharwān Shāh may well go back to Sāsānid times. The Islamic line of Arab Sharwān Shāhs began with the governor Yazīd b. Mazyad, among whose extensive territories in Armenia, north-western Persia and eastern Transcaucasia was the region of Sharwān between the south-eastern spur of the Caucasus mountains and the lower Kur river valley.

Haytham b. Muḥammad is said to have been the first governor specifically of Sharwān, one by now in effect independent and succeeding hereditarily, to assume the actual title of Sharwān Shāh. From the early fourth/tenth century, the Shāhs had their capital in Yazīdiyya, perhaps the earlier Shammākhī, but they were also often to intervene in, and at times control, Bāb al-Abwāb or Darband on the Caspian coast (see below, no. 68). Over the decades, the Shāhs had to fight off the Georgians to their west, and, in the fifth/eleventh century, incursions from northern Persia of the Turkmens. After the notable reign of Farīburz I b. Sallār, the chronology and nomenclature of the succeeding Shāhs become somewhat fragmentary and tentative, for the detailed source for the history of the earlier period, a local history of Sharwān and Bāb al-Abwāb preserved in a later Ottoman historian, comes to an end; for subsequent rulers, we depend largely on literary references from the lands outside Sharwān and the evidence from coins. These Shāhs seem to have been known as the Kasrānids (it has been suggested that this was a name or title of Farīdūn I b. Farīburz), though clearly connected with their predecessors; already, as is apparent from their onomastic, these original Arabs had by now become profoundly Iranised, and in fact claimed descent from Bahrām Gūr.

The line came to an end at the time of Tīmūr's conquests, but the later Ottoman historian Münejjim Bashï supplies details of what he calls the second line of Sharwān Shāhs, carrying these up to the late sixteenth century, and coins are known from several of these rulers. During that century, possession of Sharwān oscillated periodically between Ṣafawids and Ottomans, until by the early seventeenth century the indigenous Shāhs had finally disappeared and Sharwān became for some two centuries a governorate of the Ṣafawid empire.

Justi, 454; Sachau, 12 no. 18; Zambaur, 181–2; Album, 53.
EI² 'al-Ḳabḳ' (C. E. Bosworth); 'Shīrwān Shāhs' (W. Barthold and Bosworth).
V. Minorsky, *A History of Sharvān and Darband in the 10th–11th centuries*, Cambridge 1958.
D. K. Kouymjian, *A Numismatic History of Southeastern Transcaucasia and Adharbayjān based on the Islamic Coinage of the 5th/11th to the 7th/13th Centuries*, Columbia University Ph.D. thesis 1969, unpubl. (UMI Dissertation Services, Ann Arbor), 61–6, 136–242, with a genealogical table at p. 242.
W. Madelung, 'The minor dynasties of northern Iran', in *The Cambridge History of Iran. IV. From the Arab Invasion to the Saljuqs*, ed. R. N. Frye, Cambridge 1975, 243–9.

68

THE HĀSHIMIDS

255–468/869–1075

Bāb al-Abwāb or Darband and its hinterland

255/869	Hāshim b. Surāqa al-Sulamī, governor for the ʿAbbāsids, proclaimed himself independent
271/884	ʿUmar b. Hāshim
272/885	Muḥammad b. Hāshim
303/916	ʿAbd al-Malik b. Hāshim
327/939	Aḥmad b. ʿAbd al-Malik, first reign
(327/939	*Haytham b. Muḥammad of Sharwān, first reign)*
339/941	Aḥmad b. ʿAbd al-Malik, second reign
(330/941	*Haytham b. Muḥammad, second reign)*
(330/942	*Aḥmad b. Yazīd of Sharwān)*
(342/953	**Khashram Aḥmad b. Munabbih, of Lakz)*
342/954	Aḥmad b. ʿAbd al-Malik, third reign
366/976	Maymūn b. Aḥmad
387/997	Muḥammad b. Aḥmad
393/1003	Manṣūr b. Maymūn, first reign
(410/1019	*Yazīd b. Aḥmad of Sharwān, first reign)*
412/1021	Manṣūr b. Maymūn, second reign
(414/1023	*Yazīd b. Aḥmad of Sharwān, second reign)*
415/1024	Manṣūr b. Maymūn, third reign
425/1034	ʿAbd al-Malik b. Manṣūr, first reign
(425/1034	*ʿAlī b. Yazīd of Sharwān)*
426/1035	ʿAbd al-Malik b. Manṣūr, second reign
434/1043	Manṣūr b. ʿAbd al-Malik, first reign
446/1054	Lashkarī b. ʿAbd al-Malik
447/1055	Manṣūr b. ʿAbd al-Malik, second reign
457/1065	ʿAbd al-Malik b. Lashkarī, first reign, as vassal of Farīburz b. Sallār of Sharwān
(461/1068	*Farīburz b. Sallār, of Sharwān)*
463/1070	ʿAbd al-Malik b. Lashkarī
468/1075	Maymūn b. Manṣūr
468/1075	*Occupation of Bāb al-Abwāb by the Seljuq commander Sāwtigin*

Bāb al-Abwāb or Darband commanded the very narrow coastal route between the western shore of the Caspian and the mountains of Dāghistān, and thus enjoyed a very important strategic position. Hence it was a well-fortified bastion of Islam, a *thaghr*, against such steppe peoples to the north as the Turkish Khazars. It was furthermore a busy port, and this Caspian Sea trade plus the traffic in slaves from the South Russian steppes combined to make it highly prosperous.

The origins of the line of Hāshimids (who may have been clients of the Banū Sulaym rather than pure-born Arabs) go back to Umayyad times, when they seem first to have been appointed governors in Darband. With the internal chaos of the

ʿAbbāsid caliphate in the mid-ninth century, Hāshim b. Surāqa was able to make himself independent in Darband, and his descendants exercised power, with frequent interruptions, for over two centuries. The fortunes of Darband were indeed closely intertwined with those of neighbouring Sharwān, whose Shāhs (perhaps with the cachet of superior social status: see above, no. 67) intervened in Darband on numerous occasions. A basic cause, however, of the instability of Hāshimid rule was the strength within Darband of a strong and influential body of notables, forming an urban aristocracy, who frequently and often successfully challenged the amīrs' authority. The line was finally brought to an end, it seems, when the Seljuq sultan Alp Arslan awarded the Transcaucasian lands to his slave commander Sāwtigin, after which the Hāshimids apparently disappeared.

However, in the twelfth century, we have some sketchy knowledge of another line of Maliks of Darband (who may possibly have claimed descent from the previous dynasty), mainly from their coins. This line seems to have come to an end in the opening years of the thirteenth century when Darband came under the rule of the Sharwān Shāhs.

Sachau, 13–14 no. 21; Zambaur, 185.
EI[1] 'Derbend' (W. Barthold); EI[2] 'Bāb al-Abwāb' (D. M. Dunlop); 'al-Ḳabḳ' (C. E. Bosworth)
V. Minorsky, *A History of Sharwān and Darband.*
D. K. Kouymjian, *A Numismatic History of Southeastern Caucasia and Adharbayjān,* 66–8, 243–87, with a genealogical table at p. 287 (on the twelfth-century Maliks).
W. Madelung, in *The Cambridge History of Iran,* IV, 243–9.

69

THE JUSTĀNIDS

Late second century to fifth century/late eighth century to eleventh century

Daylam, with their centre in the Rūdbār-Shāh Rūd valleys

175/791	the 'King of Daylam' (? Justān I), sheltering 'Alids
189/805	Marzubān b. Justān I, recognised the caliph Hārūn al-Rashīd at Rayy
?	Justān II b. Marzubān, d. c. 251/c. 865
c. 251–c. 292/ c. 865–c. 905	Wahsūdān b. Justān II
c. 292/c. 905	Justān III b. Wahsūdān, killed c. 304/c. 916
307/919	'Alī b. Wahsūdān, in 'Abbāsid service at Iṣfahān and Rayy from c. 300/c. 913 onwards
?	Khusraw Fīrūz b. Wahsūdān, ruler in Rūdbār, killed after 307/919
?	Mahdī b. Khusraw Fīrūz, in Rūdbār
?	Justān IV, d. 328/940, ? father of Manādhār
336/947	Manādhar b. Justān IV, ruling in Rūdbār, ? died between 358/969 and 361/972
⊘ 361–3/972–4	Khusraw Shāh b. Manādhar, ruling in Rūdbār, ? died between 392/1002 and 396/1006
	Disappearance of the dynasty in the course of the fifth/ eleventh century

The Justānids appear as 'Kings of Daylam' towards the end of the eighth century, wih their centre in the Rūdbār of Alamūt, running into the valley of the Shāh Rūd, to become notorious two centuries or so later as the main centre of the Nizārī Ismā'īlīs in Persia (see below, no. 101); but they may well have been ruling in Daylam before this. They appear in Islamic history as part of an upsurge of the hitherto submerged indigenous peoples of north-western Persia – Daylamīs, Kurds, etc. The 'Daylamī intermezzo', of which the Justānids and several other dynasties, culminating in the Būyids (see below, no. 75), formed part, spanned the history of western and central Persia between the disintegration of the 'Abbāsid caliphate's unity and their Arab governors in western Persia and the constituting of the Great Seljuq empire (see below, no. 91, 1) across the Middle East.

After Marzubān b. Justān (I) became a Muslim in 189/805, the fortunes of the ancient family of Justānids then became connected with the Zaydī 'Alids of the Daylam region, and they seem to have adopted Shī'ism. In the tenth century, they tended to be eclipsed by the vigorous and expanding sister Daylamī dynasty of the Musāfirids or Sallārids of Ṭārum (see below, no. 71, 2), with whom the Justānids had close marriage ties, although they preserved their seat at Rūdbār in the highlands of Daylam as allies of the Būyids. In the eleventh century, the Justānids are sporadically mentioned as recognising the suzerainty of the Ghaznavids and then of the incoming Seljuqs, but thereafter they fade from history.

Justi, 440; Zambaur, 192 (both of them fragmentary and defective).
EI[2] 'Daylam' (V. Minorsky).
R. Vasmer, 'Zur Chronologie der Ǧastāniden und Sallāriden', *Islamica*, 3 (1927), 165–70, 177–9, 482–5, with a genealogical table at p. 184 correcting Zambaur.
Sayyid Aḥmad Kasravī, *Shahriyārān-i gum-nām*, Tehran 1307/1928, I, 22–34, with a genealogical table at p. 111.
W. Madelung, in *The Cambridge History of Iran*, IV, 208–9, 223–4.

70

THE SĀJIDS

276–312/889–929

Azerbaijan (Ādharbāyjān)

276/889	Muḥammad b. Abi 'l-Sāj Dīwdād I b. Dīwdast
288/901	Dīwdād II b. Muḥammad, Abu 'l-Musāfir
⊘ 288/901	Yūsuf b. Abi 'l-Sāj Dīwdād I, Abu 'l-Qāsim
⊘ 315–17/928–9	Fath b. Muḥammad b. Abi 'l-Sāj, Abu 'l-Musāfir
317/929	*End of the line of governors*

The Sājids were a line of caliphal governors in north-western Persia, the family of a commander in the ʿAbbāsid service of Soghdian descent which became culturally Arabised. Abu 'l-Sāj Dīwdād I was governor in Baghdad and Khūzistān, but with his son Muḥammad's appointment to Azerbaijan in 276/889, the family acquired what was to be its power-base for some forty years. During their tenure of power, the Sājids led numerous campaigns against such Armenian princes as the Bagratids and the Ardzrunids of Vaspurakan and extended their suzerainty over them. After the murder of Abu 'l-Musāfir Fatḥ, however, their rule in Azerbaijan ended, and control of the region passed to various Daylamī and Kurdish chiefs.

Sājid rule was thus important for the extension of Arab political and cultural influence over the Armenian provinces of eastern Transcaucasia; but, like the Ṭāhirids (see below, no. 82), the Sājids always remained faithful to their ʿAbbāsid masters and must be considered as autonomous but not independent of Baghdad.

Lane-Poole, 126; Zambaur, 179; Album, 33.

EI^{2} 'Sādjids' (C. E. Bosworth). EIr 'Banū Sāj' (W. Madelung).

C. Defrémery, 'Mémoire sur la famille des Sadjides', JA, 4th series, 9 (1847), 409–16; 10 (1847), 396–436.

W. Madelung, in *The Cambridge History of Iran*, IV, 228–32.

71

THE MUSĀFIRIDS OR SALLĀRIDS

Before 304–c. 483/before 916–c. 1090

Daylam, with their centres at Ṭārum and Samīrān, and then in Azerbaijan and Arrān also

before 304/before 916	Muḥammad b. Musāfir

Division of the family into two branches

1. The line in Azerbaijan

⊘ 330/941	Marzubān I b. Muḥammad, d. 346/957
⊘ 346–9/957–60	Justān I b. Marzubān I
⊘ 349/960	Ismāʿīl b. Wahsūdān
⊘ 351–73/962–83	Ibrāhīm I b. Marzubān I
⊘ 355/966	Nūḥ b. Wahsūdān, Abu ʾl-Ḥasan, in Ardabīl, thereafter in Samīrān until c. 379/c. 989
373/983	*Conquest of the greater part of Azerbaijan by the Rawwādids*
373–4/983–4	Marzubān II b. Ismāʿīl b. Wahsūdān, ruled over a small part of Azerbaijan (? Miyāna) until dispossessed by the Rawwādids

2. The line in Daylam

⊘ 330/941	Wahsūdān b. Muḥammad, Abū Manṣūr, first reign
(c. 354/c. 965	*Būyid occupation of Ṭārum)*
355/966	Wahsūdān b. Muḥammad, second reign
?	Marzubān II b. Ismāʿīl b. Wahsūdān
387/997	Ibrāhīm II b. Marzubān II, briefly dispossessed by the Ghaznawids in 420/1029
?	Justān II b. Ibrāhīm II, Abū Ṣāliḥ, reigning in 437/1045
?	Musāfir b. Ibrāhīm II, reigning in 454/1062
?	*Dynasty extinguished by the Ismāʿīlīs of Alamūt*

The Daylamī Musāfirids were a sister-dynasty of the Justānids and were closely linked with them (see above, no. 69), but, as a newer and, it seems, more vigorous family, were to direct their energies outside Daylam as well as within it. Whereas the Ziyārids and Būyids (see below, nos 81, 75) strove to control the rich lands of northern Persia and, in the case of the latter family, southern Persia and Iraq also, the Musāfirids expanded westwards into Azerbaijan and the eastern fringes of Armenia, where the collapse of the line of Sājid governors (see above, no. 70) had left a vacuum. 'Musāfir' is apparently an attempt to Arabise Persian Asfār/Asvār, but other names for the dynasty are found in the sources: Sallārids (< Pers. *sālār* 'military commander') and Langarids (probably from a personal name, this form being more probable, it appears, than that of Kangarids).

Muḥammad b. Musāfir, the first member of the line to appear in history, held the key fortresses of Ṭārum and Samīrān in the Safīd Rūd valley of Daylam, and from these he increased his power at the expense of the older dynasty of the Justānids. After the imprisonment of Muḥammad by his sons in 330/941, the family split into two branches, with Wahsūdān remaining in Ṭārum while his brother Marzubān extended his power northwards and westwards into Azerbaijan, Arrān, some districts of eastern Armenia and as far as Darband on the Caspian coast. Around this time, the Musāfirids seem to have espoused Ismāʿīlī Shīʿī doctrines, which were spreading within Daylam. The two branches frequently squabbled, and the latter failed to maintain itself in face of the growing power of the Rawwādids of Tabrīz (see below, no. 72). The Daylam branch was also for a while hard pressed by the Būyids, and for a time lost Shamīrān to Fakhr al-Dawla of Rayy. Their fortunes subsequently revived, and they were able to expand as far south as Zanjān. But the dynasty's history now becomes obscure and fragmentary. It survived confrontation with the Ghaznawids (see below, no. 158) and later submitted to the Seljuq Ṭoghrïl Beg. After this comes only silence, but it is probable that the last obscure Musāfirids were ended by the Ismāʿīlīs of Alamūt (see below, no. 101).

Justi, 441 (linking the Musāfirids with the Rawwādids under the common designation of Wahsūdānids); Sachau, 14 no. 23; Zambaur, 180 (defective); Album, 33–4.

EI[2] 'Musāfirids' (V. Minorsky).

R. Vasmer, 'Zur Chronologie der Ǧastāniden und Sallāriden', 170–81, with a genealogical table at p. 184 correcting Zambaur.

Sayyid Aḥmad Kasravī, *Shahriyārān-i gum-nām*, I, 52–120, with a genealogical table at p. 112.

V. Minorsky, *Studies in Caucasian History*, London 1953.

C. E. Bosworth, 'The political and dynastic history of the Iranian world (A.D. 1000–1217)', in *The Cambridge History of Iran*. V. *The Saljuq and Mongol Periods*, ed. J. A. Boyle, Cambridge 1968, 30–2.

W. Madelung, in *The Cambridge History of Iran*, IV, 232–6.

72

THE RAWWĀDIDS

Early fourth century to 463/early tenth century to 1071

Azerbaijan, with their centre at Tabriz (Tabrīz)

?	Muḥammad b. Ḥusayn al-Rawwādī
344/955	Ḥusayn I b. Muḥammad, Abu 'l-Hayjā'
⊘ 378/988	Mamlān or Muḥammad I b. Ḥusayn, Abu 'l-Hayjā'
391/1001	Ḥusayn II b. Mamlān I, Abū Naṣr
416/1025	Wahsūdān b. Mamlān I, Abū Manṣūr
451/1059	Mamlān or Muḥammad II b. Wahsūdān, Abū Naṣr
(463/1071	*Seljuq occupation of Azerbaijan)*
?	Aḥmadīl b. Ibrāhīm b. Wahsūdān, died in Marāgha 510/1116
510/1116	*Aḥmadīlī Atabegs of Marāgha*

Although Daylamīs were most prominent in the upsurge in northern Persian of Iranian peoples in the tenth century, the role of other races was not negligible. The Shaddādids of Arrān (see below, no. 73) were probably of Kurdish origin, while the Rawwādids (the form 'Rawādi' later becomes common in the sources) were in the tenth century accounted Kurdish. In reality, the family was probably Arab in origin, from the Yemeni tribe of Azd, and in the early ʿAbbāsid period they had been governors of Tabriz; but, just as the Yazīdī Sharwān Shāhs became Iranised (see above, no. 67), so the Rawwadids became Kurdicised, with such names as 'Mamlān' and 'Aḥmadīl' being characteristic Kurdish versions of the familiar Arabic names 'Muḥammad' and 'Aḥmad'.

Like their Musāfirid neighbours, the Rawwādids took advantage of the confused state of post-Sājid Azerbaijan. Despite help from the Būyids, that branch of the Musāfirids which had installed itself in Azerbaijan (see above, no. 71, 1) was gradually driven out by Abu 'l-Hayjā' Mamlān I, so that by 374/984 all the region was in Rawwādid hands. In the next century, the most outstanding member of the dynasty was Wahsudān b. Mamlān I. With the help of Kurdish neighbours, he successfully coped with the first incursions of the Oghuz Turkmens, but in 446/1054 submitted to Ṭoghrïl Beg. Thereafter, the Rawwādids ruled as Seljuq vassals until Alp Arslan returned from his Anatolian campaigns and deposed Mamlān II b. Wahsūdān. However, at least one later member of the family is known, Aḥmadīl of Marāgha, and his name was perpetuated in the twelfth century by a line of his Turkish ghulāms, called after him the Aḥmadīlīs (see below, no. 98).

Justi, 441; Zambaur, 180 (like Justi, erroneously taking the Rawwādids to be a branch of the Musāfirids); Album, 34.

EI[1] 'Tabrīz' (V. Minorsky); EI[2] 'Rawwādids' (C. E. Bosworth).

Sayyid Aḥmad Kasravī, *Shahriyārān-i gum-nām*, II, 130–58.

V. Minorsky, *Studies in Caucasian History*, 167–9, with genealogical table at p. 167.

C. E. Bosworth, in *The Cambridge History of Iran*, V, 32–4.

W. Madelung, in ibid., IV, 236–9.

73

THE SHĀDDĀDIDS
c. 340–570/c. 951–1174
Arrān and eastern Armenia

1. The main line in Ganja and Dvīn

c. 340/c. 951	Muḥammad b. Shaddād b. Q.r.t.q, in Dvīn
360/971	ʿAlī Lashkarī b. Muḥammad, in Ganja
368/978	Marzubān b. Muḥammad
⊘ 375/985	Faḍl I b. Muḥammad
422/1031	Mūsā b. Faḍl I, Abu 'l-Fatḥ
425/1034	ʿAlī Lashkarī II b. Mūsā
440/1049	Shāwur I b. Faḍl I, Abu 'l-Aswār, from 413/1022 in Dvīn, from 441/1049 in Ganja also
459/1067	Faḍl II b. Abu 'l-Aswār Shāwur I
466–8/1073–5	Faḍl III (Faḍlūn) b. Faḍl II
468/1075	*Occupation of Arrān by the Seljuq commander Sāwtigin*

2. The line in Ānī

c. 465/c. 1072	Manūchihr b. Abi 'l-Aswār Shāwur I, Abū Shujāʿ
c. 512/c. 1118	Shāwur II b. Manūchihr, Abu 'l-Aswār
518/1124	*Georgian occupation*
c. 519/c. 1125	Faḍl IV (Faḍlūn) b. Abi 'l-Aswār Shāwur II, d. 524/1130
c. 525/c. 1131	Khūshchihr b. Abi 'l-Aswār Shāwur II
?	Maḥmūd b. Abi 'l-Aswār Shāwur II
?	Shaddād b. Maḥmūd, Fakhr al-Dīn, ruling in 549/1154
550/1155	Faḍl V b. Maḥmūd
556/1161	*Georgian occupation*
⊘ 559–70/1164–74	Shāhanshāh b. Maḥmūd
570/1174	*Georgian occupation*
?	Sulṭān (? = Shāhanshāh) b. Maḥmūd, mentioned in 595/1199

The Shaddādids were another of the dynasties which arose in north-western Persia during the 'Daylamī interlude', and it is probable that they were of Kurdish origin. In such a linguistically and ethnically confused region as north-western Persia and the adjacent Caucasus, onomastic was also varied; the Shaddādids' need to find a place for themselves between the Daylamīs of Azerbaijan on one side, and the Christian Armenians and Georgians on the other, doubtless explains why Daylamī names like Lashkarī and Armenian ones like Ashūṭ/Ashot are found in the Shaddādids' genealogy.

In the middle years of the tenth century, the Kurdish adventurer Muḥammad b. Shaddād established himself at Dvīn (near Erivan in the modern Armenian Republic), a town at that time in the possession of the Musāfirids (see above, no. 71). Despite an attempt to secure Byzantine aid, Muḥammad could not prevent the Daylamīs from regaining Dvīn, but in 360/971 his sons successfully ejected the Musāfirids from Ganja in Arrān (the region of Transcaucasia between the Kur and Araxes rivers), and Ganja (the later Imperial Russian Elizavetapol, now in the Azerbaijan Republic) then became the capital of the main line of Shaddādids for a century. They now undertook with vigour the defence of Islam in this region, fighting the Georgian Bagratids, various Armenian princes, the Byzantines, the Alans or Ossetians, and the Rūs from beyond the Caucasus; in particular, Abu 'l-Aswār Shāwur I, most eminent of his house, acquired a great contemporary renown as a fighter for the faith. The Shaddādids submitted to the Seljuq Ṭoghrïl Beg when he first appeared in the Transcaucasian region, but in 468/1075 Alp Arslan's general Sāwtigin invaded Arrān and forced Faḍl III or Faḍlūn to yield up his ancestral territories. However, another branch was installed in Ānī, capital of the Armenian Bagratids, after its capture by the Seljuqs in 465/1072, and it lasted through many vicissitudes up to the Georgian resurgence in the second half of the twelfth century; a Shaddādid is still mentioned in a Persian inscription from Ānī at the end of the century.

Justi, 443; Sachau, 14 no. 22; Zambaur, 184–5 (all incomplete); Album, 34.
EI[2] 'Shaddādids' (C. E. Bosworth).
Sayyid Aḥmad Kasravī, *Shahriyārān-i gum-nām*, III, 270–332, with a genealogical table at pp. 328–9.
V. Minorsky, *Studies in Caucasian History*, with genealogical tables at pp. 6, 106.
C. E. Bosworth, in *The Cambridge History of Iran*, V, 34–5.
W. Madelung, in ibid., IV, 239–43.

74

THE DULAFIDS

Early third century to 284/early ninth century to 897
Central Jibāl, with their centre at Karaj

	al-Qāsim b. ʿĪsā al-ʿIjlī, Abū Dulaf, governor of Jibāl, d. c. 225/c. 840
⊘ c. 225/c. 840	ʿAbd al-ʿAzīz b. Abī Dulaf
⊘ 260/874	Dulaf b. ʿAbd al-ʿAzīz
⊘ 265/879	Aḥmad b. ʿAbd al-ʿAzīz, Abu ʾl-ʿAbbās
⊘ 280/893	ʿUmar b. ʿAbd al-ʿAzīz
283–4/896–7	al-Ḥārith b. ʿAbd al-ʿAzīz, Abū Laylā
284/897	*Reversion of their territories to the caliphate*

Abū Dulaf came of ancient Arab tribal stock, and from a family with a tradition of service to the ʿAbbāsids. Hārūn al-Rashīd appointed him governor of Jibāl or Media, and he served subsequent caliphs there, acquiring a reputation both as a brave military commander and as a littérateur and maecenas. His centre of power became the fief, an *īghār* or hereditary, tax-free concession, centred on Karaj between Hamadan (Hamadhān) and Isfahan (Iṣfahān), a place which henceforth became known as Karaj Abī Dulaf. His son ʿAbd al-ʿAzīz and the latter's sons, all functioning as governors for the ʿAbbāsids and exercising their military skills, succeeded him in succession, confirmed by the caliphs (to whom they remained firmly loyal) but minting their own coins, until al-Ḥārith b. ʿAbd al-ʿAzīz was killed in battle in 284/897. The district then reverted to direct ʿAbbāsid control, although descendants of the Dulafids continued to be prominent in the public affairs of the caliphate for well over a century.

Lane-Poole, 125; Zambaur, 199; Album, 32.
EI[2] 'Dulafids' (E. Marin); 'al-Ḳāsim b. ʿĪsā' (J. E. Bencheikh); EIr 'Abū Dolaf ʿEjlī' (F. M. Donner).
M. Canard, *Histoire de la dynastie des H'amdanides de Jazîra et de Syrie*, I, Algiers 1951, 311–13.

75

THE BŪYIDS OR BUWAYHIDS

320–454/932–1062

Northern, western and southern Persia and Iraq

1. The line in Jibāl

⊘ 320/932	ʿAlī b. Būya, Abu ʾl-Ḥasan ʿImād al-Dawla
⊘ 335–66/947–77	Ḥasan b. Būya, Abū ʿAlī Rukn al-Dawla

(a) The branch in Hamadan and Isfahan

⊘ 366/977	Būya b. Rukn al-Dawla Ḥasan, Abū Manṣūr Muʾayyid al-Dawla
⊘ 373/983	ʿAlī b. Rukn al-Dawla Ḥasan, Abu ʾl-Ḥasan Fakhr al-Dawla
⊘ 387/997	Fulān b. Fakhr al-Dawla ʿAlī, Abū Ṭāhir Shams al-Dawla
⊘ 412–c. 419/ 1021–c. 1028	Fulān b. Shams al-Dawla, Abu ʾl-Ḥasan Samāʾ al-Dawla, under Kākūyid suzerainty

(b) The branch in Rayy

⊘ 366/977	ʿAlī b. Rukn al-Dawla Ḥasan, Abu ʾl-Ḥasan Fakhr al-Dawla
⊘ 387–420/997–1029	Rustam b. Fakhr al-Dawla ʿAlī, Abū Ṭālib Majd al-Dawla
420/1029	*Ghaznawid conquest*

2. The line in Fars (Fārs) and Khūzistān

⊘ 322/934	ʿAlī b. Būya, Abu ʾl-Ḥasan ʿImād al-Dawla
⊘ 338/949	Fanā Khusraw b. Rukn al-Dawla Ḥasan, Abū Shujāʿ ʿAḍud al-Dawla
⊘ 372/983	Shīrzīl b. Fanā Khusraw ʿAḍud al-Dawla, Abu ʾl-Fawāris Sharaf al-Dawla
⊘ 380/990	Marzubān b. Fanā Khusraw ʿAḍud al-Dawla, Abū Kālījār Ṣamṣām al-Dawla
⊘ 388/998	Fīrūz b. Fanā Khusraw ʿAḍud al-Dawla, Abū Naṣr Bahāʾ al-Dawla
⊘ 403/1012	Abū Shujāʿ b. Fīrūz Bahāʾ al-Dawla, Sulṭān al-Dawla
⊘ 415/1024	Abū Kālījār Marzubān b. Abī Shujāʿ Sulṭān al-Dawla, ʿImād al-Dīn
⊘ 440/1048	Khusraw Fīrūz b. Marzubān ʿImād al-Dīn, Abū Naṣr al-Malik al-Raḥīm
447–54/1055–62	Fūlād Sutūn b. Marzubān ʿImād al-Dīn, Abū Manṣūr, in Fārs only
454/1062	*Power in Fars seized by the Shabānkāraʾī Kurdish chief Faḍlūya*

3. The line in Kirman (Kirmān)

324/936	Aḥmad b. Būya, Abu 'l-Ḥusayn Mu'izz al-Dawla
⊘ 338/949	Fanā Khusraw b. Ḥasan Rukn al-Dawla, Abū Shujā' 'Aḍud al-Dawla
⊘ 372/983	Marzubān b. Fanā Khusraw 'Aḍud al-Dawla, Abū Kālījār Ṣamṣām al-Dawla
⊘ 388/998	Fīrūz b. Fanā Khusraw 'Aḍud al-Dawla, Abū Naṣr Bahā' al-Dawla
⊘ 403/1012	Abu 'l-Fawāris b. Fīrūz Bahā' al-Dawla, Qawām al-Dawla
419–40/1028–48	Marzubān b. Abī Shujā' Sulṭān al-Dawla, Abū Kālījār 'Imād al-Dīn
440/1048	*Seljuq line of Qāwurd*

4. The line in Iraq

⊘ 334/945	Aḥmad b. Būya, Abu 'l-Ḥusayn Mu'izz al-Dawla
⊘ 356/967	Bakhtiyār b. Aḥmad Mu'izz al-Dawla, Abū Manṣūr 'Izz al-Dawla
⊘ 367/978	Fanā Khusraw b. Ḥasan Rukn al-Dawla, Abū Shujā' 'Aḍud al-Dawla
⊘ 372/983	Marzubān b. Fanā Khusraw 'Aḍud al-Dawla, Abū Kālījār Ṣamṣām al-Dawla
376/987	Shīrzīl b. Fanā Khusraw 'Aḍud al-Dawla, Abu 'l-Fawāris Sharaf al-Dawla
⊘ 379/989	Fīrūz b. Fanā Khusraw 'Aḍud al-Dawla, Abū Naṣr Bahā' al-Dawla
⊘ 403/1012	Abū Shujā' b. Fīrūz Bahā' al-Dawla, Sulṭān al-Dawla
412/1021	Ḥasan b. Fīrūz Bahā' al-Dawla, Abū 'Alī Musharrif al-Dawla
⊘ 416/1025	Shīrzīl b. Fīrūz Bahā' al-Dawla, Abū Ṭāhir Jalāl al-Dawla
⊘ 435/1044	Marzubān b. Abī Shujā' Sulṭān al-Dawla, Abū Kālījār 'Imād al-Dīn
440–7/1048–55	Khusraw Fīrūz b. Marzubān 'Imād al-Dīn, Abū Naṣr
447/1055	*Seljuq occupation of Baghdad*

5. The rulers of the dynasty acknowledged by local chiefs in Oman

⊘ by 361/972	Fanā Khusraw, Abū Shujā' 'Aḍud al-Dawla
⊘ 380/990	Marzubān, Abū Kalījār Ṣamṣām al-Dawla
⊘ 388/998	Fīrūz, Abū Naṣr Bahā' al-Dawla
⊘ 403/1012	Abū Shujā' Sulṭān al-Dawla
⊘ 415–42/1024–50	Marzubān, Abū Kālījār 'Imād al-Dīn
442/1050	*Power seized by a leader of the local Ibāḍīs*

Out of the Daylamī dynasties which formed in the Persian world as the 'Abbāsid grip over the provinces of the caliphate weakened, the Būyids were the most powerful and ruled over the greatest extent of territories. They began modestly enough as commanders in the army of the successful Daylami condottieri,

Mardāwīj b. Ziyār, founder of the Ziyārid dynasty (see below, no. 81). The eldest of the three sons of Būya, ʿAlī, held Iṣfahān at the time of Mardāwīj's assassination, and shortly afterwards seized the whole of Fars, while Ḥasan held Jibāl and Aḥmad held Kirman and Khūzistān. In 339/945 Aḥmad entered Baghdad, and the ʿAbbāsids began a 110-year period of tutelage under Būyid amīrs (who normally held the title in Iraq of *Amīr al-Umarā'* 'Supreme Commander'), during which the caliphate was to reach its lowest ebb. In the third quarter of the tenth century, Muʿizz al-Dawla Aḥmad's son ʿAḍud al-Dawla united under his rule what had originally been the three Būyid amirates, comprising southern and western Persia and Iraq, even extending his power across the Persian Gulf to Oman, where his successors were acknowledged as suzerains by such local chiefs as the Mukramids (see above no. 52); his reign marks the zenith of Būyid power. ʿAḍud al-Dawla pursued a vigorously expansionist policy, utilising his armies of Daylamī infantry and Turkish cavalry, in the east against the Ziyārids of Ṭabaristān and Gurgān and against the Sāmānids of Khurasan, and in the west against the Ḥamdānids of Jazīra.

However, a patrimonial conception of power, doubtless stemming from the tribal past of the Daylamīs, was strong among the various Būyid princes, with tendencies towards fragmentation apparent when strong rule was relaxed. After ʿAḍud al-Dawla's death, there was much civil strife within the dynasty. This disunity allowed petty Kurdish and Daylamī principalities to constitute themselves within the Zagros mountains and in Jibāl, and facilitated Maḥmūd of Ghazna's annexation of Rayy and much of Jibāl from the Būyids in 420/1029. It then left them weakened in the face of incursions of the Turkmen Oghuz and the westward drive of the Seljuq Ṭoghrïl Beg, who was able to arouse orthodox Sunnī religious and constitutional feeling and claim that he was liberating the western lands or Persia and Iraq from Shīʿī heretics. Baghdad was occupied in 447/1055, but the Būyid prince in Fars retained power for seven more years until his lands were seized by local Shabānkāra'ī Kurds, only to fall into the Seljuqs' hands shortly afterwards.

Like most of the Daylamīs, the Būyids were Shīʿīs, probably Zaydīs to begin with and then Twelvers or Jaʿfarīs. The traditional Shīʿī festivals and practices were introduced into their territories, and Shīʿī scholars laboured at the systematisation and intellectualisation of Shīʿī theology and law, previously somewhat vague and emotional in content. This Shīʿism may have been in part a manifestation of anti-Arab, pro-Iranian national feeling, with which attempts to provide the Būyids with a respectable genealogy going back to the Sāsānids and the adoption of an ancient Persian imperial title like *Shāhānshāh* may be connected. The Baghdad caliphs' material power and resources were inevitably circumscribed by their alleged protectors, yet the Būyids made no attempt to extinguish the caliphate and they showed themselves hostile to their rivals in the west, the Ismāʿīlī Fāṭimids. Culturally, the domination of Shīʿism in the Būyid territories was accompanied by a wide tolerance of other faiths like Christianity, Judaism and Zoroastrianism, allowing their communities to flourish and bringing about a lively intellectual ferment in the various Būyid provincial capitals; this learning was nevertheless essentially Arabic-centred, and the Būyids evinced little interest in or encouragement of the New Persian literary and cultural renaissance which was beginning in the eastern Persian lands.

Justi, 442; Lane-Poole, 139–44; Zambaur, 212–13 and Table Q; Album, 35–6.
EI[2] 'Buwayhids' (Cl. Cahen); EIr 'Buyids' (Tilman Nagel).
R. Vasmer, 'Zur Geschichte und Münzkunde von 'Omān im X. Jahrhundert', *ZfN*, 37 (1927), 274–87.
H. Bowen, 'The last Buwayhids', JRAS (1929), 229–45.
S. M. Stern and A. D. H. Bivar, 'The coinage of Oman under Abū Kālījār the Buwayhid', NC, 6th series, 18 (1958), 147–56.
H. Busse, *Chalif und Großkönig, die Buyiden im Iraq (945–1055)*, Beirut and Wiesbaden 1969, with genealogical tables at p. 610.
idem, 'Iran under the Būyids', in *The Cambridge History of Iran*, IV, 250–304.
C. E. Bosworth, in ibid., V, 36–53.

76

THE ḤASANŪYIDS OR ḤASANAWAYHIDS
c. 350–406/c. 961–1015
Southern Kurdistan

c. 350/c. 961	Ḥasanawayh b. Ḥusayn al-Barzīkānī, Abu 'l-Fawāris, d. 369/979
⊘ 370/980	Badr b. Ḥasanawayh, Abu 'l-Najm Nāṣir al-Dīn, d. 405/1014
404/1013	Ṭāhir or Ẓāhir b. Hilāl b. Badr, in Shahrazūr
405/1014	Hilāl b. Badr
405–6/1014–15	Ṭāhir b. Hilāl
406/1015	*Conquest by the ʿAnnāzids*

Ḥasanawayh was a chief of the Kurdish Barzīkānī tribe who built up for himself a principality in the region round Qarmāsīn (the later Kirmānshāh). He and his son Badr skilfully maintained their power as vassals of the Būyids (see above, no. 75) by supporting various contenders for power in the struggles between Fakhr al-Dawla of the northern Būyid amirate on the one hand and ʿAḍud al-Dawla and his successors in Fārs and Iraq on the other. They also achieved contemporary reputations for their just and beneficent rule among a Kurdish people whose very name was synonymous with violence and rapacity. Latterly, however, the Ḥasanūyids were overshadowed by a rival family of Kurdish chiefs, the ʿAnnāzids (see below, no. 77), who killed Ṭāhir b. Hilāl and generally replaced the Ḥasanūyids in central Kurdistan. The family only managed to hold on to a few fortresses like that of Sarmāj near Bīsutūn until a descendant of Badr's died there in 439/1047.

Lane-Poole, 138; Zambaur, 211; Album, 36.
EI² 'Ḥasanawayh' (Cl. Cahen).

77

THE ʿANNĀZIDS

381 to later sixth century/991 to later twelfth century
Southern Kurdistan and Luristān

381/991	Muḥammad b. ʿAnnāz, Abu ʾl-Fatḥ	
	⊘ Fāris b. Muḥammad, Abu ʾl-Shawk Ḥusām al-Dawla, in Ḥulwān, d. 437/1046	joint rulers
401/1011	Muhalhil b. Muḥammad, in Shahrazūr	joint rulers
	Surkhāb b. Muḥammad, in Bandanījīn	joint rulers
437– /1046–	Muhalhil b. Muḥammad, sporadic rule, d. c. 447/c. 1055	
438– /1046–	Saʿdī or Suʿdā b. Fāris, sporadic rule, d. after 446/1054	
447/1055	*Kurdistan under Seljuq control*	
?	Surkhāb b. Badr b. Muhalhil, d. 500/1107	
500–?/1107–?	Abū Manṣūr b. Surkhāb	
later sixth century/ later twelfth century	Surkhāb b. ʿAnnāz	

The ʿAnnāzids were another Kurdish line, like the Ḥasanūyids (see above, no. 76), with their power-base in the Shādhanjān tribe. The founder, Abu ʾl-Fatḥ Muḥammad, ruled from Ḥulwān, but his three sons and successors ruled in various other parts of southern Kurdistan, maintaining themselves against the Būyids and the Kākūyids (see below, no. 78), but with their dominions suffering increasingly from Oghuz Türkmen incursions led by the Seljuq Ibrāhīm Inal. The history of the ʿAnnāzids in these decades is confused and chaotic, for the family had several branches and the territorial extent of their rule was often shifting. After Ṭoghrïl Beg came to Iraq in 447/1055, the sources are largely silent on the ʿAnnāzids, except for occasional references which indicate that some members of the family retained a certain amount of power in Kurdistan and Luristān until some time after 570/1174.

Zambaur, 212.
EI[2] 'ʿAnnāzids' (V. Minorsky); *EIr* 'ʿAnnāzids' (K. M. Aḥmad).

78

THE KĀKŪYIDS OR KĀKAWAYHIDS

c. 398–443/c. 1008–51 independent rulers; thereafter, feudatories of the Seljuqs until the mid-sixth/mid-twelfth century
Jibāl and Kurdistan

⊘ before 398/before 1008	Muḥammad b. Rustam Dushmanziyār, Abū Ja'far 'Alā' al-Dawla, in Isfahan
⊘ 433–43/1041–51	Farāmurz b. Muḥammad, Abū Manṣūr Ẓahīr al-Dīn Shams al-Mulk, in Isfahan, d. after 455/1063
433–c. 440/1041–c. 1048	Garshāsp I b. Muḥammad, Abū Kālījār 'Alā' al-Dawla, in Hamadan and Nihāwand, d. 443/1051
? - 488/? - 1095	'Alī b. Farāmurz, Abū Manṣūr Mu'ayyid al-Dawla or 'Alā' al-Dawla, in Yazd
488–?536/1095–?1141	Garshāsp II, Abū Kālījār 'Alā' al-Dawla 'Aḍud al-Dīn *Succession of the Atabegs of Yazd*

The Kākūyids were one of the petty Kurdish and Daylamī dynasties of the Zagros region which arose when the grip of the Būyids (see above, no. 75) was becoming relaxed, only to lose their independence and be reduced to vassalage by the rising power in Persia of the Seljuqs. Dushmanziyār had been in the service of the Būyids of Rayy, and his son Muḥammad (known as Ibn Kākūya in the sources, explained as being from a Daylamī dialect word for 'maternal uncle', since Muḥammad was the maternal uncle of the Būyid Amīr Majd al-Dawla) was by 398/1008 governor of Isfahan. Soon he expanded to Hamadan and into Kurdistan, building up a principality which was of some political significance for a while and forming a court circle which included the philosopher Ibn Sīnā (Avicenna), who functioned as his vizier. Ghaznawid expansion into Jibāl after 420/1029 forced him temporarily to submit, but when the Ghaznawids found it difficult to retain these distant conquests he resumed his independence and even occupied Rayy for a while.

The invasions of the Turkmen Oghuz and their flocks changed the political and economic situation of northern Persia and forced the Kākūyids, like other Daylamī and Kurdish powers, on to the defensive. Farāmurz b. Muḥammad was obliged to yield Isfahan to Ṭoghrïl, who after 443/1051 made it the Seljuq capital but awarded Abarqūh and Yazd in compensation for the Kākūyids. His brother Garshāsp I fled from Kurdistan to the Būyids in Fars. With their little niche in central Persia, the later Kākūyids adapted themselves comfortably to the Great Seljuq régime, being frequently linked by marriage to the ruling sultans. After Garshāsp II, the history of the family becomes obscure, but Garshāsp's daughter was to be linked through marriage to the line of Turkish Atabegs which succeeded in Yazd and lasted until the thirteenth century and the time of the Il Khānids (see below, no. 133)

Justi, 445; Lane-Poole, 145; Zambaur, 216–17; Album, 36.
EI^2 'Kākūyids' (C. E. Bosworth).

G. C. Miles, 'The coinage of the Kākwayhid dynasty', *Iraq*, 5 (1938), 89–104.
idem, 'Notes on Kākwayhid coins', ANS, *Museum Notes*, 9 (1960), 231–6.
C. E. Bosworth, 'Dailamīs in central Iran: the Kākūyids of Jibāl and Yazd', *Iran*, JBIPS, 8 (1970), 73–95.

79

THE DĀBŪYID ISPAHBADHS

c. 19–144/c. 640–761

Gīlān, Rūyān and the Ṭabaristān coastlands, with their centre at Sārī

c. 19/c. 640	Gīl b. Gīlānshāh, Gāwbāra, Gīl-i Gīlān Farshwādgarshāh
c. 40/c. 660	Dābūya b. Gāwbāra
c. 56/c. 676	Khurshīd I b. Gāwbāra
⊘ 93/712	Farrukhān I b. Dābūya, Dhu 'l-Manāqib, Farrukhān-i Buzurg
⊘ after 110/after 728	Dādburzmihr b. Farrukhān I
123/741	Farrukhān II b. Farrukhān I, Farrukhān-i Kūchik, Kubālī
⊘ 131–43/749–60	Khurshīd II b. Dādburzmihr, d. 144/761
143/760	*'Abbāsid conquest of Ṭabaristān*

The Caspian coastlands of Gīlān and of Māzandarān (in earlier Islamic times, Ṭabaristān), and the massive barrier of the Elburz Mountains which separates them from the central plateau of Persia, have always been a region of Persia with a very distinct character of their own. In particular, they have been a refuge area for peoples and ideas, so that ethnic splinter-groups, old or aberrant religious beliefs, ancient languages and scripts, and social ways, have often survived there after they have disappeared from the more accessible and open parts of Persia. Islam was late arriving in the Caspian region, and for several centuries after this time various petty dynasties lingered on there, some with roots in the late Sāsānid past. One of these, the Bāwandids, endured for six or seven centuries until Il Khānid times (see below, no. 80), and the Bāduspānids (see below, no. 100) persisted from Seljuq times until the reign of the Ṣafawid Shāh 'Abbās I (i.e. until the end of the sixteenth century: see below, no. 148), when the line was suppressed and the Caspian provinces were fully integrated into the rest of the kingdom.

The Dābūyids were a line of Ispahbadhs (lit. 'military chief', here 'local prince') who apparently arose in the south-western Caspian highlands region of Gīlān in late Sāsānid times. They were local governors for the Emperors, and themselves claimed Sāsānid descent, but from the time of Farrukhān I they moved eastwards and also controlled Ṭabaristān at the south-eastern corner of the Caspian lands, residing now at Sārī. The history of the dynasty is largely known from the historian of the Caspian lands, Ibn Isfandiyār, and his information on the succession and chronology of the early Dābūyids must be regarded as only semi-historical. Arabic raids into Ṭabaristān began in the caliphate of 'Uthmān, but that of the governor of Iraq and the East, Yazīd b. al-Muhallab, in 98/716, was the first serious attack. The Dābūyid Khurshīd II aided Abū Muslim against the 'Abbāsid caliph al-Manṣūr and then the Zoroastrian rebel in Khurasan, Sunbādh. Hence in 141/758 the caliph undertook the definitive conquest of Ṭabaristān, successfully drove out Khurshīd II and ended the dynasty of the Dābūyids (who, as Zoroastrians, had never accepted Islam; they are included here as precursors of the local Caspian dynasties who did, during the years shortly afterwards, accept the new faith, and as being historically involved with the Islamic caliphs).

Justi, 430; Zambaur, 186.
EI[2] 'Dābūya' (B. Spuler); EIr 'Dabuyids' (W. Madelung).
H. L. Rabino, 'Les dynasties du Māzandarān de l'an 50 avant l'Hégire à l'an 1006 de l'Hégire (572 à 1597–1598) d'après les chroniques locales', JA, 228 (1936), 437–43, with a genealogical table at p. 438.
W. Madelung, in *The Cambridge History of Iran*, IV, 198–200.

80

THE BĀWANDID ISPAHBADHS

45–750/665–1349

The highlands of Ṭabaristān and Gīlān

1. The line of the Kāwūsiyya (Ṭabaristān), with their centre at Firrīm

45/665	Bāw, ? Ispahbadh of Ṭabaristān
60/680	*Interregnum of Walash*
68/688	Surkhāb I b. Bāw
98/717	Mihr Mardān b. Surkhāb I
138/755	Surkhāb II b. Mihr Mardān
155/772	Sharwīn I b. Surkhāb II
before 201/before 817	Shahriyār I b. Qārin
210/825	Shāpūr or Ja'far b. Shahriyār I
210–24/825–39	*Seizure of power by Māzyār b. Qārin b. Wandād-Hurmuzd*
224/839	Qārin I b. Shahriyār I, Abu 'l-Mulūk
253/867	Rustam I (? b. Surkhāb) b. Qārin
282/895	Sharwīn II b. Rustam I
318/930	Shahriyār II b. Sharwīn II
⌀ c. 353–69/c. 964–80	Rustam II b. Sharwīn II
358/969	Dārā b. Rustam II
⌀ c. 376/c. 986	Shahriyār III b. Dārā
396/1006	Rustam III b. Shahriyār III
449–66/1057–74	Qārin II b. Shahriyār III
466/1074	*Disappearance of their rule*

2. The line of the Ispahbadhiyya (Ṭabaristān and Gīlān), with their centre at Sārī

⌀ c. 466/c. 1074	Shahriyār b. Qārin, Ḥusām al-Dawla
c. 508/c. 1114	Qārin b. Shahriyār, Najm al-Dawla
511/1117	Rustam I b. Qārin, Shams al-Mulūk
⌀ 511/1118	'Alī b. Shahriyār, 'Alā' al-Dawla
⌀ c. 536/c. 1142	Shāh Ghāzī Rustam b. 'Alī, Nuṣrat al-Dīn
⌀ 560/1165	Ḥasan b. Shāh Ghāzī Rustam, 'Alā' al-Dawla Sharaf al-Mulūk
568/1173	Ardashīr b. Ḥasan, Ḥusām al-Dawla
602–6/1206–10	Rustam II b. Ardashīr
606/1210	*Khwārazmian and then Mongol rule in Ṭabaristān*

3. The line of the Kīnkhwāriyya (vassals of the Il Khānids), with their centre at Āmul

635/1238	Ardashīr b. Kīnkhwār, Ḥusām al-Dawla
after 647/after 1249	Muḥammad b. Ardashīr, Shams al-Mulūk
c. 669/c. 1271	'Alī b. Ardashīr, 'Alā' al-Dawla

c. 669/c. 1271	Yazdagird b. Shahriyār, Tāj al-Dawla
c. 700/c. 1300	Shahriyār b. Yazdagird, Nāṣir al-Dawla
c. 710/c. 1310	Kay Khusraw b. Yazdagird, Rukn al-Dawla
728/1328	Sharaf al-Mulūk b. Kay Khusraw
734–50/1334–49	Ḥasan b. Kay Khusraw, Fakhr al-Dawla
750/1349	*Succession in Māzandarān of the Afrāsiyābids*

The Bāwandids were the longest-lived of the petty Caspian dynasties, with a history extending over some six or seven centuries, a remarkable demonstration of how the region's isolation from the mainstreams of Islamic Persian life allowed a degree of family continuity unusual in the Islamic world. They claimed descent from one Bāw and traced their genealogy back beyond this to the Sāsānid emperor Kawādh. Their original centre was at Firrīm in the eastern section of the Elburz chain running through Ṭabaristān.

That part of the dynasty's history which can be reasonably well documented only begins with the Arab invasions of Ṭabaristān in the opening years of the ʿAbbāsid caliphate. This was the time when the Bāwandids and the rival house of the Qārinids were vying for power there, a rivalry which in the ninth century was to end spectacularly in the rebellion and fall of Māzyār b. Qārin (224/839). It was also at this last juncture that the Ispahbadhs at last became definitively Muslim. Subsequently, they opposed the Zaydī Imāms in lowland Ṭabaristān, and were involved during the tenth century in the struggles of the Būyids and the Ziyārids (see above, no. 75, and below, no. 81) for control of northern Persia, being linked with both these houses through marriage; it was during the times when they became vassals of the Būyids that the Bāwandids adhered to Twelver Shīʿism.

This first line faded out, and the affiliation to it of the subsequent line is not certain. These Ispahbadhiyya were firmly Twelver Shīʿīs. Within a framework of vassalage to the Great Seljuqs, they managed to preserve their local authority; at times they sheltered Seljuq claimants and made high-level marriages with the Seljuqs. The decline of Great Seljuq power in the mid-twelfth century allowed the vigorous and assertive Shāh Ghāzī Rustam to became a major, independent figure in the politics of northern Persia; he combated the Ismāʿīlīs of Alamūt (see below, no. 101) and pursued an independent policy aimed at extending his principality south of the Elburz. However, the rising power of the Khwārazm Shāhs (see below, no. 89) in the early years of the thirteenth century brought this line to an end, with direct power exercised in Māzandarān (as Ṭabaristān becomes generally called after the twelfth century).

The Bāwandids were restored after an interval of three decades in the shape of a collateral branch, the Kīnkhwāriyya, who ruled as vassals of the Mongol Il Khānids, with their capital at Āmul, until another local family of Māzandarān, that of Kiyā Afrāsiyāb Chulābī, overthrew them and ended Bāwandid rule for ever.

Justi, 431–2; Sachau, 5–7 nos 3–5; Zambaur, 187–9; Album, 34–5.
EI² 'Bāwand' (R. N. Frye); EIr 'Āl-e Bāvand' (W. Madelung).
H. L. Rabino, 'Les dynasties du Māzandarān', 409–37, with a genealogical table at p. 416.
G. C. Miles, 'The coinage of the Bāwandids of Ṭabaristān' in C. E. Bosworth (ed.), *Iran and Islam, in memory of the late Vladimir Minorsky*, Edinburgh 1971, 443–60.
W. Madelung, in *The Cambridge History of Iran*, IV, 200–5, 216–18.

81

THE ZIYĀRIDS

319–c. 483/931–c. 1090

Ṭabaristān and Gurgān

⊘ 319/931	Mardāwīj b. Ziyār, Abu 'l-Ḥajjāj
⊘ 323/935	Wushmgīr b. Ziyār, Abū Manṣūr Ẓahīr al-Dawla
⊘ 356/967	Bīsutūn b. Wushmgīr, Abū Manṣūr Ẓahīr al-Dawla
⊘ 367/978	Qābūs b. Wushmgīr, Abu 'l-Ḥasan Shams al-Ma'ālī, first reign
371–87/981–97	*Būyid occupation*
⊘ 387/997	Qābūs b. Wushmgīr, second reign
⊘ 402/1012	Manūchihr b. Qābūs, Falak al-Ma'ālī
420/1029	Anūshirwān b. Manūchihr, Abū Kālījār, d. ? 441/1049
(426/1035	Dārā b. Qābūs, governor for the Ghaznawids in Ṭabaristān and Gurgān)
441/1049	Kay Kāwūs b. Iskandar b. Qābūs, 'Unṣur al-Ma'ālī, d. c. 480/c. 1087
c. 480–c. 483/ c. 1087–c. 1090	Gīlān Shāh b. Kay Kāwūs
	Seljuq governors in lowland Ṭabaristān and Gurgān

In the early years of the tenth century, the backward and remote highland region of Daylam at the south-western corner of the Caspian Sea sent forth large numbers of its menfolk as soldiers of fortune in the armies of the caliphate and elsewhere. The Ziyārids arose out of one of the fiercest of these condottieri, Mardāwīj b. Ziyār, who was descended from the royal clan of Gīlān. On the rebellion of the commander Asfār b. Shīrūya, a general in the Sāmānid armies, Mardāwīj took the opportunity to seize most of northern Persia. His power soon extended as far south as Iṣfahān and Hamadān, but in 323/935 he was murdered by his own Turkish slave troops and his transient empire fell apart. Only in the eastern Caspian provinces did his brother Wushmgīr retain a foothold, acknowledging the Sāmānids as his overlords, and in the ensuing decades the Ziyārids were closely involved with the Sāmānid–Būyid struggle for control of northern Persia. In Qābūs b. Wushmgīr, the dynasty produced an outstanding figure of the florescence of Arabic learning in Khurasan and the East, which his seventeen-year exile in Nishapur, while the Būyids occupied his lands, facilitated. A point which marks off the Ziyārids from almost all the other Daylamī dynasties of the time was their adherence, at least latterly, to Sunnī and not Shī'ī Islam.

In the early eleventh century, the Ziyārids had to recognise the overlordship of the new and vigorous power of the Ghaznawids (see below, no. 158), and the two families became linked by marriage alliances. The incoming Seljuqs appeared in Gurgān in 433/1041 and took over the coastlands, but the Ziyārids seem to have survived, in obscure circumstances as vassals of the Seljuqs, in the highland region. One of the last amīrs, Kay Kāwūs b. Iskandar, achieved fame as the author of a celebrated 'Mirror for Princes' in Persian, the *Qābūs-nāma*, named after his illustrious grandfather. His son Gīlān Shāh was the last known member of his line to rule. He was apparently overthrown by the Nizārī Ismāʿīlīs, who were spreading their power through the Elburz region (see below, no. 101), and with him the dynasty disappears from history.

Justi, 441; Lane-Poole, 136–7; Justi, 441; Zambaur, 210–11; Album, 35.
EI[1] 'Ziyārids' (Cl. Huart); EI[2] 'Mardāwīdj' (C. E. Bosworth). (The earlier acounts of the dynasty are all confused and unreliable in their chronology of the later Ziyārids.)
C. E. Bosworth, 'On the chronology of the later Ziyārids in Gurgān and Ṭabaristān', *Der Islam*, 40 (1964), 25–34, with a genealogical table at p. 33.
G. C. Miles, 'The coinage of the Ziyārid dynasty of Ṭabaristān and Gurgān', ANS, *Museum Notes*, 18 (1972), 119–37.
W. Madelung, in *The Cambridge History of Iran*, IV, 212–16.

TEN

The Eastern Persian Lands, Transoxania and Khwārazm before the Seljuqs

82

THE ṬĀHIRIDS AND MUṢʿABIDS
205–78/821–91
Governors in Khurasan (Khurāsān) and in Baghdad and Iraq

1. The governors in Khurasan and its administrative dependencies
205–59/821–73

⊘ 205/821	Ṭāhir I b. al-Ḥusayn b. Muṣʿab b. Ruzayq al-Khuzāʿī, Abu ʾl-Ṭayyib Dhu ʾl-Yamīnayn
⊘ 207/822	Ṭalḥa b. Ṭāhir I
⊘ 213/828	ʿAbdallāh b. Ṭāhir I, Abu ʾl-ʿAbbās
⊘ 230/845	Ṭāhir II b. ʿAbdallāh
⊘ 248–59/862–73	Muḥammad b. Ṭāhir II
259/873	*Ṣaffārid occupation of Nishapur (Nīshāpūr)*
(259–67, 268– / 873–81, 882–	Muḥammad b. Ṭāhir II nominal governor of Khurasan)
(263/876	al-Ḥusayn b. Ṭāhir II, temporarily restored in Nishapur)
261– /875–	*Khurasan disputed by the Ṣaffārids and various military adventurers*

2. The military governors (*Aṣḥāb al-Shurṭa*) in Baghdad and Iraq
207–78/822–91

205/820	Ṭāhir I b. al-Ḥusayn b. Muṣʿab
207/822	Isḥāq b. Ibrāhīm b. Muṣʿab
235/849	Muḥammad b. Isḥāq
236/850	ʿAbdallāh b. Isḥāq
237/851	Muḥammad b. ʿAbdallāh b. Ṭāhir I
253/867	ʿUbaydallāh b. ʿAbdallāh b. Ṭāhir I, first governorship
255/869	Sulaymān b. ʿAbdallāh b. Ṭāhir I
266/879	ʿUbaydallāh b. ʿAbdallāh, second governorship
271/884	Muḥammad b. Ṭāhir II
276–8/890–1	ʿUbaydallāh b. ʿAbdallāh, third governorship
278/891	*The Turkish slave commanders Badr al-Muʿtaḍidī and Muʾnis al-Khādim*
c. 297/c. 910	Muḥammad b. ʿUbaydallāh, deputy *Ṣāḥib al-Shurṭa* for Muʾnis

Ṭāhir b. al-Ḥusayn was probably of Persian *mawlā* or client origin, though eulogists of the Ṭāhirids endeavoured to give them a direct lineage from the aristocratic Arab tribe of Khuzāʿa. Ṭāhir rose to favour under al-Ma'mūn as commander of the latter's forces in the fratricidal war against al-Amīn in 194/810, and after the fall of Baghdad became governor of that city and of Jazīra. Finally, he was appointed governor of the East. Just before his death shortly afterwards, he had started to omit al-Ma'mūn's name from the Friday *khuṭba* or sermon, this being tantamount to a renunciation of allegiance or declaration of independence. Nevertheless, the caliph handed on the governorship to his son Ṭalḥa, being unable to find anyone more reliable for this important office. Henceforth, the Ṭāhirids ruled from Nishapur as a hereditary line of governors but remained faithful vassals of the ʿAbbāsids, continuing to forward tribute regularly to Iraq (the Turkish military slaves in this tribute became one of the mainstays of the caliphs' professional armies), although ʿAbdallāh b. Ṭāhir was careful never to leave Khurasan for Baghdad. Hence the Ṭāhirids may be considered as a virtually autonomous line of governors but not as a separate, independent dynasty, as were their rivals the Ṣaffārids. The family's strong Sunnī orthodoxy and their favour towards the established Arab and Persian landed and military classes assured them of top-level support, while they also had a reputation for protecting the interests of the masses, of encouraging agriculture and irrigation, and of patronising scholars and poets.

In Khurasan, the main political and military efforts of the Ṭāhirids were first aimed at suppressing rebels like the Qārinid Māzyār (see above, no. 80) and keeping in check, also in the Caspian provinces, the Zaydī Shīʿīs; but latterly, their position was threatened by the rising power of the Ṣaffārids in Sistan (Sīstān) (see below, no. 84, 1), an administrative dependency of Khurasan, and this they failed to withstand. Muḥammad b. Ṭāhir II lost Nishapur to Yaʿqūb b. al-Layth in 259/873, and eventually escaped to Iraq. The caliph reappointed him to the governorship of Khurasan, but he was never able to take this up, and for the next twenty years the province was disputed by the Ṣaffārids and several local commanders.

Khurasan was, however, only one of the governorships held by the house of Muṣʿab b. Ruzayq, for other members functioned as military governors in Baghdad and Iraq until the end of the ninth century, a longer tenure of office than their kinsmen in Khurasan. After Ṭāhir I left for the East, his command in Baghdad was at first given to the parallel branch of the Muṣʿabids, but then after 237/851 the descendants of Ṭāhir I took over. The Ṭāhirids' position in Baghdad was based on their great wealth and estates there, in particular, their *Ḥarīm*, a complex of buildings and markets to the north of al-Manṣūr's Round City. The governors in Baghdad were renowned as patrons of Arabic culture, and some of them, like ʿUbaydallāh b. ʿAbdallāh, themselves enjoyed contemporary reputations as littérateurs.

Justi, 436; Lane-Poole, 128; Sachau, 19–20 no. 39; Zambaur, 197–8; Album, 32.

EI[1] 'Ṭāhirids' (W. Barthold).

Saʿīd Nafīsī, *Ta'rīkh-i khāndān-i Ṭāhirī. I. Ṭāhir b. Ḥusayn*, Tehran 1335/1956, with a genealogical table at the end.

C. E. Bosworth, 'The Ṭāhirids and Ṣaffārids', in *The Cambridge History of Iran*, IV, 90–106, 114–15.

Mongi Kaabi, *Les Ṭāhirides au Ḫurāsān et en Iraq (IIIième H./IXième J.C.)*, 2 vols, Tunis 1983, with a genealogical table at I, 409.

83

THE SĀMĀNIDS
204–395/819–1005
Transoxania and Khurasan

⊘ 204/819	Aḥmad I b. Asad b. Sāmān Khudā, originally governor of Farghāna and then of Soghdia
⊘ 250/864	Naṣr I b. Aḥmad I, ruler in Samarkand
⊘ 279/892	Ismāʿīl b. Aḥmad I, Abū Ibrāhīm al-Amīr al-Māḍī
⊘ 295/907	Aḥmad II b. Ismāʿīl, Abū Naṣr al-Amīr al-Shahīd
⊘ 301/914	Naṣr II b. Aḥmad II, al-Amīr al-Saʿīd
⊘ 331/943	Nūḥ I b. Naṣr II, al-Amīr al-Ḥamīd
⊘ 343/954	ʿAbd al-Malik I b. Nūḥ I, Abu ʾl-Fawāris al-Amīr al-Muʾayyad or al-Muwaffaq
⊘ 350/961	Manṣūr I b. Nūḥ I, Abū Ṣāliḥ al-Amīr al-Sadīd
⊘ 365/976	Nūḥ II b. Manṣūr I, al-Amīr al-Raḍī
⊘ 387/997	Manṣūr II b. Nūḥ II, Abu ʾl-Ḥārith
⊘ 389/999	ʿAbd al-Malik II b. Nūḥ II, Abu ʾl-Fawāris
⊘ 390-5/1000-5	Ismāʿīl II b. Nūḥ II, Abū Ibrāhīm al-Muntaṣir
395/1005	*Definitive division of the Sāmānid territories between the Qarakhanids and the Ghaznawids*

The founder of the Sāmānid line was one Sāmān Khudā, a *dihqān* or local landowner in the Balkh district of what is now northern Afghanistan, although the dynasty later claimed descent from the pre-Islamic Sāsānid emperors of Persia. Sāmān Khudā became a Muslim, and his four grandsons served the ʿAbbāsid caliph al-Maʾmūn as sub-governors for the Ṭāhirids of Khurasan (see above, no. 82, 1): Nūḥ was appointed governor of Samarkand (Samarqand), Aḥmad of Farghāna, Yaḥyā of Shāsh (the later Tashkent) and Ilyās of Herat (Harāt). The branch south of the Oxus did not prosper, but the others acquired a good foothold in Transoxania so that in 263/875 Naṣr b. Aḥmad received from al-Muʿtamid the governorship of that complete province. This rich region became the core of the Sāmānids' empire, and they took over also the duties of defending Transoxania's territorial integrity and its commercial interests from attack by the pagan Turks of the steppes. The northern fringes of Transoxania and Farghāna were definitely secured for Islam, and expeditions mounted into the steppes against the Qarluq and other Turkish tribes. By making their military might feared within the steppes and by keeping caravan routes across Inner Asia open, the Sāmānids assured the economic well-being of their lands; it was through their agency that many of the Turkish slaves, employed from the ninth century onwards very extensively in the armies of Muslim princes of the central and eastern lands, were imported. Backed by this prosperity, the amīrs made their court at Bukhara not only a centre of Arabic learning but also of the renaissance of New Persian language and literature, and it was under Sāmānid rule that Firdawsī began his poetic version of the Persian national epic, the *Shāh-nāma*.

In 287/900, Ismāʿīl b. Aḥmad earned the caliph's gratitude by defeating and capturing the Ṣaffārid ʿAmr b. al-Layth (see below, no. 84, 1), and was rewarded with the governorship of Khurasan in succession to the Ṭāhirids and Ṣaffārids. The Sāmānids were now the greatest power in the east, strong proponents of Sunnī orthodoxy there, and exercising suzerainty over outlying regions like Khwārazm, the upper Oxus lands and Sistan, while in northern Persia they were rivals of the Būyids (see above, no. 75), But in the middle years of the tenth century, ominous signs of instability appeared in the Sāmānid state. A series of palace revolutions showed that the military classes, opposed to the amīrs' policies of centralisation, were gaining control, while revolts in Khurasan abstracted that province from the direct authority of Bukhara. It was therefore not difficult for the Turkish Qarakhanids and Ghaznawids (see below, nos 90, 158) to take over the Sāmānid territories, and the last fugitive Sāmānid, Ismāʿīl al-Muntaṣir, was killed in 395/1005. The downfall of the dynasty meant that all the hitherto Iranian lands north of the Oxus passed under Turkish control, and there now began there a process of ethnic and linguistic Turkification, substantially completed – except in what is now the Tajikistan Republic and to a lesser extent in Uzbekistan – by modern times.

Justi, 440; Lane-Poole, 131–3; Zambaur, 202–3; Album, 33.
EI² 'Sāmānids' (C. E. Bosworth).
W. Barthold, *Turkestan down to the Mongol Invasion*, 3rd edn, London 1968.
R. N. Frye, 'The Sāmānids', in *The Cambridge History of Iran*, IV, 136–61.
W. L. Treadwell, *The Political History of the Sāmānid State*, D.Phil. thesis, Oxford 1991, unpubl.

84

THE ṢAFFĀRIDS
247–393/861–1003

Centre of their power in Sistan, with an empire extending at times into Persia and eastern Afghanistan

1. The Laythid branch

⊘ 247/861	Yaʿqūb b. al-Layth al-Ṣaffār, Abū Yūsuf
⊘ 265/879	ʿAmr b. al-Layth, Abū Ḥafṣ
⊘ *(261–8/875–82*	*Aḥmad b. ʿAbdallāh Khujistānī, Abū Shujāʿ, rebel in Nishapur)*
⊘ *(268–83/882–96*	*Rāfiʿ b. Harthama, rebel and caliphal governor in Nishapur and then Rayy)*
⊘ 287/900	Ṭāhir b. Muḥammad b. ʿAmr, Abu ʾl-Ḥasan, with his brother Yaʿqūb, Abū Yūsuf
⊘ 296/909	al-Layth b. ʿAlī b. al-Layth
298/910	Muḥammad b. ʿAlī
⊘ 298/910	al-Muʿaddal b. ʿAlī
298/911	*First Sāmānid occupation of Sīstān*
299/912	*Revolt of ⊘ Muḥammad b. Hurmuz*
299-300	ʿAmr b. Yaʿqūb b. Muḥammad b. ʿAmr, Abū Ḥafṣ
300-1/912-14	*Second Sāmānid occupation*
301-11/914-23	*Seizure of power by the local commanders Aḥmad Niyā, Kuthayyir b. Aḥmad, ⊘ Aḥmad b. Qudām and ⊘ ʿAbdallāh b. Aḥmad*

2. The Khalafid branch

⊘ 311/923	Aḥmad b. Muḥammad b. Khalaf, Abū Jaʿfar
⊘ 352–93/963–1003	Khalaf b. Aḥmad, Abū Aḥmad Walī ʾl-Dawla, d. 309/1009
⊘ (352–8/963–9	Tāhir b. Muḥammad, Abu ʾl-Ḥusayn, descendant of ʿAlī b. al-Layth, regent for Khalaf, d. 359/970)
⊘ *(359–73/970–83*	*Ḥusayn b. Ṭāhir Tamīmī, rebel)*
393/1003	*Ghaznawid occupation*

The Ṣaffārid brothers derived their name from their founder Yaʿqūb's trade of coppersmith (*ṣaffār*). Under Yaʿqūb and ʿAmr, their native province of Sistan became the centre of a vast but transient empire which covered almost all Persia except for the north-west and the Caspian region and which stretched to the frontiers of India. In the ninth century, Sistan was much disturbed by social and sectarian unrest; it had long been a refuge area for various malcontents and schismatics fleeing eastwards through Persia, including the Khārijīs, defeated and dispersed by the Umayyad governors. It may be that Yaʿqūb had been a Khārijī himself; the nucleus of his forces lay in the bands of local vigilantes defending the cause of Sunnī orthodoxy in Sistan, but his troops came to include many former Khārijīs also. With this army, Yaʿqūb expanded eastwards to Kabul (Kābul), then a pagan region on the fringe of the Indian world, and overturned the native dynasty there. In the west, he attacked the Ṭāhirids (see above, no. 82) in 259/873, wresting from them their capital Nishapur and ending their governorship over Khurasan. He was bold enough to invade Iraq and mount an attack on the heart of the caliphate itself, but this was halted on the banks of the Tigris in 262/876.

Whereas the Ṭāhirids and Sāmānids (see above, nos 82, 83) represented the interests of religious orthodoxy and the social *status quo*, the Ṣaffārid chiefs were plebeian in origin and proud of it, and they openly proclaimed their contempt for the ʿAbbāsids. Thus they effectively demolished the 'caliphal fiction' whereby provincial governors and rulers derived legitimacy for their authority from an ostensible act of delegation by the head of the Islamic community. ʿAmr b. al-Layth was recognised by the ʿAbbāsid ruler as his governor in several Persian provinces and, eventually, in Khurasan. However, not content with these extensive territories, ʿAmr coveted Transoxania also, which had been nominally under Ṭāhirid oversight. But the actual holders of power there, the Sāmānids, proved more than a match for the Ṣaffārids; ʿAmr overreached himself and was disastrously defeated. Being a personal creation of military conquerors, the Ṣaffārid empire lost its Khurasanian provinces, and in the early tenth century, after a series of weaker, ephemeral amīrs, passed temporarily under Sāmānid control.

Despite this severe check, the Ṣaffārids were to revive, and it is clear that they to some extent represented the interests and aspirations of the people of Sistan from whom they had sprung. From 311/923, the Ṣaffārids reappear as local rulers in Sistan and adjacent regions. The two amīrs of this line, from a collateral branch of the family, achieved widespread reputations as Maecenases and, in the case of Khalaf b. Aḥmad, as a scholar in his own right. In 393/1003, the aggressive and expansionist Maḥmūd of Ghazna (see below, no. 158) incorporated Sistan into his empire, an event which the patriotic anonymous author of a local history, the *Ta'rīkh-i Sīstān*, regards as a disaster for the land.

It should be noted that the convenient division of the Ṣaffārids into 'Laythids' and 'Khalafids' corresponds to the 'first line' and 'second line' in Zambaur's listing of the Ṣaffārids, but that his third and fourth lines have no demonstrable connection with the Ṣaffārid ruling house; for these, the so-called Maliks of Nīmrūz, see below, no. 106.

Justi, 439; Lane-Poole, 129–30 (ignores all but the very first Ṣaffārids); Sachau, 11 no. 16; Zambaur, 199–201 (see the remarks above); Album, 32.

EI^2 'Ṣaffārids' (C. E. Bosworth).

Milton Gold (tr.), *The Tārikh-e Sistān*, Rome 1976.

C. E. Bosworth, 'The Ṭāhirids and Ṣaffārids', in *The Cambridge History of Iran*, IV, 106–35.

idem, *The History of the Saffarids of Sistan and the Maliks of Nimruz (247/861 to 949/1542–3)*, Costa Mesa CA and New York 1994, 67–361, with genealogical tables at pp. xxiii–xxiv.

85

THE BĀNĪJŪRIDS OR ABŪ DĀWŪDIDS

c. 233–c. 295/c. 848–c. 908

Balkh and Ṭukhāristān

? Hāshim b. Bānījūr, in Khuttal, d. 243/857
⊘ 233/848 Dāwūd b. al-ʿAbbās b. Hāshim, in Balkh, d. 259/873
⊘ 260/874 Muḥammad b. Aḥmad b. Bānījūr, Abū Dāwūd, previously governor of Andarāba and Panjhīr, still ruling in 285/898 or 286/899
⊘ ? Aḥmad b. Muḥammad, in Balkh and Andarāba until c. 295/c. 908

The Bānījūrids were a line of local rulers, vassals of the Sāmānids (see above, no. 83), who ruled at Balkh and Andarāba in the region of Ṭukhāristān to the south of the middle Oxus, and generally also at Panjhīr in the Hindu Kush, famed for its silver mines. They were most probably of Iranian origin. Their ancestor Bānījūr, a contemporary of the first ʿAbbāsid caliphs, had connections with Farghāna, but both the affiliations and the chronology of his line are extremely obscure. From the early tenth century, other local chiefs seem to have controlled Ṭukhāristān, but it is possible that a line of local princes to the north of the Middle Oxus, in Khuttal, were kinsmen of the Bānījūrids.

Zambaur, 202, 204; Album, 33.

EI[2] Suppl. 'Bānīdjūrids' (C. E. Bosworth).

R. Vasmer, 'Beiträge zur muhammedanischen Münzkunde. I. Die Münzen der Abū Dā'udiden', NZ, N.F. 18 (1925), 49–62.

Muḥammad Abū-l-Faraj 'Ush, 'Dirhams Abu Dāwūdides (Banū Bānījūrī)', *Revue Numismatique*, 6th series, 15 (1973), 169–76.

86

THE SĪMJŪRIDS

300–92/913–1002

Governors in Khurasan and feudatories in Quhistān

300-1/913-14	Sīmjūr al-Dawātī, Abū ʿImrān, governor for the Sāmānids in Sistan, d. between 318/930 and 324/936
310–14/922–6	Ibrāhīm b. Sīmjūr, Abū ʿAlī, first governorship in Khurasan
333–4/945–6	Ibrāhīm b. Sīmjūr, second governorship, d. 336/948
345–9/956–60	Muḥammad I b. Ibrāhīm, Abu ʾl-Ḥasan, first governorship in Khurasan
350–71/961–82	Muḥammad I b. Ibrāhīm, second governorship, d. 378/989
⊘ 374–7/984–7	Muḥammad II b. Muḥammad I, Abū ʿAlī al-Muẓaffar ʿImād al-Dawla, Amīr al-Umarāʾ, al-Muʾayyad min al-Samāʾ, first governorship in Khurasan
385/995	Muḥammad II, second governorship, d. 387/997
?	ʿAlī b. Muḥammad I, Abu ʾl-Qāsim, commander in Khurasan until 392/1002, d. at some point thereafter

The Sīmjūrids began as Turkish military slaves of the Sāmānids (see above, no. 83), Sīmjūr being the ceremonial ink-stand bearer (*dawātī*) of Ismāʿīl b. Aḥmad. He rose to prominence when the Sāmānids temporarily drove out the Ṣaffārids (see above, no. 84) and occupied Sistan. Thereafter, the family were prominent throughout the tenth century in the warfare of the Sāmānids with their enemies in northern and eastern Persia, often as governors in Khurasan and with a territorial base in their Quhistān estates, and were finally involved in the chaos there as the Sāmānid amirate broke up, after which the family largely drops out of mention.

Sachau, 11 no. 15; Zambaur, 205.

*EI*² ʻSīmdjūridsʼ (C. E. Bosworth).

Erdoğan Merçil, *Sîmcûrîler*, n.p. n.d. = a series of articles in *Tarih Dergisi*, no. 32 (1979), 71–88; *Tarih Enstitüsü Dergisi*, nos 10–11 (1979–80), 91–6; *Tarih Dergisi*, no. 33 (1980–1), 115–32; *Belleten*, 49, no. 195 (1985), 547; and *Tarih Enstitüsü Dergisi*, no. 13 (1989), 123–38, with a genealogical table at p. 138.

87

THE ILYĀSIDS
320–57/932–68
Kirman

320–2/932–4	Muḥammad b. Ilyās, Abū ʿAlī, governor for the Sāmānids, first tenure of power
322/934	*Expulsion by Mākān b. Kākī*
324/936	Muḥammad b. Ilyās, second tenure of power, abdicated 356/967
356–7/967–8	Ilyasaʿ b. Muḥammad
357/968	*Būyid conquest of Kirman*

Muḥammad b. Ilyās was a commander, of Soghdian origin, in the service of the Sāmānid Naṣr II b. Aḥmad (see above, no. 83), who, after the failure of the rebellion of the Amīr's brothers at Bukhara in 317/929, eventually withdrew southwards to Kirman, where there was something of a power vacuum after the waning of ʿAbbāsid control in southern Persia. There he successfully established himself, fighting off the Daylamī commander Mākān and acting nominally as governor for the Sāmānids but in practice independent. He was compelled by his sons to abdicate after a reign of thirty-six years, but it was at this point that the powerful Būyid Amīr ʿAḍud al-Dawla turned his attention to Kirman, and this proved fatal for the short-lived line of the Ilyāsids, with Ilyasaʿ driven out to Transoxania. Various Ilyāsids attempted revanches, but Kirman was to remain generally under Būyid control until the advent of the Seljuqs (see below, no. 91, 3).

Sachau, 10–11 no. 14; Zambaur, 216.
*EI*² 'Ilyāsids' (C. E. Bosworth).
C. E. Bosworth, 'The Banū Ilyās of Kirmān (320–57/932–68)', in idem (ed.), *Iran and Islam, in memory of the late Vladimir Minorsky*, 107–24.

88

THE MUḤTĀJIDS

321–43/933–54

Governors in Khurasan and Amīrs of Chaghāniyān

321/933	Muḥammad b. al-Muẓaffar b. Muḥtāj, Abū Bakr, governor in Khurasan, d. 329/941
⊘ 327/939	Aḥmad b. Muḥammad, Abū ʿAlī, first governorship in Khurasan
333/945	*Governorship of Ibrāhīm b. Sīmjūr*
335/946	Aḥmad b. Muḥammad, second governorship
335/947	*Governorship of Manṣūr b. Qaratigin*
340-3/952-4	Aḥmad b. Muḥammad, third governorship, d. 344/955
late fourth/tenth and early fifth/eleventh centuries	Muḥammad b. ?, Abu 'l-Muẓaffar Fakhr al-Dawla, Amīr of Chaghāniyān, ? a Muḥtājid

The Muḥtāj family were hereditary lords of the principality of Chaghāniyān on the north bank of the middle Oxus, but whether they were descendants of the indigenous, presumably Iranian, Chaghān Khudās from the time of the Arab invasions, or possibly Persianised Arabs, is unknown. They appear as commanders for the Sāmānids, and then as governors and commanders-in-chief in Khurasan for the Amīrs, in the second quarter of the tenth century. Abū ʿAlī Aḥmad was a dominant figure there, but eventually died in exile. It seems, however, that the Muḥtājids retained their local base in Chaghāniyān, possibly into the eleventh century, since local princes there are mentioned, although their affiliation to the original line is uncertain.

Zambaur, 204; Album, 33.

EI[2] 'Muḥtādjids' (C. E. Bosworth); EIr 'Āl-e Moḥtāj' (Bosworth).

C. E. Bosworth, 'The rulers of Chaghāniyān in early Islamic times', *Iran, JBIPS*, 19 (1981), 1–20.

89

THE KHWĀRAZM SHĀHS

Pre-Islamic times to the seventh/thirteenth century

Khwārazm

1. The Afrīghids of Kāth (pre-Islamic times to 385/995)

Sixteen Shāhs are listed by al-Bīrūnī, the tenth, Arthamūkh b. Būzkār, being allegedly a contemporary of the Prophet Muḥammad. The first Shāh with an Islamic name is the seventeenth:

ʿAbdallāh b. T.r.k.s.bātha, ? early third/ninth century
Manṣūr b. ʿAbdallāh
ʿIrāq b. Manṣūr, reigning in 285/898
Muḥammad b. ʿIrāq, reigning in 309/921
ʿAbdallāh b. Ashkam, not listed by al-Bīrūnī but ruling c. 332/c. 944
⊘ Aḥmad b. Muḥammad, Abū Saʿīd, ruling in 356/967
⊘ Muḥammad b. Aḥmad, Abū ʿAbdallāh, d. 385/995
Ma'mūnid conquest

2. The Ma'mūnids of Gurgānj (385–408/995–1017)

385/995	Ma'mūn I b. Muḥammad, Abū ʿAlī
⊘ 387/997	ʿAlī b. Ma'mūn I, Abu 'l-Ḥasan
399/1009	Ma'mūn II b. Ma'mūn I, Abu 'l-ʿAbbās
407–8/1017	Muḥammad b. ʿAlī, Abu 'l-Ḥārith
408/1017	*Ghaznawid conquest*

3. The Ghaznawid governors with the title of Khwārazm Shāh (408–32/1017–41)

408/1017	Altuntash Ḥājib, Ghaznawid commander
423/1032	Hārūn b. Altuntash, lieutenant of the nominal Khwārazm Shāh, Saʿīd b. Masʿūd of Ghazna, later independent of Ghazna, probably then himself assuming the title Khwārazm Shāh
425/1034	Ismāʿīl b. Khāndān b. Altuntash, independent of Ghazna, styling himself Khwārazm Shāh
432/1041	*Conquest of Khwārazm by the Oghuz Yabghu, Shāh Malik b. ʿAlī, Abu 'l-Fawāris, of Jand, probably receiving the title Khwārazm Shāh from Masʿūd of Ghazna*

4. The line of Anūshtigin Shiḥna, originally as governors for the Seljuqs with the title of Khwārazm Shāh, from towards the mid-twelfth century often in practice largely independent rulers in Khwārazm and, at times, in Transoxania and Persia (c. 470–628/c. 1077–1231)

c. 470/c. 1077	*Anūshtigin Gharcha'ī, nominal Khwārazm Shāh*

490/1097	*Ekinchi b. Qochqar, Turkish governor with the title Khwārazm Shāh*
490/1097	Arslan Tigin Muḥammad b. Anūshtigin, Abu 'l-Fatḥ, Quṭb al-Dīn, Khwārazm Shāh
⊘ 521/1127	Qïzïl Arslan Atsïz b. Muḥammad, Abu 'l-Muẓaffar 'Alā' al-Dīn
⊘ 551/1156	Il Arslan b. Atsïz, Abu 'l-Fatḥ
⊘ 567/1172	Tekish b. Il Arslan, Abu 'l-Muẓaffar Tāj al-Dunyā wa 'l-Dīn
⊘ *567–89/1172–93*	*Maḥmūd b. Il Arslan, Abu 'l-Qāsim Sulṭān Shāh, Jalāl al-Dunyā wa 'l-Dīn, rival ruler in northern Khurasan, d. 589/1193*
⊘ 596/1200	Muḥammad b. Tekish, 'Alā' al-Dīn
⊘ 617–28/1220–31	Mengübirti (one of the usual renderings of this cryptic Turkish name; a further possibility suggested recently by Dr Peter Jackson is Mingīrinī 'having a thousand men' = the familiar Persian name Hazārmard) b. Muḥammad, Jalāl al-Dīn
	Mongol conquest of Transoxania and Persia

Khwārazm, the classical Chorasmia, was the well-irrigated, rich agricultural region on the lower Oxus, in later times the Khanate of Khiva. Surrounded as it was on all sides by steppeland and desert, it was isolated geographically, and this isolation long enabled it to maintain a separate political existence and a distinctive Iranian language and culture. Khwārazm may well have been an early home of the Iranians; certainly, the local historian and antiquary al-Bīrūnī (d. 440/1048) traced the beginnings of political life there beyond the first millennium BC. He placed the beginning of the Iranian Afrīghid dynasty in c. AD 305, and listed twenty-two Shāhs of this line down to its extinction in 385/995. Khwārazm first came into the purview of Islamic history in 93/712, when the Arab governor of Khurasan, Qutayba b. Muslim, invaded Khwārazm and wrought considerable destruction, it is reported, to the indigenous civilisation there. It thus came vaguely under Muslim suzerainty, but it was not until the end of the eighth century or the beginning of the ninth century that an Afrīghid was first converted to the new faith, appearing with the traditional convert's name of 'Abdallāh. The Islamic names of subsequent Shāhs are henceforth attested, though not their exact chronology, since al-Bīrūnī provides no dates.

In the course of the tenth century, the city of Gurgānj on the left bank of the Oxus grew in economic and political importance, largely because of its position as the terminus for the caravan trade across the steppes to the Volga and Russia. A local family, the Ma'mūnids, in 385/995 violently overthrew the Afrīghids of Kāth (which lay on the right bank of the river), and themselves assumed the traditional title of Khwārazm Shāh. The rule of the Ma'mūnids was brief but quite glorious; great scholars like the philosopher and scientist Ibn Sīnā (Avicenna) and the littérateur al-Tha'ālibī flourished under their patronage. Khwārazm had been theoretically under Sāmānid suzerainty, although in practice this had meant little; but in 408/1017, Maḥmūd of Ghazna, heir to the Sāmānids' power in Khurasan, resolved to add Khwārazm to his empire, and Ma'mūnid rule was ended there. For the next decade or so, the province was governed by Ghaznawid military commanders, and then fell into the hands of Shāh Malik, the Oghuz Turkish Yabghu or ruler of Jand at the mouth of the Syr Darya. However, very soon, in 432/1041, Shāh Malik was overthrown by his rivals from the Seljuq family of the Oghuz (see below, no. 91, 1), and soon afterwards Khwārazm passed under Seljuq control.

The Great Seljuq sultans appointed their own governors to Khwārazm, and in Malik Shāh's reign his Turkish slave commander Anūshtigin Gharcha'ī, who was keeper of the royal washing-bowls (*ṭasht-dār*) received the nominal title of Khwārazm Shāh, although he never seems to have gone there. His successors, however, became hereditary governors in Khwārazm, with the practical title of Shāh; this line of Anūshtigin was strongly Turkish in ethos, seen by the prevalence among them of Turkish names, and close connections, including by means of marriage alliances, were kept up with the Inner Asian steppes. Anūshtigin's grandson Atsïz, while remaining nominally a vassal of the sultans, had ambitions of striking out on a more independent policy. This became possible after Sanjar's disastrous defeat of 535/1141 by the Qara Khitay (see below, no. 90), but the Shāhs were in turn forced to acknowledge the suzerainty of these new invaders from the Far East. In effect, the Qara Khitay left the Shāhs largely to themselves, and the last decades of the twelfth century were taken up with a prolonged struggle for hegemony in Khurasan and the whole of the Iranian East between the Shāhs and the Ghūrids of Afghanistan (see below, no. 159). By the opening years of the thirteenth century, the Shāhs were triumphant, and were able to expand right across Persia, clearing away from there the last remnants of Great Seljuq rule and even daring to confront the ʿAbbāsid caliphs in Baghdad. They thus became masters of an empire stretching from the borders of India to those of Anatolia. Yet this impressive achievement proved transitory. In 617/1220, Chingiz Khān's Mongols conquered Transoxania, and the reign of the last Khwārazm Shāh, Jalāl al-Dīn, was spent in heroic but futile attempts to stem the Mongol influx into the Middle East.

In subsequent centuries, Khwārazm came under the rule of various Turco-Mongol and Turkish Central Asian steppe peoples, and its original Iranian character was completely overlaid, although the prestigious title of Khwārazm Shāh seems to have been borne by the governors there for the Tīmūrids as late as the fifteenth century.

Justi, 428; Lane-Poole, 176–8 (the Anūshtiginids only); Sachau, 12 no. 17 (the Ma'mūnids); Zambaur, 208–9; Album, 38–9.

E. Sachau, 'Zur Geschichte und Chronologie von Khwârazm', *SBWAW*, 73 (1873), 471–506; 74 (1873), 285–330 (includes a list of the Afrīghids as given by al-Bīrūnī).

W. Barthold, *Turkestan down to the Mongol Invasion*, 3rd edn, 144–55, 185, 275–9, 323ff.

İbrahim Kafesoğlu, *Harezmşahlar devleti tarihi (485–617/1092–1229)*, Ankara 1956 (on the Anūshtiginids).

C. E. Bosworth, in *The Cambridge History of Iran*, V, 140ff., 181ff., 185–95 (on the Anūshtiginids).

L. Richter-Bernburg, 'Zur Titulatur der Ḫwārezm-Šāhe aus der Dynastie Anūštegins', *AMI*, N.F., 9 (1976), 179–205.

90

THE QARAKHĀNIDS
382–609/992–1212
Transoxania, Farghāna, Semirechye and eastern Turkestan

'Alī b. Mūsā b. Satuq Bughra Khān (d. 388/998) and ⊘ Hārūn or Ḥasan b. Sulaymān b. Satuq Bughra Khān, Ilig, Bughra Khān, Shihāb al-Dawla (d. 382/992), joint founders of the Qarakhānid confederation in Transoxania

1. The Great Qaghans of the united kingdom

⊘ ?	'Alī b. Mūsā, Abu 'l-Ḥasan Arslan Khān Qara Khān
⊘ 388/998	Aḥmad b. 'Alī, Arslan Qara Khān, Toghan Khān, Nāṣir al-Ḥaqq Quṭb al-Dawla
⊘ 408/1017	Manṣūr b. 'Alī, Arslan Khān, Nūr al-Dawla
⊘ 415/1024	Muḥammad or Aḥmad b. Hārūn or Ḥasan Bughra Khān, Toghan Khān
⊘ 417–24/1026–32	Yūsuf b. Hārūn or Ḥasan Bughra Khān, Qadïr Khān, Nāṣir al-Dawla Malik al-Mashriq wa 'l-Ṣīn

2. The Great Qaghans of the western kingdom (Transoxania, including Bukhara and Samarkand, and Farghāna at times), with its centre at Samarkand

⊘ after c. 411/c. 1020, in control of Soghdia	'Alī Tigin b. Hārūn or Ḥasan Bughra Khān, d. 425/1034
425/1034	⊘ Yūsuf and Arslan Tigin b. 'Alī Tigin, their father's successors in Soghdia)
⊘ c. 433/c. 1042	Muḥammad b. Naṣr b. 'Alī, Arslan Qara Khān Mu'ayyid al-'Adl 'Ayn al-Dawla
⊘ c. 444/c. 1052	Ibrāhīm b. Naṣr b. 'Alī, Abu Isḥāq Böri Tigin, Tamghach or Tabghach Bughra Khān, victor over the sons of 'Alī Tigin
460/1068	Naṣr b. Ibrāhīm, Abu 'l-Ḥasan Shams al-Mulk Malik al-Mashriq wa 'l-Ṣīn
472/1080	Khiḍr b. Ibrāhīm, Abū Shujā'
?473/1081	Aḥmad b. Khiḍr
482/1089	Ya'qūb b. Sulaymān b. Yūsuf Qadïr Khān
488/1095	Mas'ūd b. Muḥammad b. Ibrāhīm
⊘ 490/1097	Sulaymān b. Dāwūd b. Ibrāhīm, Qadïr Tamghach or Tabghach Khān
⊘ 490/1097	Maḥmūd b. ... Manṣūr b. 'Alī Abu 'l-Qāsim Arslan Khān
⊘ 492/1099	Jibrā'īl b. 'Umar, Qadïr Khān
⊘ 495/1102	Muḥammad b. Sulaymān, Arslan Khān
?523/1129	Naṣr b. Muḥammad

⊘ ?523/1129	Aḥmad b. Muḥammad, Qadïr Khān
524/1130	Ḥasan b. 'Alī, Jalāl al-Dunyā wa 'l-Dīn
?526/1132	Ibrāhīm b. Sulaymān, Abu 'l-Muẓaffar Rukn al-Dunyā wa 'l-Dīn
526/1132	Maḥmūd b. Muḥammad (later, ruler of Khurasan after the Seljuq Sanjar: see below, no. 91, 1)
536/1141	*Occupation of Transoxania by the Qara Khitay*
536/1141	Ibrāhīm b. Muḥammad, Tamghach or Tabghach Khān
551/1156	'Alī b. Ḥasan, Chaghrï Khān
⊘ 556/1161	Mas'ūd b. Ḥasan, Abu 'l-Muẓaffar Tamghach or Tabghach Khān, Rukn al-Dunyā wa 'l-Dīn
566/1171	Muḥammad b Mas'ūd, Tamghach or Tabghach Khān, Ghiyāth al-Dunyā wa 'l-Dīn, d. 569/1174
574/1178	Ibrāhīm b. Ḥusayn, Arslan Khān Ulugh Sulṭān al-Salāṭīn Nuṣrat al-Dunyā wa 'l-Dīn (before 574/1178 in Farghāna, therafter in Samarkand also)
600–9/1204–12	'Uthmān b. Ibrāhīm, Ulugh Sulṭān al-Salāṭīn, vassal on various occasions of the Qara Khitay and the Khwārazm Shāhs
609/1212	*Occupation of Transoxania by the Khwārazm Shāh*

3. The Great Qaghans of the eastern kingdom (Īlāq, Talas, Shāsh, at times Farghāna, Semirechye, Kāshghar and Khotan), with its centre at Balāsāghūn, later Kāshghar

423/1032	Sulaymān b. Yūsuf, Abū Shujā' Qadïr Khan, Arslan Khān, Sharaf al-Dawla
448/1056	Muḥammad b. Yūsuf Qadïr Khān, Bughra Khān, Qawām al-Dawla
449/1057	Ibrāhīm b. Muḥammad
451/1059	Maḥmūd b. Yūsuf Qadïr Khān, Ṭoghrïl Qara Khān, Niẓām al-Dawla
467/1074	'Umar b. Maḥmūd, Ṭoghrïl Tigin
467/1075	Hārūn or Ḥasan b. Sulaymān, Abū 'Alī Tamghach or Tabghach Bughra Qara Khān, Nāṣir al-Haqq
496/1103	Aḥmad or Hārūn b. Hārūn or Ḥasan, Nūr al-Dawla
522/1128	Ibrāhīm b. Aḥmad or Hārūn
553/1158	Muḥammad b. Ibrāhīm, Arslan Khān
?	Yūsuf b. Muḥammad, Abu 'l-Muẓaffar Arslan Khān, d. 601/1205
607/1211	Muḥammad b. Yūsuf, Abu 'l-Faṭh, d. 607/1211
607/1211	*Occupation of Semirechye and Farghāna by the Nayman Mongol Küchlüg*

4. The Qaghans in Farghāna, with their centre in Uzgend

⊘ 386–403/996–1013	Naṣr b. 'Alī b. Mūsā, Tigin, Ilig Khān
⊘ 403–15/1013–24	Manṣūr b. 'Alī b. Mūsā, Abu 'l-Muẓaffar Arslan Khān, Sharaf al-Dawla

⊘ c. 432/c. 1041	Muḥammad b. Naṣr b. ʿAlī, ʿAyn al-Dawla, under the suzerainty of the eastern kingdom, d. c. 444/c. 1052
⊘ by 451/1059	Ibrāhīm b. Naṣr, Abū Isḥāq Tamghach or Tabghach Khān
?	ʿAbd al-Mu'min
?	ʿAlī b. ʿAbd al-Mu'min
?	Ḥasan (Tigin) b. ʿAlī
526/1132	Ḥusayn b. Ḥasan (Tigin), Jalāl al-Dunyā wa 'l-Dīn
⊘ 551/1156	Maḥmūd b. Ḥusayn, Toghan Khān
⊘ 559/1164	Ibrāhīm b. Ḥusayn, Arslan Khān, after 574/1178 in Samarkand also
⊘ 574/1178	Naṣr b. Ḥusayn
⊘ ?	Muḥammad b. Naṣr, d. c. 578/1182
⊘ by 606/1209	Qadïr Khān b. Ḥusayn or Naṣr, Jalāl al-Dunyā wa 'l-Dīn, vassal of the Khwārazm Shāh
⊘ ? –610/? –1213	Maḥmūd b. Aḥmad, vassal of the Khwārazm Shāh and then of Küchlüg

The Turkish dynasty of the Qarakhānids acquired this name from European orientalists because of the frequency of the word *qara* 'black' > 'northern' (the basic orientation of the early Turks) > 'powerful' in their Turkish titulature; they have also been called the Ilek (properly Ilig) Khāns, again from one of the terms in the hierarchy of this titulature, and Āl-i Afrāsiyāb 'House of Afrāsiyāb' because of a fancied connection with the ruler of Tūrān in Firdawsī's *Shāh-nāma*. It has been suggested by a leading authority on the dynasty, Omeljan Pritsak, that the Qarakhānids sprang from the Qarluq, a tribal group which had been formerly connected with the Uyghur confederation and as such had played an important role in earlier steppe history; another scholar, Elena Davidovich, has suggested a connection with the Yaghma or Chigil tribes, which were in any case components of the Qarluq.

The Qarakhānids became Muslim in the middle years of the tenth century, and their then head Satuq Bughra Khān assumed the Islamic name of ʿAbd al-Karīm. His grandson Hārūn or Ḥasan Bughra Khān was attracted southwards by the unsettled condition of Transoxania caused by the decline there of the Sāmānids, and in 392/992 temporarily occupied Bukhara. A few years later, the Ilig Khān Naṣr and Maḥmūd of Ghazna finally extinguished the authority of the Sāmānids and divided their lands. The Oxus became the boundary between the two empires, and for the next two centuries the territories of the Qarakhānids stretched from Bukhara and the lower Syr Darya in the west to Semirechye and Kashgharia in the east. The Qarakhānids formed a loose confederation rather than a monolithic, unitary state, with various members of the family holding appanages which, if they held more than one, were not necessarily contiguous. Internal quarrels soon appeared, and after c. 432/c. 1041 there were two main parts of the Qarakhānid dominions, a western Khanate centred on Samarkand in Transoxania and at times including Farghāna, while an eastern one included the lands of the middle Syr Darya valley, at times Farghāna, Semirechye, and Kashgharia in eastern Turkestan, with a military capital, the Khāns' *ordu* or encampment, near Balāsāghūn, but with Kāshghar as its religious and cultural centre. Farghāna was a substantial appanage which often had its own hereditary branch of subordinate Khāns. In general, the descendants of the Great Qaghan 'Alī b. Mūsā (the 'Alid branch, in Pritsak's convenient terminology) ruled in the west, while those of his cousin Hārūn or Ḥasan Bughra Khān b. Sulaymān (the Ḥasanid branch) ruled in the east. The boundary between these was not hard and fast, and members of each might rule in the other parts of the Qarakhānid lands; in the later twelfth century, the Ḥasanids were ruling in Samarkand. The western Khanate flourished under such rulers as Ibrāhīm Tamghach or Tabghach Khān, but in the later eleventh century fell under the suzerainty of the Seljuqs. However, after Sanjar's disastrous defeat in the Qaṭwān Steppe in 536/1141, control over the whole of Turkestan west of the T'ien Shan mountains passed to the Buddhist Qara Khitay or Western Liao from northern China. The last western Qarakhanids continued as vassals of the Qara Khitay but failed to maintain their position against the Khwārazm Shāh 'Alā' al-Dīn Muḥammad (see above, no. 89, 4), who in 609/1212 killed the last ruler there, 'Uthmān, while the eastern Khanate fell to the Mongol Küchlüg just before Chingiz Khān's hordes arrived in Central Asia.

Whereas the originally Turkish Ghaznawid sultans built up a strongly centralised state on the familiar Perso-Islamic pattern, the Qarakhānids remained closer to their tribal and steppe past and had a more diffused system of authority, with members of the ruling family allocated their own appanages and the greater part of their tribesmen remaining probably nomadic. Within the ruling family there prevailed the system, common among other Altaic peoples, of Great Qaghans and co-Qaghans, with lesser Khāns beneath them, each with his own suitable Turkish title, often combined with a totemistic title taken from the names of animals, birds, etc., for example *arslan* 'lion', *bughra* 'camel', *toghrïl* and *chaghrï* 'falcon, hawk', etc. Since members of the family were continually moving up in the hierarchy of power and acquiring new names and titles, the task of elucidating the genealogy and chronology of the Qarakhānids is exceedingly difficult; the historical sources are not numerous, and, while large numbers of Qarakhānid coins are extant, these last also present a bewildering array of names and titles. As remarked in the Introduction, Zambaur noted over seventy years ago that this was the only major Islamic dynasty whose genealogy remained obscure, and confessed that his own attempts at constructing a genealogy were necessarily sketchy; many obscurities still remain despite much recent research and many coin finds within Central Asia, the contents of which are increasingly ending up in the West. The tables given above follow the researches of Pritsak supplemented by those more recent ones of Elena Davidovich.

Zambaur, 206–7; Album, 34.

EI^2 'Ilek K͟hāns' (C. E. Bosworth).

O. Pritsak, 'Karachanidische Streitfragen 1–4', *Oriens*, 3 (1950), 209–28.

O. Pritsak, 'Die Karachaniden', *Der Islam*, 31 (1954), 17–68.

Reşat Genç, *Karahanlı devlet teşkilatı (XI. yüzyıl) (Türk hâkimiyet anlayısı ve Karahanlılar)*, Istanbul 1981.

Elena A. Davidovich, 'The Qarakhanids', in *History of the Civilisations of Central Asia*, IV/1, *The Age of Achievement*, UNESCO, Paris 1997, ch. 6.

ELEVEN
The Seljuqs, their Dependants and the Atabegs
91

THE SELJUQS
431–590/1040–1194
Persia, Iraq and Syria

1. The Great Seljuqs in Persia and Iraq 431–590/1040–1194

⊘ 431/1040 Ṭoghrïl (Ṭughril) I Beg Muḥammad b. Mīkā'īl b. Seljuq, Abū Ṭālib Rukn al-Dunyā wa 'l-Dīn, Malik al-Mashriq wa 'l-Maghrib, ruler in northern, western and southern Persia, and supreme Sultan, d. 455/1063

⊘ 431/1040 Chaghrï Beg Dāwūd b. Mīkā'īl b. Seljuq, Malik al-Mulūk, ruler in Khurāsān, d. 452/1060

⊘ 455/1063 Muḥammad Alp Arslan b. Chaghrï Beg Dāwūd, Abū Shujā' 'Aḍud al-Dawla, Ḍiyā' al-Dīn

⊘ 465/1073 Malik Shāh I b. Alp Arslan, Abu 'l-Fatḥ Mu'izz al-Dīn Jalāl al-Dawla

⊘ 485/1092 Maḥmūd I b. Malik Shāh, Nāṣir al-Dunya wa 'l-Dīn

⊘ 487/1094 Berk Yaruq (Barkiyāruq) b. Malik Shāh, Abu 'l-Muẓaffar Rukn al-Dunyā wa 'l-Dīn

⊘ 498/1105 Malik Shāh II b. Berk Yaruq, Rukn al-Dunya wa 'l-Dīn, Jalāl al-Dawla

⊘ 498/1105 Muḥammad I Tapar b. Malik Shāh, Abū Shujā' Ghiyāth al-Dunyā wa 'l-Dīn

⊘ 511–52/1118–57 Aḥmad Sanjar b. Malik Shāh I, Abu 'l-Ḥārith Mu'izz al-Dunyā wa 'l-Dīn, 'Aḍud al-Dawla, ruler in Khurasan 490–552/1097–1157, after 511/1118 supreme Sultan of the Seljuq family

552/1157 Power in Khurasan seized by various Ghuzz and Turkish slave commanders

(In Iraq and western Persia only:)

⊘ 511/1118 Maḥmūd II b. Muḥammad I, Abu 'l-Qāsim Mughīth al-Dunyā wa 'l-Dīn Jalāl al-Dawla

⊘ 525/1131 Dāwūd b. Maḥmūd II, Abu 'l-Fatḥ Ghiyāth al-Dunyā wa 'l-Dīn, in Azerbaijan and Jibāl, d. 538/1143

⊘ 526/1132 Ṭoghrïl II b. Muḥammad I, Rukn al-Dunyā wa 'l-Dīn, d. 529/1134

⊘ 529/1134 Mas'ūd b. Muḥammad I, Abu 'l-Fatḥ Ghiyāth al-Dunyā wa 'l-Dīn

⊘ 547/1152	Malik Shāh III b. Maḥmūd II, Muʿīn al-Dunyā wa 'l-Dīn
⊘ 548/1153	Muḥammad II b. Maḥmūd II, Rukn al-Dunyā wa 'l-Dīn, d. 554/1159
⊘ 555/1160	Sulaymān Shāh b. Muḥammad I, Ghiyāth al-Dunyā wa 'l-Dīn, d. 556/1161
⊘ 556/1161	Arslan (Shāh) b. Ṭoghrïl II, Abu 'l-Muẓaffar Muʿizz al-Dunyā wa 'l-Dīn
⊘ 571–90/1176–94	Ṭoghrïl III b. Arslan (Shāh), Rukn al-Dunyā wa 'l-Dīn *Khwārazmian conquest*

2. The Seljuqs of Syria 471–511/1078–1117

⊘ 471/1078	Tutush I b. Alp Arslan, Abū Saʿīd Tāj al-Dawla
⊘ 488–507/ 1095–1113	Riḍwān b. Tutush, Fakhr al-Mulk, in Aleppo, d. 507/1113
488–97/1095–1104	Duqaq b. Tutush I, Abū Naṣr Shams al-Mulūk, in Damascus, d. 497/1104
497/1104	Tutush II b. Duqaq, in Damascus, died shortly after his accession
507/1113	Alp Arslan al-Akhras b. Riḍwān } in Aleppo
⊘ 508–17/1114–23	Sulṭān Shāh b. Riḍwān } in Aleppo
517/1123	*Succession of the Börid Atabeg Ṭughtigin in Damascus; succession of the Artuqid Nūr al-Dawla Balak and then Aq Sunqur al-Bursuqī in Aleppo*

3. The Seljuqs of Kirman 440–c. 584/1048–c. 1188

⊘ 440/1048	Aḥmad Qāwurd b. Chaghrï Beg Dāwūd, Qara Arslan Beg, ʿImād al-Dīn wa 'l-Dawla
⊘ 465/1073	Kirmān Shāh b. Qāwurd
⊘ 467/1074	Ḥusayn b. Qāwurd
⊘ 467/1074	Sulṭān Shāh Isḥāq b. Qāwurd, Rukn al-Dīn wa 'l-Dawla
⊘ 477/1085	Tūrān Shāh I b. Qāwurd, Muḥyī 'l-Dīn ʿImād al-Dawla
⊘ 490/1097	Īrān Shāh b. Tūrān Shāh I, Bahā' al-Dīn wa 'l-Dawla
⊘ 494 or 495/1101	Arslan Shāh I b. Kirmān Shāh, Muḥyī 'l-Islām wa 'l-Muslimīn, d. ? 540/1145
537/1142	Muḥammad I b. Arslan Shāh I, Mughīth al-Dunyā wa 'l-Dīn
⊘ 551/1156	Ṭoghrïl Shāh b. Muḥammad I, Muḥyī 'l-Dunyā wa 'l-Dīn
⊘ 565/1170	Bahrām Shāh b. Ṭoghrïl Shāh, Abū Manṣūr, first reign
⊘ 565/1170	Arslan Shāh II b. Ṭoghrïl Shāh, first reign
c. 566/c. 1171	Bahrām Shāh b. Ṭoghrïl Shāh, second reign
c. 568/c. 1172	Arslan Shāh II, second reign
c. 571/c. 1175	Bahrām Shāh b. Ṭoghrïl Shāh, third reign
c. 571/c. 1175	Muḥammad Shāh b. Bahrām Shāh, first reign
c. 571/c. 1175	Arslan Shāh II, third reign, d. 572/1177
⊘ 572/1177	Tūrān Shāh II b. Ṭoghrïl Shāh, d. 579/1183
c. 579/c. 1183	Muḥammad Shāh, second reign
c. 584/c. 1188	*Ghuzz occupation*

The Seljuqs were originally a family of chiefs of the Qïnïq clan of the Oghuz or Ghuzz Turkish people, whose home was in the steppes north of the Caspian and Arab Seas. Becoming Muslims towards the end of the tenth century, they entered the Islamic world in Khwārazm and Transoxania in the same fashion as so many barbarian peoples all over the Old World, namely as auxiliary troops in the service of warring powers, in this case, as participants in the struggles of the last Sāmānids, the Qarakhānids and the Ghaznawids. Deflected into Khurasan, the Seljuqs, their bands of nomadic followers and their herds, gradually took over that province from the Ghaznawids, seizing the capital Nishapur temporarily in 429/1038, where their leader Ṭoghrïl Beg proclaimed himself sultan. Leaving his brother Chaghrï Beg as ruler of Khurasan, Ṭoghrïl began deliberately to associate his authority with the cause of Sunnī orthodoxy and the freeing of the 'Abbāsid caliphs from the Shī'ī Būyids' tutelage, a policy which enabled him to enlist orthodox sympathy as the Seljuqs advanced through Persia and swept aside the local Daylamī and Kurdish princes. In 447/1055, Ṭoghrïl entered Baghdad and had his title of sultan confirmed by the caliph; a few years later, the line of Būyids was finally extinguished in Fars (see above, no. 75).

The sultanate of the Great Seljuqs now evolved towards a hierarchically-organised state on the Perso-Islamic monarchic pattern, with the supreme sultan supported by a Persian and Arab bureaucracy and a multi-national army directed by Turkish slave commanders, this nucleus of professional soldiers being supplemented by the tribal contingents of the Türkmen begs or chiefs; but the continued importance within the sultanate of the Turkish elements was to mean that the Seljuq sultanate never developed into such a despotic, monolithic state as that of the Ghaznawids, much more completely cut off from the rulers' original steppe background. During the reign of Alp Arslan and his son Malik Shāh, who both depended to a great extent on their supremely able Persian minister, Niẓām al-Mulk, the empire of the great Seljuqs reached its apogee. In the east, Khwārazm and what is now western Afghanistan had been wrested from the Ghaznawids, and towards the end of his reign Malik Shāh invaded Transoxania and humbled the Qarakhānids, receiving at Uzgend the homage of the Khān of the eastern branch in Kāshghar and Khotan. In the west, the offensive was taken against the Christian Armenian princes and Georgian kings in Transcaucasia. Fāṭimid influence was excluded from Syria and Jazīra, while minor, Shī'ī-tinged dynasties like the 'Uqaylids of northern Iraq and Jazīra (see above, no. 38) were overthrown and reliable Turkish governors installed in Syria. Alp Arslan's victory over the Byzantine emperor Romanus Diogenes at Mantzikert (Malāzgird) in 463/1071 further opened up Anatolia to Turkmen incursions, and these intensified raids laid the foundations for various Turkish principalities in Asia Minor, including that of a branch of the Seljuqs in Konya (Qūnya) (see further below, Chapter Twelve). Malik Shāh's brother Tutush and the latter's sons and grandsons founded a short-lived, minor Seljuq line in Aleppo and Damascus. Seljuq arms even penetrated into the Arabian peninsula as far as Yemen and Baḥrayn. In Kirman in south-eastern Persia, Chaghrï Beg's son Qāwurd established a local Seljuq dynasty which endured for nearly a century and a half until Oghuz tribesmen from Khurasan took over the province in c. 584/c. 1188. On the cultural and intellectual plane, notable was an acceleration in the programme of the foundation of orthodox Sunnī madrasas or colleges in Iraq and the Persian lands, and the encouragement of the sultans and their servants of a synthesis of traditional theological and legal studies with the more free-ranging spirit of Ṣūfism, exemplified in the life and work of scholars like ʿAbd al-Karīm al-Qushayrī (d. 465/1072) and Muḥammad al-Ghazālī (d. 505/1111).

Centrifugal tendencies were always likely to appear within an empire like that of the Great Seljuqs, in which old Turkish patrimonial ideas about rulership and the division of territories among various members of the ruling family were still strong, once firm control from the centre was relaxed. After Malik Shāh's death, the Seljuq lands of Iraq and western Persia were racked by dissension and civil strife, although an element of continuity and stability continued in Khurasan, where Malik Shāh's son Sanjar was first governor and then, after the death in 511/1118 of his brother the supreme sultan Muḥammad, was acknowledged as senior member of the dynasty and supreme sultan. In Iraq, Seljuq authority was adversely affected by the reviving political and military power there of the ʿAbbāsid caliphs, and after 547/1152 this authority was permanently excluded from Baghdad. In the Persian lands, Transcaucasia, Jazīra and Syria, the rise of local lines of Atabegs reduced the sultans' freedom of action and their revenues which they needed for paying their troops. The Atabegs were slave commanders of the Seljuq army, who were in the first place appointed as tutor-guardians (Turkish *Atabeg* 'father-commander') to young Seljuq princes sent out as provincial governors; but in many instances they soon managed to arrogate effective power to themselves and to found hereditary lines in the provinces (see, for example, below: the Börids, Zangids, Eldigüzids, Salghurids, etc., nos 92ff.).

The entry of the Seljuqs and their nomadic followers began a long process of profound social, economic and ethnic changes to the 'northern tier' of the Middle East, namely the zone of lands extending from Afghanistan in the east through Persia and Kurdistan to Anatolia in the west; these changes included a certain increase in pastoralisation and a definitely increased degree of Turkicisation. Within the Seljuq lands there remained significant numbers of Turkish nomads, largely unassimilated to settled life and resentful of central control and, especially, of taxation. The problem of integrating such elements into the fabric of state was never solved by the Seljuq sultans; when Sanjar's reign ended disastrously in an uprising of Oghuz tribesmen whose interests had, they, felt, been neglected by the central administration, the Oghuz captured the Sultan, and, on his death soon afterwards, Khurasan slipped definitively from Seljuq control. The last Seljuq sultan in the west, Ṭoghrïl III, struggled to free himself from control by the Eldigüzid Atabegs, but unwisely provoked a war with the powerful and ambitious Khwārazm Shāh Tekish (see above, no. 89, 3) and was killed in 590/1194. Only in central Anatolia did a Seljuq line, that of the sultans of Rūm with their capital at Konya, survive for a further century or so (see below, no. 107).

Justi, 452–3; Lane-Poole, 149–54; Zambaur, 221–2 and Table R; Album, 22, 37–8.

EI² 'Kirmān. History' (A. K. S. Lambton), 'Saldjūḳids. I–IV. 1' (C. E. Bosworth), 'VIII. 1. Numismatics' (R. Darley-Doran).

Cl. Cahen, 'The Turkish invasion: the Selchükids', in K. M. Setton and M. W. Baldwin (eds), *A History of the Crusades. I. The First Hundred Years*, Philadelphia 1955, 135–76.

C. E. Bosworth, in *The Cambridge History of Iran*, V, 11–184.

Ç. Alptekin, 'Selçuklu paralari', SAD, 3 (1971), 435–591.

Gary Leiser (ed. and tr.), *A History of the Seljuks. İbrahim Kafesoğlu's Interpretation and the Resulting Controversy*, Carbondale and Edwardsville IL 1988.

92

THE BÖRIDS OR BŪRIDS
497–549/1104–54
Damascus and southern Syria

⊘ 497/1104	Ṭughtigīn, Abū Manṣūr Ẓahīr al-Dīn
⊘ 522/1128	Böri b. Ṭughtigin, Abū Sa'īd Tāj al-Mulūk
526/1132	Ismā'īl b. Böri, Shams al-Mulūk
⊘ 529/1135	Maḥmūd b. Böri, Abu 'l-Qāsim Shihāb al-Dīn
533/1139	Muḥammad b. Böri, Abū Manṣūr Jamāl al-Dīn, Shams al-Dawla
⊘ 534–49/1140–54	Abaq b. Muḥammad, Abū Sa'īd Mujīr al-Dīn, d. 564/1169
549/1154	*Succession in Damascus of the Zangid Nūr al-Dīn*

This Atabeg dynasty derived from Ṭughtigin, Atabeg to the Seljuq Amīr of Damascus Duqaq b. Tutush I (see above, no. 91, 2), who after the early death of the child Tutush II b. Duqaq became himself sole ruler in Damascus, founding a line which endured there for half a century. Ṭughtigin and his son Böri managed to maintain their power through skilful diplomacy with the Fāṭimids and timely agreements with the Frankish Crusaders, but these balancing policies were regarded with disfavour by the 'Abbāsid caliphs and the Great Seljuq sultans in Iraq. Hence the later Börids came under increased pressure from the bellicosely Sunnī orthodox Zangids of Mosul and Aleppo (see below, no. 93), who attacked Damascus in 529/1135, and in 549/1154 the last Börid Abaq had to abandon his capital to Nūr al-Dīn Maḥmūd b. Zangī.

Lane-Poole, 161; Zambaur, 225; Album, 22.
EI^2 'Būrids' (R. Le Tourneau); 'Dimashk' (N. Elisséeff).
M. Canard, 'Fāṭimides et Būrides à l'époque du calife al-Ḥāfiẓ li-dīn-illāh', *REI*, 35 (1967), 103–17.

93

THE ZANGIDS
521–649/1127–1251
Jazīra and Syria

1. The main line in Mosul and Aleppo

⊘ 521/1127	Zangī I b. Qasīm al-Dawla Aq Sunqur, ʿImād al-Dīn
541/1146	Ghāzī I b. Zangī I, Sayf al-Dīn
⊘ 544/1149	Mawdūd b. Zangī I, Quṭb al-Dīn
⊘ 565/1170	Ghāzī II b. Mawdūd, Sayf al-Dīn
⊘ 576/1180	Masʿūd I b. Mawdūd, ʿIzz al-Dīn
⊘ 589/1193	Arslan Shāh I b. Masʿūd, Abu ʾl-Ḥārith Nūr al-Dīn
⊘ 607/1211	Masʿūd II b. Arslan Shāh, al-Malik al-Qāhir ʿIzz al-Dīn
⊘ 615/1218	Arslan Shāh II b. Masʿūd II, Nūr al-Dīn
⊘ 616/1219	Maḥmūd b. Masʿūd II, al-Malik al-Qāhir Nāṣir al-Dīn
631/1234	*Rule in Mosul by the vizier Badr al-Dīn Luʾluʾ*

2. The line in Damascus and then Aleppo

⊘ 541/1147	Maḥmūd b. Zangī, Abu ʾl-Qāsim al-Malik al-ʿĀdil Nūr al-Dīn, in Aleppo and then Damascus
⊘ 569-77/1174-81	Ismāʿīl b. Maḥmūd, al-Malik al-Ṣāliḥ Nūr al-Dīn
⊘ 577/1181	Zangi II b. Mawdūd, Abu ʾl-Fatḥ al-Malik al-ʿĀdil ʿImād al-Dīn, of Sinjār
579/1183	*Conquest by the Ayyūbid Ṣalāḥ al-Dīn Yūsuf (Saladin)*

3. The line in Sinjār

⊘ 566/1171	Zangī II b. Mawdūd, 577–9/1181–3 lord of Aleppo also
⊘ 594/1197	Muḥammad b. Zangī II, Quṭb al-Dīn
616/1219	Shāhānshāh b. Muḥammad, ʿImād al-Dīn
616–17/1219–20	Maḥmūd b. Muḥammad, Jalāl al-Dīn ⊘ ʿUmar b. Muḥammad, Fatḥ al-Dīn } joint rulers
617/1220	*Ayyūbid domination*

4. The line in Jazīra

⊘ 576/1180	Sanjar Shāh b. Ghāzī II b. Mawdūd, Muʿizz al-Dīn
⊘ 605/1208	Maḥmūd b. Sanjar Shāh, al-Malik al-Muʿaẓẓam Muʿizz al-Dīn
⊘ 639–48/1241–50	Masʿūd b. Maḥmūd, al-Malik al-Ẓāhir
648/1250	*Ayyūbid domination*

5. The line in Shahrazūr

?–630/?–1233	Zangī III b. Arslan Shāh II, ʿImād al-Dīn
630–49/1233–51	Il Arslan b. Zangī III, Nūr al-Dīn

Zangī was the son of Aq Sunqur, who was a Turkish slave commander of the Great Seljuq Sultan Malik Shāh and governor of Aleppo from 479/1086 to 487/1094 (the origin of the name Zangī is unclear; an obvious meaning would be 'black African', possibly relating to a swarthy complexion, but this would be unusual for a Turk). In 521/1127, Sultan Maḥmūd b. Muḥammad appointed Zangī governor of Mosul and Atabeg of his two sons. The unsettled conditions within the Seljuq sultanate of the west, and the appearance of other, semi-independent Atabeg and Turkish principalities, such as those of the Börids and the Artuqids (see above, no. 92, and below, no. 96), facilitated the rise of the Zangids. From his base at Mosul, Zangī was well placed for expansion westwards through Jazīra into Syria and northwards into eastern Anatolia and Kurdistan. At various times, he defied the Seljuq sultan and clashed with the local Arab and Türkmen amīrs. He also fought the Byzantines and Franks, and his capture in 539/1144 of Edessa or Urfa from Count Jocelyn II, which spelt the end of the Crusader County of Edessa, made him a hero of the Sunnī world.

When Zangī died, his dominions were divided between his sons Sayf al-Dīn Ghāzī I, the elder, who inherited Mosul and its dependencies Sinjār, Irbil and Jazīra, and Nūr al-Dīn Maḥmūd, who took over Zangī's Syrian conquests. Later, a third branch of the family ruled in Sinjār for some fifty years, a fourth line continued in Jazīra after Mas'ūd b. Mawdūd in Mawṣil had become an Ayyūbid vassal (see below), while a fifth line ruled briefly at Shahrazūr in Kurdistan. Nūr al-Dīn's policy in Syria and Palestine against the Crusaders and the declining Fāṭimids paved the way for Saladin's career there and for the constituting of the Ayyūbid empire. The Syrian branch of the Zangids was later absorbed by the Mosul one, and the Zangids then inevitably came up against the Ayyūbids, who were pursuing an expansionist policy in Jazīra and Diyārbakr. Saladin twice failed to capture Mosul in 578/1182 and 581/1185, but Mas'ūd I b. Mawdūd was compelled to make terms and to recognise the Ayyūbid as his suzerain.

The end of the Zangids came with the ascendancy in Mosul of Badr al-Dīn Lu'lu', the former slave of Arslan Shāh II b. Mas'ūd II, who after that ruler's death became regent for the principality. When the last Zangid Maḥmūd b. Mas'ūd II died in 631/1234, probably murdered, Lu'lu' became Atabeg of Mosul, and he and his sons formed a short-lived line there (see below, no. 95) until the advent of Hülegü's Mongols.

Justi, 461; Lane-Poole, 162–4; Sachau, 27 no. 71; Zambaur, 226–7; Album, 40–1.
EI² 'Nūr al-Dīn Maḥmūd b. Zankī' (N. Elisséeff).
Elisséeff, *Nūr al-Dīn, un grand prince musulman de Syrie au temps des Croisades (511–569 H./1118–1174)*, Damascus 1967.
Ç. Alptekin, *The Reign of Zangi (521–541/1127–1146)*, Erzurum 1978.
D. Patton, *Badr al-Dīn Lu'lu', Atabeg of Mosul, 1211–1259*, Seattle and London 1991.
W. F. Spengler and W. G. Sayles, *Turkoman Figural Bronze Coins and their Iconography. II. The Zengids*, Lodi WI 1996.

94

THE BEGTIGINIDS

Before 529–630/before 1145–1233

North-eastern Iraq and Kurdistan, with a centre at Irbil, and at Ḥarrān in northern Syria

Before 539/before 1145	ʿAlī Küchük b. Begtigin, Zayn al-Dīn, 539/1145 governor of Mosul
563/1168	Yūsuf b. ʿAlī Küchük, Nūr al-Dīn, in Irbil, d. 586/1190
⊘ 563/1168	Gökböri b. ʿAlī Küchük, Abū Saʿīd Muẓaffar al-Dīn, in Ḥarrān until 586/1190, thereafter in Irbil, d. 630/1233
630/1233	*Succession of the ʿAbbāsid caliphs in Irbil*

Like the Lu'lu'ids of Mosul (see below, no. 95), the Begtiginids arose out of the Turkish military entourage of the Zangids, in the case of ʿAlī Küchük, that of Zangī b. Aq Sunqur. ʿAlī already controlled extensive lands on the Kurdish fringes of northern Iraq, with his capital in Irbil, when Zangī in 539/1145 gave him the governorship of Mosul also. ʿAlī remained faithful to the Zangids, and secured from them the right to transmit his territories hereditarily. Hence after his death in 583/1168, his sons succeeded at Irbil and Shahrazūr and also in his northern Syrian territories, Gökböri eventually falling sole heir to all of them. He pursued an astute policy of supporting Saladin and the Ayyūbids against the ambitions of Lu'lu', and, on his death without sons, bequeathed his lands to the ʿAbbāsid caliph al-Mustanṣir. The Begtiginids thus never functioned as a completely independent principality, but nevertheless enjoyed considerable local authority, within the framework of the surrounding greater powers, for almost a century.

Lane-Poole, 165; Zambaur, 228; Album, 41.
*EI*² 'Begteginids' (Cl. Cahen).

95

THE LU'LU'IDS
631–60/1234–62
Mosul and Jazīra

⊘ 631/1234	Lu'lu' b. ʿAbdallāh, Abu 'l-Faḍā'il al-Malik al-Raḥīm Badr al-Dīn, d. 657/1259
⊘ 657–60/1259–62	Ismāʿīl b. Lu'lu', al-Malik al-Ṣāliḥ Rukn al-Dīn, in Mosul and Sinjār, k. 660/1262
657/1259	ʿAlī b. Lu'lu', al-Malik al-Muẓaffar ʿAlā' al-Dīn, in Sinjār
657–60/1259–62	Isḥāq b. Lu'lu', al-Malik al-Mujāhid Sayf al-Dīn, in Jazīrat Ibn ʿUmar
660/1262	*Mongol conquest of Mosul and Jazīra*

Lu'lu' was a freedman of the Zangids of Mosul (see above, no. 93), apparently of Armenian servile origin. Originally regent for the last Zangid prince there, he became officially recognised, with the approval of the ʿAbbāsid caliph, as ruler of the city in 631/1234. In the ensuing years, he extended his authority into Jazīra as Ayyūbid power there waned, but latterly was forced to flee the growing pressure of Mongol raids on Iraq. Lu'lu' and the local Ayyūbid princes became tributary to the Mongols, and Lu'lu''s later rule was increasingly subordinate to them, whose overlordship he explicitly acknowledged on his coins in 652/1254. He tried to pass on his power to his sons, dividing up his dominions between them, but when after his death the Il Khān Hülegü invaded as far as Syria (658/1260), Lu'lu''s sons fled for asylum with the Mamlūks in Egypt, and Iraq and Jazīra now passed firmly under Mongol control.

Lane-Poole, 162–4; Sachau, 27 no. 72; Zambaur, 226; Album, 41.
EI[2] 'Lu'lu', Badr al-Dīn' (Cl. Cahen).
D. Patton, *Badr al-Dīn Lu'lu', Atabeg of Mosul, 1211–1259.*

96

THE ARTUQIDS

c. 494–812/c. 1101–1409

Diyār Bakr

1. The line in Ḥiṣn Kayfā and Āmid 495–629/1102–1232

	Artuq b. Ekseb or Eksek, Ẓahīr al-Dawla, Seljuq commander, d. 483/1090
495/1102	Sökmen I b. Artuq, Muʿīn al-Dawla, in Ḥiṣn Kayfā and then Mārdīn
498/1104	Ibrāhīm b. Sökmen I, in Mārdīn
502/1109	Dāwūd b. Sökmen I, Rukn al-Dawla, in Ḥiṣn Kayfā and then Khartpert
⊘ 539/1144	Qara Arslan b. Dāwūd, Fakhr al-Dīn, in Ḥiṣn Kayfā and Khartpert
⊘ 562/1167	Muḥammad b. Qara Arslan, Nūr al-Dīn, also in Āmid
⊘ 581/1185	Sökmen II b. Muḥammad, al-Malik al-Masʿūd Quṭb al-Dīn
⊘ 597/1201	Maḥmūd b. Muḥammad, al-Malik al-Ṣāliḥ Nāṣir al-Dīn
⊘ 619–29/1222–32	Mawdūd b. Maḥmūd, al-Malik al-Masʿūd Rukn al-Dīn
629–30/1232–3	*Ayyūbid conquest of Ḥiṣn Kayfā and Āmid*

2. The line in Khartpert 581-631/1185-1234

⊘ 581/1185	Abū Bakr b. Qara Arslan, ʿImād al-Dīn
600/1204	Ibrāhīm b. Abī Bakr, Niẓām al-Dīn
620/1223	Aḥmad Khiḍr b. Ibrāhīm, ʿIzz al-Dīn
631/1234	Artuq Shāh b. Aḥmad, Nūr al-Dīn
631/1234	*Seljuq conquest*

3. The line in Mārdīn and Mayyāfāriqīn c. 494–811/c. 1101–1408

c. 494/c. 1101	Yāqūtī b. Alp Yaruq b. Artuq
497/1104	ʿAlī b. Alp Yaruq
497/1104	Sökmen I b. Artuq, Muʿīn al-Dīn
507/1114 or 508/1115	Il Ghāzī I b. Artuq, Najm al-Dīn, established in Mārdīn and 512/1118 in Mayyāfāriqīn
⊘ 516/1122	Temür Tash b. Il Ghāzī I, al-Malik al-Saʿīd Ḥusām al-Dīn
⊘ 548/1154	Alpï I b. Temür Tash, Najm al-Dīn
⊘ 572/1176	Il Ghāzī II b. Alpï, Quṭb al-Dīn
⊘ 580/1184	Yülük Arslan b. Il Ghāzī II, Ḥusām al-Dīn, lost Mayyāfāriqīn in 581/1185
⊘ 599/1203	Artuq Arslan b. Il Ghāzī II, al-Malik al-Manṣūr Nāṣir al-Dīn

⊘ 637/1239	Ghāzī I b. Yülük Arslan, al-Malik al-Ẓāhir or al-Saʿīd Najm al-Dīn
658/1260	Qara Arslan b. Ghāzī I, al-Malik al-Muẓaffar Fakhr al-Dīn
691/1292	Dāwūd I b. Qara Arslan, al-Malik al-Saʿīd Shams al-Dīn
⊘ 693/1294	Ghāzī II b. Qara Arslan, al-Malik al-Manṣūr Najm al-Dīn
712/1312	ʿAlī Alpï b. Ghāzī II, al-Malik al-ʿĀdil ʿImād al-Dīn
⊘ 712/1312	Maḥmūd b. Ghāzī II, al-Malik al-Ṣāliḥ Shams al-Dīn
⊘ 765/1364	Aḥmad b. Maḥmūd, al-Malik al-Manṣūr Ḥusām al-Dīn
⊘ 769/1368	Dāwūd II b. Maḥmūd, al-Malik al-Muẓaffar Fakhr al-Dīn
⊘ 778/1376	ʿĪsā b. Dāwūd II, al-Malik al-Ẓāhir Majd al-Dīn, killed 809/1407
⊘ 809–12/1407–9	Aḥmad b. ʿĪsā, al-Malik al-Ṣāliḥ Shihāb al-Dīn
812/1409	*Qara Qoyunlu conquest*

The Turkish Artuqids of Diyār Bakr stemmed from Artuq b. Ekseb, a chief of the Döger tribe of the Oghuz. He is first heard of fighting against the Byzantines in Anatolia, and then the Great Seljuq sultan Malik Shāh (see above, no. 91, 1) sent him, like other Turkmen begs or chiefs, to fight on the peripheries of his empire – in Baḥrayn, Syria and Khurasan. He ended up as governor of Palestine and died in Jerusalem, but his sons were unable to maintain themselves there against the Fāṭimids and Crusaders, and settled instead in Diyār Bakr around Mārdīn and at Ḥiṣn Kayfā. Gradually, Il Ghāzī I b. Artuq took over Seljuq territories in that region; he was an energetic opponent of the Franks in the County of Edessa, and in 515/1121 (var. 516/1122) he also acquired Mayyāfāriqīn. There were henceforth two main branches of the family, the descendants of Sökmen I in Ḥiṣn Kayfā and later Āmid, and the descendants of his brother Il Ghāzī I in Mārdīn and Mayyāfāriqīn, with a third, subordinate branch at Khartpert which succumbed, however, after half a century of existence to the Seljuqs of Rūm.

As a Turkish dynasty in a region strongly settled by Turkmen begs and their followers, the Artuqid state retained many distinctively Turkish features, seen for example in the personal nomenclature of its princes, with such names as Alp/Alpï 'warrior, hero'. Yet Diyār Bakr was still strongly Christian also. The Artuqids, however, seem to have been tolerant towards their Christian subjects, with the Patriarch of the Syrian Jacobites periodically resident in Artuqid territory. Much attention has been focused on the distinctive artistic and iconographical features of Artuqid culture, seen for instance in the rulers' figural coinage, with its apparent classical and Byzantine motifs and representations.

The rise of the Zangids (see above, no. 93) halted the Artuqids' expansionist plans, and they had to become vassals of Nūr al-Dīn. Then the Ayyūbids whittled their power down further, and they lost Ḥiṣn Kayfā, Āmid and Mayyāfāriqīn to them. In the early thirteenth century, they were for a time vassals of the Rūm Seljuqs and of the Khwārazm Shāh Jalāl al-Dīn Mengübirti. Eventually, only the Mārdīn line survived, with Qara Arslan submitting to the Mongol Il Khān

Hülegü. The end of the dynasty a century and a half later was connected with the fresh wave of Turkmen nomads brought in the wake of the Tīmūrid invasions. The last Artuqids were enveloped by the Qara Qoyunlu confederation, and in 812/1409 Aḥmad b. ʿĪsā was forced to abandon Mārdīn to the Qara Qoyunlu chief Qara Yūsuf (see below, no. 145).

Lane-Poole, 166–9; Zambaur, 228–30; Album, 40.
İA 'Artuk Oğullari' (M. F. Köprülü); *EI*[2] 'Artuḳids' (Cl. Cahen).
O. Turan, *Doğu Anadolu Türk devletleri tarihi*, Istanbul 1973, 133–240, with list and genealogical table at 244, 281.
L. Ilisch, *Geschichte der Artuqidenherrschaft von Mardin zwischen Mamluken und Mongolen 1260–1410 AD*, diss. Münster 1984.
G. Väth, *Die Geschichte der artuqidischen Fürstentümer in Syrien und der Ǧazīra'l-Furātīya (496–812/1002* [sic]*–1409)*, Berlin 1987, with lists and genealogical table at 216–18.
W. F. Spengler and W. G. Sayles, *Turkoman Figural Bronze Coins and their Iconography. I. The Artuqids*, Lodi WI 1992.

97

THE SHĀH-I ARMANIDS
493–604/1100–1207
Akhlāṭ in eastern Anatolia

1. The Sökmenids

493/1100	Sökmen I al-Quṭbī
506/1112	Ibrāhīm b. Sökmen I, Ẓahīr al-Dīn, d. 520/1126
520 or 521/1126 or 1127	Aḥmad b. Sökmen I or Ya'qūb b. Sökmen I
522/1128	Sökmen II b. Ibrāhīm, Nāṣir al-Dīn, d. 581/1185

2. The Sökmenid slave commanders

⊘ 581/1185	Begtimur, Sayf al-Dīn
589/1193	Aq Sunqur Hazārdīnārī, Badr al-Dīn
593/1197	Qutlugh, Shujā' al-Dīn
593/1197	Muḥammad b. Begtimur, al-Malik al-Manṣūr
603–4/1207	Balabān, 'Izz al-Dīn
604/1207	*Ayyūbid occupation of Akhlāṭ*

In 493/1100, the Turkish slave commander Sökmen took over the town of Akhlāṭ or Khilāṭ on the north-western shore of Lake Van, it having passed from Armenian control to that of the Seljuqs after the battle of Malāzgird or Mantzikert. As heirs to the local Armenian princes, Sökmen and his descendants over three generations assumed the title of Shāh-i Arman. They soon made Akhlāṭ into a base for warfare against the Armenians and Georgians, and the family acquired links with neighbouring dynasties like that of the Artuqids in Mayyāfāriqīn (see above, no. 96, 3), becoming part of a nexus of Turkish principalities in Jazīra and eastern Anatolia which formed a protective screen on the western fringes of the Great Seljuq empire. However, Sökmen II was childless, and on his death in 581/1185 Akhlāṭ was seized by a series of the Sökmenids' slave commanders. But the Ayyūbids in Diyār Bakr and Jazīra had long coveted the town, and in 604/1207 it was taken over by Najm al-Dīn Ayyūb of Mayyāfāriqīn (see above, no. 30, 6).

Khalīl Ed'hem, 242; Zambaur, 229; Bosworth–Merçil–İpşirli, 85–7.
EI[2] 'Shāh-i Armanids' (C. Hillenbrand).
O. Turan, *Doğu Anadolu Türk devletleri tarihi*, 83–106, with list and genealogical table at pp. 243, 279.

98

THE AḤMADĪLĪS

c. 516 to after 617/c. 1122 to after 1220

Marāgha and Rū'īn Diz in Azerbaijan

c. 516/1122	Aq Sunqur I Aḥmadīlī
c. 528/1134	Aq Sunqur II or Arslan Aba b. Aq Sunqur I, Nuṣrat al-Dīn
c. 570/1175	Falak al-Dīn b. Aq Sunqur II
c. 584/1188	Körp Arslan, ʿAlā' al-Dīn
604/1208	? b. Körp Arslan, d. 605/1209
605/1209	*Eldigüzid occupation of Marāgha*
?	Sulāfa Khātūn, granddaughter of Körp Arslan, ruling in Marāgha and Rū'īn Diz in 617/1220

This line of Turkish Atabegs ruled in the restricted area of the town of Marāgha and the nearby fortress of Rū'īn Diz for almost a century, maintaining itself against much more powerful neighbours like the Eldigüzid Atabegs controlling the rest of Azerbaijan (see below, no. 99). Marāgha had been held in the early twelfth century by the Kurdish commander of the Seljuqs, Aḥmadīl b. Ibrāhīm, possibly a descendant of an earlier family in Azerbaijan, the Rawwādids (see above, no. 72), and Aq Sunqur Aḥmadīlī was presumably his freedman. This last became the Atabeg of the Seljuq prince Dāwūd b. Maḥmūd II, and supported him during his brief bid for the sultanate (see above, no. 91, 1). In the later decades of the century, the Aḥmadīlīs were drawn into the complex politics of Azerbaijan, involving the last Seljuqs, the Eldigüzids and other adjoining powers. Notices in the chronicles of this localised line of Atabegs are only sporadic, and numismatic evidence apparently non-existent, so that it is particularly difficult to reconstruct their chronology and genealogy; but they seem to have held Marāgha until 605/1209 and Rū'īn Diz somewhat longer, and a female member of the family, Sulāfa Khātūn, was again ruling in these places when the Mongols sacked Marāgha in 618/1221.

EI² Aḥmadīlīs' (V. Minorsky); EIr 'Atābakān-e Marāğā' (K. A. Luther).
C. E. Bosworth, in *The Cambridge History of Iran*, V, 170–1, 176–9.

99

THE ELDIGÜZIDS OR ILDEGIZIDS

c. 540–622/c. 1145–1225
Azerbaijan, Arrān and northern Jibāl

⊘ c. 530/c. 1136	Eldigüz, Shams al-Dīn, effectively independent in Azerbaijan
⊘ 571/1175	Jahān Pahlawān Muḥammad b. Eldigüz, Abū Ja'far Nuṣrat al-Dīn
⊘ 582/1186	Qïzïl Arslan 'Uthmān b. Eldigüz, Muẓaffar al-Dīn
587/1191	Qutlugh Inanch, stepson of Jahān Pahlawān Muḥammad, in Arrān and then governor of Jibāl
⊘ 587/1191	Abū Bakr b. Jahān Pahlawān Muḥammad, Nuṣrat al-Dīn, from 582/1186 ruler in Azerbaijan
⊘ 607–22/1210–25	Özbeg b. Jahān Pahlawān Muḥammad, Muẓaffar al-Dīn, from 600/1204 ruler in northern Jibāl
622/1225	*Khwārazmian conquest*

The Elgigüzids or Ildegizids were a Turkish Atabeg dynasty who controlled most of Azerbaijan (apart from the region round Marāgha held by another Atabeg line, the Aḥmadīlīs: see above, no. 98), Arrān and northern Jibāl during the second half of the twelfth century when the Great Seljuq sultanate of western Persia and Iraq was in full decay and unable to prevent the growth of virtually independent powers in the provinces.

Eldigüz (the Arabic-Persian sources write *'y.l.d.k.z*, but Armenian and Georgian transcriptions of the name seem to indicate a rendering like this) was originally a Qïpchaq military slave of the Seljuq vizier Simirumī, and then passed to Sultan Mas'ūd b. Muḥammad, who made him governor of Arrān. An adroit marriage to the widow of the Seljuq Sultan Ṭoghrïl II b. Muḥammad enabled him to champion the accession to the throne in 556/1161 of her son Arslan (Shāh), of whom he had been *de facto* Atabeg, and during Arslan's reign the Eldigüzids were the power behind the throne and effectively controlled the Great Seljuq sultanate. Their territories now stretched as far south as Iṣfahān, in the west to Akhlāṭ and in the north to the borders of Sharwān and Georgia. Sultan Ṭoghrïl III b. Arslan was for many years held in close tutelage by the Eldigüzids, who at one point claimed the sultanate for themselves, until in 587/1191 he turned the tables on Qutlugh Inanch and was able to pursue an independent policy for the last three years of his life.

In their last phase, the Eldigüzids were once more local rulers in Azerbaijan and eastern Transcaucasia, hard pressed by the aggressive Georgians, and they did not survive the troubled early decades of the thirteenth century. They continued for a while to rule in Azerbaijan, and managed to overthrow their rivals the Aḥmadīlīs, but could not withstand the superior élan of the Khwārazm Shāhs, and in 622/1225 Jalāl al-Dīn Mengübirti finally deposed Özbeg b. Jahān Pahlawān Muḥammad. The historical significance of these Atabegs thus lies in their firm control over most of north-western Persia during the later Seljuq period and also in their role in Transcaucasia as champions of Islam against the resurgent Bagratid Georgian kings.

Justi, 461; Lane-Poole, 171; Zambaur, 231; Album, 41–2.
EI[2] 'Ildeñizids or Eldigüzids' (C. E. Bosworth); EIr 'Atābakān-e Āḏarbayjān' (K. A. Luther).
Bosworth, in *The Cambridge History of Iran*, V, 169–71, 176–83.
D. K. Kouymjian, *A Numismatic History of Southeastern Caucasia and Adharbayjān*, 56–60, 288–368, with a genealogical table at p. 368.

100

THE BĀDŪSPĀNIDS

c. 493 to the tenth century/c. 1100 to the sixteenth century

The Caspian coastland districts of Rūyān and Rustamdār

1. The rulers of the united principality

⊘ ?	Naṣr b. Sharīwash (? Shahrnūsh), Sharaf al-Dīn, Nāṣir al-Dawla, ruling in 502/1109
?	Shahrīwash b. Hazārasp, ruling c. 553/1168
?	Kay Kāwūs b. Hazārasp, d. c. 580/c. 1184
c. 580–1/c. 1184–5	Hazārasp b. Shahrīwash
?	Zarrīn Kamar b. Justān b. Kay Kāwūs, d. 610/1213
610–20/1213–23	Bīsutūn b. Zarrīn Kamar, d. 620/1223
later 620s/early 1230s	Nāmāwar b. Bīsutūn, Fakhr al-Dawla, d. 640/1242
640/1242	Ardashīr b. Nāmāwar, Ḥusām al-Dawla, in Daylam, d. 640/1242
640/1242	Iskandar b. Nāmāwar, in Rūyān
640/1242	Shahrāgīm b. Nāmāwar, in Daylam and Rūyān, d. 671/1273
671/1273	Nāmāwar Shāh Ghāzī b. Shahrāgīm, Fakhr al-Dawla
701/1302	Kay Khusraw b. Shahrāgīm
712/1312	Muḥammad b. Kay Khusraw, Shams al-Mulūk
717/1317	Shahriyār b. Kay Khusraw, Nāṣir al-Dīn
725/1325	Ziyār b. Kay Khusraw, Tāj al-Dawla
734/1334	Iskandar b. Ziyār, Jalāl al-Dawla
761/1360	Shāh Ghāzī b. Ziyār, Fakhr al-Dawla
781/1379	Qubād b. Shāh Ghāzī, ʿAḍud al-Dawla, d. 783/1381
783–92/1381–90	*Rule in Rūyān by the Marʿashī Sayyids*
792/1390	Ṭūs b. Ziyār, Saʿd al-Dawla, d. 796/1394
	Tīmūrid occupation of the Caspian coastlands
c. 802/c. 1400	Kayūmarth b. Bīsutūn b. Gustahm b. Ziyār
857/1453	*Division of the kingdom into two branches*

2. The rulers in Kujūr (with the title of Malik)

c. 858/c. 1454	Iskandar b. Kayūmarth
881/1476	Tāj al-Dawla b. Iskandar
897/1492	Ashraf b. Tāj al-Dawla
915/1509	Kāwūs b. Ashraf
950/1543	Kayūmarth b. Kāwūs
963/1556	Jahāngīr b. Kāwūs
975/1568	Sulṭān Muḥammad b. Jahāngīr
998-1004 or 1006/	Jahāngīr b. Muḥammad
1590-1596 or 1598	*Direct rule by the Ṣafawids*

3. The rulers in Nūr (with the title of Malik)

c. 858/c. 1454	Kāwūs b. Kayūmarth
871/1467	Jahāngīr b. Kāwūs
904/1499	Bīsutūn b. Jahāngīr
913/1507	Bahman b. Bīsutūn
957/1550	Kayūmarth b. Bahman, d. after 984/1576
?	Sulṭān ʿAzīz b. Kayūmarth
?–1002/?–1594	Jahāngīr b. ʿAzīz
1002/1594	*Power assumed by the Ṣafawids*

The line of the Bādūspānids in the Caspian region claimed a connection, which cannot however be demonstrated with any certainty, with earlier rulers of Rūyān; these last had asserted their descent from the semi-legendary Bādūspān, a contemporary of the Dābūyids of Gīlān (see above, no. 79), hence going back to late Sāsānid times. The Bādūspānids, who are known from the late eleventh century onwards, bore the historic, local title of *Ustāndār*, and later that of Malik or king, but they seem to have been unconnected with the immediately preceding line of Ustāndārs. They first appear as vassals of the Seljuqs, and within the Caspian region they were neighbours and kinsmen by marriage of the Bāwandids (see above, no. 80) and other petty rulers there, including, latterly, the Marʿashī Sayyids of Māzandarān. They survived the Mongols and Tīmūrids, but after the mid-fifteenth century they split into two parallel branches, ruling in Kujūr and Nūr respectively, until their lands were incorporated by Shāh ʿAbbās I into the Ṣafawid empire.

Justi, 433–5; Sachau, 8–9 nos 8–10; Zambaur, 190–1, both these latter being unreliable.
EI² 'Bādūsbānids' (B. Nikitine); EIr 'Baduspanids' (W. Madelung), the most reliable account, on which the above is based.
H. M. Rabino, 'Les dynasties du Māzandarān de l'an 50 avant l'Hégire à l'an 1006 de l'Hégire (572 à 1597–1598) d'après les chroniques locales', *JA*, 228 (1936), 443–74.

101

THE NIZĀRĪ ISMĀʿĪLĪS OR ASSASSINS IN PERSIA
483–654/1090–1256
Various mountainous regions of Persia, with their main centre at Alamūt

483/1090	Ḥasan-i Ṣabbāḥ (al-Ḥasan b. ʿAlī b. al-Ṣabbāḥ), Fāṭimid and then Nizārī *dāʿī* in northern and western Persia
518/1124	Kiyā Buzurg Ummīd b. Ḥasan-i Ṣabbāḥ
⊘ 532/1138	Muḥammad I b. Kiyā Buzurg Ummīd
⊘ 557/1162	Ḥasan II b. Muḥammad I, ʿAlā Dhikrihi ʾl-Salām
561/1166	Muḥammad II b. Ḥasan II, Nūr al-Dīn
607/1210	Ḥasan III b. Muḥammad II, Jalāl al-Dīn
⊘ 618/1221	Muḥammad III b. Ḥasan III, ʿAlāʾ al-Dīn
653–4/1255–6	Khwurshāh b. Muḥammad III, Rukn al-Dīn, killed 654/1256
654/1256	*Mongol capture of Alamūt*

As noted above concerning the Syrian Ismāʿīlīs (no. 29), the Nizārī *daʿwa* arose from a split within the Fāṭimid caliphate. Ḥasan-i Ṣabbāḥ had already been spreading Ismāʿīlī teachings in Persia before the death of the caliph al-Mustanṣir in 487/1094 and the al-Mustaʿlī–Nizār split over succession to the imamate of the Ismāʿīlīs. The Persian devotees acknowledged Nizār, and Ḥasan-i Ṣabbāḥ became their leader with the title, in the absence of the Imām, of *Ḥujja* 'Proof, demonstration of the truth'. Ḥasan secured the mountain fortress of Alamūt in Daylam, in north-western Persia, where there was a long tradition of heterodoxy and sympathy for Shīʿism. From here, Ḥasan also organised the Syrian *daʿwa* (see above, no. 29), and within Persia, from the Caspian region fortresses and those in the Iṣfahān region, a series of attacks on the Great Seljuq state. Given the comparatively small numbers of the Ismāʿīlīs, these were necessarily more like guerilla actions than full-scale campaigns, and the weapon of religious and political assassination was also used, creating an atmosphere of fear and suspicion within orthodox Sunnī circles which almost certainly exaggerated the real power of the Ismāʿīlīs. Hence these last became in the popular mind the so-called Assassins of the Crusader sources (< *Ḥashīshiyyūn* or *Ḥashshāshūn* 'hashish eaters', reflecting a belief that the Ismāʿīlī agents were inspired to their daring feats of assassination through the use of hallucinatory drugs).

The Fourth Grand Master in Alamūt, Ḥasan II, assumed the more exalted religious function of Imām, but in the thirteenth century Ismāʿīlī extremism began to moderate somewhat, and the ʿAbbāsid caliph al-Nāṣir secured a great propaganda success in the contemporary Sunnī world by achieving the return of Ḥasan III to orthodoxy. However, the last Grand Master, Khwurshāh, was unable to withstand Hülegü's Mongols; Alamūt was stormed in 654/1256 and Khwurshāh seems to have been killed by the victors. Ismāʿīlism survived in some of the remoter parts of Persia in a modest and diminished fashion, but the history of the continuing imamate in Persia is very obscure until the eighteenth century.

Justi, 457; Sachau, 15 no. 26; Zambaur, 217–18 (inaccurate); Album, 42.
EI[2] 'Ismāʿīliyya' (W. Madelung).

M. G. S. Hodgson, *The Order of Assassins: The Struggle of Early Nizârî Ismâ'îlîs against the Islamic World*, The Hague 1955, 37–270, with a table at p. 42.
G. C. Miles, 'Coins of the Assassins of Alamūt', *Orientalia Lovaniensia*, 3 (1972), 155–62.
Farhad Daftary, *The Ismā'īlīs: Their History and Doctrines*, 324–434, with a table at p. 553.

102

THE HAZĀRASPIDS
543–827/1148–1424
Luristān

543–56/1148–61	Abū Ṭāhir (? b. ʿAlī) b. Muḥammad, d. 556/1161
c. 600/c. 1204	Malik Hazārasp b. Abī Ṭāhir, Nuṣrat al-Dīn, d. 626/1229 or 650/1252
	ʿImād al-Dīn b. Hazārasp, d. 646/1248 } rulers if the earlier date for their father's death is correct
	Nuṣrat al-Dīn b. Hazārasp, d. 649/1251 } rulers if the earlier date for their father's death is correct
before 655/before 1257	Tekele or Degele b. Hazārasp, killed c. 657/c. 1259
c. 657/c. 1259	Alp Arghu(n) b. Hazārasp, Shams al-Dīn
673/1274	Yūsuf Shāh I b. Alp Arghu(n)
c. 687/c. 1288	Afrāsiyāb I b. Yūsuf Shāh I, d. 695/1296
696/1296	Aḥmad b. Alp Arghu(n), Nuṣrat al-Dīn
730 or 733/1330 or 1333	Yūsuf Shāh II b. Aḥmad, Rukn al-Dīn
740/1339	Afrāsiyāb II Aḥmad b. Yūsuf Shāh II (or b. Aḥmad), Muẓaffar al-Dīn
756/1355	Nawr al-Ward b. Afrāsiyāb II
756/1355	Pashang b. ? Yūsuf Shāh II, Shams al-Din
780/1378	Pīr Aḥmad b. Pashang, challenged early in his reign by his brother Hūshang
811/1408	Abū Saʿīd b. Pīr Aḥmad
c. 820/c. 1417	Shāh Ḥusayn b. Abī Saʿīd
827/1424	Ghiyāth al-Dīn b. Kāwūs b. Hūshang
827/1424	*Tīmūrid conquest*

This line of the so-called Atabegs of Luristān ruled in Lur-i Buzurg, namely the eastern and southern parts of Luristān in western Persia from a centre at Īdhaj or Mālamīr. They were ultimately of Kurdish stock, and the founder Abū Ṭāhir traced his ancestry back to the Shabānkāra'ī chief Faḍlūya of early Seljuq times. Abū Ṭāhir himself was a commander of the Salghurid Atabegs of Fars (see below, no. 103) who eventually made himself independent in Luristān of his masters, extended his territories almost as far east as Iṣfahān and assumed the by that time prestigious Turkish title of Atabeg. Subsequent Hazāraspids ruled under the aegis of the Il Khānids, to whose army they had at times to send troops, but were later involved in the civil wars of the Muẓaffarids of Fars (see below, no. 140). When Tīmūr overran this region of south-western Persia, he confirmed them in power, but his grandson Ibrāhīm b. Shāh Rukh ended their power in 827/1424.

It should be further noted that another line of Lurī so-called Atabegs ruled in Lur-i Kūchik, that is northern and western Luristān, from the later twelfth century until the time of the Ṣafawid Shāh ʿAbbās I.

Justi, 460–1; Lane-Poole, 174–5; Zambaur, 234–5.

*EI*² 'Hazāraspids' (B. Spuler), 'Lur-i Buzurg', 'Lur-i Kūčik' (V. Minorsky); *EIr* 'Atābakān-e Lorestān' (Spuler).
Spuler, *Die Mongolen in Iran. Politik, Verwaltung und Kultur der Ilchanzeit 1220–1350*, 4th edn, Leiden 1985, 134–5.

103

THE SALGHURIDS
543–681/1148–1282
Fars

⌀ 543/1148	Sunqur b. Mawdūd, Muẓaffar al-Dīn
⌀ 556/1161	Zangī b. Mawdūd, Muẓaffar al-Dīn
⌀ 570/1175 or 574/1178	Tekele or Degele b. Zangī
⌀ 594/1198	Sa'd I b. Zangī, Abū Shujā' Muẓaffar al-Dīn
⌀ 623/1126	Qutlugh Khān b. Sa'd I, Abū Bakr Muẓaffar al-Dīn
⌀ 658/1260	Sa'd II b. Qutlugh Khān, Muẓaffar al-Dīn
658/1260	Muḥammad b. Sa'd II, 'Aḍud al-Dīn
661/1262	Muḥammad Shāh b. Salghur Shāh b. Sa'd I, Muẓaffar al-Dīn
661/1263	Seljuq Shāh b. Salghur Shāh, Muẓaffar al-Dīn
⌀ 662/1263	Ābish Khātūn b. Sa'd II, Muẓaffar al-Dīn
⌀ 663–81/1264–82	Ābish Khātūn and her husband Mengü Temür b. Hülegü, jointly
681/1282	*Direct Il Khānid rule*

The Atabeg dynasty of the Salghurids ruled in Fars for over a century as vassals first of the Seljuqs and then, in the thirteenth century, of the Khwārazm Shāhs and Mongols. They were of Türkmen origin, possibly from the Salur or Salghur tribe which had formed part of the Oghuz and which had come westwards at the time of the Seljuq invasions, playing a significant part in the establishment of the Sultanate of Rūm (see below, no. 107). The founder of the Fars line, Sunqur, took advantage of the warfare and disputes which disturbed the reign of the Great Seljuq sultan Mas'ūd b. Muḥammad in order to consolidate his position in southern Persia, after Fars had already been under the control of another Turkish Atabeg, Boz Aba. With the decline of the Great Seljuqs, the Salghurids could then enjoy uninterrupted possession of Fars, campaigning against the local Shabānkāra'ī Kurds and intervening in succession disputes among the neighbouring, last Kirman Seljuqs (see above, no. 91, 3).

Fars enjoyed considerable prosperity under Sa'd I b. Zangī, although he had latterly to acknowledge the suzerainty of the Khwārazm Shāhs and to link his family with them by means of marriage alliances. The Persian writer Sa'dī dedicated his *Bustān* and *Gulistān* to Sa'd I and his short-reigning son Sa'd II respectively, and it was from the latter that he derived his pen-name. In the reign of Sa'd I's son and successor Abū Bakr, Fars came under the suzerainty of the Mongol Great Khān Ögedey and then under that of the Il Khānid Hülegü (see below, no. 133), and it was from the Mongols that Abū Bakr acquired his title of Qutlugh Khān. After a series of ephemeral Salghurids, Sa'd II's daughter Ābish Khātūn was made Atabeg of Fars by Hülegü, with her husband, the Il Khān's son Mengü Temür, taking over *de facto* power shortly afterwards, until Salghurid power was ended completely at Mengü Temür's death and Fars was incorporated directly into the Il Khānid realm.

Justi, 460; Lane-Poole, 172–3; Zambaur, 232; Album, 42.
EI[2] 'Salghurids' (C. E. Bosworth); *EIr* 'Atābakān-e Fārs' (B. Spuler).
B. Spuler, *Die Mongolen in Iran*, 4th edn, 117–21.
Bosworth, in *The Cambridge History of Iran*, V, 172–3.
Erdoğan Merçil, *Fars Atabegleri Salgurlular*, Ankara 1975, with a genealogical table at p. 146.

104

THE ATABEGS OF YAZD
c. 536–696/c. 1141–1297

c. 536/1141	Sām b. Wardānrūz, Rukn al-Dīn, d. 590/1194
c. 584/1188	Langar b. Wardānrūz, ʿIzz al-Dīn, succeeded during his father's lifetime and reigned for nearly twenty years, d. 604/1207
604/1207	Wardānrūz b. Langar, Muḥyī ʾl-Dīn
616/1219	Isfahsālār b. Langar, Abū Manṣūr Quṭb al-Dīn
626/1229	Maḥmūd Shāh b. Abī Manṣūr Isfahsālār
639/1241	Salghur Shāh b. Maḥmūd Shāh
650/1252	Ṭogha(n) Shāh b. Salghur Shāh
⊘ 670/1272	ʿAlāʾ al-Dawla b. Ṭogha(n) Shāh
⊘ 673/1275	Yūsuf Shāh b. Ṭogha(n) Shāh
696/1297	*Mongol conquest*
c. 715–18/c. 1315–18	Ḥājjī Shāh b. Yūsuf Shāh, overthrown by local rivals
719/1319	*Muẓaffarid governor*

This line of local rulers in the central Persian town of Yazd succeeded the branch of the Kākūyids there (see above, no. 78). From the names of their earlier members at least, it seems that they were ethnically Persian, but, like the Hazāraspids (see above, no. 102), they adopted the Turkish title of Atabeg. This came about because the Great Seljuq sultan Sanjar appointed the founder of the line, Sām b. Wardānrūz, Atabeg to the daughters of the deceased last Kākūyid, Abū Kalījār Garshāsp II, in c. 536/c. 1141. Sām's successors were at first vassals of the Seljuqs and then, in the the next century, tributary to the Mongols; the Atabeg Ṭogha(n) Shāh b. Salghur Shāh had to send troops to the Mongol army attacking Alamūt and other Ismāʿīlī fortresses of northern Persia in 654/1256. The penultimate Atabeg, Yūsuf Shāh, fell into arrears of tribute, and had to flee to Sistan before an army sent out by the Il Khānid Ghazan, after which a Mongol *darugha* or police commander was appointed over Yazd. A son of his was reappointed over Yazd in c. 715/c. 1315, but was overthrown three years later by local rivals and the town soon afterwards passed under the control of the Muẓaffarids (see below, no. 140) as vassals of the Il Khānids.

Sachau, 27 no. 66; Zambaur, 231.

EIr 'Atābakān-e Yazd' (S. C. Fairbanks).

Jaʿfar b. Muḥammad b. Ḥasan Jaʿfarī, *Taʾrīkh-i Yazd*, ed. Īraj Afshār, Tehran 1338/1960, 23–9.

Aḥmad b. Ḥusayn b. ʿAlī Kātib, *Taʾrīkh-i jadīd-i Yazd*, ed. Afshār, Tehran 1345/1966, 66–79.

105

THE QUTLUGHKHĀNIDS
619–706/1222–1307
Kirman

619/1222 Baraq Ḥājib b. K.l.d.z, Abu 'l-Fawāris Qutlugh Sulṭān, Nāṣir al-Dunya wa 'l-Dīn
632/1235 Muḥammad b. ? Khamītūn, Abu 'l-Fatḥ Quṭb al-Dīn, first reign
633/1236 Mubārak b. Baraq, Rukn al-Dīn
650/1252 Muḥammad b. ? Khamītūn, second reign
655/1257 Qutlugh Terken, Quṭb al-Dīn II 'Iṣmat al-Dunyā wa 'l-Dīn, regent for Muḥammad b. ? Khamītūn's son Ḥajjāj Sulṭān
681/1282 Soyurghatmïsh b. Muḥammad, Abu 'l-Muẓaffar Jalāl al-Dīn, killed 693/1294
691/1292 Pādishāh Khātūn bt. Muḥammad, Ṣafwat al-Dīn, killed 694/1295
⊘ 695/1296 Muḥammad Shāh Sulṭān b. Ḥajjāj Sulṭān, Abu 'l-Ḥārith Muẓaffar al-Dīn
703/1304 Shāh Jahān b. Soyurghatmïsh, Quṭb al-Dīn, deposed 704/1305
706/1306 Mongol governor appointed

These local rulers in Kirman sprang from a commander in the service of the Buddhist Qara Khitay, who had migrated from the northern fringes of the Chinese empire and had overrun Transoxania in the mid-twelfth century (see above, no. 90). This founder of the Qutlughkhānid line, Baraq, whose title of Qutlugh Sulṭān was bestowed on him by the 'Abbāsid caliph, had in fact only recently been converted to Islam. He was awarded Kirman, and this became the centre of the line's power for nearly a century. His kinsmen and successors were closely connected with the Mongols, serving them in their far-flung empire and latterly governing Kirman as vassals of the Il Khānids. Notable is the role among them of two forceful women, the regent Qutlugh Terken and Pādishāh Khātūn. The last Qutlughkhānid, Shāh Jahān b. Soyurghatmïsh, fell into arrears with the tribute due to the Il Khānids, and was deposed by Öljeytü. His daughter later married Mubāriz al-Dīn Muḥammad, the real founder of Muẓaffarid power in Fars (see below, no. 140), who subsequently took possession of Kirman.

Lane-Poole, 179–80; Zambaur, 237.
EI[2] 'Kirmān. History' (A. K. S. Lambton); 'Ḳutlugh-Khānids' (V. Minorsky).

106

THE MALIKS OF NĪMRŪZ
421–c. 949/1030–c. 1542
Sistan

1. The Naṣrids

421–2/1030–1, 425–7/1034–6, 429–65/1038–73	Naṣr b. Aḥmad, Abu 'l-Faḍl Tāj al-Dīn I
465/1073	Ṭāhir b. Naṣr Tāj al-Dīn I, Bahā' al-Dawla
480/1088	Abu 'l-'Abbās b. Naṣr Tāj al-Dīn I, Badr al-Dawla
482/1090	Khalaf b. Naṣr Tāj al-Dīn I, Bahā' al-Dawla
⊘ 499/1106	Naṣr b. Khalaf, Abu 'l-Faḍl Tāj al-Dīn II
⊘ 559/1164	Muḥammad or Aḥmad b. Naṣr Tāj al-Dīn II, Shams al-Dīn
⊘ 564/1169	Ḥarb b. Muḥammad 'Izz al-Mulūk b. Naṣr, Tāj al-Dīn III
610/1213	Bahrām Shāh b. Ḥarb Tāj al-Dīn III, Yamīn al-Dīn
⊘ 618–19/1221–2	Nuṣrat or Naṣr b. Bahrām Shāh Yamīn al-Dīn, Tāj al-Dīn IV
618/1221	Maḥmūd b. Ḥarb Tāj al-Dīn III, Shihāb al-Dīn
⊘ 618–19/1221–2	Maḥmūd b. Bahrām Shāh Yamīn al-Dīn, Rukn al-Dīn
⊘ 619/1222	'Alī b. Ḥarb Tāj al-Dīn III, Abu 'l-Muẓaffar
620/1223	Aḥmad b. 'Uthmān Nāṣir al-Dīn b. Ḥarb Tāj al-Dīn III, 'Alā' al-Dīn
622/1225	'Uthmān Shāh b. 'Uthmān Nāṣir al-Dīn
622/1225	*Seizure of power by Inaltigin Khwārazmī*

2. The Mihrabānids

633/1236	'Alī b. Mas'ūd b. Khalaf b. Mihrabān, Shams al-Dīn
⊘ 653/1255	Muḥammad b. Abi 'l-Fath Mubāriz al-Dīn, Nāṣir al-Dīn
⊘ 718/1318	Muḥammad b. Muḥammad Nāṣir al-Dīn, Nuṣrat al-Dīn
⊘ 731/1330	Muḥammad b. Maḥmūd Rukn al-Dīn, Quṭb al-Dīn I
⊘ 747/1346	Tāj al-Dīn b. Muḥammad Quṭb al-Dīn I
⊘ 751/1350	Maḥmūd b. Maḥmūd Rukn al-Dīn, Jalāl al-Dīn
⊘ 753/1352	'Izz al-Dīn Karmān b. Maḥmūd Rukn al-Dīn
⊘ 782/1380	Quṭb al-Dīn II b. 'Izz al-Dīn
788/1386	Shāh-i Shāhān Abu 'l-Fatḥ b. Mas'ūd Shiḥna, Tāj al-Dīn
⊘ 806/1404	Muḥammad b. 'Alī Shams al-Dīn, Quṭb al-Dīn III
⊘ 822/1419	'Alī b. Muḥammad Quṭb al-Dīn III, Shams al-Dīn or 'Alā' al-Dīn
842/1438	Yaḥyā b. 'Ali Shams al-Dīn or 'Alā' al-Dīn, Niẓām al-Dīn, d. 885/1480
? c. 890/c. 1485	Muḥammad b. Yaḥyā Niẓām al-Dīn, Shams al-Dīn
? 900/1495 or 906/1501	Sulṭān Maḥmūd b. Yaḥyā Niẓām al-Dīn, d. in Shāh Ṭahmāsp I Ṣafawī's reign, possibly as late as 949/1542
	Incorporation of Sīstān into the Ṣafawid realm

Zambaur considered that these Maliks of Nīmrūz (an ancient name for Sistan which was revived and became increasingly used at this time) formed third and fourth lines of the earlier Ṣaffārids (see above, no. 84). However, the anonymous author of the almost contemporary local history, the *Ta'rīkh-i Sīstān*, considered that the true Ṣaffārids came to an end with the Ghaznawid occupation of his province in 993/1003. From the pages of his continuator(s) and from those of the other, later, local history of Sistan, Malik Shāh Ḥusayn's *Iḥyā' al-mulūk*, it is clear that we are now dealing with two entirely separate lines of Maliks, the Naṣrids and the Mihrabānids, with no apparent connections with earlier rulers; both must have stemmed from the local landowning families of Sistan.

The Naṣrids rose to power as discontent in Sistan with alien Ghaznawid rule increased in the early decades of the eleventh century. Content with only a local authority, the Naṣrids skilfully exchanged Ghaznawid suzerainty for that of the incoming Seljuqs, and during the twelfth century the Maliks at times provided troop contingents for the Seljuq armies. They also managed to ward off incursions by the Ismā'īlīs of neighbouring Quhistān. To Tāj al-Dīn II Abu 'l-Faḍl Naṣr is attributed the building of the fairly recently-collapsed Mīl-i Qāsimābād in Sīstān. Towards the end of the twelfth century, Sistan fell under the shadow of the Ghūrids (see below, no. 159), then in the early thirteenth century briefly under that of the Khwārazm Shāhs, but the appearance of the Mongols in Sistan in 619/1222 and the resultant destruction there spelt the end for the Naṣrids.

The first Mihrabānids were vassals of the Mongol Great Khāns and then of the Il Khānids, whose protection, in return for tribute, they needed against the expansionist policies of the Kart Maliks of Herat (see below, no. 139) and against the depredations of anarchic, plundering bands of Turco-Mongol freebooters, such as the Negüders or Nīkūdārīs. The Mihrabānids were, in any case, rarely free from internal challenges by members of rival leading families of Sistan. For these Maliks, the *Iḥyā' al-mulūk* (see above) becomes virtually the only source after c. 718/c. 1318, for Sistan now began to sink into the obscurity and the social and economic decline which have characterised it until recent times. This decay was aggravated by the ravages at the end of the fourteenth century of Tīmūr and his troops, with devastation to Sistan's irrigation system. The province was tributary to the Tīmūrids of Herat and then under pressure from the Aq Qoyunlu (see below, no. 146), and finally passed into the Ṣafawid orbit. The last decades of the Mihrabānids are obscure, but the increased threat to the Ṣafawids' eastern frontiers from the Özbegs seems to have persuaded Shāh Ṭahmāsp I to appoint his own *Qïzïl Bash* amīrs over Sistan. Because of the paucity of source material, both literary and numismatic, much in the succession and genealogical connections of the Mihrabānids still remains obscure.

Justi, 439 (the Naṣrids only); Zambaur, 200–1 (sketchy and unreliable); Album, 50.
EI² 'Sīstān' (C. E. Bosworth).
C. E. Bosworth, *The History of the Saffarids of Sistan and the Maliks of Nimruz (247/861 to 949/1542–3)*, 365–477, Costa Mesa CA and New York, 1994, with genealogical tables at pp. xxv–xxvi.

TWELVE

The Turks in Anatolia

107

THE SELJUQS OF RŪM

473–707/1081–1307

Originally in west-central Anatolia, with their capital at Konya; later, in most of Anatolia except the western fringes

473/1081	Sulaymān b. Qutalmïsh (Qutlumush) b. Arslan Yabghu	
(478/1086	Alp Arslan b. Sulaymān, in Nicaea)	
485/1092	Qïlïch Arslan I b. Sulaymān, in Nicaea, k. 500/1107	
502/1109	Malik Shāh or Shāhānshāh b. Qïlïch Arslan I, in Malatya	
⊘ 510/1116	Mas'ūd I b. Qïlïch Arslan I, Rukn al-Dīn, in Konya	
⊘ 551/1156	Qïlïch Arslan II b. Mas'ūd I, 'Izz al-Dīn, c. 581/c. 1185 divided his kingdom among his ten sons	
⊘ 588/1192	Kay Khusraw I b. Qïlïch Arslan II, Ghiyāth al-Dīn, first reign	
⊘ 593/1197	Sulaymān II b. Qïlïch Arslan II, Rukn al-Dīn	
600/1204	Qïlïch Arslan III b. Sulaymān II, 'Izz al-Dīn	
⊘ 601/1205	Kay Khusraw I, second reign	
⊘ 608/1211	Kay Kāwūs I b. Kay Khusraw I, 'Izz al-Dīn	
⊘ 616/1220	Kay Qubādh I b. Kay Khusraw I, 'Alā' al-Dīn	
⊘ 634/1237	Kay Khusraw II b. Kay Qubādh I, Ghiyāth al-Dīn	
⊘ 644/1246	Kay Kāwūs II b, Kay Khusraw II, 'Izz al-Dīn	
646/1248	Kay Kāwūs II Qïlïch Arslan IV b. Kay Khusraw II, Rukn al-Dīn	joint rulers
⊘ 647/1249	Kay Kāwūs II Qïlïch Arslan IV Kay Qubādh II b. Kay Khusraw II, 'Alā' al-Dīn	joint rulers
655/1257	Kay Khusraw II ⊘ Qïlïch Arslan IV	joint rulers
⊘ 657/1259	Qïlïch Arslan IV	
⊘ 663/1265	Kay Khusraw III b. Qïlïch Arslan IV, Ghiyāth al-Dīn	
⊘ 681/1282	Mas'ūd II b. Kay Kāwūs II, Ghiyāth al-Dīn, first reign	
⊘ 683/1284	Kay Qubādh III b. Farāmurz b. Kay Kāwūs II, 'Alā' al-Dīn, first reign	
⊘ 683/1284	Mas'ūd II, second reign	
692/1293	Kay Qubādh III, second reign	
693/1294	Mas'ūd II, third reign	
⊘ 700/1301	Kay Qubādh III, third reign, k. 702/1303	
⊘ 702/1303	Mas'ūd II, fourth reign	
707/1307	Mas'ūd III b. Kay Qubādh III, Ghiyāth al-Dīn	
707/1307	*Mongol domination*	

Soon after the Great Seljuq sultan Alp Arslan's victory over the Byzantine emperor at Mantzikert, we hear of the activities in Anatolia of the four sons of another member of the Seljuq family, Qutalmïsh or Qutlumush, and it was the descendants of one of these sons, Sulaymān, who were to establish a local Seljuq sultanate in Anatolia based on Iconium or Konya. Sulaymān reached Nicaea or Iznik in the far north-west of Asia Minor, but the emergent Byzantine dynasty of the Comneni, aided by the First Crusaders, began to re-establish the Greek position in the west, and the seat of the Seljuq sultanate was eventually fixed at Konya in west-central Anatolia as the capital of what was for long to remain a landlocked principality. Sulaymān's son Qïlïch Arslan I had ambitions in Diyār Bakr and Jazīra, but after his death his successors were left alone in Anatolia by the Great Seljuqs further to the east. The Little Armenian kingdom of Cilicia and the Franks in the county of Edessa were now attacked, and, from their base at Konya, Mas'ūd I and Qïlïch Arslan II gained the preponderance over the rival amirate of the Dānishmendids (see below, no. 108). A Byzantine attack on Konya was avenged by Qïlïch Arslan II's victory over the Greeks in 572/1176 at Myriocephalon near Lake Eğridir, after which the latter's hopes of reconquering Anatolia faded; but in his old age, the sultan lost control over his sons, his territories became fragmented and in 586/1190 the emperor Frederick Barbarossa and the Third Crusaders temporarily occupied Konya.

The Latin conquest of Constantinople in 1204 afforded the Seljuqs an opportunity to re-establish their power. From being essentially a power of the Anatolian interior, they extended to the Mediterranean, and the port of Alanya or 'Alā'iyya (thus named after 'Alā' al-Dīn Kay Qubādh I) was constructed. With this and the northern coastlands in Turkish hands, a flourishing transit trade between Egypt and the eastern Mediterranean, across Anatolia to the Black Sea, the Crimea and the lands of the Mongol Golden Horde (see below, no. 129), grew up after c. 1225, and commercial relations were begun with the Italian trading cities. The internal prosperity of the Rūm sultanate in these decades is shown by the architectural and cultural glories of Konya and other parts of Anatolia at this time. Thereafter, decline set in, with internal discontent marked by the rebellion of a charismatic dervish leader, Baba Isḥāq, in 638/1240; and, when the Mongols invaded eastern Anatolia, the Seljuqs were defeated at Köse Dagh to the east of Sivas in 641/1243. Thereafter, the Rūm sultanate became a client, tribute-paying state of the Mongol Il Khāns (see below, no. 128). After 676/1277, Mongol governors took direct control. The names of the Seljuqs continued to appear on coins up to 702/1303, but they had no real authority; the last ones may have reigned in Alanya, where Ottoman chronicles mention a Seljuq descendant in the fifteenth century. A new period in the history of Anatolia begins after 707/1307, one of fragmentation into a series of petty principalities or *beylik*s (see below, nos 106–24).

Lane-Poole, 155; Sachau, 16 no. 30; Khalīl Ed'hem, 216–17, 219; Zambaur, 143–4; Album, 29.

EI² 'Salḏjūḳids. III. 5, IV. 2, V. 2, VII. 2' (C. E. Bosworth).

Cl. Cahen, *Pre-Ottoman Turkey. A General Survey of the Material and Spiritual Culture and History c. 1071–1330*, London 1968, 73–138, 269–301.

O. Turan, *Selçuklular zamanında Türkiye. Siyasi tarih Alp Arslan'dan Osman Gazi'ye (1071–1318)*, Istanbul 1971, 45ff., with a genealogical table at the end.

108

THE DĀNISHMENDIDS

Before 490–573/before 1097–1178

Originally in north-central Anatolia, later also in eastern Anatolia

1. The line in Sivas ?–570/?–1175

	Dānishmend Ghāzī, first mentioned in 490/1097, d. 497/1104
⊘ 497/1104	Amīr Ghāzī Gümüshtigin b. Dānishmend
⊘ 529/1134	Muḥammad b. Amīr Ghāzī
⊘ 536/1142	Dhu 'l-Nūn b. Muḥammad, ʿImād al-Dīn, first reign
⊘ 537/1142	Malik Yaghïbasan b. Amīr Ghāzī Gümüshtigin
559/1164	Malik Mujāhid Ghāzī b. Yaghïbasan, Abu 'l-Maḥāmid Jamāl al-Dīn
562/1166	Malik Ibrahīm b. Muḥammad, Shams al-Dīn
⊘ 562/1166	Malik Ismāʿīl b. Ibrāhīm, Shams al-Dīn
567–70/1172–4	Malik Dhu 'l-Nūn b. Muḥammad, now with the title Nāṣir al-Dīn, second reign
570/1174	*Conquest by the Seljuqs of Rūm*

2. The line in Malatya and Elbistan

⊘ c. 537/c. 1142	Ismāʿīl b. Amīr Ghāzī Gümüshtigin, ʿAyn al-Dawla
⊘ 547/1152	Dhu 'l-Qarnayn b. Ismāʿīl
⊘ 557/1162	Muḥammad b. Ismāʿīl, Nāṣir al-Dīn, first reign
⊘ 565/1170	Qāsim b. Ismāʿīl, Fakhr al-Dīn
567/1172	Afrīdūn b. Ismāʿīl
570–3/1175–8	Muḥammad, second reign
573/1178	*Conquest by the Seljuqs of Rūm*

The centre of power of the Dānishmendids was originally in north-central Anatolia and Cappadocia, as far west as Ankara and around such centres as Tokat, Amasya and Sivas; they thus controlled the northerly route of Türkmen penetration across Asia Minor, while the Seljuqs of Rūm controlled the more southerly one. The Turkmen founder Dānishmend (Persian, 'wise, learned man, scholar') is an obscure figure who appears as a *ghāzī* or fighter for the faith in Anatolia, clashing in Cappadocia with the First Crusaders but also, in some degree, as a rival to the Seljuq Qïlïch Arslan I. He is the central figure of an epic romance, the *Dānishmend-nāme*, a mixture of genuine traditions and legendary elements written down over two centuries after the events described in it, in which he is identified with the earlier Arab frontier warrior of Malatya, Sīdī Baṭṭāl. It is accordingly difficult to disentangle fact from fiction in the elucidation of Dānishmendid origins. The Dānishmendids were at least as powerful as the Seljuqs in the early twelfth century, and Amīr Ghāzī Gümüshtigin fought the Armenians in Cilicia and the Franks in the County of Edessa, and in 521/1127 captured Kayseri and Ankara; because of his warfare against the Christians, the ʿAbbāsid caliph al-Mustarshid bestowed on him the title of *Malik* 'king', making the Amīr a legitimate Muslim sovereign prince.

However, internal disputes among the sons and brothers of the dead Malik Muḥammad brought disunity, and after 536/1142 the Dānishmendid dominions were in effect partitioned between Yaghïbasan in Sivas, his brother 'Ayn al-Dawla Ismā'īl in Malatya and Elbistan and Dhu 'l-Nūn in Kayseri. After Yaghïbasan's death, the Seljuq Qïlïch Arslan II intervened several times in the affairs of the Sivas branch, finally killing Dhu 'l-Nūn in 570/1174 and seizing his lands. At Malatya, the last Dānishmendid Muḥammad had to reign as a Seljuq vassal until Qïlïch Arslan II took over there himelf in 573/1178; according to the historian Ibn Bībī, the surviving Dānishmendids entered the service of the Seljuqs.

Justi, 455; Lane-Poole, 156 (both very fragmentary); Sachau, 15 no. 27; Khalīl Ed'hem, 220–3; Zambaur, 146–7; Album, 29.

EI² 'Dānishmendids' (Irène Mélikoff); İA 'Dânişmendliler' (M. H. Yınanç), with a genealogical table.

Cl. Cahen, *Pre-Ottoman Turkey*, 82–103.

O. Turan, *Selçuklular zamanında Türkiye*, 112–90.

109

THE MENGÜJEKIDS

Before 512 to mid-seventh century/before 1118 to mid-thirteenth century
Northern Anatolia, with centres at Erzincan, Divriği and Kemakh

?	Mengüjek Aḥmad, in Kemakh
before 512/before 1118	Isḥāq b. Mengüjek
c. 536/c. 1142	*Division of the Mengüjekid territories*

1. The line in Erzincan and Kemakh

c. 536/c. 1142	Dāwūd I b. Isḥāq
⊘ 560/1165	Bahrām Shāh b. Dāwūd, al-Malik al-Saʿīd Fakhr al-Dīn
622–5/1225–8	Dāwūd II b. Bahrām Shāh, ʿAlāʾ al-Dīn
625/1228	*Assumption of control by the Seljuqs of Rūm*

2. The line in Divriği

c. 536/c.1142	Sulaymān I b. Isḥāq
⊘ by 570/by 1175	Shāhānshāh b. Sulaymān, Abu 'l-Muẓaffar Sayf al-Dīn
c. 593/c.1197	Sulaymān II b. Shāhānshāh
c. 626/c. 1229	Aḥmad b. Sulaymān II, Abu 'l-Muẓaffar Ḥusām al-Dīn
after 640/after 1242	Malik Shāh b. Aḥmad, ruling in 650/1252
	Conquest by the Seljuqs of Rūm

This obscure *ghāzī* dynasty is not heard of until 512/1118, when Isḥāq b. Mengüjek, a relative by marriage of the Dānishmendids (see above, no. 108), menaced Malatya from his fortress at Kemakh near Erzincan. The Mengüjekid principality came to lie between those of the Dānishmendids on the west and of the Saltuqids (see below, no. 110) on the east, and included besides Kemakh and Erzincan the towns of Divriği and Kughūniya or Seben Karahisar. After Isḥāq's death in 536/1142 his possessions were divided, in accordance with the old Turkish patrimonial concepts, between his sons, so that there were thenceforth two branches of the family. Bahrām Shāh of the Erzincan branch made his court there something of a cultural centre, and he was the *mamdūḥ* or dedicatee of works by the great Persian poets Niẓāmī and Khāqānī, while the rulers in Divriği have left behind there a remarkable mosque. The Mengüjekids clashed with the Rūm Seljuqs, and sought allies in such powers as the Byzantine rulers of Trebizond, but the power of the Konya sultans prevailed, and the last ruler in Erzincan, Dāwūd II, yielded up Erzincan and Kemakh to Kay Qubādh I in 625/128, exchanging them for lands at Akşehir and İlgin. The Divriği branch lasted rather longer and apparently persisted until the middle of the thirteenth century, their end being probably linked with the appearance in eastern Anatolia of the Mongols.

Sachau, 14 no. 25; Khalīl Ed'hem, 224–6; Zambaur, 145–6; Bosworth–Merçil–İpşirli, 279–82.
*EI*² 'Mengüček' (Cl. Cahen); *IA* 'Mengücükler' (F. Sümer), with a genealogical table.
O. Turan, *Doğu Anadolu Türk devletleri tarihi*, 55–79, 242 (list), 278 (genealogical table).

110

THE SALTUQIDS

Late fifth century to 598/late eleventh century to 1202
Eastern Anatolia, with their capital at Erzurum

late fifth century/ late eleventh century	Saltuq I, Abu 'l-Qāsim
496/1102	'Alī b. Saltuq I
c. 518/c. 1124	Abu 'l-Muẓaffar Ghāzī, Ḍiyā' al-Dīn
⌀ 526/1132	Saltuq II b. 'Alī, 'Izz al-Dīn
⌀ 563/1168	Muḥammad b. Saltuq II, Nāṣir al-Dīn
between 587/1191 and 597/1201	Māmā Khātūn bt. Saltuq II
c. 597–8/c. 1201–2	Abū Manṣūr b. Muḥammad, 'Alā' al-Dīn, or Malik Shāh b. Muḥammad
598/1202	*Conquest by the Seljuqs of Rūm*

The origins of this family are obscure, but Saltuq was apparently one of the Turkmen commanders operating in Anatolia in the last decades of the eleventh century. His son 'Alī appears in history controlling a principality based on Erzurum and other towns in the district, including at times Kars (Qarṣ); the Saltuqids were to embellish Erzurum, a flourishing centre of the transit trade across northern Anatolia, with fine buildings. From 'Alī onwards, these begs enjoyed the title of *Malik*. The Saltuqids' main role in the political and military affairs of the time was in warfare with the Georgians, expanding southwards from the time of their king David the Restorer (1089–1125), often as allies of the Shāh-i Armanids (see above, no. 97); but in a curious episode, Muḥammad b. Saltuq II's son offered to convert to Christianity in order to marry the celebrated Queen T'amar of Georgia. The last years of the family are unclear, but in 598/1102 the Rūm Seljuq Sulaymān II, while en route for a campaign against the Georgians, put an end to the Saltuqids; and for some thirty years after this, Erzurum was to be ruled by two Seljuq princes as an appanage before Kay Qubādh I in 627/1230 incorporated it into his sultanate.

Khalīl Ed'hem, 227–8; Zambaur, 145; Bosworth–Merçil–İpşirli, 283–4.
EI[2] 'Saltuḳ Oghullarî' (G. Leiser).
Cl. Cahen, *Pre-Ottoman Turkey*, 106–8.
Faruk Sümer, 'Saltuklular', SAD, 3 (1971), 391–433, with a genealogical table at p. 394.
O. Turan, *Selçuklular zamanında Türkiye*, 251–4.
idem, *Doğu Anadolu Türk devletleri tarihi*, Istanbul 1973, 3–52, 241 (list), 277 (genealogical table).

111

THE QARASÏ (KARASÏ) OGHULLARÏ
c. 696–c. 761/c. 1297–c. 1360
South-western Anatolia

?	Qarasï Beg b. Qalem Beg
?	'Ajlān Beg b. Qarasï, d. c. 735/c. 1335
c. 730/c. 1330	Demir Khān, in Balıkesir
	Yakhshï Khān, Shujā' al-Dīn (? Dursun), in Bergama
c. 747/c. 1346	*Ottoman annexation*
	Sulaymān b. Demir Khān, in Trova and Çanakkale in 758/1357

This line of Begs established itself in the classical Mysia, namely the coasts and hinterland along the Asian coast of the Dardanelles and along the territory to the south, with centres at Balıkesir and Bergama. A connection of the Qarasï Begs with the Dānishmendids (see above, no. 108) is almost certainly legendary. The family probably constituted their principality in the early fourteenth century, becoming a naval power in the Aegean and the Sea of Marmora, putting pressure on Byzantium across the Dardanelles and thus paving the way for the Ottomans' crossing into Europe. After annexation by the Ottomans – the first stage in the territorial aggrandisement of that family – at least one Qarasï Beg seems to have retained some power, perhaps as a vassal, since several of the Qarasï commanders rallied to the Ottoman side; but in the absence of any inscriptions, and with few coins, much about this short-lived dynasty remains obscure.

Khalīl Ed'hem, 274–5; Zambaur, 150; Bosworth–Merçil–İpşirli, 309–11.
EI[2] 'Ḳarasi' (Cl. Cahen); *İA* 'Karası-Oğulları' (İ. H. Uzunçarşılı).
İ. H. Uzunçarşılı, *Anadolu beylikleri ve Akkoyunlu, Karakoyunlu devletleri*, Ankara 1969, 96–103.

112

THE ṢARUKHĀN OGHULLARÏ
c. 713–813/c. 1313–1410
Western Anatolia

⊘ c. 713/c. 1313	Ṣarukhān Beg b. Alpagï, d. after 749/1348
⊘ c. 749/c. 1348	Ilyās b. Ṣarukhān, Fakhr al-Dīn
⊘ by 758/by 1357	Isḥāq Chelebi b. Ilyās, Muẓaffar al-Dīn, d. c. 790/c. 1388
⊘ c. 790–2/c. 1388–90	Khiḍr Shāh b. Isḥāq, first reign
792/1390	*Ottoman annexation*
⊘ 805/1402	Orkhan b. Isḥāq
⊘ after 807–13/ after 1404–10	Khiḍr Shāh, second reign
813/1410	*Definitive Ottoman annexation*

The Ṣarukhān family of begs ruled over the agriculturally rich coastal province of classical Lydia, Ṣarukhān Beg having conquered Magnesia or Manisa in c. 713/ c. 1313. From there his family became, together with the neighbouring begs of Aydïn (see below, no. 113), a naval power in the Aegean, involved with the Genoese and Byzantines, and also, after the middle years of the century, acquiring a common frontier with the Ottomans after the latter's annexation of the principality of Qarasï (see above, no. 111). The Ottoman Bāyazīd I annexed the Ṣarukhān principality, but it was restored by Tīmūr immediately after his victory at Ankara in 804/1402 over the sultan, only to be definitively re-annexed by the Ottomans eight years later, after which Manisa became the residence of one of the Ottoman princes.

Khalīl Ed'hem, 276–8; Zambaur, 150; Bosworth–Merçil–İpşirli, 323–5.
EI[2] 'Ṣarūkhān' (Elizabeth A. Zachariadou); *IA* 'Saruhan-Oğulları' (M. Çağatay Uluçay).
İ. H. Uzunçarşılı, *Anadolu beylikleri*, 84–91.

113

THE AYDÏN OGHULLARÏ
708–829/1308–1426
Western Anatolia

⊘ 708/1308	Muḥammad Beg, Mubāriz al-Dīn Ghāzī
⊘ 734/1334	Umur I Beg b. Muḥammad, Bahā' al-Dīn Ghāzī
749/1348	Khiḍr b. Muḥammad
⊘ c. 761–92/c. 1360–90	'Īsā b. Muḥammad
792/1390	*Ottoman annexation*
805/1402	Mūsā b. 'Īsā } jointly Umur II b. 'Īsā }
⊘ 805/1403	Umur II b. 'Īsā
⊘ 808–29/1405–26	Junayd b. Ibrāhīm Bahādur b. Muḥammad
829/1426	*Definitive Ottoman annexation*

The family of Aydïn Oghlu Muḥammad Beg, who had been a commander in the army of the Germiyān Oghullarï (see below, no. 116), had their principality on the coasts and in the hinterland of western Anatolia, the classical Maeonia, with their centre at Aydïn or Tralleia, the later Güzel Hisar, a region through which ran the lower course of the Büyük Menderes river. Thus it lay between the amirates of Ṣarukhān to the north and Menteshe to the south. Umur I Beg captured Izmir or Smyrna and made the Aydïn Begs an important naval power against the Latin Christians in the Aegean, so that he became the hero of a *destān* or epic. The principality was annexed by Bāyazīd I but restored by Tīmūr. The last amīr, Junayd, supported the Ottoman counter-sultan Düzme Muṣṭafā (see below, no. 130), but was defeated by Murād II, and Aydïn was incorporated into the Ottoman empire.

Khalīl Ed'hem, 279–80; Zambaur, 151; Bosworth–Merçil–İpşirli, 287–9.
*EI*² 'Aydin-Oghlu' (Irène Mélikoff); *IA* 'Aydın' (Besim Darkot and Mükrimin Halil Yınanç).
İ. H. Uzunçarşılı, *Anadolu beylikleri*, 104–20.
E. A. Zachariadou, *Trade and Crusade: Venetian Crete and the Emirates of Menteshe and Aydin (1300–1415)*, Venice 1983.

114

THE MENTESHE OGHULLARÏ

Late seventh century to 847/late thirteenth century to 1424
South-western Anatolia

c. 679/c. 280	Menteshe Beg
by 695/by 1296	Mas'ūd b. Menteshe Beg
	Qaramān b. Menteshe Beg, in Föke or Finike in Lycia
c. 719/c. 1319	Orkhan b. Mas'ūd, Shujā' al-Dīn
⊘ c. 745/c. 1344	Ibrāhīm b. Orkhan
c. 761/c. 1360	Division of territories among Ibrāhīm's sons Mūsā (d. by 777/1375), Muḥammad and Tāj al-Dīn Aḥmad (d. 793/1391)
793/1391	*Ottoman annexation*
⊘ 805/1402	Ilyās b. Muḥammad b. Ibrāhīm, Muẓaffar al-Dīn or Shujā' al-Dīn
⊘ 824–7/1421–4	Layth b. Ilyās } jointly Aḥmad b. Ilyās }
827/1424	*Definitive Ottoman annexation*

This family occupied the coasts and hinterland of south-western Anatolia, the classical Caria, with their centres at Milas or Mylasa, Pechin, Balāṭ or Miletus, etc. Menteshe Beg's father may have been *amīr-i sawāḥil* or ruler of the coastlands for the later Seljuqs of Rūm, but the family emerges into history only towards the end of the thirteenth century. During the next century, the Menteshe amīrs were involved in maritime and land operations against the Venetians and the Knights Hospitaller in Rhodes, including a struggle over possession of Smyrna. Their principality was taken over by the Ottoman sultan Bāyazīd I after its eastern neighbours, the principalities of the Germiyān and Ḥamīd Oghullarï, had already passed into Ottoman hands, but was restored by Tīmūr. However, Ilyās Beg was forced to recognise the suzerainty of the Ottoman Muḥammad I, and in 827/1424 Murād II finally annexed Menteshe to his empire.

Khalīl Ed'hem, 283–5; Zambaur, 153–4; Bosworth–Merçil–İpşirli, 313–16.
EI[2] 'Menteshe Oghullarï' (E. Merçil); *IA* 'Menteşe-Oğulları' (İ. H. Uzunçarşılı).
P. Wittek, *Das Fürstentum Mentesche*, Istanbul 1934.
İ. H. Uzunçarşılı, *Anadolu beylikleri*, 70–83.
E. A. Zachariadou, *Trade and Crusade: Venetian Crete and the Emirates of Menteshe and Aydin*.

115

THE INANJ OGHULLARÏ
659–769/1261–1369
Deñizli in south-western Anatolia

659/1261	Muḥammad Beg, k. 660/1262
660/1262	ʿAlī Beg, k. 676/1278
675/1277	*Occupation by the Ṣāḥib Atā and Germiyān Oghullarï*
?	Inanj Beg b. ʿAlī, Shujāʿ al-Dīn, ruling in 714/1314, d. after 734/1334
⊘ c. 735/c. 1335	Murād Arslan b. Inanj Beg
⊘ by 761–by 770/ by 1360–by 1369	Isḥāq Beg b. Murād Arslan
?	*Rule of the Germiyān Oghullarï*

The town of the interior of south-western Anatolia, Lādīq or Ladik, classical Laodicea, in the fourteenth century replaced by the nearby foundation of Toñuzlu/Deñizli, was a frontier post between the amirates of Menteshe and Germiyān. It had passed into Seljuq hands from the Byzantines in 657/1259, and in the following century a local Turkmen beg, Muḥammad, made it the centre of a small *beylik*. Coming under the control of the Germiyān Oghullarï, it was granted to their kinsman Inanj Beg and held by his descendants for two more generations until the Germiyān Oghullarï took it into their own hands again shortly before their own principality was annexed by the Ottomans in 792/1390.

Khalīl Ed'hem, 295; Zambaur, 152; Bosworth–Merçil–İpşirli, 311–13.
EI[2] 'Deñizli' (Mélikoff).
İ. H. Uzunçarşılı, *Anadolu beylikleri*, 55–7.
O. Turan, *Selçuklular zamanında Türkiye*, 514–18.

116

THE GERMIYĀN OGHULLARÏ

By 699–832/by 1299–1428

Western Anatolia

by 699/by 1299	Ya'qūb I b. Karīm al-Dīn 'Alī Shīr
⊘ after 727/after 1327	Muḥammad Chakhshadān b. Ya'qūb
⊘ by 764/by 1363	Sulaymān Shāh b. Muḥammad
⊘ 789–92/1387–90	Ya'qūb II Chelebi b. Sulaymān, first reign
792/1390	*Ottoman annexation*
⊘ 805/1402	Ya'qūb II Chelebi, second reign
814/1411	*Qaramānid occupation*
816–32/1413–28	Ya'qūb II Chelebi, third reign, as an Ottoman vassal
832/1428	*Definitive Ottoman annexation*

The Germiyān were originally a Turkish tribe first heard of in the service of the Seljuqs of Rūm at Malatya. But in the late thirteenth century they moved into western Anatolia and founded a *beylik* based on Kütahya as vassals of the Seljuqs and of the latter's suzerains the Il Khanids. The decay of the Seljuqs allowed the founder of the Germiyān Oghullarï, Ya'qūb I, to form the most extensive and powerful Turkish principality of its time in western Anatolia, embracing the greater part of classical Phrygia and taking advantage of the trade routes through the Menderes basin. Also, he exercised suzerainty over neighbouring amīrs, such as those of Aydïn (see above, no. 113), and had the Emperor of Byzantium as his tributary. However, in the second half of the fourteenth century Germiyān was cut off from access to the Aegean by the growth of the maritime *beylik*s along the coast, and became squeezed between the Ottomans to the north and the Qaramānids to the south-east. The last amīr, Ya'qūb II, lost his principality to Bāyazīd I in 792/1390, but was restored by Tīmūr after the battle of Ankara; eventually, however, he bequeathed his lands to the Ottomans, so that after his death, Murād II took over Germiyān.

Khalīl Ed'hem, 292–4; Zambaur, 152; Bosworth–Merçil–İpşirli, 301–3.
*EI*² 'Germiyān-Oghullarï' (Irène Mélikoff); *İA* 'Germiyan-Oğulları' (İ. H. Uzunçarşılı).
İ. H. Uzunçarşılı, *Anadolu beylikleri*, 39–54.

117

THE ṢĀḤIB ATĀ OGHULLARÏ

c. 670–c. 742/c. 1271–c. 1341

West-central Anatolia

c. 670/c. 1271	Ḥusayn b. ʿAlī Fakhr al-Dīn Ṣāḥib Atā, Tāj al-Dīn Ḥasan b. ʿAli Fakhr al-Dīn, Nuṣrat al-Dīn	jointly
after 676/after 1277	Muḥammad b. Ḥasan Nuṣrat al-Dīn, Shams al-Dīn	
686–c. 742/1287–c. 1341	Aḥmad b. Muḥammad, Nuṣrat al-Dīn	
c. 742/c. 1341	*Annexation by the Germiyān Oghullarï*	

The Ṣāḥib Atā Oghullarï ruled a small principality centred on Afyon Karahisar and lying between the *beylik*s of the Germiyān Oghullarï and the Ḥamīd Oghullarï. They derived their name from the vizier of the Rūm Seljuqs Fakhr al-Dīn ʿAlī, called Ṣāḥib Atā (d. 687/1288), whose two sons received various march towns, including Kütahya and Akşehir, and then, more permanently, Ladik and Afyon Karahisar. Their descendants were latterly only strong enough to survive under the protection of the Germiyān Oghullarï, who towards the middle of the fourteenth century incorporated their lands into their own *beylik*.

Khalīl Ed'hem, 273; Zambaur, 148; Bosworth–Merçil–İpşirli, 321–3.
EI[2] 'Ṣāḥib Atā Oghullarï' (C. H. Imber).
İ. H. Uzunçarşılı, *Anadolu beylikleri*, 150–2.
Cl. Cahen, *Pre-Ottoman Turkey*.

118

THE ḤAMĪD OGHULLARÏ AND THE TEKKE OGHULLARÏ
c. 700–826/c. 1301–1423
West-central Anatolia and the south-western coastland

1. The Ḥamīd Oghullarï line in Eğridir

c. 700/c. 1301	Dündār Beg b. Ilyās b. Ḥamīd, Falak al-Dīn
724–8/1324–7	Occupation by the Il Khānid governor Temür Tash b. Choban
728/1327	Khiḍr Beg b. Dündār
728/1328	Isḥāq b. Dündār, Najm al-Dīn
by 745/by 1344	Muṣṭafā b. Muḥammad b. Dündār, Muẓaffar al-Dīn
?	Ilyās b. Muṣṭafā, Ḥusām al-Dīn
c. 776–93/c. 1374–91	Ḥusayn b. Ilyās, Kamāl al-Dīn
793/1391	Ottoman annexation

2. The Tekke Oghullarï line in Antalya

721/1321	Yūnus b. Ilyās b. Ḥamīd
?	Maḥmūd b. Yūnus, d. 724/1324
727/1327	Khiḍr b. Yūnus, Sinān al-Dīn
by 774/by 1372	Muḥammad b. Maḥmūd, Mubāriz al-Dīn, d. after 779/after 1378
?	ʿUthmān (ʿOthmān) Chelebi b. Muḥammad, first reign
c. 793/c. 1391	Ottoman annexation
805–26/1402–23	ʿUthmān Chelebi, second reign
826/1423	Definitive Ottoman annexation

Ilyās b. Ḥamīd was, like his father, a Turkish frontier commander of the Seljuqs, who carved out for himself a principality based on Eğridir in the classical interior region of Pisidia and also in the southern coastal regions of Lydia and Pamphylia, in the latter regions based on Antalya. The Ḥamīd Oghullarï thus came to control an important north–south trade route across western Anatolia. Two sons of Ilyās established themselves in the northern Ḥamīd principality and the southern Tekke one respectively. The first was definitively annexed by Bāyazīd I in c. 793/c. 1391, but Tekke, likewise absorbed by the Ottomans, was restored by Tīmūr, only to be finally ended in 826/1423 when the Ottomans defeated and killed the last ruler, ʿUthmān Chelebi.

Khalīl Edʻhem, 286, 289–91; Zambaur, 153; Bosworth–Merçil–İpşirli, 304–6.
EI[1] 'Teke-eli', 'Teke-oghlu' (F. Babinger), *EI*[2] 'Ḥamīd or Ḥamīd Oghullarï' (X. de Planhol);
    İA 'Hamîd-Oğulları' (İ. H. Uzunçarşılı), 'Teke-Oğulları' (M. C. Şihâbettin Tekindağ).
İ. H. Uzunçarşılı, *Anadolu beylikleri*, 62–9.

119

THE BEYS OF ALANYA

692–876/1293–1471

The southern Anatolian coastland

692/1293	Maḥmūd, Majd al-Dīn or Badr al-Dīn, governor for the Qaramānids
730–7/1330–7	Yūsuf, governor for the Qaramānids
?	Sawchï b. Muḥammad Shams al-Dīn
⊘ ?	Qaramān b. Sawchï
830/1427	*Mamlūk occupation of Alanya*
?	Luṭfī b. Sawchï, ruling in 848/1444
c. 865–76/c. 1461–71	Qïlïch Arslan b. Luṭfī
876/1471	*Ottoman annexation*

The port of Alanya received its earlier name of ʿAlāʾiyya from the Seljuq sultan ʿAlāʾ al-Dīn Kay Qubādh I, who conquered it in 617/1220. After 692/1293, it was controlled by the Qaramānids (see below, no. 124), whose representatives there bore at times the title of *amīr al-sawāḥil* 'commander of the coastlands', but on one occasion in the later fourteenth century it was controlled by the Lusignan kings of Cyprus. In the early fifteenth century it was for a while in the hands of the Mamlūks of Egypt, then governed by a descendant of the Rūm Seljuqs until in 876/1471 it was conquered by the Ottomans.

Bosworth–Merçil–İpşirli, 285–6.
EI² 'Alanya' (F. Taeschner).
İ. H. Uzunçarşılı, *Anadolu beylikleri*, 92–5.

120

THE ASHRAF (ESHREF) OGHULLARÏ
?–726/?–1326
South-central Anatolia

	Sulaymān I b. Ashraf (Eshref), Sayf al-Dīn, regent in Konya 684/1285, d. 702/1302
⊘ 702/1302	Muḥammad b. Sulaymān, Mubāriz al-Dīn
⊘ 720–6/1320–6	Sulaymān II Shāh b. Muḥammad
26/1326	*Il Khānid annexation*

Sulaymān Ashraf Oghlu was a commander in the service of the Seljuqs who, in the period of decay of the sultans in Konya, built up a a small principality centred on Beyşehir in the classical Pisidia. His successors extended to other towns in the region, such as Akşehir and Bolvadin, but the *beylik* was brought under Il Khānid obedience by the Mongols' governor for Anatolia Temür Tash b. Choban, who killed the last ruler in Beyşehir. After Temür Tash's own death, the lands of the principality were divided between the Ḥamīd Oghullarï and the Qaramānids.

Khalīl Ed'hem, 287–8; Zambaur, 154; Bosworth–Merçil–İpşirli, 299–300.
EI^2 'Ashraf Oghullarï' (İ. H. Uzunçarşılı).
İ. H. Uzunçarşılı, *Anadolu beylikleri*, 58–61.

121

THE JĀNDĀR OGHULLARÏ OR ISFANDIYĀR (ISFENDIYĀR) OGHULLARÏ
691–866/1292–1462
The Black Sea coastland

691/1292	(?) Yaman (b.) Jāndār, Shams al-Dīn
⊘ c. 708/c. 1308	Sulaymān I b. Yaman, Shujāʿ al-Dīn
c. 740/c. 1340	Ibrāhīm b. Sulaymān, Ghiyāth al-Dīn
⊘ 746/1345	ʿĀdil b. Yaʿqūb b. Yaman
⊘ c. 762/c. 1361	Bāyazīd Kötörüm b. ʿĀdil, Jalāl al-Dīn, after 786/1384 ruler in Sinop
⊘ 786/1384	Sulaymān II Shāh b. Bāyazīd, ruler in Kastamonu
787/1385	Isfandiyār (Isfendiyār) b. Bāyazīd, Mubāriz al-Dīn, ruler in Sinop, first reign
795/1393	*Ottoman annexation*
⊘ 805/1402	Isfandiyār, ruler in Kastamonu, Sinop and Samsun, second reign
⊘ 843/1440	Ibrāhīm b. Isfandiyār, Tāj al-Dīn
⊘ 847/1443	Ismāʿīl b. Ibrāhīm, Kamāl al-Dīn
⊘ 865–6/1461–2	Qïzïl Aḥmad b. Ibrāhīm
866/1462	*Ottoman annexation*

The founder of this line of beys, Shams al-Dīn (?) Yaman b. Jāndār, seized power in Kastamonu and held it under the aegis of the Il Khānids, establishing an extensive principality along the Black Sea coastland and in its hinterland, the classical Paphlagonia. After the mid-fourteenth century, the Jāndār Oghullarï threw off Il Khānid suzerainty and extended to Sinop, but lost their territories to the Ottoman sultan Bāyazīd I. The dynasty at this point also takes its additional name of Isfandiyār (Isfendiyār) Oghullarï from one of the beys of the period, Isfandiyār (and in the sixteenth century, the family were to claim the name also of Qïzïl Aḥmadlï). Restored by Tīmūr, the principality had nevertheless gradually to cede territory to the Ottomans, and was finally annexed by Muḥammad II. Under subsequent sultans, the Jāndār family were nevertheless to enjoy much favour and power in the state.

Khalīl Ed'hem, 306–7; Zambaur, 149; Bosworth–Merçil–İpşirli, 290–3.
EI^2 'Ḳasṭamūnī' (C. J. Heywood), 'Isfendiyār Oghlu' (J. H. Mordtmann*).
İ. H. Uzunçarşılı, *Anadolu beylikleri*, 121–47.

122

THE PARWĀNA OGHULLARÏ

676–722/1277–1322

Sinop, on the Black Sea coast

676/1277	Muḥammad b. Sulaymān Muʿīn al-Dīn Parwāna, Muʿīn al-Dīn
696/1297	Masʿūd b. Muḥammad, Muhadhdhib al-Dīn
700–22/1301–22	Ghāzī Chelebi b. Masʿūd
722/1322	*Annexation by the Jāndār Oghullarï*

This short-lived line was made up of the descendants of Muʿīn al-Dīn Sulaymān, who had been the virtual ruler in the weakened Seljuq sultanate of Rūm after the Seljuq defeat of Köse Dagh at the hands of the Mongols in 641/1243 (see above, no. 107), his title of *Parwāna* meaning 'personal aide to the sultan'. After his execution in 676/1277, his descendants established a small *beylik* in Sinop and Tokat, in the Black Sea coast and in its hinterland, where the Parwāna had his personal domains, and this existed until after the death in 722/1322, when the last of the line died without male heir and Sinop passed to the Jāndār Oghullarï (see above, no. 121).

Khalīl Ed'hem, 272; Zambaur, 147; Bosworth–Merçil–İpşirli, 316–18.
EI[2] 'Muʿīn al-Dīn Sulaymān Parwāna' (Carole Hillenbrand).
Cl. Cahen, *Pre-Ottoman Turkey*, 312–13.
İ. H. Uzunçarşılı, *Anadolu beylikleri*, 148–9.
O. Turan, *Selçuklular zamanında Türkiye*, 617–31.
Nejat Kaymaz, *Pervâne Muʿînü'd-Dîn Süleyman*, Ankara 1970.

123

THE CHOBĀN OGHULLARÏ

c. 624–c. 708/c. 1227–c. 1309

Kastamonu (Qasṭamūnī)

by c. 624/c. 1227	Chobān, Ḥusām al-Dīn
?	Alp Yürük b. Chobān, Ḥusām al-Dīn
before 679/1280	Yülük Arslan b. Alp Yürük, Muẓaffar al-Dīn
691–c. 709/1292–c. 1309	Maḥmūd b. Yülük Arslan, Nāṣir al-Dīn
c. 709/c. 1309	*Annexation by the Jāndār Oghullarï*

Chobān, apparently from the Qayï tribe of the Oghuz, was a commander in the service of the Seljuqs who became governor of Kastamonu, probably from 608/1211 onwards, and was entrusted by ʿAlāʾ al-Dīn Kay Qubādh I with command of an expedition against the Crimea in 622/1225. His successors seem to have enjoyed a sporadic and limited authority in Kastamonu under Seljuq and then Il Khānid suzerainty, the latter exercised through their representative Muʿīn al-Dīn Sulaymān Parwāna (see above, no. 122), but the region eventually passed to the Jāndār Oghullarï (see above, no. 121).

Zambaur, 148; Bosworth–Merçil–İpşirli, 272–3.
EI² 'Ḳasṭamūnī' (C. J. Heywood).
Cl. Cahen, *Pre-Ottoman Turkey*, 243–4, 310–12.
O. Turan, *Selçuklular zamanında Türkiye*, 608–13.

124

THE QARAMĀN OGHULLARÏ OR QARAMĀNIDS

c. 654–880/c. 1256–1475

South-central Anatolia and the Mediterranean coastland

c. 654/c. 1256	Qaramān b. Nūr al-Dīn or Nūra Ṣūfī
660/1261	Muḥammad I b. Qaramān, Shams al-Dīn
677/1278	Güneri Beg b. Qaramān, with Maḥmūd b. Qaramān as his subordinate ruler
699/1300	Maḥmūd b. Qaramān, Badr al-Dīn
707/1307	Yakhshï b. Maḥmūd
c. 717/c. 1317	Ibrāhīm I b. Maḥmūd, Badr al-Dīn, vassal of the Mamlūks, with other Qaramānid princes governing various towns of the principality
between 745/1344 and 750/1349	Aḥmad b. Ibrāhīm I, Fakhr al-Dīn, d. by 750/1349
⊘ by 750/by 1349	Shams al-Dīn b. Ibrāhīm I
753/1352	Sulaymān b. Khalīl b. Maḥmūd b. Qaramān
⊘ 762–800/1361–98	'Alā' al-Dīn b. Khalīl
800/1398	*Ottoman annexation*
⊘ 804/1402	Muḥammad II b. 'Alā' al-Dīn, first reign
⊘ 822/1419	'Alī b. 'Alā' al-Dīn, first reign
⊘ 824/1421	Muḥammad II, second reign
⊘ 826/1423	'Alī, second reign
⊘ 827/1424	Ibrāhīm II b. Muḥammad II, Tāj al-Dīn
⊘ 869/1464	Isḥāq b. Ibrāhīm II } jointly Pīr Aḥmad b. Ibrāhīm II }
⊘ 870–80/1465–75	Pīr Aḥmad
880/1475	*Definitive Ottoman annexation* (Qāsim b. Ibrāhīm, Ottoman vassal until his death in 888/1483)

The Qaramānids were the most powerful and enduring of the Turkish dynasties of Anatolia which grew up alongside the Ottomans but were eventually absorbed by them. It seems that they arose from the Afshār tribe of Turkmens and that the father of Qaramān, Nūr al-Dīn, was a well-known Ṣūfī shaykh; the dynasty would thus resemble certain other Anatolian lines which sprang from dervish origins. Their original centre was in the Ermenek-Mut region in the north-western Taurus Mountains, where they were somewhat rebellious vassals of the Seljuq sultan of Konya, Rukn al-Dīn Qïlïch Arslan IV, and then tenacious opponents of the Mongol Il Khānid attempts to dominate Anatolia. These endeavours continued into the fourteenth century, and by then the Qaramānids, definitely an independent power which, as heir to the Seljuqs, controlled much of southern and central Anatolia, at one point acknowledged the suzerainty of the Mamlūks of Egypt and Syria, who were their neighbours on the east after the Mamlūk reduction of the Little Armenian kingdom of Sis. Larande or Karaman

(Qaramān), the original capital of the Qaramānids before their acquisition of Konya, became an important centre of literary and artistic activity, and, in modern Turkish eyes at least, the Qaramānids have achieved some fame for their encouragement of Turkish instead of Persian as the language of administration.

Relations with the Ottomans were inevitably uneasy, and after ʿAlāʾ al-Dīn b. Khalīl was defeated and killed by Bāyazīd, the Qaramānid territories fell to the Ottomans. However, they were restored by Tīmūr, and after the Ottomans' absorption of the Germiyān Oghullarï of north-western Anatolia in 832/1428 and the Jāndār or Isfandiyār Oghullarï of the Black Sea coastlands in 866/1462 (see above, nos 116, 121), they formed the Ottomans' most serious rivals for power in Anatolia. The last great Qaramānid ruler, Tāj al-Dīn Ibrāhīm II, was drawn into the nexus of Mediterranean powers, Christian and Muslim, opposing Ottoman expansionism. The alliance of the 'Grand Caraman' was sought by Venice and the Papacy and by their eastern neighbours, the Aq Qoyunlu of Uzun Ḥasan (see below, no. 146), and the Ottoman pretender Prince Jem was later supported. But internal disputes favoured Ottoman intervention, with Sultan Muḥammad II's goal being the absorption of the Qaramānid lands, and this was achieved by 880/1475, when the dynasty was extinguished.

It should be noted that, from 692/1293 onwards, a branch of the Qaramānids controlled Alanya or ʿAlāʾiyya (see above, no. 114).

Lane-Poole, 184; Khalīl Ed'hem, 296–302; Zambaur, 158, 160.
EI[2] 'Ḳaramān-Og͟hullarï' (F. Sümer); IA 'Karamanlılar' (M. C. Şihâbeddin Tekindağ).
Cl. Cahen, *Pre-Ottoman Turkey*.
İ. H. Uzunçarşılı, *Anadolu beylikleri*, 1–38.

125

THE ERETNA OGHULLARĪ

736–82/1336–80

North-eastern Anatolia

ø 736/1336 Eretna b. Ja'far, 'Alā' al-Dīn
ø 753/1352 Muḥammad I b. Eretna, Ghiyāth al-Dīn
ø 767/1366 'Alī b. Muḥammad, 'Alā' al-Dīn
782/1380 Muḥammad II Chelebi b. 'Alī
782/1380 Rule and eventual succession in Sinop (Ṣīnūb) of Qāḍī Burhān al-Dīn

Eretna (whose name has been explained as possibly stemming ultimately from Sanskrit *ratna* 'jewel') was a commander of Uyghur origin (hence from eastern Turkestan), probably in the service of the Chobanids and their suzerains the last Il Khānids. After the fall of Temür Tash b. Chobān (see above, no. 120), Eretna was able to assemble an extensive principality stretching from Ankara in the west and Samsun (Ṣāmsūn) in the north to Erzincan (Erzinjān) in the east, with its capital first at Sivas (Sīwās) and then at Kayseri (Qayṣariyye), and under the protection of the Mamlūks of Egypt and Syria. After his death, however, the lands of Eretna were nibbled away by the Ottomans in the west and the Aq Qoyunlu in the east, and authority in their lands was effectively exercised by Qāḍī Burhān al-Dīn, who in 782/1380 ended the line of Eretna and instituted his own short-lived *beylik* based on Sivas (see below, no. 126).

Khalīl Ed'hem, 384–6; Zambaur, 155; Bosworth–Merçil–İpşirli, 297–9.
EI² 'Eretna' (Cl. Cahen); IA 'Eretna' (İ. H. Uzunçarşılı).
İ. H. Uzunçarşılı, *Anadolu beylikleri*, 155–61.

126

THE QĀḌĪ BURHĀN AL-DĪN OGHULLARÏ
783–800/1381–98
North-eastern Anatolia

⊘ 783/1391 Aḥmad b. Muḥammad Shams al-Dīn, Qāḍī Burhān al-Dīn
800/1398 ʿAlī Zayn al-ʿĀbidīn b. Aḥmad, ʿAlāʾ al-Dīn
800/1398 Ottoman annexation

Qāḍī Burhān al-Dīn stemmed from an originally Oghuz family settled in Kayseri, and became vizier and atabeg to the weak, later rulers of the Eretna Oghullarï (see above, no. 125) until, shortly after the demise of the last of that line, he personally assumed power in their dominions. In the midst of a life spent in ceaseless military activity, defending his *beylik* against the Ottomans, Qaramānids and other local rivals, and also against the Mamlūks and Aq Qoyunlu, he found time to function actively as a scholar and poet. However, after his death at the hands of the Aq Qoyunlu, the notables of Sivas eventually handed over the city to the Ottoman Bāyazīd I.

Khalīl Ed'hem, 387–8; Zambaur, 155; Bosworth–Merçil–İpşirli, 307–9.
EI[2] 'Sīwās' (S. Faroqhi); İA 'Kadı Bürhaneddin' (Mirza Bala).
İ. H. Uzunçarşılı, *Anadolu beylikleri*, 162–8.
Yaşar Yücel, *Kadı Burhaneddin ve devleti (1344–1398)*, Ankara 1970.

127

THE TĀJ AL-DĪN OGHULLARĪ

c. 749–831/c. 1348–1428

The region of Canik (Jānīk), in the hinterland of the Black Sea coast

c. 749/c. 1348	Tāj al-Dīn b. Doghan Shāh	
789–800/1387–98	Maḥmūd b. Tāj al-Dīn, in Niksar, d. 826/1423	
796/1394	Alp Arslan b. Tāj al-Dīn, in part of the Niksar district	
796/1396	Ḥasan b. Alp Arslan, Ḥusām al-Dīn Muḥammad Yavuz b. Alp Arslan, Ḥusām al-Dīn	jointly in the Samsun and Çarşamba districts, first reigns
800/1398	*Ottoman annexation*	
805–31/1402–28	Ḥasan b. Alp Arslan Muḥammad b. Alp Arslan	jointly in the Samsun and Çarşamba districts, second reigns
831/1428	*Definitive Ottoman annexation*	

The region of Canik lay to the south of Samsun, and it was at Niksar, on the southern slopes of the Pontic range, that the Türkmen beg Tāj al-Dīn, whose father Doghan Shāh had been influential under the Il Khānids in eastern Anatolia, established a small principality on his father's death. He contracted a protective marriage alliance with the Byzantine kingdom of Trebizond on his eastern borders, but was unable to fend off the attacks of Qāḍī Burhān al-Dīn of Sivas (see above, no. 126), and his son submitted to the Ottomans. Tāj al-Dīn's grandsons were restored by Tīmūr, but eventually handed over their principality to Sultan Murād II.

Bosworth–Merçil–İpşirli, 326–8.
İ. H. Uzunçarşılı, *Anadolu beylikleri*, 153–4.

128

THE RAMAḌĀN OGHULLARÏ
c. 780–1017/c. 1378–1608
Cilicia and Little Armenia

	Ramaḍān Beg, mentioned in 754/1353
by 780/by 1378	Ibrāhīm I b. Ramaḍān Beg, Ṣārim al-Dīn
785/1383	Aḥmad b. Ramaḍān Beg, Shihāb al-Dīn
819/1416	Ibrāhīm II b. Aḥmad, Ṣārim al-Dīn
821/1418	Ḥamza b. Aḥmad, 'Izz al-Dīn
832/1429	Muḥammad I b. Aḥmad
?	Eylük, d. 843/1439
in 861/1457	Dündār
?	'Umar
885/1480	Khalīl b. Dāwūd b. Ibrāhīm II, Ghars al-Dīn
916/1510	Maḥmūd b. Dāwūd
922/1516	*Ottoman suzerainty imposed*
922/1516	Selīm b. 'Umar
922/1516	Qubādh b. Khalīl
c. 923/c. 1517	Pīrī Muḥammad b. Khalīl
976/1568	Darwīsh b. Pīrī Muḥammad
977/1569	Ibrāhīm III b. Pīrī Muḥammad
994/1586	Muḥammad II b. Ibrāhīm III
1014–17/1605–8	Pīr Manṣūr b. Muḥammad II
1017/1608	*Ottoman annexation*

The eponym Ramaḍān Beg is said to have been from the Oghuz, but this line of rulers in Cilicia, with its capital at Adana, only comes into historical focus with Ramaḍān Beg's son Ṣārim al-Dīn Ibrāhīm I, who helped the Dulghadïr Oghullarï and Qaramānids (see below, no. 129, and above, 124) against the Mamlūks. Subsequently, the Ramaḍān Oghullarï oscillated between support for the Mamlūks and the Qaramānids but with generally a pro-Mamlūk policy, and they formed a buffer-state between the Mamlūks and the Ottomans. But the Ottoman sultan Selīm I, en route for his campaign against Mamlūk Syria in 922/1516, brought the Ramaḍān Oghullarï into submission, and the later rulers of the family functioned as governors for the Ottomans in Adana, until at the opening of the seventeenth century Adana was fully incorporated into the Ottoman empire as an *eyālet* or province, with a governor appointed from Istanbul.

Sachau, 16 no. 29; Khalīl Ed'hem, 313–17; Zambaur, 157; Bosworth–Merçil–İpşirli, 318–20.

EI[2] 'Adana' (F. Taeschner), 'Ramaḍān Og̲h̲ullarï' (F. Babinger*); İA 'Ramazan-Oğulları' (F. Sümer).

İ. H. Uzunçarşılı, *Anadolu beylikleri*, 176–9.

129

THE DULGHADÏR OGHULLARÏ OR DHU 'L-QADRIDS
738–928/1337–1521
South-eastern Anatolia

738/1337	Qaraja b. Dulghadïr, al-Malik al-Ẓāhir Zayn al-Dīn
754/1353	Khalīl b. Qaraja, Ghars al-Dīn
788/1386	Sha'bān Sūlī b. Qaraja
800/1398	Muḥammad b. Khalīl, Nāṣir al-Dīn
846/1442	Sulaymān b. Muḥammad
858/1454	Malik Arslan b. Sulaymān
870/1465	Shāh Budaq, first reign
871/1466	Shāh Suwār b. Sulaymān
877/1472	Shāh Budaq, second reign
884/1479	Bozqurd b. Sulayman, 'Alā' al-Dawla
921–8/1515–21	'Alī b. Shāh Suwār
928/1521	*Ottoman annexation*

The founder of this line of rulers in the Taurus Mountains and upper Euphrates region, with its centres at Maraş (Mar'ash) and Elbistan (Albistān), was an Oghuz chief, Qaraj b. Dulghadïr (the latter Turkish name, of uncertain meaning, being later Arabised or rendered by folk etymology as Dhu 'l-Qadr 'Powerful, mighty'), who led Turkmen bands into the region of Little Armenia. His successors maintained their position, at times as vassals of the Mamlūks, and survived the attacks of Tīmūr. In the fifteenth century they maintained good relations with both the Ottomans, as enemies of the Qaramānids, and the Mamlūks, and resisted pressure from the Aq Qoyunlu ruler Uzun Ḥasan (see below, no. 146). The potentates of Istanbul and Cairo struggled for influence in this region of south-eastern Anatolia and supported rival candidates for power in Elbistan and Maraş. But Selīm I's victories over the Mamlūks in 922–3/1516–17 tipped the scales decisively in favour of the Ottomans, who ended the Dulghadïr line shortly afterwards and transformed their *beylik* into the Dhu 'l-Qadriyya governorate.

Sachau, 15–16 no. 28; Khalīl Ed'hem, 308–12; Zambaur, 158; Bosworth–Merçil–İpşirli, 294–6.

*EI*² 'Dhu 'l-Ḳadr' (J. H. Mordtmann and V. L. Ménage); *İA* 'Dulkadırlılar' (J. H. Mordtmann and Mükrimin Halil Yınanç).

İ. H. Uzunçarşılı, *Anadolu beylikleri*, 169–75.

130

THE OTTOMANS OR OSMANLIS

Late seventh century to 1342/late thirteenth century to 1924

Original nucleus in north-western Anatolia, subsequently rulers of an empire embracing all Anatolia, the Balkans and the Arab lands from Iraq to Algeria and southwards to Eritrea

?	Ertoghrul, d. c. 679/c. 1280
⊘ 680/1281	'Uthmān ('Othmān) I b. Ertoghrul, Ghāzī
⊘ 724/1324	Orkhan b. 'Uthmān I
⊘ 761/1360	Murād I b. Orkhan
⊘ 791/1389	Bāyazīd (Bāyezīd) I b. Murād I, Yïldïrïm ('the Lightning shaft')
804/1402	*Tīmūrid invasion*
⊘ 805/1403	Muḥammad (Meḥemmed) I Chelebi b. Bāyazīd I, at first in Anatolia only, after 816/1413 in Rumeli also
⊘ 806/1403	Sulaymān (Süleymān) I b. Bāyazīd I, in Rumeli only until 814/1411
⊘ 814/1411	Mūsā Chelebi b. Bāyazīd I, counter-sultan in Rumeli until 816/1413
⊘ 824/1421	Murād II b. Muḥammad I, first reign
⊘ 824/1421	Muṣṭafā Chelebi b. Muḥammad I, Düzme, counter-sultan in Rumeli until 825/1422
⊘ 848/1444	Muḥammad II b. Murād II, Fātiḥ ('the Conqueror'), first reign
⊘ 850/1446	Murād II, second reign
⊘ 855/1451	Muḥammad II, second reign
⊘ 886/1481	Bāyazīd II b. Muḥammad II
⊘ 918/1512	Salīm (Selīm) I b. Bāyazīd II, Yavuz ('the Grim')
⊘ 926/1520	Sulaymān II b. Selīm I, Qānūnī ('the Lawgiver'; also called, in Western usage, 'the Magnificent')
⊘ 974/1566	Salīm II b. Sulaymān II
⊘ 982/1574	Murād III b. Selīm II
⊘ 1003/1595	Muḥammad III b. Murād III
⊘ 1012/1603	Aḥmad (Aḥmed) I b. Muḥammad III
⊘ 1026/1617	Muṣṭafā I b. Muḥammad III, first reign
⊘ 1027/1618	'Uthmān II b. Aḥmad I
⊘ 1031/1622	Muṣṭafā I, second reign
⊘ 1032/1623	Murād IV b. Aḥmad I
⊘ 1049/1640	Ibrāhīm b. Aḥmad I
⊘ 1058/1648	Muḥammad IV b. Ibrāhīm
⊘ 1099/1687	Sulaymān III b. Ibrāhīm
⊘ 1102/1691	Aḥmad II b. Ibrāhīm
⊘ 1106/1695	Muṣṭafā II b. Muḥammad IV
⊘ 1115/1703	Aḥmad III b. Muḥammad IV
⊘ 1143/1730	Maḥmūd I b. Muṣṭafā II

⊘ 1168/1754	ʿUthmān III b. Muṣṭafā II
⊘ 1171/1757	Muṣṭafā III b. Aḥmad III
⊘ 1187/1774	ʿAbd al-Ḥamīd (ʿAbd ül-Ḥamīd) I b. Aḥmad III
⊘ 1203/1789	Salīm III b. Muṣṭafā III
⊘ 1222/1807	Muṣṭafā IV b. ʿAbd al-Ḥamīd I
⊘ 1223/1808	Maḥmūd II b. ʿAbd al-Ḥamīd I
⊘ 1255/1839	ʿAbd al-Majīd (ʿAbd ül-Mejīd) I b. Maḥmūd II
⊘ 1277/1861	ʿAbd al-ʿAzīz b. Maḥmūd II
⊘ 1293/1876	Murād V b. ʿAbd al-Majīd I
⊘ 1293/1876	ʿAbd al-Ḥamīd II b. ʿAbd al-Majīd I
⊘ 1327/1909	Muḥammad V Rashād (Reshād) b. ʿAbd al-Majīd I
⊘ 1336/1918	Muḥammad VI Waḥīd al-Dīn b. ʿAbd al-Majīd I, last sultan
1341–2/1922–4	ʿAbd al-Majīd II b. ʿAbd al-ʿAzīz, as caliph only
1342/1924	*Republican régime of Muṣṭafā Kemāl*

The beginnings of the Ottomans are shrouded in legend, and few firm historical facts are known before 1300. Numismatic evidence now seems to show that Ertoghrul actually existed, but the name ʿUthmān or ʿOthmān, which gave its designation to the dynasty, may well be an adaptation to the prestigious name of the third Rightly-Guided Caliph (see above, no. 1) from an originally Turkish name like Atman. According to one tradition, the family stemmed from the Qayï clan of the Oghuz and led a nomadic group in Asia Minor. Whatever their exact origins, they were clearly part of the prolonged wave of Turkmens who came in from the east and gradually pushed the Byzantines back. The Ottomans had been loosely attached to the Seljuq sultans of Konya, but the appearance in Anatolia of the Mongol Il Khānids and the consequent decline of the Seljuqs during the later thirteenth century probably impelled various Turkmen groups to move westwards into the remaining lands in north-western Asia Minor of the Byzantines, who had been desperately weakened by the Latin occupation of Constantinople. An older view, embodying the views of the Austrian scholar Paul Wittek, was that the Ottomans, whose lands were in the classical Bithynia (the later Ottoman province of Hüdavendigâr (Khudāwendigār)), acquired a particular dynamism from their role there as frontier *ghāzīs*, so that this superior élan and zeal for the spreading of the Islamic faith enabled them eventually to triumph over all the other *beylik*s of Anatolia and to put an end to the Byzantine empire. But the Ottomans seem rather to have been just the most successful of several *beylik*s of Turkmen origin established in western Anatolia and involved in the intricate politics of the region, inspired more by secular love of plunder than by Islamic fervour.

At all events, they were able to expand against the Greeks and Italians of the Aegean and Marmara seas region, and from a base at Gelibolu or Gallipoli, captured in 755/1354, the Ottomans began the conquest of south-eastern Europe, taking advantage of the disunity of the Balkan Slavs and the religious emnities there of Orthodox and Catholics. Soon they had overrun a large part of the Balkans, and these conquests were eventually formed into the province of Rūmeli or Rumelia. Indicative of the Ottomans' new concentration on Europe rather than on Asia was the removal of their capital from Bursa to Edirne or Adrianople in 767/1366. Militarily, they came to depend less and less on their Türkmen followers, whose religious sympathies were often heterodox. There arose a feudal cavalry element which was allotted estates off which to live, but most important in creating an image for Christian Europe of Ottoman ferocity and invincibility were the Janissaries (*Yeñi Cheri* 'New Troops'), who were recruited from the children of the subject Christian population of the Balkans, converted to Islam and trained as an élite military force. In 796/1394, Bāyazīd I secured from the *fainéant* ʿAbbāsid caliph in Cairo, al-Mutawakkil I (see above, no. 3, 3), the title of Sultan of Rūm, thereby formally making himself heir to the Seljuqs in Anatolia; but his Asiatic empire was suddenly shattered by the onslaught of Tīmūr and his Turco-Mongol forces, who defeated the sultan at Ankara in 805/1402. Tīmūr restored many of the *beylik*s recently swallowed up by Bāyazīd, and it was some decades before the Ottoman empire in Anatolia was reconstituted, the Qaramānids (see above, no. 124) being the last major rival to be absorbed; meanwhile, Muḥammad II the Conqueror had finally captured Constantinople in 857/1453.

The sixteenth century was the golden age of the empire. In 922–3/1516–17, Salīm I the Grim conquered Syria and Egypt from the decadent rule of the Mamlūks; after the victory of Mohács in 932/1526, Sulaymān the Magnificent brought most of Hungary under Turkish rule for over a century and a half; footholds were secured in southern Italy, and corsair principalities established in Tunis and Algiers. On the eastern borders, the Shīʿī Ṣafawids, bitter rivals of the Ottomans (see below, no. 148), were defeated at Chāldirān in north-western Azerbaijan in 920/1514 and Azerbaijan itself invaded; in the Indian Ocean, Turkish naval forces operated from South Arabian bases against the incoming Portuguese.

The Ottomans ruled over a multi-ethnic empire, and at the peak of their strength they maintained an attitude of detached tolerance towards the *millet*s or religious and ethnic minorities within their lands, so that Jews, for instance, resorted thither from persecution in Christian Central Europe and the Iberian peninsula. It was only towards the end of the seventeenth century that the tide began to turn definitely against the Turks in eastern Europe. They had failed to take much advantage of the European powers' preoccupation with the Thirty Years' War, and their only major success at this time was the capture of Crete from Venice. Yet the Ottomans were only just repulsed from Vienna in 1094/1683, and the losses of Hungary and Transylvania still left them in control of the Slav, Greek, Albanian and Rumanian parts of the Balkans. European political and diplomatic divisions and jealousies masked the Ottomans' decline and preserved their empire for two more centuries, at a time when European technical skills had by then given them a clear military and naval superiority. The sultans endeavoured tentatively to modernise their forces, but it was not until 1241/1826 that Maḥmūd II was able to break the power of the Janissaries, by now an undisciplined force hostile to all military reform. Economically, the Turkish and Arab lands began to suffer from the competition of western manufactured goods and superior commercial techniques; indigenous production declined, internal sources of revenue decreased and, in the nineteenth century, as the sultans contracted expensive European-type tastes, the empire at times tottered on the edge of bankruptcy.

Russian expansionism was an especial threat, for by the end of the eighteenth century the Russians had subdued the Ottomans' allies, the Crimean Tatars (see below, no. 135, 1), so that the Black Sea was no longer a Turkish lake, and the Tsars were anxious to gain control of Istanbul and the Straits, thus acquiring access to the Mediterranean. In the opening years of the nineteenth century, the commander Muḥammad ʿAlī became governor and virtually autonomous ruler in Egypt (see above, no. 34); the Greeks revolted and by 1829 had their independence recognised; and Algeria was lost to the French. The growth of nationalist and ethnic sentiment engendered by the French Revolution and its aftermath led the Balkan peoples to rebel against Turkish rule, and, by the end of the Second Balkan War of 1912–13, Turkey in Europe was reduced to its present region of eastern Thrace. Turkey's ill-advised participation in the First World War on the side of the Central Powers caused the loss of the Arab provinces, so that the terms of the Treaty of Sèvres (1920) brought about a major redrawing of boundaries in the Near East. Also, European powers were tempted to make claims on what was genuinely ethnic Turkish territory, and a Greco–Turkish War was provoked. All these events brought about a reaction of Turkish national feeling, one aspect of which was a weariness with the Ottoman ruling house, by now largely dominated by the European powers' control in Istanbul; the dynasty was increasingly felt by those Turkish Nationalists who rallied in Ankara, away from the cosmopolitan atmosphere of the capital, as a bar to progress and as inextricably bound up with the reverses and humiliations of the previous two centuries. Under the stimulus of the Nationalist leader Muṣṭafā Kemāl (the later Atatürk 'Father of the Turkish nation'), first the Ottoman sultanate was abolished in 1922 and then, in 1924, the caliphate was ended and the last Ottoman, ʿAbd al-Majīd II, deposed and exiled.

Lane-Poole, 186–97; Khalīl Ed'hem, 320–30; Zambaur, 160–1 and Table O.
*EI*² 'ʿOth̲mānli. 1. Political and dynastic history' (C. E. Bosworth, E. A. Zachariadou and J. H. Kramers*).
A. D. Alderson, *The Structure of the Ottoman Dynasty*, Oxford 1956.
Halil Inalcik, *The Ottoman Empire: The Classical Age 1300–1600*, London 1973.
M. A. Cook (ed.), *A History of the Ottoman Empire*, Cambridge 1976.
S. J. and Ezel Kural Shaw, *History of the Ottoman Empire and Modern Turkey*, Cambridge 1976–7.
R. Mantran (ed.), *Histoire de l'empire Ottoman*, Paris 1989.

THIRTEEN
The Mongols and their Central Asia and Eastern European Successors

THE MONGOLS OR CHINGIZIDS

The recorded history of the Mongols begins only at the end of the twelfth and the beginning of the thirteenth centuries, for it is only with the thirteenth-century *Secret History of the Mongols* and some Persian and Chinese sources of that time that any historical records become available. It seems, however, that the Mongols were originally a forest people, inhabiting the Siberian and Outer Mongolian forest fringes around Lake Baikal and the river basins to the south-east of it, rather than steppe nomads, even though it is as steppe conquerors, moving swiftly on horseback across vast distances, that they first appear in history. It also seems that the Mongols were, from the outset, intermingled and intermarried with the Turkish tribes of what is now Mongolia, so that the whole of the movements and conquests of the Mongols ought more properly to be described as those of the Turco-Mongols.

The father of Chingiz (in Mongolian, Chinggis), Yesügey, was the minor chieftain of a Mongol clan. Chingiz was perhaps born around 1167, and originally had the name Temüjin (= 'blacksmith'). He rose to prominence in Mongolia through the patronage of a chief of the Turkish Kereyt tribe, Toghrïl, Wang or Ong Khān (Qa'an) (the Prester John of Marco Polo). Later, Temüjin quarrelled with Toghrïl, and defeated in battle first Toghrïl and then a Mongol rival Jamuqa. He had already acquired the title of Chinggis (? < Turkish *tengiz* 'sea' = 'Oceanic, Universal [Qa'an or Khān]'), and at a *Quriltay* or assembly of Turco-Mongol chiefs in 1206 was acclaimed as Supreme Chief of all the Turco-Mongol peoples. He now expanded beyond the confines of Mongolia, and undertook campaigns against the Tibetan Tanguts of the Kansu and Ordos regions of north-western China, and in 1213 invaded China proper, sacking the northern capital of the Chin Emperors in 1215 and undermining their position. Turning westwards now, an invasion of Semirechye in 1218 gave Chingiz a common frontier with the territories of the Islamic Khwārazm Shāhs (see above, no. 89, 4). There had already been peaceful diplomatic contacts, but the incident at Utrār on the Syr Darya in 615/1218, when the Khwārazmian governor there massacred Chingiz's envoys and a whole caravan of Muslim merchants accompanying them, precipitated the Mongol invasion of the Islamic lands. In 616–17/1219–20, Transoxania was conquered; Chingiz's son Toluy was sent into Khurasan, and, after a momentary reverse at Parwān in Afghanistan, the last Khwārazm Shāh, Jalāl al-Dīn, was pursued into India (618/1221). Meanwhile, two other sons, Jochi and Chaghatay, were operating in the region of the lower Syr Darya and Khwārazm, destroying the homeland of the Shāhs; for the last years of his life, Jalāl al-Dīn was a fugitive, fleeing ever westwards before the Mongols.

It was the custom of Mongol chiefs to distribute sections of their territories to other members of their families, and this Chingiz had done before his death in 624/1227, allotting each of them a stretch of pasture ground (a *yurt* or *nuntuq*) for their followers and herds. The territories which the Mongols had already overrun were too vast to be ruled as a centralised state, and the Mongols themselves were politically and administratively quite unsophisticated; the Mongol language was not yet at this time a written one. Hence a bureaucracy had to be hastily improvised for the conquered lands, if only to divide up booty and to collect taxation for the khāns. The official classes of these lands, Khitan, Uyghur, Chinese and Persian, were drawn upon, and the Buddhist Uyghur Turkish secretaries, the *bitikchis*, were especially noteworthy. It is from two Persian Muslims in the Mongol service, ʿAṭāʾ Malik Juwaynī and Rashīd al-Dīn Faḍl Allāh, that much of our knowledge of the early Mongols and their history comes.

Chingiz's lands were accordingly divided among his four sons or their heirs in the following way.

(1) The eldest, Jochi, in fact died just before his father; it was the traditional steppe nomad practice to grant the pasture grounds farthest away from the home camp to the eldest son. Jochi's inheritance now passed to his own son Batu. Jochi's allocation had been of western Siberia and the Qïpchaq steppe, extending into southern Russia and including also Khwārazm, which had always been linked culturally and commercially with the lower Volga lands. His son Batu founded the Blue Horde in South Russia, nucleus of the later Golden Horde, while Jochi's eldest son, Orda, founded the White Horde in western Siberia, these two groups being united in the fourteenth century. At a later date, various khanates in Russia and Siberia evolved from the Hordes (see below, nos 136–8), while in the fifteenth and sixteenth centuries, the descendants of another of Jochi's sons, Shïban, namely the Shïbānids or Özbegs, made themselves masters of Khwārazm and Transoxania (see below, no. 153).

(2) The second son, Chaghatay, was given the Central Asian lands to the north of Transoxania, roughly those which had been held by the Qara Khitay and which came to be known now as Mogholistan, and extending into Eastern or the later Chinese Turkestan; to these were added Transoxania itself during Ögedey's reign. The western branch of Chaghatay's descendants in Transoxania soon came within the Islamic religious and cultural sphere of influence, but was brought under the control of Tīmūr Lang; the eastern branch in Semirechye, the Ili basin and across the T'ien Shan mountains in the Tarim basin, was more resistant to Islam. However, the eastern descendants of Chaghatay eventually helped to spread Islam in Eastern Turkestan, and they ruled there until the later seventeenth century (see below, no. 132).

(3) The third son Ögedey had been favoured by Chingiz during his lifetime as his future successor as Great Khān, and this was confirmed in 627/1229 by a *Quriltay* of Mongol chiefs. But within a generation the Supreme Khanate fell into the hands of the descendants of Toluy, although Ögedey's grandson Qaydu retained his territories in the Pamirs and T'ien Shan, was recognised by the Chaghatayids and remained hostile to the Tolu'id Great Khān Qubilay until Qaydu's death in 703/1304.

(4) The youngest son Toluy had received, following traditional steppe practice as *otchigin* 'guardian of the hearth', the heartland of the empire, Mongolia itself. His sons Möngke and Qubilay followed Ögedey's line as Great Khāns, but only Möngke retained the newly-built centre of Qaraqorum in Mongolia as his capital. The Great Khāns' possessions included the Chinese conquests, where the Mongols became known as the Yüan dynasty and reigned until the second half of the fourteenth century. The cultural and religious attractions of Chinese civilisation proved strong for the Great Khāns in their northern Chinese capital of Peking; they became Buddhists, and their adherence to this faith, which was to become the dominant one in Mongolia itself, gradually opened up a breach with the subordinate Mongol khāns in western Asia and Russia, who adopted Islam in varying stages. It was one of Qubilay's brothers, Hülegü, who launched a fresh wave of conquest upon the Islamic world and who founded the Il Khānid line in Persia; thus the khanates of western Asia ceased, for all practical purposes, to acknowledge the authority of the Great Khāns back in Mongolia and in Peking.

EI[2] 'Mongols' (D. O. Morgan).
R. Grousset, *L'empire des steppes*, Paris 1939, Eng. tr. *The Empire of the Steppes. A History of Central Asia*, New Brunswick NJ 1970.
J. J. Saunders, *The History of the Mongol Conquests*, London 1971.
B. Spuler, *The Mongols in History*, London 1971.
D. O. Morgan, *The Mongols*, Oxford 1986.

131

THE MONGOL GREAT KHĀNS, DESCENDANTS OF ÖGEDEY AND TOLUY,
LATER THE YÜAN DYNASTY OF CHINA

602–1043/1206–1634

Mongolia and the conquests made from there, then in Mongolia and China, then in Mongolia alone

⊘ 602/1206	Chinggis (Chingiz), son of Yesügey, d. 624/1227
⊘ 626/1229	Ögedey Khān, son of Chingiz
⊘ 639/1241	Töregene Khātūn, widow of Ögedey, as regent
644/1246	Güyük, son of Ögedey
646/1248	Oghul Ghaymish, widow of Güyük, as regent
⊘ 649/1251	Möngke (Mengü), son of Toluy, d. 657/1259
⊘ 658/1260	Qubilay, son of Toluy
⊘ (658–62/1260–4	Ariq Böke, son of Toluy, rival Khān in Mongolia)
693/1294	Temür Öljeytü, son of Chen-chin (Jim Gim) and grandson of Qubilay
706/1307	Qayshan Gülük (Hai-shan), son of Darmabala, son of Chen-chin, and great-grandson of Qubilay
711/1311	Ayurparibhadra (Ayurbarwada) or Buyantu, son of Darmabala
720/1320	Suddhipala Gege'en or Gegen (Shidebala), son of Buyantu
723/1323	Yesün Temür, son of Kammala, son of Chen-chin
728/1328	Arigaba (Aragibag), son of Yesün Temür
728/1328	Jijaghatu Toq Temür, son of Qayshan Gülük, first reign
729/1329	Qoshila Qutuqtu, son of Qayshan Gülük
729/1329	Jijaghatu Toq Temür, second reign
733/1332	Rinchenpal (Irinchinbal), son of Qoshila
733–71/1333–70	Toghan Temür, son of Qoshila
	The Great Khāns in China replaced by the Ming dynasty in 770/1368, but the line of Toluy's descendants continuing in Mongolia until the seventeenth century

Ögedey's reign was one of resumed, triumphal conquest. That of northern China and what is now Manchuria, with the overthrow of the Chin dynasty and the annexation of Korea, was achieved, though it was not until 1279 that the Sung rulers of southern China were finally extinguished. At the other end of the Old World, Batu was raiding the South Russian steppes and central Europe, terrorising mediaeval Christendom (see below, no. 134, 1). Although Ögedey's son Güyük had numerous offspring, the supreme khanate passed on Güyük's death in April 1248 eventually to another line, that of Möngke and the descendants of Toluy. When Möngke's brother Qubilay was hailed as Great Khān by a *Quriltay* in Mongolia which rival branches of the family did not attend, the descendants of Ögedey broke out in revolt, and under Qaydu and his son Chapar were for long an embarassment to the Great Khāns. They submitted in the end to the family of Toluy, but in later times various members of the house of Ögedey were raised to power in periods of revolution and unrest, and the great Tīmūr (see below, no.

144) set up two of these in Transoxania, Soyurghatmïsh and his son Maḥmūd, to replace the Chaghatayids there.

The Great Khāns in Qaraqorum and, after Möngke's time, in Peking or Khān balïq (= 'City of the Khāns') led a life of a certain barbarian splendour, as the accounts of travellers and vistors from Western Europe like Marco Polo and from the Near East like the Armenian king Hayton show. Material wealth and plunder gained from the Mongol conquests flowed into the capital; artisans and craftsmen were gathered there; scholars, writers and religious leaders made their way to the khāns' encampment. The Mongols displayed the traditional steppe tolerance of religions, or indifference to them, and were willing to give a hearing to the arguments of Latin and Nestorian Christians, Muslims, Buddhists and Confucianists. Inevitably, in Mongolia and northern China, the original animistic shamanism of the Mongols gave way to one of the higher religions, in fact to Buddhism in the Tibetan Lamaist form. This became and has remained the dominant religion of the Mongols of Eastern Asia, and was even carried westwards to the Volga and Kuban river regions by the Oyrot Mongols or Kalmucks in their great migration of the early seventeenth century.

The Mongol Great Khāns gradually settled down to being yet another Chinese dynasty of barbarian origin, the Yüan, considered in traditional Chinese historiography as the Twentieth Official Dynasty and as ruling from 1280 onwards. They ruled in China until in 1368 they were replaced by the native Ming, but well before that they had ceased to have much influence over the Mongol khanates of central and western Asia. Only in Mongolia did the descendants of the Great Khāns survive with some independence, though under the general suzerainty of the Ming emperors.

Lane-Poole, 201–16; Zambaur, 241–3; Album, 43.

EI² 'Čingiz-Khān' (J. A. Boyle), 'Ḳubilay' (W. Barthold and J. A. Boyle), 'Öldjeytü' (D. O. Morgan); EIr 'Čengīz' (D. O. Morgan).

L. Hambis, *Le chapitre CVII du Yuan Che, les généalogies impériales mongoles dans l'histoire chinoise officielle de la dynastie mongole* (= Supplement to TP, 38, Leiden 1945), 51–2, 71–3, 85–9, 106–9, 114–17, 128–32, 136–44. 153–5, 157–8 (tables based on both Chinese and Persian sources).

F. W. Cleaves, 'The Mongol names and terms in the *History of the Nation of Archers* by Grigor of Akanc'', HJAS, 12 (1949), 400–43.

J. A. Boyle, 'On the titles given in Juvainī to certain Mongol princes', HJAS, 19 (1956), 146–54.

idem, *The Successors of Genghis Khan, translated from the Persian of Rashīd al-Dīn*, New York and London 1971, with a genealogical table at p. 342.

D. O. Morgan, *The Mongols*, with genealogical tables at pp. 222–3.

132

THE CHAGHATAYIDS, DESCENDANTS OF CHAGHATAY

624–764/1227–1363

Transoxania, Mogholistan including Semirechye, and eastern Turkestan

⊘ 624/1227	Chaghatay, son of Chingiz
⊘ 642/1244	Qara Hülegü, son of Mö'etüken, son of Chingiz, first reign
⊘ 644/1246	Yesü Möngke, son of Chaghatay
649/1251	Qara Hülegü, second reign
⊘ 650/1252	Orqina Khātūn, widow of Qara Hülegü
⊘ 658/1260	Alughu, son of Baydar, son of Chaghatay
664/1266	Mubārak Shāh, son of Qara Hülegü
⊘ c. 664/c. 1266	Baraq, Ghiyāth al-Dīn, son of Yesūn Du'a, son of Mö'etüken
670/1271	Negübey (Nīkpāy), son of Sarban, son of Chaghatay
⊘ 670/1272	Buqa or Toqa Temür, son of Qadaqchi Sechen and great-grandson of Mö'etüken
⊘ c. 681/c. 1282	Du'a (Duwa), son of Baraq
706/1306	Könchek, son of Du'a
708/1308	Taliqu, son of Qadaqchi Sechem and great-grandson of Mö'etüken
709/1309	Kebek (Köpek), son of Du'a, first reign
⊘ 709/1309	Esen Buqa, son of Du'a
⊘ c. 720/c. 1320	Kebek, second reign
⊘ 726/1326	Eljigedey, son of Du'a
726/1326	Du'a Temür, son of Du'a
⊘ 726/1326	Tarmashīrīn, 'Alā' al-Dīn, son of Du'a
734/1334	Buzan, son of Du'a Temür
⊘ 734/1334	Changshi, son of Ebügen, son of Du'a
⊘ c. 739/c. 1338	Yesün Temür, son of Ebügen
⊘ (742–4/1341–3	'Alī Khalīl (Allāh), descendant of Ögedey)
⊘ c. 743/c. 1342	Muḥammad, son of Pūlād, son of Könchek
⊘ 744/1343	Qazan, son of Yasa'ur, son of Du'a, k. 747/1347
⊘ 747/1346	Dānishmendji, son of 'Alī Sulṭān, descendant of Ögedey
⊘ 749/1358	Buyan Quli, son of Surughu Oghul, son of Du'a, k. 759/1358
760/1359	Shāh Temür b. 'Abdallāh b. Qazghan
⊘ 760–4/1359–63	Tughluq Temür, ? son of Esen Buqa
764/1363	*Domination of Tīmūr Lang over the Western Chaghatay Khanate, with the Eastern Khanate remaining in power until the later seventeenth century*

After Chingiz's death, Chaghatay had great prestige as the oldest surviving son and as an acknowledged expert on the Mongol tribal law, the *Yasa*; he was, indeed, strongly anti-Muslim and insisted on enforcing those prescriptions of the *Yasa* which ran counter to the Muslim *Sharī'a*, for example over the slaughtering of animals for meat and over ablutions in running water. Chaghatay's appanage straddled the T'ien Shan mountains from the Uyghur lands in the east to Soghdia in the west, but the Chaghatay khanate was not really founded until after Chaghatay's own death. His sons and grandsons quarrelled among themselves and conspired against the Great Khān Möngke, and according to William of Rubruck, the Flemish friar who travelled to the Mongol court at Qaraqorum, the whole Mongol empire was divided c. 1250 between Möngke and Batu, son of Jochi. The real founder of the Chaghatay khanate was Chaghatay's grandson Alughu, who took advantage of the civil war between Möngke's sons Qubilay and Arïgh Böke to seize Khwārazm, western Turkestan and Afghanistan, nominally for Arïgh Böke but in fact for himself. These territories became the nucleus of the khanate, which continued now in a slightly reduced form, nominally subject to the Great Khāns but in fact until the end of the thirteenth century sharing influence in Central Asia with Qaydu, the grandson of Ögedey, until the latter's death in 702/1303.

From their geographical position, the Chaghatayids were less directly under the influence of Islam than their relatives in Persia, the Il Khānids (see below, no. 133), and preserved their tribal and nomadic ways much longer. These facts may have contributed to the general decline of urban life and agriculture in Central Asia outside the oases of Transoxania and Eastern Turkestan. The short-reigned Mubārak Shāh (664/1266) was the first Chaghatayid definitely to adopt Islam, but from c. 681/c. 1282 Du'a and his descendants were fiercely pagan and resided in the eastern territories of the khanate. Kebek was the first to return to Transoxania, where he built a palace at Nakhshab or Qarshi (< Mongol 'palace'). Tarmashīrīn (whose name in this Persianised form enshrines a Buddhist Sanskrit one like *Dharmasīla* 'Having the habit of the Dharma or Buddhist law') became a Muslim, but the strongly anti-Islamic nomadic Mongols of the eastern part of the khanate rose against him and killed him in 734/1334.

The unity of the Chaghatayids began to disintegrate soon after this, as Tīmūr Lang rose to power in Transoxania. Various Chaghatayids were placed on the throne in Transoxania by the Turkish amīrs, and then after 764/1363 some descendants of Ögedey were set up by Tīmūr. The Chaghatayids nevertheless survived, and after Tīmūr's death their fortunes revived in Mogholistan and endured there until the mid-fifteenth century under Esen Buqa II b. Uways Khān (r. 833–67/1429–62), a dangerous enemy of the later Tīmūrids; but the Chaghatayids' Transoxanian territories fell to the Shībānids (see below, no. 153) by the beginning of the sixteenth century. Only the eastern branch persisted in Semirechye, with its capital at first at Almalïgh in the upper Ili region, and in the Tarim basin, where it expanded towards Turfan and shared power in Kāshghar with the Dughlat tribe of Turks until the final extinction of the Chaghatayids in 1089/1678 and their replacement in Eastern Turkestan by a line of local Naqshbandī religious leaders, the Khōjas.

Lane-Poole, 241–2; Sachau, 30 no. 77; Zambaur, 248–50; Album, 43–4.

EI^2 'Čaghatay Khān', 'Čaghatay Khānate' (W. Barthold and J. A. Boyle); EIr 'Chaghatayid dynasty' (P. Jackson).

L. Hambis, *Le chapitre CVII du Yuan Che*, 56–64.

J. A. Boyle, *The Successors of Genghis Khan*, with a genealogical table at p. 345.

133

THE IL KHĀNIDS, DESCENDANTS OF QUBILAY'S BROTHER HÜLEGÜ
654–754/1256–1353
Persia, Iraq, eastern and central Anatolia

⊘ 654/1256	Hülegü (Hūlākū), son of Toluy
⊘ 663/1265	Abaqa, son of Hülegü, d. 680/1282
⊘ 681/1282	Aḥmad Tegüder (Takūdār), son of Hülegü
⊘ 683/1284	Arghun, son of Abaqa
⊘ 690/1291	Gaykhatu, son of Abaqa
⊘ 694/1295	Baydu, son of Taraqay, son of Hülegü
⊘ 694/1295	Maḥmūd Ghazan (Ghāzān) I, son of Arghun
⊘ 703/1304	Muḥammad Khudābanda Öljeytü (Ūljāytū), Ghiyāth al-Dīn, son of Arghun
⊘ 716/1316	Abū Sa'īd, 'Alā' al-Dunyā wa 'l-Dīn, Bahādur, son of Öljeytü
⊘ 736/1335	Arpa Ke'ün (Gawon), descendant of Arïgh Böke, son of Toluy
⊘ 736/1336	Mūsā, son of 'Alī, son of Baydu
⊘ 737–8/1337–8	Muḥammad, descendant of Hülegü's son Möngke Temür
⊘ (739–54/1338–53	Togha(y) Temür, descendant of one of Chingiz Khān's brothers, either Ötken or Jochi, in control of western Khurasan and Gurgān
754–90/1353–88	Luqmān b. Togha(y) Temür, sporadic claimant in Khurasan)
738–54/1338–53	*Period of several rival khāns in various parts of Persia nominated by the Jalāyirid Amīr Ḥasan Buzurg (⊘ Toghay Temür, see above; ⊘ Jahān Temur) and the Chobanid Amīr Ḥasan Küchük (⊘ Sati Beg Khātūn; ⊘ Sulaymān; ⊘ Anūshirwān; ⊘ Ghazan II); thereafter, Persia divided among local dynasties such as the Jalāyirids, the Muẓaffarids and the Sarbadārids*

The Great Khān Möngke entrusted his brother Hülegü with the task of recovering and consolidating the Mongol conquests in Western Asia, for in the interval since Ögedey's death direct control of much of the Islamic world south of the Oxus had slipped out of Mongol hands. Hülegü accordingly came westwards. He overcame the resistance of the Ismā'īlīs or Assassins of northern Persia (see above, no. 101) (654/1256); routed a caliphal army in Iraq and murdered the last 'Abbāsid caliph al-Musta'ṣim (656/1258); and advanced into Syria where, however, the Mongols were defeated and halted at 'Ayn Jālūt in Palestine by the Mamlūks of Egypt and Syria (see above, no. 31) (658/1260). Even so, Hülegü now became ruler on behalf of the Great Khān of all the regions of Persia, Iraq, Transcaucasia and Anatolia, and assumed the title of *Il Khān*, namely territorial khān, implying subordination to the Great Khān.

The Il Khānid kingdom was now definitely constituted, but it had many external enemies, including the Mamlūks, who had destroyed the popular belief in Mongol invincibility and were now the standard-bearers of Islam against the scourge of the pagans. The other Mongol houses of the Chaghatayids (see above, no. 132) and the Golden Horde (see below, no. 134) were also hostile over disputed territories in the Caucasus region and on the north-eastern Persian fringes respectively. It was common hostility towards the Il Khānids that brought about a political and commercial alliance of the Mamlūks and the Golden Horde, whereas the Il Khānids for their part sought to conclude an anti-Muslim coalition with the European Christian powers, with the surviving Crusaders in the Levant coastal towns and with the Little Armenian kingdom in Cilicia. Hülegü's wife Doquz Khātūn was a Nestorian Christian, and the first Il Khānids were favourably inclined towards Christianity and Buddhism.

The Il Khānids managed to hold their own against external foes, but, after the Great Khān Qubilay's death in 693/1294, links with the senior members of the Mongol family in Mongolia and China became very loose, especially as the cultural and religious pressures of the Persian environment brought about the conversion to Islam of Ghazan (his short-reigned predecessor Aḥmad Tegüder had also been converted) and his successors. Abū Saʿīd was the last great Il Khānid. He made peace with the Mamlūks in 723/1323 and thus ended the fighting over possession of Syria, but relations with the Golden Horde and disputes over the Caucasus region continued throughout his reign. It was unfortunate that he died without an heir and, indeed, without any close relations to succeed him. The two decades after his death were filled with a succession of ephemeral khans, raised to the throne by the rival Jalāyirid and Chobanid Amīrs, until finally the Il Khānid empire fell apart and was replaced by local dynasties across Persia. It was left to Tīmūr Lang a generation later to reunite the Persian lands under one sovereign.

Despite much warfare and internal disturbance, the Il Khānid period was a prosperous one for Persia. After Ghazan became a Muslim, there began tentatively a reconciliatory process between the Mongol-Turkish military and ruling class and their Persian subjects. The Il Khānid capitals of Tabrīz and Marāgha in Azerbaijan became centres of learning, with the natural sciences, astronomy and historical writing especially flourishing. After 707/1307, Öljeytü planned a new capital at Sulṭāniyya near Qazwīn; artists, architects and craftsmen were encouraged, and distinctive styles of, for example, Il Khānid architecture and painting emerged. The internationalist attitudes of the Mongols and their connections with such ancient cultures as the Chinese brought fresh intellectual, commercial and artistic influences into the Persian world. Colonies of Italian traders now appeared in the capital Tabrīz, and the Il Khānid empire played a significant connecting rôle in trade with the Far East and India.

Lane-Poole, 217–21; Zambaur, 244–5; Album, 45–8.
EI[2] 'Īlkhāns' (B. Spuler).
L. Hambis, *Le chapitre CVII du Yuan Che*, 90–4.
J. A. Boyle, *The Successors of Genghis Khan*, with a genealogical table at p. 343.
B. Spuler, *Die Mongolen in Iran. Politik, Verwaltung und Kultur der Ilchanzeit 1220–1350*, 4th edn, Leiden 1985, with a genealogical table at p. 382.
D. O. Morgan, *The Mongols*, with a genealogical table at p. 225.

134

THE KHĀNS OF THE GOLDEN HORDE, DESCENDANTS OF JOCHI
624–907/1227–1502
Western Siberia, Khwārazm and South Russia

1. The line of Batu'ids, Khāns of the Blue Horde in South Russia, Khwārazm and the western part of the Qïpchaq steppe

624/1227	Batu, son of Jochi, d. ?653/?1255
654/1256	Sartaq, son of Batu
655/1257	Ulaghchi, son or brother of Sartaq
655/1257	Berke (Baraka), son of Jochi
⊘ 665/1267	Möngke (Mengü) Temür, son of Toqoqan, son of Batu
⊘ 679/1280	Töde Möngke (Mengü), son of Toqoqan
⊘ 687/1287	Töle Buqa, son of Tartu, son of Toqoqan
⊘ 690/1291	Toqta, son of Möngke Temür, Ghiyāth al-Dīn
⊘ 713/1313	Muḥammad Özbeg, son of Toghrïlcha, son of Möngke Temür, Ghiyāth al-Dīn
742/1341	Tīnī Beg, son of Özbeg
⊘ 743/1342	Jānī Beg (Jambek), son of Özbeg
758–82/1357–80	*Period of anarchy, with several rival claimants, including ⊘ Muḥammad Berdi Beg, ⊘ Qulpa, ⊘ Muḥammad Nawrūz Beg, ⊘ Khiḍr, ⊘ Murād, ⊘ Muḥammad Bolaq, etc.*

2. The line of Orda, Khāns of the White Horde in western Siberia and the eastern part of the Qïpchaq steppe, and, after 780/1378, of the Blue and White Hordes united into the Golden Horde of South Russia

623/1226	Orda, son of Jochi
679/1280	Köchü
701/1302	Buyan
708/1309	Sāsibuqa (? Sarïgh Buqa)
c. 715/c. 1315	Ilbasan
720/1320	Mubārak Khwāja
745/1344	Chimtay
776/1374	Urus, son of Chimtay
778/1376	Toqtaqiya, son of Urus
778/1377	Temür Malik, son of Urus
⊘ 778/1377	Toqtamïsh, son of Toli Khwāja or descendant of Orda's brother Toqa Temür, Ghiyāth al-Dīn
⊘ 797/1395	Temür Qutlugh, son of Temür Malik
⊘ 803/1401	Shādī Beg, son of Temür Malik
⊘ 810/1407	Pūlād (Bolod) Khān, son of Temür Malik
813/1410	Temür, son of Temür Qutlugh
⊘ 815/1412	Jalāl al-Dīn, son of Toqtamïsh
815/1412	Karīm Berdi, son of Toqtamïsh
⊘ 817/1414	Kebek, son of Toqtamïsh

820/1417	Yeremferden (? Jabbār Berdi), son of Toqtamïsh	
⊘ 822/1419	Ulugh Muḥammad, first reign	rival khāns
⊘ 823/1420	Dawlat Berdi	
825/1422	Baraq	
832/1427	Ulugh Muḥammad, second reign (later in Qazan)	
c. 838/c. 1433	Sayyid Aḥmad I	
⊘ c. 840/c. 1435	Küchük Muḥammad, son of Temür	
c. 871/c. 1465	Aḥmad, son of Temür	
886–903/1481–98, 904–7/1499–1502	Shaykh Aḥmad, d. 911/1505	sons of Aḥmad, as co-rulers
886– /1481–	Sayyid Aḥmad II	
886–904/1481–99	Murtaḍā	
907/1502	*Defeat of Shaykh Aḥmad by the Giray Khāns of the Crimea and absorption of the Golden Horde into the Crimean Tatar Horde*	

Chingiz's eldest son Jochi had been allotted as his appanage western Siberia and the Qïpchaq Steppe, and on his death in 624/1227 the eastern part of all this, namely western Siberia, fell to his eldest son Orda, who became titular head of the descendants of Jochi and who founded in his territories the White Horde. Little is known about the early White Horde khāns, but the forceful and energetic Toqtamïsh (d. 809/1406) is a figure of major importance in steppe and eastern European history. He united the Batu'id Blue Horde (by now known as the Golden Horde) with the White Horde, and once more made the Golden Horde a power of importance in Russia, sacking Nizhniy Novgorod and Moscow in 784/1382. However, he had the misfortune to come up against Tīmūr Lang, who drove him out of his capital Saray on the Volga, so that Toqtamïsh was forced to flee into exile with Vitold (Vitautas), Grand Duke of Lithuania.

The western half of Jochi's appanage, Khwārazm and the Qïpchaq Steppe of South Russia, went to his second son Batu. Batu ravaged Russia almost as far as Novgorod, captured Kiev and attacked Poland and Hungary. Christian Europe was only saved from further molestation after Batu's Liegnitz victory of 638/1241 and the pursuit of the Hungarian King Béla IV to the shores of the Adriatic by the news of the Great Khān Ögedey's death. Based on the capital Saray, Batu's Blue Horde became the nucleus of the Golden Horde (a name apparently given to them by the Russians, *Zolotaya Orda*, although Russian and Polish-Lithuanian sources most usually refer to it simply as 'the Great Horde'). From Özbeg onwards (d. 742/1341), the khāns of the Golden Horde were all Muslims, and this meant that there was a religious gulf fixed between the ruling Golden Horde and the mass of their Orthodox Christian Russian subjects, although Latin Christian missionaries continued to work for some time in the Qïpchaq Steppe. The Horde had important commercial links with Anatolia and the Mamlūk empire in Syria and Egypt; slave replenishments were sent to the Mamlūks, while the culture of the Horde received a definite Islamic-Mediterranean impress, in contrast to the Persianised Il Khānids. However, the growth of Ottoman Turkish power and the Ottoman control of the Dardanelles after 755/1354 cut the Horde off from the Mediterranean and contact with the Mamlūks and made them purely a power within Russia.

After Toqtamïsh's death, real power in the Golden Horde was held by the capable 'Mayor of the Palace' Edigü, but after the latter's death in 822/1419 a process of disintegration, involving much internal discord, set in. Already in the later fourteenth century, the rise of Poland-Lithuania and the Princedom of Muscovy had seriously checked the authority of the khāns, and the Ottomans and their allies the Crimean Tatars were also hostile. It was, indeed, the Crimean khān, Mengli Giray, who in 907/1502 defeated the leader of the Horde and incorporated the major part of its manpower into his own forces. But before that date, other khanates had split off from the Golden Horde, under various descendants of a third son of Jochi, Toqa Temür; these included the khanates of Astrakhan (until the Russian conquest of 961/1554: see below, no. 136), of Kazan (until the Russian conquest of 959/1552: see below, no. 137); of Qāsimov (around Ryazan, until c. 1092/c. 1681: see below, no. 138); and of the Crimea (see below, no. 135).

Lane-Poole, 222–31 and table at p. 240; Zambaur, 244, 246–7 and Table S; Album, 44.
L. Hambis, *Le chapitre CVII du Yuan Che*, 52–7.
B. Spuler, *Die Goldene Horde. Die Mongolen in Russland 1223–1502*, 2nd edn, Wiesbaden 1965, with genealogical tables and lists at pp. 453–4.
J. A. Boyle, *The Successors of Genghis Khan*, with a genealogical table at p. 344.
D. O. Morgan, *The Mongols*, with a genealogical table at p. 224.

135

THE GIRAY KHĀNS OF THE CRIMEA, DESCENDANTS OF JOCHI

853–1208/1449–1792

The Crimea and the southern Ukraine

1. The Khāns of the Crimea

early ninth/ fifteenth century	Dawlat Birdi Giray (Kerey) b. Tash Temür and, after 830/ 1427, Ḥājjī Giray b. Ghiyāth al-Dīn b. Tash Temür, rulers in the Crimea under the Golden Horde khāns
⊘ 853/1449	Ḥājjī Giray I b. Ghiyāth al-Dīn b. Tash Temür, independent ruler, first reign
860/1456	Ḥaydar Giray b. Ḥājji I
860/1456	Ḥājjī Giray I, second reign
⊘ 870/1466	Nūr Dawlat Giray b. Ḥājjī I, first reign
⊘ 871/1467	Mengli Giray b. Ḥājji I, first reign
879/1474	Nūr Dawlat, second reign
880/1475	Mengli Giray, second reign
881/1476	Nūr Dawlat Giray, third reign
883/1478	Mengli Giray, third reign
⊘ 920/1514	Muḥammad Giray I b. Mengli
931/1523	Ghāzī Giray I b. Muḥammad I
⊘ 932/1524	Saʿādat Giray I b. Mengli
939/1532	Islām Giray I b. Muḥammad I
⊘ 939/1532	Ṣāḥib Giray I b. Mengli
⊘ 958/1551	Dawlat Giray I b. Mubārak b. Mengli
⊘ 985/1577	Muḥammad Giray II b. Dawlat I
⊘ 992/1584	Islām Giray II b. Dawlat I
⊘ 998/1588	Ghāzī Giray II b. Dawlat I, first reign
1005/1596	Fatḥ Giray I b. Dawlat I
1006/1596	Ghāzī Giray II, second reign
1016/1608	Toqtamïsh Giray b. Ghāzī II
⊘ 1017/1608	Salāmat Giray I b. Dawlat I
1019/1610	Muḥammad Giray III b. Saʿādat b. Muḥammad II, first reign
⊘ 1019/1610	Jānī Beg Giray b. Mubārak b. Dawlat I, first reign
1032/1623	Muḥammad Giray III, second reign
⊘ 1033/1624	Jānī Beg Giray, second reign
1033/1624	Muḥammad Giray III, third reign
⊘ 1036/1627	Jānī Beg Giray, third reign
1044/1635	ʿInāyat Giray b. Ghāzī II
1046/1637	Bahādur Giray I b. Salāmat I
1051/1641	Muḥammad Giray IV b. Salāmat I, Ṣofu, first reign
⊘ 1054/1644	Islām Giray III b. Salāmat I
⊘ 1064/1654	Muḥammad Giray IV, second reign
⊘ 1076/1666	ʿĀdil Giray b. Dawlat b. Fatḥ I

⊘ 1082/1671	Salīm Giray I b. Bahādur, first reign
⊘ 1089/1678	Murād Giray b. Mubārak b. Salāmat I
1094/1683	Ḥājjī Giray II b. Qïrïm b. Salāmat I
⊘ 1095/1684	Salīm Giray I, second reign
1103/1691	Sa'ādat Giray II b. Qïrïm b. Salāmat I
⊘ 1103/1691	Ṣafā' Giray b. Ṣafā' b. Salāmat I
⊘ 1104/1692	Salīm Giray I, third reign
⊘ 1110/1699	Dawlat Giray II b. Salīm I, first reign
1114/1702	Salīm Giray I, fourth reign
⊘ 1116/1704	Ghāzī Giray III b. Salīm I
⊘ 1119/1707	Qaplan Giray I b. Salīm I, first reign
⊘ 1120/1708	Dawlat Giray II, second reign
⊘ 1125/1713	Qaplan Giray I, second reign
1128/1716	Dawlat Giray III b. 'Ādil b. Salāmat I
⊘ 1129/1717	Sa'ādat Giray III b. Salīm I
⊘ 1137/1724	Mengli Giray II b. Salīm I, first reign
⊘ 1143/1730	Qaplan Giray I, third reign
⊘ 1149/1736	Fatḥ Giray II b. Dawlat II
1150/1737	Mengli Giray II, second reign
⊘ 1152/1740	Salāmat Giray II b. Salīm I
⊘ 1156/1743	Salīm Giray II b. Qaplan I
⊘ 1161/1748	Arslan Giray b. Dawlat II, first reign
⊘ 1169/1756	Ḥalīm Giray b. Sa'ādat III
⊘ 1172/1758	Qïrïm Giray b. Dawlat II, first reign
⊘ 1178/1764	Salīm Giray III b. Fatḥ II, first reign
1180/1767	Arslan Giray, second reign
⊘ 1181/1767	Maqṣūd Giray b. Salāmat II, first reign
⊘ 1182/1768	Qïrïm Giray, second reign
⊘ 1182/1769	Dawlat Giray IV b. Arslan, first reign
⊘ 1183/1769	Qaplan Giray II b. Salīm II
1184/1770	Salīm Giray III, second reign
1185/1771	Maqṣūd Giray, second reign
⊘ 1186/1772	Ṣāḥib Giray II b. Salīm III
⊘ 1189/1775	Dawlat Giray IV, second reign
⊘ 1191/1777	Shāhīn Giray b. Aḥmad b. Dawlat II, first reign
1196–7/1782–3	Bahādur II Giray b. Aḥmad b. Dawlat II
1197/1783	*Russian annexation of the Crimea*
1197–1201/1783–7	Shāhīn Giray, second reign, as a Russian vassal

2. The Khāns of the Tatars of Bujaq or Bessarabia, as Ottoman nominees

1201/1787	Shāhbāz Giray b. Arslan
1203–6/1789–92	Bakht Giray

Among the descendants of Jochi's son Toqa Temür, one branch established itself in the Crimea during the course of the internecine strife which convulsed the Golden Horde after 760/1359. At first they were vassals of Toqtamïsh, but then in the early fifteenth century they gradually became independent under the progeny of Tash Temür, with Ḥājjī Giray formally declaring himself ruler of

Qïrïm in 853/1449. The family name Giray derives possibly from that of the Kerey, a component clan of the Golden Horde which had supported Ḥājjī Giray. The Crimean khanate now became one of the most enduring states to arise under the descendants of Chingiz Khān, and by the end of the fifteenth century it also controlled the lands of the Noghays on the northern Black Sea coast as far west as Bujaq or Bessarabia.

The Ottomans were the natural allies of the Girays, at first against the Golden Horde, whose khans continued to regard the Crimea as one of their own dependencies, and then, from the sixteenth century onwards, against the Russians. The Girays claimed to be heirs of the Golden Horde after they had defeated its leader and incorporated the greater part of its fighting manpower into their own forces (see above, no. 134), and did for part of the sixteenth century rule at Kazan (see below, no. 137). Their increased military strength after 907/1502, and the fact that the pasture grounds of the Girays were nearer to Moscow than the Golden Horde's more usual centre on the lower Volga, now meant increased military pressure on Muscovy, with attacks and raids continuing until the eighteenth century. From the later sixteenth century, the khans ruled from their capital at Baghche Saray (Simferopol) over much of the southern part of the Ukraine and the lower Don-Kuban region, acting as a buffer-state between the Ottomans and the Christian powers of Eastern Europe; in fact, during the early seventeenth century they were at times allied with Poland-Lithuania against the Russian Tsars. The Ottomans regarded the Crimean Tatars as their dependents, requiring the presence of a hostage Giray prince at their court, although rarely intermarrying with the Girays; there was a vague feeling that, should the Ottoman dynasty die out (as seemed not impossible at one point in the seventeenth century), the Girays would have a claim on the succession in Turkey.

Russian expansionism southwards brought about Peter the Great's capture of Azov in 1699, which cut the lands of the Crimean Tatars in two. In the eighteenth century, Russian pressure increased, with the enfeebled Ottoman empire unable to help, and by 1197/1783 Catherine the Great's troops had occupied and annexed the Crimea. Two of the Girays were, however, appointed by the Porte to head the Tatars in Bessarabia for a few years.

Lane-Poole, 235–7 and table at p. 240; Zambaur, 247–8 and Table S; Album, 44–5.
İA 'Giray' (Halil İnalcık), with a genealogical table; *EI*² 'Girāy' (idem), 'Ḳirim' (B. Spuler), with a list of rulers.
Alan W. Fisher, *The Crimean Tatars*, Stanford CA 1978, 1–69.

136

THE KHĀNS OF ASTRAKHAN (ASTRAKHĀN, ASHTARKHĀN)

871–964/1466–1557

The lower Volga and the adjacent steppelands

871/1466	Qāsim b. Maḥmūd b. Küchük Muḥammad
895/1490	ʿAbd al-Karīm b. Maḥmūd b. Küchük Muḥammad
909/1504	Qāsim or Qasay b. Sayyid Aḥmad
938/1532	Aq Köbek b. Murtaḍā, first reign
941/1534	ʿAbd al-Raḥmān b. ʿAbd al-Karīm
945/1538	Shaykh Ḥaydar b. Shaykh Aḥmad
948/1541	Aq Köbek, second reign
951/1544	Yaghmurchi b. Birdi Beg
961/1554	*Russian conquest*
961–4/1554–7	Darwīsh ʿAlī b. Shaykh Ḥaydar, as a Russian nominee
964/1557	*Incorporation of the khanate into Russia*

During the decline of the Golden Horde (see above, no. 134), there arose at Astrakhan near the mouth of the Volga (a town long important from its position on the trade route down the Volga to the Caspian Sea and beyond) a line of Noghay Tatar khāns stemming from Orda's White Horde through Toqtamïsh. The lands of the first khāns extended as far as the Kazan khanate (see below, no. 137) in the north, to Orenburg or Chkalov in the east and the lands of the Crimean Tatar khāns in the west. By the 1530s, ʿAbd al-Raḥmān Khān was being pressed by the khāns of Crimea and the Noghays, and appealed for help to the Russian Tsar; but in 961/1554 Ivan IV ('The Terrible') conquered Astrakhan, and three years later deposed the puppet Darwīsh ʿAlī Khān when he began seeking support from his Tatar Muslim neighbours, and Astrakhan was incorporated into the Russian empire.

Lane-Poole, 229 and table at p. 240; Zambaur, 247 (fragmentary) and Table S.
İA 'Astırhan, Astraḫan' (R. Rahmeti Arat); *EI*[2] 'Astra<u>kh</u>ān' (B. Spuler).

137

THE KHĀNS OF KAZAN (QĀZĀN)
840–959/1437–1552
The middle Volga region

1. The line of Ulugh Muḥammad

840/1437	Ulugh Muḥammad b. Jalāl al-Dīn b. Toqtamïsh
849/1445	Maḥmūd (Maḥmūdak) b. Ulugh Muḥammad
866/1462	Khalīl b. Maḥmūd
871/1467	Ibrāhīm b. Maḥmūd
884/1479	ʿAlī b. Ibrāhīm, first reign
889/1484	Muḥammad Amīn b. Ibrāhīm, first reign
890/1485	ʿAlī b. Ibrāhīm, second reign
892/1487	Muḥammad Amīn b. Ibrāhīm, second reign
(900/1495	Mamūq b. Ibaq, Khān of the Tatars of Siberia)
901/1496	ʿAbd al-Laṭīf b. Ibrāhīm
907–24/1502–18	Muḥammad Amīn b. Ibrāhīm, third reign

2. Khāns from various outside lines

925/1519	Shāh ʿAlī b. Sayyid Awliyār, from the Khāns of Qāsimov, first reign
927/1521	Ṣāḥib Giray (I) b. Mengli I, from the Khāns of Crimea
930/1524	Ṣafāʾ Giray b. Fatḥ, from the Khāns of Crimea, first reign
937/1531	Jān ʿAlī b. Sayyid Awliyār, from the Khāns of Qāsimov
939/1533	Ṣafāʾ Giray b. Fatḥ, second reign
953/1546	Shāh ʿAlī b. Sayyid Awliyār, second reign
953/1546	Ṣafāʾ Giray b. Fatḥ, third reign
956/1549	Ötemish b. Ṣafāʾ Giray, from the Khāns of Crimea, regent for Süyün Bike
958/1551	Shāh ʿAlī b. Sayyid Awliyār, third reign
959/1552	Yādigār Muḥammad b. Qāsim, from the Khāns of Astrakhan
959/1552	*Russian conquest*

The Kazan khanate was another of the groupings founded by a Jochid epigone. Toqtamïsh's grandson Ulugh Muḥammad rose to power in what later became eastern Russia as the Golden Horde decayed, and his son Maḥmūd in 849/1445 seized the actual town of Kazan from a local prince, possibly of Bulghār descent, ʿAlī Beg. It was likewise around this time that the sister khanate of Qāsimov (see below, no. 138) emerged. The khanate spanned the middle Volga basin around the confluence of the Volga and Kama rivers and in the south bordered on the khanate of Astrakhan (see above, no. 136). It thus covered a region which had been exposed to Islamic influences since the constituting of the Bulghār kingdom towards the opening of the tenth century. Kazan's position gave it a considerable commercial importance, not least as a mart for slaves.

All through the khanate's life, its history was bound up with that of the Princedom of Muscovy, its western neighbour, now reasserting itself after some two centuries of thraldom to the Golden Horde and its successors. From the outset, the Princes interfered in succession disputes within Kazan. This intervention intensified after the end of the family of Ulugh Muḥammad, and the last three decades or so of the khanate saw rulers installed at Kazan from various outside Chingizid lines, with internal tensions between the partisans of an accommodation with Muscovy and those hoping to preserve Kazan's independence through links with the Crimean Tatars and the Noghay Horde. Finally, the army of Tsar Ivan IV captured Kazan in 959/1552, and a systematic Russian occupation and colonisation of the lands of the former khanate began. A considerable proportion of the Muslim Tatar population has nevertheless survived over the centuries, and a reduced part of the khanate formed under the Soviets the Tatar Autonomous SSR.

Lane-Poole, genealogical table at p. 240; Zambaur, 249 and Table S.
İA 'Kazan' (Reşid Rahmati Arat), with a genealogical table; *EI*[2] 'Ḳāzān' (W. Barthold and A. Bennigsen).
Azade-Ayşe Rorlich, *The Volga Tatars. A Profile in National Resilience*, Stanford CA 1986, 3–33.

138

THE KHĀNS OF QĀSIMOV

c. 856–1092/c. 1452–1681

The region of Ryazan, to the south-east of Moscow

1. The Khāns from the line of rulers of Kazan

c. 856/c.1452	Qāsim b. Ulugh Muḥammad
873–91/1469–86	Dāniyār b. Qāsim

2. The Khāns from the line of the rulers of the Crimea

891/1486	Nūr Dawlat Giray b. Ḥājjī I
c. 905/c. 1500	Satïlghan b. Nūr Dawlat
912/1506	Jānay b. Nūr Dawlat

3. The Khāns from the line of the rulers of Astrakhan

918/1512	Sayyid Awliyār b. Bakhtiyār Sulṭān b. Küchük Muḥammad
922/1516	Shāh ʿAlī b. Sayyid Awliyār, first reign
925–38/1519–32	Jān ʿAlī b. Sayyid Awliyār
944–58/1537–51	Shāh ʿAlī b. Sayyid Awliyār, second reign
959/1552	Shāh ʿAlī, third reign
974/1567	Sayïn Bulāt b. Bik Bulāt (Simeon Bekbulatovich), d. 1025/1616
981–1008/1573–1600	Muṣṭafā ʿAlī b. Aq Köbek

4. Kazakh Khān

1008–19/1600–10	Uraz Muḥammad
(1019–23/1610–14	*the throne vacant in Qāsimov)*

5. The Khāns from the line of the rulers of Siberia

1023/1614	Arslan or Alp Arslan b. ʿAlī b. Kuchum
1036/1627	Sayyid Burhān b. Arslan (Vassili)
1090–2/1679–81	Fāṭima Sulṭān Bike, widow of Arslan
1092/1681	*Annexation to Russia*

The khanate of Qāsimov was another of the distant successors to the *ulus* of Jochi and Batu. It was founded by a member of the ruling family in Kazan, Qāsim, who had fled to Moscow for protection. The Grand Prince Vassili I granted to him the town of Gorodets or Gorodok Meshchevskiy, later named after its ruler Qāsimov, on the Oka river to the south-east of Moscow. This became the centre of a principality which has been described as 'a historical curiosity' but which survived for over two centuries as a petty state, with ill-defined frontiers. The khāns bore in Russian the titles of Tsar and Tsarevitch, and were, in effect, feudal vassals of the Grand Princes and Emperors. Qāsimov was often a refuge for dissident Chingizids and was ruled at different times by members of the various Jochid lines. Latterly, some of the ruling family in Qāsimov became Christian and entered Russian service, and the khanate was eventually annexed to the Russian crown.

Lane-Poole, 234–5 and genealogical table at p. 240; Zambaur, 249 and Table S.
İA 'Kasım hanlığı' (Reşid Rahmeti Arat); *EI*[2] 'Ḳāsimov' (A. Bennigsen).

FOURTEEN

Persia after the Mongols

139

THE KARTS OR KURTS

643–791/1245–1389

Eastern Khurasan and northern Afghanistan

643/1245	Muḥammad b. Abī Bakr Rukn al-Dīn b. ʿUthmān Marghānī, Shams al-Dīn I, k. 676/1278
676/1277	Rukn al-Dīn or Shams al-Dīn II b. Muḥammad Shams al-Dīn I, d. 705/1305
694/1295	Fakhr al-Dīn b. Rukn al-Dīn or Shams al-Dīn II
707/1308	Ghiyāth al-Dīn I b. Rukn al-Dīn or Shams al-Dīn II
729/1329	Shams al-Dīn III b. Ghiyāth al-Dīn I
730/1330	Ḥāfiẓ b. Ghiyāth al-Dīn I
⊘ 732/1332	Pīr Ḥusayn Muḥammad b. Ghiyāth al-Dīn I, Muʿizz al-Dīn
⊘ 772–91/1370–89	Pīr ʿAlī b. Pīr Ḥusayn Muḥammad Muʿizz al-Dīn, Ghiyāth al-Dīn II
791/1389	*Annexation by Tīmūr*

The Karts (a presumably Iranian name of unknown significance) were an indigenous line of Maliks of Afghan stock, from the clan or family of the Shansabānīs of Ghūr (see below, no. 159); the founder, Shams al-Dīn Muḥammad I, had married a Ghūrid princess, so that the Karts could claim to be, in some measure, heirs of the Ghūrids, ruling also as they did from the former centres of the Ghūrids, Herat and fortresses within Ghūr.

The incoming Mongols allowed Shams al-Dīn I Muḥammad to retain his lands as a vassal prince, and, ensconced in their nucleus of territories in Herat and the inaccesible mountains of Ghūr, the Karts generally remained loyal allies of the Il Khāns. The decay of Il Khānid power in Khurasan after Abū Saʿīd's death enabled Muʿizz al-Dīn Pīr Ḥusayn Muḥammad to raise his principality, which now reached to western Khurasan and the Sarbadārid territories (see below, no. 143), to new heights of power and splendour. But the rise of Tīmūr cut short Kart power, and, on the death of his tributary Ghiyāth al-Dīn II Pīr ʿAlī, Tīmūr annexed the Kart territories to his empire.

Lane-Poole, 252; Zambaur, 256–7; Album, 50.

EI^2 'Kart' (T. W. Haig and B. Spuler); EIr 'Āl-e Kart' (B. Spuler).

B. Spuler, *Die Mongolen in Iran. Politik, Verwaltung und Kultur der Ilchanzeit 1220–1350*, 4th edn, 129–33.

L. G. Potter, *The Kart Dynasty of Herat. Religion and Politics in medieval Iran*, Ph.D diss., Columbia University, New York 1992, unpubl. (UMI Dissertation Services, Ann Arbour).

140

THE MUẒAFFARIDS
713–95/1314–93
Southern and western Persia

⊘ 713/1314	Muḥammad b. Muẓaffar Sharaf al-Dīn, Mubāriz al-Dīn, d. 765/1363	
⊘ 759/1358	Shāh-i Shujāʿ b. Muḥammad Mubāriz al-Dīn, Abu ʾl-Fawāris Jamāl al-Dīn, first reign	
⊘ 765/1364	Shāh Maḥmūd b. Muḥammad Mubāriz al-Dīn, Quṭb al-Dīn, d. 776/1375	
767/1366	Shāh-i Shujāʿ, second reign	
⊘ 786/1384	Zayn al-ʿĀbidīn ʿAlī b. Shāh-i Shujāʿ, Mujāhid al-Dīn	
789/1387	Shāh Yaḥyā b. Shāh Muẓaffar b. Muḥammad Mubāriz al-Dīn, in Shīrāz	vassals of Tīmūr
	⊘ Sulṭān Aḥmad b. Muḥammad Mubāriz al-Dīn, ʿImād al-Dīn, in Kirmān	vassals of Tīmūr
	Sulṭān Abū Isḥaq b. Sulṭān Uways b. Shāh-i Shujāʿ, in Sīrajān	vassals of Tīmūr
⊘ 793–5/1391–3	Shāh Manṣūr b. Shāh Muẓaffar	
795/1393	*Tīmūrid conquest*	
before 810/1407 or 812/1409	Sulṭān Muʿtaṣim b. Zayn al-ʿĀbidīn, attempted to seize Iṣfahān	

The Muẓaffarids, distantly of Khurasanian Arab origin, rose to power in Kirman, Fars and ʿIrāq-i ʿAjam or Jibāl as the Il Khānid empire declined. Sharaf al-Dīn Muẓaffar was in the service of the Mongols, and was appointed by the Il Khān Ghazan to be commander of 1,000, with military and police duties in southern Persia. His son Mubāriz al-Dīn Muḥammad was the second founder of the dynasty. From a base at Yazd, during the chaos attendant on Abū Saʿīd's death he expanded his possessions into Fars after protracted strugles with the Inju'id Abū Isḥāq (see below, no. 141). A marriage to the daughter of the last Qutlugh Khānid ruler of Kirman (see above, no. 105) brought that province to him. By 758/1356 he was undisputed master of Fars and Iraq, and was tempted into invading Azerbaijan, where he captured Tabriz (Tabrīz) but was unable to hold on to it. Muḥammad was deposed by his own son Shāh-i Shujāʿ, but Shāh Shujāʿ was involved in disputes with his brother Shāh Maḥmūd, governor in Iṣfahān, until the latter's death. Shāh Maḥmūd had sought the help of the Muẓaffarids' old enemies, the Jalāyirids (see below, no. 142), and, when he had at last secured Iṣfahān, Shāh-i Shujāʿ led an expedition into Azerbaijan against the Jalāyirid Ḥusayn b. Uways. But the shadow of Tīmūr was now falling across Persia. Shāh-i Shujāʿ hastened to submit to the great conqueror. His successors, however, were less circumspect. Before his death in 786/1384 Shāh-i Shujāʿ had divided his Kirman and Fars dominions among his relatives, and dynastic disputes were now fatally to weaken the dynasty. In Fars, Zayn al-ʿĀbidīn ʿAlī submitted at first to Tīmūr, but Tīmūr later sacked Iṣfahān after his tax-collectors there had been killed in a popular uprising. The last Muẓaffarid, Shāh Manṣūr, was ruler over all Fars and Iraq when Tīmūr in 795/1393 resolved to extinguish the independent powers of western Persia; Shāh Manṣūr was killed in battle and most of the surviving Muẓaffarids massacred.

Although much of the Muẓaffarid period was racked by family strife, they were nevertheless patrons of such great figures as the poet Ḥāfiẓ and the theologian ʿAḍud al-Dīn Ījī, so that their cultural significance well outweighs their mediocre political aptitudes.

Justi, 460; Lane-Poole, 249–50; Zambaur, 254; Album, 48–9.
EI[2] 'Muẓaffarids', 'Shāh-i Shudjāʿ' (P. Jackson).
H. R. Roemer, 'The Jalayirids, Muẓaffarids and Sarbadārs', in *The Cambridge History of Iran. VI. The Timurid and Safavid Periods*, Cambridge 1986, 11–16, 59–64.

141

THE INJU'IDS
c. 725–54/c. 1325–53
Fars

c. 725/c. 1325	Maḥmūd Shāh Inju, Sharaf al-Dīn
736/1336	Mas'ūd Shāh b. Maḥmūd Shāh, Jalāl al-Dīn, with his power contested until 739/1338 by Ghiyāth al-Dīn Kay Khusraw b. Maḥmūd Shāh
739/1339	Muḥammad b. Maḥmūd Shāh, Shams al-Dīn, k. 740/1340
⊘ 743–54/1343–53	Abū Ishāq b. Maḥmūd Shāh, Jamāl al-Dīn, k. 758/1357
754/1353	*Occupation of Shiraz (Shīrāz) by the Muẓaffarids*

The Inju'ids derived their name from the fact that the founder of this short line, Sharaf al-Dīn Maḥmūd, was sent to Fars by the Il Khān Öljeytü to administer the royal states there (called in Turkish, and thence in Mongolian, *injü*). During Abū Sa'īd's reign, he consolidated his power at Shiraz and made himself virtually the independent ruler of Fars before being executed by the new Il Khān, Arpa Ke'ün (see above, no. 133). His sons squabbled over possession of Fārs, and when the last one, Jamāl al-Dīn Abū Isḥāq, tried to extend his power to Yazd and Kirman, he came up against the Muẓaffarids (see above, no. 140), who captured Shiraz in 754/1353, the fugitive Abū Isḥāq being killed shortly afterwards.

Sachau, 28 no. 73; Zambaur, 255; Album, 48.
EI^2 'Indjū' (J. A. Boyle).
B. Spuler, *Die Mongolen in Iran*, 4th edn, 122.

142

THE JALĀYIRIDS
740–835/1340–1432
Iraq, Kurdistan and Azerbaijan

⊘ 740/1340	Shaykh Ḥasan-i Buzurg b. Ḥusayn, Tāj al-Dīn
⊘ 757/1356	Shaykh Uways I b. Ḥasan-i Buzurg
⊘ 776/1374	Ḥusayn I b. Shaykh Uways I, Jalāl al-Dīn
⊘ 784/1382	Sulṭān Aḥmad b. Shaykh Uways I, Ghiyāth al-Dīn, k. 813/1410
(784–5/1382–3	Bāyazīd b. Shaykh Uways I, in Kurdistan)
813/1410	Shāh Walad b. ʿAlī b. Shaykh Uways I
814/1411	Maḥmūd b. Shāh Walad, first reign, under the tutelage of Tandu Khātūn
⊘ 814/1411	Uways II b. Shāh Walad
⊘ 824/1421	Muḥammad b. Shāh Walad
824/1421	Maḥmūd b. Shāh Walad, second reign
⊘ 828–35/1425–32	Ḥusayn II b. ʿAlāʾ al-Dawla b. Sulṭān Aḥmad
835/1432	*Qara Qoyunlu conquest of southern Iraq*

The Jalāyirids were one of the successor-states to the Il Khānids, succeeding to their territories in Iraq and Azerbaijan. The Jalāyir were, it seems, originally a Mongol tribe in Hülegü's following. The founder of the dynasty's fortunes was Ḥasan-i Buzurg (called 'Great' to distinguish him from his enemy and rival from the Chopanid family of Amīrs, Ḥasan-i Kūchik 'the Small'), who had been governor of Anatolia under the Il Khān Abū Saʿīd. He eventually prevailed over the Chopanids and made Baghdad the centre of his power; nevertheless, he continued to recognise various Il Khānid *fainéants* up to 747/1346, and it was left to his son Shaykh Uways to assume full personal sovereignty.

Shaykh Uways at first recognised the dominion of the Golden Horde (see above, no. 134) over Azerbaijan, but then in 761/1360 conquered it for himself. He also imposed his overlordship in Fars on the disputing Muẓaffarids (see above, no. 140), but his successors had to cope with the rising power of the Qara Qoyunlu Turkmens in Diyār Bakr (see below, no. 145) and an invasion through the Caucasus into Azerbaijan of the Golden Horde Khāns. Shaykh Uways's son Sulṭān Aḥmad opposed Tīmūr when the latter appeared in northern Persia and Iraq, and had to flee into exile with the Mamlūks in Syria, and he only returned permanently to his capital Baghdad after Tīmūr's death in 807/1405. However, the shock of the Tīmūrid invasions had much weakened the Jalāyirids' position. Azerbaijan quickly fell to the Qara Qoyunlu, and Baghdad itself was captured by them in 814/1411. Only in Lower Iraq, at Wāsiṭ, Baṣra and Shushtar, did minor Jalāyirid princes survive as vassals of the Tīmūrid Shāh Rukh, until Ḥusayn II was killed at Ḥilla in 835/1432.

The Jalāyirids, on the evidence of their preferences for personal names, may have had some Shīʿī sympathies, although this evidence is not in general strong. Their rule and patronage in Baghdad and Tabriz was of considerable cultural sigificance, especially in such spheres as architecture and miniature painting, traditions which were regrettably uprooted by the devastations and deportations of Tīmūr.

Lane-Poole, 246–8; Zambaur, 253; Album, 49.
EI[2] 'D̲j̲alāyir, D̲j̲alāyirid' (J. M. Smith Jr).
H. R. Roemer, in *The Cambridge History of Iran*, VI, 5–10, 64–7.

143

THE SARBADĀRIDS
737–88/1337–86
Western Khurasan

737/1332	ʿAbd al-Razzāq b. Faḍl Allāh	
738/1338	Masʿūd b. Faḍl Allāh, Wajīh al-Dīn	
743/1343	Muḥammad Ay Temür, k. 747/1346	
⊘ 748/1347	ʿAlī b. Shams al-Dīn Chishumī, Khwāja Tāj al-Dīn	
⊘ 752/1351	Yaḥyā Karāwī, k. 759/1357	
	Luṭf Allāh b. Masʿūd Wajīh al-Dīn; Amīr Walī, in Astarābād; Ḥaydar Qaṣṣāb; Ḥasan Dāmghānī, k. 763/1362	Confused period, with various rivals for power
⊘ 763/1362	Khwāja ʿAlī b. Mu'ayyad, first reign	
778/1376	Rukn al-Dīn	
781–8/1379–86	Khwāja ʿAlī, second reign	
788/1386	*Division of territories among several commanders of the Tīmūrids*	

The Sarbadārids (roughly interpretable as 'reckless ones') ruled in the Bayhaq or Sabzawār district of Khurasan during the period between the death of the Il Khānid Abū Saʿīd and the steep decline of his dynasty's power (see above, no. 133) and the rise of Tīmūr. Rather than being a 'bandit state' or a millenarian Shīʿī movement, the Sarbadārids represented an attempt by the local populations of western Khurasan to preserve some order and security there in the aftermath of Mongol rule over Persia; thus in some ways they form a later, and shorter-lived, counterpart to the earlier constituting of the Kart Maliks' principality in eastern Khurasan (see above, no. 139).

The Sarbadārid movement began as a rising in 737/1332 against fiscal oppression under the Chingizid Toqay Temür. The rebels soon afterwards made an uneasy alliance with local Shīʿī shaykhs. In 754/1353 they succeeded in overthrowing and killing Toqay Temür, the last of his line. Leadership within the Sarbadār movement was unstable and often contested. Under the last leader, Khwāja ʿAlī, Shīʿism was explicitly adopted, but Khwāja ʿAlī also submitted to Tīmūr. When the former died in 788/1386, the Sarbadārid lands were divided among several commanders who also served Tīmūr.

Lane-Poole, 251; Zambaur, 258; Album, 50.

*EI*² 'Sarbadārids' (C. P. Melville).

J. Masson Smith Jr, *The History of the Sarbadār Dynasty 1336–1381 A.D. and its Sources*, The Hague 1970, with a list and discussion of the confused chronology of the Sarbadārid commanders, and the contradictory information of the sources, at pp. 52–4.

A. H. Morton, 'The history of the Sarbadārs in the light of new numismatic evidence', *NC*, 7th series, 16 (1976), 255–8.

H. R. Roemer, in *The Cambridge History of Iran*, VI, 16–39.

144

THE TĪMŪRIDS
771–913/1370–1507
Transoxania and Persia

1. The rulers in Samarkand

⊘ 771/1370	Tīmūr-i Lang (Tamerlane) b. Taraghay Barlas, Küreken
⊘ 807–9/1405–7	Pīr Muḥammad b. Jahāngīr b. Tīmūr, in Kandahar (Qandahār)
⊘ 807–11/1405–9	Khalīl Sulṭān b. Mīrān Shāh b. Tīmūr, in Samarkand, d. 814/1411
⊘ 807–11/1405–9	Shāh Rukh b. Tīmūr, in Khurasan only
⊘ 811/1409	Shāh Rukh, in Transoxania, eastern and central Persia and then western Persia
⊘ 850/1447	Ulugh Beg b. Shāh Rukh, in Transoxania and Khurasan
⊘ 853/1449	ʿAbd al-Laṭīf b. Ulugh Beg, in Transoxania
⊘ 854/1450	ʿAbdallāh b. Ibrāhīm b. Shāh Rukh, in Transoxania
⊘ 855/1451	Abū Saʿīd b. Muḥammad b. Mīrān Shāh, in Transoxania, eastern, central and western Persia as far as ʿIrāq-i ʿAjam
⊘ 873/1469	Sulṭān Aḥmad b. Abī Saʿīd, in Transoxania
⊘ 899/1494	Maḥmūd b. Abī Saʿīd, in Transoxania
900–6/1495–1500	⊘ Baysonqur b. Maḥmūd ⊘ Masʿūd b. Maḥmūd ⊘ ʿAlī b. Maḥmūd } in Transoxania
906/1500	*Özbeg conquest of Transoxania and Farghāna*

2. The rulers in Khurasan after Ulugh Beg's death

⊘ 851/1447	Bābur b. Baysonqur, Abu 'l-Qāsim
⊘ 861/1457	Shāh Maḥmūd b. Bābur
⊘ 861/1457	Ibrāhīm b. ʿAlāʾ al-Dawla b. Baysonqur
⊘ 863/1459	Abū Saʿīd b. Muḥammad b. Mīrān Shāh
⊘ 873/1469	Ḥusayn b. Manṣūr b. Bayqara b. ʿUmar Shaykh b. Tīmūr, first reign
⊘ 875/1470	Yādgār Muḥammad b. Sulṭān Muḥammad b. Baysonqur, protégé of the Aq Qoyunlu Uzun Ḥasan in Herat, k. 875/1470
⊘ 875/1470	Ḥusayn b. Manṣūr b. Bayqara, second reign
911/1506	⊘ Badīʿ al-Zamān b. Ḥusayn, d. 923/1517 ⊘ Muẓaffar Ḥusayn b. Ḥusayn } co-rulers
913/1507	*Özbeg conquest of Herat*

3. The rulers in western Persia and Iraq after Tīmūr

795/1393	Mīrān Shāh b. Tīmūr, Jalāl al-Dīn, governor of ʿIrāq-i ʿAjam and Azerbaijan, 806/1404 in ʿIrāq-i ʿArab, k. 810/1408

807–12/1404–9	Pīr Muḥammad b. ʿUmar Shaykh b. Tīmūr, in Fars
807–12/1404–9	Rustam b. ʿUmar Shaykh, in southern ʿIrāq-i ʿAjam
812/1409	Khalīl Sulṭān b. Mīrān Shāh, in Rayy, d. 814/1411
812/1409	Bayqara b. ʿUmar Shaykh, in Fars
815–17/1412–14	Iskandar b. ʿUmar Shaykh, in Fars and then ʿIrāq-i ʿAjam
817/1414	Shāh Rukh b. Tīmūr, uniting western and central Persia with his Transoxanian and Khurasanian territories

Tīmūr arose from the Barlas clan of Turkicised Mongols which had nomadised within the Chaghatayid *ulus* (see above, no. 132). Although his family may subsequently have claimed Chingizid descent, Tīmūr personally never did, and always contented himself with the Arab-Islamic title of Amīr, and not the Turkish one of Khān. He did, however, acquire the title *güregen/küreken*, in Mongolian 'royal son-in-law', by virtue of his marriage to a Chingizid princess. He put together a vast military empire in central, western and southern Asia. But Tīmūr's interests were in the settled lands of ancient Islamic or Indian culture rather than in the steppes and mountains of Inner Asia, thus marking him off from the earlier Mongol steppe conquerors. He eventually built himself a permanent capital, Samarkand; and though clearly not a religious man, he found the religious ideology of Islam a useful aid in his campaigns into such regions as the Caucasus and India.

Tīmūr's rise to power took place in a fragmented Transoxania, weakened by the decay of the Chaghatayids of the west, during which various attempts from Mogholistan to re-establish the *ulus* failed. There was still a certain feeling, however, for the legitimacy of Mongol rule, and when Tīmūr first came to power he installed puppet Chingizid khāns in Transoxania, including a descendant of the Great Khan Ögedey, Soyurghatmïsh, and his son.

His first campaigns were in Khwārazm and Khurasan, after which he began the conquest of Persia in earnest. During the 'Five Years' War' beginning 797/1395, the Muẓaffarids of Fars were destroyed and the Jalāyirid Aḥmad b. Shaykh Uways driven from Iraq. Tīmūr's northern frontier was an open one, and his great rival in the steppes was Toqtamïsh, Khān of the White Horde, by now supreme across the whole Qïpchaq steppe of South Russia and south-western Siberia (see above, no. 134). Tīmūr accordingly invaded Qïpchaq in 797/1395, penetrating as far as Astrakhan and Muscovy. But his main efforts were directed aganst the Islamic heartlands, where his campaigns had a cataclysmic effect on the political structures of the time. During the Indian campaign of 800/1398–9, Delhi was sacked and the end of the Tughluqids hastened (see below, no. 160, 3), facilitating in the fifteenth century the rise of independent provincial sultanates such as those of Jawnpūr, Gujarāt, Mālwa and Khāndesh (see below, Chapter Sixteen). In the west, Tīmūr's defeat of Sultan Bāyazīd I at Ankara in 805/1402 meant the restoration for a few decades longer of many of the Anatolian *beylik*s absorbed by the Ottomans (see above, Chapter Twelve).

Before his death, which occurred just as he was about to leave for China, Tīmūr had divided up his territories among his sons and grandsons. The steppe tradition that an empire was not the personal property of the supreme ruler, but belonged to all male members of the ruling family, meant the parcelling-out of the Tīmūrid empire among its numerous princes, and in the absence of a clear succession principle left the field open for disputes and fragmentation. Three lines of Tīmūrids are listed above, but there were several other members of the family ruling either with varying degrees of independence or as vassals of other Tīmūrids in regions as far apart as the Caspian provinces, Kirman, and Kabul and Kandahar in eastern Afghanistan. And although possession of Tīmūr's old capital Samarkand conferred prestige within the dynasty, it did not automatically entail headship or supremacy; thus Ḥusayn b. Manṣūr Bayqara was, in his time, the greatest ruler among the later Tīmūrids, but reigned at Herat and not Samarkand.

Once the terror inspired by Tīmūr was gone, the later Tīmūrids eventually sank to the status of local rulers in Khurasan and Transoxania, with the western lands abandoned to the rising power of Türkmen dynasties like the Qara Qoyunlu and Aq Qoyunlu (see below, nos 145, 146). At first, there were two great kingdoms, in western Persia and Iraq, and in Khurasan and Transoxania, these latter two regions being first united by Tīmūr's son Shāh Rukh and then with his suzerainty extended over the western lands as well. Shāh Rukh's great-nephew Abū Sa'īd was, next to the Ottoman Muḥammad the Conqueror, the most powerful monarch of his age, although he was unable to prevent the Özbegs, the ultimate destroyers of Tīmūrid power, from raiding across the Oxus (see below, no. 153), and his campaign of 872/1468 to help the Qara Qoyunlu against the rising power of the Aq Qoyunlu leader Uzun Ḥasan, with the hope also of regaining the former western territories of the Tīmūrids, ended in disaster.

The Tīmūrids were the last great Islamic dynasty of steppe origin. After their time, the rise of powerful settled states like those of the Ottomans, the Ṣafawids and the Mughals, all employing firearms and more advanced military techniques, tilted the balance against any further large-scale invasions by horsemen from the Inner Asian steppes. The Tīmūrid period of Transoxanian and Persian history, essentially the fifteenth century, was also one of the most glorious ones of mediaeval Islamic art and culture, with outstanding schools of Persian and Chaghatay Turkish literature and of architecture, painting and book production, and with a final flowering at the court in Herat of Ḥusayn b. Manṣūr b. Bayqara, where the poets Jāmī and 'Alī Shīr Nawā'ī and the painter Bihzad worked.

Justi, 472–5; Lane-Poole, 265–8; Sachau, 30–1, nos 78–83; Zambaur, 269–70 and Table T; Album, 50–3.

R. M. Savory, 'The struggle for supremacy in Persia after the death of Tīmūr', *Der Islam*, 40 (1964), 35–54.

H. R. Roemer, 'Tīmūr in Iran', 'The successors of Tīmūr', in *The Cambridge History of Iran*, VI, 42–146, with genealogical tables at p. 146.

Beatrice Forbes Manz, *The Rise and Rule of Tamerlane*, Cambridge 1989, with a genealogical table at p. 166.

Robert C. Grossman, 'A numismatic "King-List" of the Timurids', *Oriental Numismatic Society Information Sheet* no. 27, September 1990.

145

THE QARA QOYUNLU

752–874/1351–1469

Eastern Anatolia, Azerbaijan, Iraq and western Persia

752/1351	Bayram Khōja, vassal of the Jalāyirids in northern Iraq and eastern Anatolia
782/1380	Qara Muḥammad b. Türemish, nephew of Bayram Khōja, after 784/1382 independent of the Jalāyirids, k. 791/1389
c. 792/c. 1390	Qara Yūsuf b. Qara Muḥammad, Abū Naṣr, first reign
802/1400	*Invasion of Tīmūr*
⊘ 809/1406	Qara Yūsuf, second reign, d. 823/1420
⊘ (814–21/1411–18	Pīr Budaq b. Qara Yūsuf, governor of Azerbaijan under his father's regency)
⊘ 823–41/1420–38	Iskandar b. Qara Yūsuf, k. 841/1438
(832–3/1429–30	Abū Sa'īd b. Qara Yūsuf, vassal of the Tīmūrids in Azerbaijan
⊘ 836/1433	Ispan (?) b. Qara Yūsuf, Tīmūrid vassal in Iraq
⊘ 837/1434	Jahān Shāh b. Qara Yūsuf, Tīmūrid vassal in eastern Anatolia)
⊘ 843/1439	Jahān Shāh b. Qara Yūsuf, up to 853/1449 as a Tīmūrid vassal
⊘ 872/1467	Ḥasan 'Alī b. Jahān Shāh
⊘ 873–4/1469	Abū Yūsuf b. Jahān Shāh, ruler in Fars only
874/1469	*Aq Qoyunlu conquest*

The confederation of the Qara Qoyunlu '[those with] black sheep' arose out of Türkmen elements pushed westwards by the Mongol invasions. Their ruling family seems to have come from the Yïwa or Iwa clan of the Oghuz, and the seats of their power in the fourteenth century lay to the north of Lake Van and in the Mosul region of northern Iraq.

The confederation was in many ways similar to that of the Jalāyirids (see above, no. 142), and came to think of itself as the successor to the Jalāyirids, with their traditions and connections going back to Chingizid times. The first Qara Qoyunlu leaders were vassals of the older Türkmen line, until in 784/1382 Qara Muḥammad made himself independent of the Jalāyirids, basing his power on Tabriz in Azerbaijan and on eastern Anatolia. The greatest ruler of the dynasty, Qara Yūsuf, opposed Tīmūr, and had to flee first to the Ottomans and then to Mamlūk Syria, only returning in 809/1406 and then ending the power of the Jalāyirids in Azerbaijan and Iraq. Qara Yūsuf now undertook warfare against his Aq Qoyunlu rivals (see below, no. 146) in Diyār Bakr, against the Georgians and the later Shīrwān Shāhs (see above, no. 67, 2) in the Caucasus, and against the Tīmūrid suzerains in western Persia. Once the forceful Shāh Rukh was dead, Jahān Shāh extended his rule to Fars, Kirman and even Oman, and made the Qara Qoyunlu an imperial power, adopting for himself such titles as *khān* and *sulṭān*. Finally, he attacked the redoubtable Aq Qoyunlu ruler Uzun Ḥasan, but was defeated and lost his life. His son Ḥasan 'Alī was unable to secure his position as leader of the Qara Qoyunlu, and killed himself in 873/1469, so that all the Qara Qoyunlu territories passed into the hands of the Aq Qoyunlu.

The constituting of the Qara Qoyunlu confederation was part of the interlude of Türkmen domination over the central part of the northern tier of the Middle East, from Anatolia to Khurasan, during the period between the decay of the Il Khānids and the rise of the Ottomans, Ṣafawids and Özbegs. Ethnically, the rule of Türkmens accelerated the process, already well advanced, whereby Azerbaijan and parts of Fars became strongly Turkish in race and speech. As to the religious affiliations of the Qara Qoyunlu, although some of the later members of the family had Shīʿī-type names and there were occasional Shīʿī coin legends, there seems no strong evidence for definite Shīʿī sympathies beyond possible influences from a general climate of such sympathies among many Türkmen elements of the time.

Lane-Poole, 253; Zambaur, 257; Album, 53.
İA 'Kara-Koyunlular' (Faruk Sümer), with a detailed genealogical table; *EI*[2] 'Ḳarā-Ḳoyunlu' (F. Sümer), with a detailed genealogical table.
R. M. Savory, 'The struggle for supremacy in Persia after the death of Tīmūr', 35–50.
Faruk Sümer, *Kara-Koyunlular (başlangıştan Cihan-Şah'a kadar)*, I, Ankara 1967.
H. R. Roemer, 'The Türkmen dynasties', in *The Cambridge History of Iran*, VI, 150–74.

146

THE AQ QOYUNLU

798–914/1396–1508

Diyār Bakr, Eastern Anatolia, Azerbaijan and, later, western Persia, Fars and Kirman

c. 761/c. 1360	Qutlugh b. Ṭūr ʿAlī b. Pahlawān, Fakhr al-Dīn
791/1389	Aḥmad b. Qutlugh, nominal head of the confederation until 805/1403
⊘ 805/1403	Qara Yoluq ʿUthmān b. Qutlugh, Fakhr al-Dīn, *de facto* head of the confederation since 798/1396
⊘ 839/1435	ʿAlī b. Qara ʿUthmān, Jalāl al-Dīn, in dispute with his brothers Ḥamza and Yaʿqūb
⊘ 841/1438	Ḥamza b. Qara ʿUthmān, Nūr al-Dīn, in dispute with Yaʿqūb and Jaʿfar b. Yaʿqūb
⊘ 848/1444	Jahāngīr b. ʿAlī, Muʿizz al-Dīn
(855–6/1451–2	Qïlïch Arslan b. Aḥmad b. Qutlugh, in eastern Anatolia)
⊘ 861/1457	Uzun Ḥasan b. ʿAlī, Abu ʾl-Naṣr
⊘ 882/1478	Sulṭān Khalīl b. Uzun Ḥasan, Abu ʾl-Fatḥ
⊘ 883/1478	Yaʿqūb b. Uzun Ḥasan, Abu ʾl-Muẓaffar
⊘ 896/1490	Baysonqur b. Yaʿqūb, Abu ʾl-Fatḥ, in dispute with Masīḥ Mīrzā b. Uzun Ḥasan, k. 896/1491
⊘ 898/1493	Rustam b. Maqṣūd b. Uzun Ḥasan, Abu ʾl-Muẓaffar
⊘ 902/1497	Aḥmad Gövde b. Ughurlu Muḥammad b. Uzun Ḥasan, Abu ʾl-Naṣr
⊘ 903/1497	Alwand b. Yūsuf b. Uzun Ḥasan, Abu ʾl-Muẓaffar, in Diyār Bakr and then in Azerbaijan until 908/1502, d. 910/1504
⊘ 903/1497	Muḥammadī b. Yūsuf b. Uzun Ḥasan, Abu ʾl-Makārim, in Iraq and southern Persia, k. 905/1500
⊘ 905–14/1500–8	Sulṭān Murād b. Yaʿqūb b. Uzun Ḥasan, Abu ʾl-Muẓaffar, in Fars and Kirman until 914/1508, d. 920/1514
⊘ 910–14/1504–8	Zayn al-ʿĀbidīn b. Aḥmad b. Ughurlu Muḥammad, in Diyār Bakr
914/1508	*Ṣafawid conquest*

The Aq Qoyunlu '[those with] white sheep' were a nomadic confederation of Türkmens centred on Diyār Bakr, with their ruling stratum drawn from the ancient Oghuz clan of the Bayundur. Already in the mid-fourteenth century they were raiding the Byzantine principality of Trebizond and were able to force marriage alliances on the Greek rulers. It was from the Türkmen–Byzantine marriage of 753/1352 that there arose the real founder of the confederation's fortunes, Qara Yoluq ʿUthmān, and relations between the two powers remained close for a century. Unlike their rivals the Qara Qoyunlu (see above, no. 145), the Aq Qoyunlu submitted to Tīmūr, and Qara ʿUthmān fought for him against the Ottoman Bāyazīd I at Ankara, being rewarded by the grant of Diyār Bakr. Expansion eastwards was blocked first by the Jalāyirids (see above, no. 142) and then by the Qara Qoyunlu, but Uzun Ḥasan, a military commander and statesman of genius, at last crushed Jahān Shāh in 872/1467 and incorporated many of the Qara Qoyunlu sub-tribes into his own horde, and after defeating the Tīmūrid Abū Sa'īd was able to extend his rule as far as Khurasan and down to Iraq and the Persian Gulf shores.

Uzun Ḥasan's prime enemy in the west was, however, the Ottomans, who were at this time mopping up the remaining *beylik*s of Anatolia (see above, Chapter Twelve) and pressing eastwards. Anti-Ottoman common interest made him ally with the Qaramānids (see above, no. 124), and he also tried to save Trebizond, to whose rulers he was related through his Byzantine wife Despina, from the attacks of Muḥammad the Conqueror. The Aq Qoyunlu were now a power of international significance. In 868/1464, diplomatic relations were opened up with the Ottomans' Venetian enemies, and arms and munitions were despatched from Venice via southern Anatolia. Yet Uzun Ḥasan's cavalrymen were no match for Ottoman firepower at Tercan (Terjān) in 878/1473, and the Aq Qoyunlu leader was crushingly defeated. His son Ya'qūb carried on the struggle, but the dynasty went into a terminal period of division, internecine strife and succession disputes. The Qaramānids had fallen to the Ottomans, and, despite the fact that there had been a marriage link between Uzun Ḥasan and the head of the Ṣafawiyya order, Shaykh Junayd (see below, no. 148), Shī'ī propaganda was being spread among the Sunnī Aq Qoyunlu's Türkmen followers in eastern Anatolia. In 906/1501, Alwand was defeated by the Ṣafawid Shāh Ismā'īl I, and the last Aq Qoyunlu, Sulṭān Murād, was forced to flee to the Ottomans. The dynasty's rule was now finished everywhere, but had left behind in such places as Uzun Ḥasan's capital at Tabriz a distinguished tradition of cultural and literary patronage.

Lane-Poole, 254; Zambaur, 258–9; Album, 53–4.

IA 'Aḳ Ḳoyunlular' (M. H. Yınanç), with a genealogical table; *EI*² 'Aḳ Ḳoyunlu' (V. Minorsky).

R. M. Savory, 'The struggle for supremacy in Persia after the death of Tīmūr', 50–65.

John E. Woods, *The Aqquyunlu. Clan, Confederation, Empire. A Study in 15th/9th Century Turko-Iranian Politics*, Minneapolis and Chicago 1976, with Appendix C of genealogical tables.

H. R. Roemer, in *The Cambridge History of Iran*, VI, 147–88.

147

THE MUSHAʿSHAʿIDS

839–1342/1435–1924

ʿArabistān, in south-western Persia

839/1435	Sayyid Muḥammad b. Falāḥ b. Haybat Allāh, *walī* of the Mahdī or Twelfth Imām, d. 870/1466, first period of rule
(857–61/1453–7)	Sayyid Sulṭān ʿAlī b. Muḥammad, as his father's deputy)
861/1457	Sayyid Muḥammad b. Falāḥ, second period of rule
870/1466	Sayyid Sulṭān Muḥsin b. Muḥammad, d. 905/1500 or c. 914/c. 1508
ø ?	Sayyid Falāḥ b. Muḥsin, d. 920/1514
920/1514	Sayyid Badrān b. Falāḥ, Shujāʿ al-Dīn, d. soon after 988/1580
c. 988/c. 1580	Sayyid Sajjād b. Badrān
before 992/1584	Sayyid ʿAlī b. Sajjād
992/1584	Sayyid Zunbūr ʿAlī b. ʿAlī, in Khūzistān until 998/1590
995/1587	Sayyid Mubārak b. (ʿAbd al–) Muṭṭalib b. Badrān, in Ḥuwayza, with the additional title of Khān
1025/1616	Sayyid Nāṣir b. Mubārak
1025/1616	Sayyid Rāshid b. Salīm b. Muṭṭalib, k. shortly after his appointment
1030/1621	Sayyid Manṣūr b. Muṭṭalib, first governorship
1033/1624	Sayyid Muḥammad b. Mubārak
after 1042/1632	Sayyid Manṣūr, second governorship
1053/1643	Sayyid Baraka b. Manṣūr
1060/1650	Sayyid ʿAlī b. Khalaf b. Muṭṭalib, d. 1092/1681
1097/1686	Sayyid Ḥaydar (? or ʿAbdallāh) b. Khalaf
1097/1686	Sayyid Faraj Allāh b. ʿAlī
1112/1700	Sayyid ʿAlī, nephew of Faraj Allāh, first governorship
1114/1707	Sayyid ʿAbdallāh b. Faraj Allāh
1127/1715	Sayyid ʿAlī, second governorship
1132/1720	Sayyid Muḥammad b. ʿAbdallāh
1150/1737	Sayyid Faraj Allāh, in Dawraq, until 1160/1747
1060/1747	Sayyid Muṭṭalib b. Muḥammad, in Ḥuwayza, k. 1176/1762
?	Sayyid Mawlā Jūd Allāh, cousin of Muṭṭalib
?	Sayyid Mawlā Ismāʿīl
c. 1193/c. 1779	Sayyid Mawlā Muḥsin b. Jūd Allāh
?	Sayyid Mawlā Muḥammad b. Jūd Allāh
after 1212/1797	Sayyid Mawlā Muṭṭalib b. Muḥammad
?	Sayyid Mawlā ʿAbd al-ʿAlī
1257/1841	Sayyid Mawlā Faraj Allāh, governor of Khūzistān
1289/1872	Sayyid Mawlā Muḥammad b. Naṣr Allāh
1298/1881	Sayyid Mawlā Muṭṭalib b. Naṣr Allāh, after c. 1312/c. 1895 in Dizfūl
c. 1305/c. 1888	Sayyid Mawlā Naṣr Allāh, in Ḥuwayza
?	Sayyid Mawlā ʿAbd al-ʿAlī, to 1328/1910

1328–42/1910–24 Musha'sha'ī nominee in Ḥuwayza of Shaykh Khaz'al of Muḥammara
1342/1924 Restoration of 'Abd al-'Alī as Shaykh of Ḥuwayza by Riḍā Khān

The Musha'sha'ī movement arose in the fifteenth century in southern Khūzistān, in the region which in more recent times has come to be known as 'Arabistān. Although this region at the head of the Persian Gulf was ethnically Arab, it became the home of a typically Persia extremist Shī'ī millenarian movement; and the Musha'sha' family, throughout nearly 500 years of its existence, was always linked politically with the rulers of Persia rather than with those in Iraq (latterly, in fact, the Ottomans). Sayyid Muḥammad b. Falāḥ proclaimed his *ẓuhūr* or manifestation as the *ḥijāb* or 'shield' of the Expected Imām, in opposition to the Qara Qoyunlu rulers of Iraq (see above, no. 145); the name Musha'sha' seems to have connotations (cf. *shu'ā'* 'ray of light') of illuminationism, a perceptible strain within Shī'ism as it was to develop in Ṣafawid Persia.

During the fifteenth century, the Musha'sha' were independent local rulers based on Ḥuwayza or Ḥawīza, and this was their heyday as a religio-political movement. Once the Ṣafawid Shāh Ismā'īl I (see below, no. 148) had extended his power into Khūzistān in 920/1514, the Musha'sha' were reduced to submission, and over the next centuries generally functioned as *wālī*s or governors for the Persian monarchs. At the end of the nineteenth century, their local influence was overshadowed by the rise of the rulers of Muḥammara from the Arab Banū Kalb, but the Musha'sha' family nevertheless managed to survive up to the time of Riḍā Shāh Pahlawī (see below, no. 152).

Album, 54.
*EI*² 'Mu<u>sh</u>a'<u>sh</u>a'' (P. Luft).
W. Caskel, 'Ein Mahdī des 15. Jahrhunderts. Saijid Muḥammad ibn Falāḥ und seine Nachkommen', *Islamica*, 4 (1931), 48–93, with a genealogical stem at p. 75.
idem, 'Die Wālī's von Ḥuwēzeh', *Islamica*, 6 (1934), 415–34, with a genealogical stem and list at pp. 424–32.

148

THE ṢAFAWIDS

907–1135/1501–1722, thereafter as *fainéants* and pretenders until 1179/1765

Persia

⊘ 907/1501	Ismāʿīl I b. Ḥaydar b. Junayd, Abu 'l-Muẓaffar
⊘ 930/1524	Ṭahmāsp I b. Ismāʿīl I
⊘ 984/1576	Ismāʿīl II b. Ṭahmāsp I
⊘ 985/1578	Muḥammad Khudābanda b. Ṭahmāsp I, d. 1003/1595 or 1004/1596
⊘ 995/1587	ʿAbbās I b. Muḥammad Khudābanda
⊘ 1038/1629	Ṣafī I, Sām Mīrzā b. Ṣafī Mīrzā
⊘ 1052/1642	ʿAbbās II, Sulṭān Muḥammad Mīrzā b. Ṣafī I
⊘ 1077/1666	Ṣafī II b. ʿAbbās II, re-enthroned in 1078/1668 as Sulaymān I
⊘ 1105/1694	Ḥusayn I b. Sulaymān I, Mullā
1135/1722	*Afghan invasion*
⊘ 1135/1722	Ṭahmāsp II b. Ḥusayn I, k. 1153/1740
⊘ 1145/1732	ʿAbbās III b. Ṭahmāsp II, k. 1153/1740
1148/1736	*Nādir Shāh Afshār*
1161/1748	*Shāh Rukh, Afshārid, first reign*
⊘ 1163/1750	Sulaymān II, Sayyid Muḥammad, grandson of Sulaymān I, at Mashhad
1163/1750	*Shāh Rukh, second reign, in Khurāsān*
⊘ 1163–79/1750–65	Ismāʿīl III b. Sayyid Murtaḍā, Abū Turāb, in Iṣfahān as a puppet of the Zands, d. 1187/1773

The origins of the Ṣafawids are obscure, and their elucidation is not helped by the production, by at least the first half of the sixteenth century, of an 'official' version of Ṣafawid genealogy and early history. It does, however, seem probable that they hailed from Persian Kurdistan, and, as Turkish speakers, they seem to be part of the Türkmen resurgence of post-Mongol times. The family headed a Ṣūfī order, the Ṣafawiyya, based on Ardabīl in Azerbaijan, originally orthodox Sunnī in complexion, but in the mid-fifteenth century the leader of the order, Shaykh Junayd, embarked on a campaign for material power in addition to spiritual authority. In the atmosphere of heterodoxy and Shīʿī sympathies among the Türkmen of Anatolia and Azerbaijan, the Ṣafawiyya gradually became Shīʿī in emphasis.

The political ambitions of the first Ṣafawids brought them up against the other Türkmen powers of eastern Anatolia, Iraq and Persia, but in 905/1501 Ismāʿīl I defeated the Aq Qoyunlu (see above, no. 146), seized Azerbaijan and brought the whole of Persia under his control during the ensuing ten years, and thus established the Ṣafawid theocracy, for not only did Ismāʿīl and his successors claim to be lineal descendants of ʿAlī through the Seventh Imām Mūsā al-Kāẓim, but Ismāʿīl, at least, on the evidence of his poetry, also claimed divine status in the extremist Shīʿī *ghulāt* tradition. Their Türkmen tribal followers, the so-called *Qïzïl Bash* or 'red heads' (from the red caps which they wore) thus owed a spiritual as well as a political allegiance. Shīʿism was imposed as the state religion on a country which up until then had been, at least officially, predominantly Sunnī. The Ṣafawid period is thus of supreme importance in Persian history because of this consolidation of Shīʿism there; in the process, Persia acquired a new sense of solidarity and nationhood which enabled her to survive into modern times with her national spirit and the integrity of Persian territory substantially unimpaired.

Militarily, the early Ṣafawids had to face the strenuous hostility of their Sunnī neighbours, the Ottomans in the west and the Özbegs in the north-east. On the north-eastern frontier, the Shāhs just managed to hold their own, with cities like Herat, Mashhad and Sarakhs frequently changing hands; but Türkmen incursions for plunder and slaves continued well into the nineteenth century. The Ottomans were especially dangerous, being at the peak of their military strength in the sixteenth century. Sultan Selīm I's victory over the Ṣafawids at Chāldirān in 920/1514 was a triumph of logistics and superior firepower for the Ottomans (like the Mamlūks of Egypt, the Ṣafawids were slow to adopt artillery and handguns), and also impaired the Ṣafawids' supporters' beliefs in the divine invincibility of their masters. Soon afterwards, Kurdistan, Diyār Bakr and Baghdad passed into Ottoman hands, and Azerbaijan was frequently invaded; later, the Ṣafawid capital was moved from vulnerable Tabriz to Qazwīn and then to Iṣfahān.

The reign of Shāh ʿAbbās I, near-contemporary of such great rulers as Elizabeth I of England, Philip II of Spain, Ivan IV ('The Terrible') of Russia and the Mughal emperor Akbar, marks the apex of Ṣafawid military power and also Ṣafawid culture and civilisation, some of whose manifestations are visible in the architectural glories of Iṣfahān. During his reign, the Ottomans were ejected from Azerbaijan, and Persian control over the Caucasus and the Gulf strengthened. Diplomatic contacts with Europe were established (although a Ṣafawid–European grand alliance against the Ottomans never materialised), and commercial and cultural contacts grew. In order to counteract the influence in the state of the *Qïzïl Bash*, ʿAbbās recruited Georgian and Circassian converts as slave guards, and favoured the formation of a group of Türkmen owing allegiance to himself personally and not to the tribal chiefs (the *Shāh seven* or 'Lovers of the Shāh').

After the death of Shāh ʿAbbās II in 1077/1666, there was a perceptible decline in the personal qualities of the rulers. Ṣafawid authority had at times stretched as far as eastern Afghanistan, but Sunnī Afghan sentiment was opposed to the strongly Shīʿī policies of the Shāhs, and in the early eighteenth century the governor for the Ṣafawids there, Mīr Uways, declared himself independent. In 1135/1722, his son Maḥmūd invaded Persia; Ṣafawid resistance collapsed, and for several years until the rise of Nādir Shāh Afshār (see below, no. 149), the Ghilzay Afghans occupied much of Persia. The subsequent holders of power in Persia at times felt a need to nominate Ṣafawid descendants or claimants as puppet rulers, but the effective rule of the dynasty disappeared with Ṭahmāsp II.

Justi, 479; Lane-Poole, 255–9; Zambaur, 261–2; Abum, 54–7.
EI[2] 'Ṣafawids. 1. Dynastic, political and military history' (R. M. Savory).
J. R. Perry, 'The last Ṣafavids, 1722–1773', *Iran*, JBIPS, 9 (1971), 59–69.
Roger Savory, *Iran under the Safavids*, Cambridge 1980.
H. R. Roemer, 'The Safavid period', in *The Cambridge History of Iran*, VI, 189–350.

149

THE AFSHĀRIDS
1148–1210/1736–96
Persia

⊘ 1148/1736	Nadr Qulī b. Imām Qulī, Ṭahmāsp Qulī, Nādir Shāh Afshār, since 1144/1732 regent for Shāh Ṭahmāsp II
⊘ 1160/1747	ʿAlī Qulī b. Muḥammad Ibrāhīm b. Imām Qulī, ʿĀdil Shāh, k. 1160/1747
⊘ 1161/1748	Ibrāhīm b. Muḥammad Ibrāhīm, in central and western Persia
⊘ 1163/1750	Shāh Rukh b. Riḍā Qulī b. Nādir Shāh, in Khurasan, first reign, deposed 1163/1750
⊘ 1163/1750	Shāh Rukh, second reign
1168–1210/1755–96	Shāh Rukh, third reign, at first as the puppet of the Abdālī or Durrānī Afghans
1210/1796	*Succession of the Qājārs*
(1210–18/1796–1803	Nādir Mīrzā b. Shāh Rukh, holder of power in Mashhad)

Nadr or Nādir was a chieftain of the Afshār, a Türkmen tribe settled in northern Khurasan; it was in this home territory that he later constructed his stronghold and treasury, the Qalʿat-i Nādirī. In this period of Ṣafawid decay, when much of Persia was in the hands of the Ghilzays, the national unity of Persia, which had been built up by the earlier Ṣafawids, seemed likely to disintegrate. It was to be Nādir's achievement temporarily to restore the territorial integrity of Persia, albeit at the price of leaving the country financially and economically exhausted. His ascent to power began through service with the ineffective Ṣafawid Shāh Ṭahmāsp II (whence the name which he adopted, 'slave of Ṭahmāsp'). He began systematically to clear the Afghan invaders from Persia, and when by 1140/1727 this had been achieved, the Shāh rewarded him wth the governorship of Khurasan, Kirman, Sistan and Māzandarān. With such extensive lands under his personal control, Nādir began to act like an independent ruler, now minting his own coins. Turning to external enemies, he drove the Ottomans out of Azerbaijan and Kurdistan, and penetrated through the Caucasus as far as Dāghistān. Ṭahmāsp's conclusion of a treaty with Turkey and Russia unfavourable to Persia's interests provided Nādir with a pretext to depose him, setting up another Ṣafawid prince as puppet ruler, until in 1148/1736 he was himself proclaimed Shāh. Nādir seems at this point to have sought an end to the ancient Shīʿī–Sunnī hostility between Persia and Turkey, and he announced the abandonment of Twelver Shīʿism as the state religion and the establishment instead of much-attenuated form of Shīʿism whose spiritual head was to be the Sixth Imām, Jaʿfar al-Ṣādiq; in practice, this conciliatory move pleased no-one and did not bring about détente with the Ottomans.

The expense of continual warfare drove Nādir into his brilliantly successful Indian campaign of 1151–2/1738–9, as a result of which the Mughal emperor Muḥammad Shāh (see below, no. 175) had to cede all his provinces north and west of the Indus and to pay an enormous tribute; because of this last, Nādir declared the people of Persia exempt from taxation for three years. An assassination attempt on him in 1154/1741, in which Nādir suspected the complicity of his son Riḍā Qulī, caused a deterioration in his character, so that his policies became more and more cruel and erratic. Rebellions broke out in the provinces against his exactions, and in 1160/1747 a group of Afshār and Qājār Türkmen chiefs finally murdered him. Two of his nephews reigned briefly, and then his blinded grandson Shāh Rukh ruled as a puppet of military commanders in Khurasan, until Agha Muḥammad Qājār (see below, no. 151) extended his power eastwards from northern Persia in 1210/1796 and ended what remained of the authority of the Afshārids.

Lane-Poole, 257–9; Zambaur, 261; Album, 57–8.
EI^2 'Nādir Shāh Afshār' (J. R. Perry).
Peter Avery, 'Nādir Shāh and the Afsharid legacy', in *The Cambridge History of Iran. VII. From Nadir Shah to the Islamic Republic*, Cambridge 1991, 3–62.

150

THE ZANDS
1164–1209/1751–94
Persia, excepting Khurasan

⊘ 1164/1751	Muḥammad Karīm Khān b. Inaq Khān, as *wakīl* or regent for Ismā'īl III Ṣafawī
⊘ 1193/1779	Abu 'l-Fatḥ b. Muḥammad Karīm } nominal rulers in Shiraz Muḥammad 'Alī b. Muḥammad Karīm }
⊘ 1193/1779	Muḥamad Ṣādiq b. Inaq, in Shiraz
⊘ 1195/1781	'Alī Murād b. Allāh Murād or Qaydar Khān, in Isfahan
⊘ 1199/1785	Ja'far b. Muḥammad Ṣādiq, at first in Isfahan, latterly in Shiraz
⊘ 1204–9/1789–94	Luṭf 'Alī b. Ja'far, in Shiraz
1209/1794	*Succession of the Qājārs*

In the chaos which followed Nādir Shāh's death, various military chiefs seized power in the provinces of Persia. His Afghan commander Aḥmad Abdālī founded in Kandahar an important Afghan state, whose territories included Nādir's conquests in north-western India (see below, no. 175). In Khurasan, the Afshārid Shāh Rukh retained a precarious power as the puppet of local commanders. In the Caspian provinces, the Qājārs maintained their power-base (see below, no. 151), while in Azerbaijan another of Nādir's Afghan generals, Āzād, established himself. In southern Persia, the main force was initially the Bakhtiyārī leader 'Alī Mardān, who had taken Isfahan and raised to the throne there a *fainéant* Ṣafawid, Ismā'īl III (1163/1750) (see above, no. 148). 'Alī Mardan's lieutenant and *sardār* or commander of the forces was Muḥammad Karīm Zand, from a minor tribe of Lurs in the central Zagros Mountains; and when 'Alī was murdered, Muḥammad Karīm made himself sole ruler in southern Persia.

He still had a lengthy struggle with the Qājār Muḥammad Ḥasan Khān before his authority over the greater part of Persia outside Khurasan was made firm. Muḥammad Karīm never himself assumed the title of Shāh, but reigned from Shiraz as *wakīl al-dawla* or regent for Ismā'īl III. His reign of almost thirty years was one of clemency and moderation, and the land flourished under his enlightened rule; among other things, commercial relations with Britain via Bushire (Būshahr) on the Persia Gulf were encouraged. But his death was the signal for disastrous succession disputes to break out within the Zand family. 'Alī Murād finally secured the throne, but died soon afterwards, and in the reign of Ja'far the power of the Zands' rivals the Qājārs grew until the Zands had to abandon Iṣfahān to them. The last Zand, Luṭf 'Alī Khān, a popular ruler and an able general, took up arms against the Qājārs and was successful for a while. But in 1209/1794 he was captured at Kirmān by Agha Muḥammad Khān Qājār and brutally murdered; the whole of Persia now became united under one monarch for the first time since the brief career of Nādir Shāh and the heyday of the Ṣafawids.

Lane-Poole, 260, 262; Zambaur, 261, 264; Album, 58–9.

John R. Perry, *Karim Khan Zand. A History of Iran, 1747–1779*, Chicago and London 1979, with a genealogical table at p. 296.

idem, 'The Zand dynasty', in *The Cambridge History of Iran*, VII, 63–103, and Gavin R. G. Hambly, 'Āghā Muḥammad Khān and the establishment of the Qājār dynasty', in ibid., 104–26, with a genealogical table at p. 961.

151

THE QĀJĀRS
1193–1344/1779–1925
Persia

	Fatḥ ʿAlī Khān, k. 1139/1726	tribal chiefs in Gurgān and Māzandarān
	⊘ Muḥammad Ḥasan b. Fatḥ ʿAlī, k. 1172/1759	
	Ḥusayn Qulī b. Muḥammad Ḥusayn, Jahānsūz, d. 1191/1777	
⊘ 1193/1779	Agha Muḥammad b. Muḥammad Ḥasan, ruler in northern and central Persia, after 1209/1794 ruler in southern Persia also, after 1210/1796 ruler in Khurasan also	
⊘ 1212/1797	Fatḥ ʿAlī b. Ḥusayn Qulī, Bābā Khān	
⊘ 1250/1834	Muḥammad b. ʿAbbās Mīrzā b. Fatḥ ʿAlī	
⊘ 1264/1848	Nāṣir al-Dīn b. Muḥammad	
⊘ 1313/1896	Muẓaffar al-Dīn b. Nāṣir al-Dīn	
⊘ 1324/1907	Muḥammad ʿAlī b. Muẓaffar al-Dīn, d. 1343/1925	
⊘ 1327–44/1909–25	Aḥmad b. Muḥammad ʿAlī, d. 1347/1929	
1344/1925	*Succession of the Pahlawīs*	

The Qājār tribe of Türkmens had probably been settled near Astarābād in the Caspian coastlands since Mongol times; later, they were one of the seven great Türkmen tribes supporting the early Ṣafawids and comprising the *Qïzïl Bash.* With the disintegration of the Ṣafawid empire in the early eighteenth century, the Qājārs began to play a more-than-local part in Persian affairs. The chiefs of the Qoyunlu clan of the Qājārs expanded across northern Persia in an endeavour to take over Nādir Shāh's western territories, but it was not until 1209/1794 that Agha Muḥammad was finally victorious over the Zands (see above, no. 150); soon afterwards, Persian suzerainty was re-established, albeit temporarily, over Georgia, and the last Afshārid removed from Khurasan (see above, no. 149). The frightful Agha Muḥammad, whose excesses are doubtless in part explicable by the fact that, as a boy, he had been castrated by Nādir's nephew ʿĀdil Shāh, was thus the founder of the dynasty under which Persia was to move definitely into the modern world, acquiring an important strategic and economic rôle in the international states-system. It was also under the first Qājār Shāh that Tehran (Ṭihrān), previously a town of only modest importance, became the capital (1200/1786); in this way began the movement of all life towards the centre which has characterised modern Persia.

Regular diplomatic relations with the European powers date from Fatḥ ʿAlī Shāh's reign, when Persia was courted by Britain on one side and by Napoleonic France on the other on account of her strategic position across the routes to the East. A by-product of this attention from the West was the introduction of European techniques and training into the Persian army. This was all the more necessary for Persia in that, during the nineteenth century, Imperial Russia, advancing now into the Caucasus and into Central Asia, was a continuing threat; by the humiliating Treaty of Turkmanchay in 1243/1828, Persia had had to relinquish all claims to territories in eastern Armenia and the Caucasus and had had to facilitate Russian commercial penetration of Persia. For their part, the Qājārs were for long reluctant to renounce the heritage of eastern conquests made by the Ṣafawids and by Nādir, and disputes with Afghanistan continued until the later nineteenth century (see below, no. 180).

Through the mutual rivalries of the European powers and the astuteness of Nāṣir al-Dīn Shāh, the geographically-compact land of Persia was much more successful than the disparate Ottoman empire in maintaining its territorial integrity. Nevertheless, the cost of warfare and royal extravagance were plunging the nation deeply into foreign indebtedness, thereby increasing the economic stranglehold of the European creditor nations. During the reign of Muẓaffar al-Dīn Shāh, there arose a movement demanding some degree of political liberalism and the granting of a constitution, demands which had to be met in 1906. The prestige and power of the Qājārs were now perceptibly failing. During the First World War, Persia remained officially neutral, but despite this, Turkish, Russian and British troops fought over her soil, and, at the end of the war, various local rebellions and separatist movements arose in the provinces. Accordingly, it was not difficult for a decisive military leader like Riḍā Khan to get the National Assembly to depose the Qājārs in 1925 (see below, no. 152).

Lane-Poole, 260; Zambaur, 261–3; Album, 59–61.

EI² 'Ḳādjār' (A. K. S Lambton).

Gavin R. G. Hambly, 'Āghā Muḥammad Khān and the establishment of the Qājār dynasty', idem, 'Iran during the reigns of Fatḥ 'Alī Shāh and Muḥammad Shāh', and Nikki Keddie and Mehrdad Amanat, 'Iran under the later Qājārs, 1848–1922', in *The Cambridge History of Iran*, VII, 104–212, with a genealogical table at p. 962.

152

THE PAHLAWĪS
1344–98/1925–79
Persia

⊘ 1344/1925 Riḍā b. ʿAbbās ʿAlī, d. 1365/1944
⊘ 1360–98/1941–79 Muḥammad b. Riḍā, d. 1399/1980
1398/1979 Islamic Republic

Riḍā Khān was a soldier in the Persian army who had participated in the *coup d'état* of 1921 which began the process of the ousting of the Qājārs (see above, no. 151). In December 1925, the *Majlis* or National Assembly voted him in as Shāh in succession to Aḥmad Qājār, who had left the country two years previously; Riḍā had already assumed the family name of Pahlawī, redolent of ancient Persian glories.

Riḍā's sixteen-year rule in many ways resembled other military dictatorships which emerged in both the Middle East (such as that of Muṣṭafā Kemāl Atatürk in Turkey) and Europe. His driving aim was the modernisation of his country so that it could stand on its own feet against outside pressures, and this involved the centralisation of power and the bureaucratisation of many aspects of Persian life. During his reign, the country made immense strides in industrialisation, the provision of modern communications and the introduction of modern, secular educational and legal systems; but all this was at the price of individual liberty and freedom of expression. Riḍā Shāh's pro-German stance in the early part of the Second World War led to his deposition under British and Russian pressure and his replacement by his son Muḥammad. Muḥammad wished to continue his father's policies, but was involved in disputes with his *Majlis* and with both nationalist and communist factions. Educational and land reforms were nevertheless successful while Persia was benefiting from rising oil revenues, but after 1975 lower oil prices brought inflation and economic hardship to the country. Popular discontent was utilised by a wide spectrum of opposition forces, including the Shīʿī clergy, and, unwilling to use military force against his own people, the Shāh, already very sick, left his throne for exile in January 1979. The Pahlawī monarchy was then replaced by an Islamic Republic hostile to virtually everything which the Pahlawīs had sought to achieve.

*EI*² 'Muḥammad Riḍā Shāh Pahlawī' (R. M. Savory), 'Riḍā Shāh' (G. R. G. Hambly).
Gavin R. G. Hambly, 'The Pahlavī autocracy: Rizā Shāh, 1921–1941', idem, 'The Pahlavī autocracy: Muḥammad Rizā Shāh, 1941–1979', in *The Cambridge History of Iran*, VII, 213–93.

FIFTEEN

Central Asia after the Mongols

153

THE SHĪBĀNIDS (SHAYBĀNIDS) OR ABU 'L-KHAYRIDS
906–1007/1500–99
Transoxania and northern Afghanistan

c. 842–72/c. 1438–68	Abu 'l-Khayr b. Dawlat Shaykh b. Ibrāhīm, khān at Tura (Tiumen) in Western Siberia, then ruler also in northern Khwārazm
⊘ 906/1500	Muḥammad Shībānī b. Shāh Budaq b. Abi 'l-Khayr, Abu 'l-Fatḥ, Shāh Beg Özbeg, conqueror of Transoxania, k. 916/1510
⊘ 918/1512	Köchkunju Muḥammad b. Abi 'l-Khayr
⊘ 937/1531	Abū Sa'īd b. Köchkunju, Muẓaffar al-Dīn
⊘ 940/1534	'Ubaydallāh b. Maḥmūd b. Shāh Budaq, Abu 'l-Ghāzī
⊘ 946/1539	'Abdallāh I b. Köchkunju
⊘ 947/1540	'Abd al-Laṭīf b. Köchkunju
⊘ 959/1552	Nawrūz Aḥmad or Baraq b. Sunjuq b. Abi 'l-Khayr
⊘ 963/1556	Pīr Muḥammad I b. Jānī Beg, great-grandson of Abu 'l-Khayr
⊘ 968/1561	Iskandar b. Jānī Beg
⊘ 991/1583	'Abdallāh II b. Iskandar
⊘ 1006/1598	'Abd al-Mu'min b. 'Abdallāh II
⊘ 1006–7/1598–9	Pīr Muḥammad II b. Sulaymān b. Jānī Beg
1007/1599	*Succession in Bukhārā of the Toqay Temürids or Jānids, descendants of the Khāns of Astrakhan*

When Toqtamïsh and his White Horde moved westwards and united with the Golden Horde in South Russia, Western Siberia fell to the descendants of Jochi's youngest son Shïban. Later, these descendants came to be known as the Shībānids (Arabised, perhaps with a hope of suggesting a fictitious connection with the ancient Arab tribe of Shaybān of Bakr, as Shaybānids). One branch of them remained in Siberia as Khāns of Tura or Tümen (Tiumen) until extinguished in the late sixteenth century, but much of the Horde of Shïban moved into Transoxania, where its members acquired the name of Özbegs (presumably after the famous Golden Horde Khān Muḥammad Özbeg, 713–42/1313–41, see above, no. 134), becoming the progenitors of the greater part of the indigenous inhabitants of the present-day Uzbek Republic.

Abu 'l-Khayr took over northern Khwārazm and unsuccessfully attacked the Tīmūrids (see above, no. 144) in Transoxania, but his grandson Muḥammad conquered Transoxania by 906/1500 from the last Tīmūrids and temporarily occupied Khurasan also. This last was retaken by Shāh Ismā'īl Ṣafawī (see above, no. 148), but for much of the sixteenth century the Sunnī orthodox Shībānids carried on warfare against the Shīʿī Ṣafawids of Persia, and their alliance was courted by other Sunnī empires such as those of the Ottomans and the Mughals of India. The Shïbānid khanate in fact formed a loose family confederacy, with powerful appanages granted out by the ruling supreme khān to various junior members. These appanages were centred upon Balkh, Bukhara, Tashkent and Samarkand, and these local centres became the capital of the whole khanate when their holders moved up and became recognised as supreme ruler.

Abu 'l-Khayrid power reached its peak under ʿAbdallāh II b. Iskandar, effective ruler for nearly forty years, under whom Transoxania experienced much cultural and commercial progress. This Shïbānid clan ruled until 1007/1599, when its last member, Pīr Muḥammad II, was killed by his rival for control of Transoxania, Bāqī Muḥammad b. Jāni Muḥammad, a descendant of Jochi's son Orda and a connection of the Shïbānids in the female line. The family of Bāqī Muḥammad, the Toqay Temürids or Jānids, then assumed power in Bukhara (see below, no. 154).

However, a collateral line of Shïbānids, the ʿArabshāhids, ruled in Khwārazm during this period. These were the descendants of ʿArabshāh b. Pūlād, Pūlād being the great-grandfather of Abu 'l-Khayr. One of them, Ilbars b. Büreke, became khān at Ürgench in 917/1511. The ʿArabshāhids soon controlled the whole of Khwārazm as far south as northern Khurasan. In c. 1008/c. 1600 the khāns moved their capital to Khiva (Khīwa), and thus there began the khanate of that name which was to endure until the early twentieth century; the ʿArabshāhid line itself seems to have ended around the end of the seventeenth or the beginning of the eighteenth century.

Lane-Poole, 238–40, 270–3; Zambaur, 270–1, 274–5; Album, 62–3.

EI[1] 'Shaibānī Khān' (W. Barthold), EI[2] 'Shībānids' (R. D. McChesney); EIr ''Arabšāhī' (Y. Bregel), 'Central Asia. VI. In the 10th–12th/16th–18th centuries' (Robert D. McChesney), with a genealogical table of the Abu 'l-Khayrids.

W. Barthold, *Histoire des Turcs d'Asie Centrale*, Paris 1945, 184–8.

N. M. Lowick, 'Shaybānid silver coins', NC, 7th series, 6 (1966), 251–330, with a genealogical table and a list of rulers at pp. 255–6.

154

THE TOQAY TEMÜRIDS OR JĀNIDS OR ASHTARKHĀNIDS

1007–1160/1599–1747

Transoxania and northern Afghanistan

⊘ 1007/1599	Jānī Muḥammad b. Yār Muḥammad
⊘ 1012/1603	Bāqī Muḥammad b. Jānī Muḥammad
⊘ 1014/1605	Walī Muḥammad b. Jānī Muḥammad
⊘ 1020/1611	Imām Qulī b. Dīn Muḥammad b. Jānī Muḥammad as Great Khān in Transoxania, with Nadhr Muḥammad b. Dīn Muḥammad as lesser Khān in Balkh
⊘ 1051/1641	Nadhr Muḥammad, as ruler of the reunited khanate, then 1055–61/1645–51 in Balkh only
⊘ 1055/1645	ʿAbd al-ʿAzīz b. Nadhr Muḥammad, Khān in Transoxania only, after 1061/1651 Great Khān, with Ṣubḥān Qulī b. Nadhr Muḥammad as lesser Khān in Balkh
⊘ 1092/1681	Ṣubḥān Qulī as ruler of the reunited khanate
1114/1702	ʿUbaydallāh b. Ṣubḥān Qulī
⊘ 1123–60/1711–47	Abu ʾl-Fayḍ b. Ṣubḥān Qulī
1160/1747	De facto *transfer of power to the Mangïts*
(1160–c. 1163/ 1747–c. 1750	ʿAbd al-Muʾmin b. Abi ʾl-Fayḍ } nominal khāns under the Mangïts
1164–5/1751–2	ʿUbaydallāh b. Abi ʾl-Fayḍ } nominal khāns under the Mangïts
⊘ after 1172/1758	Abu ʾl-Ghāzī b. ʿAbd al-Muʾmin, deposed shortly after 1203/1789) } nominal khāns under the Mangïts

It was a Toqay Temürid force which killed the last Abu ʾl-Khayrid Pīr Muḥammad (see above, no. 153). This group, under the leadership of Jānī Muḥammad, descendant of a prince from the ruling house of Astrakhan (see above, no. 131) (whence the name of Ashtarkhānids given to the family which was now to rule in Transoxania and the lands along the upper Oxus), then assumed the khanate for itself, with the general acquiescence of the Özbeg amīrs of Transoxania and Balkh, who regarded its members as being suitable continuers of the Chingizid system. Members of the Jānī Begid family of the Abu'l-Khayrids were elbowed aside. As in previous régimes, appanages were distributed to princes of the new ruling family; but for two considerable stretches during the seventeenth century, there was something like a double khanate system, with one brother in Transoxania as Great Khān and another brother in Balkh as lesser Khān. The Khāns in Bukhara had to preserve their authority against internal elements such as the Qazaqs and external powers like the ʿArabshāhids of Khwārazm (see above, no. 153), activist and aggressive in the mid-seventeenth century under Abu ʾl-Ghāzī and his son Anūsha Muḥammad, while those in Balkh were involved in relations with the Ṣafawids and the Mughals.

Latterly, the rise of powerful Özbeg chiefs and the ravages of the Qazaqs led to a serious decline in order and prosperity in Transoxania. After the death of the last powerful and significant Jānid ruler, Subḥān Qulī, real political power at

Bukhara fell more and more into the hands of the Khāns' *Atalïq* or Chief Minister Muḥammad Ḥakīm Biy Mangït and his son, and it was from the Mangïts that the ultimate line of Khāns of Bukhara was to arise (see below, no. 155). But at least two puppet khāns from the Jānid family were retained by the Mangïts after Abu 'l-Fayd b. Subḥān Qulī's time (sc. after 1160/1747), and such *fainéants* seem to have continued on the throne at Bukhara until almost the end of the eighteenth century.

Lane-Poole, 274–5; Zambaur, 273; Album, 63.

EI[2] 'Djānids' (B. Spuler); EIr 'Central Asia. VI. In the 10th–12th/16th–18th centuries' (Robert D. McChesney). 'VII. In the 12th–13th/18th–19th centuries' (Y. Bregel).

Hélène Carrère d'Encausse, *Islam and the Russian Empire. Reform and Revolution in Central Asia*, London 1988, with a list of the rulers in Bukhara at p. 193.

155

THE MANGÏTS

1166–1339/1753–1920

The Khanate of Bukhara

1160/1747 Muḥammad Raḥīm *Atalïq* b. Muḥammad Ḥakīm Biy, at first with puppet khāns, after 1166/1753 as sole ruler and Amīr, in 1170/1756 Khān

⊘ 1172/1758 Dāniyāl Biy *Atalïq* b. Muḥammad, uncle of Muḥammad Raḥīm, at first as regent for his nephew Fāḍil Tora, then with puppet Jānid khāns

⊘ 1199/1785 Shāh Murād b. Dāniyāl Biy, Amīr-i Maʿṣūm

⊘ 1215/1800 Sayyid Ḥaydar Tora b. Shāh Murād

⊘ 1242/1826 Sayyid Ḥusayn b. Ḥaydar Tora

1242/1827 ʿUmar b. Ḥaydar Tora

⊘ 1242/1827 Naṣr Allāh b. Ḥaydar Tora

⊘ 1277/1860 Muẓaffar al-Dīn b. Naṣr Allāh

⊘ 1303/1886 ʿAbd al-Aḥad b. Muẓaffar al-Dīn

⊘ 1328–39/1910–20 Sayyid ʿĀlim Khān b. ʿAbd al-Aḥad

1339/1920 Overthrow of the Khanate

The Mangïts of Bukhara arose from an Özbeg tribe of the same name which became influential under the Toqay Temürids or Jānids (see above, no. 154), so that in the early eighteenth century Khudāyār Biy Mangït became *Atalïq* or Chief Minister to Abu 'l-Fayḍ Khān, being followed in this office by his son Muḥammad Ḥakīm and his grandson Muḥammad Raḥīm. Very soon the family became the real rulers in Bukhara, although they continued to enthrone puppet khāns from the Jānids until the end of the eighteenth century. Shāh Murād, however, ended this pretence and himself reigned as fully sovereign Amīr; this last title was borne by all the remaining members of his line, indicating that they saw themselves as Islamic monarchs *par excellence* and not as khāns in the Turkish steppe tradition.

The greatest single event in the history of Central Asia during the nineteenth century was, of course, the territorial and military advance of Imperial Russia. The Amīr Muẓaffar al-Dīn was crushingly defeated by the Russians, lost some of his territory and in effect lost his independence (1285/1868). The Khanate survived, within somewhat shrunken boundaries, with little Russian interference in its internal affairs, so that the Amīrs remained as despotic and capricious and the religious classes as fanatical and ignorant as before. But in September 1920 the Amīr's rule was overthrown and a 'People's Republic of Bukhara' set up, soon to be replaced by a forcibly imposed Bolshevism; the last ruler, ʿĀlim Khān, fled to exile in Kabul.

Lane-Poole, 276–7; Zambaur, 273–4; Album, 63.

EI² 'Mangïts' (Y. Bregel); EIr 'Central Asia. VII. In the 12th–13th/18th–19th centuries' (Yuri Bregel).

Hélène Carrère d'Encausse, *Islam and the Russian Empire*, with a list of rulers at p. 193.

Edward A. Allworth, *Central Asia: 130 Years of Russian Dominance*, 3rd edn, Durham NC and London.

156

THE QUNGRATS OR ÏNAQIDS
1184–1338/1770–1920
The Khanate of Khiva (Khīwa)

1184/1770	Muḥammad Amīn as *Ïnaq* for puppet khāns of the Qazaq Chingizids
1204/1790	ʿAwaẓ b. Muḥammad Amīn, *Ïnaq*
1218/1803	Eltüzer b. ʿAwaẓ, *Ïnaq* and then in 1219/1804 Khān
⊘ 1221/1806	Muḥammad Raḥīm b. ʿAwaẓ
⊘ 1240/1825	Allāh Qulī b. Muḥammad Raḥīm
1258/1842	Raḥīm Qulī b. Allāh Qulī
⊘ 1261/1845	Muḥammad Amīn b. Allāh Qulī, Abu 'l-Ghāzi, called Medemīn
1271/1855	ʿAbdallāh b. ʿUbaydallāh, great-grandson of ʿAwaẓ
1272/1856	Qutlugh Murād b. ʿUbaydallāh
⊘ 1272/1856	Sayyid Muḥammad Bahādur b. Muḥammad Raḥīm
⊘ 1281/1864	Sayyid Muḥammad Raḥīm b. Sayyid Muḥammad Bahādur
1328/1910	Isfandiyār b. Sayyid Muḥammad Raḥīm
⊘ 1336–8/1918–20	Saʿīd ʿAbdallāh
1338/1920	*Overthrow of the Khanate*

By the mid-eighteenth century, power in the Khanate of Khiva, covering essentially the older province of Khwārazm, was disputed by two powerful families of the Qazaq Chingizids. In 1176/1763, the leader of the Qungrat tribe of the Özbegs, Muḥammad Amīn *Ïnaq* (the old title *ïnaq* 'trusted adviser [of the ruler]' was by now given to tribal chiefs), became chief of all the local Özbeg tribal chiefs. As Ataliq of Khiva, he subdued the Yomud Turkmens and became virtual ruler, installing puppet khāns from the Qazaq Chingizids. He and his son ʿAwaẓ nevertheless did not themselves assume the title of Khān, but Eltüzer b. ʿAwaẓ felt strong enough to dispense with Chingizid puppets and proclaim himself Khān, founding a new, and the ultimate, line of rulers in Khiva. As in the other two Central Asian khanates, the rulers were by now able to behave more despotically through a declining reliance on Özbeg and other tribal forces and the use of their own personal forces of guards. The Khāns of Khiva were for a while able to expand as far south as Merv (Marw); they continually raided Persian territory in northern Khurasan; and they expanded northwards into the Qazaq Steppe.

But the Khāns were totally unable to withstand Russian pressures. In 1290/1873, a Russian army occupied Khiva with minimal resistance, and stringent peace terms were imposed on what now became a vastly-reduced khanate. The Russians did not interfere internally at Khiva, but the Khāns had no independent status and were far more circumscribed than their fellow-Khāns of Bukhara. In April 1920 the last Khān Saʿīd ʿAbdallāh was deposed and a 'People's Republic of Khiva' proclaimed, to be replaced a year later by a Bolshevik régime.

Lane-Poole, 278–9; Zambaur, 275–6; Album, 64.
EI[2] 'Khīwa' (W. Barthold and M. M. Brill), Suppl. 'Īnaḳ' (Y. Bregel); *EIr* 'Central Asia. VII. In the 12th–13th/18th–19th centuries' (Yuri Bregel).
Edward A. Allworth, *Central Asia: 130 Years of Russian Dominance*, 3rd edn.

157

THE MINGS
1213–93/1798–1876
The Khanate of Khokand (Khoqand)

1213/1798	ʿĀlim b. Nārbūta Biy	
⊘ 1225/1810	Muḥammad ʿUmar b. Nārbūta Biy	
⊘ 1238/1822	Muḥammad ʿAlī b. Nārbūta Biy	
1258/1842	Shīr ʿAlī b. Ḥājjī Biy	
⊘ 1261/1845	Murād b. ʿĀlim	
1261/1845	Muḥammad Khudāyār b. Shīr ʿAlī, first reign	
⊘ 1274/1858	Mallā b. Shīr ʿAlī	
⊘ 1278/1862	Shāh Murād, nephew of Mallā	
1278/1862	Muḥammad Khudāyār, second reign	
⊘ 1280/1863	Sayyid Sulṭān or Sulṭān (Mīr) Sayyid b. Mallā	
⊘ 1281/1865	Muḥammad Khudāyār, third reign	
1292–3/1875–6	⊘ Naṣr al-Dīn b. Khudāyār	rival claimants
	⊘ Isḥāq Mullā or Muḥammad Pūlād	rival claimants
1293/1876	*Suppression of the Khanate by Russia*	

During the later eighteenth century, a third Özbeg khanate, in addition to those of Bukhara and Khiva (see above, nos 155–6), emerged under leaders of the Ming tribe in Farghāna. The rise of the ruling family is usually traced back to Shāh Rukh Ataliq (d. between 1121 and 1133/1709–21). His son ʿAbd al-Karīm Biy in 1153/1740 founded the town of Khokand, which was to become the capital of his family's khanate. His grandson Nārbūta united Farghāna under Ming rule, so that his son and successor ʿĀlim could assume the title of Khān and formally begin the dynasty. His brother and successor Muḥammad ʿUmar went even further and claimed the title of Amīr al-Muʾminīn on his coins. The Mings soon came to control very extensive territories, beginning with the capture of Tashkent, of great strategic and commercial importance, in 1224/1809, and continuing with expansion northwards into the Qazaq Steppe and across the T'ien Shan into Eastern Turkestan, where the Khāns controlled customs duties from the so-called 'six towns' there, and into the Pamirs region. Khokand thus became greater in territory than its two fellow-khanates, if not in population.

Like the other khanates, Khokand was racked by internal tribal and other feuds, and was at one point briefly occupied by Bukhara. It was also threatened by Russian imperial expansion. In 1282/1865, Tashkent was captured and a commercial treaty imposed by Russia on Khokand. In 1292/1875, an internal rebellion brought the Russian army into the Khanate, and early in the next year it was suppressed and its territories annexed to the governorate-general of Turkestan as its Farghānan province.

Lane-Poole, 280; Zambaur, 276; Album, 64.
EI^2 'Khoḳand' (W. Barthold and C. E. Bosworth); EIr 'Central Asia. VII. In the 12th–13th/18th–19th centuries' (Yuri Bregel).
Edward A. Allworth, *Central Asia: 120 Years of Russian Rule*, 3rd edn.

SIXTEEN

Afghanistan and the Indian Subcontinent

158

THE GHAZNAWIDS

366–582/977–1186

Afghanistan, Khurasan, Baluchistan and north-western India

⊘ 366/977	Sebüktigin b. Qara Bechkem, Abū Manṣūr Nāṣir al-Dīn wa 'l-Dawla, governor in Ghazna for the Sāmānids
⊘ 387/997	Ismāʿīl b. Sebüktigin
⊘ 388/998	Maḥmūd b. Sebüktigin, Abu 'l-Qāsim Sayf al-Dawla, Yamīn al-Dawla wa-Amīn al-Milla
⊘ 421/1030	Muḥammad b. Maḥmūd, Abū Aḥmad Jalāl al-Dawla, first reign
⊘ 421/1031	Masʿūd I b. Maḥmūd, Abū Saʿīd Shihāb al-Dawla
432/1040	Muḥammad b. Maḥmūd, second reign
⊘ 432/1041	Mawdūd b. Masʿūd, Abu 'l-Fath Shihāb al-Dawla
? 440/1048	Masʿūd II b. Mawdūd, Abū Jaʿfar
? 440/1048	ʿAlī b. Masʿūd, Abu 'l-Ḥasan Bahā' al-Dawla
⊘ ? 440/1049	ʿAbd al-Rashīd b. Maḥmūd, Abū Manṣūr ʿIzz al-Dawla wa-Zayn al-Milla
⊘ *443/1052*	*Usurpation in Ghazna of the slave commander Abū Saʿīd Ṭoghrïl, Qiwām al-Dawla*
⊘ 443/1052	Farrukhzād b. Masʿūd I, Abū Shujāʿ Jamāl al-Dawla wa-Kamāl al-Milla
⊘ 451/1059	Ibrāhīm b. Masʿūd, Abu 'l-Muẓaffar Ẓahīr al-Dawla wa-Nāṣir al-Milla
⊘ 492/1099	Masʿūd III b. Ibrāhīm, Abū Saʿd Abu 'l-Mulūk ʿAlā' al-Dawla wa 'l-Dīn
508/1115	Shīrzād b. Masʿūd III, ʿAḍud al-Dawla, Kamāl al-Dawla
⊘ 509/1116	Malik Arslan or Arslan Shāh b. Masʿūd III, Sulṭān al-Dawla
510/1117	*Seljuq occupation of Ghazna*
⊘ 511/1117	Bahrām Shāh b. Masʿūd III, Abu 'l-Muẓaffar Yamīn al-Dawla wa-Amīn al-Milla, first reign
545/1150	*Ghūrid occupation of Ghazna*
547/1152 or after	Bahrām Shāh b. Masʿūd III, second reign
⊘ ? 552/1157	Khusraw Shāh b. Bahrām Shāh, Muʿizz al-Dawla, latterly in north-western India only
⊘ 555–82/1160–86	Khusraw Malik b. Khusraw Shāh, Abu 'l-Muẓaffar Tāj al-Dawla, in north-western India, k. 587/1191
582/1186	*Ghūrid conquest*

On the death in 350/961 of the Sāmānid Amīr ʿAbd al-Malik (see above, no. 83), the Turkish slave commander of the Sāmānid army in Khurasan, Alptigin, attempted to manipulate the succession at Bukhara in his own favour. He failed, and was obliged to withdraw with some of his troops to Ghazna in what is now eastern Afghanistan. Here on the periphery of the Sāmānid empire, and facing the pagan subcontinent of India, a series of Turkish commanders followed Alptigin, governing nominally for the Sāmānids, until in 366/977 Sebüktigin came to power. Under him, the Ghaznawid tradition of raiding the plains of India in search of treasure and slaves was established, but it was his son Maḥmūd who became fully independent and who achieved a reputation throughout the eastern Islamic world as hammer of the infidels, penetrating down the Ganges valley to Muttra (Mat'hurā) and Kanawj and into the Kathiawar (Kāṭīāwār) peninsula to attack the famous idol temple there of Somnath (Sūmanāt). In the north, he set up the Oxus as his frontier with the rival power of the Qarakhānids (see above, no. 90), and annexed Khwārazm. The former Sāmānid province of Khurasan was taken over and, towards the end of his life, Maḥmūd's armies marched into northern and western Persia and overthrew the Būyid amirate there (see above, no. 75, 1).

Maḥmūd's empire at his death was thus the most extensive and imposing edifice in eastern Islam since the time of the Ṣaffārids (see above, no. 84), and his army the most effective military machine of the age. With the adoption of Persian administrative and cultural ways, the Ghaznawids threw off their original Turkish steppe background and became largely integrated with the Perso-Islamic tradition. But under his son Masʿūd I, Maḥmūd's empire – essentially a personal creation – could not be maintained in the west against the Seljuqs (see above, no. 91), and Khwārazm, Khurasan and northern Persia were lost to the incomers. The middle years of the eleventh century were largely spent in warfare with the Seljuqs over possession of Sistan and western Afghanistan. At the accession of Ibrāhīm b. Masʿūd in 451/1059, a *modus vivendi* was worked out with the Seljuqs, and peace reigned substantially for over half a century.

Reduced as it now was to eastern Afghanistan, Baluchistan and north-western India, the Ghaznawid empire was still an imposing and powerful one. It inevitably acquired a more pronounced orientation towards India, but the courts of the sultans of the twelfth century were centres of a splendid Persian culture, with such luminaries as the mystical poet Sanā'ī. In the early part of that century, the Ghaznawid Bahrām Shāh became tributary to the Seljuqs, for Sanjar had helped Bahrām Shāh secure his throne. Towards the end of the latter's reign, the capital Ghazna suffered a frightful sacking by the 'World Incendiary', the Ghūrid ʿAlā' al-Dīn Ḥusayn (see below, no. 159). The rise of the Ghūrids in fact reduced the power of the last Ghaznawids, and their rule was latterly confined to the Punjab (Panjāb) until the Ghūrid Muʿizz al-Dīn Muḥammad finally extinguished the line in 582/1186.

Justi, 444; Lane-Poole, 285–90; Zambaur, 282–3; Album, 36–7.
EI[2] 'Ghaznawids' (B. Spuler); EIr 'Ghaznavids' (C. E. Bosworth).
C. E. Bosworth, 'The titulature of the early Ghaznavids', *Oriens*, 15 (1962), 210–33.
idem, *The Ghaznavids. Their Empire in Afghanistan and Eastern Iran 994:1040*, Edinburgh 1963.
idem, 'The early Ghaznavids', in *The Cambridge History of Iran*, IV, 162–97.
idem, *The Later Ghaznavids: Splendour and Decay. The Dynasty in Afghanistan and Northern India 1040–1186*, Edinburgh 1977.

159

THE GHŪRIDS

Early fifth century to 612/early eleventh century to 1215

Ghūr, Khurasan and north-western India

1. The main line in Ghūr and then also in Ghazna

?	Muḥammad b. Sūrī Shansabānī, chief in Ghūr
401/1011 until the 420s/1030s	Abū ʿAlī b. Muḥammad, Ghaznavid vassal
?	ʿAbbās b. Shīth
after 451/1059	Muḥammad b. ʿAbbās
?	Ḥasan b Muḥammad, Quṭb al-Dīn
493/1100	Ḥusayn I b. Ḥasan, Abu 'l-Mulūk ʿIzz al-Dīn
540/1146	Sūrī b. Ḥusayn I, Sayf al-Dīn, in Fīrūzkūh as Malik al-Jibāl
544/1149	Sām I b. Ḥusayn I, Bahā' al-Dīn
⊘ 544/1149	Ḥusayn II b. Ḥusayn I, ʿAlā' al-Dīn Jahān-sūz
⊘ 556/1161	Muḥammad b. Ḥusayn II, Sayf al-Dīn
⊘ 558/1163	Muḥammad b. Sām I Bahā' al-Dīn, Abu 'l-Fath Shams al-Dīn, Ghiyāth al-Dīn, supreme sultan in Fīrūzkūh
⊘ (569–99/1173–1203	Muḥammad b. Sām I, Shihāb al-Dīn, Muʿizz al-Dīn, ruler in Ghazna)
⊘ 599/1203	Muḥammad b. Sām I, supreme sultan in Ghūr and India
⊘ 602/1206	Maḥmūd b. Muḥammad Ghiyāth al-Dīn, Ghiyāth al-Dīn
⊘ (602–11/1206–15	Yïldïz Muʿizzī, Tāj al-Dīn, governor in Ghazna for Maḥmūd Ghiyāth al-Dīn)
609/1212	Sām II b. Maḥmūd, Bahā' al-Dīn
610/1213	Atsïz b. Ḥusayn II, ʿAlā' al-Dīn, vassal of the Khwārazm Shāh
611–12/1214–15	Muḥammad b.ʿAlī Shujāʿ al-Dīn b. ʿAlī ʿAlā' al-Dīn b. Ḥusayn I, Ḍiyā' al-Dīn, ʿAlā' al-Dīn, vassal of the Khwārazm Shāh
612/1215	*Khwārazmian conquest*

2. The line in Bāmiyān, Ṭukhāristān and Badakhshān

⊘ 540/1145	Masʿūd b. Ḥusayn I ʿIzz al-Dīn, Fakhr al-Dīn
⊘ 558/1163	Muḥammad b. Masʿūd Fakhr al-Dīn, Shams al-Dīn
⊘ 588/1192	Sām b. Muḥammad Shams al-Dīn, Bahā' al-Dīn
⊘ 602–12/1206–15	ʿAlī b. Sām Bahā' al-Dīn, Jalāl al-Dīn
612/1215	*Khwārazmian conquest*

The remote, mountainous region of what is now Afghanistan, called Ghūr, was almost wholly *terra incognita* to the early Islamic geographers, known only as a source of slaves and as the home of a race of bellicose mountaineers who remained pagan until well into the eleventh century. At this time, the Ghaznawids (see above, no. 158) led raids into Ghūr and made the local chiefs of the

Shansabānī family their vassals; but in the early twelfth century, the fortunes of the Ghaznawids waned and Seljuq influence now spread through Ghūr, so that 'Izz al-Dīn Ḥusayn, the first fully historical figure of the family, paid tribute to Sultan Sanjar (see above, no. 91, 1). Attempts by Sultan Bahrām Shāh to reassert Ghaznawid influence led to the Ghūrids' sack of Ghazna in 545/1150 and the eventual acquisition by them of all the Ghaznawid possessions on the Afghan plateau. In the west, Ghūrid expansionist policies were at first checked by Sanjar, but the collapse of Seljuq power in Khurasan allowed the Sultans to establish an empire, centred on Fīrūzkūh in Ghūr, stretching almost from the Caspian Sea to northern India, where the Ghaznawid traditions of *jihād* against the infidels were inherited and kept up.

The joint architects of this achievement were the two brothers Ghiyāth al-Dīn Muḥammad and Mu'izz al-Dīn Muḥammad, the former campaigning mainly in the west and the latter in India. Bāmiyān and the lands along the upper Oxus were ruled by another branch of the Ghūrid family. Ghiyāth al-Dīn contested possession of Khurasan with the Khwārazm Shāhs and the latter's suzerains, the Qara Khitay (see above, no. 89, 4); at one point he invaded Khwārazm itself, and by his death held all Khurasan as far west as Bisṭām.

Yet it seems that the Ghūrids' resources of manpower were inadequate for holding this empire together, whereas their Khwārazmian adversaries could draw freely on the Inner Asian steppes for troops. After Mu'izz al-Dīn Muḥammad's death in 602/1206, the dynasty was rent by internal squabbles. A group of their Turkish soldiers made themselves independent in Ghazna under Tāj al-Dīn Yïldïz, and could not be dislodged by the sultans in Fīrūzkūh and Bāmiyān. The Khwārazm Shāh Jalāl al-Dīn was therefore able to step in and incorporate the Ghūrid lands into his own empire. But this Khwārazmian domination was only of brief duration, for the whole eastern Islamic world was shortly afterwards overwhelmed by Chingiz Khān's Mongols (see above, no. 131). Moreover, the Turkish generals of Mu'izz al-Dīn Muḥammad continued to uphold Ghūrid policies and traditions in northern India, where Quṭb al-Dīn Aybak was installed as ruler in Lahore (Lāhawur) by one of the last Ghūrids (see below, no. 160, 1).

The coinage of the Ghūrids is particularly interesting, in that Mu'izz al-Dīn Muḥammad minted coins for his Indian lands with the Islamic *shahāda* and its proclamation of *tawḥīd*, the indivisible unity of God, on one side, and on the other side Sanskrit inscriptions and the likeness of the Hindu goddess Lakśmi.

Justi, 455–6; Lane-Poole, 291–4; Zambaur, 280–1, 284; Album, 39–40.

EI² 'G͟hūrids' (C. E. Bosworth); EIr 'Ghurids' (C. E. Bosworth).

G. Wiet, in André Maricq and Gaston Wiet, *Le minaret de Djam. La découverte de la capital des sultans ghorides (XIIe–XIIIe siècles)*, Méms DAFA, 16, Paris 1959, 31–54.

C. E. Bosworth, 'The eastern fringes of the Iranian world: the end of the G͟haznavids and the upsurge of the G͟hūrids', in *The Cambridge History of Iran*, IV, 157–66.

160

THE DELHI SULTANS

602–962/1206–1555

Northern India and, at times, the northern Deccan

1. The Muʿizzī or Shamsī Slave Kings

⊘ 602/1206	Aybak, Quṭb al-Dīn, Malik of Hindūstān in Lahore for the Ghūrids
607/1210	Ārām Shāh, protégé, dubiously the son, of Aybak, in Lahore
⊘ 607/1211	Iltutmish b. Ilam Khān, Shams al-Dīn, sultan in Delhi (Dihlī)
⊘ 633/1236	Fīrūz Shāh I b. Iltutmish, Rukn al-Dīn
⊘ 634/1236	Raḍiyya Begum b. Iltutmish, Jalālat al-Dīn
⊘ 637/1240	Bahrām Shāh b. Iltutmish, Muʿizz al-Dīn
⊘ 639/1242	Masʿūd Shāh b. Fīrūz Shāh I, ʿAlāʾ al-Dīn
⊘ 644/1246	Maḥmūd Shāh I b. Nāṣir al-Dīn b. Iltutmish, Nāṣir al-Dīn
⊘ 664/1266	Balban, Ulugh Khān, Ghiyāth al-Dīn, already viceroy (*nāʾib-i mamlakat*) in the previous reign
⊘ 686/1287	Kay Qubādh b. Bughra Khān b. Balban, Muʿizz al-Dīn
⊘ 689/1290	Kayūmarth b. Muʿizz al-Dīn Kay Qubādh, Shams al-Dīn

2. The Khaljīs

⊘ 689/1290	Fīrūz Shāh II Khaljī b. Yughrush, Jalāl al-Dīn
⊘ 695/1296	Ibrāhīm Shāh I Qadīr Khān b. Fīrūz Shāh II, Rukn al-Dīn
⊘ 695/1296	Muḥammad Shāh I ʿAlī Garshāsp b. Masʿūd b. Yughrush, ʿAlāʾ al-Dīn
⊘ 715/1316	ʿUmar Shāh b. Muḥammad Shāh I, Shihāb al-Dīn
⊘ 716–20/1316–20	Mubārak Shāh b. Muḥammad Shāh I, Quṭb al-Dīn
⊘ *720/1320*	*Usurpation of Khusraw Khān Barwārī, Nāṣir al-Dīn*

3. The Tughluqids

⊘ 720/1320	Tughluq Shāh I b. ? Ghāzī, Ghiyāth al-Dīn
⊘ 725/1325	Muḥammad Shāh II b. Tughluq Shāh I, Abu ʾl-Mujāhid Ulugh Khān Jawna Ghiyāth al-Dīn
⊘ 752/1351	Fīrūz Shāh III b. Rajab b. Tughluq Shāh I, Kamāl al-Dīn
⊘ (752/1351	Maḥmūd, Ghiyāth al-Dīn, alleged son of Muḥammad Shāh II, puppet of the rebel Khwāja-yi Jahān Aḥmad Ayāz)
(789/1387	Muḥammad Shāh III b. Fīrūz Shāh III, Nāṣir al-Dīn, as co-ruler with his father)
⊘ 790/1388	Tughluq Shāh II b. Fatḥ Khan b. Fīrūz Shāh III, Ghiyāth al-Dīn, k. 791/1389
⊘ (? 791/1389	? Fīrūz Shāh Ẓafar b. Fīrūz Shāh III; identical with the next ruler?)

⊘ 791–3/1389–91	Abū Bakr Shāh b. Ẓafar b. Fīrūz Shāh III, in Delhi
⊘ 791–6/1389–94	Muḥammad Shāh III b. Fīrūz Shāh III, Nāṣir al-Dīn, in the provinces and then Delhi
⊘ 796/1394	Sikandar Shāh I b. Muḥammad III, ʿAlāʾ al-Dīn
⊘ 796/1394	Maḥmūd Shāh II b. Muḥammad III, Nāṣir al-Dīn, first reign
⊘ (797/1395	Nuṣrat Shāh b. Fatḥ Khān, in Fīrūzābād, d. 801/1399)
804/1401	Mahmūd Shāh II b. Muḥammad III, second reign
815–17/1412–14	*Succession of Dawlat Khān Lōdī*

4. The Sayyids

817/1414	Khiḍr Khān b. Sulaymān, *Rāyat-i Aʿlā*
⊘ 824/1421	Mubārak Shāh II b. Khiḍr, Muʿizz al-Dīn
⊘ 837/1434	Muḥammad Shāh IV b. Farīd b. Khiḍr
⊘ 847–55/1443–51	ʿĀlam Shāh b. Muḥammad IV, ʿAlāʾ al-Dīn, 855–83/1451–78 ruler in Badaon (Badāʾūn)

5. The Lōdīs

⊘ 855/1451	Bahlūl b. Kālā b. Bahrām Lōdī
⊘ 894/1489	Sikandār II Niẓām Khān b. Bahlūl
⊘ 923–32/1517–26	Ibrāhīm II b. Sikandar II
932/1526	*Mughal victory*

6. The Sūrīs

⊘ 947/1540	Shīr Shāh Sūr b. Miyān Ḥasan, Farīd al-Dīn
⊘ 952/1545	Islām Shāh Sūr b. Shīr Shāh
⊘ 961/1554	Muḥammad V Mubāriz Khān ʿĀdil Shāh b. Niẓām Khān b. Ismāʿīl
⊘ 961/1554	Ibrāhīm Khān III b. Ghāzī b. Ismāʿīl
⊘ 962/1555	Aḥmad Khān Sikandar Shāh III b. Ismāʿīl, in Lahore
962/1555	*Mughal conquest*

Islam was first implanted in the lower Indus valley by the Arab governors of the East for the Umayyad caliphs; in 92/711, Sind was conquered by the commander Muḥammad b. al-Qāsim al-Thaqafī. This foothold was retained during the next three centuries, a period in which some of the Muslim communities there were affected by the propaganda of Ismāʿīlī Shīʿī missionaries, who were working intensively on behalf of the Fāṭimids (see above, no. 27) in many parts of the Islamic world, from North Africa to Yemen and the fringes of India. There were also trade contacts between Arabia and the Persian Gulf region and the coastlands of peninsular India, namely Gujarāt, Bombay and the Deccan coasts, just as there had been in classical times; but these sporadic and superficial contacts hardly affected the interior, the overwhelming land mass of the subcontinent.

It was the Turkish Ghaznawids who first brought the full weight of Muslim military power into northern India, overthrowing powerful native dynasties like the Hindūshāhīs of Wayhind, reducing many of the Rājput rulers to tributary status and raiding as far as Somnath and Benares (Banāras, Varanasi), although most of those rulers who submitted threw off their obligations as soon as the Ghaznawid armies went back. Maḥmūd of Ghazna became an Islamic hero for his attacks on infidel Hindustan, but it is clear that the sultan was not a fanatical zealot, bent on the conversion or extermination of the Hindus – a palpably impossible task – since he used Indian troops in his own armies, and it does not seem that conversion to Islam was a condition of recruitment. The Ghaznawids' interest in India was primarily financial, the subcontinent being regarded as an almost inexhaustible reservoir of slaves and treasure; but they did take over the Punjab and make it a permanent base for the extension of Muslim power through northern India, and towards the end of the dynasty's life Lahore became the sultans' capital (see above, no. 158).

Hence there existed there a springboard for the Indian conquests of Muʿizz al-Dīn Muḥammad Ghūrī and his Turkish slave generals in the last years of the twelfth century and at the beginning of the thirteenth. After eliminating the last Ghaznawids, he expanded into the Gangetic plain, attacking local Rājput princes, such as the Chāhamāna or Chawhān king of Ajmer and Delhi (Dihlī) and then the Gāhadavāla king of Benares and Kanawj. Among Muʿizz al-Dīn's commanders, Quṭb al-Dīn Aybak was placed in charge of the Indian conquests during his master's lifetime, when the sultan was involved in Khurasan and elsewhere. Aybak held on to the Ghūrid conquests in the Punjab and the Ganges-Jumna Do'āb, and raided as far as Gujarāt. Another general, Ikhtiyār al-Dīn Muḥammad Khaljī, penetrated into Bihār and Bengal (Bangāla), making Gawr or Lakhnawatī his base there, and he even attacked Assam (see below, no. 161, 1). It is thus in the period of the Ghūrids and their commanders that the permanent establishment of Islam in northern India begins: long-established Hindu dynasties were humbled and the foundations of various Muslim sultanates laid. On the other hand, throughout the period of the Delhi Sultanate and after, many local Hindu chiefs retained their power, especially away from the main centres of Turco-Afghan military concentration, and Hindus always played important roles in the administrations and armies of Muslim potentates.

When Muʿizz al-Dīn died in 602/1206, Aybak assumed power in Lahore as *Malik* or ruler on behalf of the Ghūrid sultan in Fīrūzkūh. Henceforth, Ghazna and the Afghan provinces of the Ghūrid empire were severed from India, falling briefly to the Khwārazm Shāhs and then to the Mongols, but Ghūrid traditions of both civil authority and military organisation lived on in northern India under the succeeding Muslim rulers there. Aybak and his successors up to 689/1290 are often called the Slave Kings, although only three of them, Aybak, Iltutmish and Balban, were of servile origin and all had in any case been manumitted by their masters before achieving power. Nor did these rulers belong to a single line, but to three distinct ones. Under Iltutmish, the real architect of an independent sultanate in Delhi, Sind, formerly in the hands of the Muʿizzī general Nāṣir al-Dīn Qabācha, was added to the Delhi Sultanate. He also managed to keep the Khwārazmians out of his dominions, but the Mongols overran the Punjab in 639/1241, sacking Lahore and advancing as far as Uch (Uchchh). A succession of weaker sultans brought internal discord, and the unity of the Sultanate was only assured first by the regency and then by the independent rule of the capable Balban, who had been originally one of the famous band of Turkish miltary slaves, the *Chihilgān* (in the surmise of Dr Peter Jackson, so called because they each themselves commanded forty military slaves) of Iltutmish. Balban continued the work of his master, placing the Sultanate on a firm military and governmental basis by his reforms, and exalting the authority of the sovereign on traditional Perso-Islamic lines. Spiritual links with the rest of the Islamic world were strengthened. Already, Iltutmish had sought investiture from the ʿAbbāsid caliph al-Mustanṣir; after the demise of the last caliph in Baghdad, al-Mustaʿṣim, the Muʿizzī sultans long continued to keep his name on their coins. In this way, one can discern the motif of identification with the wider world of Sunnī Islam and acknowledgement of the moral leadership of the caliphate; such threads run through much of the history of Indian Islam and reflect its struggle to maintain its identity against the pressures of the enveloping Hindu environment. Important, too, as a fertilising influence in the culture of this period were the waves of refugees – scholars and religious figures – from Transoxania and Persia, who fled before the Mongols and found their way to India during such reigns as those of Iltutmish and Balban; and in later times also, such as the reign of Muḥammad II b. Tughluq, infusions of fresh blood continued to revitalise Indo-Muslim religious life and culture.

In 689/1290, the Muʿizzī sultans were succeeded by the line of Jalāl al-Dīn Fīrūz Shāh II Khaljī. The Khalaj were originally a Turkish people (or perhaps a Turkicised people of a different ethnic origin) inhabiting eastern Afghanistan; it seems likely that the later Ghilzay Afghans were descended from them. During the reign of Muʿizz al-Dīn Muḥammad Ghūrī, the Khalaj had played a prominent part in the invasions of India, with Ikhtiyār al-Dīn Muḥammad Khaljī especially notable for bringing Islam to eastern India and Bengal (see above). The pressing task for Fīrūz Shāh II was to keep out the Mongols; it was, nevertheless, during his reign that large numbers of Mongols converted to Islam were allowed to settle in the Delhi area. The outstanding figure of the dynasty is undeniably ʿAlāʾ al-Dīn Muḥammad Shāh I, who considered himself a second Alexander the Great and had grandiose dreams of assembling a vast empire. In actuality, he had to cope with the threat from the Chaghatayid Mongols, who several times raided as far as Delhi, but his ambitions found their main outlet in South India, the rich area south of the Vindhya Mountains as yet untouched by Muslim arms. An attack in 695/1296 on Deogīr or Devagiri in the north-western Deccan, capital of the Yādavas, brought him the wealth which he afterwards used to win the sultanate for himself, and when he was firmly established on the throne he sent further armies to the southernmost tip of the Deccan. ʿAlāʾ al-Dīn Muḥammad continued to use the traditional designation of *Nāṣir Amīr al-Muʾminīn* 'Helper of the Commander of the Faithful'; the first and last Indo-Muslim ruler to appropriate for himself the caliphal title of *Amīr al-Muʾminīn* was his son Quṭb al-Dīn Mubārak Shāh I.

The Khaljī line collapsed when Khusraw Khān, a Gujarātī convert from Hinduism and favourite of the last Khaljī sultan, possibly apostasised from Islam and certainly briefly usurped the throne in Delhi. Muslim control was re-established by the Turco-Indian Tughluq Shāh I and his son Muḥammad Shāh II, who in 720/1320 inaugurated the reign of the Tughluqid sultans. The first did much to restore the stability of the Sultanate and to reimpose Muslim control over the Deccan. Muḥammad Shāh II is an enigmatic figure: a skilful general whose behaviour was nevertheless often erratic and his judgement poor. Increases of taxation necessary to run the sultanate and to finance warfare made him unpopular, but his decision of 727/1327 to transfer the capital from Delhi southwards to Deogīr, now renamed Dawlatābād, proved disastrous. On the other hand, he did successfully repel a Chaghatayid invasion from Transoxania, but his project for taking advantage of Chaghatayid weakness, perhaps in concert with the Il Khānids, and for invading Central Asia via the Pamirs (if such really was his intention, the sources being vague over this), was a chimera. Muḥammad Shāh II had diplomatic relations with the Islamic world outside India, including with the Mamlūks of Egypt (see above, no. 31), and sought investiture from the ʿAbbāsid puppet caliph in Cairo (see above, no. 3, 3). The diversion of energies to unrealistic military projects on the northern frontiers of the subcontinent led to a weakening of the Tughluqid hold over the Deccan. An independent Muslim sultanate arose in Maʿbar or Madura in the extreme south (see below, no. 166), and in 748/1347 the Bahmanid kingdom of the central Deccan was founded by ʿAlāʾ al-Dīn Ḥasan Bahman Shāh (see below, no. 167, 1). Later, Fīrūz Shāh III restored sultanal authority in Sind and Bengal, but made no attempt to touch the Deccan. The last Tughluqids were weaklings, so that Tīmūr was able to invade India in 801/1398–9 and wreak great devastation; as a result, the political unity of the Sultanate was dissolved, and various Muslim leaders seized independent power in the provinces.

For rather less than forty years, power was in the hands of the line of Khiḍr Khān, former governor of Multan (Multān), first for the last Tughluqids and then for Tīmūr. Khiḍr Khān ruled in the names of Tīmūr and his son Shāh Rukh, contenting himself with the title *Rāyat-i Aʿlā* 'Exalted Banner'; because of their claim to a fictitious descent from the Prophet, his line acquired the name of Sayyids. The effective authority of the Sayyids was reduced to a small area round Delhi, and with their initial dependence on the Tīmūrids they were unpopular with the Turkish and Afghan military classes in the capital. In 855/1451, their line was replaced by that of Bahlūl Khān, a chief of the Afghan tribe of the Lōdīs and formerly governor of Sirhind and Lahore. Bahlūl was the equal in vigour of the great Tughluqī sultans, and did much to restore Muslim prestige in India; the authority of Delhi was imposed over much of Central India, and the Sharqī rulers of Jawnpur (see below, no. 164) overthrown in 881/1477. His son Sikandar II conducted operations against the Rājput princes with some success, and moved his capital to Agra as being a better base for these attacks. However, the last Lōdī, Ibrāhīm II, alienated many of his nobles and commanders, and certain of these invited the Chaghatayid Mughal Bābur, then in Kabul, to intervene.

Bābur's victory at the first battle of Pānīpat, to the north of Delhi, in 932/1526 resulted in Ibrāhīm's death, the end of the Lōdī line and the first appearance of the dynasty of the Mughals in India. But this did not mean the permanent establishment yet of Bābur's line, for his son Humāyūn's reign was interrupted by the fifteen-year restoration of Afghan rule in India by Shīr Shāh Sūr. Operating from Bihār, Shīr Shāh defeated Humāyūn at Kanawj, thus negating all Bābur's work. As well as being a fine general, Shīr Shāh introduced important fiscal and land reforms. But for his premature death, a strong Afghan sultanate might have been implanted in India; discouraging Humāyūn from trying his fortunes once more; as it was, the weakness of Shīr Shāh's ephemeral successors facilitated a successful Mughal revanche.

Justi, 464–5; Lane-Poole, 295–303; Sachau, 32 no. 87 (Khaljīs), 33 no. 93 (Sūrīs); Zambaur, 285–8.

EI[2] 'Dihlī Sultanate' (P. Hardy), 'Hind. IV. History' (J. Burton-Page); 'Khaldjīs' (S. Moinul Haq), 'Lōdīs' (S. M. Imamuddin), 'Sayyids' (K. A. Nizami), 'Sūrīs' (I. H. Siddiqi).

H. Nelson Wright, *The Coinage and Metrology of the Sulṭāns of Dehlī, Incorporating a Catalogue of the Coins in the Author's Cabinet now in the Dehlī Museum*, Delhi 1936.

K. S. Lal, *History of the Khaljis A.D. 1290–1320*, revised edn, New Delhi 1980.

(Agha) Mahdi Husain, *Tughluq Dynasty*, Calcutta 1963.

Abd ul-Halim, *History of the Lodi Sultans of Delhi and Agra*, Dacca 1961.

I. H. Siddiqi, *History of Sher Shah Sur*, Aligarh 1971.

R. C. Majumdar, A. D. Pusalker and A. K. Majumdar (eds), *The History and Culture of the Indian People. V. The Struggle for Empire*, Bombay 1957, chs 4–5.

eidem (eds), *VI. The Delhi Sultanate*, Bombay 1960, chs 2–9, 14.

Majumdar (ed.), *VII. The Mughul Empire*, Bombay 1974, ch. 4.

Mohammad Habib and Khaliq Ahmad Nizami (eds), *A Comprehensive History of India. V. The Delhi Sultanat (A.D. 1206–1526)*, Delhi 1970, chs 2–7.

161

THE GOVERNORS AND SULTANS OF BENGAL

594–984/1198–1576

Bengal and Bihār

1. The governors for the Delhi Sultans, often ruling as independent sovereigns

⊘ 594/1198	Muḥammad Bakhtiyār Khaljī, Ikhtiyār al-Dīn, conqueror of Bihār and Bengal
603/1206	ʿAlī Mardān, first term of office
603/1207	Muḥammad Shirān Khān, ʿIzz al-Dīn
⊘ 604/1208	ʿIwaḍ, Ḥusām al-Dīn, first term of office
607/1210	ʿAlī Mardān, ruling title ʿAlāʾ al-Dīn, second term of office
⊘ 610/1213	ʿIwaḍ, Ḥusām al-Dīn, ruling title Ghiyāth al-Dīn
⊘ 624/1227	Maḥmūd b. Iltutmish, Nāṣir al-Dīn, Malik al-Sharq
626/1229	Bilge Khan b. Mawdūd, Ikhtiyār al-Dīn, ruled as Dawlat Shāh
629/1232	Masʿūd Jānī, ʿAlāʾ al-Dīn, first term of office
⊘ 630/1233	Aybak Khitāʾī, Sayf al-Dīn
633/1236	Āʾor Khan Aybak
633/1236	Ṭoghrïl Toghan Khān, ʿIzz al-Dīn
642/1244	Temür Qirān Khān, Qamar al-Dīn
645/1247	Masʿūd Jānī b. Masʿūd Jānī, Jalāl al-Dīn, first term of office
⊘ 649/1251	Yuzbak, Ikhtiyār al-Dīn, with the ruling title Abu ʾl-Muẓaffar Ghiyāth al-Dīn
655/1257	Balban Yuzbakī, ʿIzz al-Dīn, first term of office
657/1259	Masʿūd Jānī b. Masʿūd Jānī, second term of office
657/1259	Balban Yuzbakī, second term of office
657/1259	Muḥammad Arslan Khān Sanjar, Tāj al-Dīn
663/1265	Tātār Khān b. Muḥammad Arslan
666/1268	Shīr Khān
670–80/1272–81	Ṭoghrïl, with the ruling title Mughīth al-Dīn

2. The governors, and then independent rulers, of Balban's line

681/1282	Bughra b. Balban, Nāṣir al-Dīn
⊘ 690/1291	Kay Kāwūs b. Bughra, Rukn al-Dīn
⊘ 701–22/1302–22	Fīrūz Shāh, Shams al-Dīn, latterly in Bihār only
⊘ c. 709/c. 1309	Maḥmūd b. Fīrūz Shāh, Jalāl al-Dīn, in Bengal
⊘ c. 717–18/c. 1317–18	Bughra b. Fīrūz Shāh, Shihāb al-Dīn, in Bengal
⊘ 722/1322	Bahādur b. Fīrūz Shāh, Ghiyāth al-Dīn, also a provincial ruler during his father's lifetime, first term of office
⊘ 724/1324	Ibrāhīm b. Fīrūz Shāh, Nāṣir al-Dīn, governor for the Delhi Sultan in Lakhnawatī, d. after 728/1328
⊘ 726–39/1326–38	Pindar or Bīdar Qadïr Khān, in Lakhnawatī

726–41/1326–40	Yaḥyā, ʿIzz al-Dīn, in Sātgā'on
727–39/1327–39	Bahrām, Tātār Khān, in Sonārgā'on
⊘ 727–8/1327–8	Bahādur b. Fīrūz Shāh, Ghiyāth al-Dīn, in Sonārgā'on jointly with Tātār Khān
⊘ 739–50/1339–49	Mubārak Shāh, Fakhr al-Dīn, in Sonārgā'on
⊘ 740–3/1339–42	ʿAlī Mubārak, ʿAlā' al-Dīn, in Lakhnawatī
⊘ 750–3/1349–52	Ghāzī Shāh (?) b. Mubārak Shāh, Ikhtiyār al-Dīn, in Sonārgā'on until its conquest by Ilyās Shāh

3. The line of Ilyās Shāh

⊘ 740/1339	Ilyās Shāh, Shams al-Dīn, originally in Sātgā'on
⊘ 759/1358	Sikandar Shāh I b. Ilyās Shāh
⊘ 792/1390	Aʿẓam Shāh b. Sikandar Shāh I, Ghiyāth al-Dīn
⊘ 813/1410	Ḥamza Shāh b. Aʿẓam Shāh, Sayf al-Dīn
⊘ 815/1412	Bāyazīd Shāh b. Aʿẓam Shāh, Sayf al-Dīn
⊘ 817/1414	Fīrūz Shāh b. Bāyazīd Shāh

4. The line of Rājā Gaṇeśa (Ganesh)

817/1414	Jadu, son of Rājā Gaṇeśa, first reign under the regency of his father
⊘ 819/1416	Rājā Gaṇeśa, as Danūj Mardan Deva
⊘ 821/1418	Mahendra Deva, son of Rājā Gaṇeśa
⊘ 821/1418	Jadu, now Muḥammad Shāh, Jalāl al-Dīn, second reign
⊘ 836–40/1433–7	Aḥmad Shāh b. Muḥammad Shāh

5. The line of Ilyās Shāh restored

⊘ 841/1437	Maḥmūd Shāh, descendant of Ilyās Shāh, Abu 'l-Muẓaffar Nāṣir al-Dīn
⊘ 864/1460	Barbak Shāh b. Maḥmūd Shāh, Rukn al-Dīn
⊘ 879/1474	Yūsuf Shāh b. Barbak Shāh, Shams al-Dīn
⊘ 886/1481	Sikandar Shāh II (b) b. Yūsuf Shāh
⊘ 886–92/1481–7	Ḥusayn Fatḥ Shāh b. Maḥmūd Shāh, Jalāl al-Dīn

6. The domination of the Ḥabashīs

⊘ 892/1487	Sulṭān Shāhzāda Barbak Shāh
⊘ 892/1487	ʿAndil, ruled as Aḥmad Fīrūz Shāh Sayf al-Dīn
⊘ 895/1490	Maḥmūd Shāh (?) b. Aḥmad Fīrūz Shāh, Nāṣir al-Dīn
⊘ 896–8/1491–3	Dīwāna, ruled as Muẓaffar Shams al-Dīn

7. The line of Sayyid Ḥusayn Shāh

⊘ 898/1493	Sayyid Ḥusayn Shāh, ʿAlā' al-Dīn
⊘ 925/1519	Nuṣrat Shāh b. Ḥusayn Shāh, Nāṣir al-Dīn
⊘ 939/1533	Fīrūz Shāh b. Ḥusayn Shāh, ʿAlā' al-Dīn
⊘ 940–4/1534–7	Maḥmūd Shāh b. Ḥusayn Shāh, Ghiyāth al-Dīn

8. The Sūrīs

944/1537	Shīr Shāh Sūr
(947/1540	Khiḍr Khān, governor for Shīr Shāh)
⊘ 952/1545	Muḥammad Khān Sūr, Shams al-Dīn, independent in 960/1553
⊘ 962/1555	Khiḍr Khān Bahādur Shāh b. Muḥammad Khān Sūr, Ghiyāth al-Dīn
⊘ 968–71/1561–4	Jalāl Shāh b. Muḥammad Khān Sūr, Abu 'l-Muẓaffar Ghiyāth al-Dīn

9. The Kararānīs

971/1564	Sulaymān Kararānī
980/1572	Bāyazīd Kararāni b. Sulaymān
⊘ 980–4/1572–6	Dāwūd Kararānī b. Sulaymān
984/1576	*Mughal conquest*

The conquest of the easternmost provinces of India, Bihār and Bengal, was the achievement of Mu'izz al-Dīn Muḥammad Ghūrī's commander Muḥammad Bakhtiyār Khaljī, who raided as far as the mountain barrier beyond which lay Tibet, and founded a capital at Lakhnawatī or Gawr in the frontier zone between Bihār and Bengal. Subsequently, governors of the Delhi Sultans made other towns into centres of government, Sātgā'on in south-western Bengal and Sonārgā'on in the east (near modern Dacca or Ḍhākā), until Ilyās Shāh integrated all these into the independent Bengal sultanate. Because of the province's richness and its distance from Delhi, Bengal had always been difficult for the Sultans to administer, and central government control was often sporadic. In the first half of the fourteenth century, Muslim troops penetrated across the Brahmaputra into Sylhet (Silhet) and Assam and to Chittagong on the Bay of Bengal, and it was from this time that a steady process of conversion to Islam of low-caste Hindus began, leading to the eventual preponderance of Muslims over much of Bengal.

In the time of Muḥammad b. Tughluq, Bengal came to be ruled by Fakhr al-Dīn Mubārak Shāh at Sonārgā'on in the east and 'Alā' al-Dīn 'Alī at Lakhnawatī in the west, and henceforth for over two centuries independent sultans controlled Bengal. Under the Ilyāsids, the Islamic arts and sciences flourished, and commerce in Bengal's textiles and foodstuffs was encouraged. In the first decade of the fifteenth century, Ghiyāth al-Dīn A'ẓam Shāh renewed old diplomatic and cultural links with China, and the growth of the port of Chittagong probably reflects increased trade with the lands farther east. The reign of the Ilyāsids was interrupted for over twenty years by the seizure of power by Rājā Gaṇeśa, a local Hindu landlord of Bengal; his son became a Muslim and ruled as Jalāl al-Dīn Muḥammad, and despite their Hindu origins the family was able to rule with some Muslim support. Under the restored Ilyāsids, the influence of Ḥabashī or black palace guards grew, until in 892/1487 their commander, the eunuch Sulṭān Shāhzāda, murdered the last Ilyāsid and seized power for himself.

Order was eventually restored by Sayyid 'Alā' al-Dīn Ḥusayn Shāh, whose enlightened rule came opportunely after the chaos of the Ḥabashī period. Bihār was annexed; asylum given to the Sharqī ruler of Jawnpur, dispossessed by the Lōdīs of Delhi (see below, no. 164, and above, no. 160, 5), and the Jawnpur troops added to the Bengal army. The growth of a vernacular Bengali literature was a process continuing during these centuries, and royal encouragement is seen in Nuṣrat Shāh b. Sayyid Ḥusayn's patronage of a Bengali translation of the *Mahābhārata*. The line of Sayyid Ḥusayn was ended by the meteoric rise of the Afghan chief Shīr Shāh Sūr, who took over Bengal and used it as a base from which to eject the Mughal Humāyūn from India (see above, no. 160, 6, and below, no. 175). But once the Mughals were firmly re-established in Lahore and Delhi and the Afghans defeated, Mughal influence began to be felt in Bengal. Sulaymān Kararānī, the former governor of southern Bihār, acknowledged the suzerainty of Akbar, and in 984/1576 Bengal was overrun and incorporated in the Mughal empire, becoming one of its *ṣūba*s or provinces.

Lane-Poole, 305–8; Zambaur, 286, 289.
EI[2] 'Bangāla' (A. H. Dani); 'Hind. IV. History' (J. Burton-Page).
R. C. Majumdar et al. (eds), *The History and Culture of the Indian People. VI. The Delhi Sultanate*, ch. 10 E.
M. Habib and K. A. Nizami (eds), *A Comprehensive History of India. V. The Delhi Sultanat (A.D. 1206–1526)*, chs 2 iv and 19.
Sir Jadu-Nath Sarkar, *The History of Bengal, Muslim Period 1200–1757*, Patna 1973, chs 2–7.
Mohammad Yusuf Siddiq, *Arabian and Persian Texts of the Islamic Inscriptions of Bengal*, Watertown MA 1991.
idem, *al-Nuqūsh al-ʿarabiyya fī 'l-Banghāl wa-atharuhā al-ḥaḍarī*, Beirut 1996.

162

THE SULTANS OF KASHMĪR
739–996/1339–1588

1. The line of Shāh Mīr Swātī

739/1339	Shāh Mīr Swātī, Shams al-Dīn
743/1342	Jamshīd b. Shāh Mīr
745/1344	ʿAlī Shīr b. Shāh Mīr, ʿAlāʾ al-Dīn
755/1354	Shīrāshāmak b. ʿAlī Shīr, Shihāb al-Dīn
775/1374	Hindal b. ʿAlī Shīr, Quṭb al-Dīn
792/1390	Sikandar b. Hindal, But-shikan, until 795/1393 under the regency of his mother Sura
⊘ 813/1410	ʿAlī Mīr Khān b. Sikandar, ruled as ʿAlī Shāh
⊘ 823/1420	Shāhī Khān b. Sikandar, ruled as Sultan Zayn al-ʿĀbidīn, called Bud Shāh 'Great King'
⊘ 875/1470	Ḥājjī Khān b. Zayn al-ʿĀbidīn, ruled as Ḥaydar Shāh
⊘ 876/1472	Ḥasan Shāh b. Ḥaydar
889/1484	Muḥammad Shāh b. Ḥasan, first reign
⊘ 892/1487	Fatḥ Shāh b. Ad'ham Khān b. Zayn al-ʿĀbidīn, first reign
⊘ 904/1499	Muḥammad b. Ḥasan, second reign
910/1505	Fatḥ Shāh b. Ad'ham Khān, second reign
922/1516	Muḥammad Shāh b. Ḥasan, third reign
934/1528	Ibrāhīm Shāh b. Muḥammad, first reign
935/1529	Nāzūk or Nādir Shāh b. Fatḥ
⊘ 936/1530	Muḥammad Shāh b. Ḥasan, fourth reign
943/1537	Shams al-Dīn b. Muḥammad
947/1540	Ismāʿīl Shāh b. Muḥammad, first reign
947–58/1540–51	*Mīrzā Ḥaydar Dughlat, governor for the Mughal Humāyūn*
958/1551	Nāzūk Shāh b. Ibrāhīm, second reign
⊘ 959/1552	Ibrāhīm Shāh b. Muḥammad, second reign
⊘ 962/1555	Ismāʿīl Shāh b. Muḥammad, second reign
964–8/1557–61	Ḥabīb Shāh b. Ismāʿīl, deposed by Ghāzī Khān Chak

2. The line of Ghāzī Shāh Chak

968/1561	Ghāzī Khān Chak, ruled as Muḥammad Nāṣir al-Dīn
971/1563	Ḥusayn Shāh, Nāṣir al-Dīn, brother of Muḥammad Ghāzī
978/1570	Muḥammad ʿAlī Shāh, Ẓahīr al-Dīn, brother of Muḥammad Ghāzī and Ḥusayn
⊘ 987/1579	Yūsuf Shāh b. ʿAlī, Nāṣir al-Dīn, d. in Bihār 1000/1592
994–6/1586–8	Yaʿqūb Shāh b. Yūsuf, d. 1001/1593
996/1588	*Definitive Mughal conquest*

Because of its geographical position, separated by high mountain barriers from the plains of northern India, Kashmīr was long sheltered from Muslim raids. It remained under its own dynasty of Hindu rulers long after most of northern India had passed under Muslim control. Maḥmūd of Ghazna (see above, no. 158) made two attempts to invade Kashmīr from the south, but was held up on both occasions by the fortress of Lohkot. However, Muslim Turkish mercenaries (*Turuśka*) began to be employed by the Hindu kings of Kashmīr, and the process of Islamisation, which has given the province today an overwhelmingly Muslim population, must have tentatively begun.

In 735/1335, the throne there was seized by Shāh Mīr Swātī, a Muslim adventurer who was probably of Pathan origin and who had been minister to Rājā Sinha Deva. The régime of Shams al-Dīn (this being the honorific which Shāh Mīr adopted) was tolerant and mild towards the majority Hindus, but his grandson Sikandar was a Muslim zealot who patronised the *'ulamā'* and scholars and who persecuted the Hindus, destroying their temples and earning for himself the epithet *But-shikan* 'Idol-breaker'. Already before this, the Kubrawī Ṣūfī saint 'Alī Hamadhānī and many Sayyids had arrived in Kashmīr, and during Sikandar's reign the group of Bayhaqī Sayyids, who were to play a prominent role in the religious and intellectual life of the province, migrated from Delhi to Kashmīr. However, his son Zayn al-'Ābidīn reversed this rigorist policy, and his long and enlightened reign was something of a Golden Age for Kashmīr; under his patronage, the *Mahābhārata* and Kalhaṇa's twelfth-century metrical chronicle of Kashmīr, the *Rājatarangiṇī*, were translated into Persian. Unfortunately, his descendants were lesser men, and much internecine strife now followed; various provincial chiefs took advantage of the mountainous and difficult terrain and established a virtual independence. In particular, the influence of the powerful Chak tribe, originally immigrants from Dardistān, grew, its leaders serving as ministers and commanders for the last feeble *fainéant* rulers of Shāh Mīr's line. The Mughal prince Ḥaydar Dughlat invaded Kashmīr in 947/1540, and ruled in Srinagar for ten years on behalf of his kinsman Humāyūn, until he was killed in an uprising. The Chak family was now again in the ascendant, and after 968/1561 they ruled as sovereigns themselves, assuming the title *Pādishāh* 'Monarch' in imitation of the Mughals; their religious inclinations were towards Shī'ism. However, the last two Chaks had to rule as vassals of Akbar until they were finally deposed and Kashmīr fully incorporated into the Mughal empire.

Justi, 478; Sachau, 32–3 nos 89 and 90; Zambaur, 293–4.

EI[2] 'Hind. IV. History' (J. Burton-Page), 'Kashmīr. I. Before 1947' (Mohibbul Hasan), Suppl. 'Čaks' (idem).

Sir T. W. Haig, 'The chronology and genealogy of the Muhammadan Kings of Kashmir', JRAS (1918), 451–68.

Mohibbul Hasan, *Kashmir under the Sultans*, Calcutta 1959.

R. C. Majumdar et al. (eds), *The History and Culture of the Indian People. VI. The Delhi Sultanate*, ch. 13 C.

M. Habib and K. A. Nizami (eds), *A Comprehensive History of India. V. The Delhi Sultanat (A.D. 1206–1526)*, ch. 9.

163

THE SULTANS OF GUJARĀT
806–980/1403–1573
Western India

(793/1391	Ẓafar Khān b. Wajīh al-Mulk, governor with the title of Muẓaffar Khān)
806/1403	Tātār Khān b. Muẓaffar, proclaimed himself Sultan with the title of Muḥammad Shāh (I)
810/1407	Muẓaffar Khān, proclaimed Sultan with the title of Muẓaffar Shāh (I)
⊘ 814/1411	Aḥmad Shāh I b. Muḥammad b. Muẓaffar, Shihāb al-Dīn
⊘ 846/1442	Muḥammad Shāh II Karīm b. Aḥmad
⊘ 855/1451	Jalāl Khān b. Muḥammad II, succeeded as Aḥmad Shāh (II), Quṭb al-Dīn
862/1458	Dāwūd Khān b. Aḥmad I
⊘ 862/1458	Fatḥ Khān b. Muḥammad II, succeeded as Maḥmūd Shāh I, Begṛā, Sayf al-Dīn
⊘ 917/1511	Khalīl Khān b. Maḥmūd, succeeded as Muẓaffar Shāh II
932/1526	Sikandar b. Muẓaffar II
932/1526	Nāṣir Khān b. Muẓaffar II, succeeded as Maḥmūd Shāh (II)
⊘ 932/1526	Bahādur Shāh b. Muẓaffar II, first reign
941–2/1535–6	*Mughal occupation*
942–3/1536–7	Bahādur Shāh, second reign
⊘ 943/1537	Maḥmūd Shāh III b. Laṭīf Khān b. Muẓaffar II
⊘ 962/1554	Aḥmad Shāh III, descendant of Aḥmad I, Raḍī 'l-Mulk
⊘ 968/1561	Muẓaffar Shāh III b. ? Maḥmūd III, first reign
980/1573	*Mughal conquest*
⊘ (991/1583	Muẓaffar Shāh III, brief second reign, d. 1001/1593)
991/1583	*Definitive Mughal conquest*

The mediaeval province of Gujarāt on the western coastland of India comprised both a mainland section lying to the east of the Rann of Cutch (Kachchh) and also the peninsula of Kathiawar. Because of its commercial and maritime connections with the other shores of the Indian Ocean, Gujarāt was a particularly rich province; but although Maḥmūd of Ghazna had marched through it en route for Somnath (see above, no. 158), permanent Muslim conquest was quite long delayed. Only in 697/1298 did the troops of ʿAlāʾ al-Dīn Muḥammad Khaljī defeat the main local Hindu dynasty, the Vāghelās of Anahilwāra. During the fourteenth century, Gujarāt was ruled by governors appointed by the Delhi Sultans, until in 793/1391 the Tughluqid Muḥammad III sent out Ẓafar Khān. As the Tughluqids fell into palpable decline, Ẓafar Khan became in effect independent, and his son and he claimed the insignia of royalty and the title of Shāh. The new sultanate was consolidated by the founder's grandson Aḥmad I, much of whose reign was occupied by warfare against the Hindu Rājās of Gujarāt and Rājputānā and against his fellow-Muslim sovereigns of Mālwa, Khāndesh and the Deccan.

It was he who built for himself the new capital of Aḥmadābād, which replaced that of Anahilwāra. The fifty-five years of Maḥmūd Begṛā's reign (862–917/1458–1511) were the greatest in the history of the Gujarāt Sultanate. Campaigns against the Hindu princes led, among other things, to the capture of the fortress of Chāmpānēr, now renamed Maḥmūdābād and made the sultan's capital; indeed, during his reign the Sultanate attained its greatest extent before the subsequent annexation of Mālwa (see below, no. 165)

A new factor in the politics of western and southern India appeared before the end of Maḥmūd's reign, namely the Portuguese. After Vasco da Gama appeared at Calicut (Kalikat) in 1498, the Portuguese began to divert much of the Indian Ocean commerce into their own hands, thus bypassing the traders of Egypt and Gujarāt. Hence in 914/1508 Maḥmūd allied with the Mamlūk Sultan Qānṣūh al-Ghawrī (see above, no. 31, 2), but despite the initial Muslim naval victory near Bombay over Dom Lourenço de Almeida, the Portuguese captured Goa from the neighbouring ʿĀdil Shāhīs of Bījapur (see below, no. 170) and Maḥmūd was compelled to make peace. The last great sultan of Gujarāt was Maḥmūd's grandson Bahādur Shāh, who assumed the offensive against the Hindus and also conquered Mālwa, only to lose it and part of his own dominions to the Mughal Humāyūn. The menace from the Portuguese revived, and despite the grant to them of Diu (Dīw) they treacherously killed Bahādur Shāh in 943/1537. The unity of Gujarāt now crumbled; dynastic quarrels broke out, and the kingdom began to split up among various nobles. In despair, the Mughals were called in so that Akbar took over Gujarāt in 980/1572–3 and made it into a province of his empire, although the last sultan of Gujarāt, Muẓaffar III, made several attempts at a revanche up to his death in 1001/1593.

Justi, 476; Lane-Poole, 312–14; Zambaur, 296.
EI[2] 'Gudjarāt' (J. Burton-Page), 'Hind. IV. History' (idem).
G. P. Taylor, 'The coins of the Gujarāt salṭanat', JBBRAS, 21 (1903), 278–338, with a genealogical table at p. 308.
M. S. Commissariat, *History of Gujarat. Including a Survey of its Chief Architectural Monuments and Inscriptions. I. From A.D. 1297–8 to A.D. 1573*, Bombay etc. 1938, with a chronological table and chronological list of rulers at pp. 564–5.
R. C. Majumdar et al. (eds), *The History and Culture of the Indian People. VI. The Delhi Sultanate*, ch. 10 A.
M. Habib and K. A. Nizami (eds), *A Comprehensive History of India. V. The Delhi Sultanat (A.D. 1206–1506)*, ch. 11.

164

THE SHARQĪ SULTANS OF JAWNPUR
796–888/1394–1483
East-central northern India

796/1394	Malik Sarwar, Khwāja-yi Jahān
⊘ 802/1399	Malik Qaranful Mubārak Shāh, adopted son of Malik Sarwar
⊘ 804/1401	Ibrāhīm, Shams al-Dīn, brother of Mubārak Shāh
⊘ 844/1440	Maḥmūd Shāh b. Ibrāhīm
⊘ 862/1458	Bhikan Khān b. Maḥmūd Shāh, ruled as Muḥammad Shāh
⊘ 862–88/1458–83	Ḥusayn Shāh b. Mahmūd Shāh, d. 911/1505
888/1483	*Conquest by the Delhi Sultans*

Jawnpur lies on the Gumtī river to the north of Benares, between what were later the provinces of Bihār and Oudh (Awadh), hence in what is now the eastern part of Uttar Pradesh State, and is traditionally said to have been founded in 762/1359 by the Tughluqid Fīrūz Shāh III and named after his cousin and patron Muḥammad b. Tughluq, one of whose names was Jawna (< *Yāvana* 'foreigner') Shāh. In the fifteenth century it became the centre of a powerful Muslim state, situated between the Sultanates of Delhi and Bengal, and the Sultans of Jawnpur played a significant rôle in developing the Islamic culture of the region; Jawnpur, indeed, became known as 'the Shīrāz of the East'.

The dynasty was founded by one Malik Sarwar, the eunuch slave minister of the last Tughluqid Maḥmūd Shāh II, who conquered Oudh on behalf of his master in 796/1394 and then remained there as virtual ruler, persuading the sultan to grant him the title of *Malik al-Sharq* 'King of the East', whence the name of the dynasty. Helped by the chaos which followed Tīmūr's invasion of India, his adopted son Mubārak Shāh behaved as a fully independent ruler, minting his own coins and having the bidding prayers in the *khuṭba* or Friday sermon made in his own name alone. His brother Ibrāhīm was the greatest of the Sharqīs, and during his reign of nearly forty years the dynasty reached a peak of affluence and power. A particularly fine school of Indo-Muslim architecture developed in Jawnpur, and, being himself a man of culture, Ibrāhīm encouraged scholars and literary men at his court. His successors were drawn into warfare with the Lōdī Sultans of Delhi and raided Gwalior (Gwāliyār), but were most successful in attacking Orissa (Uṙīsā). According to Muslim chronicles, Jawnpur had at this time one of the largest armies in India. The last Sharqī sultan, Ḥusayn Shāh, reached the gates of Delhi on one occasion, but Bahlūl and Sikandar Lōdī were in the end too much for him. Sikandar defeated Ḥusayn, who fled to Bengal and lived out his life in a small district granted to him by the Bengal Sultan ʿAlāʾ al-Dīn Ḥusayn Shāh (see above, no. 161, 7). Jawnpur thus passed under the control of the Lōdī Sultan, who deliberately destroyed the city's fine buildings left by the Sharqīs. Ḥusayn Shāh's descendants had irredentist hopes of regaining the kingdom, hopes which the Mughals were not disposed to satisfy, although Bābur and Humāyūn did permit them to style themselves sultans.

Lane-Poole, 309; Zambaur, 292.
EI[2] 'D̲j̲awnpur' (J. Burton-Page), 'Hind. IV. History' (idem), 'S̲h̲arḳīs' (K. A. Nizami).
H. M. Whittell, 'The coinage of the Sharqī Kings of Jaunpūr', JASB, new series, 18 (1922), Numismatic Suppl., pp. N.10–N.35.
M. M. Saeed, *The Sharqi Sultanate of Jaunpur: A Political and Cultural History*, Karachi 1972, with Appx A on coinage at pp. 293–301 and a genealogical table as Appx C at pp. 306–7.
R. C. Majumdar et al. (eds), *The History and Culture of the Indian People. VI. The Delhi Sultanate*, ch. 10 D.
M. Habib and K. A. Nizami (eds), *A Comprehensive History of India. V. The Delhi Sultanat (A.D. 1206–1506)*, ch. 8.

165

THE SULTANS AND RULERS OF MĀLWA
804–969/1402–1562
Central India

1. The line of the Ghūrīs

(793/1391	Dilāwar Khān Ḥasan Ghūrī, governor for the Delhi Sultans)
804/1402	Dilāwar Khān, as ʿAmīd Shāh Dāwūd
⊘ 809/1406	Alp Khān b. Dilāwar, succeeded as Hūshang Shāh
838/1435	Ghaznī Khān b. Alp, succeeded as Muḥammad Shāh Ghūrī
839/1436	Masʿūd Khān b. Muḥammad

2. The line of the Khaljīs

⊘ 839/1436	Maḥmūd Khān, succeeded as Maḥmūd Shāh (I) Khaljī
⊘ 873/1469	Ghiyāth al-Dīn Shāh b. Maḥmūd
⊘ 906–16/1501–10	Nāṣir al-Dīn Shāh b. Ghiyāth al-Dīn, ʿAbd al-Qādir
⊘ 917–37/1511–31	Maḥmūd Shāh II b. Nāṣir al-Dīn, after 924/1518 as a vassal of the Sultans of Gujarāt
937–41/1531–5	*Occupation by Gujarāt*

3. Various governors and independent rulers

939/1533	Mallū Khān, governor for Gujarāt in 939/1533 and then independent as Qādir Shāh
949/1542	Shajāʿat Khān, governor for the Delhi Sultan Shīr Shāh Sūr, first period of power
952/1545	ʿĪsā Khān, governor for Islām Shāh Sūr
961/1554	Shajāʿat Khān, governor for Muḥammad ʿĀdil Shāh Sūr, second period of power, independent in 962/1555
⊘ 962–9/1555–62	Miyān Bāyazīd b. Shajāʿat Khān, Bāz Bahādur
969/1562	*Definitive Mughal conquest*

Mediaeval Indian Mālwa was the plateau region of western Central India, which formed a triangle with the Vindhya range as its base, hence it corresponded to what is now largely within the westernmost part of Madhya Pradesh State. Muslim rule was only established there after long and bloody struggles with the local Rājput rulers of Chitōr and Ujjain. In 705/1305, the Delhi Sultan ʿAlāʾ al-Dīn Khaljī despatched an army which subjugated Mālwa, and thereafter governors were sent out to the region from Delhi. The Afghan governor Dilāwar Khān Ghūrī sheltered the refugee Tughluqid Maḥmūd Shāh II during Tīmūr's invasion of northern India in 801/1398–9, but the shock to the fabric of the Delhi Sultanate at this time permitted Dilāwar Khān shortly afterwards to declare his independence and assume the insignia of royalty. The circumstances of Mālwa's achievement of independence thus parallel those of the rise of the Sharqīs in Jawnpur (see above, no. 164). The Mālwa Sultans made their capital the inaccessible and heavily-defended fortress of Māndū, and adorned the city which grew up there with many splendid buildings.

At one point, the Ghūrī sultans undertook a raid as far as Hindu Orissa, but most of their military activity was against nearby Rājput chiefs and neighbouring Muslim rulers, including the Sharqīs, the Gujarāt Sultans, the Sayyid Sultans of Delhi and the Bahmanids of the Deccan; in this warfare against Muslim rivals, they did not hesitate to ally with Hindu princes. In 839/1436, the chief minister Maḥmūd Khān took over the throne in Mālwa (the last Ghūrī sultan fleeing to Gujarāt) and began the line of the Khaljīs there. Maḥmūd I Khaljī was the greatest of the Mālwa Sultans, and despite several setbacks in his campaigns against the Rājputs of Chitōr and the Bahmanids he expanded his territories considerably. His fame spread beyond the subcontinent; he received a formal investiture of power from the *fainéant* ʿAbbāsid caliph in Cairo al-Mustanjid (see above, no. 3, 3), and embassies were exchanged with the Tīmūrid sultan in Herat, Abū Saʿīd (see above, no. 144, 1). But during the reign of his great-grandson Maḥmūd II, there arose an ascendancy of Rājput ministers and courtiers in the state, such as that of the sultan's vizier Mēdinī Rā'ī, and tensions between Muslim and Hindu elements grew. At one point, Maḥmūd was captured by the Rājā of Chitōr, and, though he was restored in Mālwa, his kingdom fell in 937/1531 to Bahādur Shāh of Gujarāt (see above, no. 163).

During the next three decades, there were several governors acting for the Gujarāt Sultans and then the Delhi Sultans, some of whom managed to make themselves at times independent, until the last such ruler, Bāz Bahādur, was defeated by Akbar's forces and Mālwa was incorporated into the Mughal empire as one of its provinces.

Justi, 477; Lane-Poole, 310–11; Zambaur, 292.

EI[2] 'Hind. IV. History' (J. Burton-Page), 'Mālwā' (T. W. Haig and Riazul Islam).

L. White King, 'History and coinage of Malwa', NC, 4th series, 3 (1903), 356–98, with a genealogical table and a chronological list of rulers at pp. 359–60; also 4 (1904), 62–100.

U. N. Day, *Medieval Malwa: A Political and Cultural History 1401–1557*, Delhi 1965.

R. C. Majumdar et al. (eds), *The History and Culture of the Indian People. VI. The Delhi Sultanate,* ch. 10 C.

M. Habib and K. A. Nizami (eds), *A Comprehensive History of India. V. The Delhi Sultanat (A.D. 1206–1526)*, ch. 12.

166

THE SULTANS OF MAʿBAR OR MADURA

734–79/1334–77

The southernmost Deccan

⊘ 734/1334	Sharīf Aḥsan, Jalāl al-Dīn, governor since 723/1323, then independent
⊘ 739/1338	ʿAlāʾ al-Dīn Udayji
⊘ 740/1339	Fīrūz Shāh, Quṭb al-Dīn, nephew and son-in-law of ʿAlāʾ al-Dīn
⊘ 740/1339	Muḥammad Dāmghān Shāh, Ghiyāth al-Dīn, son-in-law of Sharīf Aḥsan
⊘ 745/1344	Maḥmūd Dāmghān Shāh, Nāṣir al-Dīn, nephew and son-in-law of Muḥammad Dāmghān Shāh
⊘ by 757/1356	ʿĀdil Shāh, Abu ʾl-Muẓaffar Shams al-Dīn
⊘ by 761/1360	Mubārak Shāh, Fakhr al-Dīn, possibly a Bahmanid
⊘ c. 774–9/c. 1372–7	Sikandar Shāh, ʿAlāʾ al-Dīn
c. 779/c. 1377	*Conquest by Vijayanagara*

The region known to the mediaeval Islamic geographers as Maʿbar covered the lower south-eastern coastland of the Deccan, roughly corresponding to the later Coromandel. Madura, which became its capital, was conquered by an army sent by the Delhi Sultan Muḥammad b. Tughluq in 723/1323, and the governor installed there began some years later an independent line of Sultans of Maʿbar. The Moroccan traveller Ibn Baṭṭūṭa stayed there in 743/1342 after being at the Tughluqid court in Delhi, en route for China, and married a princess of the Maʿbar ruling family. By the mid-fourteenth century, the Sultans seem also to have controlled the southern tip of the Deccan round westwards as far as Cochin. The Sultanate was always under threat from powerful Hindu neighbours, in particular, from the early 1350s onwards, from the kingdom of Vijayanagara situated to its north, and this last seems to have overwhelmed the Sultanate by 779/1377 or shortly afterwards.

EI^2 'Hind. IV. History' (J. Burton-Page), 'Maʿbar' (A. D. W. Forbes).

R. C. Majumdar et al. (eds), *The History and Culture of the Indian People. VI. The Delhi Sultanate*, ch. 10 H.II.

M. Habib and K. A. Nizami (eds), *A Comprehensive History of India. V. The Delhi Sultanat (A.D. 1206–1526)*, ch. 15.

Haroon Khan Sherwani and P. M. Joshi (eds), *History of Medieval Deccan (1295–1724)*, Hyderabad 1973, I, 57–75.

167

THE BAHMANIDS
748–934/1347–1528
The northern Deccan

1. The rulers at Aḥsanābād-Gulbargā

(746/1346	Ismāʿīl Mukh, elected king as Abu 'l-Fatḥ Ismāʿīl Shāh Nāṣir al-Dīn)
⊘ 748/1347	Ẓafar Khān, elected king as Abu 'l-Muẓaffar Ḥasan Gangu ʿAlāʾ al-Dīn Bahman Shāh
⊘ 759/1358	Muḥammad I Shāh b. Ḥasan Gangu Bahman Shāh, Abu 'l-Muẓaffar Ẓafar Khān
⊘ 776/1375	Mujāhid b. Muḥammad I, Abu 'l-Maghāzī ʿAlāʾ al-Dīn Mujāhid Shāh
780/1378	Dāwūd I Shāh, cousin of Mujāhid
⊘ 780/1378	Muḥammad II Shāh, grandson of Ḥasan Gangu Bahman Shāh
⊘ 799/1397	Ghiyāth al-Dīn Tahamtan b. Muḥammad II, Abu 'l-Muẓaffar
⊘ 799/1397	Dāwūd II Shāh, step-brother of Tahamtan Ghiyāth al-Dīn, Shams al-Dīn
⊘ 800/1397	Fīrūz Shāh, son-in-law of Muḥammad II, Tāj al-Dīn

2. The rulers in Muḥammadābād-Bīdar

⊘ 825/1422	Aḥmad I Shāh, son-in-law of Muḥammad II, Walī Shihāb al-Dīn	
⊘ 839/1436	Aḥmad II b. Aḥmad I, Abu 'l-Muẓaffar ʿAlāʾ al-Dīn Ẓafar Khān	
⊘ 862/1458	Humāyūn Shāh b. Aḥmad II, Abu 'l-Maghāzī ʿAlāʾ al-Dīn Ẓālim	
⊘ 865/1461	Aḥmad III Shāh b. Humāyūn, Abu 'l-Muẓaffar Niẓām al-Dīn	
⊘ 867/1463	Muḥammad III Shāh b. Humāyūn, Shams al-Dīn Lashkarī	
⊘ 887/1482	Maḥmūd Shāh b. Muḥammad III, Abu 'l-Maghāzī Shihāb al-Dīn	
924/1518	Aḥmad IV b. Maḥmūd	nominal sultans under the control of the chief minister, Amīr ʿAlī Barīd of Bīdar
927/1520	ʿAlāʾ al-Dīn b. Aḥmad IV	
927/1521	Walī Allāh b. Maḥmūd	
⊘ 932–4/1526–8	Kalīm Allāh b. Maḥmūd, d. 945/1538	
934/1528	*Dissolution of the Bahmanid Sultanate into five local sultanates of the Deccan*	

As the authority of Muḥammad b. Tughluq waned in the second half of his reign, the recently-conquered parts of the Deccan began to fall away from the control of Delhi. The governor of Maʿbar in the extreme south proclaimed himself independent and founded the Sultanate of Maʻbar or Madura (see above, no. 166). Much more powerful and enduring was the state founded on the table-land of the northern Deccan by the Amīr Ḥasan Gangu. Ḥasan's origins are very obscure, but they seem to have been humble ones; the claim to Persian descent, seen in his assumption of the old Iranian name of Bahman (in the Iranian national epic, son of Isfandiyār), should not be taken seriously. After his successful rebellion in Dawlatābād, Ḥasan transferred his capital southwards to Gulbargā, and for over eighty years this remained the Bahmanid capital.

The rise of the Bahmanids meant that a strong and aggressive Muslim power now confronted the two chief Hindu kingdoms of the southern Decca, Warangal and Vijayanagar. For the next century or so, warfare was frequent, ending in the case of Warangal by its overthrow in 830/1425 by Aḥmad Shāh I and its incorporation into the Bahmanid Sultanate; Vijayanagar, on the other hand, which had already overwhelmed the Sultanate of Maʻbar or Madura (see above, no. 166), was never conquered at this time.

A point of note in this warfare was the use from the second half of the fourteenth century onwards of artillery and firearms, knowledge of these weapons being acquired through South India's connections with lands further west. After the conquest of Warangal, Aḥmad moved his capital to the more central Bīdar, and he also carried the war northwards against the Muslim rulers of Gujarāt and Mālwa. The Bahmanid Sultanate was until the second half of the fifteenth century essentially a land-locked kingdom of the northern Deccan, but Muḥammad Shāh III's energetic chief minister, the Khwāja-yi Jahān Maḥmūd Gāwān, who was of Persian origin, allied with Gujarāt against the Sultanate's enemies, intervened successfully in Orissa and extended the kingdom's eastern boundary to the Bay of Bengal, and extended its western one over the Western Ghats to Goa and the Arabian Sea coast.

The Bahmanids thus acquired considerable fame in the Islamic world at large, especially as they made their court a great centre of learning; it was also under them that a specific Deccani style of Indo-Muslim architecture evolved. The Bahmanids were the first power of the subcontinent to exchange ambassadors with the Ottomans (between Muḥammad Shāh III and Muḥammad II Fātiḥ). The Bahmanid state, as well as being militarily powerful, had an effective civil administrative system. There was, accordingly, a need for skilled personnel, and many Turks, Persians, Arabs, etc., entered the sultans' service. It was through this influx that there arose in the fifteenth century tensions between the native Deccani Muslims (the *Dakhnīs* or *Deshīs*) and the 'outsiders' (the *Āfāqīs* or *Gharībān* or *Pardeshīs*). Mounting internal chaos in the state and increasing ineffectiveness of the rulers are in part explicable by these rivalries. Toward the end of the fifteenth century, after the unwise execution by the sultan of Maḥmūd Gāwān, signs of disintegration began to appear. The last four sultans were *fainéants* under the tutelage of the Turkish amīr ʻAlī Barīdī; the fourth of these, Kalīm Allāh, appealed unsuccessfully to the Mughal Bābur for help in throwing off the yoke of the Barīdīs, and finally had to abandon his dominions for exile in Bījapur.

From the ruins of the Bahmanid Sultanate there emerged in the Muslim Deccan five successor states, all sprung from the commanders or officials of the Bahmanids: the ʻImād Shāhīs of Berār, the Barīd Shāhīs of Bīdar, the ʻĀdil Shāhīs of Bījapur, the Niẓām Shāhīs of Aḥmadnagar and the Quṭb Shāhīs of Golconda (Golkonḍā) (see below, nos 169–73). The ʿImād Shāhīs were absorbed by the Niẓām Shāhīs in the later sixteenth century, but the other four sultanates continued into the seventeenth century, in two instances until the time of the Mughal Awrangzīb, all of them eventually forming part of that Emperor's vast but ephemeral empire.

Justi, 470; Lane-Poole, 316–21; Zambaur, 297–9.

EI[2] 'Bahmanīs' (H. K. Sherwani).

E. E. Speight, 'The coins of the Bahmani Kings of the Deccan', *IC*, 9 (1935), 268–307.

Haroon Khan Sherwani, *The Bahmanis of the Deccan: An Objective Study*, Hyderabad-Deccan 1953, with a chronology of events and the rulers at pp. 435–44 and a detailed genealogical table at the end.

R. C. Majumdar et al. (eds), *The History and Culture of the Indian People. VI. The Delhi Sultanate*, ch. 11.

M. Habib and K. A. Nizami (eds), *A Comprehensive History of India. V. The Delhi Sultanat (A.D. 1206–1526)*, ch. 14.

H. K. Sherwani and P. M. Joshi (eds), *History of Medieval Deccan (1295–1724)*, I, 141–222, with a detailed genealogical table at p. 142, II, 432–9.

168

THE FĀRŪQĪ RULERS OF KHĀNDESH
c. 784–1009/c. 1382–1601
The north-west Deccan

c. 784/c. 1382	Malik Rājā Aḥmad Fārūqī b. ? Khwāja-yi Jahān A'ẓam Humāyūn
⌀ 801/1399	Nāṣir Khān b. Rājā Aḥmad
841/1437	Mīrzā 'Ādil Khān I b. Nāṣir
844/1441	Mīrān Mubārak Khān I b. 'Ādil I
861/1457	'Ādil Khān II 'Aynā b. Mubārak
907/1501	Dāwūd Khān b. Mubārak
914/1508	Ghaznī Khān b. Dāwūd
914/1508	'Ālam Khān, of Aḥmadnagar
914/1509	'Ādil Khān III 'Ālam Khān A'ẓam Humāyūn b. Aḥsan Khān, descendant of Nāṣir Khān's brother Iftikhār Khān Ḥasan b. Rājā Aḥmad
926/1520	Mīrān Muḥammad Shāh I b. 'Ādil III
943/1537	Aḥmad Shāh b. Muḥammad I
943/1537	Mubārak Shāh II b. 'Ādil III
974/1566	Mīrān Muḥammad Shāh II b. Mubārak II
984/1576	Rājā 'Ali Khān 'Ādil Shāh IV
1005–9/1597–1601	Bahādur Shāh b. 'Ādil Shāh IV, d. 1033/1624
1009/1600–1	*Mughal conquest*

Mediaeval Islamic Khāndesh was essentially the region in the north-west of the Deccan south of the Narbadā river and straddling the middle and upper basin of the Tāptī; its neighbours on the north were Gujarāt and Mālwa, and on the south the Bahmanids and their successors. It owed its name 'Land of the Khāns' to its Fārūqī rulers, who were not admitted to the rank of Sultan by their more powerful neighbours but were known by the lesser title of Khān and often referred to by the other powers as *ḥākim* or *wālī*. Before the first Muslim conquest, the region had been held by the Yādavas or the Chawhāns.

The founder of the Muslim line, Malik Rājā Aḥmad, had a background of service with the Bahmanids, but then transferred to the court of the Delhi Sultan Fīrūz Shāh III and was appointed by the latter governor over certain districts in the northern Deccan. In the confusion of the declining years of the Tughluqids, Malik Rājā followed the example of his neighbour in Mālwa, Dilāwar Khān (see above, no. 165), and asserted his independence. Since he claimed descent from the second caliph 'Umar b. al-Khaṭṭāb, who had the by-name *al-Fārūq* 'the Just' (see above, no. 1), his successors called themselves the Fārūqīs. His son Nāṣir Khān captured the fortress of Asīrgaṙh from its Hindu chief, and built close by it the town of Burhānpur, henceforth the capital of the rulers of Khāndesh. Under 'Ādil Khān II, Khāndesh flourished exceedingly; he failed to throw off the suzerainty of the Sultans of Gujarāt, but he did extend his power eastwards against the Hindu Rājās of Gondwāna and Jhārkand, and his exploits earned him the title *Shāh-i Jhārkand* 'King of the Forest'.

In the early years of the sixteenth century, Khāndesh was racked by succession disputes, which conduced to the intervention of outside powers, especially of the Gujarāt Sultans and the successors of the Bahmanids in Aḥmadnagar, the Niẓām Shāhis of Berār (see below, no. 171). With limited manpower and economic resources available to them, the Fārūqīs only survived while they could pursue an adroit diplomatic policy between their mightier neighbours. This often involved conciliating the Sultans of Gujarāt, and at one point Mīrān Muḥammad I was designated heir-presumptive to the throne in Gujarāt; he died, however, before this claim could be consolidated. The first clash of the Fārūqīs with the Mughals came in 962/1555, and ten years later the Fārūqīs became vassals of Akbar. After c. 993/c. 1585, direct Mughal pressure grew. Bahādur Shāh offended the Mughals, and his fortress of Asīrgaṛh was in 1009/1600 captured by Akbar and the surviving Fārūqīs carried off into exile. Khāndesh now became a province of the Mughal empire, for a time renamed Dāndesh after Akbar's son Dāniyāl.

Justi, 477; Lane-Poole, 315; Zambaur, 295.

EI[2] 'Fārūḳids' (P. Hardy), 'Hind. IV. History' (J. Burton-Page), 'Khāndēsh' (idem).

T. W. Haig, 'The Faruqi dynasty of Khandesh', *The Indian Antiquary*, 47 (1918), 113–24, 141–9, 178–86.

R. C. Majumdar et al. (eds), *The History and Culture of the Indian People. VI. The Delhi Sultanate*, ch. 10 B.

M. Habib and K. A. Nizami (eds), *A Comprehensive History of India. V. The Delhi Sultanat (A.D. 1206–1526)*, ch. 11.

H. K. Sherwani and P. M. Joshi (eds), *History of Medieval Deccan*, I, 491–516, with a genealogical table at p. 493.

169

THE BARĪD SHĀHĪS
c. 892–1028/c. 1487–1619
Bīdar

(892/1487	Qāsim I Barīd, chief minister of the Bahmanid Sultan)
910/1504	Amīr Barīd I b. Qāsim, nominal vassal of the last Bahmanids
950/1543	ʿAlī b. Amīr Barīd, proclaimed his independence as Malik al-Mulūk
⊘ 987/1579	Ibrāhīm b. ʿAlī
⊘ ?997/1589	Qāsim II
?1000/1592	Mīrzā ʿAlī b. Qāsim II
⊘ ?1018/1609	Amīr Barīd II
?1018–28/1609–19	Mīrzā Walī Amīr Barīd III
1028/1619	*Annexation by the ʿĀdil Shāhīs*

Bīdar lay in the central Deccan, to the north-west of Hyderabad City, and is now just within the north-eastern tip of Karnataka State. Qāsim Barīd was originally a Turkish slave in the service of the Bahmanids, but towards the end of the fifteenth century rose to become one of the dominating influences in the decaying Sultanate. His family continued to recognise the last titular rulers of the Bahmanids, until ʿAlī Barīd finally proclaimed himself an independent prince. Bīdar had a strategically important situation, and the Bahmanids had adorned it with fine buildings, a process continued by the Barīd Shāhīs. The fortunes of these last – who remained, unlike some others of their fellow-princes of the Deccan, resolutely Sunnī in faith – declined after ʿAlī's death, and the ʿĀdil Shāhīs of Bījapur (see below, no. 170) seized Bīdar in 1028/1619 and ended the Barīd Shāhīs; thirty-seven years later, Bīdar fell to the Mughal Awrangzīb.

Lane-Poole, 318, 321; Zambaur, 298.

*EI*² 'Barīd Shāhīs' (H. K. Sherwani), 'Bīdar' (H. K. Sherwani and J. Burton-Page); 'Hind. IV. History' (Burton-Page).

Gulam Yazdani, *Bidar: Its History and Monuments*, Oxford 1947, ch. 1.

H. K. Sherwani and P. M. Joshi (eds), *History of Medieval Deccan (1295–1724)*, I, 289–394, with a genealogical table at p. 290, II, 446–7.

R. C. Majumdar (ed.), *The History and Culture of the Indian People. VII. The Mughul Empire (1526–1707 A.D.)*, Bombay 1974, ch. 14 V.

170

THE ʿĀDIL SHĀHĪS
895–1097/1490–1686
Bījapur

895/1490	Yūsuf ʿĀdil Khān, previously governor for the Bahmanids in Dawlatābād by 874/1470
916/1510	Ismāʿīl b. Yūsuf
941/1534	Mallū b. Ismāʿīl
941/1535	Ibrāhīm I b. Ismāʿīl
⌀ 965/1558	ʿAlī I b. Ibrāhīm I
⌀ 987/1579	Ibrāhīm II b. Ṭahmāsp b. Ibrāhīm I
⌀ 1035/1626	Muḥammad b. Ibrāhīm II
1066/1656	ʿAlī II b. Muḥammad
1083–97/1672–86	Sikandar b. ʿAlī, d. 1111/1700
1097/1686	*Mughal conquest*

Bījapur was situated in the western part of the Bahmanid Sultanate, and is now near the northern boundary of Karnataka State. Like the founder of the ʿImād Shāhīs, Daryā Khān (see below, no. 172), Yūsuf Khān was a commander and provincial governor for the Bahmanids, originally a slave in the service of Muḥammad III's minister Maḥmūd Gāwān (see above, no. 167), who proclaimed his independence in 895/1489. He may well have been of Persian origin, though the story in historians partial to the ʿĀdil Shāhīs that he was of Ottoman royal blood is fanciful. He was certainly the first ruler to introduce Shīʿism into South India, and this became the faith of three out of the five successor-states to the Bahmanids there.

The history of the ʿĀdil Shāhīs is one of almost continuous warfare with their Muslim neighbours and with the Hindu kingdom of Vijayanagar. The capital Bījapur nevertheless became a splendid centre for learning and the arts, adorned with fine buildings erected by the Shāhs, while the florescence there of Persian literature accelerated the process whereby much of Muslim South India became culturally Persianised. By the mid-seventeenth century, Bījapur was under pressure from the militant Marāṭhās, and from 1046/1636 its rulers had to acknowledge Mughal suzerainty; then in 1097/1686 Awrangzīb captured Bījapur, brought the line of Shāhs to an end and incorporated their dominions into his own empire.

Justi, 470; Lane-Poole, 318, 321; Zambaur, 298–9.

EI[2] 'ʿĀdil-Shāhīs' (P. Hardy), 'Bīdjāpūr' (A. S. Bazmee Ansari), 'Hind. IV. History' (J. Burton-Page).

H. K. Sherwani and P. M. Joshi (eds), *History of Medieval Deccan (1295–1724)*, I, 289–394, with a genealogical table at p. 290, II, 441–3.

R. C. Majumdar (ed.), *The History and Culture of the Indian People. VII. The Mughul Empire*, ch. 14 III.

171

THE NIẒĀM SHĀHĪS
895–1046/1490–1636
Aḥmadnagar

895/1490	Aḥmad Niẓām Shāh Baḥrī b. Timma Bhaṭṭ Niẓām al-Mulk Ḥasan, minister of the Bahmanids, proclaimed his independence
915/1509	Burhān I b. Aḥmad
961/1554	Ḥusayn I b. Burhān
972/1565	Murtaḍā I b. Ḥusayn I
997/1589	Ḥusayn II b. Murtaḍā I
998/1590	Ismāʿīl b. Burhān II, cousin of Ḥusayn II
999/1591	Burhān II b. Ḥusayn b. Burhān I
1003/1595	Ibrāhīm b. Burhān II
1004–9/1595–1600	Bahādur b. Ibrāhīm
1009/1600	*Mughal capture of Aḥmadnagar*
1009/1600	Murtaḍā II b. ʿAlī b. Burhān I
1019/1610	Burhān III
1041–3/1632–3	Ḥusayn III b. Murtaḍā II
1046/1636	*Division of the Niẓām Shāhī territories between the Mughals and the ʿĀdil Shāhīs*

Aḥmadnagar is on the Deccan plateau to the east of Bombay in what is now Maharashtra State. It was founded as the capital of the Bahmanid successor state by Aḥmad Niẓām, son of the vizier to Maḥmūd Bahman Shāh, and named after himself. Aḥmad asserted his independence at Aḥmadnagar during the years of the dynasty's decline. His son Burhān adopted Shīʿism, thus aligning his principality with those of the ʿĀdil Shāhīs and Quṭb Shāhīs, and the ruling family was henceforth intermittently Shīʿī. During the sixteenth century, the Niẓām Shāhīs were involved in fighting with their Muslim rivals and with Vijayanagar, but from the end of that century decline set in, there was a rapid turnover of rulers, and the Mughals captured Aḥmadnagar in 1009/1600. The last Niẓām Shāhīs ruled under the ascendancy of the Ḥabashī or black African slave commander Malik ʿAmbar, under whose able direction the Niẓām Shāhī fortunes revived. But after his death in 1035/1626, Mughal pressure became intense, and in 1046/1636 the Emperor Shāh Jahān and Muḥammad ʿĀdil Shāhī, alarmed at the Marāṭhā threat, divided the Niẓām Shāhī territories between themselves.

Justi, 471; Lane-Poole, 318, 329; Zambaur, 298–9.
EI[2] 'Hind. IV. History' (J. Burton-Page), 'Niẓām Shāhīs' (Marie H. Martin).
Radhey Shyam, *The Kingdom of Ahmadnagar*, Varanasi 1966.
H. K. Sherwani and P. M. Joshi (eds), *History of Medieval Deccan (1295–1724)*, I, 223–77, with a genealogical table at p. 225, II, 439–41.
R. C. Majumdar (ed.), *The History and Culture of the Indian People. VII. The Mughul Empire*, ch. 14 II.

172

THE ʿIMĀD SHĀHĪS
896–982/1491–1574
Berār

890/1485	Fatḥ Allāh Daryā Khān, ʿImād al-Mulk, governor for the Bahmanīs in Berār since 876/1471
890/1485	ʿAlāʾ al-Dīn b. Fatḥ Allāh, assumed the title of Shāh in 896/1491
939/1533	Daryā b. ʿAlāʾ al-Dīn
969–82/1562–74	Burhān b. Daryā, under the regency of Tufāl Khān Dakhnī
982/1574	*Conquest by the Niẓām Shāhīs*

The extensive district of Berār comprised the northern region of the Bahmanid Sultanate, now the easternmost part of Maharashtra State. The founder of the ʿImād Shāhī principality there, Daryā Khān, was a Hindu convert in the service of the Bahmanids, who was made governor of Berār and who became latterly one of the powers behind the throne as the Sultanate became increasingly enfeebled. He eventually asserted his independence as ruler of Berār, with his capital at Elichpur. Together with that of the Barīd Shāhīs (see above, no. 169), Daryā Khān's was the only Sunnī principality among the Deccani successor-states to the Bahmanids. The history of the ʿImād Shāhīs during the eighty years or so of their independence was filled with warfare with their neighbours, such as the ʿĀdil Shāhīs and Niẓām Shāhīs. Eventually, the Niẓām Shāhīs absorbed the ʿImād Shāhīs, but in the early seventeenth century Berār was conquered by Akbar and passed into Mughal hands.

Lane-Poole, 318, 320; Zambaur, 298.

EI² 'Berār' (C. Collin Davies), 'Hind. IV. History' (J. Burton-Page), ''Imād Shāhīs' (A. S. Bazmee Ansari), Suppl. 'Eličpur' (C. E. Bosworth).

H. K. Sherwani and P. M. Joshi (eds), *History of Medieval Deccan (1295–1724)*, I, 278–87, with a genealogical table at p. 278.

R. C. Majumdar (ed.), *The History and Culture of the Indian People. VII. The Mughul Empire*, ch. 14 IV.

173

THE QUṬB SHĀHĪS
901–1098/1496–1687
Golconda-Muḥammadnagar

901/1496	Sulṭān Qulī Khawāṣṣ Khān Bahārlu, Quṭb al-Mulk
⊘ 950/1543	Yār Qulī Jamshīd b. Sulṭān Qulī
⊘ 957/1550	Ṣubḥān b. Jamshīd
⊘ 957/1550	Ibrāhīm b. Sulṭān Qulī
⊘ 988/1580	Muḥammad Qulī b. Ibrāhīm
⊘ 1020/1612	Muḥammad b. Muḥammad Amīn b. Ibrāhīm
⊘ 1035/1626	ʿAbdallāh b. Muḥammad
⊘ 1083–98/1672–87	Abu ʾl-Ḥasan, son-in-law of ʿAbdallāh
1098/1687	*Mughal conquest*

The Quṭb Shāhīs ruled over the east-central, largely Telugu-speaking part of the Deccan (now Andhra Pradesh State) from the ancient hill-fort of Golconda and then from their new city of Hyderabad (Ḥaydarābād), which was adjacent to the fortress and planned by Muḥammad Qulī in 997/1589, and to which the state capital was moved some time afterwards.

The founder of the line, Sulṭān Qulī, was a Türkmen from western Persia who was descended from the Qara Qoyunlu (see above, no. 145) and who migrated to seek his fortune in South India soon after the fall of the Türkmen dynasty. He became one of Maḥmūd Shāh Bahmanī's chief ministers and governor of Tilang Andhra or Telingana, the eastern part of the Bahmanid Sultanate and nucleus of the future Quṭb Shāhī principality. His successors turned what had been *de facto* independence into the reality of sovereign power. Sulṭān Qulī Quṭb Shāh had vigorously proclaimed his Twelver Shīʿism, eventually recognising the Ṣafawid Shāh Ismāʿīl I (see above, no. 148) as his spiritual suzerain, and the Quṭb Shāhī court became a vigorous centre for Persian literature and culture in general. The Quṭb Shāhīs were almost continuously involved in warfare with the other successor-states to the Bahmanids, the ʿĀdil Shāhīs and the Niẓām Shāhīs (see above, nos 170, 171), and with Vijayanagar, until Shāh Jahān intervened in 1045/1636 and forced on the Quṭb Shāhīs their recognition of Mughal suzerainty, in the shape of tribute and a treaty of submission (*inqiyād-nāma*) which, *inter alia*, banned the public celebration of Shīʿī practices and festivals. Some fifty years later, Awrangzīb ended the Shāhs' semi-independent status completely and incorporated their lands into his empire.

Justi, 471; Lane-Poole, 318, 321; Zambaur, 298–9.
EI[2] 'Golkonḍa' (H. K. Sherwani), 'Ḥaydarābād. a. City' (J. Burton-Page), 'Hind. IV. History' (idem), 'Ḳuṭb Shāhī' (R. M. Eaton).
H. K. Sherwani and P. M. Joshi (eds), *History of Medieval Deccan (1295–1724)*, I, 411–90, with a genealogical table at p. 413, II, 446–7.
Haroon Khan Sherwani, *History of the Qutb Shāhī Dynasty*, New Delhi 1974, with a genealogical table at the end.
R. C. Majumdar (ed.), *The History and Culture of the Indian People. VII. The Mughul Empire*, ch. 14 IV.

174

THE ARGHŪNS
926–99/1520–91
Multan and Sind

1. The line of Dhu 'l-Nūn Beg

c. 880/c. 1475	Dhu 'l-Nūn Beg Arghūn, governor of Kandahar and north-eastern Baluchistan for the Tīmūrids
⊘ (913/1507	Shāh Beg b. Dhi 'l-Nūn, governor in Kandahar for the Shībānids)
926/1520	Shāh Beg, now as ruler in Upper Sind and then the whole province
930–61/1524–54	Shāh Ḥusayn b. Shāh Beg, d. 963/1556

2. The line of Muḥammad 'Īsā Tarkhān

961/1554	Muḥammad 'Īsā Tarkhān b. 'Abd al-'Alī, in Lower Sind (Maḥmūd Gokaltāsh, in Upper Sind until 982/1574)
975/1567	Muḥammad Bāqī b. Muḥammad 'Īsā
993–9/1585–91	Jānī Beg b. Muḥammad Bāqī, d. 1008/1599
999/1591	*Mughal conquest of Lower Sind*

Sind and the Indus valley as far up as Multan had been invaded and settled by the Arabs at the beginning of the eighth century (see above, no. 160). But even after the Ghaznawids and Ghūrids had extended over much of north-western India, Sind remained a comparatively isolated region, cut off from the major trends and events affecting Muslim India. In the eleventh century, Sind fell under the control of the Rājput tribe of the Sumerās. Their power was challenged in the early fourteenth century by the rival tribe of Sammās who, unlike the Sumerās, became firm Muslims and who emerged triumphant in the later part of the century. With the collapse of the Tughluqids (see above, no. 160, 3) and the shrinkage of the Delhi Sultans' authority, the ruling Jāms of the Sammās were able to dominate Sind from their capital Ṫhaṫṫā in Lower Sind until the early sixteenth century.

The Arghūns were a Turkish or Turco-Mongol tribe prominent under the Il Khānids and then the Tīmūrids. Dhu 'l-Nūn Beg Arghūn was appointed governor over what were later the eastern and southern parts of Afghanistan by the sultan in Herat, Ḥusayn b. Manṣūr b. Bayqara (see above, no. 144, 2), and speedily became in effect independent there. The rise in the eastern Iranian world of powerful states like those of the Shībānids and the Ṣafawids made the Arghūns' base of Kandahar increasingly untenable, so Shāh Beg and his son continued Dhu 'l-Nūn Beg's process of expansion southwards, conquering Multan and eventually defeating the last Sammā Jām and taking over the whole of Sind. After 961/1554, the Tarkhāns, a senior branch of the Arghūns, took over, but Akbar first annexed Upper Sind and then, finally, Lower Sind, so that Sind became incorporated into the province of Multan in the Mughal empire.

EI² 'Arghūn' (C. Collin Davies), 'Hind. IV. History' (J. Burton-Page), 'Sind. 1. History' (T. W. Haig and C. E. Bosworth).

R. C. Majumdar et al. (eds), *The History and Culture of the Indian People. VI. The Delhi Sultanat*, ch. 10 F, G.

M. Habib and K. A. Nizami (eds), *A Comprehensive History of India. V. The Delhi Sultanat (A.D. 1206–1526)*, ch. 18.

175

THE MUGHAL EMPERORS
932–1274/1526–1858
India

⊘ 932/1526	Bābur b. ʿUmar Shaykh, Muḥammad Ẓahīr al-Dīn, ruler in Farghāna 899/1494
(936–60/1530–53	Kāmrān b. Bābur, in Kandahar, d. 964/1557)
⊘ 937/1530	Humāyūn b. Bābur, Nāṣir al-Dīn, first reign
947–62/1540–55	*Sūrī Sultans of Delhi*
⊘ 962/1555	Humāyūn, second reign
⊘ 963/1556	Akbar I b. Humāyūn, Abu ʾl-Fatḥ Muḥammad Jalāl al-Dīn
⊘ 1014/1605	Jahāngīr b. Akbar, Abu ʾl-Muẓaffar Muḥammad Sālim Nūr al-Dīn
⊘ 1037/1627	Dāwar Bakhsh b. Khusraw b. Jahāngīr
⊘ 1037/1628	Shāh Jahān I Khusraw b. Jahāngīr, Shihāb al-Dīn, d. 1076/1666
⊘ (1068/1657	Murād Bakhsh b. Shāh Jahān, in Gujarāt, k. 1072/1661)
⊘ (1068–9/1657–9	Sulṭān or Shāh Shujāʿ b. Shāh Jahān I, in Bengal, k. 1071/1660)
(1068–9/1657–9	Dārā Shikūh b. Shāh Jahān I, in Agra, k. 1069/1659)
⊘ 1068/1658	Awrangzīb b. Shāh Jahān I, Abu ʾl-Muẓaffar Muḥammad ʿĀlamgīr I Muḥyī ʾl-Dīn
⊘ (1118/1707	Aʿẓam Shāh b. Awrangzīb, in northern India)
⊘ (1118–20/1707–9	Kām Bakhsh b. Awrangzīb, in the Deccan)
⊘ 1118/1707	Shāh ʿĀlam I Bahādur b. Awrangzīb, Muḥammad Muʿaẓẓam Quṭb al-Dīn
⊘ (1124/1712	ʿAẓīm al-Shaʾn Muḥammad ʿAẓīm b. Shāh ʿĀlam I, claimant)
⊘ 1124/1712	Jahāndār b. Shāh ʿĀlam I, Abu ʾl-Fatḥ Muʿizz al-Dīn, k. 1125/1713
⊘ 1124/1713	Farrukh-siyar b. Muḥammad ʿAẓīm
⊘ 1131/1719	Rāfiʿ al-Darajāt b. Rāfiʿ al-Shaʾn b. Shāh ʿĀlam I, Shams al-Dīn
⊘ 1131/1719	Shāh Jahān II b. Rāfiʿ al-Shaʾn, Rāfiʿ al-Dawla
⊘ 1131/1719	Nīkū-siyar Muḥammad b. Muḥammad Akbar b. Awrangzīb
⊘ (1132–3/1720	Ibrāhīm b. Rāfiʿ al-Shaʾn)
⊘ 1131/1719	Muḥammad Shāh b. Jahān Shāh b. Shāh ʿĀlam I, Rawshan Akhtar Nāṣir al-Dīn
⊘ 1161/1748	Aḥmad Shāh Bahādur b. Muḥammad Shāh
⊘ 1167/1754	ʿĀlamgīr II b. Jahāndār, ʿAzīz al-Dīn
⊘ (1173/1759	Shāh Jahān III b. Muḥammad b. Kām Bakhsh)
⊘ 1173/1759	Shāh ʿĀlam II b. ʿĀlamgīr II, ʿAlī Jawhar Jalāl al-Dīn, first reign

⊘ 1202/1788 Bīdār Bakht b. Aḥmad Shāh
⊘ 1203/1788 Shāh ʿĀlam II, second reign
⊘ 1221/1806 Akbar II b. Shāh ʿĀlam II, Abū Naṣr Muḥammad Muʿīn al-Dīn
⊘ 1253–74/1837–58 Bahādur Shāh II b. Akbar II, Abu 'l-Muẓaffar Muḥammad Sirāj al-Dīn, d. 1279/1862
1274/1858 Mughal rule ended by the British

Bābur, the founder of the Mughal dynasty, was a Chaghatay Turk of Central Asia, separated from Tīmūr by five generations on his father's side and from Chingiz Khān on his mother's. His father ʿUmar Shaykh b. Abī Saʿīd ruled a small Tīmūrid principality in the Central Asian region of Farghāna, but Bābur found that the rising power of the Shībānid Özbegs (see above, no. 151) made it difficult for him to retain a foothold there after his father's death. Accordingly, in 910/1514 he moved southwards and occupied Kabul, and very soon afterwards made his first raid into India as far as the Indus. It seems that Bābur only turned to India when his repeated attempts to regain power in his Central Asian homeland had failed, but eventually a discontented faction at the court of the Lōdī Sultans of Delhi (see above, no. 160, 5) invited him to intervene. He defeated Ibrāhīm II Lōdī at the first battle of Pānīpat in 932/1526 and, in the next year, a coalition of Rājput chiefs at Khānwa near Agra. Yet these victories were only a beginning. There was as yet no solid structure of Mughal power, and the strong reaction of the Afghan military leaders in India, led by Shīr Shāh Sūr (see above, no. 160, 6), caused Bābur's son Humāyūn to flee from northern India to Sind, Afghanistan and Persia for fifteen years. Only the weakness of Shīr Shāh's successors allowed Humāyūn to return in 962/1555 and establish himself in Delhi and Agra.

The fifty-year reign of Akbar the Great now followed. The Mughal hold on northern and central India was made firm: Mālwa and the independent Rājput states, Gujarāt and Khāndesh, were secured, and by 984/1576 Bengal was restored once more to the control of Delhi. The north-western frontier, gateway to India for so many invaders, was secured by the acquisition of Kabul and Kandahar, although the latter town was to be a bone of contention with the rulers of Persia for a long time to come. In the Deccan, the princedoms of the northern tier of the Bahmanid successor-states were either directly annexed or made to acknowledge Akbar's supremacy, but the military and administrative structures of the Empire were not yet strong enough for full authority to be established all through the Deccan; this was to be the work of Awrangzīb, in whose reign almost all India – with the exceptions of the parts of western India controlled by the Marāṭhās and the southernmost tip of peninsular India – passed under Mughal control. On the diplomatic level, the initially friendly relations with the Ṣafawids were exchanged for an agreement with the Özbeg ʿAbdallāh Khan II (see above no. 153) over the demarcation of the respective territories of the Mughals and the Shībānids. There was also diplomatic contact with the Ottomans over the common threat to both empires from the Portuguese in the seas around Arabia and the Indian Ocean, but the distance between Delhi and Istanbul was too vast for a Sunnī Grand Alliance to emerge, and no concrete naval or military cooperation proved possible.

Akbar was thus undeniably a great general and statesman, but he is equally interesting as a wide-ranging thinker on religious questions. His syncretistic *Dīn-i Ilāhī* or Divine Faith, though it was restricted in membership to an élite court circle, shows his deep intellectual curiosity about religions in general. Hindus participated to a greater extent than usual in the administration and direction of the empire. It was under Akbar that the governmental structure of the Mughal empire took shape, and he welded together into a governing class diverse ethnic elements, comprising Turks, Afghans, Persians and Hindus. This class formed the *manṣabdār*s, holders of official appointments who were obliged to provide a certain number of troops. Official salaries were in part paid by *jāgīr*s or assignments of the revenues from estates, which were not, however, hereditary like the *iqṭā*'s and *soyurghal*s of the Islamic lands west of India. Although the ruler himself had theoretically unbridled secular authority, the early Mughals at least were benevolent rather than tyrannical despots; in any case, the very vastness of the empire made over-centralisation and the extension of the ruler's autocracy into every corner of it difficult to achieve.

Akbar's successors Jahāngīr and Shāh Jahān continued the policy of enforcing obedience over outlying parts – over the Rājput rulers of Mēwāŕ, the Shī'ī sultanates of the Deccan, the Portuguese on the coasts of Bengal – but Shāh Jahān's ambitions of uniting Central Asia and India in a grand Sunnī empire only ended in failure and loss of prestige (1057/1647). When he abdicated in 1068/1657, a savage succession struggle broke out among his four sons. In the course of this, Awrangzīb twice defeated and then executed his brother Dārā Shikūh, and began a fifty-year reign. An orthodox reaction against the liberal and eclectic attitudes of Akbar and his son, spearheaded by the increasingly influential Naqshbandī Ṣūfī order, had been gathering momentum during the preceding decades. Awrangzīb now espoused in large measure this rigorist programme, attacking lax social and religious practices which had grown up in Muslim India under the all-pervading influence of the surrounding Hindu majority society and attempting a reformation along the lines to be enunciated in the eighteenth and early nineteenth century by such figures as Shāh Walī Allāh of Delhi and Sayyid Aḥmad of Bareilly and his *mujāhidīn*. In part, Awrangzīb's policy was a reaction against the renewed vigour, intellectual and material, of Hinduism; yet he continued to let Hindus form an integral part of the Mughal military and administrative structures. His military efforts were at first directed at strengthening the north-western frontier, where fierce fighting was necessary to exert control over the Pathan tribes. Latterly, he became increasingly concerned with the Deccan; the remaining Shī'ī sultanates, those of the 'Ādil Shāhīs and the Quṭb Shāhīs, were extinguished, and the Marāṫhās curbed; yet this last check was only a temporary one, and the high point of Muslim power in the Deccan was never to be reached again.

Awrangzīb's death in 1118/1707 began the agonising decline of the Mughals. A series of ephemeral rulers followed, and the longer reign of Muḥammad Shāh did not prevent the outlying provinces of the empire from falling into the hands of such groups as the Marāṫhās, the Jāṫs, the Sikhs and the Rohilla Afghans. Nādir Shāh's invasion of India in 1151–2/1738–9 (see above, no. 149) and the sacking and occupation of Delhi, and the subsequent campaigns of Aḥmad Shāh Abdālī or Durrānī (see below, no. 180, 1), dealt the empire material and moral blows from which it never recovered. On several sides, Hindu fortunes were reviving, and the factor of the British presence was now significant in the interior as well as in the coastlands. While the British were extending their power through Bengal to Oudh (see below, nos 176, 178), Central India and Rājputānā, the Mughals, whose practical authority reached little beyond Delhi, could only look on helplessly. Shāh ʿĀlam II and his successors were British pensioners, and in 1274/1858 the last Mughal was deposed and exiled to Rangoon for complicity in the Sepoy Mutiny.

Justi, 472–5; Lane-Poole, 322–9; Zambaur, 300 and Table U.

EI[2] 'Mughals. 1. History, 11. Numismatics' (J. Burton-Page).

G. P. Taylor, 'Some dates relating to the Mughal Emperors of India', JASB, new series, 3 (1907), Numismatic Suppl., 57–64.

W. Irvine, *The Later Mughals*, I–II, Calcutta 1921–2, ed. and augmented Jadunath Sarkar, Allahabad 1974.

R. C. Majumdar (ed.), *The History and Culture of the Indian People. VII. The Mughul Empire*, chs 2–3, 5–8, 10.

idem (ed.), *VIII. The Maratha Supremacy*, Bombay 1977, ch. 5.

Ishwari Prasad, *India in the Eighteenth Century*, Allahabad 1973.

idem, *The Mughal Empire*, Allahabad 1974.

J. F. Richards, *The New Cambridge History of India, I.5, The Mughal Empire*, Cambridge 1993.

176

THE NAWWĀB-VIZIERS AND NAWWĀB-NĀẒIMS OF BENGAL
1116–1274/1704–1858
Bengal

1116/1704 Murshid Qulī Khān, Jaʿfar Khān ʿAlāʾ al-Dawla
1138/1725 Shujāʿ Khān, Shujāʿ al-Dawla, Murshid Qulī Khān's son-in-law
1151/1739 Sarfarāz Khān b. Shujāʿ al-Dawla, ʿAlāʾ al-Dawla
1153/1740 ʿAlīwirdī Khān, Mīrzā Muḥammad ʿAlī Mahābat Jang Hāshim al-Dawla
1169/1756 Mīrzā Maḥmūd b. Zayn al-Dīn Aḥmad, Sirāj al-Dawla, grandson of ʿAlīwirdī Khān
1170/1757 Mīr Jaʿfar Muhammad Khān b. Sayyid Ahmad Najafī, Hāshim al-Dawla, nephew by marriage of ʿAlīwirdī Khān, first reign
1174/1760 Mīr Qāsim ʿAlī, son-in-law of Mīr Jaʿfar, d. 1191/1777
1177–8/1763–5 Mīr Jaʿfar ʿAlī, second reign
1178/1765 Incorporation of Bengal into British India; continuation of the line of Nawwābs in Murshidābād as local figures until the present day

The Nawwāb-Nāẓims of Bengal arose, like the Niẓāms of Hyderabad (see below, no. 178) and the Nawwāb-Viziers of Oudh (see below, no. 177), out of the Mughal empire, and, until Britain formally took over Bengal (see below), ruled theoretically as governors for the Emperors in Delhi. Murshid Qulī Khān became *dīwān* or governor for Bengal under Awrangzīb, making his capital at Makhṣūṣābād in West Bengal, which was now named after him Murshidābād; and his descendants, Shīʿī like himself, held on to the governorship of Bengal with the title Nawwāb. They managed to repel several Marāṭhā raids and incursions, but lost Orissa to them.

The middle years of the eighteenth century were, however, the time of transition from the East India Company's trading posts in Bengal to the acquisition of actual territory there. At the Battle of Plassey in 1170/1757, Clive defeated Sirāj al-Dawla and placed his own candidate, Mīr Jaʿfar, on the throne of Bengal. A final attempt by Mīr Qāsim and his allies, the Mughal Emperor Shāh ʿĀlam II and the Nawwāb-Vizier of Oudh Shujāʿ al-Dawla, to overthrow British power failed at the Battle of Buxar (Baksar) in 1178/1764. After the battle, Shāh ʿĀlam was compelled to make a formal grant of the revenues of Bengal, Bihar and Orissa to the British, and there was then constituted out of them a Presidency with supreme powers of superintendence over the other two Presidencies of British India, Bombay and Madras. Mīr Jaʿfar's son Mahābat Jang Najm al-Dawla and his descendants accordingly ruled only as petty local chiefs at Murshidābād in British Bengal. They became pensioners, first of the British Government of India, and then, after Partition, of the Government of the Indian Union.

Zambaur, 301.
Purna Ch. Majumdar, *The Musnud of Murshidabad (1704–1904). A Synopsis of the History of Murshidabad for the Last Two Centuries*, Murshidabad 1905, with a genealogical table at p. 13 and a list of the rulers, including the post-1178/1765 Nawwābs, 13–20.
R. C. Majumdar (ed.), *The History and Culture of the Indian People. VIII. The Maratha Supremacy*, ch. 10.
idem (ed.), *IX. British Paramountcy and Indian Renaissance*, Part I, Bombay 1963, ch. 4 E.6.
P. J. Marshall, *The New Cambridge History of India. II.2. Bengal, the British Bridgehead. Eastern India 1740–1828*, Cambridge 1987.

177

THE NAWWĀB-VIZIERS AND KINGS OF OUDH (AWADH)
1134–1272/1722–1856
North India

1134/1722	Sayyid Muḥammad Amīn Saʿādat Khān Bahādur, Burhān al-Mulk
1152/1739	Abū Manṣūr Khān, Ṣafdār Jang
⊘ 1167/1754	Ḥaydar b. Ṣafdār Jang, Shujāʿ al-Dawla Jalāl al-Dīn
⊘ 1189/1775	Āṣaf al-Dawla b. Ḥaydar
1212/1797	Wazīr ʿAlī, adopted son of Aṣaf al-Dawla, d. 1232/1817
⊘ 1213/1798	Saʿādat ʿAlī Khān b. Āṣaf al-Dawla
⊘ 1229/1814	Ḥaydar I b. Saʿādat ʿAlī, Ghāzī ʾl-Dīn, after 1234/1819 with the title of King
⊘ 1243/1827	Ḥaydar II Sulaymān Jāh b. Ḥaydar I
⊘ 1253/1837	Muḥammad ʿAlī b. Saʿādat ʿAlī, Muʿīn al-Dīn
⊘ 1258/1842	Amjad ʿAlī Thurayyā Jāh b. Muḥammad ʿAlī b. Saʿādat ʿAlī
⊘ 1263–72/1847–56	Wājid ʿAlī b. Amjad, d. 1304/1887
1272/1856	*Annexation to British India*
⊘ (1273/1857	Barjīs Qadīr b. Wājid ʿAlī, raised to the throne during the Sepoy Mutiny)

The region of Oudh was part of the great Gangetic plain and comprised what is now the central region of Uttar Pradesh State, the Madhya Deśa or 'middle land' of Hindu epic times. In the Islamic period, its main cities were Lucknow (Lakhnaw) and Cawnpore (Kānpur).

The decline of the Mughal empire after Awrangzīb's death in 1118/1707 allowed Saʿādat Khān, whose family stemmed from Khurasan in eastern Persia, and his successors as Nawwābs or governors, to assume virtual independence, although right to the end they acknowledged the theoretical suzerainty of the Mughal emperors in Delhi. During the eighteenth century, Oudh had a strategic importance in British eyes as a bulwark against Marāṭhā encroachments from the west and south, and after 1178/1764 it was willy-nilly drawn into alliance with the East India Company in its base of Bengal. By the opening of the nineteenth century, however, Oudh was surrounded by British territory except for the frontier with Nepal on the north. The introduction of sound government was a proviso of the 1801 treaty with Oudh, and it was on grounds of misgovernment that the Governor-General Lord Dalhousie deposed Wājid ʿAlī in 1272/1856, thus putting an end to the kingdom of Oudh. Fears aroused by its annexation turned out, in fact, to be a major contributory cause of the Sepoy Mutiny of 1857–8.

Under its local rulers, Oudh, and especially the capital Lucknow, with its court circle, witnessed a burgeoning of Shīʿī religiosity, Urdu literature and Indo-Muslim architecture, and Lucknow remains today an important centre of North Indian Shīʿism.

Zambaur, 302.
EI[2] 'Awadh' (C. Collin Davies), 'Burhān al-Mulk' (A. S. Bazmee Ansari), 'Kānpur' (C. E. Bosworth), 'Lakhnaw' (Abdus Subhan).
G. P. Taylor, 'The coins of the Kings of Awadh', JASB, new series, 8 (1912), Numismatic Suppl., 249–74.
R. C. Majumdar (ed.), *The History and Culture of the Indian People. VIII. The Maratha Supremacy*, ch. 5 (b).
idem (ed.), *IX. British Paramountcy and Indian Renaissance*, Part I, ch. 4 C.
R. D. Barnett, *North India between Empires. Awadh, the Mughals and the British 1720–1801*, Berkeley CA 1980.

178

THE NIẒĀMS OF HYDERABAD (ḤAYDARĀBĀD)
1137–1367/1724–1948
South India

1132/1720 Chin Qïlïch Khān, Qamar al-Dīn Niẓām al-Mulk, Mughal governor of the Deccan, independent 1137/1724 with the title Āṣaf Jāh

1161/1748 Nāṣir Jang b. Niẓām al-Mulk

1164/1751 Muẓaffar Jang, Niẓām al-Mulk's son-in-law

1165/1752 Ṣalābat Jang b. Niẓām al-Mulk

1175/1762 Niẓām ʿAlī Khān b. Niẓām al-Mulk

⊘ 1218/1803 Sikandar Jāh b. Niẓām ʿAlī

⊘ 1244/1829 Farkhanda ʿAlī Khān b. Sikandar, Nāṣir al-Dawla

⊘ 1273/1857 Mīr Maḥbūb ʿAlī I b. Farkhanda ʿAlī, Afḍal al-Dawla

⊘ 1285/1869 Mīr Maḥbūb ʿAlī II b. Maḥbūb ʿAlī I, until 1301/1884 under the regency of (Sir) Nawwāb Sālār Jang

⊘ 1329–67/1911–48 Mīr ʿUthmān ʿAlī Khān Bahādur Fatḥ Jang b. Mīr Maḥbūb ʿAlī II

1367/1948 Annexation by India

By the end of the seventeenth century, the Mughals had absorbed all the lands of the former South Indian sultanates (see above, nos 164–8). The whole of the Muslim Deccan – excepting those parts of it conquered by the Marāṭhās – was now formed into a single vast province of the Deccan under a *ṣūbadār* or governor.

In the confusion and decay within the Mughal empire after Awrangzīb's death in 1118/1707, Chin Qïlïch Khān became governor of the Deccan in 1132/1720, and soon became independent at the former Quṭb Shāhī capital of Hyderabad. The Mughal emperor Muḥammad Shāh granted him the further title of Āṣaf Jāh, henceforth borne by all the members of Chin Qïlïch Khān's line, together with that of Niẓām, derived from his honorific of Niẓām al-Mulk. By the early nineteenth century, Hyderabad State was surrounded by British territory and had become an ally of Britain, although the Niẓāms continued to acknowledge the puppet Mughal Emperors on their coins until the final demise of the latter. The theoretical suzerainty of the Mughals was nevertheless recognised until the final demise of the latter in 1274/1858 (see above, no. 175), and British sovereignty not explicitly acknowledged until 1926. At the time of the Partition of India in 1947, the Niẓām's government opted for accession to Pakistan, but the state was forcibly integrated into the Indian Union in 1948 and the rule of the Niẓāms ended.

Zambaur, 303.
EI[2] 'Ḥaydarābād. b. Ḥaydarābād State' (J. Burton-Page).
R. C. Majumdar (ed.), *The History and Culture of the Indian People. VIII. The Maratha Supremacy*, ch. 12.

179

THE MUSLIM RULERS IN MYSORE (MAHISUR, MAYSŪR)
1173–1213/1760–99
South India

⊘ 1173/1760 Ḥaydar ʿAlī Khān Bahādur b. Fatḥ Muḥammad, effective ruler in Mysore
⊘ 1197–1213/1782–99 Tīpū Sulṭān b. Ḥaydar ʿAlī, sole ruler in Mysore after 1210/1796
1213/1799 Restoration of the line of Hindu Rājās

Mysore had been within the Hindu state of Vijayanagar, traditional foe of the Muslim sultanates of South India, in the extreme south of the Deccan, until the sultanates' victory over Vijayanagar in 972/1565 at Tālīkoṭa. Descendants of the Rājās of Vijayanagar established themselves in Mysore as the Rāma Rājā dynasty, managing to withstand the power of the ʿĀdil Shāhīs (see above, no. 170) and coming to a *modus vivendi* with the Mughal Awrangzīb. In the mid-eighteenth century, their Muslim general Ḥaydar ʿAlī, who claimed noble Arab descent, achieved fame for repelling the Marāṭhās and then seized real power in the state, retaining the Rājās only as figureheads. His hostility to the British and to the Niẓāms of Hyderabad drew him closer to the French, and this policy was continued by his son and successor Tīpū, who eventually dispensed with the Rājās, received French envoys at his capital Seringapatam and was admitted as 'Citizen Tipu' to membership of the French Republic. The forces of Britain and Hyderabad defeated Tīpū in 1213/1799, and he died in the fighting at Seringapatam. He had been a zealous enforcer of Islam on the Hindu majority of his subjects, including forcible conversions and circumcisions, and in the modern hagiography of Pakistan is revered as 'the Martyr Sultan'. On his death, the old line of Hindu Rājās was restored in Mysore under British protection.

EI[1] 'Tīpū Sulṭān' (T. W. Haig), *EI*[2] 'Ḥaydar ʿAlī Khān Bahādur' (Mohibbul Hasan), 'Mahisur, Maysūr. 1. Geography and history' (C. E. Bosworth).

R. C. Majumdar (ed.), *The History and Culture of the Indian People. VIII. The Maratha Supremacy*, chs 12–13.

180

THE ABDĀLĪ OR DURRĀNĪ RULERS AND KINGS OF AFGHANISTAN
1160–1393/1747–1973

1. The Sadōzays or Popalzays

⊘ 1160/1747	Aḥmad Khān Abdālī b. Muḥammad Zamān Khān, in Kandahar and Kabul
⊘ 1184/1773	Tīmūr Shāh b. Aḥmad, in Herat, after 1189/1775 in Kabul
⊘ 1207/1793	Zamān Shāh b. Tīmūr, in Kabul and Kandahar, after 1211/1797 in Herat
⊘ 1215/1800	Maḥmūd Shāh b. Tīmūr, in Kabul and Kandahar, first reign
⊘ (1218/1803	Qayṣar b. Zamān Shāh, in Kabul and Kandahar)
⊘ 1218/1803	Shāh Shujāʿ b. Tīmūr, Shujāʿ al-Mulk, in Kabul and Kandahar, first reign, after 1233/1818 a pensioner of Britain in India
⊘ (1222–3/1807–8	Qayṣar, in Kashmir)
⊘ 1224/1809	Maḥmūd Shāh, in Kabul and Kandahar, in Herat until 1245/1829, second reign
⊘ 1233–41/1818–26	Period of civil war, with Bārakzay *Sardār*s in control and a series of puppet rulers in Kabul: ʿAlī Shāh b. Tīmūr, ⊘ Ayyūb Shāh b. Tīmūr, Ḥabīb Allāh b. ʿAẓīm Khān
⊘ 1233–58/1818–42	Kāmrān b. Maḥmūd Shāh, in Herat
⊘ (1241/1826	Dūst Muḥammad b. Pāyinda Khān Bārakzay, in Kabul, after 1250/1834 with the title of Amīr, first reign)
⊘ 1255/1839	Shāh Shujāʿ, second reign, with British military support
⊘ 1258/1842	Fatḥ Jang b. Shāh Shujāʿ, in Kabul

2. The Bārakzays or Muḥammadzays

⊘ 1259/1843	Dūst Muḥammad, in Kabul, in Kandahar 1272/1855 and in Herat 1279/1863
⊘ 1279/1863	Shīr ʿAlī b. Dūst Muḥammad, in Kabul, first reign
⊘ 1283/1866	Muḥammad Afḍal b. Dūst Muḥammad, in Kabul
⊘ 1284/1867	Muḥammad Aʿẓam b. Dūst Muḥammad, in Kabul
⊘ 1285/1868	Shīr ʿAlī, in Kabul, second reign, d. 1296/1879
⊘ 1295–6/1878–9	Muḥammad Yaʿqūb Khān b. Shīr ʿAlī, regent for his father and then Amīr in Kabul after his death
1296–7/1879–80	*British occupation of eastern Afghanistan*
⊘ 1297/1880	ʿAbd al-Raḥmān b. Muḥammad Afḍal
⊘ 1319/1901	Ḥabīb Allāh b. ʿAbd al-Raḥmān
1337/1919	Naṣr Allāh b. ʿAbd al-Raḥmān, d. 1339/1921
⊘ 1337/1919	Amān Allāh b. Ḥabīb Allāh, d. 1379/1960
⊘ *(1347/1929*	*Bachcha-yi Saqqa(w), as Ḥabīb Allāh II, k. 1348/1929)*
⊘ 1348/1929	Muḥammad Nādir b. Muḥammad Yūsuf b. Yaḥyā
⊘ 1352–93/1933–73	Muḥammad Ẓāhir b. Nādir
1393/1973	*Republican régime established*

The Ghilzay Afghans had played a leading part in Persian affairs during the declining years of the Ṣafawids, overrunning and occupying much of Persia during the third decade of the eighteenth century (see above, no. 148). Although Nādir Shāh ended this Afghan domination, he recruited large numbers of Afghans into his forces. One of his leading commanders was Aḥmad Khān of the Sadōzay section of the Abdālī tribe of Afghans, a tribe which was originally from the Herat region but which Nādir allowed to settle around Kandahar. After Nādir's assassination in 1160/1747, the Afghan troops aclaimed Aḥmad as their leader and as Shāh, and he assumed the title *Durr-i Durrān* 'Pearl of Pearls', whence the name Durrānī which then became applied to the Abdālīs in general and to the dynasty which he now proceeded to found in particular. It is roughly from this time, also, that, under the stimulus of Aḥmad's imperial ambitions and conquests, the name and the concept of 'Afghanistan' comes into existence and, for the first time, into literary and historical usage.

Aḥmad Shāh regarded himself as heir to Nādir's eastern conquests, and invaded India several times, clashing with the Mughals, the Marāṫhās and the Sikhs, and in 1170/1757 sacking Delhi and Agra. A great empire was built up in north-western India, including Sind, Baluchistan, much of the Panjab and Kashmīr, and his victory at the third battle of Pānīpat in 1174/1761 checked the ambitions of the Marāṫhās and, among other things, indirectly enabled the British to consolidate their power in India from their Bengal base. In Khurasan, Aḥmad established a protectorate over Nādir's descendant, the blind Shāh Rukh (see above, no. 149), although in the reign of Aḥmad's grandson Zamān Shāh the Afghans were powerless to stem the Qājār annexation of Khurasan and the deposition of Shāh Rukh. The last years of the eighteenth century and the early decades of the nineteenth were, indeed, disastrous for the Durrānī empire. The family was rent by internal feuds, with members of it at odds with each other from bases in the three key cities of the land, Kabul, Kandahar and Herat, and the Marāṫhās and Sikhs were able to eject the Afghans from most of their Indian possessions.

Meanwhile, the star of another branch of the Abdālīs, the Bārakzays or Muḥammadzays, was already rising. In 1233/1818, Dūst Muḥammad controlled Kabul, where he set up a puppet Sadōzay ruler, himself assuming the title of Amīr of Kabul some sixteen years later. With the loss of the Indian possessions, the Afghan kingdom was now a geographically compact unit, essentially one of mountains and plateaux, prolonged occupation of which by outside powers was extremely difficult to achieve, as British expeditions were to find during the course of the nineteenth century. Hence Afghanistan survived intact into the twentieth century, fighting off Persian ambitions regarding Herat, pressure from Imperial Russia in the north and two wars with Britain. Dūst Muḥammad resisted temptations to intervene in India, and remained indifferent to the rebels' cause during the Indian Sepoy Mutiny. After the Second Afghan–British War, ʿAbd al-Raḥmān Khān established careful and correct relations with the Great Powers, and this policy was only broken by the impetuousness of Amān Allāh in 1337/1919, provoking the Third Afghan–British War. His later, over-hasty attempts at the modernisation of a profoundly conservative and traditionalist Islamic society led to his abdication. The throne passed to another branch of the family, which retained power until monarchical rule was replaced in 1393/1973 by a republican régime under the last king's cousin Muḥammad Dāwūd b. Muḥammad ʿAzīz b. Muḥammad Yūsuf, the prelude to a Communist takeover of the country and its being plunged into a period of bloody warfare which still continues today.

Lane-Poole, 330–5; Zambaur, 304–5.
EI[2] 'Afg̲h̲ānistān. V. History' (M. Longworth Dames).
M. Longworth Dames, 'The coins of the Durrānīs', NC, 3rd series, 8 (1888), 325–63.
L. White King, 'History and coinage of the Bārakzai dynasty of Afghānistān', NC, 3rd series, 16 (1896), 276–344.
W. K. Fraser-Tytler, *Afghanistan. A Study of Political Developments in Central and Southern Asia*, 3rd edn, London 1967, with a genealogical table of the Bārakzays on p. 346.
Louis Dupree, *Afghanistan*, Princeton 1973, Parts III–IV.
Vartan Gregorian, *The Emergence of Modern Afghanistan. Politics of Reform and Modernization, 1880–1946*, Stanford CA 1969.

SEVENTEEN

South-East Asia and Indonesia

181

THE RULERS OF MALACCA (MELAKA)

c. 805–1111/c. 1403–1699

The south-western coast of the Malay peninsula

by 805/1403	Parameśvara
817/1414	Megat Iskandar Shāh b. Parameśvara
827/1424	Śri Maharājā Sultan Muḥammad Shāh, son of Megat Iskandar Shāh
? 849/1445	Rājā Ibrāhīm, Śri Parameśvara Deva Shāh, son of Muḥammad Shāh
⊘ 850/1446	Rājā Qāsim, Sultan Muẓaffar Shāh, son of Muḥammad Shāh
863/1459	Rājā ʿAbdallāh, Sultan Manṣūr Shāh, son of Muẓaffar Shāh
882/1477	Sultan ʿAlāʾ al-Dīn Riʿāyat, Manṣūr Shāh
⊘ 893–934/1488–1528	Sultan Maḥmūd Shāh b. Riʿāyat Shāh, first reign
⊘ 916/1510	Sultan Aḥmad Shāh b. Maḥmūd Shāh
916–34/1510–28	Sultan Maḥmūd Shāh, second reign
(917/1511	*Portuguese conquest of Malacca)*
	Continuance of members of the Malaccan dynasty in the Riau-Lingga archipelago and in peninsular Malaysia, for example
934/1528	Sultan ʿAlāʾ al-Dīn b. Maḥmūd Shah, in Johor
934/1528	Sultan Muẓaffar Shāh b. Maḥmūd Shāh, in Perak

The origins of the kingdom of Malacca are obscure; it has been suggested that it was in existence well before the fifteenth century, but the majority view is that it was founded by Parameśvara (literally, 'prince-consort', i.e. he was the husband of a princess of the Hindu kingdom of Majapahit in Java) at the opening of the fifteenth century. It grew rapidly in importance as a trading centre and as a nest of corsairs, and from the ability of its rulers to levy transit dues on shipping through the Straits of Malacca. Parameśvara seems to have become a Muslim through a further marriage to a daughter of the Sultan of Pasè or Pasai in the northern tip of Sumatra, Muslim since the fourteenth century. The names of the subsequent rulers of Parameśvara's line and their regnal dates are known partly from written sources and partly from their gravestones, but the dates in several cases must be regarded as only approximate. In the mid-fifteenth century, the rulers followed a lively expansionist policy, warding off Siamese attacks, extending their power within peninsular Malaya and across the Straits to Sumatra, and entertaining diplomatic relations with the Ming Emperors of China. At this time,

Malacca became not only the chief trading-centre for South-East Asia but also the main diffusion-centre there for the Islamic faith. Thus local rulers within the Malay peninsula became vassals of Malacca and Muslims at the same time, while Brunei, in northern Borneo (see below, no. 186), came to accept the faith through its trading connections with Malacca, as did various ports along the north coast of Java.

The end of the line of Parameśvara came from the attacks of the Portuguese under Afonso de Albuquerque, so that Malacca passed into Portuguese hands in 917/1511 and became a centre for Portuguese trade in East Asia. But scions of the native Malayan dynasty continued in the islands to the south of Malaya, the kingdom of Riau-Lingga (whose last sultan reigned until as recently as 1911; now within Indonesia), and still survive on the Malayan mainland in the present-day sultanates of Johor, Pahang and Trengganu.

EI² 'Malacca' (Barbara Watson Andaya).

D. G. E. Hall, *A History of South-East Asia*, 4th edn, London 1981, 221ff., 366ff., with a genealogical table at p. 973.

Saran Singh, *The Encyclopaedia of the Coins of Malaysia, Singapore and Brunei 1400–1986*, Kuala Lumpur 1986.

182

THE SULTANS OF ACHEH (ATJÈH, ACEH)

c. 901–1321/c. 1496–1903

The northern tip of Sumatra

c. 854/c. 1450	ʿInāyat Shāh
?	Muẓaffar Shāh, d. 902/1497
?	Shams al-Dīn Shāh
c. 901/c. 1496	ʿAlī Mughāyat Shāh
⊘ c. 936/c. 1530	Ṣalāḥ al-Dīn b. ʿAlī
⊘ c. 944/c. 1537	Riʿāyat Shāh b. ʿAlī, ʿAlāʾ al-Dīn al-Qahhār
⊘ 979/1571	ʿAlī or Ḥusayn Riʿāyat Shāh
987/1579	Sultan Muda
987/1579	Sultan Śri ʿĀlam
987/1579	Zayn al-ʿĀbidīn
⊘ 987/1579	Manṣūr Shāh, ʿAlāʾ al-Dīn, originally of Perak, son-in-law of ʿAlāʾ al-Dīn Riʿāyat Shāh
⊘ c. 994/c. 1586	ʿAlī Riʿāyat Shāh or Rājā Buyung
⊘ c. 996/c. 1588	Riʿāyat Shāh, ʿAlāʾ al-Dīn
1013/1604	ʿAlī Riʿāyat Shāh or Sultan Muda
⊘ 1016/1607	Iskandar Muda, posthumously called Makota ʿĀlam 'Crown of the World'
⊘ 1046/1636	Mughāyat Shāh, Iskandar Thānī ʿAlāʾ al-Dīn
⊘ 1051/1641	Ṣafiyyat al-Dīn Shāh bt. Iskandar Muda, Tāj al-ʿĀlam, queen, widow of Iskandar Thānī
1086/1675	Naqiyyat al-Dīn Shāh, Nūr al-ʿĀlam, queen
⊘ 1089/1678	Zakiyyat al-Dīn Shāh, ʿInāyat, queen
⊘ 1099/1688	Zīnat al-Dīn Kamālat Shāh, queen
1111/1699	Sharīf Hāshim Jamāl al-Dīn Badr al-ʿĀlam
⊘ 1114/1702	Perkasa ʿĀlam Sharīf Lamtuy b. Sharīf Ibrāhīm
1115/1703	Badr al-Munīr, Jamāl al-ʿĀlam
1138/1726	Amīn al-Dīn Shāh, Jawhar al-ʿĀlam
1138/1726	Shams al-ʿĀlam or Wandi Tĕbing
1139/1727	Aḥmad Shāh or Maharājā Lela Mĕlayu, ʿAlāʾ al-Dīn
⊘ 1148/1735	Jahān Shāh or Pòtjut Auk, ʿAlāʾ al-Dīn
1173–95/1760–81	Maḥmūd Shāh or Tuanku Raja
(1177–8/1764–5	Badr al-Dīn
1187/1773	Sulaymān Shāh or Raja Udahna Lela)
1195/1781	Muḥammad Shāh or Tuanku Muḥammad, ʿAlāʾ al-Dīn
1209–39/1795–1824	Jawhar al-ʿĀlam Shāh, ʿAlāʾ al-Dīn
(1230–5/1815–20	Sharīf Sayf al-ʿĀlam)
1239/1824	Muḥammad Shāh b. Jawhar al-ʿĀlam Shāh
⊘ 1252/1836	Manṣūr Shāh
1287/1870	Maḥmūd Shāh
1291/1874	*Capture of the capital Kutaraja by the Dutch*
1291–1321/1874–1903	Muḥammad Dāwūd Shāh, ʿAlāʾ al-Dīn
1321/1903	*Definitive Dutch conquest of Acheh*

Acheh is the most northerly part of Sumatra, and it became the centre of a powerful Muslim sultanate which at times controlled much also of the coastlands of Sumatra to the south. Sustained Islamic activity in the region, brought from western India, certainly dates from the thirteenth century. Marco Polo found a Muslim town Ferlec (Pĕrlak) on the north-eastern coast of Sumatra and along the Malaccan Straits; Ibn Baṭṭūṭa landed at Muslim ports there some forty years later; and the names of various Muslim rulers, for some of whom there are coins extant, are known from c. 1300.

When the sultanate of Acheh was established in the early sixteenth century, it rapidly gained control of much trade with Gujarāt and with China, and in this expansionist phase confronted the Portuguese in Malacca and such Malayan states as Johor and Pĕrlak, with its sultans soliciting and receiving aid from the Ottoman Turks. A three-cornered struggle ensued between the Portuguese, Acheh and Johor, complicated in the seventeenth century by the appearance of the Dutch and English. By then, the sultans of Acheh were dealing substantially with the Dutch over the export trade in tin from Pĕrak, but in the later seventeenth century Acheh declined in power under the nominal rule of a series of female rulers, with the real authority exercised by the great chiefs. Acheh nevertheless remained a strong religious and cultural centre for Indonesian Islam, with such famous scholars as Ḥamza Fanṣūrī (*flor.* in the later sixteenth century) as proponents of an Indian-type Ṣūfī mysticism in Indonesia.

In the nineteenth century, tensions became acute with the Dutch government, by now controlling southern and central Sumatra, largely because of Achenese piracy and slave trading in the waters around northern Sumatra. These led to a lengthy and costly guerilla war extending from 1873 to 1903, by the end of which the Acheh sultanate was swept away and the last claimant to its throne exiled; members of the family still survive, however, in contemporary Indonesia.

Zambaur, 308.

*EI*² 'Atjèh' (Th. W. Juynboll and P. Voorhoeve).

Jan M. Pluvier, *A Handbook and Chart of South-East Asian History*, Kuala Lumpur 1967, 25–7 (recent period only).

T. Ibrahim Alfian, *Mata ugang emas kerajaan-kerajaan di Aceh*, Aceh Museum, Aceh 1977.

D. G. E. Hall, *A History of South-East Asia*, 4th edn, 367–72, 618–22, with a genealogical table at pp. 973–4.

M. C. Ricklefs, *A History of Modern Indonesia since* c. *1300*, 2nd edn, London 1993, 32–6, 133–8.

183

THE RULERS OF MATARAM
c. 983–1168/c. 1575–1755
Central Java

c. 983/c. 1575	Mas Ngabehi Sutavijaya Senapati, son of Kjai Gede Pamanahan
1009/1601	Panembahan Seda Krapyak, Mas Jolang
1022/1613	Tjakrakusuma Ngabdurrahman, Sultan Agung, after 1034/1625 with the title Susuhunan
1055/1645	Prabu Amangkurat I, Sunan Tegalwangi
1088/1677	Amangkurat II
1115/1703	Amangkurat III, Sunan Mas
1117/1705	Pakubuwana I, Sunan Puger
1131/1719	Amangkurat IV, Jawa
1137/1725	Pakubuwana II, Kombul
1162–8/1749–55	Pakubuwana III, Swarga
1168/1755	*Division of the kingdom into the states of Surakarta and Jogjakarta (Yogyakarta)*

Mataram was the third Muslim sultanate to arise in Java after those of Demak in north-central Java (917–57/1511–50) and Bantam at the extreme western end of the island (932–1228/1526–1813). It was centred on what is now Surakarta, and was founded by the father of Senepati (literally, 'commander', i.e. of his original overlord the Sultan of Pajang), around whose origins a cloud of legend grew up in an attempt to connect him, probably speciously, with earlier royal families such as those of Majapahit. With his grandson Sultan Agung, the dynasty produced one of Indonesia's greatest rulers, who captured the rival city of Surabaya and extended his power as far as the island of Madura and Borneo; in 1625 he assumed the title *Susuhunan* (literally, 'royal foot', i.e. placed on the head of a vassal paying homage, not very felicitously rendered by the Dutch as 'emperor', since the term has more a religious connotation, being associated with the legendary *walī*s or saints who are said first to have brought Islam to Java).

The Dutch in Batavia were in fact becoming a power in Java, and were opposed to Agung's strongly Islamic policies of forging closer links with Arabia and of reviving the former Javanese empire of Majapahit. Agung's weaker successors eventually came to terms with the Dutch, and a treaty of 1684 made the sultanate practically a dependency of the Dutch East India Company (VOC), which now controlled a block of territory in western Java cutting the island into two parts. In the early eighteenth century, the Dutch were called into the internal quarrels of Mataram, the so-called First and Second Javanese Wars of Succession (1116–17/1704–5 and 1133–4/1721–2), and further disputes led to a partition of Mataram between rival claimants in 1168/1755, with two subsequent sultanates at Surakarta and Jogjakarta (see below, nos 184, 185).

EI[1] 'Java' (A. W. Nieuwenhuis), 'Surakarta' (C. C. Berg).

D. G. E. Hall, *A History of South-East Asia*, 4th edn, 303–8, 337–8, 341–2, 346–54, 359–60, with a genealogical table at p. 972.
M. C. Ricklefs, *A History of Modern Indonesia since* c. *1300*, 2nd edn, 39–48, 69–93.

184

THE SUSUHUNANS OF SURAKARTA
1168–1368/1755–1949
Central Java

1168/1755	Pakubuwana III, Swarga, of Mataram
1202/1788	Pakubuwana IV, Bagus
1235/1820	Pakubuwana V, Sugih
1238/1823	Pakubuwana VI, Bangun Tapa
1245/1830	Pakubuwana VII, Purbaya
1274/1858	Pakubuwana VIII, Angabehi
1277/1861	Pakubuwana IX, Bangun Kadaton
1310/1893	Pakubuwana X, Wicaksana
1358/1939	Pakubuwana XI
1363–/1944–	Pakubuwana XII
(1368/1949	*Republic of Indonesia proclaimed)*

In the course of the Third Javanese War of Succession (1162–70/1749–57), a partition of the Mataram territories was made in 1168/1755. Pakubuwana III continued as ruler of the eastern half of the kingdom, with Surakarta as his capital and with himself and his descendants bearing the title of *Susuhunan*, one higher than that of Sultan. A portion of Mataram, Mangku-Negara, went to a third claimant, Mas Said, now styled Mangkunegara, the nephew of Pakubuwana II and his brother, Mangkubumi, this last now sultan in Jogjakarta. These were in effect vassal states of the VOC and then of the Dutch government, but the two rival states of Surakarta and Jogjakarta had to work out a system of living in harmony and administering the divided lands within a Javanese political tradition which had known only a sole ruler. Once this understanding was achieved, both states survived the nineteenth century, with its bursts of violence such as the Javanese War of 1825–30, into the twentieth century, through the Japanese occupation of 1942–5 and into the constituting of the Indonesian Republic after the Second World War. The long-reigning Susuhunan Pakubuwana XII still retains his social position at Surakarta within contemporary Indonesia.

EI[2] 'Surakarta' (O. Schumann).
Jan M. Pluvier, *A Handbook and Chart of South-East Asian History*, 29, 31.
D. G. E. Hall, *A History of South-East Asia*, 4th edn, 359–60, 502ff., with a genealogical table at pp. 972–3.
M. C. Ricklefs, *A History of Modern Indonesia since* c. *1300*, 2nd edn, 94–103, 110–11.

185

THE SULTANS OF JOGJAKARTA
1168–1368/1755–1949
South-central Java

1168/1755	Abdurrahman Mangkubuwana or Hămengkubuwana I, Swarga
1206/1792	Abdurrahman Mangkubuwana or Hămengkubuwana II, Sepuh, first reign
1225/1810	Abdurrahman Mangkubuwana or Hămengkubuwana III, Rājā, first reign
1226/1811	Abdurrahman Mangkubuwana or Hămengkubuwana II, Sepuh, second reign
1227/1812	Abdurrahman Mangkubuwana or Hămengkubuwana III, Rājā, second reign
1229/1814	Abdurrahman Mangkubuwana or Hămengkubuwana IV, Seda Pesiyar
1237/1822	Abdurrahman Mangkubuwana or Hămengkubuwana V, Menol, first reign
1241/1826	Abdurrahman Mangkubuwana or Hămengkubuwana II, Sepuh, third reign
1243/1828	Abdurrahman Mangkubuwana V, Menol, second reign
1271/1855	Abdurrahman Mangkubuwana or Hămengkubuwana VI, Mangkubumi
1294/1877	Abdurrahman Mangkubuwana or Hămengkubuwana VII, Angabehi
1339/1921	Abdurrahman Mangkubuwana or Hămengkubuwana VIII
1358–1408/1939–88	Abdurrahman Mangkubuwana or Hămengkubuwana IX
1368/1949	*Republic of Indonesia proclaimed*
1408–/1988–	Abdurrahman Mangkubuwana or Hămengkubuwana X

The sultanate of Jogjakarta arose out of the partition of Mataram in 1168/1755 (see above, nos 183, 184). Relations with the sister state of Surakarta were at times strained, with the respective rulers endeavouring on occasion to use the Dutch and, in the early nineteenth century, the British, as their allies. Leadership in the Javanese War of 1825–30 came from a prince of the royal house of Jogjakarta, Dipanagara, who himself claimed the title of sultan and protector of Islam. Like its sister state, the sultanate of Jogjakarta has endured until the present day and the constituting of the Republic of Indonesia. Sultan Mangkubuwana IX played a role in resistance to the Dutch attempts at reimposing their colonial rule after the Second World War and was a member of the first Indonesian cabinet after independence; his son Mangkubuwana X has succeeded him, retaining his social position in Jogjakarta at the present time.

EI[1] 'D̲jokyakarta' (A. W. Nieuwenhuis).
Jan M. Pluvier, *A Handbook and Chart of South-East Asian History*, 29, 31.
D. G. E. Hall, *A History of South-East Asia*, 4th edn, 502ff., with a genealogical table at p. 973.
M. C. Ricklefs, *A History of Modern Indonesia since* c. *1300*, 2nd edn, 95–104, 109–18.

186

THE SULTANS OF BRUNEI
? seventh century AD onwards
Northern Borneo

early tenth century/ early sixteenth century	Muhammad, of the Bendahara family, became a Muslim in 920/1514
c. 927/c. 1521	Ahmad, brother of Muhammad
c. 932/c. 1526	Sharif Ali, Sultan Berkat, son-in-law of Ahmad
?	Sulaiman b. Sharif Ali
?	Bolkiah b. Sulaiman
?	Abdul Kahhar b. Bolkiah, d. 986/1578
ruling in 986/1578	Saiful Rijal b. Abdul Kahhar, d. c. 998/c. 1590
c. 998/c. 1590	Shah Brunei b. Saiful Rijal
c. 1008/c. 1600	Raja Ghafur b. Shah Brunei, under the regency of his uncle Muhammad Hasan
1009/1601	Muhammad Hasan b. Saiful Rijal
1026/1617	Abdul Jalilul Akbar b. Muhammad Hasan, posthumously called Marhum Tuha
c. 1047/c. 1637	Abdul Jalilul Jabbar b. Abdul Jalilul Akbar
c. 1052/c. 1642	Haji Muhammad Ali b. Muhammad Hasan
c. 1058/c. 1648	Abdul Hakk Mubin, grandson of Saiful Rijal
1065/1655	Muhyiddin, probably first acclaimed sultan in 1058/1648, d. c. 1081/c. 1670
⊘ decade 1081–91/ 1670–80	Nasruddin Husin Kamaluddin
⊘ c. 1091/c. 1680	Muhammad Aliuddin, son-in-law of Husin Kamaluddin
1101 to mid-twelfth century/ 1690-mid-eighteenth century	*Period of usurpation and civil warfare, followed by the restoration of the Bendaharas:*
c. 1163/c. 1750	Omar Ali Saifuddin I, d. 1209/1795
1194/1780	Muhammad Tajuddin b. Omar Ali Saifuddin I, first reign
1206/1792	Muhammad Jamalul Alam b. Muhammad Tajuddin
1207/1793	Muhammad Tajuddin. second reign
1221/1806	Muhammad Kanzul Alam b. Omar Ali Saifuddin I
c. 1237/c. 1822	Raja Api b. Muhammad Kanzul Alam
c. 1237/c. 1822	Omar Ali Saifuddin II, nephew of Raja Api
⊘ 1268/1852	Abdul Mumin
⊘ 1302–24/1885–1906	Hashim b. Omar Ali Saifuddin II
1324/1906	*British Residency established*
1324/1906	Muhammad Jamalul Alam b. Omar Ali Saifuddin II
1342/1924	Ahmad Tajuddin b. Muhammad Jamalul Alam
1369/1950	Daughter of Ahmad Tajuddin

⊘ 1369/1950 Sir Omar Ali Saifuddin III b. Muhammad Jamalul Alam
⊘ 1387–/1967– Sir Hassanal Bolkiah b. Omar Ali Saifuddin

Brunei, on the north coast of Borneo, is an old-established sultanate which has survived until today as the State of Brunei. It has been surmised that emigrants from the South-East Asian mainland may have founded Brunei as far back as the seventh century AD, and there are sporadic mentions of it in Chinese sources of the next few centuries, since there were clearly trade contacts with China. Official Brunei wisdom today holds that the Brunei sultanate has been perpetually Muslim, and official genealogies and lore place the first Muslim rulers in the fourteenth or early fifteenth century. In fact, while Islam was doubtless established along the north Borneo littoral from an early time as a result of commercial contacts with Malaysia, Sumatra, etc., there is evidence that the sultans may not have been converted from the indigenous paganism until the early sixteenth century. The chronology for the Muslim rulers followed in the table above is essentially that of Robert Nicholl, what might be called a 'shorter' chronology; but, as noted above, official Bruneian historiography favours a 'longer' chronology going back 100 or 150 years earlier. It is nevertheless the case that only in the eighteenth century does the chronology becomes more or less certain.

The first Muslim sultans made Brunei the centre of a considerable empire, embracing most of Borneo itself, Celebes (modern Sulawesi) and the Sulu archipelago and even the southern Philippines. It was this empire which was first encountered by Spanish and Portuguese voyagers in South-East Asian waters; their reports and narratives, from those of Magellan's expedition onwards, are a prime source for the history and chronology of the Brunei sultanate against which the indigenous tradition can be tested. The sultanate was torn by internal strife thereafter and became constricted by European pressures, with its authority confined now to northern Borneo. In 1841, much of this last had to be ceded to Sir James Brooke as Rajah of Sarawak, and in 1877 Brunei's portion of north-eastern Borneo was leased to British trading interests, eventually to the British North Borneo Company, reducing the sultanate to its present size. In 1888, Brunei became a British protectorate, and from 1906 a British Resident was installed. The exploitation of large reserves of oil and natural gas has revived the fortunes of Brunei in the twentieth century. It decided in 1973 not to join the Malaysian Federation; the sultanate became a constitutional monarchy under British protection, but since 1984 has been a fully-independent state known officially as Negara Brunei Darussalam.

The coins of the Sultans of Brunei are (like those of many other Indonesian dynasties) difficult to utilise as historical evidence, since dates are frequently not given on the coins, and titles of rulers are often recorded in an abbreviated or cursory manner, hence applicable to more than one ruler.

EI^2 Suppl. 'Brunei' (O. Schumann).
D. E. Brown, *Brunei: The Structure and History of a Bornean Malay Sultanate*, Monograph of the Brunei Museum Journal, no. II/2, Brunei 1970, 130–63.
Saran Singh, 'The coinage of the Sultanate of Brunei, 1400–1980', *Brunei Museum Journal*, 4:4 (1980), 38–103, with a genealogical table at p. 45.

idem, *The Encyclopaedia of the Coins of Malaysia, Singapore and Brunei 1400–1986.*
Sylvia C. Engelen Krausse and Gerald H. Krausse, *Brunei*, World Bibliographical Series no. 93, Oxford 1988, Introd., with a genealogical table at pp. xlii–xliii.
Robert Nicholl, 'Some problems of Brunei chronology', *Journal of Southeast Asian Studies*, 20 (Singapore 1989), 175–95.

INDEXES

(A) PERSONAL NAMES

The listing and indexing of Islamic names present difficulties because of the frequent complexity of the complete name and titles of a ruler or other leading person (see Introduction, pp. xxii–xxiii). Also, a person may be best known by one particular element of the complete name, hence al-Mutawakkil rather than Ja'far b. Abī Isḥāq al-Mu'taṣim, Sayf al-Dawla rather than 'Alī b. 'Abdallāh, and al-Malik al-Kāmil rather than Muḥammad b. Muḥammad or Aḥmad.

Faced with this problem – but on a much greater scale than in the present book – the two compilers of the standard works on Arabic biobibliography, Carl Brockelmann and Fuat Sezgin, opted in their extensive indexes to their respective *Geschichte der arabischen Litterature* and *Geschichte des arabischen Schrifttums* for listing everyone under *ism* plus further *isms* of the *nasab*, patronymics and honorifics as required for distinguishing purposes. Ordering essentially by *ism* has seemed to be the best procedure here, but an endeavour has been made to give well-known honorifics also, hence al-Rashīd as well as Hārūn b. Muḥammad al-Mahdi and al-Malik al-Kāmil as well as Muḥammad b. al-'Ādil I Muḥammad, and also to give conventional European forms like Boabdil and Saladin. Even so, as users of the *GAL* and *GAS* have always found, a certain amount of detective work may be necessary as the price of not excessively and tediously overloading an index of personal names.

The arrangement is in word-by-word alphabetical order, hyphens being treated as spaces but diacritics and other punctuation being ignored. The references are to the pages on which names appear in the dynastic lists.

Abaq, Börid, 189
Abaqa, Il Khānid, 250
Abba Muṣṭafā I and II, Mais of Dikwa, 128
'Abbād, 'Abbādid of Seville, 17
'Abbās
  I, II and III, Ṣafawids, 279
  (or Ya'qūb) b. al-Mutawakkil I, 'Abbāsid caliph in Cairo, 7
  Ghūrid, 298
'Abbās Ḥilmī I and II, House of Muḥammad 'Alī, 83
al-'Abbās al-Mahdī, Zaydī Imām, 97
al-'Abbās al-Mukarram, Zuray'id, 104
'Abd al-Aḥad, Mangīt, 292
'Abd al-'Aziz
  I, Āl Su'ūd, 116, 118
  II, amīr in Riyāḍ, King of Ḥijāz and Najd, and King of Su'ūdī Arabia, 116
  I and II, Marīnids, 41
  Āl Rashīd, 120
  'Alawid Sharīf, 53
  Dulafid, 153
  Ḥafṣid, 45
  al-Manṣūr, 'Āmirid, 19
  al-Manṣūr of Valencia and Almería, 17, 20
  Ottoman, 240
  Toqay Temürid, 290
('Abd) al-Ḥafīẓ, 'Alawid Sharīf, 53
'Abd al-Ḥalīm, Marīnid, 41
'Abd al-Ḥamīd I and II, Ottomans, 240
'Abd al-Ḥaqq I and II, Marīnids, 41, 48
'Abd al-Jalīl (Jīl) or Selema, ruler of Kanem, 126
'Abd al-Karīm
  'Abbāsid caliph in Baghdad, 6
  Khān of Astrakhan, 258
  Sultan of Harar, 138
'Abd al-Laṭīf
  Khān of Kazan, 259
  Shībānid, 288
'Abd al-Majīd
  I and II, Ottomans, 240
  Fāṭimid, 63
'Abd al-Malik
  I and II, Sāmānids, 170
  'Alawid Sharīf, 53
  'Āmirid, 19
  b. Hāshim, Hāshimid of Darband, 143
  b. Lashkarī, Hāshimid of Darband, 143
  b. Maḥammad al-Shaykh, al-Mu'taṣim, Sa'did Sharīf, 50
  b. Manṣūr, Hāshimid of Darband, 143
  b. Zaydān al-Nāṣir, Abū Marwān, Sa'did Sharīf, 50
  'Imād al-Dawla, Hūdid, 19
  Jahwarid of Cordova, 18
  Umayyad caliph, 3
'Abd al-Mu'min
  Almohad, 39
  Ḥafṣid, 45
  Marīnid, 41
  Qarakhānid, 183
  Shībānid, 288
  Toqay Temürid, 290
'Abd al-Muṭṭalib, Hāshimite Sharīf, 118
'Abd al-Nabī, Mahdid, 107
'Abd al-Raḥmān
  I, II and III, 'Abd al-Wādids, 43
  I–V, Spanish Umayyads, 11
  'Alawid Sharīf, 53
  Bārakzay, 341
  (Danyen Kasko), Fulani, 130
  governor of Riyāḍ, Āl Su'ūd, 116
  Kanembu Shehu of Bornu, 127
  Khān of Astrakhan, 258

Marīnid, 41
Rustamid, 27
Sultan of Harar, 138
'Abd al-Rashīd, Ghaznawid, 296
'Abd al-Razzāq, Sarbadārid, 269
'Abd al-Shakūr Muḥammad I, Sultan of Harar, 138
'Abd al-Wahhāb, Rustamid, 27
'Abd al-Wāḥid
'Abd al-Wādid, 43
b. Idrīs I, Almohad, 39
b. Yūsuf I, Almohad, 39
'Abdallāh
I, 'Abd al-Wādid, 43
II, 'Abd al-Wādid, 43
I and II, Aghlabids, 31
I and II, Shībānids, 288
I and II, Sultans of Harar, 138
I, II and III, Su'ūdīs, 116
(Abdallahi), Fulani, 130
Abū Fāris al-Wāthiq, Sa'did Sharīf, 50
Afṭasid of Badajoz, 18
'Alawid Sharīf, 53
Almohad, 39
b. Aḥmad, Mazrū'ī, 136
b. 'Alī, Āl Rashīd, 120
b. 'Alī, Ibn Ashqīlūla, ruler of Murcia, 20
b. Ashkam, Afrīghid Khwārazm Shāh, 178
b. Faraj al-Thaghrī, ruler of Murcia, 20
b. al-Ḥasan, Mahdali Sultan of Kilwa, 133
b. Ḥusayn, Amīr and later King of Transjordan, Hāshimite Sharīf, 118
b. Isḥāq, Ṭāhirid of Khurasan, 168
b. 'Iyāḍ, ruler of Murcia, 20
b. Kade, Sultan of Kanem, 126
b. Maḥammad, al-Shaykh, Abū Muḥammad al-Ghālib, Sa'did Sharīf, 50
b. Maḥammad, al-Shaykh al-Ma'mūn, al-Ghālib, Sa'did Sharīf, 50
b. Muḥammad, Abu 'l-Qāsim al-Muqtadī, 'Abbāsid caliph in Baghdad, 6
b. Muḥammad, Hāshimite Sharīf, 118
b. Muḥammad, al-Imām, Abu 'l-'Abbās al-Saffāḥ, 'Abbāsid caliph in Baghdad, 6
b. Muḥammad, al-Imām, Abū Ja'far al-Manṣur, 'Abbāsid caliph in Baghdad, 6
b. Muḥammad, Mazrū'ī, 136
b. Muḥammad, ruler of the Banū Ghāniya, 21
b. al-Muktafī, 'Abbāsid caliph in Baghdad, 6
b. al-Mustanṣir, 'Abbāsid caliph in Baghdad, 7
b. Mut'ab II, Āl Rashīd, 120
b. al-Qādir, 'Abbāsid caliph in Baghdad, 6
b. al-Rashīd, 'Abbāsid caliph in Baghdad, 6
b. Ṭāhir I, Ṭāhirid of Khurasan, 168
b. T.r.k.s.bātha, Afrīghid Khwārazm, 178
b. 'Umar, Sultan of Kanem, 126
b. Yūsuf, Fāṭimid, 63
Āl Bū Sa'īd, 137
Bikur, ruler of Kanem, 126
Ḥamdānid, 85
Hamdānid, 106
Isḥāq, ruler of the Banū Ghāniya, 21
Kalbid, 33
al-Mahdī, Zaydī Imām, 97
al Manṣur, Zaydī Imām, 96
Marīnid, 41
Midrārid, 29
al-Murtaḍā, ruler of Majorca, 18
al-Muẓaffar, Tujībid, 19
Qungrat, 293
Quṭb Shāhī, 328
Sāmānid commander in Sīstān, 172
Sayfī of Bornu, 127
Spanish Umayyad, 11
Tīmūrid, 270
('Ubaydallāh) b. Ḥusayn, Fāṭimid, 63
Yu'firid, 100
Zīrid of Granada, 17
Ziyādid, 99
Abdul Hakk Mubin, Sultan of Brunei, 353
Abdul Jalilul Akbar, posthumously called Marhum Tuha, Sultan of Brunei, 353
Abdul Jalilul Jabbar, Sultan of Brunei, 353
Abdul Kahhar, Sultan of Brunei, 353
Abdul Mumin, Sultan of Brunei, 353
'Abdūn Ibn Khazrūn, Khazrūn of Arcos, 17
Abdurrahman Mangkubuwana or Hămengkubuwana I–X, Sultans of Jogjakarta, 351
Ābish Khātūn, Muẓaffar al-Dīn, Salghurid, 207
Abū 'l-'Abbās, Badr al-Dawla, Naṣrid Malik, 211
Abū 'Abdallāh Muḥammad, Rey Lobo or Lope, ruler of Valencia, 19
Abū 'Abdallāh al-Shī'ī, propagandist, 63
Abū 'Alī, Ghūrid, 298
Abū 'l-'Arab, Ya'rubid, 113
Abū Bakr or Bakari, King of Songhay, 124
Abū Bakr
I and II, Ḥafṣids, 45
I and II, Sultans of Harar, 138
b. 'Abd al-Ḥaqq I, Marīnid, 41
b. Dāwūd, Sultan of Kanem, 126
b. Fāris, Marīnid, 41
b. Muḥammad, Nabhānī of Pate (840/1346), 134
b. Muḥammad, Nabhānī of Pate (900/1495), 134
b. Shehu, Fulani, 130
b. 'Umar, Almoravid, 37
governor of Sharwān for the Ottomans, 141
'Imād al-Dīn, Artuqid, 194
Kanembu Shehu of Bornu, 127
King of Songhay, 124
al-Manṣūr, 'Āmirid, 19
Nuṣrat al-Dīn, Eldigüzid, 199
Rustamid, 27
Sharwān Shāh, 141
Abū Bakr 'Atīq (Atiku) b. 'Uthmān, called Mai Katuru, Fulani, 130
Abū Bakr 'Atīq (Atiku na Rabah) b. Muḥammad Bello, Fulani, 130
Abū Bakr Bwana Gogo, Nabhānī of Pate, 134
Abū Bakr Shāh, Tughluqid Sultan of Delhi, 301
Abū Bakr al-Ṣiddīq, 'Rightly-Guided' Caliph, 1

Abū 'l-Fatḥ, Nizārī Ismā'īlī, 68
Abū 'l-Fatḥ, Zand, 283
Abū 'l-Fatḥ al-Daylamī al-Nāṣir, Zaydī Imām, 96
Abū 'l-Fatḥ Ismā'īl Shāh Nāṣir al-Dīn (Ismā'īl Mukh), Bahmanid, 319
Abū 'l-Fawāris, Būyid in Kirman, 155
Abū 'l-Fayḍ, Toqay Temürid, 290
Abū 'l-Ghanā'im, 'Uqaylid, 91
Abū 'l-Ghārāt, Zuray'id, 104
Abū Ghashshām, 'Uqaylid, 91
Abū 'l-Ghāzī, Toqay Temürid, 290
Abū 'l-Ḥasan, Quṭb Shāhī, 328
Abū Ibrāhīm Isḥāq b. Muḥammad, ruler of the Banū Ghāniya, 21
Abū Ishāq, Jamāl al-Dīn, Inju'id, 266
Abū 'l-Jaysh, Mukramid, 112
Abū Kālījār Marzubān 'Imād al-Dīn, Būyid in Fars and Khūzistān, 154
Abū 'l-Khayr, khān at Tura and ruler in northern Khwārazm, 288
Abū 'l-Ma'ālī, Raḍī 'l-Dīn, Nizārī Ismā'īlī, 68
Abū Manṣūr
'Alā' al-Dīn, or Malik Shāh, Saltuqid, 218
'Annāzid, 159
Nizārī Ismā'īlī, 68
Abū Manṣūr Khān, Nawwāb of Oudh, 337
Abū Muḥammad, Nizārī Ismā'īlī, 68
Abū Muḥammad II, Mukramid, 112
Abū 'l-Muẓaffar Ghāzī, Ḍiyā' al-Dīn, Saltuqid, 218
Abū 'l-Muẓaffar Ghiyāth al-Dīn (Yuzbak, Ikhtiyār al-Dīn), governor of Bengal, 306
Abū 'l-Muẓaffar Ḥasan Gangu 'Alā' al-Dīn Bahman Shāh (Ẓafar Khān), Bahmanid, 319
Abū 'l-Rayyān, 'Uqaylid, 91
Abū Sa'id
Hazāraspid, 205
Il Khānid, 250
Muẓaffar al-Dīn, Shībānid, 288
Qara Qoyunlu, 273
Tīmūrid, 270
Abū Sa'id al-Za'īm, 'Abd al-Wādid, 43
Abū Sa'id Ṭoghrïl, Qiwām al-Dawla, slave commander of the Ghaznawids, 296
Abū Shujā', Sulṭān al-Dawla, Būyid in Fars, Khūzistān, Iraq and Oman, 154–5
Abū 'l-Su'ūd, Zuray'id, 104
Abū Ṭāhir, Hazāraspid, 205
Abū Ṭāhir al-Ṣā'igh, Nizārī Ismā'īlī, 68
Abū Tāshufīn, 'Abd al-Wādid, 43
Abū Yūsuf, Qara Qoyunlu, 273
al-'Āḍid, Fāṭimid, 63
'Ādil, Jāndār Oghullarï, 229
'Ādil Giray, Khān of the Crimea, 255
'Ādil Khān II and III, Fārūqīs, 322
'Ādil Shāh, Sultan of Ma'bar, 318
Aflaḥ, Rustamid, 27
Afrāsiyāb I and II, Hazāraspids, 205
Afrīdūn, Dānishmendid, 213
Agha Muḥammad, Qājār, 285
al-Aghlab, Aghlabid, 31
Aḥmad
I and II, 'Abd al-Wādids, 43
I–IV, Bahmanids, 319
I, II and III, Ḥafṣids, 45
I and II, Hūdids, 19
I and II, Ḥusaynid Beys, 55
I and II, Marīnids, 41
II, Qaramānlī, 57
I and II, Sāmānids, 170
III, Sayf al-Dawla, Hūdid, 18, 20
I, II and III, Sultans of Harar, 138
'Abbāsid caliph in Aleppo, Ḥarrān and northern Syria, 7
Abū Bakr Ibn Ṭāhir, ruler of Murcia, 20
Abū Ja'far, ruler of Murcia, 20
Afrīghid Khwārazm Shāh, 178
Aghlabid, 31
(Ahmadu) or Zaraku b. Abī Bakr 'Atīq, called Mai Cimola, Fulani, 130
(Ahmadu Rafaye) b. 'Uthmān, Fulani, 130
(Aḥmed) I, II and III, Ottomans, 239
'Alā' al-Dīn, Naṣrid Malik of Sistan, 211
'Alawid Sharīf, 53
Aq Qoyunlu, 275
al-A'raj, Sa'did Sharīf, 50
b. Abd al-Malik, Hāshimid of Darband, 143
b. Abī 'Umāra, Ḥafṣid usurper, 45
b. 'Alī, Qarakhānid, 181
b. al-Ḥasan, 'Abbāsid caliph in Cairo, 7
b. al-Ḥasan, Kalbid, 33
b. al-Ḥasan, Zaydī Imām, 97
b. al-Ḥusayn, Zaydī Imām, 97
b. Isḥāq, 'Abbāsid caliph in Baghdad, 6
b. Ismā'īl al-Dhahabī, 'Alawid Sharīf, 53
b. Khiḍr, Qarakhānid, 181
b. Maḥammad al-Shaykh, Sa'did Sharīf, 50
b. Muḥammad, 'Abbāsid caliph in Baghdad, 6
b. Muḥammad, Nabhānī of Pate, 134
b. Mulḥim, Ma'n Amīr, 81
b. al-Muqtadī, 'Abbāsid caliph in Baghdad, 6
b. al-Mustaḍī, 'Abbāsid caliph in Baghdad, 6
b. al-Mustakfī I, 'Abbāsid caliph in Cairo, 7
b. al-Mutawakkil, 'Abbāsid caliph in Baghdad, 6
b. al-Muwaffaq, 'Abbāsid caliph in Baghdad, 6
b. al-Qāsim, Abu 'l-'Aysh, Idrīsid at Aṣīlā, 25
b. Qudām, commander in Sistan, 172
b. Shehe b. Fumo Luti, Nabhānī of Pate (1224/1809), 134
b. Shehe b. Fumo Luti, Nabhānī of Pate (1262/1846), 134
b. Sulaymān, Nabhānī of Pate, 134
b. 'Umar, Nabhānī of Pate, 134
b. al-Wazīr Abrām, Sultan of Harar, 138
b. Yazīd of Sharwān, Hāshimid, 143
b. al-Ẓāhir, 'Abbāsid caliph in Cairo, 7
b. Zaydān al-Nāṣir, Sa'did Sharīf, 50
Bānījūrid, 174
Būyid in Iraq and Kirman, 155
Bwana Waziri, Nabhānī of Pate, 134

Carmathian, 94
Dulafid, 153
Fakhr al-Dīn, Qaramān Oghullarï, 232
Fāṭimid, 63
Golden Horde Khān, 253
(Hārūn), Nūr al-Dawla, Qarakhānid, 182
Ikhshīdid, 62
Imām of the Ibāḍiyya, 114
Khalafid Ṣaffārid, 172
Laythid Ṣaffārid, 172
Mahdali, 133
al-Malik al-Manṣūr Ḥusām al-Dīn, Artuqid, 195
al-Malik al-Ṣāliḥ Shihāb al-Dīn, Artuqid, 195
Marwānid, 89
Mazrū'ī, 136
Mengüjekid, 217
Menteshe Oghullarï, 222
Midrārid, 29
(Muḥammad), Shams al-Dīn, Naṣrid Malik of Sistan, 211
(Muḥammad), Toghan Khān, Qarakhānid, 181
Muḥtājid governor of Khurasan, 177
Mu'izz al-Dawla, of the Banū Ṣumādiḥ of Almería, 17
al-Nāṣir, Zaydī Imām, 96
Nuṣrat al-Dīn, Hazāraspid, 205
Nuṣrat al-Dīn, Ṣāḥib Atā Oghullarï, 225
Qāḍī Burhān al-Dīn Oghullarï, 234–5
Qadïr Khān, Qarakhānid, 182
Qājār, 285
Sāmānid commander in Sīstān, 172
Sayf al-Islām, Zaydī Imām, 97
Sayfī of Bornu, 127
Shihāb al-Dīn, Ramaḍān Oghullarï, 237
Ṣulayḥid, 102
Sultan of Brunei, 353
Ṭūlūnid, 60
Waṭṭāsid, 48
(Ya'qūb), Sökmenid, 197
Yazīdī Sharwān Shāh, 140
Aḥmad al-'Abbās, Sa'did Sharīf, 50
Aḥmad al-Akḥal, Kalbid, 33
Aḥmad Bey I, Qaramānlī, 57
Aḥmad Fīrūz Shāh Sayf al-Dīn ('Andil), ruler of Bengal, 307
Aḥmad Fu'ād I and II, House of Muḥammad 'Alī, 83
Aḥmad Gövde, Aq Qoyunlu, 275
Aḥmad Grāñ, Walashma' Sultan in Harar, 138
Aḥmad Khān Abdālī, Sadōzay, 341
Aḥmad Khān Sikandar Shāh III, Sūrī Delhi Sultan, 301
Aḥmad Khiḍr, 'Izz al-Dīn, Artuqid, 194
Aḥmad al-Mahdī al-Mūṭi', Zaydī Imām, 96
Aḥmad al-Mutawakkil, Zaydī Imām, 96–7
Aḥmad Niyā, Sāmānid commander in Sistan, 172
Aḥmad Niẓām Shāh Baḥri, minister of the Bahmanids and first Niẓām Shāhī, Burhān I, 326
Aḥmad Qāwurd, Seljuq of Kirman, 186
Aḥmad Sanjar, 'Aḍud al-Dawla, ruler in Khurasan and supreme Sultan of the Seljuqs, 185
Aḥmad Shāh
I, II and III, Sultans of Gujarāt, 312
Fārūqī, 322
(Maharājā Lela Mēlayu), Sultan of Acheh, 346
ruler of Bengal, 307
Aḥmad Shāh Bahādur, Mughal, 331
Aḥmad Simba, Nabhānī of Pate, 134
Aḥmad Tajuddin, Sultan of Brunei, 353
Aḥmad Tegüder (Takūdār), Il Khānid, 250
Aḥmadīl b. Ibrāhīm, Rawwādid, 150
Ahmadu b. Abī Bakr 'Atīq, called Mai Cimola, Fulani, 130
Ahmadu Rafaye b. 'Uthmān, Fulani, 130
'Ajlān Beg, Qarasï Oghullarï, 219
Akbar I and II, Mughals, 331–2
Akhsitān I and II, Yazīdī Sharwān Shāhs, 140–1
'Alā' al-Dawla, Atabeg of Yazd, 209
'Alā' al-Dīn
Bahmanid, 319
'Imād Shāhī, 327
Qaramān Oghullarï, 232
Seljuq of Rūm, 213
Udayji, Sultan of Ma'bar, 318
'Ālam Khān of Aḥmadnagar, Fārūqī, 322
'Ālam Shāh, 'Alā' al-Dīn, Sayyid ruler in Delhi, 301
'Ālamgīr II, 'Azīz al-Dīn, Mughal, 331
Alfonso I el Batallador, 20
Alfonso VI of León and Castile, 18
'Alī
I and II, 'Ādil Shāhīs, 325
I and II, Ḥamdānids, 85
I, II and III, Ḥusaynid Beys, 55
I and II, Idrīsids, 25
I and II, Mazyadids, 87
I and II, Qaramānlīs, 57
'Abbāsid caliph in Baghdad, 6
Aḥmad, Ṣulayḥid, 102
(Aliyu) Babba, called Mai Cinaka, Fulani, 130
b. 'Abd al-Mu'min, Qarakhānid, 183
b. 'Abdallāh, Hāshimite Sharīf, 118
b. Abī Ṭālib, 'Rightly-Guided' Caliph, 1
b. Ardashīr, Bāwandid Ispahbadh, 164
b. Basha, Shīrāzī Sultan of Kilwa, 132
b. Būya, Abu 'l-Ḥasan 'Imād al-Dawla, first of the Būyids, 154
b. Dāwūd, Shīrāzī Sultan of Kilwa (433–93/1042–1110), 132
b. Dāwūd, Shīrāzī Sultan of Kilwa (661–5/1263–7), 132
b. Ḥamdūn, Sayfī of Bornu, 127
b. Ḥammūd, Āl Bū Sa'id, 137
b. Ḥammūd, al-Nāṣir, Ḥammūdid of Málaga, 16
b. al-Ḥasan, Mahdali Sultan of Kilwa, 133
b. Haytham, Yazīdī Sharwān Shāh, 140
b. Ḥusayn, Hāshimite Sharīf, 118
b. al-Ḥusayn, Shīrāzī Sultan of Kilwa, 132
b. Ibrāhīm, Sayfī of Bornu, 127

b. Idrīs, Sayfī of Bornu, 127
b. Mas'ūd, Mihrabānid Malik of Sistan, 211
b. Muḥammad, Abu 'l-Ḥasan Janāḥ al-Dawla, 'Uqaylid, 91
b. Muḥammad, 'Alā' al-Dīn, Eretna Oghullarï, 234
b. Muḥammad, Mihrabānid Malik of Sistan, 211
b. Muḥammad, Zuray'id, 104
b. Muḥammad II, Abu 'l-Ḥasan or Abū Ḥassūn, Waṭṭāsid, 48
b. Muḥammad al-Ṣulayḥī, Ṣulayḥid, 102
b. Mūsā b. Satuq Bughra Khān, joint founder of the Qarakhānid confederation, 181
b. Muslim, 'Uqaylid, 91
b. Rukn al-Dawla Ḥasan, Būyid, 154
b. Saba', al-A'azz, Zuray'id, 104
b. Sa'd, Abu 'l-Ḥasan (Muley Hácen), Naṣrid, 22
b. Sa'id, Āl Bū Sa'id, 137
b. Shahriyār, Bāwandid Ispahbadh, 164
b. 'Uthmān, Mazrū'ī, 136
b. Yazīd, Abū Manṣūr, Yazīdī Sharwān Shāh, 140
b. Yazīd of Sharwān, Hāshimid, 143
b. Yūsuf, Almoravid, 37
b. Yūsuf, Waṭṭāsid, 48
b. Zayd, Zaydī Imām, 96
Dulghadïr Oghullarï, 238
Fāṭimid, 63
Ghaznawid, 296
Ikhshīdid, 62
Justānid, 145
Kākūyid, 160
Kalbid, 33
Lu'lu'id, 193
Mahdid, 107
al-Malik al-'Ādil 'Imād al-Dīn, Artuqid, 195
al-Manṣūr, Zaydī Imām, 97
Marīnid, 41
Ma'mūnid Khwārazm Shāh, 178
Mukramid, 112
al-Nāṣir, Ḥammūdid of Ceuta, 16
Naṣrid Malik of Sistan, 211
Qarakhānid, 181
Qaramān Oghullarï, 232
ruler of the Banū Ghāniya, 21
Saltuqid, 218
Sīmjūrid, 175
son of Si Ma Gogo or Maḥmūd Da'o, King of Songhay, 124
Sultan of Harar, 138
Tīmūrid, 270
al-Waḥīd, Hamdānid, 106
Zīrid of Kairouan, 35
'Alī Beg, Inanj Oghullarï, 223
'Alī Chaghrï Khan, Qarakhānid, 182
'Alī Fannami, Sayfī of Bornu, 127
'Alī Ghāzī Kanuri, Sayfī of Bornu, 127
'Alī Golom, King of Songhay, 124
'Alī Ibn Ḥammūd, al-Nāṣir, Spanish Umayyad, 11
'Alī Iqbāl al-Dawla, Mujāhid of Denia and Majorca, 17
'Alī Jalāl al-Dīn, Aq Qoyunlu, 275
'Alī Jalāl al-Dīn, Ghūrid, 298
'Alī Jarād, son of Aḥmad Grāñ, joint ruler of Harar, 138
'Alī Karām (Aliyu Karami), Fulani, 130
'Alī Khalīl (Allāh), Chaghatayid, 248
'Alī Khān of Kazan, 259
'Alī Khwāja Tāj al-Dīn, Sarbadārid, 269
'Alī Kolon, King of Songhay, 124
'Alī Küchük, Begtiginid, 192
'Alī Lashkarī I and II, Shaddādids, 151
'Alī Malik al-Mulūk, Barīd Shāhī, 324
'Alī Mardān, governor of Bengal, 306
'Alī Mīr Khān (ruling title 'Alī Shāh), Sultan of Kashmīr, 310
'Alī Mubārak, 'Alā' al-Dīn, ruler of Bengal, 307
'Alī Mughāyat Shāh, Sultan of Acheh, 346
'Alī Murād, Zand, 283
'Alī or Ḥusayn Ri'āyat Shāh, Sultan of Acheh, 346
'Alī Qulī, Afshārid, 281
'Alī Ri'āyat Shāh
(Rājā Buyung), Sultan of Acheh, 346
(Sultan Muda), Sultan of Acheh, 346
'Alī Sayfī of Bornu (1055–95/1645–84), 127
'Alī Shāh
('Alī Mīr Khān), Sultan of Kashmīr, 310
Sadōzay, 341
'Alī Shīr, 'Alā' al-Dīn, Sultan of Kashmīr, 310
'Alī Tigin, Qarakhānid, 181
'Alī Zayn al-'Ābidīn
'Alawid Sharīf, 53
Qāḍī Burhān al-Din Oghullarï, 235
'Ālim, Ming, 295
'Alīwirdī Khān, Nawwāb of Bengal, 335
Aliyu Babba, Fulani, 130
Aliyu Karami, Fulani, 130
Allāh ('Alī Khalīl), Chaghatayid, 248
Allāh Qulī, Qungrat, 293
Alp Arghu(n), Shams al-Dīn, Hazāraspid, 205
Alp Arslan
al-Akhras, Seljuq in Aleppo, 186
Great Seljuq, 185
Seljuq of Rūm, 213
Tāj al-Dīn Oghullarï, 236
Alp Khān (ruling title Hūshang Shāh), Sultan of Mālwa, 316
Alp Yürük, Ḥusām al-Dīn, Chobān Oghullarï, 231
Alpï I, Najm al-Dīn, Artuqid, 194
Altuntash Ḥājib, Ghaznawid commander, 178
Alughu, Chaghatayid, 248
Alwand, Aq Qoyunlu, 275
Alyaman, King of Songhay, 124
Amān Allāh, Bārakzay, 341
Amangkurat I–IV, rulers of Mataram, 348
Amarma, Sultan of Kanem, 127
Amer, Sultan of Kanem, 127
'Amīd Shāh Dāwūd (Dilāwar Khān), Ghūrī, 316
al-Amīn, 'Abbāsid caliph in Baghdad, 6
Amīn al-Dīn Shāh, Jawhar al-'Ālam, Sultan of Acheh, 346

al-'Āmir, Fāṭimid, 63
Amīr Barīd I and II, Barīd Shāhīs, 324
Amīr Ghāzī Gümüshtigin, Dānishmendid, 215
Amīr Walī, Sarbadārid, 269
Amjad 'Alī Thurayyā Jāh, Nawwāb of Oudh, 337
'Amr
  b. al-Layth, Laythid Ṣaffārid, 172
  b. Ya'qūb, Laythid Ṣaffārid, 172
  Marīnid, 41
'Andil (ruling title Aḥmad Fīrūz Shāh Sayf al-Dīn), ruler of Bengal, 307
Anūshirwān, Ziyārid, 166
Ā'or Khan Aybak, governor of Bengal, 306
Aq Kābek, Khān of Astrakhan, 258
Aq Sunqur
  I Aḥmadīlī, 198
  II (Arslan Aba), Nuṣrat al-Dīn, Aḥmadīlī, 198
  al-Bursuqī, ruler in Aleppo, 186
  Hazārdīnārī, Badr al-Dīn, Sökmenid slave commander, 197
Aragibag (Arigaba), Mongol Great Khān, 246
Ārām Shāh, Mu'izzī Delhi Sultan,300
Ardashīr
  b. Ḥasan, Bāwandid Ispahbadh, 164
  b. Kīnkhwār, Bāwandid Ispahbadh, 164
  Ḥusām al-Dawla, Bādūspānid, 201
Arghun, Il Khānid, 250
Arigaba (Aragibag), Mongol Great Khān, 246
Ariq Böke, Mongol Great Khān, 246
Arp Arslan (Arslan), Khān of Qāsimov, 261
Arpa Ke'ün (Gawon), Il Khānid, 250
Arslan
  (Alp Arslan), Khān of Qāsimov, 261
  (Aq Sunqur II), Nuṣrat al-Dīn, Aḥmadīlī, 198
  Giray, Khān of the Crimea, 256
  Shāh I and II, Seljuqs of Kirman, 186
  Shāh I and II, Zangids, 190
  (Shāh), Great Seljuq, 186
  Shāh (Malik Shāh), Ghaznawid, 296
  Tigin, Qarakhānid, 181
  Tigin Muḥammad, Khwārazm Shāh, 179
Arthamūkh, Afrīghid Khwārazm Shāh, 178
Artuq, Ẓahīr al-Dawla, Seljuq commander, 194
Artuq Arslan, al-Malik al-Manṣūr Nāṣir al-Dīn, Artuqid, 194
Artuq Shāh, Nūr al-Dīn, Artuqid, 194
As'ad, Yu'firid, 100
Āṣaf al-Dawla, Nawwāb of Oudh, 337
Āṣaf Jāh (Chin Qïlïch Khān), Niẓām, 339
Ashraf, Bādūspānid, 201
'Aṭiyya, Mirdāsid, 66
Atsïz, 'Alā' al-Dīn, Ghūrid, 298
'Awaẓ, Qungrat, 293
'Awn al-Rafāq, Hāshimite Sharīf, 118
Awrangzīb, Mughal, 331
Aybak, Quṭb al-Dīn, Mu'izzī Delhi Sultan, 300
Aybak Khitā'ī, Sayf al-Dīn, governor of Bengal, 306
Ayurparibhadra (Ayurbarwada) or Buyantu, Mongol Great Khān, 246
Ayyūb Shāh, Sadōzay, 341
A'ẓam Shāh
  Ghiyāth al-Dīn, ruler of Bengal, 307
  Mughal, 331
'Aẓīm al-Sha'n Muḥammad 'Aẓīm, Mughal claimant, 331
al-'Azīz
  (al-'Izz), Birzāl of Carmona, 17
  b. 'Abd al-Malik, Ḍiyā' al-Dawla, ruler of Murcia, 20
  Fāṭimid, 63
  Ḥammādid, 35
'Azzān, Āl Bū Sa'id, 114

Bābur
  Abu 'l-Qāsim, Tīmūrid, 270
  Mughal, 331
Bachcha-yi Saqqa(w) (ruling title Ḥabīb Allāh II), usurper in Afghanistan, 341
Bādh al-Kurdī, Kurdish chief and founder of the Marwānids, 89
Badī' al-Zamān, Tīmūrid, 270
Bādīs
  Ḥammādid, 35
  al-Muẓaffar al-Nāṣir, Zīrid of Granada, 17
  Zīrid of Kairouan, 35
Badr
  al-Dīn, Sultan of Acheh, 346
  al-Dīn Lu'lu', vizier, ruler in Mosul, 190
  Ḥasanūyid, 158
  al-Munīr, Jamāl al-'Ālam, Sultan of Acheh, 346
  al-Mu'taḍidī, Turkish slave commander, 168
  Ḥasanūyid, 158
  Zaydī Imām, 97
Bahādur
  I and II Giray, Khāns of the Crimea, 255–6
  Ghiyāth al-Dīn, ruler of Bengal, 306–7
  Niẓām Shāhī, 326
  Shāh
    II, Mughal, 332
    Fārūqī, 322
    Sultan of Gujarāt, 312
Bahlūl, Lōdī, 301
Bahman, Bādūspānid, 202
Bahrām
  leader of the Syrian Ismā'īlī community, 68
  Shāh
    Ghaznawid, 296
    Mengüjekid, 217
    Mu'izz al-Dīn, Mu'izzī Delhi Sultan, 300
    Seljuq of Kirman, 186
    Yamīn al-Dīn, Naṣrid Malik of Sistan, 211
  Tātār Khān, ruler of Bengal, 307
Bakht Giray, Khān of the Tatars, 256
Bakhtiyār, Būyid in Iraq, 155
Balabān, 'Izz al-Dīn, Sökmenid slave commander, 197
Balban, Ulugh Khān, Ghiyāth al-Dīn, Mu'izzī Delhi Sultan, 300
Balban Yuzbakī, 'Izz al-Dīn, governor of Bengal, 306
Bandar, Āl Rashīd, 120

Bāqī Muḥammad, Toqay Temürid, 290
Baraka
(Berke), Batu'id, 252
'Uqaylid, 91
Baraq
Ghiyāth al-Dīn, Chaghatayid, 248
Golden Horde Khān, 253
Baraq Ḥājib, Nāṣir al-Dunya wa 'l-Dīn, Qutlughkhānid, 210
Barbak Shāh, Rukn al-Dīn, ruler of Bengal, 307
Barghash, Āl Bū Sa'id, 137
Bāri, Börid, 189
Barjīs Qadïr, Nawwāb of Oudh, 337
Barkiyāruq (or Berk Yaruq), Seljuq in Persia and Iraq, 185
Bashīr I, II and III, Shihāb Amīrs, 82
Bata-Mande-Bori, Keita of Mali, 122
Bat'iah Dël Wanbarā, widow of Aḥmad Grāñ, joint ruler of Harar, 138
Batu, Batu'id, 252
Bāw of Ṭabaristān, Bāwandid Ispahbadh, 164
Bāyazīd
(Bāyezīd) I, Yïldïrïm ('the Lightning shaft'), Ottoman, 239
II, Ottoman, 239
Jalāyirid, 267
Kararāni b. Sulaymān, ruler of Bengal, 308
Kötörüm, Jalāl al-Dīn, Jāndār Oghullarï, 229
Shāh, Sayf al-Dīn, ruler of Bengal, 307
Baydu, Il Khānid, 250
Bayqara, Tīmūrid, 271
Bayram, Sharwān Shāh, 141
Bayram Khōja, Qara Qoyunlu, 273
Baysonqur
Aq Qoyunlu, 275
Tīmūrid, 270
Begtimur, Sayf al-Dīn, Sökmenid slave commander, 197
Ber the Great, King of Songhay, 124
Berk Yaruq (Barkiyāruq), Seljuq in Persia and Iraq, 185
Berke (Baraka), Batu'id, 252
Bhikan Khān (ruling title Muhammad Shāh), Sharqī, 314
Bīdār Bakht, Mughal, 332
Bīdar Qadïr Khān (or Pindar), ruler of Bengal, 306
Bilge Khan, Ikhtiyār al-Dīn, governor of Bengal, 306
Biri
b. Dunama, Sultan of Kanem, 126
Ibrāhīm, Sultan of Kanem, 126
Bīsutūn
Bādūspānid, 201–2
Ziyārid, 166
Boabdil, Muḥammad XII, Naṣrid, 22
Bolkiah, Sultan of Brunei, 353
Bolod (Pūlād) Khān, Golden Horde Khān, 252
Bozqurd, 'Alā' al-Dawla, Dulghadïr Oghullarï, 238
Bud Shāh (or Shāh Khān or Zayn al-'Ābidīn), ruler of Kashmīr, 310
Bughra
Nāṣir al-Dīn, ruler of Bengal, 306
Shihāb al-Dīn, ruler of Bengal, 306
Bukar
I Kura, Kanembu Shehu of Bornu, 127
Garbai, Shehu of Dikwa and later Bornu, 128
Mai of Dikwa, 128
Bukhtnaṣṣar 'Alī, Yazīdī Sharwān Shāh, 140
Buluggīn II, Ḥammādid, 35
Buqa (Toqa Temür), Chaghatayid, 248
Burhān
I, II and III, Niẓām Shāhīs, 326
'Alī, Sharwān Shāh, 141
'Imād Shāhī, 327
Būya b. Rukn al-Dawla Ḥasan, Būyid in Hamadan and Isfahan, 154
Buyan, White Horde Khān, 252
Buyan Quli, Chaghatayid, 248
Buyantu (or Ayurparibhadra or Ayurbarwada), Mongol Great Khān, 246
Buzan, Chaghatayid, 248
Bwana
Bakari I and II, Nabhānīs of Pate, 134
Fumo Madi, Muḥammad, Nabhānī of Pate, 134
Mkuu
I and II, Nabhānī of Pate, 134
b. Shehe, Nabhānī of Pate, 134
Shehe
b. Aḥmad, Nabhānī of Pate, 134
b. Muḥammad Bwana Fumo Madi, Nabhānī of Pate, 134
Tamu Mkuu, Abū Bakr, Nabhānī of Pate, 134
Tamu Mtoto, Abū Bakr, Nabhānī of Pate, 134

Chaghatay, Chaghatayid, 248
Chaghrï Beg Dāwūd, Seljuq ruler in Khurāsān, 185
Changshi, Chaghatayid, 248
Charles V, Emperor, 45
Chimtay, White Horde Khān, 252
Chin Qïlïch Khān (ruling title Āṣaf Jāh), Niẓām of Hyderabad, 339
Chinggis (Chingiz), Mongol Great Khān, 246
Chobān, Ḥusām al-Dīn, Chobān Oghullarï, 231

Dābūya b. Gāwbāra, Dābūyid Ispahbadh, 162
Dādburzmihr b. Farrukhān I, Dābūyid Ispahbadh, 162
Dānishmendji, Chaghatayid, 248
Dāniyāl Biy Atalïq, Mangït, 292
Dāniyār, Khān of Qāsimov, 261
Danūj Mardan Deva (Rājā Gaṇeśa), ruler of Bengal, 307
Danyen Kasko, Fulani, 130
Dārā
Bāwandid Ispahbadh, 164
Ziyārid, 166
Dārā Shikūh, Mughal, 331
Darwīsh
'Alī, Khān of Astrakhan, 258
Ramaḍān Oghullarï, 237

Daryā, 'Imād Shāhī, 327
Dāwar Bakhsh, Mughal, 331
Dawlat Berdi, Golden Horde Khān, 253
Dawlat Birdi Giray (Kerey), Khān of the Crimea, 255
Dawlat Giray I–IV, Khāns of the Crimea, 255–6
Dawlat Khān Lōdī, Delhi Sultan, 301
Dāwūd
I and II, Artuqids, 195
I and II, Mengüjekids, 217
I and II Shāh, Bahmanids, 319
'Abbāsid caliph in Cairo, 7
Askiya of Songhay, 124
b. 'Alī, Shīrāzī Sultan of Kilwa, 132
b. Ibrāhīm Nikale, Sultan of Kanem, 126
b. Sulaymān, Shīrāzī Sultan of Kilwa (525/1131), 132
b. Sulaymān, Shīrāzī Sultan of Kilwa (585/1189), 132
Bānījūrid, 174
Mahdali Sultan of Kilwa, 132
Rukn al-Dawla, Artuqid, 194
Seljuq in Persia and Iraq, 185
Dāwūd Kararānī b. Sulaymān, ruler of Bengal, 308
Dāwūd Khān
Fārūqī, 322
Sultan of Gujarāt, 312
Ḍayfa Khātūn, Ayyūbid regent in Aleppo, 71
Degele (or Tekele)
Hazāraspid, 205
Salghurid, 207
Demir Khān, Qarasī Oghullarī, 219
Dhu 'l-Nūn, 'Imād al-Dīn, Dānishmendid, 213
Dhu 'l-Nūn Beg Arghūn, governor of Kandahar and first of the Arghūns, 329
Dhu 'l-Nūnid Yaḥyā, puppet ruler of Valencia, 19
Dhu 'l-Qarnayn, Dānishmendid, 213
Dilāwar Khān Ḥasan Ghūrī, governor and then ruler of Mālwa, 316
Dirke Kelem b. Dunama, Sultan of Kanem, 126
Dīwāna (ruling title Muẓaffar Shams al-Dīn), ruler of Bengal, 307
Dīwdād II, Sājid, 147
Don John of Austria, 46
Du'a (Duwa), Chaghatayid, 248
Du'a Temür, Chaghatayid, 248
Dubays I and II, Mazyadids, 87
Dulaf, Dulafid, 153
Dunama
b. 'Alī, Sayfī of Bornu, 127
b. Biri, Sultan of Kanem, 126
b. Ibrāhīm, Sultan of Kanem, 126
b. 'Umar, Sultan of Kanem, 126
Dunama Dibalemi, Muḥammad, ruler of Kanem, 126
Dunama Gana, Sayfī of Bornu, 127
Dunama Lefiami, Sayfī of Bornu, 127
Dunama Muḥammad, Sayfī of Bornu, 127
Dunama Umemi Muḥammad, ruler of Kanem, 126
Dündār, Ramaḍān Oghullarī, 237
Dündār Beg, Falak al-Dīn, Ḥamīd Oghullarī, 226
Duqaq, Seljuq in Damascus, 186
Dūst Muḥammad, Bārakzay, 341

Ekinchi b. Qochqar, Khwārazm Shāh, 179
Eldigüz, Shams al-Dīn, Eldigüzid, 199
Eljigedey, Chaghatayid, 248
Eltüzer, Qungrat, 293
Eretna, 'Alā' al-Dīn, Eretna Oghullarī, 234
Esen Buqa, Chaghatayid, 248
Eylük, Ramaḍān Oghullarī, 237

al-Fāḍil
b. al-Muqtadir, 'Abbāsid caliph in Baghdad, 6
Carmathian ruler, 94
Zaydī Imām, 96
Fāḍil Tora, Mangīt, 292
Faḍl I–V, Shaddādids, 151
Faḍl Allāh, Ḥamdānid, 85
Faḍlūya, Kurdish chief in Fars, 154
Fahd, Āl Su'ūd, 116
al-Fā'iz, Fāṭimid, 63
Fakhr al-Dīn
II b. Qorqmaz II, Ma'n Amīr, 81
Kart, 263
Falak al-Dīn, Aḥmadīlī, 198
Fanā Khusraw, 'Aḍud al-Dawla, Būyid, 154–5
Farāmurz, Kākūyid, 160
Farīburz
II and III, Yazīdī Sharwān Shāhs, 141
b. Sallār of Sharwān, Hāshimid, 143
Yazīdī Sharwān Shāh, 140
Farīdūn I and II, Yazīdī Sharwān Shāhs, 140
Fāris
'Annāzid, 159
Marīnid, 41
Farkhanda 'Alī Khān, Nāṣir al-Dawla, Niẓām of Hyderabad, 339
Farrukh-siyar, Mughal, 331
Farrukhān I and II, Dābūyid Ispahbadhs, 162
Farrukhsiyar, Sharwān Shāh, 141
Farrukhzād
I and II, Yazīdī Sharwān Shāhs, 141
Ghaznawid, 296
Fārūq, House of Muḥammad 'Alī, 83
Fatḥ, Sājid, 147
Fatḥ 'Alī Khān, Qājār, 285
Fatḥ 'Alī Shāh, Bābā Khān, Qājār, 285
Fatḥ Allāh Daryā Khān, 'Imād al-Mulk, first of the 'Imād Shāhīs, 327
Fatḥ Giray I and II, Khāns of the Crimea, 256
Fatḥ Jang, Sadōzay, 341
Fatḥ Khān (ruling title Maḥmūd Shāh I, Begṛā, Sayf al-Dīn), Sultan of Gujarāt, 312
Fatḥ Shāh, Sultan of Kashmīr, 310
Fātik I, II and III, Najāḥids, 101
Fāṭima Sulṭān Bike, Khān of Qāsimov, 261
Fayṣal
I b. Ḥusayn b. 'Alī, King of Greater Syria and subsequently of Iraq, 118
II b. Ghāzī, Hāshimite King of Iraq, 118

I and II, Su'ūdīs, 116
Āl Bū Sa'id, 114
Ferdinand II of Aragon, 43
Fīrūz, Būyid, 154–5
Fīrūz Shāh
III, Kamāl al-Dīn, Tughluqid Delhi Sultan, 300
I, Rukn al-Dīn, Mu'izzī Delhi Sultan, 300
II Khaljī, Jalāl al-Dīn, Khaljī Delhi Sultan, 300
b. Bāyazīd Shāh, ruler of Bengal, 307
b. Ḥusayn Shāh, 'Alā' al-Dīn, ruler of Bengal, 307
Quṭb al-Dīn, Sultan of Ma'bar, 318
Shams al-Dīn, ruler of Bengal, 306
Tāj al-Dīn, Bahmanid, 319
Ẓafar, Tughluqid Delhi Sultan, 300
Fuḍayl, Mahdali Sultan of Kilwa, 133
Fūlād Sutūn, Būyid in Fars, 154
Fumo Bakari
b. Aḥmad, Nabhānī of Pate, 134
b. Bwana Shehe, Nabhānī of Pate, 134
Fumo Luti b. Shehe, Nabhānī of Pate, 134
Fumo Luti Kipanga, Nabhānī of Pate, 134
Fumo Omari b. Aḥmad b. Shehe, Nabhānī of Pate, 134

Garshāsp
I and II, Kākūyids, 160
I and II, Yazīdī Sharwān Shāhs, 141
Gawon (Arpa Ke'ün), Il Khānid, 250
Gaykhatu, Il Khānid, 250
Gharīb, 'Uqaylid, 91
Ghāzān (or Maḥmūd Ghazan) I, Il Khānid, 250
Ghāzī
I and II, Najm al-Dīn, Artuqids, 195
I and II, Sayf al-Dīn, Zangids, 190
Hāshimite King of Iraq, 118
Sharwān Shāh, 141
Sultan of Kanem, 127
Ghāzī Chelebi, Parwāna Oghullarï, 230
Ghāzī Giray I, II and III, Khāns of the Crimea, 256
Ghāzī Khān Chak (ruling title Muḥammad Nāṣir al-Dīn), Sultan of Kashmīr, 310
Ghāzī Shāh, Ikhtiyār al-Dīn, ruler of Bengal, 307
Ghaznī Khān
Fārūqī, 322
Sultan of Mālwa, 316
Ghiyāth al-Dīn
I and II, Karts, 263
Hazāraspid, 205
('Iwaḍ, Ḥusām al-Dīn), governor of Bengal, 306
Kay Khusraw, Inju'id, 266
Shāh, Khaljī Delhi Sultan, 316
Tahamtan, Bahmanid, 319
Gīl, Dābūyid Ispahbadh, 162
Gīlān Shāh, Ziyārid, 166
Gökbori, Begtiginid, 192
'Great Sanūsī', the, Sayyid Muḥammad b. 'Alī, 58
Güneri Beg, Qaramān Oghullarï, 232
Gushnāsp or Garshāsp II, Yazīdī Sharwān Shāh, 141
Güyük, Mongol Great Khān, 246

Ḥabbūs, Zīrid of Granada, 17
Ḥabīb Allāh
I Bārakzay, 341
II, or Bachcha-yi Saqqā(w), usurper in Afghanistan, 341
Sadōzay, 341
Ḥabīb Shāh, Sultan of Kashmīr, 310
al-Hādī, Mūsā, 'Abbāsid caliph in Baghdad, 6
al-Ḥāfiẓ, Fāṭimid, 63
Ḥāfiẓ, Kart, 263
Hai-shan (or Qayshan Gülük), Mongol Great Khān, 246
Haji Muhammad Ali, Sultan of Brunei, 353
Ḥajjāj Sulṭān, Qutlughkhānid, 210
Ḥājjī Giray I and II, Khāns of the Crimea, 255–6
Ḥājjī Khān (ruling title Ḥaydar Shāh), Sultan of Kashmīr, 310
Ḥājjī Shāh, Atabeg of Yazd, 209
al-Ḥakam I and II, Spanish Umayyads, 11
al-Ḥakim
I, 'Abbāsid caliph in Aleppo and then Cairo, 7
II, 'Abbāsid caliph in Cairo, 7
Fāṭimid, 63
al-Hakīm al-Munajjim, Nizārī Ismā'īlī, 68
Ḥalīm Giray, Khān of the Crimea, 256
Ḥamdān, chief in Mārdīn and Mosul, founder of the Ḥamdānids, 85
Ḥamdīn, al-Manṣūr, ruler in Cordova, 18
Ḥamdūn, Sayf of Bornu, 127
Ḥāmid
Āl Bū Sa'id, 114, 137
Sultan of Harar, 138
Ḥammād, Ḥammādid, 35
Ḥammūd, Āl Bū Sa'id, 137
Ḥam(m)ūda Pasha, Ḥusaynid Bey, 55
Ḥamza
'Abbāsid caliph in Cairo, 7
Aq Qoyunlu, 275
'Izz al-Dīn, Ramaḍān Oghullarï, 237
Zaydī Imam, 96
Ḥamza Shāh, Sayf al-Dīn, ruler of Bengal, 307
Ḥarb, Tāj al-Dīn III, Naṣrid Malik of Sistan, 211
al-Ḥārith, Dulafid, 153
Hārūn
(Aḥmad), Nūr al-Dawla, Qarakhānid, 182
b. al-Mahdī, 'Abbāsid caliph in Baghdad, 6
b. al-Mu'taṣim, al-Rashīd, 'Abbāsid caliph in Baghdad, 6
(Ḥasan), joint founder of the Qarakhānid confederation, 181
(Ḥasan), Nāṣir al-Haqq, Qarakhānid, 182
Khwārazm Shāh, 178
Ṭūlūnid, 60
Ḥasan
II and III, Nizārī Ismā'īlīs, 203
b. Alp Arslan Muḥammad, Tāj al-Dīn Oghullarï, 236
b. Būya, Abū 'Alī Rukn al-Dawla, Būyid in Jibāl, 154

b. Kay Khusraw, Fakhr al-Dawla, Bāwandid Ispahbadh, 165
Bāwandid Ispahbadh, 164
Būyid in Iraq, 155
Fulani, 130
(Hārūn), joint founder of the Qarakhānid confederation, 181
Ḥusām al-Dīn, Tāj al-Dīn Oghullarï, 236
Jalāl al-Dunyā wa 'l-Dīn, Qarakhānid, 182
al-Mustanṣir, Ḥammūdid of Ceuta, 16
Numayrid, 93
Quṭb al-Dīn, Ghūrid, 298
Ṣāḥib Atā Oghullarï, 225
(Tigin) b. 'Alī, Qarakhānid, 183
Tīmūrid, 270
al-Ḥasan
I and II, 'Alawid Sharīfs, 53
'Abbāsid caliph in Baghdad, 6
'Abd al-Wādid, 43
Abū 'Alī al-A'ṣam, Carmathian ruler, 94
Abū Sa'id, Carmathian ruler, 94
b. 'Abdallāh, Kalbid, 33
b. Dāwūd, Shīrāzī Sultan of Kilwa, 132
b. Ismā'īl, al-Khaṭīb, Mahdali Sultan of Kilwa, 133
b. Muḥammad, Idrīsid at al-Ḥajjām, 25
b. al-Qāsim, Idrīsid at Ḥajar al-Nasr, 25
b. Sulaymān
Abu 'l-Mawāhib, Mahdali Sultan of Kilwa (710/1310), 132
Mahdali Sultan of Kilwa (884/1479, 891–4/1468–9), 133
Shīrāzī Sultan of Kilwa, 132
b. Ṭālūt, Mahdali Sultan of Kilwa, 132
Ḥafṣid, 45
Ḥamdānid, 85
Kamāl al-Dīn, Nizārī Ismā'īlī, 68
Marwānid, 89
al-Mustanṣir, Ḥammūdid of Málaga, 16
Nāṣir al-Dīn, Baḥrī Mamlūk, 77
al-Ṣamṣām, Kalbid, 33
'Uqaylid, 91
Zaydī Imām, 96
Zīrid of Kairouan, 35
Ḥasan 'Alī, Qara Qoyunlu, 273
Ḥasan Dāmghānī, Sarbadārid, 269
Ḥasan-i Ṣabbāḥ (al-Ḥasan), Fāṭimid agent and Nizārī Ismā'īlī, 203
Ḥasan Shāh, Sultan of Kashmīr, 310
Ḥasanawayh, Ḥasanūyid, 158
Hāshim
b. Surāqa al-Sulamī, governor of Darband and first of the Hāshimids, 143
Bānījūrid, 174
Kanembu Shehu of Bornu, 128
Sultan of Brunei, 353
Sultan of Harar, 138
Hassanal Bolkiah, Sultan of Brunei, 354
Ḥātim
Aḥmad, Ḥāmid al-Dawla, Hamdānid, 106
b. al-Ghashīm al-Hamdānī, Hamdānid, 96, 106
b. al-Ḥumās, Hamdānid, 106
Ḥaydar
I and II, Nawwābs of Oudh, 337
'Alī Khān Bahādur, ruler in Mysore, 340
Shihāb Amīr, 82
Shujā' al-Dawla Jalāl al-Dīn, Nawwāb of Oudh, 337
Ḥaydar Giray, Khān of the Crimea, 255
Ḥaydar Qaṣṣāb, Sarbadārid, 269
Ḥaydar Shāh (Ḥājjī Khān), Sultan of Kashmīr, 310
Haytham
b. Muḥammad, Yazīdī Sharwān Shāh, 140
b. Muḥammad of Sharwān, Hāshimid, 143
Khālid, Yazīdī Sharwān Shāh, 140
Hazārasp, Bādūspānid, 201
Hilāl
Ḥasanūyid, 158
Ibn Mardanīsh, ruler of Valencia, 19
Hindal, Quṭb al-Dīn, Sultan of Kashmīr, 310
Hishām
I, II and III, Spanish Umayyads, 11
'Alawid Sharīf, 53
Hamdānid, 106
Umayyad caliph, 3
Hülegü (or Hūlākū), Il Khānid, 250
al-Ḥumās, Hamdānid, 106
Humāyūn, Nāṣir al-Dīn, Mughal, 331
Humāyūn Shāh, Bahmanid, 319
Hume or Ume Jilmi, first Yazanī ruler of Kanem, 126
Ḥusayn
I and II, Ghūrids, 298
I and II, Jalāyirids, 267
I, II and III, Niẓām Shāhīs, 326
I and II, Rawwādids, 150
I, Ṣafawid, 279
'Alawid Sharīf, 53
b. 'Alī, Sharīf of Mecca and Ḥijāz and King of Ḥijāz, Hāshimite Sharīf, 118
b. Ṭalāl, Hāshimite King of Jordan, 118
Jalāl al-Dunyā wa 'l-Dīn, Qarakhānid, 183
Kamāl al-Dīn, Ḥamīd Oghullarï, 226
al-Naṣr, Ḥusaynid Bey, 55
rebel against Khalafid Ṣaffārids, 172
Ṣāḥib Atā Oghullarï, 225
Seljuq of Kirman, 186
Tīmūrid, 270
al-Ḥusayn
I and II, Ḥusaynid Beys, 55
b. Khalīl II, Ayyūbid in Diyār Bakr, 73
b. al-Qāsim, Zaydī Imām, 96
b. Sulaymān (757/1356), Mahdali Sultan of Kilwa, 132
b. Sulaymān (791/1389), Mahdali Sultan of Kilwa, 132
Ḥamdānid, 85
Hāshimite Sharīf, 118
Mukramid, 112
Ṭāhirid, 168
Ḥusayn Fatḥ Shāh, Jalāl al-Dīn, ruler of Bengal, 307
Ḥusayn Kāmil, House of Muḥammad 'Alī, 83
al-Ḥusayn al-Mahdī, Zaydī Imām, 96
al-Ḥusayn al-Manṣūr, Zaydī Imām, 97
Ḥusayn Qulī, Qājār, 285

Ḥusayn Shāh
Nāṣir al-Dīn, Sultan of Kashmīr, 310
Sharqī, 314
Hūshang, Yazīdī Sharwān Shāh, 141
Hūshang Shāh (Alp Khān), Sultan of Mālwa, 316

Ibn al-Mu'tazz al-Murtaḍā al-Muntaṣif, 'Abbāsid caliph in Baghdad, 6
Ibrāhīm
I and II, 'Ādil Shāhīs, 325
I and II, Aghlabids, 31
I and II, Ḥafṣids, 45
II, Lōdī Delhi Sultan, 301
I and II, Musāfirids, 148
I and II, Qaramān Oghullarï, 232
I, II and III, Ramaḍān Oghullarï, 237
I and II, Yazīdī Sharwān Shāhs, 141
'Abbāsid caliph in Cairo, 7
('Abdallāh) b. 'Abdallāh, Ziyādid, 99
Afshārid, 281
Arslan Khān Ulugh Sulṭān al-Salāṭīn Nuṣrat al-Dunyā wa 'l-Dīn, Qarakhānid, 182
b. Abī Bakr, Almoravid ruler in Sijilmāsa, 37
b. Abī Bakr, Niẓām al-Dīn, Artuqid, 194
b. Aḥmad, Sayfī of Bornu, 127
b. Aḥmad (Hārūn), Qarakhānid, 182
b. Ḥusayn, Arslan Khān, Qarakhānid, 183
b. Idrīs, Sayfī of Bornu, 127
b. al-Mahdī, 'Abbāsid caliph in Baghdad, 6
b. Muḥammad (449/1057), Qarakhānid, 182
b. Muḥammad, Ziyādid, 99
b. al-Muqtadir, 'Abbāsid caliph in Baghdad, 6
b. Naṣr, Qarakhānid, 183
b. Sökmen I, Artuqid, 194
b. Sulaymān, Qarakhānid, 182
b. Tāshufīn, Almoravid, 37
b. 'Uthmān, Sultan of Kanem, 126
Barīd Shāhī, 324
Ghaznawid, 296
Ghiyāth al-Dīn, Jāndār Oghullarï, 229
Ḥamdānid, 85
Kanembu Shehu of Bornu, 127
Khān of Kazan, 259
Mahdali Sultan of Kilwa, 133
Marīnid, 41
Menteshe Oghullarï, 222
Mughal, 331
Muḥtājid, 177
Nāṣir al-Dīn, ruler of Bengal, 306
Niẓām Shāhī, 326
Ottoman, 239
Pasha of Egypt, 82
Quṭb Shāhī, 328
Shams al-Dīn, Sharqī, 314
Shehu of Dikwa, 128
Sīmjūrid, 175
Tāj al-Dīn, Jāndār Oghullarï, 229
Tamghach (Tabghach) Bughra Khān, Ibrāhīm, Qarakhānid, 181
Tamghach (Tabghach) Khān (536/1141), Qarakhānid, 182
Tīmūrid, 270
Umayyad caliph, 3
'Uqaylid, 91
Yu'firid, 100
Ẓahīr al-Dīn, Sökmenid, 197
Ibrāhīm Kabayao, King of Songhay, 124
Ibrāhīm Khān III, Sūrī Delhi Sultan, 301
Ibrāhīm Nikale b. Biri, Sultan of Kanem, 126
Ibrāhīm Pasha, House of Muḥammad 'Alī, 83
Ibrāhīm Shāh
I Qadïr Khān, Rukn al-Dīn, Khaljī Delhi Sultan, 300
Sultan of Kashmīr, 310
Idrīs
II, Almohad, 39
I, disputant for authority in Morocco, 39
I, II and III, Ḥammūdids, 16
I and II, Idrīsids, 25
'Abbāsid caliph in Cairo, 7
b. Dāwūd, Sultan of Kanem, 126
b. Ibrāhīm Nikale, Sultan of Kanem, 126
Idrīs Alawma, Sayfī of Bornu, 127
Idrīs Katagarmabe, Sayfī of Bornu, 127
Il Arslan
Khwārazm Shāh, 179
Nūr al-Dīn, Zangid, 190
Il Ghāzī I and II, Artuqids, 194
Ilbasan, White Horde Khan, 252
Iltutmish, Shams al-Dīn, Mu'izzī Delhi Sultan, 300
Ilyās
Fakhr al-Dīn, Ṣarukhān Oghullarï, 220
Ḥusām al-Dīn, Ḥamīd Oghullarï, 226
Muẓaffar al-Dīn or Shujā' al-Dīn, Menteshe Oghullarï, 222
Ilyās Shāh, Shams al-Dīn, ruler of Bengal, 307
Ilyasa'
b. Muḥammad, Ilyāsid, 176
Midrārid, 29
'Imād al-Dīn, Hazāraspid, 205
Imām Qulī, Toqay Temürid, 290
Imām 'Umar Dīn, Sultan of Harar, 138
'Imrān b. Muḥammad, Zuray'id, 104
Inanj Beg, Shujā' al-Dīn, Inanj Oghullarï, 223
'Ināyat Giray, Khān of the Crimea, 255
'Ināyat Shāh, Sultan of Acheh, 346
Īrān Shāh, Seljuq of Kirman, 186
'Irāq, Afrīghid Khwārazm Shāh, 178
Irinchinbal (Rinchenpal), Mongol Great Khān, 246
'Īsā
Aydïn Oghullarï, 221
Fāṭimid, 63
al-Malik al-Ẓāhir Majd al-Dīn, Artuqid, 195
'Uqaylid, 91
'Īsā Khān, governor of Mālwa, 316
Isfahsālār, Atabeg of Yazd, 209
Isfandiyār
(Isfendiyār), Mubāriz al-Dīn, Jāndār Oghullarï, 229
Qungrat, 293
Isḥāq
I and II, Askiyas of Songhay, 124

Almoravid, 37
Birzāl of Carmona, 17
Lu'lu'id, 193
Mengüjekid, 217
Najm al-Dīn, Ḥamīd Oghullarï, 226
Qaramān Oghullarï, 232
Ṭāhirid in Baghdad and Iraq, 168
Ziyādid, 99
Isḥāq Beg, Inanj Oghullarï, 223
Isḥāq Chelebi, Muẓaffar al-Dīn, Ṣarukhān Oghullarï, 220
Isḥāq Mullā or Muḥammad Pūlād, Ming, 295
Iskandar
b. Kayūmarth, Bādūspānid, 201
b. Nāmāwar, Bādūspānid, 201
b. Ziyār, Jalāl al-Dawla, Bādūspānid, 201
Qara Qoyunlu, 273
Shībānid, 288
Tīmūrid, 271
Iskandar Muda, posthumously called Makota 'Ālam (Crown of the World), Sultan of Acheh, 346
Islām Giray I, II and III, Khāns of the Crimea, 255
Islām Shāh Sūr, Sūrī Delhi Sultan, 301
Ismā'īl
I and II, Abu 'l-Walīd, Naṣrids, 22
I, II and III, Ṣafawids, 279
II b. Nūḥ II, Sāmānid, 170
'Ādil Shāhī, 325
al-'Ajamī, Nizārī Ismā'īlī, 68
Askiya of Songhay, 124
'Ayn al-Dawla, Dānishmendid, 213
b. Aḥmad I, Sāmānid, 170
b. al-'Azīz Tughtigin, Ayyūbid in Yemen, 73
b. al-Ḥāfiẓ, Fāṭimid, 63
b. al-Qā'im, Fāṭimid, 63
Dhu 'l-Nūnid of Toledo, 18
Ghaznawid, 296
Kamāl al-Dīn, Jāndār Oghullarï, 229
Khwārazm Shāh, 178
Lu'lu'id, 193
Mahdali Sultan of Kilwa, 133
Musāfirid, 148
al-Mutawakkil, Zaydī Imām, 97
Najm al-Dīn, Nizārī Ismā'īlī, 68
Niẓām Shāhī, 326
Shams al-Mulūk, Börid, 189
'Uthmān, Rasūlid, 108
Zangid, 190
Ismā'īl Mukh (ruling title Abu 'l-Fatḥ Ismā'īl Shāh Nāṣir al-Dīn), Bahmanid, 319
Ismā'īl Pasha, House of Muḥammad 'Alī, 83
Ismā'īl al-Samīn, 'Alawid Sharīf, 53
Ismā'īl Shāh, Sultan of Kashmīr, 310
Ispan, Qara Qoyunlu, 273
'Iwaḍ, Ḥusām al-Dīn (ruling title Ghiyāth al-Dīn), governor of Bengal, 306
'Izz al-Dīn Karmān, Mihrabānid Malik, 211

? Jabbār Berdi (or Yeremferden), Golden Horde Khān, 253
Jadu, later Muẓaffar Shams al-Dīn, ruler of Bengal, 307
Ja'far
Aq Qoyunlu, 275
b. Muḥammad, Kalbid, 33
b. al-Mu'taḍid, 'Abbāsid caliph in Baghdad, 6
b. al-Mu'taṣim, 'Abbāsid caliph in Baghdad, 6
Bāwandid Ispahbadh, 164
Tāj al-Dawla, Kalbid, 33
Zand, 283
Zaydī Imām, 96
Jahān Pahlawān Muḥammad, Eldigüzid, 199
Jahān Shāh
(Pòtjut Auk), Sultan of Acheh, 346
Qara Qoyunlu, 273
Jahāndār, Mughal, 331
Jahāngīr
Aq Qoyunlu, 275
b. 'Azīz, Bādūspānid, 202
b. Kāwūs, Bādūspānid, 201–2
b. Muḥammad, Bādūspānid, 201
Mughal, 331
Jāhir, Kalbid, 33
Jahwar, Jahwarid of Cordova, 18
Jalāl al-Dīn, Golden Horde Khān, 252
Jalāl Khān (ruling title Aḥmad Shāh (II), Quṭb al-Dīn), Sultan of Gujarāt, 312
Jalāl Shāh, Sūrī ruler of Bengal, 308
Jalīl, Sultan of Kanem, 126
Jambek (Jānī Beg), Batu'id, 252
Jamshīd
Āl Bū Sa'īd, 137
Sultan of Kashmīr, 310
Jān 'Alī, Khān of Kazan and Qāsimov, 259, 261
Jānay, Khān of Qāsimov, 261
Jānī Beg
Arghūn, 329
(Jambek), Batu'id, 252
Jānī Beg Giray, Khān of the Crimea, 255
Jānī Muḥammad, Toqay Temürid, 290
Jawhar, Fāṭimid general, 62
Jawhar al-'Ālam Shāh, Sultan of Acheh, 346
Jawhar al-Mu'aẓẓamī, Ṣulayḥid regent, 102
Jaysh, Ṭūlūnid, 60
Jayyāsh, Najāḥid, 101
Jibrā'īl, Qarakhānid, 181
Jijaghatu Toq Temür, Mongol Great Khān, 246
Jil, Sultan of Kanem, 126
al-Julandā, first Ibāḍī Imām in Oman, 111
Junayd, Aydïn Oghullarï, 221
Justān
II, III and IV, Justānids, 145
I and II, Musāfirids, 148

Kade
b. Dunama, Sultan of Kanem, 126
b. Idrīs, Sultan of Kanem, 126
b. 'Uthmān, Sultan of Kanem, 126
Kāfūr al-Lābī, Ikhshīdid, 62
Kalīm Allāh, Bahmanid, 319
Kām Bakhsh, Mughal, 331
Kāmrān
Mughal, 331
Sadōzay, 341

Kanafa, King of Songhay, 124
Karīm Berdi, Golden Horde Khān, 252
Kathīr, 'Uqaylid, 91
Kawkaw, Askiya of Songhay, 124
Kāwūs
 b. Ashraf, Bādūspānid, 201
 b. Kayūmarth, Bādūspānid, 202
Kay Kāwūs, Bādūspānid, 201
 I and II, 'Izz al-Dīn, Seljuqs of Rūm, 213
 Rukn al-Dīn, ruler of Bengal, 306
 Yazīdī Sharwān Shāh, 141
 Ziyārid, 166
Kay Khusraw
 I, II and III, Seljuqs of Rūm, 213
 b. Yazdagird, Rukn al-Dawla, Bāwandid Ispahbadh, 165
 Bādūspānid, 201
Kay Qubādh
 I, II and III, Seljuqs of Rūm, 213
 Mu'izz al-Dīn, Mu'izzī Delhi Sultan, 300
 Yazīdī Sharwān Shāh, 141
Kayūmarth
 b. Bahman, Bādūspānid, 202
 b. Bīsutūn, Bādūspānid, 201
 Shams al-Dīn, Mu'izzī Delhi Sultan, 300
Kebek
 (Köpek), Chaghatayid, 248
 Golden Horde Khān, 252
Khalaf
 Bahā' al-Dawla, Naṣrid Malik of Sistan, 211
 Khalafid Ṣaffārid, 172
 Sultan of Harar, 138
Khālid
 I and II, Ḥafṣids, 45
 b. 'Abd al-'Azīz, Āl Su'ūd, 116
 b. Sulaymān, Shīrāzī Sultan of Kilwa, 132
 b. Su'ūd I, Āl Su'ūd, 116
 b. Yazīd, precursor of the Yazīdī Sharwān Shahs, 140
Khalīfa
 b. Barghash, Āl Bū Sa'id, 137
 b. Kharūb, Āl Bū Sa'id, 137
Khalīl
 I and II, Sharwān Shāhs, 141
 Ghars al-Dīn, Dulghadïr Oghullarï, 238
 Ghars al-Dīn, Ramaḍān Oghullarï, 237
 Khān of Kazan, 259
Khalīl Khān (ruling title Muẓaffar Shāh II), Sultan of Gujarāt, 312
Khalīl Sulṭān, Tīmūrid, 270
Khamīs, 'Uqaylid, 91
Khashram Aḥmad, ruler of Lakz, 143
Khayr al-Dīn Barbarossa, 45
Khayrān al-Ṣaqlabī, of Almería, 17, 20
Khiḍr
 Aydïn Oghullarï, 221
 Batu'id, 252
 Qarakhānid, 181
 Sinān al-Dīn, Tekke Oghullarï, 226
Khiḍr Beg, Ḥamīd Oghullarï, 226
Khiḍr Khān
 Bahādur Shāh, Ghiyāth al-Dīn, Sūrī governor and then ruler of Bengal, 308
 Rāyat-i A'lā, Sayyid ruler of Delhi, 301
Khiḍr Shāh, Ṣarukhān Oghullarï, 220
Khumārawayh, Ṭūlūnid, 60
Khurshīd I and II, Dābūyid Ispahbadhs, 162
Khūshchihr, Shaddādid, 151
Khusraw Fīrūz
 Būyid, 154–5
 Justānid, 145
Khusraw Khān Barwārī, usurper in Delhi, 300
Khusraw Malik, Ghaznawid, 296
Khusraw Shāh
 Justānid, 145
 Mu'izz al-Dawla, Ghaznawid, 296
Khwāja 'Alī
 Nizārī Ismā'īlī, 68
 Sarbadārid, 269
Khwāja-yi Jahān Aḥmad Ayāz, Tughluqid rebel, 300
Khwurshāh, Rukn al-Dīn, Nizārī Ismā'īlī, 203
Kirmān Shāh, Seljuq of Kirman, 186
Kiyā Buzurg, Nizārī Ismā'īlī, 203
Köchkunju Muḥammad, Shïbānid, 288
Köchü, White Horde Khān, 252
Könchek, Chaghatayid, 248
Köpek (or Kebek), Chaghatayid, 248
Körp Arslan, 'Alā' al-Dīn, Aḥmadīlī, 198
Kosoy (or Kosay) Muslim Dam, King of Songhay, 124
Küchük Muḥammad, Golden Horde Khān, 253
Kure Gana, Sultan of Kanem, 126
Kure Kura, Sultan of Kanem, 126
Kuthayyir b. Aḥmad, commander in Sistan, 172

Labīb al-Ṣaqlabī, ruler in Valencia, 19
Langar, 'Izz al-Dīn, Atabeg of Yazd, 209
Lashkarī, Hāshimid of Darband, 143
al-Layth, Laythid Ṣaffārid, 172
Layth, Menteshe Oghullarï, 222
Luqmān, Il Khānid, 250
Luṭf 'Alī, Zand, 283
Luṭf Allāh, Sarbadārid, 269
Luṭfī, Bey of Alanya, 227
Lu'lu'
 Lu'lu'id Atabeg, 193
 regent in Aleppo and northern Syria for the Ḥamdānids, 85

Ma'add
 Abu 'l-Ḥasan al-Zahir, Fāṭimid, 63
 Abū Tamīm al-Mustanṣir, Fāṭimid, 63
Maghā I, Keita of Mali, 122
Maḥammad al-Shaykh
 al-Aṣghar or al-Ṣaghīr, Sa'did Sharīf, 50
 al-Ma'mūn, Sa'did Sharīf, 50
 b. Muḥammad al-Mahdi, Sa'did Sharīf, 50
Maharājā Lela Mĕlayu (or Aḥmad Shāh), Sultan of Acheh, 346
Mahdī
 Justānid, 145
 Mahdid, 107
al Mahdī
 'Abbāsid caliph in Baghdad, 6
 Fāṭimid, 63
Mahendra Deva, ruler of Bengal, 307

Maḥmūd
I and II, Ottomans, 239–40
I and II, Seljuqs in Persia and Iraq, 185
b. Aḥmad, vassal of the Khwārazm Shāh and then of Küchlüg, Qarakhānid, 183
b. Dāwūd, Ramaḍān Oghullarï, 237
b. Ḥusayn, Toghan Khān, Qarakhānid, 183
b. Zangī, Zangid ruler in Aleppo and then Damascus, 190
Badr al-Dīn, Qaramān Oghullarï, 232
Börid, 189
Ghaznawid, 296
Ghiyāth al-Dīn
Ghūrid, 298
Tughluqid, 300
Ḥusaynid Bey, 55
Jalāl al-Dīn
Mihrabānid Malik of Sistan, 211
ruler of Bengal, 306
Zangid, 190
Jalāl al-Dunyā wa 'l-Dīn, Sulṭān Shāh, Anūshtiginid Khwārazm Shāh, 179
Jalāyirid, 267
(Maḥmūdak), Khān of Kazan, 259
Majd al-Dīn (Badr al-Dīn), Bey of Alanya, 227
al-Malik al-Mu'aẓẓam Mu'izz al-Dīn, Zangid, 190
al-Malik al-Qāhir Nāṣir al-Dīn, Zangid, 190
al-Malik al-Ṣāliḥ
Nāṣir al-Dīn, Artuqid, 194
Shams al-Dīn, Artuqid, 195
Mirdāsid, 66
Nāṣir al-Dīn
Chobān Oghullarï, 231
Malik al-Sharq, governor of Bengal, 306
Qarakhānid, 181–2
Rukn al-Dīn, Naṣrid Malik of Sistan, 211
Shaddādid, 151
Shihāb al-Dīn, Naṣrid Malik of Sistan, 211
Tāj al-Dīn Oghullarï, 236
Tekke Oghullarï, 226
Tīmūrid, 270
Ṭoghrïl Qara Khān, Niẓām al-Dawla, Qarakhānid, 182
Yazīdī Sharwān Shāh, 141
Maḥmūd Dāmghān Shāh, Nāṣir al-Dīn, Sultan of Ma'bar, 318
Maḥmūd Ghazan (Ghāzān) I, Il Khānid, 250
Maḥmūd Gokaltāsh, Arghūn, 329
Maḥmūd Khān (ruling title Maḥmūd Shāh (I) Khaljī), Sultan of Mālwa, 316
Maḥmūd Shāh
II, Khaljī Sultan of Mālwa, 316
I, Nāṣir al-Dīn, Mu'izzī Sultan of Delhi, 300
II, Nāṣir al-Dīn, Tughluqid Sultan of Delhi, 301
I, II and III, Sultans of Gujarāt, 312
Abu 'l-Muẓaffar Nāṣir al-Dīn, ruler of Bengal, 307
Atabeg of Yazd, 209
Bahmanid, 319
Ghiyāth al-Dīn, ruler of Bengal, 307
Inju, Sharaf al-Dīn, Inju'id, 266
Nāṣir al-Dīn, ruler of Bengal, 307
Sadōzay, 341
Sharqī, 314
Sultan of Acheh (1287/1870), 346
(Tuanku Raja), Sultan of Acheh (1173–95/1760–81), 346
Mai Cimola, Fulani, 130
Mai Cinaka, Fulani, 130
Mai Katuru, Fulani, 130
Mai Turare, Fulani, 130
Mai Wurno, Fulani, 130
Majd al-Dīn' Muẓaffar, Nizārī Ismā'īlī, 68
Majīd, Āl Bū Sa'id, 137
Mākān, Daylamī commander, 176
Makota 'Ālam (Iskandar Muda), Sultan of Acheh, 346
Malāq Ādam, Sultan of Harar, 138
al-Malik al-'Ādil
I and II, Ayyūbids in Damascus, 70
I, III and IV, Ayyūbids in Diyār Bakr, 72
II Abū Bakr, Ayyūbid in Egypt, 70
VI Khalaf b. Muḥammad, Ayyūbid in Diyār Bakr, 73
I Muḥammad or Aḥmad, Ayyūbid in Aleppo and Egypt, 70–1
V Sulaymān I, Ayyūbid in Diyār Bakr, 73
al-'Abbās or Ya'qūb, 'Abbāsid caliph and Mamlūk sultan, 77
'Abdallāh Jakam, Burjī Mamlūk, 77
Baydarā, Badr al-Dīn, Baḥrī Mamlūk, 76
Kitbughā, Zayn al-Dīn, Baḥrī Mamlūk, 76
Salāmish or Süleymish, Badr al-Dīn, Baḥrī Mamlūk, 76
Ṭūmān Bay I, Sayf al-Dīn, Burjī Mamlūk, 78
al-Malik al-Afḍal
al-'Abbās, Rasūlid, 108
'Alī, Ayyūbid in Damascus, 70
Muḥammad, Ayyūbid in Ḥamāt, 72
Muḥammad, Rasūlid, 108
Malik al-Jibāl, Sūrī b. Ḥusayn I, Ghūrid, 298
Malik al-Mulūk ('Alī), Barīd Shāhī, 324
Malik Arslan, Dulghadïr Oghullarï, 238
Malik Arslan (or Arslan Shāh), Ghaznawid, 296
al-Malik al-Ashraf
II Aḥmad, Ayyūbid in Diyār Bakr, 73
I Mūsā, Ayyūbid in Damascus and Diyār Bakr, 72
II Mūsā, Ayyūbid in Egypt, 70
Barsbay, Burjī Mamlūk, 77
Ināl al-'Alā'ī al-Ẓāhirī, Burjī Mamlūk, 78
Ismā'īl I, II and III, Rasūlids, 108
Jānbulāṭ, Burjī Mamlūk, 78
Khalīl, Ṣalāḥ al-Dīn, Baḥrī Mamlūk, 76
Kūjūk, 'Alā' al-Dīn, Baḥrī Mamlūk, 76
Mūsā, Ayyūbid in Ḥimṣ, 71
Mūsā, Baḥrī Mamlūk, 76
Qānṣawh II al-Ghawrī, Burj Mamlūk, 78
Qāyit Bay al-Ẓāhirī, Burjī Mamlūk, 78
Sha'bān II, Nāṣir al-Dīn, Baḥrī Mamlūk, 77
Ṭūmān Bay II, Burjī Mamlūk, 78
'Umar II, Rasūlid, 108
al-Malik al-Awḥad Ayyūb, Ayyūbid in Diyār Bakr, 72

al-Malik al-ʿAzīz
I ʿUthmān, Ayyūbid in Egypt, 70
Muḥammad, Ayyūbid in Aleppo, 71
Tughtigin, Ayyūbid in Yemen, 73
Yūsuf, Jamāl al-Dīn, Burjī Mamlūk, 77
Malik Dhu ʾl-Nūn, Dānishmendid, 213
Malik Hazārasp, Nuṣrat al-Dīn, Hazāraspid, 205
Malik Ibrahīm, Shams al-Dīn, Dānishmendid, 213
Malik Ismāʿīl, Shams al-Dīn, Dānishmendid, 213
al-Malik al-Kāmil
II and III, Ayyūbids in Diyār Bakr, 72
I Muḥammad, Ayyūbid in Damascus and Egypt, 70
(al-ʿĀdil Aḥmad), Ayyūbid in Diyār Bakr, 73
Khalīl II, Ayyūbid in Diyār Bakr, 73
Shaʿbān I, Sayf al-Dīn, Baḥrī Mamlūk, 77
Sunqur al-Ashqar, Sayf al-Dīn, Baḥrī Mamlūk, 76
al-Malik al-Manṣūr
I and II Muḥammad, Ayyūbids in Ḥamāt, 71–2
Abd al-ʿAzīz, ʿIzz al-Dīn, Burjī Mamlūk, 77
ʿAbd al-Wahhāb, Tāj al-Dīn, Ṭāhirid of Yemen, 110
ʿAbdallāh, Rasūlid, 108
Abū Bakr, Sayf al-Dīn, Baḥrī Mamlūk, 76
ʿAlī I and II, ʿAlāʾ al-Dīn, Baḥrī Mamlūks, 76–7
Ibrāhīm, Ayyūbid in Ḥimṣ, 71
Lāchīn or Lājīn al-Ashqar, Ḥusām al-Dīn, Baḥrī Mamlūk, 76
Muḥammad II, Ṣalāḥ al-Dīn, Baḥrī Mamlūk, 77
Muḥammad, Ayyūbid in Egypt, 70
Qalāwūn al-Alfī, Abu ʾl-Maʿālī Sayf al-Dīn, Baḥrī Mamlūk, 76
ʿUmar I, Rasūlid, 108
ʿUthmān, Fakhr al-Dīn, Burjī Mamlūk, 77
al-Malik al-Masʿūd
Rasūlid, 108
Yūsuf, Ayyūbid in Yemen, 73
al-Malik al-Muʾayyad
Aḥmad III, Shihāb al-Dīn, Burjī Mamlūk, 78
Dāwūd, Rasūlid, 108
al-Ḥusayn, Rasūlid, 108
Shaykh al-Maḥmūdī al-Ẓāhirī, Sayf al-Dīn, Burjī Mamlūk, 77
al-Malik al-Muʿaẓẓam
ʿĪsā, Sharaf al-Dīn, Ayyūbid in Damascus, 70
Sulaymān, Ayyūbid in Yemen, 73
Tūrān Shāh, Ayyūbids in Damascus, Diyār Bakr, Egypt and Yemen, 70–3
al-Malik al-Muʿizz Aybak al-Turkumānī, ʿIzz al-Dīn, Baḥrī Mamlūk, 76
al-Malik al-Mujāhid
ʿAlī, Rasūlid, 108
ʿAlī, Shams al-Dīn, Ṭāhirid of Yemen, 110
Sanjar, ʿAlam al-Dīn, Baḥrī Mamlūk, 76
Shīrkūh II, Ayyūbid in Ḥimṣ, 71
Malik Mujāhid Ghāzī, Dānishmendid, 213
al-Malik al-Muwaḥḥid ʿAbdallāh, Ayyūbid in Diyār Bakr, 72
al-Malik al-Muẓaffar
II and III Maḥmūd, Ayyūbids in Ḥamāt, 72
I ʿUmar, Ayyūbid in Ḥamāt, 71
Aḥmad II, Burjī Mamlūk, 77
Baybars II al-Jāshnakīr, Rukn al-Dīn (Burjī), Baḥrī Mamlūk, 76
Ghāzī, Ayyūbid in Diyār Bakr, 72
Ḥājjī I and II, Ṣalāḥ al-Dīn, Baḥrī Mamlūk, 77
Quṭuz al-Muʿizzī, Sayf al-Dīn, Baḥrī Mamlūk, 76
Yūsuf I, Shams al-Dīn, Rasūlid, 108
al-Malik al-Nāṣir
II Dāwūd, Ayyūbid in Damascus, 70
I Ṣalāḥ al-Dīn (Saladin), Ayyūbid in Diyār Bakr, 72
I and II Yūsuf, Ayyūbids in Aleppo, Damascus and Egypt, 70–1
Aḥmad I, Shihāb al-Dīn, Baḥrī Mamlūk, 76
Aḥmad b. Ismāʿīl I, Rasūlid, 108
Aḥmad b. Yaḥyā, Rasūlid, 108
Ayyūb, Ayyūbid in Yemen, 73
Faraj, Nāṣir al-Dīn, Burjī Mamlūk, 77
al-Ḥasan, Nāṣir al-Dīn, Baḥrī Mamlūk, 77
Muḥammad IV, Burjī Mamlūk, 78
Muḥammad I, Nāṣir al-Dīn, Baḥrī Mamlūk, 76
Qilij Arslan, Ayyūbid in Ḥamāt, 71
al-Malik al-Qāhir Muḥammad, Ayyūbid in Ḥimṣ, 71
Malik Qaranful Mubārak Shāh, Sharqī, 314
Malik Rājā Aḥmad Fārūqī, Fārūqī, 322
al-Malik al-Saʿīd Baraka or Berke Khān, Nāṣir al-Dīn, Baḥrī Mamlūk, 76
al-Malik al-Ṣāliḥ
I and II, Ayyūbids in Damascus, 70–1
III Abū Bakr, Ayyūbid in Diyār Bakr, 73
II Ayyūb, Ayyūbid in Diyār Bakr and Egypt, 70, 72
IV Khalīl, Ayyūbid in Diyār Bakr, 73
Ismāʿīl, ʿImād al-Dīn, Baḥrī Mamlūk, 76
(al-Manṣūr Ḥājjī II), Ṣalāḥ al-Dīn, Baḥrī Mamlūk, 77
al-Muʾayyad Ismāʿīl, Ayyūbid in Ḥamāt, 72
Muḥammad III, Nāṣir al-Dīn, Burjī Mamlūk, 77
Ṣalāḥ al-Dīn, Baḥrī Mamlūk, 77
Malik Sarwar, Khwāja-yi Jahān, Sharqī, 314
Malik Shāh
I, II and III, Seljuqs in Persia and Iraq, 185–6
(Abū Manṣūr, ʿAlī al-Dīn), Saltuqid, 218
Mengüjekid, 217
(Shāhānshāh), Seljuq of Rūm, 213
Malik Yaghībasan, Dānishmendid, 213
al-Malik al-Ẓāfir ʿĀmir II, Ṣalāḥ al-Dīn, Ṭāhirid of Yemen, 110
al-Malik al-Ẓāhir
Barqūq al-Yalbughāwī, Sayf al-Dīn, Mamlūk, 77
Baybars I al-Bunduqdārī, Rukn al-Dīn, Baḥrī Mamlūk, 76

Chaqmaq or Jaqmaq, Sayf al-Dīn, Burjī Mamlūk, 77
Khushqadam, Sayf al-Dīn, Burjī Mamlūk, 78
Qānṣawh I, Burjī Mamlūk, 78
Ṭāṭār, Sayf al-Dīn, Burjī Mamlūk, 77
Timurbughā, Burjī Mamlūk, 78
Yaḥyā, Rasūlid, 108
Yalbay, Sayf al-Dīn, Burjī Mamlūk, 78
al-Malik al-Ẓāhir Ghāzī, Ayyūbid in Aleppo, 71
Mallā, Ming, 295
Mallū, 'Ādil Shāhī, 325
Mallū Khān, governor of Mālwa, 316
Māmā Khātūn, Saltuqid, 218
Mamlān or Muḥammad I and II, Rawwādids, 150
al-Ma'mūn, 'Abbāsid caliph in Baghdad, 6
Ma'mūn I and II, Ma'mūnids Khwārazm Shāhs, 178
Mamūq, Khān of Kazan, 259
Ma'n
'Alam al-Dīn, Ma'n Amīr, 81
Hamdānid, 106
of the Banū Ṣumādiḥ of Almería, 17
Zayn al-Dīn, Ma'n Amīr, 81
Manādhar, Justānid, 145
Manī', Numayrid, 93
Mansā Abū Bakr I and II, Keitas of Mali, 122
Mansā Gaw or Qū, Keita of Mali, 122
Mansā Kamba or Qanba or Qāsā, Keita of Mali, 122
Mansā Khalīfa, Keita of Mali, 122
Mansā Maghan I, II and III, Keitas of Mali, 122
Mansā Mamadu or Muḥammad, Keita of Mali, 122
Mansā Mari Dyāta or Mārī Jāṭa II, Keita of Mali, 122
Mansā Mūsā I, II and III, Keitas of Mali, 122
Mansā Qanba or Qāsā *see* Mansā Kamba
Mansā Sulaymān, Keita of Mali, 122
Mansā Ulī or Ule, Keita of Mali, 122
Mansā Wātī, Keita of Mali, 122
Manṣūr
I and II, Sāmānids, 170
Abū Naṣr Murtaḍā al-Dawla, Ḥamdānid, 85
Afrīghid Khwārazm Shāh, 178
Arslan Khān, Nūr al-Dawla, Qarakhānid, 181
b. 'Abd al-Malik, Hāshimid of Darband, 143
b. Maymūn, Hāshimid of Darband, 143
Marwānid, 89
Mazyadid, 87
Muḥtājid, 177
Qāḍī, ruler of Valencia, 19
Sharaf al-Dawla, Qarakhānid, 182
Shihāb Amir, 82
al-Manṣūr
'Abbāsid caliph in Baghdad, 6
b. Abī 'Āmir, Almanzor, Ḥājib in Spain, 12–13
b. al-'Azīz, Fāṭimid, 63
b. al-Musta'lī, Fāṭimid, 63
b. al-Mustarshid, 'Abbāsid caliph in Baghdad, 6
b. al-Ẓāhir, 'Abbāsid caliph in Baghdad, 7
Fāṭimid, 63
Ḥammādid, 35
Najāḥid, 101
Saba', Ṣulayḥid, 102
'Uqaylid, 91
Zīrid governor of the Maghrib, 35
Manṣūr Shāh
'Alā' al-Dīn, Sultan of Acheh (987/1579), 346
Sultan of Acheh (1252/1836), 346
Manūchihr
I, II and III, Yazīdī Sharwān Shāhs, 140
Shaddādid, 151
Ziyārid, 166
Maqṣūd Giray, Khān of the Crimea, 256
Mardāwīj, Ziyārid, 166
Marhum Tuha (Abdul Jalilul Akbar), Sultan of Brunei, 353
Mari Sun Dyāta (Mārī Jāṭa) I, Keita of Mali, 122
Marwān
I, Umayyad caliph, 3
II, al-Ḥimār, Umayyad caliph, 3
Marzubān
I and II, Musāfirids, 148
Abū Kālījār 'Imād al-Dīn, Būyid, 155
Abū Kālījār Ṣamṣām al-Dawla, Būyid, 155
b. Abī Shujā' Sulṭān al-Dawla, Būyid, 155
Justānid, 145
Shaddādid, 151
Mas Ngabehi Sutavijaya Senapati, ruler of Mataram, 348
Masīḥ Mīrzā, Aq Qoyunlu, 275
Masta
b. Muḥammad Amīn Kiari, Mai of Dikwa, 128
b. Shehu Sanda Mandarama, Mai of Dikwa, 128
Mas'ūd
I, II and III, Ghaznawids, 296
I and II, 'Izz al-Dīn, Zangids, 190
I, II and III, Seljuqs of Rūm, 213
b. Ḥsan, Qarakhānid, 182
b. Muḥammad, Qarakhānid, 181
Fakhr al-Dīn, Ghūrid, 298
al-Malik al-Ẓāhir, Zangid, 190
Mazrū'ī, 136
Menteshe Oghullarï, 222
Muhadhdhib al-Dīn, Parwāna Oghullarï, 230
Seljuq in Persia and Iraq, 185
Tīmūrid, 270
Wajīh al-Dīn, Sarbadārid, 269
al-Mas'ūd, Zuray'id, 104
Mas'ūd Jānī
'Alā' al-Dīn, governor of Bengal, 306
Jalāl al-Dīn, governor of Bengal, 306
Mas'ūd Khān, Sultan of Mālwa, 316
Mas'ūd Shāh
'Alā' al-Dīn, Mu'izzī, 300
Jalāl al-Dīn, Inju'id, 266
Mawdūd
Ghaznawid, 296
al-Malik al-Mas'ūd Rukn al-Dīn, Artuqid, 194

Quṭb al-Dīn, Zangid, 190
Maymūn
b. Aḥmad, Hāshimid of Darband, 143
b. Manṣūr, Hāshimid of Darband, 143
Ibn Thaqiyya, al-Amīr, Midrārid, 29
Māzyār, Bāwandid Ispahbadh, 164
Medemīn (Muḥammad Amīn, Abu 'l-Ghāzi), Qungrat, 293
Megat Iskandar Shāh, ruler of Malacca, 344
Meḥemmed *see* Muḥammad, Ottomans, 239
Menelik, Emperor of Ethiopia, 138
Mengli Giray, Khān of the Crimea, 255–6
Mengü
(Möngke) Temür, Batu'id, 252
(Töde Möngke), Batu'id, 252
Mengü Temür, Salghurid, 207
Mengübirti, Jalāl al-Dīn, Anūshtiginid Khwārazm Shāh, 179
Mengüjek Aḥmad, Mengüjekid, 217
Menteshe Beg, Menteshe Oghullarï, 222
Midrār (al-Muntaṣir), Midrārid, 29
Mihr Mardān, Bāwandid Ispahbadh, 164
?Mingīrinī *see* Mengübirti, Jalāl al-Dīn
Mīr Ja'far Muhammad Khān, Nawwāb of Bengal, 335
Mīr Maḥbūb 'Alī I and II, Niẓāms of Hyderabad, 339
Mīr Qāsim 'Alī, Nawwāb of Bengal, 335
Mīr 'Uthmān 'Alī Khān Bahādur Fatḥ Jang, Niẓām of Hyderabad, 339
Mīrān Mubārak Khān I, Fārūqī, 322
Mīrān Muḥammad Shāh I and II, Fārūqīs, 322
Mīrān Shāh, Jalāl al-Dīn, Tīmūrid, 270
Mīrzā 'Ādil Khān I, Fārūqī, 322
Mīrzā 'Alī, Barīd Shāhī, 324
Mīrzā Ḥaydar Dughlat, Mughal prince in Kashmīr, 310
Mīrzā Maḥmūd, Nawwāb of Bengal, 335
Mīrzā Walī Amīr Barīd III, Barīd Shāhī, 324
Mit'ab I and II, Āl Rashīd, 120
Miyān Bāyazīd, Bāz Bahādur, ruler of Mālwa, 316
Mö'etüken, son of Chingiz Khāh, 248
Möngke (Mengü)
Mongol Great Khān, 246
Temür, Batu'id, 252
Moyasa Ahmadu, Fulani, 130
al-Mu'addal, Laythid Ṣaffārid, 172
Mu'ādh (Mu'azu, Moyasa) Ahmadu, Fulani, 130
Mu'āwiya I and II, Umayyad caliphs, 3
Mu'azu Ahmadu, Fulani, 130
Mubārak
Qutlughkhānid, 210
Ṣārim al-Dīn, Nizārī Ismā'īlī, 68
Mubārak al-Ṣaqlabī, ruler in Valencia, 19
Mubārak Khwāja, White Horde Khān, 252
Mubārak Shāh
II, Fārūqī, 322
II, Mu'izz al-Dīn, Sayyid ruler of Delhi, 301
Chaghatayid, 248
Fakhr al-Dīn, ruler of Bengal, 307
Fakhr al-Dīn, Sultan of Ma'bar, 318
Quṭb al-Dīn, Khaljī Delhi Sultan, 300
Mubashshir, Nāṣir al-Dawla, ruler of Majorca, 18
Mughāyat Shāh, Iskandar Thāni 'Alā' al-Dīn, Sultan of Acheh, 346
Mughīth al-Dīn (Ṭoghrïl), governor of Bengal, 306
Muhalhil
Annāzid, 159
Mazyadid, 87
Muḥammad
I and II, 'Abbādids of Seville, 17
I–VIII, 'Abd al-Wādids, 43
I and II, Aghlabids, 31
I–V, Alawid Sharīfs, 53
III, Askiya of Songhay, 124
II Fātiḥ ('the Conqueror'), Ottoman, 239
I, Ghiyāth al-Dīn, Eretna Oghullarï, 234
I–VI, Ḥafṣids, 45
I and II, Ḥammūdids of Málaga, 16
I–VIII, Ḥusaynid Beys, 55
I–V, Marīnids, 41
I, Mughīth al-Dunyā wa 'l-Dīn, Seljuq of Kirman, 186
I–XII, Naṣrids, 22
I, II and III, Nizārī Ismā'īlīs, 203
III–V and VI, Ottomans, 239–40
I and II, Qaramān Oghullarï, 232
I and II, Ramaḍān Oghullarï, 237
I and II, Sa'did Sharīfs, 50
II, Seljuq in Persia and Iraq, 186
I and II, Sīmjūrids, 175
I, II and III, Spanish Umayyads, 11
II, Sultan of Harar, 138
I, II and III, Waṭṭāsids, 48
II Benkan, Askiya of Songhay, 124
I Chelebi, Ottoman, 239
II Chelebi, Eretna Oghullarï, 234
V Mubāriz Khān 'Ādil Shāh, Sūrī Delhi Sultan, 301
I, II and III Shāh, Bahmanids, 319
I Tapar, Seljuq in Persia and Iraq, 185
'Abbāsid caliph in Cairo, 7
Afṭasid of Badajoz, 18
(Aḥmad)
Shams al-Dīn, Naṣrid Malik of Sistan, 211
Toghan Khān, Qarakhānid, 181
Amīr of Chaghāniyān, ? Muḥtājid, 177
Amīr of Dir'iyya, Āl Su'ūd, 116
'Annāzid, 159
Arslan Khān, Qarakhānid, 181–2
Arslan Qara Khān Mu'ayyid al-'Adl 'Ayn al-Dawla, Qarakhānid, 181
b. 'Abbās, Ghūrid, 298
b. 'Abdallāh, Āl Rashīd, 120
b. 'Abdallāh, Sultan of Kanem, 126
b. 'Abdallāh, Ṭāhirid of Khurasam, 168
b. 'Abdallāh Ibn Rashīd of Ḥā'il, conqueror of Riyāḍ, 116
b. Abī Bakr, Nabhānī of Pate (875/1470), 134
b. Abī Bakr, Nabhānī of Pate (973/1565), 134
b. Abī Ja'far Muḥammad, ruler of Murcia, 20
b. Abi 'l-Ghārāt, Zuray'id, 104
b. Aḥmad, Afrīghid Khwārazm Shāh, 178

b. Aḥmad, Hāshimid of Darband, 143
b. Aḥmad, Nabhānī of Pate, 134
b. Aḥmad, Yazīdī Sharwān Shāh, 140
b. Aḥmad ʿAtīq, called Mai Turare, Fulani, 130
b. Aḥmad Ibn Ṭāhir, ruler of Murcia, 20
b. ʿAlī b. Yūsuf al-Massūfī, Ibn Ghāniya, governor of the Balearics, 21
b. Amīr Ghāzī, Dānishmendid, 213
b. ʿArafa, ʿAlawid Sharīf, 53
b. Begtimur, al-Malik al-Manṣūr, Sökmenid slave commander, 197
b. Fayṣal I, al-Muṭawwiʿ, vassal governor of Riyāḍ, Āl Suʿūd, 116
b. Hāshim, Hāshimid of Darband, 143
b. Haytham, Yazīdī Sharwān Shāh, 140
b. Ḥusayn al-Rawwādī, Rawwādid, 150
b. Ibrāhīm, Yuʿfirid, 100
b. Ibrāhīm II, ʿĀdil Shāhī, 325
b. Idrīs, Sayfī of Bornu (931/1525), 127
b. Idrīs, Sayfī of Bornu (c.1012/c.1603), 127
b. Idrīs, Sultan of Kanem, 126
b. Idrīs II, al-Muntaṣir, Idrīsid, 25
b. ʿIrāq, Afrīghid Khwārazm Shāh, 178
b. Isḥāq, ruler of the Banū Ghāniya under Almohad suzerainty, 21
b. Isḥāq, Ṭāhirid of Khurasan, 168
b. Ismāʿīl, Nāṣir al-Dīn, Dānishmendid, 213
b. Jaʿfar, Zaydī Imām, 96
b. Kade, Sultan of Kanem, 127
b. Khālid, governor of Armenia, precursor of Sharwān Shahs, 140
b. Khamītūn, Qutlughkhānid, 210
b. Kiwāb, usurper of Mahdali Sultanate of Kilwa, 133
b. al-Manṣūr, ʿAbbāsid caliph in Baghdad, 6
b. Maymūn, Midrārid, 29
b. Muḥammad, called Tambari, Fulani, 130
b. Muḥammad, ruler of Murcia, 20
b. Muḥammad, Sultan of Kanem, 127
b. Musāfir, founder of the Musāfirids, 148
b. al-Musayyab, Abu ʾl-Dhawwād, ʿUqaylid, 91
b. al-Musayyab al-ʿUqaylī, ʿUqaylid, 91
b. al-Mustaẓhir, ʿAbbāsid caliph in Baghdad, 6
b. al-Muʿtaḍid, ʿAbbāsid caliph in Baghdad, 6
b. al-Mutawakkil, Abū ʿAbdallāh al-Muʿtazz, ʿAbbāsid caliph in Baghdad, 6
b. al-Mutawakkil, Abū Jaʿfar al-Muntaṣir, ʿAbbāsid caliph in Baghdad, 6
b. al-Nāṣir, ʿAbbāsid caliph in Baghdad, 7
b. Nāṣir, Sultan of Harar, 138
b. Naṣr, Qarakhānid, 183
b. Rāfiʿ, ʿUqaylid, 91
b. al-Rashīd, Abū Isḥāq al-Muʿtaṣim, ʿAbbāsid caliph in Baghdad, 6
b. al-Rashīd, Abū Mūsā al-Amīn, ʿAbbāsid caliph in Baghdad, 6
b. Sabaʾ, al-Muʿaẓẓam, Zurayʿid, 104
b. Saʿd, Naṣrid, 23
b. Saʿd, Rey Lobo or Lope, ruler of Murcia, 20
b. Saʿid al-Maʿāmirī, Mazrūʿī, 136
b. Sām I, supreme sultan in Ghūr and India, Ghūrid, 298
b. Sārū, Midrārid, 29
b. Sulaymān, al-ʿĀdil, Mahdali Sultan of Kilwa, 132
b. Sulaymān, Nabhānī of Pate, 134
b. Sūrī Shansabānī, Ghūrid, 298
b. Suʿūd II, Āl Suʿūd, 116
b. Ṭāhir II, Ṭāhirid of Khurasan, 168
b. Ṭalāl, Āl Rashīd, 120
b. Tūmart, Almohad, 39
b. ʿUbaydallāh, Ṭāhirid of Baghdad and Iraq, 168
b. ʿUmar, Nabhānī of Pate, 134
b. ʿUthmān, Mazrūʿī, 136
b. Wāsūl al-Fatḥ, al-Shākir, Midrārid, 29
b. al-Wāthiq, ʿAbbāsid caliph in Baghdad, 6
b. Yaʿqūb, Almohad, 39
b. Yazīd, Yazīdī Sharwān Shāh, 140
b. Yuʿfir, Yuʿfirid, 100
b. Yūsuf, Abu ʾl-Fatḥ, Qarakhānid, 182
b. Yūsuf Ibn Hūd, ruler of Murcia, 20
b. Ziyād, Ziyādid, 99
Bānījūrid, 174
Bāwandid Ispahbadh, 164
Birzāl of Carmona, 17
Bughra Khān, Qawām al-Dawla, Qarakhānid, 182
Chaghatayid, 248
Ḍiyāʾ al-Dīn, ʿAlāʾ al-Dīn, Ghūrid, 298
Fāṭimid, 63
Ghaznawid, 296
Ghiyāth al-Dīn, Ghūrid, 298
Ḥamīd al-Dīn al-Manṣūr, Zaydī Imam, 97
Hāshimite Sharīf, 118
Il Khānid, 250
Ilyāsid, 176
Jahwarid of Cordova, 18
Jalāyirid, 267
Kākūyid, 160
Khazrūn of Arcos, 17
Laythid Ṣaffārid, 172
Mazyadid, 87
(Mamlān) I and II, Rawwādids, 150
Maʾmūnid Khwārazm Shāh, 178
Menteshe Oghullarï, 222
al-Muʾayyad, Zaydī Imām, 96
Mubāriz al-Dīn
  Ashraf Oghullarï, 228
  Muẓaffarid, 264
  Tekke Oghullarï, 226
Muḥtājid governor of Khurasan, 177
Muʿīn al-Dīn, Parwāna Oghullarï, 230
Muẓaffar al-Dīn, Salghurid, 207
Nāṣir al-Dīn
  Dulghadïr Oghullarï, 238
  Mihrabānid Malik of Sistan, 211
Nūr al-Dīn, Artuqid, 194
Nuṣrat al-Dīn, Mihrabānid Malik, 211
of the Banū Ṣumādiḥ of Almería, 17
of the Bendahara family, Sultan of Brunei, 353
Pahlawī, 287

Qājār, 285
Qaramānlī, 57
Quṭb al-Dīn
I and III, Mihrabānid Maliks of Sistan, 211
Khwārazm Shāh, 179
Zangid, 190
Quṭb Shāhī, 328
Rustamid, 27
Sājid, 147
Sayf al-Dīn, Ghūrid, 298
Shaddādid, 151
Shams al-Dawla, Börid, 189
Shams al-Dīn
I, Kart, 263
Ghūrid, 298
Inju'id, 266
Mihrabānid Malik of Sistan, 211
Mu'izz al-Dīn, Ghūrid, 298
Ṣāḥib Atā Oghullarï, 225
Shams al-Mulūk, Bādūspānid, 201
Shīrāzī Sultan of Kilwa, 132
Sultan of Kanem (853/1449), 126
Tamghach (Tabghach Khān), Ghiyāth al-Dunyā wa 'l-Dīn, Qarakhānid, 182
Ya'rubid, 113
Muḥammad Abū Bakr al-Ikhshīd, Ikhshīdid, 62
Muḥammad 'Aḍud al-Dawla, Hūdid, 19
Muḥammad 'Aḍud al-Dīn, Salghurid, 207
Muḥammad Afḍal, Bārakzay, 341
Muḥammad 'Alī
Ming, 295
Mu'īn al-Dīn, Nawwāb of Oudh, 337
Pasha, 83
Qājār, 285
Zand, 283
Muḥammad 'Alī Shāh, Ẓahīr al-Dīn, Sultan of Kashmīr, 310
Muḥammad Aliuddin, Sultan of Brunei, 353
Muḥammad Alp Arslan, Seljuq in Persia and Iraq, 185
Muḥammad Amīn
Abu 'l-Ghāzi, called Medemīn, Qungrat, 293
Khān of Kazan, 259
Muḥammad Amīn al-Kānemī, Shehu Laminu, Kanembu Shehu of Bornu, 127
Muḥammad Amīn Kiari, Kanembu Shehu of Bornu, 128
Muḥammad Arslan Khān Sanjar, Tāj al-Dīn, governor of Bengal, 306
Muḥammad Ay Temür, Sarbadārid, 269
Muḥammad A'ẓam, Bārakzay, 341
Muḥammad Bakhtiyār Khaljī, Ikhtiyār al-Dīn, conqueror of Bihār and Bengal, 306
Muḥammad Bāqī, Arghūn, 329
Muḥammad Beg
Inanj Oghullarï, 223
Mubāriz al-Dīn Ghāzī, Aydïn Oghullarï, 221
Muḥammad Bello, called Mai Wurno, Fulani, 130
Muḥammad Berdi Beg, Batu'id, 252
Muḥammad Bolaq, Batu'id, 252
Muḥammad Chakhshadān, Germiyān Oghullarï, 224
Muḥammad Dāmghān Shāh, Ghiyāth al-Dīn, Sultan of Ma'bar, 318
Muḥammad Dāwūd Shāh, Sultan of Acheh, 346
Muḥammad Ergama, Sayf of Bornu, 127
Muḥammad Gao or Kawkaw, Askiya of Songhay, 124
Muḥammad Giray I–IV, Khāns of the Crimea, 255
Muḥammad Hasan
Qājār, 285
regent of Brunei, 353
Sultan of Brunei, 353
Muḥammad Ibn Hūd, ruler of Murcia, 20
Muḥammad Ibn Khazrūn, Khazrūn of Arcos, 17
Muḥammad 'Īsā Tarkhān, Arghūn, 329
Muḥammad 'Izz al-Dīn al-Nāṣir, Zaydī Imām, 96
Muḥammad Jamalul Alam
b. Muhammad Tajuddin, Sultan of Brunei, 353
b. Omar Ali Saifuddin II, Sultan of Brunei, 353
Muḥammad Jāsā, Sultan of Harar, 138
Muḥammad Kanzul Alam, Sultan of Brunei, 353
Muḥammad Karīm Khān, Zand, 283
Muḥammad Khān Sūr, Shams al-Dīn, Sūrī ruler of Bengal, 308
Muḥammad Khudābanda
Öljeytü (Uljāytū), Il Khānid, 250
Ṣafawid, 279
Muḥammad Khudāyār, Ming, 295
Muḥammad al-Maẓlūm, Mahdali Sultan of Kilwa, 133
Muḥammad al-Murtaḍā, Zaydī Imām, 96
Muḥammad al-Mustaḍī', 'Alawid Sharīf, 53
Muḥammad al-Mutawakkil, Zaydī Imām, 97
Muḥammad Nādir, Bārakzay, 341
Muḥammad Nāṣir al-Dīn (Ghāzī Khān Chak), Sultan of Kashmīr, 310
Muḥammad al-Nāṣir al-Hādi al-Mahdī, Zaydī Imām, 97
Muḥammad Nawrūz Beg, Batu'id, 252
Muḥammad Ngileruma, Sayfī of Bornu, 127
Muḥammad Özbeg, Ghiyāth al-Dīn, Batu'id, 252
Muḥammad Pūlād or Isḥāq Mullā, Ming, 295
Muḥammad Qulī, Quṭb Shāhī, 328
Muḥammad Raḥīm
Atalïq, Mangït, 292
Qungrat, 293
Muḥammad Ṣādiq, Zand, 283
Muḥammad Sa'īd Pasha, House of Muḥammad 'Alī, 83
Muḥammad Shāh
III, Nāṣir al-Dīn, Tughluqid Delhi Sultan, 301
IV, Sayyid ruler of Delhi, 301
I and II, Sultans of Gujarāt, 312

II and III, Tughluqid Delhi Sultans, 300
I 'Alī Garshāsp, 'Alā' al-Dīn, Khaljī Delhi Sultan, 300
b. Jawhar al-'Ālam Shāh, Sultan of Acheh, 346
(Bhikan Khān), Sharqī, 314
Mughal, 331
Seljuq of Kirman, 186
Sultan of Kashmīr, 310
(Tuanku Muḥammad), Sultan of Acheh, 346
Muḥammad Shāh Ghūrī (Ghaznī Khān), Sultan of Mālwa, 316
Muḥammad Shāh Sulṭān, Qutlughkhānid, 210
Muḥammad Shībānī, Abu 'l-Fatḥ, Shāh Beg Özbeg, conqueror of Transoxania, 288
Muḥammad Shirān Khān, 'Izz al-Dīn, governor of Bengal, 306
Muḥammad Ṭāhir I and II, Fulani, 130
Muḥammad Tajuddin, Sultan of Brunei, 353
Muḥammad Tawfīq, House of Muḥammad 'Alī, 83
Muḥammad Ture, Askiya of Songhay, 124
Muḥammad 'Umar, Ming, 295
Muḥammad al-Walīd, Sa'did Sharīf, 50
Muḥammad Yaḥya, al-Mutawakkil, Zaydī Imām, 97
Muḥammad Ya'qūb Khān, Bārakzay, 341
Muḥammad Yavuz, Ḥusām al-Dīn, Tāj al-Dīn Oghullarï, 236
Muḥammad Ẓāhir, Bārakzay, 341
Muḥammadī, Aq Qoyunlu, 275
Muḥsin, Ḥammādid, 35
al-Muhtadī, 'Abbāsid caliph in Baghdad, 6
Muhyiddin, Sultan of Brunei, 353
al-Mu'izz
Fāṭimid, 63
Zīrid of Kairouan, 35
Mujāhid
Bahmanid, 319
Mujāhid, 17
ruler of Murcia, 20
al-Mukarram al-Aṣghar, Ṣulayḥid, 102
al-Muktafī, 'Abbāsid caliph in Baghdad, 6
Muley Hácen ('Alī b. Sa'd, Abu 'l-Ḥasan), Naṣrid, 22
Mulḥim
Shihāb Amīr, 82
Yūnus, Ma'n Amīr, 81
al-Mundhir
I and II, Tujībids, 19
b. Aḥmad, 'Imād al-Dawla, Hūdid, 19
b. Sulaymān, Hūdid, 19
Spanish Umayyad, 11
Mu'nis al-Khādim, Turkish slave commander, 168
al-Muntaṣir, 'Abbāsid caliph in Baghdad, 6
al-Muntaṣir (Midrār), Midrārid, 29
al-Muqallad, 'Uqaylid, 91
al-Muqtadī, 'Abbāsid caliph in Baghdad, 6
al-Muqtadir, 'Abbāsid caliph in Baghdad, 6
al-Muqtafī, 'Abbāsid caliph in Baghdad, 6
Murād
I–V, Ottomans, 239–40
Batu'id, 252
Ming, 295
Murād Arslan, Inanj Oghullarï, 223
Murād Bakhsh, Mughal, 331
Murād Giray, Khān of the Crimea, 256
Murshid Qulī Khān, Nawwāb of Bengal, 335
Murtaḍā
I and II, Niẓām Shāhīs, 326
Golden Horde Khān, 253
Mūsā
I, II and III, 'Abd al-Wādids, 43
Askiya of Songhay, 124
Aydïn Oghullarï, 221
b. Abi 'l-Āfiya, Fāṭimid governor of Morocco, 25
al-Hādī, 'Abbāsid caliph in Baghdad, 6
Il Khānid, 250
Marīnid, 41
Menteshe Oghullarï, 222
Shaddādid, 151
Mūsā Chelebi, Ottoman, 239
Muṣ'ab, 'Uqaylid, 91
Musāfir, Musāfirid, 148
Mushārī, Āl Su'ūd, 116
Muslim, 'Uqaylid, 91
al-Mustaḍi, 'Abbāsid caliph in Baghdad, 6
Muṣṭafā
I–IV, Ottomans, 239–40
'Alī, Khān of Qāsimov, 261
Ḥusaynid Bey, 55
Muẓaffar al-Dīn, Ḥamīd Oghullarï, 226
Muṣṭafā Chelebi, Ottoman, 239
Muṣṭafā Kemāl, 240
al-Must'īn
'Abbāsid caliph in Baghdad, 6
'Abbāsid caliph in Cairo and sultan, 7
al-Mustakfī
I and II, , 'Abbāsid caliphs in Cairo, 7
'Abbāsid caliph in Baghdad, 6
al-Musta'lī, Fāṭimid, 63
al-Mustamsik, 'Abbāsid caliph in Cairo, 6
al-Mustanjid,
'Abbāsid caliph in Baghdad, 6
'Abbāsid caliph in Cairo, 7
al-Mustanṣir,
'Abbāsid caliph in Baghdad, 7
'Abbāsid caliph in Cairo, 7
Fāṭmid, 63
al-Mustarshid, 'Abbāsid caliph in Baghdad, 6
al-Musta'ṣim, , 'Abbāsid caliph in Baghdad, 7
al-Mustaẓhir, , 'Abbāsid caliph in Baghdad, 6
Mut'ab (Mit'ab) I and II, Āl Rashīd, 120
al-Mu'taḍid
I and II, 'Abbāsid caliphs in Cairo, 7
'Abbāsid caliph in Baghdad, 6
Muṭā'in, Numayrid, 93
al-Mu'tamid, 'Abbāsid caliph in Baghdad, 6
al-Mu'taṣim,
'Abbāsid caliph in Baghdad, 6
'Abbāsid caliph in Cairo, 7
al-Mutawakkil
'Abbāsid caliph in Baghdad, 6
I, II and III, 'Abbāsid caliphs in Cairo, 7
al-Mu'tazz, 'Abbāsid caliph in Baghdad, 6

al-Muṭīʻ, ʻAbbāsid caliph in Baghdad, 6
al-Muttaqī, ʻAbbāsid caliph in Baghdad, 6
al-Muẓaffar
  Ṣulayḥid, 102
  Yūsuf II, Rasūlid, 108
Muẓaffar al-Dīn
  Mangït, 292
  Qājār, 285
Muẓaffar al-Ṣaqlabī, ruler in Valencia, 19
Muẓaffar Ḥusayn, Tīmūrid, 270
Muẓaffar Jang, Niẓām of Hyderabad, 339
Muẓaffar Khān, Sultan of Gujarāt, 312
Muẓaffar Shāh
  I, II and III, Sultans of Gujarāt, 312
  Sultan of Acheh, 346
Muẓaffar Shams al-Dīn
  (Dīwāna), ruler of Bengal, 307
  (formerly Jadu), ruler of Bengal, 307
Mwana Khadīja, Nabhānī of Pate, 134

Nadhr Muḥammad, Toqay Temürid, 290
Nādir (or Nāzūk) Shāh, Sultan of Kashmīr, 310
Nādir Mīrzā, Afshārid, 281
Nādir Shāh Afshār, Ṣafawid, 279
Nadr Qulī, Nādir Shāh Afshār, Afshārid, 281
Nāmāwar, Fakhr al-Dawla, Bādūspānid, 201
Nāmāwar Shāh Ghāzī, Fakhr al-Dawla, Bādūspānid, 201
Naqiyyat al-Dīn Shāh, Nūr al-ʻĀlam, Queen of Acheh, 346
Nāṣir
  Mazrūʻī, 136
  Sultan of Harar, 138
al-Nāṣir
  ʻAbbāsid caliph in Baghdad, 6
  ʻAbd al-Raḥmān III, Spanish Umayyad in Spain, 11
  Ḥammādid, 35
  Muḥammad Nāsir al-Dīn, Mamlūk ruler of Ḥamāt, 72
Nāṣir al-Dīn Shāh, Qājār, 285
Nāṣir al-Dīn Shāh, Sultan of Mālwa, 316
Nāṣir Jang, Niẓām of Hyderabad, 339
Nāṣir Khān
  Fārūqī, 322
  Sultan of Gujarāt, 312
Naṣr
  I and II, Mirdāsids, 66
  I and II, Sāmānids 170
  b. Aḥmad, Naṣrid Malik of Sistan, 211
  b. Ibrāhīm, Qarakhānid, 181
  b. Khalaf, Naṣrid Malik of Sistan, 211
  b. Muḥammad, Qarakhānid, 181
  Marwānid, 89
  Naṣrid, 22
  (Nuṣrat), Tāj al-Dīn IV, Naṣrid Malik of Sistan, 211
  Qarakhānid, 183
  Sharaf al-Dīn, Nāṣir al-Dawla, Bādūspānid, 201
  Tigin, Ilig Khān, Qarakhānid, 182
  ʻUqaylid, 91
Naṣr al-Dīn, Ming, 295
Naṣr Allāh
  Bārakzay, 341
  Mangït, 292
Nasruddin Husin Kamaluddin, Sultan of Brunei, 353
Nawr al-Ward, Hazāraspid, 205
Nawrūz Aḥmad or Baraq, Shïbānid, 288
Nawwāb Sālār Jang, regent for the Niẓām of Hyderabad, 339
Nāzūk or Nādir Shāh, Sultan of Kashmīr, 310
Negübey (Nīkpāy), Chaghatayid, 248
Nīkpāy (or Negübey), Chaghatayid, 248
Nīkū-siyar Muḥammad, Mughal, 331
Niẓām ʻAlī Khān, Niẓām of Hyderabad, 339
Nizār, Fāṭimid, 63
Nūḥ
  I and II, Sāmānid, 170
  Musāfirid, 148
  Sultan of Harar, 138
Nūr al-Dawla Balak, ruler in Aleppo, 186
Nūr Dawlat Giray
  Khān of Crimea, 255
  Khān of Qāsimov, 261
Nuṣrat (Naṣr), Tāj al-Dīn IV, Naṣrid Malik of Sistan, 211
Nuṣrat al-Dīn
  Hazāraspid, 205
  Ṣāḥib Atā Oghullarï, 225
Nuṣrat Shāh
  ruler of Bengal, 307
  Tughluqid, 301

Ögedey, Mongol Great Khān, 246
Oghul Ghaymish, Mongol regent, 246
Omar Ali Saifuddin I, II and III, Sultans of Brunei, 353–4
Orda, White Horde Khān, 252
Orkhan
  Ottoman, 239
  Ṣarukhān Oghullarï, 220
  Shujāʻ al-Dīn, Menteshe Oghullarï, 222
Orqina Khātūn, Chaghatayid, 248
Ötemish, Khān of Kazan, 259
ʻOthmān (or ʻUthmān)
  Chelebi, Tekke Oghullarï, 226
  Ghāzī, Ottoman, 239
Özbeg, Muẓaffar al-Dīn, Eldigüzid, 199

Pādishāh Khātūn, Ṣafwat al-Dīn, Qutlughkhānid, 210
Pakubuwana
  I, II and III, rulers of Mataram, 348
  III–XII, Susuhunans, 350
Panembahan Seda Krapyak, Mas Jolang, ruler of Mataram, 348
Parameśvara, ruler of Malacca, 344
Pashang, Shams al-Din, Hazāraspid, 205
Perkasa ʻĀlam Sharīf Lamtuy, Sultan of Acheh, 346
Pindar or Bīdar Qadïr Khān, ruler of Bengal, 306
Pīr Aḥmad
  Hazāraspid, 205
  Qaramān Oghullarï, 232
Pīr ʻAlī, Ghiyāth al-Dīn II, Kart, 263

Pīr Budaq, Qara Qoyunlu, 273
Pīr Ḥusayn Muḥammad, Kart, 263
Pīr Manṣūr, Ramaḍān Oghullarï, 237
Pīr Muḥammad
I and II, Shïbānids, 288
b. Jahāngīr, Tīmūrid, 270
b. 'Umar Shaykh, Tīmūrid, 271
Pīrī Muḥammad, Ramaḍān Oghullarï, 237
Pòtjut Auk or Jahān Shāh, Sultan of Acheh, 346
Prabu Amangkurat I, Sunan Tegalwangi, ruler of Mataram, 348
Pūlād (Bolod) Khān, Golden Horde Khān, 252

Qābūs
Āl Bū Sa'īd, 114
Ziyārid, 166
Qāḍī Burhān al-Dīn, 234
al-Qādir, 'Abbāsid caliph of Baghdad, 6
Qadïr Khān, Jalāl al-Dunyā wa 'l-Dīn, Qarakhānid, 183
Qādir Shāh (formerly Mallū Khān), governor and then Sultan of Mālwa, 316
al-Qāhir, 'Abbāsid caliph of Baghdad, 6
al-Qā'id, Ḥammādid, 35
al-Qā'im
'Abbāsid caliph of Baghdad, 6
'Abbāsid caliph in Cairo, 7
Fāṭimid, 63
Qaplan Giray I and II, Khāns of the Crimea, 256
Qara Arslan
b. Dawūd, Artuqid, 194
b. Ghāzī, Artuqid, 195
Qara Hülegü, Chaghatayid, 248
Qara Khitay, Qarakhānid, 182
Qara Muḥammad, Qara Qoyunlu, 273
Qara Yūsuf, Abū Naṣr, Qara Qoyunlu, 273
Qaraj b. Dulghadir, founder of Dulghadir Oghullarï, 238
Qaraja, al-Malik al-Ẓāhir Zayn al-Dīn, Dulghadïr Oghullarï, 238
Qaraj b. Dulghadir, founder of Dulghadir Oghullarï, 238
Qaramān
Bey of Alanya, 227
Menteshe Oghullarï, 222
Qaramān Oghullarï, 232
Qarasï Beg, Qarasï Oghullarï, 219
Qārin I and II, Bāwandid Ispahbadhs, 164
Qāsim
I Barīd, chief minister of the Bahmanid Sultan, 324
II, Barīd Shāhī, 324
b. Maḥmūd, Khān of Astrakhan, 258
Fakhr al-Dīn, Dānishmendid, 213
Khān of Qāsimov, 261
Qaramān Oghullarï, 232
(Qasay) b. Sayyid Aḥmad, Khān of Astrakhan, 258
al-Qāsim
b. 'Alī al-'Iyānī, Abu 'l-Ḥusayn al-Manṣūr, Zaydī Imām, 96
b. Ibrāhīm al-Ḥasanī al-Rassī, Zaydī Imām, 96
Gannūn b. Muḥammad, Idrīsid, 25
governor of Jibāl and first of the Dulafids, 153
Ibn Ḥammūd, al-Ma'mūn, Spanish Umayyad, 11
al-Mahdī, Zaydī Imām, 97
al-Ma'mūn, Ḥammūdid of Ceuta and Málaga, 16
al-Manṣūr, Zaydī Imām, 96
al-Mu'ayyad, Zaydī Imām, 97
al-Mutawakkil, Zaydī Imām, 97
Qawām, Numayrid, 93
Qayṣar, Sadōzay, 341
Qayshan Gülük (Hai-shan), Mongol Great Khān, 246
Qazan, Chaghatayid, 248
Qïlïch Arslan
I–IV, Seljuqs of Rūm, 213
Aq Qoyunlu, 275
Bey of Alanya, 227
Qïrïm Giray I and II, Khāns of the Crimea, 256
Qirwāsh, 'Uqaylid, 91
Qïzïl Aḥmad, Jāndār Oghullarï, 229
Qïzïl Arslan Atsïz, Anūshtiginid Khwārazm Shāh, 179
Qïzïl Arslan 'Uthmān, Eldigüzid, 199
Qorqmaz I and II, Ma'n Amīrs, 81
Qoshila Qutuqtu, Mongol Great Khān, 246
Qubād, 'Aḍud al-Dawla, Bādūspānid, 201
Qubādh
Ramaḍān Oghullarï, 237
Yazīdī Sharwān Shāh, 140
Qubilay, Mongol Great Khān, 246
Qulpa, Batu'id, 252
Quraysh, 'Uqaylid, 91
Quṭb al-Dīn II, Mihrabānid Malik of Sistan, 211
Qutlugh
Fakhr al-Dīn, Aq Qoyunlu, 275
Shujā' al-Dīn, Sökmenid slave commander, 197
Qutlugh Inanch, Eldigüzid, 199
Qutlugh Khān, Salghurid, 207
Qutlugh Murād, Qungrat, 293
Qutlugh Terken, Qutlughkhānid regent, 210

Rābiḥ b. Faḍl Allāh, conqueror of Bornu and Dikwa, 128
al-Rāḍī, 'Abbāsid caliph in Baghdad, 6
Raḍiyya Begum, Jalālat al-Dīn, Mu'izzī queen in Delhi, 300
Rāfi'
rebel and caliphal governor in Nishapur and then Rayy, 172
'Uqaylid, 91
Rāfi' al-Darajāt, Shams al-Dīn, Mughal, 331
Raḥīm Qulī, Qungrat, 293
Rājā 'Abdallāh, Sultan Manṣūr Shāh, ruler of Malacca, 344
Rājā 'Ali Khān 'Ādil Shāh IV, Fārūqī, 322
Raja Api, Sultan of Brunei, 353
Rājā Buyung or 'Alī Ri'āyat Shāh, Sultan of Acheh, 346
Rājā Gaṇeśa (Danūj Mardan Deva), ruler of Bengal, 307

Raja Ghafur, Sultan of Brunei, 353
Rājā Ibrāhīm, Śri Parameśvara Deva Shāh, ruler of Malacca, 344
Rājā Qāsim, Sultan Muẓaffar Shāh, ruler of Malacca, 344
Raja Udahna Lela or Sulaymān Shāh, Sultan of Acheh, 346
Ramaḍān Beg, Ramaḍān Oghullarï, 237
Ramiro II of Aragon, 20
Rashād al-Mahdī, King of the Tunisians, 55
Rashīd, Āl al-Julandā, 111
al-Rāshid
'Abbāsid caliph in Baghdad, 6
'Alawid Sharif, 53
Hārūn, 'Abbāsid caliph in Baghdad, 6
Ri'āyat Shāh
'Alā' al-Dīn, Sultan of Acheh, 346
b. 'Alī, 'Alā' al-Dīn al-Qahhār, Sultan of Acheh, 346
Riḍā Khān, later Shah, Pahlawī, 278, 287
Riḍā Khan, 278
Riḍwān, Seljuq in Aleppo, 186
Rinchenpal (Irinchinbal), Mongol Great Khān, 246
Rukn al-Dīn
Sarbadārid, 269
Shams al-Dīn II, Kart, 263
Rustam
I, II and III, Bāwandid Ispahbadhs, 164
Aq Qoyunlu, 275
b. Fakhr al-Dawla 'Alī, Būyid in Rayy, 154
Tīmūrid, 271

Sa'ādat 'Alī Khān, Nawwāb of Oudh, 337
Sa'ādat Giray I, II and III, Khāns of the Crimea, 255–6
Saba' b. Abi 'l-Su'ūd, Zuray'id, 104
Sabakura or Sākūra, Keita of Mali, 122
Sabhat, Mahdali Sultan of Kilwa, 133
Sābiq, Mirdāsid, 66–7
Ṣabr al-Dīn, Sultan of Harar, 138
Sābūr al-Ṣaqlabī, governor of Badajoz, 18
Sa'd I and II, Salghurids, 207
Sa'd al-Dīn, Sultan of Harar, 138
Ṣadaqa I and II, Mazyadids, 87
Sa'dī, 'Annāzid, 159
Ṣādiq, Sultan of Harar, 138
Ṣafā' Giray
Khān of Kazan, 259
Khān of the Crimea, 256
al-Saffāh, 'Abbāsid caliph in Baghdad, 6
Ṣafī I and II, Ṣafawids, 279
Ṣafiyyat al-Dīn Shāh, Tāj al-'Ālam, Queen of Acheh, 346
Ṣāḥib Atā, 223
Ṣāḥib Giray
I and II, Khāns of the Crimea, 255–6
Khān of Kazan, 259
Sa'id
'Abd al-Wādid, 43
'Abdallāh, Qungrat, 293
Abu 'l-Qāsim, Carmathian ruler, 94
Āl al-Julandā, 111
b. Aḥmad, Āl Bū Sa'īd, 114
b. Idrīs, Sultan of Kanem, 126
b. Mas'ūd, Ghaznawid Khwārazm Shāh, 178
b. Sulṭān, Bū Sa'īd, 114
b. Taymūr, Bū Sa'īd, 114
Bū Sa'īd, 137
Hamdānid, 85
Mahdali Sultan of Kilwa, 133
Marwānid, 89
Sa'id al-Aḥwal, Najāḥid, 101
Saiful Rijal, Sultan of Brunei, 353
Sākūra (or Sabakura), Keita of Mali, 122
Ṣalābat Jang, Niẓām of Hyderabad, 339
Ṣalāḥ al-Dīn
Rasūlid, 108
Sultan of Acheh, 346
Ṣalāḥ al-Dīn Yūsuf (Saladin), 63, 72, 190
Ṣalāḥ Re'īs Pasha of Algiers, 43
Salāmat Giray I and II, Khāns of the Crimea, 255
Salghur Shāh, Atabeg of Yazd, 209
Ṣāliḥ
b. Mirdās, Asad al-Dawla, Amīr of Raḥba, Mirdāsid, 66
Mazrū'ī, 136
Salīm
II and III, Ottomans, 239–40
Bū Sa'īd, 114
Mazrū'ī, 136
(Selīm) I, Yavuz ('the Grim'), Ottoman, 239
Salīm Giray I, II and III, Khāns of the Crimea, 256
Sallār, Yazīdī Sharwān Shāh, 140
Salmān Nari, King of Songhay, 124
Saltuq I and II, Saltuqids, 218
Sām
I and II, Ghūrids, 298
b. Muḥammad Shams al-Dīn, Ghūrid, 298
Rukn al-Dīn, Atabeg of Yazd, 209
Samā' al-Dawla, Būyid in Hamadan and Isfahan, 154
Samgū, al-Muntaṣir, Midrārid, 29
Sanda Limanambe Wuduroma, Kanembu Shehu of Bornu, 128
Sanjar, ruler in Khurasan and supreme sultan of the Seljuqs, 185
Sanjar Shāh, Mu'izz al-Dīn, Zangid, 190
Sarfarāz Khān, 'Alā' al-Dawla, Nawwāb of Bengal, 335
Sarïgh Buqa (or Sāsibuqa), White Horde Khān, 252
Sartaq, Batu'id, 252
Ṣarukhān Beg, Ṣarukhān Oghullarï, 220
Sāsibuqa (? Sarïgh Buqa), White Horde Khān, 252
Satïlghan, Khān of Qāsimov, 261
Sawchï, Bey of Alanya, 227
Sāwtigin, Seljuq commander, 143, 151
Sayf
I and II, Ya'rubids, 113
governor of Mombasa, 136
Sayf al-Dawla,
Ḥamdānid, 85
Zīrid of Granada, 17

Sayïn Bulāt, Khān of Qāsimov, 261
Sayyid 'Abdallāh, Musha'sha'id, 277
Sayyid Aḥmad
I and II, Golden Horde Khāns, 253
Sayyid Aḥmad al-Sharīf, 58–9
Sayyid 'Alī
b. Khalaf, Musha'sha'id, 277
b. Sajjād, Musha'sha'id, 277
nephew of Faraj Allāh, Musha'sha'id, 277
Sayyid 'Ālim Khān, Mangït, 292
Sayyid Awliyār, Khān of Qāsimov, 261
Sayyid Badrān, Shujā' al-Dīn, Musha'sha'id, 277
Sayyid Baraka, Musha'sha'id, 277
Sayyid Burhān, Khān of Qāsimov, 261
Sayyid Falāḥ, Musha'sha'id, 277
Sayyid Faraj Allāh, Musha'sha'id, 277
Sayyid Ḥaydar ('Abdallāh), Musha'sha'id, 277
Sayyid Ḥaydar Tora, Mangït, 292
Sayyid Ḥusayn, Mangït, 292
Sayyid Ḥusayn Shāh, 'Alā' al-Dīn, ruler of Bengal, 307
Sayyid Manṣūr, Musha'sha'id, 277
Sayyid Mawlā 'Abd al-'Alī, Musha'sha'id, 277
Sayyid Mawlā Faraj Allāh, Musha'sha'id, 277
Sayyid Mawlā Ismā'īl, Musha'sha'id, 277
Sayyid Mawlā Jūd Allāh, Musha'sha'id, 277
Sayyid Mawlā Muḥammad
b. Jūd Allāh, Musha'sha'id, 277
b. Naṣr Allāh, Musha'sha'id, 277
Sayyid Mawlā Muḥsin, Musha'sha'id, 277
Sayyid Mawlā Muṭṭalib
b. Muḥammad, Musha'sha'id, 277
b. Naṣr Allāh, Musha'sha'id, 277
Sayyid Mawlā Naṣr Allāh, Musha'sha'id, 277
Sayyid Mubārak, Musha'sha'id, 277
Sayyid Muḥammad
b. 'Abdallāh, Musha'sha'id, 277
b. 'Alī, founder of Sanūsiyya dervish order, the 'Great Sanūsi', 58
b. Falāḥ, Musha'sha'id, 277
b. Mubārak, Musha'sha'id, 277
Sayyid Muḥammad al-Mahdī, 58
Sayyid Muḥammad Amīn Sa'ādat Khān Bahādur, Nawwāb of Oudh, 337
Sayyid Muḥammad Bahādur, Qungrat, 293
Sayyid Muḥammad Idrīs, 58–9
Sayyid Muḥammad Raḥīm, Qungrat, 293
Sayyid Muṭṭalib, Musha'sha'id, 277
Sayyid Nāṣir, Musha'sha'id, 277
Sayyid Rāshid, Musha'sha'id, 277
Sayyid Sajjād, Musha'sha'id, 277
Sayyid Sulṭān 'Alī, Musha'sha'id, 277
Sayyid Sulṭān Muḥsin, Musha'sha'id, 277
Sayyid Sulṭān or Sulṭān (Mīr) Sayyid, Ming, 295
Sayyid Zunbūr 'Alī, Musha'sha'id, 277
al-Sayyida Arwā, Ṣulayḥid queen, 102
Sebüktigin, governor in Ghazna for the Sāmānids, 296
Selema, Sultan of Kanem, 126
Selīm
Ramaḍān Oghullarï, 237
(Salīm) I, Yavuz ('the Grim'), Ottoman, 239
(Salīm) II and III, Ottomans, 239–40
Seljuq Shāh, Salghurid, 207
Sha'bān Sūlī, Dulghadïr Oghullarï, 238
Shabīb, Numayrid, 93
Shaddād, Shaddādid, 151
Shādī Beg
Arghūn, 329
Golden Horde Khān, 252
Shāh 'Ālam I and II, Mughals, 331
Shāh 'Alī, Khān
of Kazan, 259
of Qāsimov, 261
Shāh Brunei, Sultan of Brunei, 353
Shāh Budaq, Dulghadïr Oghullarï, 238
Shāh Ghāzī, Fakhr al-Dawla, Bādūspānid, 201
Shāh Ghāzī Rustam, Bāwandid Ispahbadh, 164
Shāh Ḥusayn
Arghūn, 329
Hazāraspid, 205
Shāh Jahān
I, II and III, Mughals, 331
Quṭb al-Dīn, Qutlughkhānid, 210
Shāh Maḥmūd
Quṭb al-Dīn, Muẓaffarid, 264
Tīmūrid, 270
Shāh Malik of Jand, Khwārazm Shāh, 178
Shāh Manṣūr, Muẓaffarid, 264
Shāh Mīr Swātī, Shams al-Dīn, Sultan of Kashmīr, 310
Shāh Murād
Amīr-i Ma'ṣūm, Mangït, 292
Ming, 295
Shāh Rukh
Afshārid, 279, 281
Sharwān Shāh, 141
Tīmūrid, 270, 271
Shāh Shujā', Sadōzay, 341
Shāh Suwār, Dulghadïr Oghullarï, 238
Shāh Temür, Chaghatayid, 248
Shāh Walad, Jalāyirid, 267
Shāh Yaḥyā, Muẓaffarid, 264
Shāh-i Shāhān Abu 'l-Fatḥ, Mihrabānid Malik of Sistan, 211
Shāh-i Shujā', Muẓaffarid, 264
Shāhanshāh or Shāhānshāh
'Imād al-Dīn, Zangid, 190
(Malik Shāh), Seljuq of Rūm, 213
Mengüjekid, 217
Shaddādid, 151
Yazīdī Sharwān Shāh, 140
Shāhbāz Giray, Khān of the Tatars, 256
Shāhī Khān (ruling title Zayn al-'Ābidīn), called Bud Shāh (Great King), of Kashmīr, 310
Shāhīn Giray, Khān of the Crimea, 256
Shahrāgīm, Bādūspānid, 201
Shahrīwash, Bādūspānid, 201
Shahriyār
I, II and III, Bāwandid Ispahbadhs, 164
Nāṣir al-Dīn, Bādūspānid, 201
Yazdagird, Nāṣir al-Dawla, Bāwandid Ispahbadh, 165
Shajā'at Khān, governor of Mālwa, 316
Shajar al-Durr, Baḥrī Mamlūk, 76

Shams al-'Ālam or Wandi Tēbing, Sultan of Acheh, 346
Shams al-Dawla, Būyid in Hamadan and Isfahan, 154
Shams al-Dīn
II and III, Karts, 263
Nizārī Ismā'īlī, 68
Qaramān Oghullarï, 232
Sultan of Kashmīr, 310
Shams al-Dīn Shāh, Sultan of Acheh, 346
Shāpūr, Bāwandid Ispahbadh, 164
Sharaf al-Mulūk b. Kay Khusraw, Bāwandid Ispahbadh, 165
Sharīf I, Ḥamdānid, 85
Sharīf Aḥsan, Jalāl al-Dīn, governor and later Sultan of Ma'bar, 318
Sharif Ali, Sultan Berkat, Sultan of Brunei, 353
Sharīf Hāshim Jamāl al-Dīn Badr al-'Ālam, Sultan of Acheh, 346
Sharīf Sayf al-'Ālam, Sultan of Acheh, 346
Sharwīn I and II, Bāwandid Ispahbadhs, 164
Shāwur I and II, Shaddādids, 151
Shaybān, Ṭūlūnid, 60
Shaykh Aḥmad, Golden Horde Khān, 253
Shaykh Ḥasan-i Buzurg, Tāj al-Dīn, Jalāyirid, 267
Shaykh Ḥaydar, Khān of Astrakhan, 258
Shaykh Khaz'al of Muḥammara, 278
Shaykh Shāh or Ibrāhīm, Sharwān, 141
Shaykh Uways I, Jalāyirid, 267
Shidebala (or Suddhipala Gege'en or Gegen), Mongol Great Khān, 246
Shīr 'Alī
Bārakzay, 341
Ming, 295
Shīr Khān, governor of Bengal, 306
Shīr Shāh Sūr, Sūrī Delhi Sultan and ruler in Bengal, 301, 308
Shīrāshāmak, Shihāb al-Dīn, Sultan of Kashmīr, 310
Shīrzād, Ghaznawid, 296
Shīrzīl
b. Fanā Khusraw 'Aḍud al-Dawla, Būyid, 154–5
b. Fīrūz Bahā' al-Dawla, Būyid, 155
Shujā' Khān, Shujā' al-Dawla, Nawwāb of Bengal, 335
Sikandar
II Niẓām Khān, Lōdī Delhi Sultan, 301
'Ādil Shāhī, 325
But-shikan, Sultan of Kashmīr, 310
Sultan of Gujarāt, 312
Sikandar Jāh, Niẓām of Hyderabad, 339
Sikandar Shāh
I, 'Alā'l al-Dīn, Tughluqid Delhi Sultan, 301
I and II, rulers of Bengal, 307
'Alā' al-Dīn, Sultan of Ma'bar, 318
Sīmjūr al-Dawātī, governor for the Sāmānids in Sistan and founder of the Sīmjūrids, 175
Sinān, Nizārī Ismā'īlī, 68
Sinān Pasha, 46
Sirāj al-Dīn' Abu 'l-Futūḥ, Nizārī Ismā'īlī, 68
Sökmen
I and II, Artuqids, 194
I and II, Sökmenids, 197
Soyurghatmïsh, Qutlughkhānid, 210
Śri Maharājā Sultan Muḥammad Shāh, ruler of Malacca, 344
Ṣubḥān, Quṭb Shāhī, 328
Ṣubḥān Qulī, Toqay Temürid, 290
Su'dā, 'Annāzid, 159
Suddhipala Gege'en or Gegen (Shidebala), Mongol Great Khān, 246
Sulāfa Khātūn, ruler of Marāgha and Rū'īn Diz, Aḥmadīlī, 198
Sulaiman, Sultan of Brunei, 353
Sulaymān
I and II, Mengüjekids, 217
(Süleymān) I, II and III, Ottomans, 239
I, Sayf al-Dīn, Ashraf Oghullarï, 228
II, Sayyid Muḥammad, Ṣafawid, 279
I and II, Seljuqs of Rūm, 213
I, Shujā' al-Dīn, Jāndār Oghullarï, 229
II b. Khalīl II, Ayyūbid in Diyār Bakr, 73
II Shāh, Ashraf Oghullarï, 228
II Shāh, Jāndār Oghullarï, 229
Abū Ṭāhir, Carmathian ruler, 94
Āl al-Julandā, 111
'Alawid Sharīf, 53
Arslan Khān, Sharaf al-Dawla, Qarakhānid, 182
b. Dāwūd, Mahdali Sultan of Kilwa, 132
b. al-Ḥākim I, 'Abbāsid caliph in Cairo, 7
b. al-Ḥasan, Mahdali Sultan of Kilwa, 132
b. al-Ḥasan b. Dāwūd, Shīrāzī Sultan of Kilwa, 132
b. al-Ḥusayn, Mahdali Sultan of Kilwa, 132
b. Muḥammad, Mahdali Sultan of Kilwa, 132
b. Muḥammad Ibn Hūd al-Judhāmī, Hūdid, 19
b. al-Mundhir, Sayyid al-Dawla, Hūdid, 19
b. al-Mutawakkil I, 'Abbāsid caliph in Cairo, 7
Dulghadïr Oghullarï, 238
Marīnid, 41
Mazrū'ī, 136
al-Musta'īn, Spanish Umayyad, 11
Nabhānī of Pate, 134
Qadïr Tamghach or Tabghach Khān, Qarakhānid, 181
Qānūnī ('the Lawgiver' and 'the Magnificent'), Ottoman, 239
Qaramān Oghullarï, 232
Qarasï Oghullarï, 219
Shīrāzī Sultan of Kilwa (523/1129), 132
Ṭāhirid in Baghdad and Iraq, 168
Tāj al-Dawla, Hūdid, 19
Umayyad caliph, 3
Sulaymān Dama or Dandi, King of Songhay, 124
Sulaymān Kararānī, ruler of Bengal, 308
Sulaymān Shāh
Germiyān Oghullarï, 224
(Raja Udahna Lela), Sultan of Acheh, 346
Seljuq in Persia and Iraq, 186

Sulṭān
I and II, Ya'rubids, 113
Āl Bū Sa'īd, 114
Āl Rashīd, 120
rival to Ya'rubid Imāms, 113
Shaddādid, 151
Sulṭān Abū Isḥaq, Muẓaffarid, 264
Sulṭān Aḥmad
Ghiyāth al-Dīn, Jalāyirid, 267
'Imād al-Dīn, Muẓaffarid, 264
Tīmūrid, 270
Sultan Aḥmad Shāh, ruler of Malacca, 344
Sultan 'Alā' al-Dīn, ruler of Malacca, 344
Sultan 'Alā' al-Dīn Ri'āyat, Manṣūr Shāh, ruler of Malacca, 344
Sulṭān 'Azīz b. Kayūmarth, Bādūspānid, 202
Sulṭān Khalīl, Aq Qoyunlu, 275
Sulṭān Maḥmūd, Mihrabānid Malik of Sistan, 211
Sultan Maḥmūd Shāh, ruler of Malacca, 344
Sultan Muda ('Alī Ri'āyat Shāh), Sultan of Acheh, 346
Sulṭān Muḥammad, Bādūspānid, 201
Sulṭān Murād, Aq Qoyunlu, 275
Sulṭān Mu'taṣim, Muẓaffarid, 264
Sultan Muẓaffar Shāh, ruler of Malacca, 344
Sulṭān Qulī Khawāṣṣ Khān Bahārlu, Quṭb al-Mulk, Quṭb Shāhī, 328
Sulṭān Shāh, Seljuq in Aleppo, 186
Sulṭān Shāh Isḥāq, Seljuq of Kirman, 186
Sulṭān Shāhzāda Barbak Shāh, ruler of Bengal, 307
Sultan Śri 'Ālam, Sultan of Acheh, 346
Sunqur, Salghurid, 207
Sūrī, Sayf al-Dīn, Ghūrid, 298
Surkhāb
I and II, Bāwandid Ispahbadhs, 164
b. 'Annāz, 'Annāzid, 159
b. Badr, 'Annāzid, 159
b. Muḥammad, 'Annāzid, 159
Susuhunan (Tjakrakusuma Ngabdurrahman, Sultan Agung), ruler of Mataram, 348
Su'ūd
I and II, Āl Rashīd, 120
I, II and III, Su'ūdīs, 116

Tāhir
I and II, Ṭāhirid of Khurasan, 168
Bahā' al-Dawla, Naṣrid Malik of Sistan, 211
Ḥasanūyid, 158
Khalafid Ṣaffārid regent, 172
Laythid Ṣaffārid, 172
Ṭahmāsp I and II, Ṣafawids, 279
al-Ṭā'i', 'Abbāsid caliph in Baghdad, 6
Tāj al-Dawla, Bādūspānid, 201
Tāj al-Dīn
I, Mihrabānid Malik of Sistan, 211
Oghullarī, 236
Tāj al-Dīn Aḥmad, Menteshe Oghullarī, 222
Takūdār (or Aḥmad Tegüder), Il Khānid, 250
Ṭalāl
Āl Rashīd, 120
Hāshimite King of Jordan, 118
Ṭalḥa
b. 'Abbās al-Wazīr, Sultan of Harar, 138
b. 'Abdallāh, Sultan of Harar, 138
Ṭāhirid of Khurasam, 168
Taliqu, Chaghatayid, 248
Ṭālūt
b. al-Ḥusayn, Mahdali Sultan of Kilwa, 132
b. Sulaymān, Shīrāzī Sultan of Kilwa, 132
Tambari, Fulani, 130
Tamerlane *see* Tīmūr
Tamīm
Zīrid of Granada, 17
Zīrid of Kairouan, 35
Tandu Khātūn, 267
Tarmashīrīn, 'Alā' al-Dīn, Chaghatayid, 248
Tāshufīn
Almoravid, 37
Marīnid, 41
Tātār Khān
governor of Bengal, 306
(Muḥammad Shāh (I)), Sultan of Gujarāt, 312
Tekele or Degele
Hazāraspid, 205
Salghurid, 207
Tekish, Anūshtiginid Khwārazm Shāh, 179
Temür, Golden Horde Khān, 252
Temür Malik, White Horde Khān, 252
Temür Öljeytü, Mongol Great Khān, 246
Temür Qirān Khān, Qamar al-Dīn, governor of Bengal, 306
Temür Qutlugh, Golden Horde Khān, 252
Temür Tash
Artuqid, 194
Il Khānid governor of Eğridir, 226
Tharwān, 'Uqaylid, 91
Thimāl, Mirdāsid, 66
Thuwaynī, Āl Bū Sa'īd, 114
Tīmūr-i Lang (Tamerlane), Küreken, Tīmūrid, 270
Tīmūr Shāh, Sadōzay, 341
Tīnī Beg, Batu'id, 252
Tīpū Sulṭān, ruler in Mysore, 340
Tjakrakusuma Ngabdurrahman, Sultan Agung (ruling title Susuhunan), ruler of Mataram, 348
Töde Möngke (Mengü), Batu'id, 252
Ṭogha(n) Shāh, Atabeg of Yazd, 209
Toghan Temür, Mongol Great Khān, 246
Togha(y) Temür, Il Khānid, 250
Ṭoghrïl
II and III, Seljuqs in Persia and Iraq, 185–6
(Mughīth al-Dīn), governor of Bengal, 306
(Ṭughril) I Beg Muḥammad, supreme Sultan, Seljuq, 185
Ṭoghrïl Shāh, Muḥyī 'l-Dunyā wa 'l-Dīn, Seljuq of Kirman, 186
Ṭoghrïl Toghan Khān, 'Izz al-Dīn, governor of Bengal, 306
Töle Buqa, Batu'id, 252
Toqa or Buqa Temür, Chaghatayid, 248
Toqta, Ghiyāth al-Dīn, Batu'id, 252
Toqtamïsh, Ghiyāth al-Dīn, White Horde and then Golden Horde Khān, 252
Toqtamïsh Giray, Khān of the Crimea, 255

Toqtaqiya, White Horde Khān, 252
Töregene Khātūn, Mongol regent, 246
Tuanku Muḥammad or Muḥammad Shāh, Sultan of Acheh, 346
Tuanku Raja or Maḥmūd Shāh, Sultan of Acheh, 346
Tufāl Khān Dakhnī, 'Imād Shāhī regent, 327
Tughluq Shāh I and II, Ghiyāth al-Dīn, Tughluqid Delhi Sultans, 300
Tughluq Temür, Chaghatayid, 248
Ṭughril (or Ṭughrïl) I Beg Muḥammad, ruler in Persia and supreme Sultan, Seljuq, 185
Ṭughtigin
  Börid, 189
  ruler in Damascus, 186
Tūrān Shāh I and II, Seljuqs of Kirman, 186
Turkī
  Āl Bū Sa'īd, 114
  Āl Su'ūd, 116
Ṭūsr, Sa'd al-Dawla, Bādūspānid, 201
Tutush I and II, Seljuqs, 186

'Ubaydallāh
  ('Abdallāh) b. Ḥusayn, Fāṭimid, 63
  Abu 'l-Ghāzī, Shībānid, 288
  b. Abi 'l-Fayḍ, Toqay Temürid, 290
  b. Ṣubḥān Qulī, Toqay Temürid, 290
  Ṭāhirid in Baghdad and Iraq, 168
Ulaghchi, Batu'id, 252
Uljāytū (or Muḥammad Khudābanda Öljeytü), Il Khānid, 250
Ulugh Beg, Tīmūrid, 270
Ulugh Muḥammad
  Golden Horde Khān, 259
  Khān of Kazan, 259
'Ulūj 'Alī, Turkish conqueror of Tunis, 45
'Umar
  I and II, Ḥafṣids, 45
  (II), Umayyad caliph, 3
  I b. al-Khaṭṭāb, al Fārūq, 'Rightly-Guided' Caliph, 1
  'Abbāsid caliph in Cairo, 7
  Afṭasid of Badajoz, 18
  Almohad, 39
  Dulafid, 153
  Fatḥ al-Dīn, Zangid, 190
  Hāshimid of Darband, 143
  Kanembu Shehu of Bornu, 127
  Mangīt, 292
  Nabhānī of Pate, 134
  Ramaḍān Oghullarï, 237
  Sanda Mandarama, Shehu of Dikwa, 128
  Ṭoghrïl Tigin, Qarakhānid, 182
  (Umaru), Fulani, 130
'Umar Abba Yarema, Mai of Dikwa, 128
'Umar b. 'Abdallāh, Sultan of Kanem, 127
'Umar b. Idrīs, Sayfī of Bornu, 127
'Umar b. Idrīs, Sultan of Kanem, 126
'Umar Sanda Kiarimi, Shehu of Dikwa and later Bornu, 128
'Umar Sanda Kura, Shehu of Dikwa and Bornu, 128
'Umar Shāh, Shihāb al-Dīn, Khaljī Delhi Sultan, 300
Ume, Sultan of Kanem, 127
Ume Jilmi, first Yazanī ruler of Kanem, 126
Umur I and II, Aydïn Oghullarï, 221
Ūnūjūr, Ikhshīdid, 62
Uraz Muḥammad, Khān of Qāsimov, 261
Urus, White Horde Khān, 252
Usumanu dan Fodio ('Uthmān), Fulani, 130
'Uthmān
  I and II, 'Abd al-Wādids, 43
  I, II and III, Marīnids, 41
  III b. Muṣṭafā II, Ottoman, 240
  ('Othmān) II and III, Ottomans, 239
  b. 'Affān, 'Rightly-Guided' Caliph, 1
  b. Dāwūd, Sultan of Kanem, 126
  b. Idrīs, Sultan of Kanem (767/1366), 126
  b. Idrīs, Sultan of Kanem (792/1390), 126
  b. Kade, Sultan of Kanem, 127
  Ḥafṣid, 45
  Ḥusaynid Bey, 55
  Kachim Biri, Sultan of Kanem, 126
  ('Othmān) Chelebi, Tekke Oghullarï, 226
  ('Othmān) I Ghāzī, Ottoman, 239
  al-Qāḍī, 'Āmirid, 19
  Sultan of Harar, 138
  Ulugh Sulṭān al-Salāṭīn, Qarakhānid, 182
  (Usumanu dan Fodio), Fulani, 130
'Uthmān Biri, ruler of Kanem, 126
'Uthmān Gifo, King of Songhay, 124
'Uthmān Kalinumuwa, Sultan of Kanem, 126
'Uthmān Ma'n, Ma'n Amīr, 81
'Uthmān Shāh, Naṣrid Malik of Sistan, 211
Uways II, Jalāyirid, 267
Uzun Ḥasan, Aq Qoyunlu, 275

Wahsūdān
  Justānid, 145
  Musāfirid, 148
  Rawwādid, 150
Wājid 'Alī, Nawwāb of Oudh, 337
Walī Allāh, Bahmanid, 319
Walī Muḥammad, Toqay Temürid, 290
al-Walīd, I and II Umayyad caliphs, 3
Wandi Tēbing or Shams al-'Ālam, Sultan of Acheh, 346
Wardānrūz, Muḥyī 'l-Dīn, Atabeg of Yazd, 209
Wāsūl al-Fatḥ, Midrārid, 29
al-Wāthiq
  I and II, 'Abbāsid caliphs in Cairo, 7
  'Abbāsid calif in Baghdad, 6
Waththāb, Numayrid, 93
Wazīr 'Alī, Nawwāb of Oudh, 337
Wushmgīr, Zīyārīd, 166

Yādgār Muḥammad, Tīmūrid, 270
Yādigār Muḥammad, Khān of Kazan, 259
Yaghmurāsan, 'Abd al-Wādid, 43
Yaghmurchi, Khān of Astrakhan, 258
Yaḥyā
  I and II, Dhu 'l-Nūnids of Toledo, 18
  I, II and III, Ḥafṣids, 45
  I and II, Ḥammūdids, 16
  I, II, III and IV, Idrīsids, 25
  I and II, Waṭṭāsids, 48
  Afṭasid of Badajoz, 18

Almohad, 39
b. Aḥmad, Zaydī Imām, 96
b. Ibrāhīm al-Gudālī or al-Jaddālī, Almoravid, 37
b. Muḥammad, Abū Ṭālib, Zaydī Imām, 96
b. ʿUmar al-Lamtūnī, Almoravid, 37
Ḥammādid, 35
Ibn Ghāniya, ruler in Cordova, 18
ʿIzz al-Dīn, ruler of Bengal, 307
al-Muʿtalī, Spanish Umayyad, 11
Najm al-Dīn al-Hādī ilā ʾl-Ḥaqq, Zaydī Imām, 96
Niẓām al-Dīn, Mihrabānid Malik of Sistan, 211
Tujībid, 19
Zīrid of Kairouan, 35
Yaḥyā al-Hādī ilā ʾl-Ḥaqq, Zaydī Imām, 96
Yaḥyā al-Mutawakkil, Zaydī Imām, 97
Yaḥyā Karāwī, Sarbadārid, 269
Yaʿīsh, Dhu ʾl-Nūnid of Toledo, 18
Yakhshï, Qaramān Oghullarï, 232
Yakhshï Khān, Shujāʿ al-Dīn, Qarasï Oghullarï, 219
Yaman, Shams al-Dīn, Jāndār Oghullarï, 229
Yaʿqūb
I and II, Germiyān Oghullarï, 224
Abū Yūsuf, Laythid Ṣaffārid, 172
(Aḥmad), Sökmenid, 197
Almohad, 39
Aq Qoyunlu, 275
b. al-Mutawakkil I and II, ʿAbbāsid caliphs in Cairo, 7
Marīnid, 41
Qarakhānid, 181
Rustamid, 27
Yaʿqūb Shāh, Sultan of Kashmīr, 310
Yāqūtī, Artuqids, 194
Yaqẓān, Rustamid, 27
Yār Qulī Jamshīd, Quṭb Shāhī, 328
Yaʿrub, Yaʿrubid, 113
Yazdagird b. Shahriyār, Tāj al-Dawla, Bāwandid Ispahbadh, 165
Yazīd
I, II and III, Umayyad caliphs, 3
ʿAlawid Sharīf, 53
b. Aḥmad, Yazīdī Sharwān Shāh, 140, 143
b. Mazyad al-Shaybānī, governor of Armenia, precursor of the Sharwān Shahs, 140
b. Muḥammad, Yazīdī Sharwān Shāh, 140
Yeremferden (? Jabbār Berdi), line of Orda, 253
Yesü Möngke, Chaghatayid, 248
Yesün Temür
Chaghatayid, 248
Mongol Great Khān, 246
Yïldïz Muʿizzī, Tāj al-Dīn, governor for the Ghūrids, 298
Yuʿfir, Yuʿfirid, 100
Yülük Arslan
Ḥusām al-Dīn, Artuqid, 194
Muẓaffar al-Dīn, Chobān Oghullarï, 231
Yūnus, Tekke Oghullarï, 226
Yūnus Maʿn, Maʿn Amīr, 81
Yūsuf
I and II, ʿAbd al-Wādids, 43
I and II, Almohads, 39
I–V, Naṣrids, 22
ʿAbbāsid caliph
in Baghdad, 6
in Cairo, 7
Abū Yaʿqūb, Carmathian ruler, 94
ʿAlawid Sharīf, 53
Almoravid, 37
b. Muḥammad, Qarakhānid, 182
Begtiginid, 192
Bey of Alanya, 227
Kalbid, 33
Marīnid, 41
al-Muʾtamin, Hūdid, 19
Qadïr Khān, Nāṣir al-Dawla Malik al-Mashriq wa ʾl-Ṣīn, Qarakhānid, 181
Qaramānlī, 57
Rustamid, 27
Sājid, 147
Shihāb Amir, 82
Sultan of Harar, 138
Zaydī Imam, 96
Yūsuf ʿĀdil Khān, governor of Dawlatābād, 325
Yūsuf Buluggīn I, Zīrid governor of the Maghrib, 35
Yūsuf Shāh
I and II, Rukn al-Dīn, Hazāraspids, 205
Atabeg of Yazd, 209
Shams al-Dīn, ruler of Bengal, 307
Sultan of Kashmīr, 310
Yuzbak (ruling title Abu ʾl-Muẓaffar Ghiyāth al-Dīn), governor of Bengal, 306

Za Bisi Baro or Ber, King of Songhay, 124
Ẓafar Khān
(Abu ʾl-Muẓaffar Ḥasan Gangu ʿAlāʾ al-Dīn), Bahmanid, 319
governor of Gujarāt with the title of Muẓaffar Khān, 312
al-Ẓāfir, Fāṭimid, 63
al-Ẓāhir
ʿAbbāsid caliph in Baghdad, 7
Fāṭimid, 63
Ẓāhir, Ḥasanūyid, 158
Zakariyyāʾ
I and II, Ḥafṣids, 45
ʿAbbāsid caliph in Cairo, 7
Zakiyyat al-Dīn Shāh, ʿInāyat, Queen of Acheh, 346
Zamān Shāh, Sadōzay, 341
Zangi
I, II and III, Zangids, 190
Salghurid, 207
Zaraku b. Abī Bakr ʿAtīq, called Mai Cimola, Fulani, 130
Zarrīn Kamar, Bādūspānid, 201
Zāwī, Zīrid of Granada, 17
Zaydān, Saʿdid Sharīf, 50
Zayn al-ʿĀbidīn
ʿAlī, Mujāhid al-Dīn, Muẓaffarid, 264
Aq Qoyunlu, 275
(Shāhī Khān or Bud Shāh), ruler of Kashmīr, 310

Sultan of Acheh, 346
Zīnat al-Dīn Kamālat Shāh, Queen of Acheh, 346
Zīrī, Zīrid governor of the Maghrib, 35
Ziyād
b. Ibrāhīm, Ziyādid, 99
b. Isḥāq, Ziyādid, 99
Ziyādat Allāh I, II and III, Aghlabids, 31
Ziyār, Tāj al-Dawla, Bādūspānid, 201
Zuhayr al-Ṣaqlabī, of Almería, 17, 20
Zuray', Zuray'id, 104

(B) DYNASTIES, PEOPLES, TRIBES ETC.

'Abbādids, 17
'Abbāsid caliph, in Aleppo, 7
'Abbāsid caliphs, in Baghdad, 6
'Abbāsid caliphs, in Cairo, 7
'Abd al-Wādids, 43
Abdālīs or Durrānīs, 341
Abū Dāwūdids, 174
Abu 'l-Khayrids, 288
Abū Sa'īd al-Jannābī, line of, or Carmathians, 94
Acheh, Sultans of, 346
'Ādil Shāhīs, 325
Afrīghids, line of Khwārazm Shāhs, 178
Afshārids, 281
Afṭasids, 18
Aghlabids, 31
Aḥmad Grāñ, line of, in Harar and Ausa, 138
Aḥmar, Banū, 'l-, 22
Aḥmadīlīs, 198
Āl al-Julandā, 111
Āl Bū Sa'īd, 114, 137
Āl Rashīd, 120
Āl Su'ūd (Sa'ūd), 115
'Alawid Sharīfs, 53
'Alī b. Dāwūd, line of, in Harar, 138
Almohads (al-Muwaḥḥidūn), 39
Almoravids (al-Murābiṭūn), 37
'Āmirids, 19
Ānī, line of Shaddādids in, 151
'Annāzids, 159
Anūshtigin Shiḥna, line of Khwārazm Shāhs, 178
Aq Qoyunlu, 275
Arghūns, 329
Artuqids, 194
Ashraf Oghullarï, 228
Ashtarkhānids, 290
Askiyas, Kings of Songhay, 124
Assassins of Persia, or Ismā'īlīs, 203
Assassins of Syria, or Ismā'īlīs, 68
Atabegs of Yazd, 209
'Awn family, 116
Aydïn Oghullarï, 221
Ayyūbids, 70

Bāduspānids, 201
Bahmanids, 319
Baḥrīs Mamlūks, 76
Balban, line of rulers in Bengal , 306
Bānījūrids, 174
Bārakzays (Muḥammadzays), 341
Barīd Shāhīs, 324
Batu'ids (Blue Horde), 252
Bāwandid Ispahbadhs, 164
Begtiginids, 192
Birzāl, Banū, 17
'Black' sultans of Kanem, 126
Börids (Burids), 189
Burjī Mamlūks, 77
Būyids (Buwayhids), 154

Carmathians or Qarmaṭīs of Abū Sa'īd al-Jannābī's line, 94
Chaghatayids, 248
Chingizids, 246
Chobān Oghullarï, 231

Dābūyid Ispahbadhs, 162
Dānishmendids, 215
Delhi Sultans, 300
Dhu 'l-Nūn Beg, line of Arghūns, 329
Dhu 'l-Nūnids, 18
Dulafids, 153
Dulghadïr Oghullarï (Dhu 'l-Qadrids), 238
Durrānīs or Abdālīs, 341

Eldigüzids, 199
Eretna Oghullarï, 234
Eshref Oghullarï, 228

Fārūqīs, 322
Fāṭimids, 63
Filālī Sharīfs, 53
Fulanis, 130

Ganja and Dvīn, line of Shaddādids in, 151
Germiyān Oghullarï, 224
Ghāniya, Banū, 21
Ghāzī Shāh Chak, line of Kashmir Sultans, 310
Ghaznawids, 178, 296
Ghūrids, 298
Ghūrī, line of Mālwa Sultans, 316
Giray Khāns, 255
Golden Horde, the, Khāns of, 252

Ḥabashīs, rulers in Bengal, 307
Ḥafṣids, 45
Ḥamdānids, in Jazīra and Syria, 85
Ḥamdānids, in Yemen, 106
Ḥamid Oghullarï, 226
Ḥammādids, 35
Ḥammūdids, 16
Harar, sultans of, 138

Ḥasanūyids (Ḥasanawayhids), 158
Hāshimids of Darband, 143
Hāshimite Sharīfs, 116
Ḥātim, Banū, 106
Hazāraspids, 205
Hūdids, 19–20
Ḥusaynid Beys, 55

Idrīsids, 25
Ikhshīdids, 62
Il Khanids, 250
Ildegizids, 199
Ilyās Shāh, line of Bengal Sultans, 307
Ilyāsids, 176
'Imād Shāhīs, 327
Inanj Oghullarï, 223
Inaqids (Qungrats), 293
Inju'ids, 266
Isfandiyār (Isfendiyār) Oghullarï or Jāndār Oghularï, 229

Jahwarids, 18
Jalāyirids, 267
Jāndār Oghullarï or Isfaniyār Oghullarï, 229
Jānids, 290
Jogjakarta, sultans of, 351
Justānids, 145

Kākūyids (Kākawayhids), 160
Kalbids, 33
Kanembu line of Shaykhs or Shehus of Bornu and Dikwa, 127, 128
Karam, Banū, 'l-, 104
Kararānīs, 308
Karasï Oghullarï, 219
Karts (Kurts), 263
Keita kings, of Mali, 122
Khalafids, line of Ṣaffāvids, 172
Khaljīs, line of Delhi Sultans, 300
Khaljīs, line of Mālwa Sultans, 316
Khazrūn, Banū, 17
Khwārazm Shāhs, 178
Kilwa, Sultans of, 132

Laythids, line of Ṣaffārids, 172
Lōdīs, line of Delhi Sultans, 301
Lu'lu'ids, 193

Mahdali Sayyids, Sultans of Kilwa, 132
Mahdids, 107
Mais of Bornu and Dikwa, 127, 128
Malacca, rulers of, 344
Maliks of Nīmrūz, 211
Mālwa Sultans, 316
Mamlūks, 76
Ma'mūnids, line of Khwārazm Shāhs, 178
Ma'n amīrs, 81
Mangïts, 292
Marīnids, 41
Marwānids, in Diyār Bakr, 89
Marwānids, line of Umayyad califs, 3
Mataram, rulers of, 348
Mazruis (Mazrū'īs), 136
Mazyadids, 87
Mengüjekids, 217
Menteshe Oghullarï, 222
Midrārids, 29
Mihrabānids, line of Maliks of Nīmrūz, 211
Mings, 295
Mirdāsids, 66
Mongols, 246
Mughal Emperors, 331
Muḥammad 'Alī, House of, 83
Muḥammad Īsā Tarkhān, line of Arghūns, 329
Muḥammadzays (Barakzays), 341
Muḥtājids, 177
Mu'izzī or Shamsī Slave Kings of Delhi, 300
Mujahid, Banū, 17
Mukramids, 112
Mulūk al-Ṭawā'if (Reyes da Taifas), in Spain, 14
Muṣ'abids, line of Ṭāhirids in Baghdad and Iraq, 168
Musāfirids (Sallārids), 148
Musha'sha'ids, 277
Muẓaffarids, 264

Nabhānīs, rulers of Pate, 134
Najaḥids, 101
Naṣrids line of Maliks of Nīmrūz, 211
Naṣrids of Granada, 22
Nawwāb-Viziers and Kings of Oudh, 337
Nawwāb-Viziers and Nawwāb-Nāẓims of Bengal, 335
Niẓām Shāhīs, 326
Niẓāms of Hyderabad, 339
Nizārī Isma'īlīs, 68, 203
Numayrids, 93

Orda, line of (White Horde and then Golden Horde), 252
'Orthodox' or Rightly-Guided caliphs, 1
Ottomans (Osmanlis), 239

Pahlawīs, 287
Parwāna Oghullarï, 230
'Patriarchal' or Rightly-Guided or 'Orthodox' Caliphs, 1
Popalzays (Sadōzays), 341

Qāḍī Burhān al-Dīn Oghullarï, 235
Qājārs, 285
Qara Qoyunlu, 273
Qarakhānids (Ilig Khāns), 181
Qaramān Oghullarï (Qaramānids), 232
Qaramānlīs, 57
Qarasï Oghullarï, 219
Qarmaṭīs (Carmathians), 94
Qāsimids, line of Zaydī Imāms in Yemen, 96
Qubayb, Banū, 'l-, 106
Qungrats (Inaqids), 293
Quṭb Shāhīs, 328
Qutlughkhānids, 210

Rājā Gaṇeśha, line of Bengal sultans, 307
Ramaḍan Oghullarï, 237
Rassids, line of Zaydī Imāms, in Yemen, 96
Rasūlids, 108
Rawwādids, 150

Reyes de Taifas (Mulūk al-Ṭawā'if), 14
Rightly-Guided or 'Patriarchal' or 'Orthodox' Caliphs, 1
Rustamids, 27

Sa'did Sharīfs, 50
Sadōzays (Popalzays), 341
Ṣafawids, 279
Ṣaffārids, 172
Ṣaḥib Atā Oghullarï, 225
Sājids, 147
Salghurids, 207
Sallārids (Musāfirids), 148
Saltuqids, 218
Sāmānids, 170
Sanūsīs, 58
Sarbadārids, 269
Ṣarukhan Oghullarï, 220
Sayfī (Sefuwa) rulers of Kanem and Bornu, 126, 127
Sayyid Ḥusayn Shāh, line of, in Bengal, 307
Sayyids, rulers in Delhi, 301
Seljuqs, 185, 213
Shaddādids, 151
Shāh Mīr Swātī, line of Kashmir Sultans, 310
Shāh-iArmanids, 197
Shamsī or Mu'izzi Slave Kings of Delhi, 300
Sharqī Sultans, 314
Sharwān Shāhs, 140
Shïbānids (Shaybānids), 288
Shihāb Amīrs, 82
Shīrāzī sultans of Kilwa, 132
Sīmjūrids, 175
Sis (Sonnis), Kings of Songhay, 124
Sökmenids, 197
Spanish Umayyads, 11
Sufyānids, line of Umayyad caliphs, 3
Ṣulayḥids, 102
Ṣumādiḥ, Banū, 17
Sūrīs, line of Delhi Sultans, 301
Sūrīs, rulers in Bengal, 308
Susuhunans of Surakarta, 350

Ṭāhirids, of Khurasan and in Baghdad and Iraq, 168
Ṭāhirids, of Spain, 20
Ṭāhirids, of Yemen, 110
Tāj al-Din Oghullarï, 236
Tekke Oghullarï, 226
Tīmūrids, 270
Toqay Temürids, 290
Tughluqids, line of Delhi Sultans, 300
Tujībids, 19
Ṭūlūnids, 60

Ulugh Muḥammad, line of, 259
Umayyad caliphs, 3
'Uqaylids, 91

Waṭṭāsids, 48
White Horde (line of Orda), 252

Ya'rubids, 113
Yazanīs, rulers of Kanem, 126
Yüan dynasty, the Mongol Great Khans in China, 246
Yu'firids (or Ya'furids), 100

Zands, 283
Zangids, 190
Zas (Zuwas), Kings of Songhay, 124
Zaydī Imāms in Yemen, 96
Zayyānids (Ziyānids), 43
Zīrids, 17, 35
Ziyādids, 99
Ziyānids (Zayyanids), 43
Ziyārids, 166
Zuray'ids, 104

(C) PLACES

Acheh (Atjèh, Aceh), 346
Aden, 104
Afghanistan, 172, 263, 288, 290, 296, 341
Africa, Horn of, 132
Aḥmadnagar, 326
Aḥsanābād-Gulbargā, 319
Akhlāt, 197
al-Ḥadītha, 91
al-Miqrāna, 110
al-Rustāq, 113
Alamūt, 203
Albarracin, 14
Aleppo, 7, 71, 85, 190
Algeciras, 14
Algeria, 31, 35, 43, 45, 239
Almería, 14, 17
Alpuente, 14
Āmid, 194
Āmul, 164
Āna, 91
Anatolia, 197, 213, 215, 217–28, 232, 234–5, 238–9, 250, 273, 275
Ānī, 151
Antalya, 226
'Arabistān, 277
Arcos, 14, 17
Armenia, 151
Arrān, 148, 151, 199
Astrakhan, 258
Ausa, 138
Azerbaijan (Ādharbāyjān), 147–8, 150, 198–9, 267, 273, 275

Badajoz, 14, 18
Badakhshān, 298
Balad, 91
Balāsāghūn, 182
Ba'lbakk, 73

Balearic Islands, 14, 21
Balkans, 239
Balkh, 174
Baluchistan, 296
Bāmiyān, 298
Bāniyās, 73
Baza, 14
Bengal, 306, 335
Berār, 327
Bīdar, 324
Bihār, 306
Bījapur, 324
Black Sea coastland, 229–30, 236
Borneo, 353
Bornu (Borno), 126–8
Brunei, 353
Bukhara, 181, 292
Buṣrā, 73

Calatayud, 14, 19
Calatrava, 14
Canik (Jānīk), 236
Carmona, 14, 17
Caucasus, the, 140
Ceuta, 14, 16
Chaghāniyān, 177
China, 246
Cilicia, 79, 237, 251
Cordova, 14, 18
Crimea, the, 255

Damascus, 70, 189–90
Darband, 143
Daylam, 145, 148
Deccan, 300, 318–19, 322
Denia, 14, 17, 19
Deñizli, 223
Dhū Jibla, 102
Dikwa, 127–8
Divriği, 217
Diyār Bakr, 70, 72, 89, 194, 275
Dvīn, 151

Eğridir, 226
Egypt, 60, 62–3, 70, 76, 83
Elbistan, 215
Eritrea, 239
Erzincan, 217
Erzurum, 218
Ethiopia, 138

Farghāna, 181–2
Fars (Fārs), 154, 207, 266, 275
Firrīm, 164

Gambia, 122
Ganja, 151
Gao, 124
Ghazna, 298
Ghūr, 298
Gīlān, 162, 164
Golconda-Muḥammadnagar, 328
Granada, 14, 17, 22
Guinea, 122
Gujarāt, 312
Gurgān, 166
Gurgānj, 178

Ḥamāt, 71
Harar, 138
Harrān, 7, 93, 192
Hausaland, 130
Ḥijāz, 118
Ḥilla, 87
Ḥimṣ, 71
Ḥiṣn al-Ashrāf, 15
Ḥiṣn Kayfā, 194
Hīt, 91
Huelva, 14
Huesca, 14, 19
Hyderabad (Haydarābād), 339

Ifrīqiya, 31
Īlāq, 182
India, 296, 298, 300, 312, 314, 316, 331, 337, 339–40
Indonesia, 344
Iraq, 6, 87, 91, 94, 118, 129, 154–5, 168, 185, 192, 250, 267, 270, 273
Irbil, 192

Jaén, 14
Janad, 100
Java, 348, 350–1
Jawnpur, 314
Jazīra, 70, 85, 89, 190, 193
Jibāl, 153–4, 160, 199
Jogjakarta, 351
Jordan, 118
Juban, 110

Kairouan, 35
Kanem, 126
Karaj, 153
Karak, 73
Kāshghar, 182
Kashmīr, 310
Kastamonu (Qasṭamūnī), 231
Kāth, 178
Kazan, 259
Kemakh, 217
Kenya, 134
Khāndesh, 322
Khartpert, 194
Khiva (Khīwa), 293
Khokand (Khoqand), 295
Khotan, 182
Khurasan (Khurāsān), 168, 170, 175, 177, 263, 269–70, 283, 296, 298
Khūzistān, 154
Khwārazm, 178, 252
Kilwa, 132
Kirman (Kirmān), 155, 176, 186, 210, 275
Konya, 213
Kujūr, 201
Kurdistan, 158–60, 192, 267

La Sahla, 15

Lebanon, 81–2
Lérida, 14, 19
Libya, 58
Little Armenia, 237
Luristān, 159, 205

Ma'bar (Madura), 318
Majorca, 14, 17
Malacca (Melaka), 344
Málaga, 14, 16
Malatya, 215
Malay peninsula, 344
Mali, 122
Mālwa, 316
Marāgha, 198
Mārdīn, 194
Mataram, 348
Mayyāfāriqīn, 194
Mecca, 118
Medinaceli, 14
Mértola, 14
Mombasa, 136
Mongolia, 246
Morocco, 25, 29, 48, 50, 53
Morón, 14
Moscow, 260, 261
Mosul, 85, 91, 190, 193
Muḥammadābād-Bīdar, 319
Multan, 329
Murcia, 14, 20
Murviedro, 14
Muscat, 114
Mysore (Mahisur, Maysūr), 340

Najd, 116, 120
Niebla, 14
Nigeria, 130
Niṣībīn, 91
Nūr, 202

Oman ('Umān), 111–14, 155
Oudh (Awadh), 337

Pate, 134
Pemba, 136
Persia, 140, 154, 168, 172, 185, 203, 250, 264, 270, 273, 275, 277, 279, 281, 283, 285, 287

Qal'at Banī Ḥammad, 35
Qal'at Ja'bar, 91, 93
Qāsimov (Goradets Meshehevskiy), 261
Qïpchaq steppe, 252
Quhistān, 175
Raqqa, 93
Rayy, 154
Ronda, 15
Rūdbār-Shāh Rūd valleys, 145
Rū'īn Diz, 198
Rustamdār, 201
Rūyān, 162, 201
Ryazan, 261

Ṣa'da (Ṣan'ā'), 96, 100, 102, 106
Samarkand, 181, 270
Samīrān, 147
Santa Maria de Algarve, 15
Saragossa, 15, 19–20
Sārī, 162, 164
Sarūj, 93
Segura, 15
Semirechye, 181–2
Senegal, 122
Seville, 15, 17
Shahrazūr, 190
Sharwān, 140
Shāsh, 182
Siberia, 252
Sicily, 31, 33
Silves, 15
Sind, 329
Sinjār, 190
Sinop, 230
Sistan, 172, 211
Sivas, 215
Sokoto, 130
Spain, 7, 14, 37, 39
Subayba, 73
Sudan, 58, 126
Sumatra, 346
Surakarta, 350
Syria, 7, 60, 62–3, 66, 68, 70, 76, 85, 89, 94, 118, 186, 189–90, 192

Ṭabaristān, 162, 164, 166
Tabriz (Tabrīz), 150
Tahert, 27
Ta'izz, 108
Takrīt, 91
Talas, 182
Tanzania, 132
Tārum, 147
Tihāma, 108, 110
Toledo, 15, 18
Tortosa, 15, 19
Transcaucasia, 140
Transjordan, 118
Transoxania, 168, 170, 181, 288, 290
Tripolitania, 57
Tudela, 15, 19
Ṭukhāristan, 174, 298
Tunisia, 35, 45, 55
Turkestan, 181

'Ukbarā, 91
Ukraine, 255
Uzgend, 182

Valencia, 15, 19
Vilches, 15
Volga region, 258–9

Yazd, 209
Yazīdiyya, 140
Yemen, 70, 73, 96, 99–102, 104, 106–8, 110

Zabīd, 99, 101, 107
Zanzibar, 114, 137